Issues of Legal Ethics in the Practice of Environmental Law

By Irma S. Russell

Defending Liberty
Pursuing Justice

Section of Environment, Energy, and Resources
Book Publications Committee, 2002-2003

John P. Manard, Jr., chair
Kathleen Marion Carr
James W. Checkley, Jr.
Sam Kalen

John D. Levin
Jay G. Martin
Karen McGaffey
Cary R. Perlman

The publications of the Section of Environment, Energy, and Resources have a commitment to quality. Our authors and editors are outstanding professionals and active practitioners in their fields. In addition, prior to publication, the contents of all of our books are rigorously reviewed by the Section's Book Publications Committee and outside experts to ensure the highest quality product and presentation.

The materials contained herein represent the opinions of the authors and editors and should not be construed to be the action of either the American Bar Association or the Section of Environment, Energy, and Resources unless adopted pursuant to the bylaws of the Association.

Nothing contained in this book is to be considered as the rendering of legal advice for specific cases, and readers are responsible for obtaining such advice from their own legal counsel. This book and any forms and agreements herein are intended for educational and informational purposes only.

© 2003 American Bar Association. All rights reserved.
Printed in the United States of America.

07 06 05 04 03 5 4 3 2 1

Library of Congress Cataloging-in-Publication Data

Russell, Irma S.
  Issues of legal ethics in the practice of environmental law / by Irma S. Russell.
    p. cm.
  ISBN 1-59031-166-3
    1. Environmental lawyers—Professional ethics—United States. 2. Legal ethics—United States. I. American Bar Association. Section of Environment, Energy, and Resources. II. Title.

KF306.R87 2003
174'.3—dc21   2003009533

Discounts are available for books ordered in bulk. Special consideration is given to state bars, CLE programs, and other bar-related organizations. Inquire at Book Publishing, ABA Publishing, American Bar Association, 750 North Lake Shore Drive, Chicago, Illinois 60611.

www.ababooks.org

CONTENTS

Acknowledgments ix

About the Author xi

Foreword xiii

CHAPTER 1
Regulation of Lawyers 1
Regulation of Government Lawyers 3
Unauthorized Practice of Law 10
Peer Evaluation 12
The Disciplinary Process 14
History of ABA Rules 16
Statutory Controls 18
Judicial Controls 19
Limiting Use of Rules: 2002 Revision 20
Tort Liability 21
Lawyer Conduct Subject to Regulation 28
Nonlegal Services Provided by a Lawyer 29
Moral Judgment 30
Application of Rules to Lawyers Acting in Nonprofessional Capacity
(2002 Revision) 31
Forum and Laboratory Shopping 31
Taking Advantage of an Opponent's Mistakes 32
Indeterminacy in the Law 34
Indeterminacy in Lawyering 35
Indeterminacy: Environmental Example 36
Indeterminacy: Example of Endocrine Disrupters 37

CHAPTER 2
The Duty of Competence 41
Model Rule 1.1 41
Environmental Context 41
Lawyer's Duty of Diligence 42
The Limits of Diligence 42

iv ISSUES OF LEGAL ETHICS IN THE PRACTICE OF ENVIRONMENTAL LAW

CHAPTER 3
The Lawyer-Client Relationship 47
The Client's Objectives 49
The Lawyer's Role as Advisor 56
Client Status 58
Prospective Clients 62
Former Clients 64
The Environmental Context 65
Attorney-Client Privilege 67
The Organizational Client 73
Corporate Clients: Environmental Example 83

CHAPTER 4
Confidentiality 89
Society's Interest in Disclosure of Dangerous Conditions 91
Background Principles 92
History of Confidentiality 92
Model Rule 1.6 99
Disclosure of Confidential Client Information 105
Organizational Clients 108
Client Wrongdoing: 1983 Version of Model Rule 1.6 108
Recognition of Other Law 110
The Effect of Deletion of References to Other Law 112
The Tension With Other Law: Environmental Examples 113
The Tension With the Lawyer's Duty of Candor 114
Government Lawyers 116
The Environmental Lawyer's Nightmare 119
Preemptive Self-Defense 122
Reporting Obligations: Environmental Examples 124
Protection of Confidential Business Information 128
Interpretation and Enforcement of Environmental Statutes 129
Complying With Law 132
Misprision 136
State Environmental Laws: Mandatory Sanctions 137
Environmental Audits 138
Securities Act Requirements 138
Confidentiality and the Common Law: Environmental Issues 143
Relevant Common-Law Developments 147
Lawyer Liability to Nonclients 147
The Professional's Duty to Warn 153
Attorney-Client Privilege 159
Work Product Rule 171
Inadvertent Disclosure of Client Information 175

Contents   v

Termination of In-House Counsel 179
Other Common Issues 191
Requirement of Complying with Discovery Requests 195

CHAPTER 5
Basic Conflicts Concerns 199
Organization and Terminology 200
Overview and General Principles 201
The Duty of Loyalty 203
The 1983 Model Rules Approach 204
Current Clients 209
Determining Adversity Standard (2002 Revision) 215
Generally Adverse Interests: Environmental Example 215
The Model Code Approach 216
The Restatement Approach 217
Multiple Representation 218
The Use of a Conflict to Seek Disqualification 222
Consequences and Sanctions 223
Avoiding Conflicts 224
Curative Measures 224
Close Cases and Consent: Environmental Example 228
Nonwaivable Conflicts 229
Nonwaivable Conflicts (2002 Revision) 231
Curative Measures 232
Prospective Clients 238
Former Clients 245

CHAPTER 6
Special Conflicts Concerns 261
Imputed Conflicts 261
Private Lawyers 263
The Mobile Lawyer 264
Disease Metaphors 267
Disqualification: Model Rules Provision 267
Imputed Conflicts (2002 Revision) 268
Firm Size 268
Environmental Example 271
Curative Measures 272
Government Lawyers 278
Federal Statute 292
Corporate Clients 294
Criminal Defendants 302
Positional or Issue Conflicts 306

vi   ISSUES OF LEGAL ETHICS IN THE PRACTICE OF ENVIRONMENTAL LAW

Business Dealings with a Client   310
Settlements   312
Joint Plaintiff Groups   318
The Lawyer Witness   319
Client Witness   320
Serving as a Neutral   323

CHAPTER 7
The Lawyer's Duty of Candor to the Tribunal   327
Duty of Candor to Tribunal   330
Duty of Candor to Tribunal (2002 Revision)   331
Duty of Candor: Environmental Example   331

CHAPTER 8
The Lawyer's Duties to Nonclients   333
Duty of Fairness and Truthfulness   333
Respect for the Rights of Third Persons   334
Respect for the Rights of Third Persons (2002 Revision)   335
Duty of Candor: Environmental Example   335
Duty to Third Persons   337
Rescission: Environmental Examples   337
Duty of Candor to the Profession   339
Lawyer Misconduct Generally   342
Lawyer Misconduct Generally (2002 Revision)   343

CHAPTER 9
Alternative Dispute Resolution   345
ADR in Environmental Matters   345
Third-Party Neutrals   348
Third-Party Neutrals (2002 Revision)   349

CHAPTER 10
The Anticontact Rule—Represented Persons   351
Anticontact Rule (2002 Revision)   357
Anticontact Rule: Environmental Examples   358
Corporate Entities   359
Application to Employees and Agents   359
Former Employees   360
Corporate Clients: Environmental Examples   362
Former Employees: Environmental Example   364
Knowledge of Representation   365
Client Contact with Opposition   365
Government Agencies   366

Contents vii

Government Agencies (2002 Revision) 368
Contact by Government Prosecutors 368
Unrepresented Persons 369
Unrepresented Persons: Environmental Example 371
Unrepresented Person (2002 Revision) 372

CHAPTER 11
Multidisciplinary Practice 373
Confidentiality 375
The Potential Professional Cognitor 376
Commission on Multidisciplinary Practice 377
Environmental Practice 379

CHAPTER 12
Multijurisdictional Practice 381
Unauthorized Practice of Law 383
2002 Revisions 386

CHAPTER 13
Pro Bono Representations 389
2002 Revision 389

CHAPTER 14
Lawyer Advertising 391
Solicitation of Clients 391
Technology 396
Solicitation of Clients (2002 Revision) 399

CHAPTER 15
Lawyer Fees 401
Billing and Collection Practices 405
Advance Fees 406
Lawyer Fees (2002 Revision) 407
Retainer Agreement 408
Contingent Fees 410
Contingent Fees (2002 Revision) 411
Environmental Public Interest Groups 411
Payment of Fees as a Sanction 412
Collection 412
Fees in the Environmental Context 413
Referral Fees: Environmental Practice 413
Fee Sharing 415
Fee Division (2002 Revision) 416

viii ISSUES OF LEGAL ETHICS IN THE PRACTICE OF ENVIRONMENTAL LAW

CHAPTER 16
The Lawyer's Role in Working with Consultants 419
Model Rule 5.3 420
Model Rule 5.3 (2002 Revision) 422
Model Rule 7.2 (2002 Revision) 422

CHAPTER 17
The Lawyer's Role in Working With the Media 423
Environmental Example 425

CHAPTER 18
Termination and Withdrawal from Representation 427
Mandatory Bases for Withdrawal 428
Permissive Bases for Withdrawal 429
Confidentiality 433
Impact on Other Parties 433
Withdrawal (2002 Revision) 435

Conclusion 437

Glossary 439

Appendix A
Acronym List 449

Appendix B
Frequently Asked Questions 451

Appendix C
Sample Letters Relating to Professional Legal Services 457

Table of Cases 465

Index 481

ACKNOWLEDGMENTS

The author gratefully acknowledges the financial support of a grant by the Plough Corporation, which was administered by the University of Memphis Foundation. The author expresses sincere appreciation for the comments of colleagues, practitioners, and students on earlier drafts of this book; those comments were of invaluable help in determining the scope and content of this work. The author would also like to thank the ABA Section on Environment, Energy, and Resources and the ABA Section of Administrative Law and Regulatory Practice, as well as the members of these sections. The author thanks especially the staff lawyers for the ABA Standing Committee on Ethics and Professional Responsibility, and Professors Amanda K. Esquibel, Janet L. Richards, Rodney Smith, Ernest Lidge III, Ralph Brashier, Carl Pierce, Edward Brewer, Ellen Y. Suni, and Bradley W. Wendel. Many practitioners, professors, and students also shared their views on hypothetical fact patterns and analysis of the points raised here. In particular, the author thanks Kelly Rayne Brayton, Allan Gates, Kathleen S. Hall, Michael Gerrard, Mark Squillace, Lucian Pera, Albert Harvey, Brian J. Redding, Mark Tuft, Blake Biles, Cynthia Drew, Chris W. Dodson, Hal Lieberman, Walter Mugdan, Cynthia F. Covell, Bradley F. Tellum, Rebecca Feichtl, Phillip Hilliard, and David Hunter. The author also acknowledges Ethics and Lawyering Today, an e-mail newsletter published by William Freivogel and Lucian Pera, available at http://www.ethicsandlawyering.com, and, additionally, the participants on the Washburn Law School legal ethics listserv, legalethics-l@lawlib.wuacc.edu, for information, insights, and cites to important cases. She thanks Joseph Bean, Adrian Bohnenberger, Stephenie Booher, Gwyn R. Fisher, Sharon Russo, Melinda A. Troeger, Susanne Lissant, John J. Winkler, and John Houseal for their helpful research. She thanks Karol Usmani and Alissa Marriott for their tireless efforts in preparing the manuscript for publication. Finally, she gives thanks to and for Tom, Nat, and Anna.

ABOUT THE AUTHOR

Irma S. Russell is a professor of law at the University of Memphis School of Law, Memphis, Tennessee, where she teaches Environmental Law and Contracts. She is currently a Visiting Professor of Law at the University of Missouri–Kansas City. In practice, Professor Russell has represented potentially responsible parties on issues arising under the Comprehensive Environmental Response, Compensation and Liability Act (CERCLA) in Superfund negotiations as well as representing government entities, lenders, and other clients on issues involving the National Environmental Policy Act (NEPA), wetlands designation and site mitigation, the Clean Water Act, asbestos regulation, and other environmental issues. She is currently a council member of the ABA Section on Environment, Energy, and Resources, and serves as Section liaison to the American Association of Law Schools and to the ABA Standing Committee on Ethics and Professional Responsibility. She served as a vice-chair of the Ethics Committee of the ABA Section on Environment, Energy, and Resources for one year (1998-99) and as chair of that Committee for two years (1999–2000 and 2000–01). She was founding chair of the Memphis Bar Association Environmental Law Section and also has served as chair of the Tennessee Bar Association Environmental Section.

Professor Russell's legal publications include a chapter on Legal Ethics in *The Law of Environmental Justice*, a book published by the American Bar Association; *Unreasonable Risk: Model Rule 1.6, Environmental Hazards, and Positive Law*, 55 WASH. & LEE L. REV. 117 (1998); *Cries and Whispers: Environmental Hazards, Model Rule 1.6, and the Attorney's Conflicting Duties to Clients and Others*, 72 WASH. L. REV. 409 (1997).

Professor Russell received her J.D. from the University of Kansas School of Law. She served as judicial clerk to the Honorable James K. Logan on the U.S. Court of Appeals for the Tenth Circuit. She is a member of the American Law Institute, the Judicial Conference of the Tenth Judicial Circuit, the Memphis Bar Association, the American Bar Association, and the ABA Section of Environment, Energy, and Resources.

FOREWORD

The purpose of this book is to identify and explore questions of legal ethics that environmental lawyers may encounter in representing industrial clients, government agencies, individuals, public interest groups, and others. One might ask why a book on ethics in the environmental area is necessary. After all, the rules of ethics apply to all lawyers regardless of their area of practice. This book examines the evolving responsibilities and problems of lawyers practicing environmental law, addressing fundamental principles of ethics to apply these rules to the difficult context of environmental practice. Thus, the book focuses primarily on those rules of ethics that raise significant concerns for the environmental practitioner. Additionally, the commentary presented here seeks to provide sufficient background on the ethics rules to facilitate meaningful analysis of the ethical issues arising in the environmental context.

The Detailed Discussion summarizes fundamental ethical principles that present problems for environmental practitioners, even though not all of these problems are unique to environmental practice. It also provides discussion of the cautious or prudent course of action for lawyers concerned about particular ethics issues. What constitutes the "best" practice in a given situation is frequently open to debate. Indeed, the Ethics 2000 Commission originally planned to include a statement of best practices applicable to each rule. It ultimately abandoned that effort as unworkable, however.[1]

While this text sometimes refers to the "best practice," the use of this term is not intended as an assertion that there is only one appropriate answer or response to the question at hand. Rather, the intent is to identify a prudent course of conduct and to raise the issue of what other courses might serve the purposes of the lawyer, his clients, and the administration of justice.[2] The discussion frequently draws on cases that have arisen in the environmental

---

1. Notes of telephone conference with Professor Carl Pierce, Reporter of the Ethics 2000 Commission (July 25, 2002).

2. Since 2001, the Clinical Legal Education Association (CLEA) has been working on a project intended to "identify best practices for preparing new lawyers for law practice." Rather than trying to state a "single best answer," the project seeks to pull together "a variety of proposals for improving the preparation of new lawyers. The work of CLEA on this project, named the Best Practices Project, is ongoing at the time of this publication. It can be accessed at: http://professionalism.law.sc.edu in the "news" section. E-mail of Roy Stuckey (Aug. 1, 2002) (copy on file with author).

xiii

field. In resolving issues as they arise, lawyers are likely to consult a particular section of this text rather than reading the book cover to cover. To facilitate this process, some sections briefly repeat background or foundational information to set the stage for the point at hand.

The approach of anticipating and analyzing difficult ethics issues in a particular practice area has great potential benefits. A proactive approach to ethics helps lawyers avoid problems by making reasoned decisions before ethical problems arise in urgent or complicated contexts. Moreover, the environmental context provides a testing ground for the ethics rules. This is because issues of public health and safety often arise in environmental controversies, creating high-stakes choices for the lawyers forced to make ethical decisions in such situations.

The Precautionary Principle

The approach of this work can be described by reference to the precautionary principle.[3] This work does not discuss all of the Model Rules or all cases involving ethical issues in the environmental arena. Rather, it seeks to identify the issues, and some of the judicial responses to those issues, most likely to arise in environmental practice, with the goal of helping lawyers avoid liability or other negative consequences. Scientists use the precautionary principle to make conclusions that are consistent with protecting human life and the environment. In other words, a margin of safety should be incorporated into scientific conclusions when the health and safety of people can be affected by that conclusion. Similarly, legislatures and agencies include a margin of safety in the rules they adopt for regulating hazardous wastes, for example.

The precautionary principle is well known in environmental law. Application of this principle may have merit in the context of liability as well as physical safety. In explaining the risks of liability to clients, lawyers often use the precautionary principle approach. They note when a trend may exist toward finding liability in particular situations. Moreover, even when only one case exists that would result in liability, lawyers make this case known to their clients. For example, the *Fleet Factors* case generated both scholarly work and lawyer comment, although it was only one approach to liability for lending institutions that foreclosed on contaminated property. Similarly, this work attempts to draw to the attention of the environmental practitioner cases as well as trends and possible interpretations that could result in lawyer liability or other sanctions.

In deciding questions of legal ethics in the practice of law, the controlling authority is the applicable rule of ethics promulgated by the lawyer's jurisdic-

---

3. *See generally* Frank B. Cross, *Paradoxical Perils of the Precautionary Principle*, 53 WASH. & LEE L. REV. 851 (1996).

tion of licensure relevant to the particular case involved.[4] Additionally, lawyers may be subject to other ethical duties, such as those imposed by the Code of Ethics for Arbitration.[5] While the principles explored here have general acceptance, commentary should not be treated as a substitute for the study of the particular rules applicable in the individual lawyer's jurisdiction of licensure. Accordingly, readers should regard works such as this, the Model Rules, and the Model Code promulgated by the ABA as the starting point rather than the end point of a particular inquiry into legal ethics.

Executive Summary

Environmental law presents ample opportunities for exploring legal ethics, policy, morality, and public interest. Indeed, at times environmental practice may seem to present an unending series of ethical dilemmas. Is it ethical for the lawyer to set up meetings to educate and solicit residents as plaintiffs in a toxic tort case? To oppose siting a hazardous waste site? May a lawyer agree in a settlement to bring no similar actions against the defendant? If a defendant offers the plaintiffs named in an action a lump-sum settlement to drop the suit (and thereby defeat standing), what is the lawyer's ethical obligation? May a lawyer accept representation with a potentially responsible party (PRP) when a partner in his firm represents a different PRP at the same Superfund site? Does the attorney-client privilege attach to reports from environmental consultants? May the lawyer for a corporate defendant disclose environmental violations by her client that she discovers while working on an environmental case? What should a lawyer do when she becomes convinced that her client's position, though colorable, is legally wrong? What if she sees the claim as morally wrong?

This book explores these and other questions of legal ethics. It examines judicial decisions, formal and informal ABA Opinions, opinions of state advisory committees or committees on professional responsibility, and the American Bar Association Model Rules of Professional Conduct (Model Rules). In some cases, it considers provisions of the ABA Model Code of Professional Responsibility (Model Code), the American Law Institute's Restatement of the Law Governing Lawyers, and the revisions of the Model Rules drafted by the ABA Commission on Evaluation of the Rules of Professional Conduct and adopted as amended by the ABA House of Delegates in February 2002. The revised rules constitute the ABA's current statement of the rules of legal ethics. This discussion includes explanation of the rules as revised in 2002 that have special significance for environmental lawyers.

---

4. *See, e.g., Tennessee Adopts ABA Model Rules, Making Numerous Changes to Model,* 71 U.S. Law Wk. 2197 (Sept. 24, 2002) (noting that, like other jurisdictions, the new Tennessee rules alter or omit parts of the model rules).

5. *See* Model Rules of Prof'l Conduct R. 2.2 cmt. 2.

At the time of this publication, no state has yet debated or adopted the ethics rules embodied in the Model Rules revised in February 2002.[6] Thus, the basic template for the current applicable law governing lawyers through the rules adopted by states is the 1983 version of the Model Rules of Professional Conduct. For this reason, this discussion focuses on the 1983 rules as well as the revised rules of 2002. Over 80 percent of jurisdictions in the United States use the Model Rules of 1983 as the basis of the law governing lawyers for the jurisdiction.[7] Although the Model Rules superseded the ABA Model Code of Professional Responsibility of 1969, a few jurisdictions have retained the Model Code as the basis for their rules of ethics.[8] Some differences between the Code and the Model Rules are taken up here as background for understanding the current Model Rules and for noting the different approaches. The Code had superseded the ABA Canons of Professional Ethics, the first statement of the rules of legal ethics, which the ABA adopted in 1908. No jurisdictions continue to use the canons as a model for the rules of legal ethics. Nevertheless, this discussion refers to some of the canons as a way of providing historical perspective. Although states do not use the Restatement as a basis for ethics rules in lieu of the Model Rules or Model Code, courts have followed Restatement provisions in deciding cases and determining the applicable standard of care to apply to lawyers in considering malpractice and other claims.[9] For this reason, this book discusses some provisions of the Restatement.

---

6. A few courts incorporate the Model Rules as rules of the court. *See, e.g.,* Southern District of Georgia (Rule 83.5(d)) (stating that the Model Rules are "included" as rules of the court); V. I. Terr. Ct. R. 303 (2001) (declaring the ABA Rules of Professional Conduct to be the rules pertaining to discipline of lawyers practicing in the Virgin Islands). The rules do not indicate whether the incorporation refers to the current rules in force at the time of the passage of the rule or whether amendment to the ABA rules results in the automatic amendment of the rules for lawyers practicing in the jurisdiction. On the related question of which rule controls in the case of a conflict, *see* Model Rule 8.5.
7. *See Tennessee Adopts ABA Model Rules, Making Numerous Changes to Model,* 71 U.S. Law. Wk. 2197 (Sept. 24, 2002) (noting that 45 of the jurisdictions have based their rules on the Model Rules).
8. For this reason, this work refers to the Code in the present tense rather than the past tense.
9. *See, e.g.,* Zachair, Ltd. v. Driggs, 965 F. Supp. 741 (D. Md. 1997) (following Restatement approach in disqualifying plaintiff's counsel for ex parte interview of former employee of corporate defendant). Courts may turn to other authority in determining conflicts issues or other issues of professional ethics. *See In re* Dresser Industries, Inc., 972 F.2d 540 (5th Cir. 1992) (considering ABA Model Rules of Professional Conduct, Code of Professional Responsibility and drafts of the American Law Institute's Restatement of the Law Governing Lawyers for guidance in addition to state rules of ethics).

The rules of states and those formulated by the ABA continue to evolve.[10] The ABA Commission on Evaluation of the Rules of Professional Conduct, known informally as the "Ethics 2000 Commission," studied the Model Rules for four years and proposed revisions. During that time, the Commission surveyed lawyers and scholars, reviewed formal opinions by the ABA Standing Committee on Professionalism Ethics and Professional Responsibility and opinions from state disciplinary boards, conducted hearings, and drafted proposed revisions to the Model Rules.

The Commission's work is an example of the continuing study and evaluation necessary to ensure that the rules of legal ethics continue to evolve in response to changes in the law and society. The revisions can be accessed at the Commission's Web site: http://www.abanet.org/cpr/ethics2k.html. After its study, the Commission presented proposed revisions to the Model Rules to the ABA House of Delegates. In August 2001 and February 2002, the American Bar Association House of Delegates debated the merits of proposed amendments to the ABA Model Rules of Professional Conduct and adopted amended versions of the proposed rules. In August 2002, they completed the work of updating the Model Rules of Professional Conduct, by passage of the rules relating to multijurisdictional practice and the unauthorized practice of law (UPL).[11]

Scope

Environmental Ethics: The Philosophical Movement

Ethical issues in environmental law have both philosophical and practical dimensions. Lawyers engaged in environmental practice note ethical and philosophical questions in their practice. Each lawyer is called upon to practice within the constraints of his conscience. Indeed, philosophical issues permeate decision making. Environmental laws reflect philosophical values and the need to conserve and protect the environment for its inherent value as well as for utilitarian reasons. Policies relating to sustainable use of resources reflect the need to enhance the quality of the air, water, and the natural environment. Many laws also serve the goal of preserving the environment for future generations. The philosophical movement of environmental ethics has been termed a "second generation" phenomenon, which

---

10. Tennessee, Vermont, and Virginia are in the process of considering adoption of the Model Rules. *See generally* A. Jeffry Taylor, *Work in Progress: The Vermont Rules of Professional Conduct*, 20 VT. L. REV. 901 (1996); PROPOSED MODEL RULES OF PROFESSIONAL CONDUCT, VA. LAW., Mar. 1997; TENNESSEE PROPOSED RULES, Nov. 1, 1997, 957 S.W.2d Ct.R-37 (1997).

11. *See* http://www.abanet.org/cpr/mjp-home.html (last visited April 15, 2002).

has resulted in an impressive body of scholarship and legal thought in recent years.[12]

Perhaps the concern for ethical aspects of environmentalism and environmental law is evidence of the maturity of the field. Broad ethical issues were rarely articulated at the beginning. Early environmental concerns were very immediate, addressing crisis situations that needed to be resolved to prevent the destruction of resources that, once lost, could not be recovered. In the early 1960s, particular threats called for rapid responses, usually by immediate recourse to litigation, without much opportunity to ponder broad philosophical issues. By now, however, the ethical dimensions of environmentalism have been examined, and although major philosophical issues may not be articulated in environmental litigation or environmental legislation, their presence underlies a great deal of current thinking and activity.[13]

The environmental philosophy movement and public demand have led to environmental legislation and regulation that have changed the face of American business, influencing both industrial practices and business values. Most major universities now offer courses and degrees in environmental study and environmental philosophy. The literature of environmental law explores philosophy openly, juxtaposing chemistry and biology with philosophical and moral inquiries.[14] Coverage in this area is broad-ranging. Scholars provide practical insights into the environmental movement[15] and into the difficult political and personal choices inherent in today's world.[16]

---

12. *See, e.g.*, CHRISTOPHER D. STONE, EARTH AND OTHER ETHICS: THE CASE FOR MORAL PLURALISM (1987); CHRISTOPHER D. STONE, THE GNAT IS OLDER THAN THE MAN (1993); F. FERRY & P. HARTEL, ETHICS AND ENVIRONMENTAL POLICY (1994); H. ROLSTON, III, ENVIRONMENTAL ETHICS: DUTIES TO THE VALUES IN THE NATURAL WORLD (1988); E. C. HARGROVE, FOUNDATIONS OF ENVIRONMENTAL ETHICS (1989); R. ATTFIELD, THE ETHICS OF ENVIRONMENTAL CONCERN (2d ed. 1991).

13. FRANK P. GRAD & JOEL A. MINTZ, ENVIRONMENTAL LAW 7 (4th ed. 2000).

14. *SEE, E.G.*, MARK SAGOFF, THE ECONOMY OF EARTH: PHILOSOPHY, LAW AND THE ENVIRONMENT (1988); CHRISTOPHER D. STONE, THE GNAT IS OLDER THAN MAN (1993); CHRISTOPHER STONE, EARTH AND OTHER ETHICS: THE CASE FOR MORAL PLURALISM (1987); R. LAZARUS, *Pursuing Environmental Justice: The Distributional Effects of Environmental Protection*, 87 NW. U.L. REV. 101 (1993); RODERICK F. NASH, THE RIGHTS OF NATURE (1989); PETER S. WENZ, ENVIRONMENTAL JUSTICE (1988); ERIC T. FREYFOGLE, JUSTICE AND THE EARTH: IMAGES FOR OUR PLANETARY SURVIVAL (1993).

15. *See, e.g.*, ANNA LISA PETERSON, BEING HUMAN: ETHICS, ENVIRONMENT, AND OUR PLACE IN THE WORLD; Robert R.M. Verchick, *In a Greener Voice: Feminist Theory and Environmental Justice*, 19 HARV. WOMEN'S L.J. 23 (1996).

16. *See, e.g.,* NICHOLAS LOW, GLOBAL ETHICS AND ENVIRONMENT (1999); J. BAIRD CALLICOTT, FERNANDO J. R. ROCHA, EARTH SUMMIT ETHICS: TOWARD A RECONSTRUCTIVE POSTMODERN PHILOSOPHY OF ENVIRONMENTAL EDUCATION (1996); HILKKA PIETILÄ, DAUGHTERS OF MOTHER EARTH: WOMEN'S CULTURE AS AN ETHICAL AND PRACTICAL BASIS FOR SUSTAINABLE DEVELOPMENT (1989).

A separate category of ethical questions could be called "metaethical." Such questions explore policy and normative issues of ethical propositions. Many of the law review articles that raise questions of ethics in the environmental area focus on this type of question. A third type of ethics inquiry concerns the psychology of "doing the right thing," including the motivation that people feel to fulfill obligations.

Additionally, many industry groups have ethics statements and governing bodies, as well as certification processes similar to those in the legal field. The clients, as members of their respective industries, should carefully comply with peer standards as well as governmental requirements relating to ethical obligations of the particular industry. Lawyers should be aware of the ethical principles of their client's industry to serve the client well.

While the environmental philosophy movement and other ethical explorations of ethics present legitimate and compelling insights on the ethical and moral questions that impact the natural world and particular occupations and industries, the focus of this work is a different sort of ethics (that is, the principles of legal ethics that require, permit, or prohibit specific conduct of lawyers in the practice of law). The rules that form the body of legal ethics in this country have a moral and ethical basis, although they do not pretend to deal exhaustively with the moral questions that arise in legal practice. The ethics rules that apply to the legal profession should also serve the public interest generally and should survive the scrutiny of a philosophical inquiry. The drafters of the rules of ethics recognize the predominance of the public good. They also recognized that for the legal profession to retain the privilege of self-regulation, it must recognize its ultimate responsibility to the public good. The drafters of the ABA Model Rules noted the duty of lawyers and the legal profession to serve the public interest, cautioning against allowing self-interest to influence the drafting of ethics rules. "The legal profession's relative autonomy carries with it special responsibilities of self-government. The profession has a responsibility to assure that its regulations are conceived in the public interest and not in furtherance of parochial or self-interested concerns of the bar."[17] Like the overriding policies of conservation and preservation found in the philosophy of environmental ethics and the adoption of modern laws, the policies of legal ethics must serve the public good.

Application of Ethics Rules to All Lawyers

The obligations of the rules of ethics of each jurisdiction apply to all lawyers practicing within that jurisdiction, whether they are in private, corporate, or government practice. The Preliminary Statement of the Model Code

---

17. ABA Model Rules of Prof'l Conduct Preamble ¶ 11.

of Professional Responsibility states: "Disciplinary Rules should be uniformly applied to all lawyers, regardless of the nature of their professional activities." Thus, the rules apply to the lawyer who works as corporate, "in-house" counsel or practices for many clients in a firm setting. Ethics rules generally apply to government lawyers as well as to private practitioners.[18] Of course, special concerns and considerations may arise because of the context of a type of practice.[19] While lawyers generally are charged with duties to the court as officers of the court, government lawyers are often seen as having a greater responsibility in this regard.

The context within which lawyers work sometimes presents interesting challenges for application of the rules of ethics.[20] Lawyers in some specialties have gone on record as stating the need for wider discretion for lawyers because of the particular type of practice engaged in. For example, the American College of Trust and Estate Counsel has noted the custom and need for trust and estate counsel to represent more than one individual.[21] Similarly, the American Academy of Matrimonial Lawyers has argued for the need to moderate the rule on confidentiality when the welfare of a child is at risk.[22] The Ethics 2000 Commission recognized that prosecutors and other government lawyers have investigative authority that may limit or trump rules of ethics.[23]

---

18. The Preliminary Statement of the MODEL CODE OF PROFESSIONAL RESPONSIBILITY states: "Disciplinary Rules should be uniformly applied to all lawyers, regardless of the nature of their professional activities." *See also* United States *ex rel.* O'Keefe v. McDonnell Douglas Corp., 961 F. Supp. 1288 (E.D. Mo. 1997) (holding Department of Justice lawyers are not exempt from state ethics rules concerning ex parte communications); Comments of Walter Mugdan, U.S. EPA Regional Counsel, New York, N.Y. Comments from 2000 ABA Annual Meeting, July 7, 2000, at presentation "Ethics Issues for Environmental Practitioners."

19. *See generally* Catherine J. Lanctot, *The Duty of Zealous Advocacy and the Ethics of the Federal Government Lawyer: The Three Hardest Questions,* 64 S. CAL. L. REV. 951 (1998); *see also Utah Panel Advises That Government Lawyers May Participate in Lawful Covert Operations,* 70 U.S. LAW WK. 2662 (April 23, 2002) (Utah State Bar Ethics Advisory Opinion Comm., No. 20-05, 3/18/02, determining that Rule 8.4(c) was not meant to prohibit prosecutors or other government attorneys from taking part in covert operations involving deceit).

20. MODEL RULES Scope ¶ 2; *see also* MODEL RULE 1.16(a)(1) (prohibiting representations that "will result in violation of . . . law").

21. American College of Trust and Estate Counsel Commentaries on the Model Rules of Professional Conduct (3d ed. 1999).

22. American Academy of Matrimonial Lawyers, Goals for Family Lawyers, comments on MR 1.6.

23. Posting of Margaret Love, Apr 8 2001 to legalethics-l@lawlib.wuacc.edu.

Foreword   xxi

In fact, numerous examples in the comments to the Model Rules note issues and special considerations arising in corporate[24] and governmental practice.[25]

Need for Guidance

Rules of ethics provide guidance on both general and specific questions. Both the Model Rules and the Model Code of Professional Responsibility refer lawyers to their conscience for the process of resolving ethics issues.[26] The Model Rules state: "Many of a lawyer's professional responsibilities are prescribed in the Rules of Professional Conduct, as well as in substantive and procedural law. However, a lawyer is also guided by personal conscience and the approbation of professional peers."[27] Nevertheless, the lawyer should be wary of allowing his conscience to trump rules of professional conduct. The strong preference should be to comply with the rule. Listening to one's inner voice may not always provide a clear-cut decision in difficult cases. While the ethics rules generally have common sense to recommend them, they are not entirely intuitive. Moreover, it is impossible for any system of ethics rules to address exhaustively the issues of ethics that arise in practice. The lawyer considering a course of action that has ethical implications should think and read broadly, considering the rules, her own conscience, and the approbation of her peers. Even though the sources for ethical inquiries are broad, it makes sense to give special consideration to the ethics rules of her jurisdiction of licensure because, as a practical matter, the power to sanction the lawyer rests with the courts and the disciplinary board of her jurisdiction, and these decision makers will rely on the jurisdiction's rules of ethics.

---

24. For example, the comments to MODEL RULES 1.7, 1.10, 1.13, and other rules deal specifically with situations involving corporate clients. Concerns often arise in the context of representing multiple corporate clients in a single matter in either litigation or nonlitigation matters. *See, e.g.*, Brooklyn Navy Yard Cogeneration Partners, L.P. v. PMNC, 663 N.Y.S.2d 499 (N.Y. Sup. Ct. 1997) (law firm representing subsidiary corporation not disqualified from representing plaintiff suing parent corporation, as work performed for subsidiary was highly specialized and not relevant to present controversy; law firm was highly structured and formal, and work for subsidiary was performed by geographically isolated firm member, rendering remote and speculative any risk of acquisition of parent corporation's confidential information).
25. *See, e.g.*, MODEL RULES OF PROF'L CONDUCT R. 1.11 cmt. 2.
26. *See* Center for Prof'l Responsibility, American Bar Ass'n, THE LEGISLATIVE HISTORY OF THE MODEL RULES OF PROFESSIONAL CONDUCT: THEIR DEVELOPMENT IN THE ABA HOUSE OF DELEGATES 12 (1987); MODEL CODE OF PROF'L RESPONSIBILITY Preamble (1983) ("Each lawyer must find within his own conscience the touchstone against which to test the extent to which his actions should rise above minimum standards.").
27. MODEL RULES Preamble ¶ 6.

Need for Guidance for Environmental Lawyers

The need for additional guidance relating to the rules of legal ethics seems particularly strong in the environmental arena, in part because public safety is often an issue underlying environmental laws. J. William Futrell, president of the Environmental Law Institute, has argued forcefully that environmental lawyers have "heightened duties" because of their role in helping clients comply with the sweeping requirements of environmental law.[28] These heightened duties create a "need for more explicit ethical guidance drafted with environmental lawyers in mind."[29] He also points out that the current ethics rules of the profession fail to take into consideration transactional practice and much of the work of environmental law because they assume as a starting place that all legal representation involves litigation.

> Both the Model Code and the Model Rules implicitly assume that the adversarial system is the lawyer's proper arena. The paradigm case on which most of the rules were modeled is that of the lone criminal defendant, for whom a lawyer is the only means of asserting innocence and who seeks to prevail against the system by stonewalling the government.[30]

Reevaluation of the ABA Rules: Ethics 2000

The American Bar Association responded to the acceleration of change in the practice of law by forming a commission to study and reevaluate the ABA Model Rules of Professional Conduct. Since 1997, the Ethics 2000 Commission has been studying the Model Rules. The ABA House of Delegates adopted some of the revisions to the rules proposed by the Ethics 2000 Commission in February 2002, changing the existing rules significantly in some cases in ways that may affect environmental practice. Consequently, the Detailed Discussion section includes references to the revised rules, though no state has yet adopted the changes. The discussion also retains references to the ABA Model Rules as they existed prior to February 2002 because the state rules currently incorporate the approach of these rules.

Detailed Discussion: Introduction

Throughout the Detailed Discussion, the reader will find comparisons of

---

28. *See generally* William Futrell, *Environmental Ethics, Legal Ethics, and Codes of Professional Responsibility*, 27 Loy. L.A. L. Rev. 825 (1994); Douglas R. Williams, *Loyalty, Independence and Social Responsibility in the Practice of Environmental Law*, 44 St. Louis U. L.J. 1061 (2000); Tanina Rostain, *Ethics Lost: Limitations of Current Approaches to Lawyer Regulation*, 71 S. Cal. L. Rev. 1273 (1998); Sara Beth Watson, *Ethical Issues in Environmental Law Practice*, 55 A.L.I. 253 (2000).

29. Futrell, *supra* at 835.

30. *Id.*

symmetries and asymmetries and tensions between different ethics rules and between the ethics rules and the mandates of other law. This discussion draws attention to potential dangers and pitfalls in legal practice and examines steps that lawyers should consider taking as a matter of prudent practice. The Detailed Discussion also discusses sample letters that can be found in the appendices to the book. Some of the hypotheticals noted in this discussion present extreme or worst-case scenarios. Others seek to dramatize ordinary, day-to-day problems that are likely to arise in environmental practice. Within each part, the Detailed Discussion presents general principles, relevant rules, discussion of relevant decisional law, and hypothetical fact scenarios that illustrate the rules.

Dimensions of Ethical Questions

Questions of legal ethics arise in the practice of law in various ways. Accordingly, when a lawyer consults a particular case or intends to rely on case law, he should take careful note of the context of the decision. For example, disciplinary boards address ethical issues in hearings. They issue opinions and sanctions based on the facts established before them. Ethics committees raise ethics questions and issue advisory opinions on those questions to clarify the rules for practicing lawyers.[31] Additionally, ethics issues arise in court cases in a variety of contexts. A party may allege malpractice based on an argument that the lawyer failed to abide by the rules of ethics. A party may seek to remove opposing counsel through a disqualification motion. A dissatisfied client may bring an action seeking a fee forfeiture or refund based on an argument that the lawyer had a conflict of interest during the representation at issue or was not licensed to practice in the state at the time of the representation.[32]

Each of these modes or settings deals with ethical issues. The context in which the question has arisen may affect the holding or reasoning of the decision maker. For example, in a motion to disqualify counsel, the court dealing with a conflict of interest issue will consider not only the Model Rules but also the conduct of the parties in the case. A court may apply the conflict rules in a way that seems more lenient than opinions from ethics committees and the ABA ethics opinions if, for example, the party raising the disqualification motion failed to raise it in a timely manner. Consider, for example, an environmental suit involving (as is often the case) thousands

---

31. Most bar associations provide that their advisory opinions are an educational service and "should not be relied upon as a substitute for individual legal advice." *See, e.g.,* Illinois Bar Ass'n Op. No. 762 (1982).

32. *See* Koscove v. Bolt, 2001 WL 125900 (Colo. Ct. App. Feb. 15, 2001) (requiring Wisconsin lawyer to refund fees for services in Colorado prior to grant of pro hac vice admission).

of pages of documents and a long history of depositions of experts and witnesses. The lawyer on the case has background that is essentially irreplaceable. If, despite early knowledge of an apparent conflict, a party waits until the eve of trial to seek disqualification of the opponent's lawyer in such a case, a court will consider the reason for the timing of the motion. Failing to raise the issue of a conflict when it becomes known could result in loss of the ability to disqualify opposing counsel.[33] In such a case, the court may find that the opponent's failure to act in a timely fashion and the resulting prejudice justify a denial of the motion to disqualify.

---

33. *See* Lopez v. Precision Papers, Inc., 470 N.Y.S.2d 678 (A.D. 1984) (finding disqualification of lawyers unwarranted and noting delay of movant in seeking disqualification of opposing counsel).

CHAPTER I

Regulation of Lawyers

The regulation of lawyers is often referred to as within the inherent power of courts.[1] Courts have the power to discipline lawyers appearing before them directly or to refer cases of lawyer discipline to the state disciplinary boards.[2] Local, state, and national law associations also play a role in the regulation of lawyers, as do administrative tribunals. Each jurisdiction establishes the rules of ethics related to the practice of law in that jurisdiction, drawing primarily on either the ABA Model Rules or the ABA Model Code. Additionally, agencies, commissions, and other tribunals have inherent authority to discipline lawyers and other professionals that appear before the tribunal.[3] Moreover, the criminal justice system also exerts control on lawyers.[4] "[L]awyers . . . are neither exempt from the reach of the criminal law nor immune from criminal prosecution, the criminal law plays a significant role in regulating lawyers."[5] A

---

1. *See* Nemours Found. v. Gilbane, Aetna Federal Ins. Co., 632 F. Supp. 418 (D. Del. 1986); CHARLES W. WOLFRAM, MODERN LEGAL ETHICS, at 2.2.1 (1986).
2. In *Ausherman v. Bank of America Corp.*, 212 F. Supp. 2d 435 (D.Md. 2002), the trial court referred the issue of a lawyer's conduct to the bar disciplinary committee rather than invoking its inherent authority to discipline lawyers, reasoning that the lawyer's allegedly deceitful conduct in connection with settlement negotiations was not closely connected to the issues before the court. After long and frustrating refusals by the lawyer for plaintiffs in an action alleging misuse of credit information, the court ordered the lawyer to be deposed and to respond personally to appropriate discovery requests. In the deposition, the lawyer acknowledged that he had lied in a letter offering to settle the case. *Id.* at 439.
3. *See, e.g.*, Herman v. Dulles, 205 F.2d 715, 716 (D.C. Cir. 1953) (recognizing the implied power of International Claims Commission to prescribe rules setting standards of practice and disciplining lawyers and affirming revocation after fair investigation, notice, hearing, and opportunity to answer to provide due process).
4. *See* Bruce A. Green, *The Criminal Regulation of Lawyers*, 67 FORDHAM L. REV. 327 (1998).
5. *Id.* at 327 (noting the danger of overcriminalization of lawyer conduct that violates professional norms).

lawyer who could face criminal liability for conduct in connection with a representation may refuse to testify under the Fifth Amendment.[6] In disciplinary proceedings, however, such a refusal to testify may create an adverse inference.

Scholars speak of the U.S. system of regulating lawyers as a matter of "self-regulation." Movements toward placing more controls on lawyers and establishing more uniform controls have been common, however.[7] For example, currently, the U.S. Judicial Conference has under consideration proposals for a uniform rule of professional conduct in federal courts.[8] Despite the efforts of the ABA to foster uniformity of approach throughout the states and despite the influence of the ABA Model Rules, numerous examples of divergent authority exist—another reason careful study of the rules of individual jurisdictions is essential. As a practical matter, courts have the power to recognize the role of the lawyer as something more than a "hired gun."[9] The best practice for the lawyer who has an ethical problem or concern is to talk with the office in charge of lawyer discipline in the state. Nevertheless, the study of the principles that inform the rules of each jurisdiction is a worthy endeavor and a more practical approach than attempting to exhaustively analyze the rules of each jurisdiction.

The Preamble to the Model Rules acknowledges the power of courts over lawyers: "ultimate authority over the legal profession is vested largely in the courts."[10] Nevertheless, the Model Rules seek to insulate the lawyer from evaluation by a court or disciplinary board for a decision to maintain client confidences. For example, the Scope section states that the lawyer's "exercise of discretion not to disclose information under Rule 1.6 should not be subject to

---

6. *See* Geoffrey C. Hazard, Jr. & Cameron Beard, *A Lawyer's Privilege Against Self-Incrimination in Professional Disciplinary Proceedings*, 96 YALE L.J. 1060, 1066–67 (1987).

7. David B. Wilkens, *Who Should Regulate Lawyers?*, 105 HARV. L. REV. 799 (1992) (analyzing disciplinary, liability, enforcement, and legislative systems to enforce professional norms against lawyers, rejecting the ABA's view that a properly functioning disciplinary process can effectively control lawyer misconduct, and concluding that multiple systems are needed to effectively manage lawyers).

8. *See Federal Judges Study New Option for Uniform Rule on Attorney Conduct,* 68 U.S. LAW WEEK 2614.

9. *See, e.g.*, Transcraft, Inc. v. Galvin Stalmack Kirschner & Clark, 39 F.3d 812, 817 (7th Cir. 1994) (noting that lawyer "who takes Law Day rhetoric seriously, who sincerely believes that he has a dual duty, to his client and to the law, and acts on his belief, may lose some clients to his less scrupulous competitors but he should not be deemed to be courting a tort judgment").

10. *See* Preamble to MODEL RULES OF PROF'L CONDUCT [hereinafter MODEL RULES].

reexamination."[11] This statement is not content-neutral. It advocates protecting the lawyer from review by courts or state disciplinary boards of professional responsibility, but only when the lawyer maintains the code of silence, choosing not to reveal client information. Similarly, Comment 21 to Model Rule 1.6 recognizes the power of other law but counsels against applying other law. "[A] lawyer may be obligated or permitted by other provisions of law to give information about a client. Whether another provision of law supersedes Rule 1.6 is a matter of interpretation beyond the scope of these rules, but a presumption should exist against such a supersession."[12] Despite these admonitions from the drafters of the Model Rules, control of lawyers is properly within the realm of courts, boards, and legislatures. While bar associations have had significant influence in this area, courts are the official arbiters of disputes and it is their role to consider both statutory and common law in determining disputes—even when the disputant is a lawyer.

Regulation of Government Lawyers

Many environmental lawyers represent governmental agencies at the federal, state, and local level. EPA, the Army Corps of Engineers, the Soil Conservation Service, the Bureau of Land Management, and other agencies hire numerous lawyers to conduct the business of the agencies and to represent the agencies in disputes. Moreover, the National Environmental Policy Act (NEPA) places responsibility on all federal agencies to ensure that their actions do not create significant adverse impacts on the environment, creating a need for each agency to allocate time and legal expertise to environmental issues. Many states have created similar duties on the part of state agencies.[13] These and other laws create a need for environmental lawyers in government representation. Like all lawyers, these lawyers are subject to the rules of legal ethics imposed by their jurisdictions.[14] Like other government lawyers, environmen-

---

11. *See* MODEL RULES Scope 20 (1983).

12. MODEL RULE 1.6 cmt. 21 (1983).

13. *See* Jonathan Poisner, *A Civic Republican Perspective on the National Environmental Policy Act's Process for Citizen Participation*, 26 ENVTL. L. 53, 55 (1996) (noting the state's adoption of NEPA process for state agencies); J.B. Ruhl, *Biodiversity Conservation and the Ever-Expanding Web of Federal Laws Regulating Nonfederal Lands: Time for Something Completely Different?*, 66 U. COLO. L. REV. 555 (1995) (noting that projects that do not receive federal funding are subject to scrutiny by virtue of state legislation that presents similar mandates at the state level).

14. Comment 2 to Model Rule 1.11 provides: "A lawyer representing a government agency, whether employed or specially retained by the government, is subject to the Rules of Professional Conduct." The Model Rules make clear that the requirements of Model Rule

4 ISSUES OF LEGAL ETHICS IN THE PRACTICE OF ENVIRONMENTAL LAW

tal lawyers who work for the government often are regarded as having special responsibilities to the public and to the individuals involved in disputes with the government. These factors combine to make the context of government legal work an important segment of environmental law, one that demands considerable care in balancing the competing interests at issue in ethics rules as well as in legal issues. For these reasons, this work focuses separately on the issues of confidentiality, candor, conflicts, client status, the anticontact rule, and other ethical issues as they apply specifically to lawyers representing governmental entities.

While it is clear that the Model Rules apply to government lawyers as well as nongovernment lawyers,[15] it is also clear that the role of the government lawyer differs from that of the non-government lawyer in some cases, often in complicated ways. For example, in the area of confidentiality, the Revised Model Rule 1.13 notes that "when the client is a governmental organization, a different balance may be appropriate between maintaining confidentiality and assuring that the wrongful official act is prevented or rectified because public business is involved."[16] Government lawyers are often charged with protecting the public interest, a mission that can be difficult to decipher in some cases.

> The fact that agency life is often marked by inter-agency rivalries (Agriculture may be warring with the EPA on land use) is no argument for maintaining that a lawyer should be responsible to the agency in its role as part-protector of the public interest. Although there are specific jobs to be done, often under specific legislative mandates, that is no reason to think of a government agency as responsible only to one or another aspect of the public interest. Such thinking allows the internecine warfare to continue instead of fostering a spirit of cooperation among multitudinous government groups.[17]

1.13 apply to government lawyers as well as corporate lawyers. *See* MODEL RULE 1.13 cmt. 6.

15. *See* Catherine J. Lanctot, *The Duty of Zealous Advocacy and the Ethics of the Federal Government Lawyer: The Three Hardest Questions*, 64 S. CAL. L. REV. 951, 968 (1991) (noting that the ABA declined to create different ethical rules for government lawyers despite a request from the Federal Bar Association); MODEL RULE 1.13 cmt. 6.

16. MODEL RULE 1.13 cmt. 7, cited favorably by RESTATEMENT (THIRD) OF THE LAW GOVERNING LAWYERS § 97 cmt. j.

17. Robert P. Lawry, *Who Is the Client of the Federal Government Lawyer? An Analysis of the Wrong Question*, 37 FED. CIR. BAR J. 61 (1978).

While the Model Rules regulate all lawyers, they seem to be drafted with the private lawyer in mind rather than counsel for the government. The mismatch between assumptions about the lawyer role in the world of private representation and that of government work can lead to difficulties. For example, the obligation of a lawyer to invoke the attorney-client privilege to protect a client from compelled disclosure of information is more difficult to apply when the client is the United States government or another governmental entity.[18] The government lawyer's duty of confidentiality may allow greater leeway for protection of government information in some cases and less than the ordinary setting requires in other cases. For example, in *Frost v. Perry*, plaintiffs alleged violations of the Resource Conservation and Recovery Act (RCRA) in the storage and disposal of classified waste at a classified Air Force facility.[19] Counsel for the plaintiffs sent a letter to the government requesting the specific name and location of the site. The government refused to supply the information, but stipulated that the site may be called "the operating location near Groom Lake." In ruling on the plaintiffs' motion to compel an answer, the court held that plaintiffs could not compel government defendants to reveal the name of an operation in violation of RCRA where the information was considered to be a matter of national security. The court also found that Congress did not intend to supersede this privilege through statutory language allowing the President to exempt certain facilities if it is in the interest of the United States.[20] On the other hand, laws that mandate transparency in government operations provide access to a great deal of information held by the federal government.[21]

The question of what rule governs a government lawyer's conduct can present difficult questions as well. "[F]ederal lawyers are generally subject to the profession's ethics codes in two different forms: one of the model codes adopted by the American Bar Association is directly applicable by agency regulation, and a state code (either of the state of admission or that of practice or perhaps both) is applicable through the state's disciplinary mechanism."[22] Likewise, government lawyers sometimes face difficult issues regarding what person to listen to for client decisions.

---

18. Michael Stokes Paulsen, *Who "Owns" the Government's Attorney-Client Privilege?*, 83 MINN. L. REV. 473 (1998) (arguing that, like corporate entities, the federal government has the right to protect communications of its officers and employees under the attorney-client privilege).

19. Frost v. Perry, 161 F.R.D. 434 (D. Nev. 1995).

20. *Id.*

21. *See, e.g.,* Freedom of Information Act (FOIA), 5 U.S.C. § 552.

22. Roger C. Cramton, *The Lawyer As Whistleblower: Confidentiality and the Government Lawyer*, 5 GEO. J. LEGAL ETHICS 291, 293 (1991).

6 ISSUES OF LEGAL ETHICS IN THE PRACTICE OF ENVIRONMENTAL LAW

Numerous difficulties come with representation of governmental entities. The special role of government lawyers heightens the difficulty of balancing the lawyer's duty in such varied contexts as the duty of candor owed by the lawyer to the court and to opponents, the lawyer's duty of confidentiality to the government client and his duty of disclosure to the public, and other puzzles of balancing rights. The duty of confidentiality applies to government lawyers as well as other lawyers. The government lawyer's duty of confidentiality is subject to numerous instances of the need to balance duties to the client and to the public. For example, the Freedom of Information Act presents a statutory balancing of the government's right to retain information with the right of the public to obtain information in the possession of the government. In some circumstances, the need for secrecy to protect public safety or national security may prevail, however.[23] Likewise, the question of whether a government lawyer may be required or permitted to withdraw from representation may be considerably more difficult than in the private sphere. The existence of a conflict or knowledge that the client is engaged in an ongoing crime or a fraud applies to government lawyers as well as private practice lawyers. The significance of the decisions of governmental entities can raise profound policy debates that may mean a lawyer will withdraw from the representation because the lawyer disagrees with the initiatives of the current administration.[24] Additionally, the prohibition against contacts with persons represented by counsel is qualified with respect to government entities in order to accommodate the constitutional right of citizens and residents to petition the government.

Higher Responsibilities of Government Lawyers

Numerous courts and scholars suggest that government lawyers have a higher ethical duty than their private counterparts.[25] Both the Model Rules and Re-

---

23. *See, e.g.,* Frost v. Perry, 161 F.R.D. 434 (D. Nev. 1995) (holding that plaintiffs may not compel federal agency to reveal classified information when confidentiality is in interest of national security). This issue is discussed further in the section on confidentiality.

24. *See, e.g.,* Elizabeth Shogren, *A Natural Split With Bush, and Many Quit,* L.A. TIMES, June 3, 2002, at A1 (reporting resignation of Michele Merkel, EPA staff attorney, who departed EPA, asserting that Administrator Christine Whitman told her EPA would downplay enforcement in favor of encouraging companies to stop polluting voluntarily); Faye Fiore, *Top EPA Enforcement Official Quits, Blasts Bush Policy,* L.A. TIMES, Mar. 1, 2002, at A17 (resigning as director of EPA Office of Regulatory Enforcement, accusing Bush administration of delay on Clean Air Act lawsuits filed against nine power companies and interfering with EPA's ability to enforce law).

25. *See, e.g.,* Silverman v. Ehrlich Beer Corp., 687 F. Supp. 67, 69–70 (S.D.N.Y. 1987);

Chapter 1: Regulation of Lawyers 7

statement note that the role of the government lawyer may differ from that of the nongovernment lawyer in some cases. "[W]hen the client is a governmental organization, a different balance may be appropriate between maintaining confidentiality and assuring that the wrongful official act is prevented or rectified because public business is involved."[26] The Scope section of the Model Rules also suggests that government lawyers have additional powers and responsibility as compared with private lawyers. A government lawyer "may also have authority to represent the 'public interest' in circumstances where a private lawyer would not be authorized to do so. These rules do not abrogate any such authority."[27]

Lawyer Client Relationship (Government Lawyers): Special Issues

The question of client status can present novel issues in environmental actions as a result of the involvement of multiple government agencies in an action. To explore this point, note that CERCLA specifically provides for liability of government entities by including such entities in its definition of "person."[28] Assume that EPA sues potentially responsible parties at a Superfund site. The named defendants bring a third-party action against a governmental agency such as the Department of Defense or the Department of Energy, alleging that the agencies discharged hazardous substances at the site. In such a cost recovery action, the United States is both a plaintiff and a defendant. At first blush, it may seem that the additional agencies joined as defendants create a conflict of interest for the lawyer representing EPA. Such a representation goes forward, nevertheless, presumably because the government agencies consented to the representation based on a judgment that the representation is not adversely affected. This problem does not surface in litigation often, perhaps because the agencies often deal with the issue without litigation by such means as memoranda of understanding.

Gray v. Rhode Island Dept. of Children, Youth and Families, 937 F. Supp. 153 (D.R.I. 1996); State v. Irizarry, 639 A.2d 305 (N.J. Super. 1994); *In re* City of Newark, 346 N.J. Super. 460 (N.J. Super. Jan. 14, 2002); Douglas v. Donovan, 704 F.2d 1276, 1279–80 (D.C. Cir. 1983) (noting that government lawyers "have special responsibilities to both this court and the public at large"); EEOC v. Waterfront Comm'n of New York Harbor, 665 F. Supp. 197, 201 (S.D.N.Y. 1987) (stating that government lawyers should be held to "highest standards of the Bar").

26. MODEL RULE 1.13 cmt. 7, cited favorably by RESTATEMENT (THIRD) OF THE LAW GOVERNING LAWYERS § 97 cmt. j.

27. MODEL RULES Scope.

28. *See* 42 U.S.C. § 9601(21); § 9607(a).

8 ISSUES OF LEGAL ETHICS IN THE PRACTICE OF ENVIRONMENTAL LAW

The arrangement may also be seen as violating the principle that a party cannot sue himself.[29] This principle does not necessarily result in a bar to a case involving governmental agencies, however. For example, in the case of *United States v. Interstate Commerce Commission*,[30] the United States sued the Interstate Commerce Commission seeking to have an order of the Commission set aside. The District Court for the D.C. Circuit dismissed the case on the basis that Government could not maintain a suit against itself.[31] The United States Supreme Court noted the problem but reversed the district court's decision, holding that the principle against suing oneself did not apply.[32] The Supreme Court also rejected this argument in *United States v. Nixon*.[33]

Similarly, courts have held that the government may represent different interest in litigation, particularly when the obligation arises from legislation. In *Nevada v. United States*, the United States Supreme Court held that the federal government acted properly in representing both a tribal reservation and the water project in actions for allocation of water rights. (The United States had acted on behalf of an Indian reservation in a prior action.) The defendants asserted that the plaintiffs were precluded from requesting additional water rights by a previous suit. The court of appeals held that the case lacked the required adversity because the United States represented both the tribe and the project landowners. The Supreme Court reversed, holding that when Congress creates statutory obligations for the government, it may properly perform multiple tasks.[34]

If it is assumed that the lawyers for different agencies all work for one client, then the government lawyers would seem to have a duty to reveal information to each other.[35] This theory, referred to here as the "unitary client theory," suggests that defense agreements that seek confidentiality between the agencies named as potentially responsible parties (PRPs) and other PRPs may result in withholding information from the client, the United States government.[36] For example, PRPs at a Superfund site sometimes reveal information about their contributions at a site as a way of determining their appropriate allocation for cleanup costs. Before sharing information to establish quantities

---

29. *See* Globe & Rutgers Fire Ins. Co. v. Hines, 273 F. 774 (2d Cir. 1921).
30. 337 U.S. 426 (1949).
31. 78 F. Supp. 580 (D.D.C. Cir. 1948).
32. 337 U.S. 426, 431.
33. United States v. Nixon, 418 U.S. 683 (1974); *see also* Dean v. Harrington, 668 F. Supp. 646 (E.D. Tenn. 1987).
34. Nevada v. United States, 463 U.S. 110 (1983).
35. This is the view expressed by lawyers for DOJ at ethics seminars. Notes of author on file.
36. *See* 31 TRENDS 11–12 (Mar./Apr. 2000).

of the contribution, PRPs will ordinarily enter a confidentiality agreement, promising not to reveal the information disclosed for the purposes of a negotiated settlement. The Department of Defense or any other department included as a defendant would seem to be unable to honor the confidentiality agreement under the view that all federal lawyers represent one client. If a government lawyer enters an agreement to exchange confidential information with nonfederal defendants and to refrain from revealing that information to other agencies, the lawyer may have seriously compromised her client's interests or misrepresented her ability to maintain confidentiality of the information. In other words, lawyers for the agency could not hold such information secret from the EPA. They must share with the EPA any information they learned in the settlement conferences about the other PRPs and their contributions to the site since, under the unitary theory, the EPA (like the other agency) is the lawyer's client.[37]

The environmental citizen suit of *Kasza v. Browner* presented a claim of conflict of interest because the same lawyers represented different government agencies. In this case, former workers at a classified facility operated by the United States Air Force brought actions under the Resource Conservation and Recovery Act of 1976 (RCRA) against the Air Force[38] and the Environmental Protection Agency, alleging violations by the government entities.[39] The plaintiffs brought two separate actions, one against the Air Force, in *Frost v. Perry*, and another against the Environmental Protection Agency, in *Kasza v. Browner*.[40] The same team of lawyers represented the two federal agencies in the cases. The district court granted summary judgment in favor of the Air Force in *Frost* and held the action in *Kasza* was moot because the EPA complied with the regulations after the action was filed. On appeal, the plaintiffs argued that the trial court erred in denying their motion to disqualify the DOJ lawyers, contending that the DOJ lawyers were guilty of a conflict of interest in representing both federal defendants. On appeal, the court held the plaintiffs in *Frost* lacked standing to assert conflict of interest. "We have difficulty seeing how Frost has standing to complain about a possible conflict of interest arising out of common representation of defendants in different civil actions, having nothing to do with her own representation."[41] Noting that the typical

---

37. Walter Mugdan, U.S. EPA Regional Counsel, New York, N.Y. Comments from 2000 ABA Annual Meeting, July 7, 2000, at presentation "Ethics Issues for Environmental Practitioners."
38. Frost v. Perry, 161 F.R.D. 434 (D. Nev. 1995).
39. Kasza v. Browner, 133 F.3d 1159 (1998).
40. *Id.*
41. *Id.* at 1171.

10 ISSUES OF LEGAL ETHICS IN THE PRACTICE OF ENVIRONMENTAL LAW

disqualification motion is lodged by a former client who has standing because he is affected by the representation of another client, the court found no evidence that plaintiffs were affected by the common representation.[42]

Unauthorized Practice of Law

The risk of running afoul of the rule on unauthorized practice is particularly pronounced in areas such as environmental law where lawyers represent numerous corporate clients with offices and facilities in far-flung locations both within the country and in other countries. Many U.S. law firms maintain offices in several cities and states and countries. These major firms often include a division specializing in environmental law for national and international clients. Corporations increasingly use in-house corporate counsel for as much of their legal work as possible, sometimes giving in-house counsel projects that relate to business properties in states other than that of the in-house counsel's state of licensure.[43] The frequency with which lawyers represent corporations and individuals who are located outside the state in which the lawyers are licensed has increased along with business dealings across great distances. Lawyers travel to other states to meet with business clients, to interview witnesses, or to negotiate or arbitrate disputes. In some states, pro hac vice admission is not available. One scholar has suggested that in the modern world a lawyer should be allowed to practice throughout the country as long as she has a valid license in one state and complies with the requirement of procuring local counsel and other requirements of the state in which the matter is located.[44]

The issue of unauthorized practice is controlled by state statute as well as ethics rules. State statutes prohibit the practice of law both by nonlawyers and by lawyers who are not licensed in the state. The issue of unauthorized practice has arisen more frequently in recent years. The Model Rules deal with the issue in Model Rules 5.5 and 8.5 on unauthorized practice of law and choice of law. Model Rule 5.5 not only prohibits the unauthorized practice of law, it

---

42. *Id.*
43. *See, e.g.,* Tennessee Formal Ethics Opinion 85-F-91 (4/29/85) (finding lawyers admitted to practice in other jurisdictions but not in Tennessee may not practice law in state); Tennessee Formal Ethics Opinion 95-F-139 (3/8/96) (holding lawyer's employment by estate-planning company specializing in selling living trusts would violate Code of Professional Responsibility).
44. Ronald C. Minkoff, *One License for Life: A Paradigm for Multijurisdictional Practice,* 11 THE PROFESSIONAL LAWYER 1 (2000); *see also* Mary C. Daly, *Resolving Ethical Conflicts in Multijurisdictional Practice—Is Model Rule 8.5 The Answer, An Answer, or No Answer At All?*, 36 S. TEX. L. REV. 715 (1995).

Chapter 1: Regulation of Lawyers   11

also prohibits lawyers from assisting another person "who is not a member of the bar in the performance of activity that constitutes the unauthorized practice of law."[45] Model Rule 8.5 makes clear that a lawyer is subject to the ethics rules of his jurisdiction of practice for conduct within and without that jurisdiction. The rule states: "A lawyer admitted to practice in this jurisdiction is subject to the disciplinary authority of this jurisdiction, regardless of where the lawyer's conduct occurs. A lawyer may be subject to the disciplinary authority of both this jurisdiction and another jurisdiction where the lawyer is admitted for the same conduct."[46] The rule indicates lawyers are subject to the rules of their jurisdiction of licensure. The effect of this policy is that it creates the possibility that a lawyer could engage in conduct that is a violation in the state in which the conduct occurs but escape discipline because the conduct is not a violation in his state of licensure. The 2002 Revision makes clear that a lawyer is subject to the rules of ethics of any jurisdiction in which he practices.[47] Recognizing the potential of inconsistent mandates to the lawyer, the rule indicates that a lawyer's conduct may have effects in more than one jurisdiction in some cases and seeks to minimize confusion and uncertainty by noting that the conduct of a lawyer should be subject to only one set of rules.[48] Rule 8.5 specifies which set of rules applies in such cases, declaring the choice of law standard. The rule specifies the law to be applied as the jurisdiction of the court in court proceedings. In cases not before a court, Rule 8.5 states that ethics rules of the jurisdiction in which the lawyer principally practices apply. However, the Rule also indicates that when the "predominant effect" of the lawyer's conduct occurs in a jurisdiction other than the jurisdiction in which the lawyer principally practices, the rules of the jurisdiction with the predominant effect apply.[49]

The ABA finalized its deliberations on the issue of multijurisdictional practice in August 2002.[50] After considering the final report of the ABA Commission on Multijurisdictional Practice, the House of Delegates adopted revised Model Rules 5.5 and 8.5, liberalizing the rules in significant ways, permitting practice in jurisdictions other than the lawyer's state of licensure in carefully described situations. Revised Model Rule 5.5 permits a lawyer to engage in activities outside his state of licensure, including pro hac vice appearances and activities undertaken in anticipation of a pro hac vice admission

---

45. MODEL RULE 5.5 (1983).
46. MODEL RULE 8.5(a) (1983).
47. MODEL RULE 8.5 (2002)
48. MODEL RULE 8.5, cmt. 3 (1983).
49. MODEL RULE 8.5 (1983).
50. *See* http://www.abanet.org/cpr/mjp-home.html (last visited Mar. 22, 2003).

12   ISSUES OF LEGAL ETHICS IN THE PRACTICE OF ENVIRONMENTAL LAW

when local counsel is involved in a substantive way. It also allows practice reasonably related to a lawyer's practice in his home jurisdiction, participation in ADR proceedings, and certain activities by in-house counsel. Revised Model Rule 8.5 made clear that the states have the right to discipline lawyers who are not licensed in the state. It notes the "authority of a jurisdiction to discipline lawyers licensed in another jurisdiction who practice law within their jurisdiction pursuant to the provisions of Rule 5.5 or other law."[51] The issues raised here are discussed in depth in the section on Multijurisdictional Practice.

Problems of unauthorized practice of law arise frequently as a result of the way both lawyers and clients do business in a modern and increasingly global world. The court's or jurisdiction's rule on unauthorized practice can have dramatic results. For example, in *Wellmore Coal Corporation v. Harman Mining Corporation*, the Virginia Supreme Court dismissed a company's appeal of a $6 million judgment based on the failure of lawyers to include a signature of a lawyer licensed in Virginia. The court held failure to include a signature of a Virginia lawyer violated the rules on notice of appeal. Additionally, the court held that this failure was not merely clerical error. When the lawyers amended the notice of appeal to include a signature of a Virginia lawyer, the court rejected the notice stating that "an amendment presupposes a valid instrument as its object." The court denied the party the right to amend on this basis.[52]

Peer Evaluation

Each state has a disciplinary board that hears complaints lodged against lawyers. Bar associations (local, state, and national associations) sponsor continuing legal education (CLE) programs and have ethics committees that provide opinions on issues of legal ethics. The environmental law sections of some bars also present CLE in which lawyers in environmental practice share information and views on topics relating to the particular ethics problems that frequently arise in environmental law. These entities form another kind of informal regulation, providing feedback and peer review of lawyers in all fields and those who focus their practice in the environmental arena. Such sections also provide education geared to help members understand the law of the area and acquire skills needed for the practice in this particular area.

Role of Bar Associations

The ABA has played an active role in the regulation of lawyers by enunciating

---

51. *Report of the ABA Commission on Multijurisdictional Practice* (Aug. 2002).
52. Wellmore Coal Corp. v. Harman Mining Corp., 568 S.E.2d 671 (Va. 2002).

Chapter 1: Regulation of Lawyers   13

standards of professional conduct for over a decade. The ABA Model Rules of Professional Conduct and the ABA Model Code of Professional Responsibility, which preceded it, are prime examples of this sort of regulation. The models are adopted by states either through the court system or by legislation. The ethical precepts stated in these rules provide the primary means for regulating lawyers. When lawyers violate the prescriptive rules, they are subject to sanctions.[53] The ABA Standing Committee on Ethics and Professional Responsibility issues Formal Opinions that explain the application of the rules and principles of legal ethics in response to specific problems or questions.[54] The Committee issues advisory opinions rather than decisions in actual disciplinary cases, taking up issues that it believes need clarification.[55] These formal ethics opinions are widely available in law libraries. They can also be found using hypertext links to the ABA ETHICSearch Web site, on an annotated list of Internet ethics research sites located on the ABA Center for Professional Responsibility Web site, and by online research services such as Westlaw and LEXIS.[56]

In recent years, many states have formed professionalism commissions, stimulated in part by a 1996 conference of chief justices of state courts that developed "a national action plan on lawyer conduct and professionalism."[57] While such committees are not directly involved in lawyer discipline, they provide resources for lawyers and help strengthen norms of the profession.

---

53. *See* MODEL RULES Scope.
54. In the past, the ABA Standing Committee on Ethics and Professional Responsibility issued both formal and informal ethics opinions. In recent years, the Committee has issued all opinions in the form of formal opinions.
55. The formal opinions of the ABA Standing Committee on Ethics and Professional Responsibility appear in compilations available from the ABA Service Center (800-285-2221).
56. The following Westlaw databases include formal opinions and other information on ethics rules and opinions: ABA-BNA (the ABA-BNA Lawyers' Manual on Professional Conduct); METH-EO (the full text of ethics opinions from approximately 20 states); METH-CS (state caselaw that focuses on ethics and professional discipline); ETH-TP (a collection of law review articles/publications that focus on legal ethics); ABA-MRPC (the ABA Model Rules of Professional Conduct); and ABA-ETHOP (ABA ethics opinions). LEXIS has two sources: The National Reporter on Legal Ethics and Professional Responsibilities, which provides state bar formal and informal opinions on legal ethics and professional responsibility, and the ABA formal and informal opinionate. The ABA databases include: ETHICS;ETHICS (ABA Codes and Ethics Opinions Combined); ETHCS;FOPIN (ABA Formal Ethics Opinions); ABA;INFOP (ABA Information Ethics Opinions); and ABA;CODES (ABA Code of Professional Conduct & Code of Judicial Conduct).
57. A GUIDE TO PROFESSIONALISM COMMISSIONS ix (2001).

14 ISSUES OF LEGAL ETHICS IN THE PRACTICE OF ENVIRONMENTAL LAW

Such professionalism commissions also provide mentoring programs for new lawyers, promote continuing legal education, and develop proposals for reforming the law and the judicial system.[58] In 2000, the ABA published *A Guide to Professionalism Commissions* to assist in the establishment of professional commissions in all states.[59]

The Role of State Boards of Professional Responsibility[60]

Most states have a board, committee, or a panel that deals with claims relating to lawyer compliance with the state's rules of professional conduct. Such a body (herein "board") conducts hearings, finds facts, makes conclusions of law, and determines or recommends sanctions when it finds that the respondent lawyer has failed to comply with the state's rules of legal ethics. The decisions possible range from a finding in favor of the lawyer to sanctions, including a recommendation of disbarment. These boards are made up of lawyers who serve as fact finders in claims brought against lawyers. The disciplinary system also has staff lawyers who may answer questions addressed to them by lawyers of the jurisdiction and who undertake investigations of lawyers in response to complaints.

Additionally, boards or ethics committees of state bar associations issue formal and informal opinions to assist and guide lawyers regarding specific issues of legal ethics, at times in response to questions addressing such issues. These boards are typically a separate entity from the board or committee that conducts hearings in response to specific complaints. In many states, the bar association is the entity that issues ethics opinions. In some of these states, the disciplinary office provides informal guidance to lawyers seeking advice on ethics issues. In some states, the disciplinary office issues informal advisory opinions and the advisory committee of the bar issues formal opinions.

The Disciplinary Process

An Overview

A lawyer may be subject to an investigation based on a written complaint from a client or other person alleging that the lawyer violated an ethical obligation. A Board of Professional Responsibility or disciplinary counsel may also initiate an investigation of a lawyer as a result of other information. In

---

58. *Id.*

59. *Id.*

60. Background on this section was provided by Sara Rittman, Deputy Chief Disciplinary Counsel, Office of the Chief Disciplinary Counsel of the Supreme Court of Missouri.

Chapter 1: Regulation of Lawyers   15

any case, the staff lawyer or Board normally provides a written statement to the lawyer who is the subject of the investigation. Typically, the staff lawyer sends a copy of the complaint from the client to the subject lawyer. After an investigation, the staff lawyer in charge of the investigation reports to the Board or Disciplinary Counsel, recommending some disposition of the matter. The recommendation could be dismissal of the complaint, admonition, or a formal hearing. If the disciplinary counsel issues an informal private admonition, the lawyer ordinarily has the option of requesting a formal hearing rather than accepting the admonition. A formal hearing may be held as the result of the recommendation by disciplinary counsel, a determination by the Board, or a request by the lawyer investigated. Before the hearing, the Board ordinarily will provide formal written charges to the lawyer, and the lawyer may file a response to the charges. Generally, the rules of procedure of the state of licensure are applicable to the disciplinary proceeding. These include some degree of discovery, pretrial conferences, and the ability to subpoena witnesses. After discovery, the Board conducts a nonjury trial and issues its written findings. In some jurisdictions, the lawyer may file an appeal to the findings. Generally, a judge appointed by the supreme court of the state will hear the appeal. In many jurisdictions the supreme court of the state makes the final decision. In the event that discipline is imposed, it may be in the form of a reprimand, a public censure, probation, suspension, or disbarment.[61]

Readmission

In recent years, lawyers have been disbarred from the practice of law in increasing numbers.[62] For example, F. Lee Bailey was disbarred by the Florida Supreme Court for mishandling $6 million in stock for one of his clients, a drug trafficker now serving a life sentence. In May 2002, Bailey's disbarment was upheld by the U.S. Supreme Court. Bailey may reapply for his license after five years.[63] Similarly, Maryland lobbyist Bruce C. Bereano was dis-

---

61. *See* Elizabeth J. Cohen, *The Scarlet 'L': A Suspended or Disbarred Lawyer Has a Tough Time Getting Any Legal Work*, 87 A.B.A. J. 70 (Apr. 2001).

62. Disbarments and suspensions appear to have increased at a greater pace than the number of private practitioners. *See* Robert W. Emerson, *Rule 2(e) Revisited: SEC Disciplining of Attorneys Since In re Carter*, 29 Am. Bus. L.J. 155 (1991) (relying on American Bar Ass'n Standing Comm. on Professional Discipline & Center for Professional Responsibility, Survey on Lawyer Disciplinary Systems—1988 Data (1989), at I ("Trends 1986-1988"), n. 95-96 & 98-99 to compare the suspension rate in state court in 1977 (620), 1984 (989), and 1988 (1,384).

63. *Bailey Can't Have License*, Orlando Sentinel Tribune, May 14, 2002, LEXIS, News, News Group File, Most Recent 60 Days.

barred after being convicted in Maryland Federal District Court for mail fraud.[64] Bereano received a sentence of five years' probation on each of seven counts of mail fraud for his practice of using money from clients to make illicit campaign contributions and billing the clients for "legislative entertainment."[65]

In most jurisdictions, a lawyer who has been suspended or disbarred may seek readmission to practice after a specified period of time has elapsed, typically five years. The decision of whether to grant the request for readmission is scrutinized under a different standard than the admission process for a new law graduate seeking admission. Courts generally place a higher burden on the disbarred lawyer who seeks readmission. The standard of proof in such cases is generally clear and convincing evidence that the lawyer should be readmitted.[66]

History of ABA Rules

In 1908, the ABA promulgated the Canons of Professional Ethics, grouping 32 canons as a nonexclusive statement of the duties of lawyers.[67] In 1922, the ABA authorized the Committee on Professional Ethics to interpret the ethics rules and to hear charges of professional misconduct against members of the association. In 1958, the Association divided this committee into two committees: the Committee on Professional Ethics and the Committee on Professional Grievances.[68] In 1969, the ABA superseded the Canons with the ABA Model Code of Professional Responsibility. Again, in 1983, the ABA revised its model with the promulgation of the Model Rules of Professional Conduct. During these years, the ABA adopted individual amendments to the rules. Finally, in 2002, the ABA debated the revisions proposed by the Ethics 2000 Commission and, with changes, adopted the revisions.[69]

---

64. *See In re Bereano*, 719 A.2d 98 (D.C. 1998).
65. *See* United States v. Bereano, 161 F.3d 3 (4th Cir. 1998), *cert. denied,* 526 U.S. 1130 (1999).
66. *See* WOLFRAM, *supra* note 1, 3.5.5, at 132; *see also* Cohen, *The Scarlet 'L', supra* note 61.
67. "The following canons of ethics are adopted by the American Bar Association as a general guide, yet the enumeration of particular duties should not be construed as a denial of the existence of others equally imperative, though not specifically mentioned." ABA CANONS OF PROFESSIONAL ETHICS Preamble.
68. Paul R. Rice, *Attorney-Client Privilege: The Eroding Concept of Confidentiality Should Be Abolished,* 47 DUKE L.J. 853 (1998).
69. For a thorough discussion of the changes proposed by the Commission, see MARGARET COLGATE LOVE, "ABA ETHICS 2000 COMMISSION FINAL REPORT—SUMMARY OF RECOMMENDATIONS (June 9, 2001), *available at* http://www.abanet.org/cpr/e2k-mlove_article.html.

Chapter 1: Regulation of Lawyers 17

The 1969 ABA Model Code included coverage of ethical issues under sections entitled Ethical Considerations. The Code stated that the ethical considerations are "aspirational in character and represent the objectives toward which every member of the profession should strive."[70] Unlike the Ethical Considerations, the Disciplinary Rules are mandatory in nature. The ABA Model Rules of Professional Conduct abandoned this system for marking the boundary between required norms and aspirational principles. While the Model Rules deleted coverage of aspirational principles relating to the practice of law, they expressly recognize the need for application of moral and ethical judgment.[71]

The ABA Model Rules present a system for guiding, inspiring, and judging lawyer conduct through general principles. As with most prospective endeavors, rule making that exhausts all questions of application is impossible. Accordingly, the principles set down in the rules must be interpreted under a rule of reason approach. Certainly, application to the environmental area requires such a reasonable approach to discern a workable rule. For example, Model Rule 1.8 prohibits an aggregate settlement of two or more clients "unless each client consents after consultation" to the settlement. When negotiating on behalf of a public interest group, regarding each member of an organization as the lawyer's client would result in an unworkable rule; it would give a veto power to each individual member of the organization.[72] On the other hand, if the claim brought on behalf of a number of clients is for individual harms rather than for an aggregate harm and aggregate remedy, a reasonable interpretation of the rule seems to require that a lawyer obtain informed consent of each client to settle the case ethically.[73]

The requirement of Rule 1.8(g) that a lawyer proceed to settlement only after all parties he represents have agreed to the settlement can raise difficult factual questions. In *Quintero v. Jim Walter Homes, Inc.*, for example, the court overturned a settlement on the basis that the lawyer had failed to inform his clients "of the nature and settlement amounts of the claims involved." The settlement at issue involved nearly 350 claims of misrepresentation against a builder. The lawyer had failed to inform the parties that they had won a separate judgment against the opponent prior to consenting to a significantly smaller settlement. In the case of *Scamardella v. Illiano*, however, the court

---

70. *See* MODEL CODE OF PROFESSIONAL RESPONSIBILITY Preliminary Statement ¶ 4 .
71. MODEL RULES Preamble & Scope.
72. MODEL RULE 1.13 also makes clear that when an organization is the designated client, the lawyer owes duties to the organizational entity itself rather than to its officers, directors, or other constituent members.
73. *See* MODEL RULE 1.8(g); ABA-BNA Lawyers' Manual on Professional Conduct 51:378.

18   ISSUES OF LEGAL ETHICS IN THE PRACTICE OF ENVIRONMENTAL LAW

refused to overturn a settlement based on the argument that the lawyer did not provide sufficient information about the settlement before the parties agreed to it. The *Scamardella* case involved a wrongful death action in which a lawyer represented the decedent's parents, husband, and child, as well as the decedent's estate. The settlement was for the maximum amount of insurance. The parents of the decedent attacked the settlement, arguing that the lawyer violated a duty to disclose information under Rule 1.8(g). Although the lawyer informed each party of the involvement of other clients in the settlement, the parents argued that the lawyer failed to inform them of the exact share each would have of the settlement proceeds. The court held that the lawyer did not violate Rule 1.8(g).

Statutory Controls

Lawyers, like others, have been held accountable under statutes. For example, in *Bennet v. Berg*,[74] the court refused to dismiss a civil action against lawyers under the Racketeer Influenced and Corrupt Organizations provisions of the Organized Crime Control Act of 1970.[75] Absent a violation of the constitutional doctrine of Separation of Powers, statutory mandates, like common law mandates, may apply to lawyers as well as their clients. The interpretive issue of whether a statute is applicable to lawyers presents a separate question that is dealt with in the section on confidentiality (see pages 129-37). Congress recently passed the Sarbanes-Oxley Act, which requires a new SEC rule speaking directly to lawyers. The Act addresses corporate practices generally and the role of the lawyer in responding to corporate wrongdoing. It charges the SEC with the duty to issue a rule requiring lawyers to report evidence of securities violations "to the chief legal counsel or the chief executive of the company,"[76] and, if necessary, "to the audit committee of the board of directors of the issuer or to another committee of the board of directors comprised solely of directors not employed directly or indirectly by the issuer, or to the board of directors."[77] In March 2002, the ABA appointed a task force to consider amending the Model Rules to enhance the protection of the public against corporate fraud.[78]

---

74. 710 F.2d 1361, 1363–64 (8th Cir. 1983).

75. *See* 18 U.S.C. 1961–68 (1988).

76. 15 U.S.C. § 7245 (2002).

77. *Id.*

78. The ABA Task Force on Corporate Responsibility is chaired by James H. Cheek of Nashville. In its preliminary report, the Task Force recommended amendment of MODEL RULES 1.13 and 1.6 to permit disclosure of corporate misconduct likely to result in substantial injury to financial or property interests.

Judicial Controls

The supreme court of each state regulates lawyers practicing within the state. Courts have inherent power to control admission of lawyers to practice.[79] For example, the Pennsylvania Constitution states that "the Supreme Court shall have the power to prescribe general rules governing . . . admission to the bar and to practice law."[80] Typically, the supreme court of each jurisdiction adopts the rules of legal ethics based on one of the models created by the ABA. In some states, the legislature of the state adopts the rules. Courts and other tribunals have inherent power to regulate the conduct of lawyers who appear in matters before them.[81] Additionally, courts often promulgate local rules of conduct or rules of civility for lawyers practicing within the forum. Judicial control of lawyers has noteworthy significance in the case of environmental laws by virtue of the fact that the judicial system has served as one of the most often used ways to enforce environmental laws.[82] Courts may impose sanctions on both lawyers and their clients in response to violations of discovery or procedural rules, and they may disqualify a lawyer from representing clients in litigation when the court determines that the lawyer's representation results in a conflict of interest.[83] Neither the Model Code nor the Model Rules provides for a cause of action against a lawyer. The ethics rules provide a basis for Boards of Professional Responsibility in making disciplinary decisions. The Scope section of the ABA Model Rules notes the relationship of the Model Rules to the disciplinary procedures of each jurisdiction of licensure. "Failure to comply with an obligation or prohibition imposed by a rule is a basis for invoking the disciplinary process."[84] The Scope section of the Model

---

79. Anderson v. Dunn, 19 U.S. 204 (1821); Link v. Wabash R.R. Co., 370 U.S. 626 (1962).

80. *See* P.A. Const. art. V, § 10; *see also* Haymond v. Lundy, 2000 WL 1824174 (E.D. Pa. Dec. 12, 2000) (holding unconstitutional state statute creating private action against lawyers aiding nonlawyer practice as an infringement of the state supreme court's power to regulate lawyers).

81. *See, e.g., In re* First City Bancorporation, 282 F.3d 864 (5th Cir. 2002) (affirming sanction against lawyer for obnoxious and unprofessional conduct).

82. Margaret Graham Tebo, *Fertile Waters*, 87 ABA J. 36 (Feb. 2001) (noting favorable law to environmental plaintiffs and new trial tactics that plaintiffs' lawyers developed in the big tobacco cases).

83. *See* Darryl Van Duch, *Harvard Adversary Slammed: Employee's Counsel Sanctioned $94,718*, NAT'L L. J. (Apr. 10, 2001) (ordering lawyer to pay Harvard University legal fees expended in moving for sanctions for the lawyer's attempts to use "informal" discovery to attempt to prove that its client, Kathleen Stanford, had been passed over for promotions in violation of law).

84. *See* MODEL RULES Scope [17].

ISSUES OF LEGAL ETHICS IN THE PRACTICE OF ENVIRONMENTAL LAW

Rules also attempts to limit the use of the rules to disciplinary matters, stating that a "violation of a rule should not give rise to a cause of action nor should it create any presumption that a legal duty has been breached."[85] The Scope section also indicates a desire to insulate lawyers from judicial scrutiny. It states that "exercise of discretion not to disclose information under Rule 1.6 should not be subject to reexamination."[86] This statement encourages courts and state boards of professional responsibility to refuse to judge a lawyer's decision to remain silent in the face of peril to a nonclient. Similarly, the Model Code discourages the use of its disciplinary rules to determine civil liability.[87]

Despite this attempt by the drafters of ethics rules to insulate lawyers from the use of the Model Rules to establish liability against a lawyer, courts have the power to rely on the rules of the applicable jurisdiction of licensure or other statements of professional standards in assessing and determining a tort cause of action brought against a lawyer by a client or others.[88] Courts also look to professional standards in making determinations of duty and liability in causes of action against other professionals.[89]

Limiting Use of Rules: 2002 Revision

The 2002 version of the Model Rules continues to maintain the position that violation of the rules should not give rise to a cause of action against a lawyer. The Preamble to the Rules states: "Violation of a rule should not *itself* give rise to a cause of action *against a lawyer* nor should it create any presumption *in such a case* that a legal duty has been breached. *In addition, violation of a rule does not necessarily warrant any other nondisciplinary remedy, such as disqualification of a lawyer in pending litigation.*"[90] As with the 1983 version, the 2002 Preamble seeks to insulate the lawyer from use of the rules by opponents. Both versions state: "The fact that a rule is a just basis for a lawyer's self-assessment, or for sanctioning a lawyer under the administration of a

---

85. *See* MODEL RULES Scope [18].

86. *See* MODEL RULES Scope [20].

87. *See* MODEL CODE Preamble (1980).

88. *See also* Charles Wolfram, *The Code of Professional Responsibility as a Measure of Attorney Liability in Civil Litigation*, 30 S.C. L. REV. 281 (1979).

89. *See, e.g.*, Horne v. Patton, 287 So. 2d 824, 827–31 (Ala. 1973) (finding that doctors may not reveal confidences patients disclosed to them in the course of medical treatment); Hammonds v. Aetna Cas. & Sur. Co., 243 F. Supp. 793, 795-99 (C.D. Ohio 1965) (holding that public policy requires that doctors not reveal patient confidences).

90. MODEL RULES Preamble ¶ 20 (2002) (italics indicate added language).

Chapter 1: Regulation of Lawyers 21

disciplinary authority, does not imply that an antagonist in a collateral proceeding or transaction has standing to seek enforcement of the rule."[91]

The 2002 version of the rules also recognizes, however, that the standards have relevance to actions other than disciplinary proceedings. The revision of paragraph 20 of the Preamble adds the following statement: "Nevertheless, since the rules do establish standards of conduct by lawyers, a lawyer's violation of a rule may be evidence of breach of the applicable standard of conduct."[92]

Tort Liability

Another sort of sanction on lawyers is administered through the judicial system by means of awards of damages in legal malpractice suits.[93] Tort liability is of enhanced concern to lawyers practicing environmental law, in part because of the staggering awards associated with environmental litigation and the high costs of cleaning up hazardous waste sites or remediating other environmental problems.[94] Additionally, there has been speculation about the potential for claims in the environmental area against lawyers themselves.[95] Traditionally, clients have been able to sue their lawyers for legal malpractice or professional negligence.[96] The number of such lawsuits has increased dra-

---

91. *Id.*
92. *Id.*
93. *See* Wolfram, *supra* note 1, at 2.1.
94. In *Houchens v. Rockwell Int'l Corp.*, a jury ordered Rockwell to pay $8 million in actual damages and $210 million in punitive damages for polluting the Mud River with polychlorinated biphenyls. *See* Houchens v. Rockwell Int'l Corp., No.93-CI-00158 (Ky. Cir. Ct. May 31, 1996), discussed in *Riparian Owners Awarded $218 Million in Kentucky Pollution Suit Against Rockwell*, 11 Toxics L. Rep. (BNA) 14, 14–15 (June 5, 1996). The court rendered the verdict in spite of an absence of proof on emotional damages. *See also PG&E to Pay $333 Million to Settle Lawsuit over Environmental Exposures*, 11 Toxics L. Rep. (BNA) 173, 173–74 (July 10, 1996) (discussing case in which 650 plaintiffs alleged health problems due to chromium exposure from natural gas).
95. *See, e.g.,* James R. Arnold & Gerald J. Buchwald, *Superfund = Superliability: Are Lawyers the Next Deep Pocket?*, A.B.A. J. (Sept. 1993), at 117 (noting the risk that "the next professional liability crisis may focus on environmental lawyers as the deep pocket"); Don J. Benedictus, *Hazardous Advice: Lawyer, Firm Prosecuted for Telling Client Not to Clean Up Waste*, A.B.A. J. (Sept. 1991), at 16 (discussing felony charges filed against eight people, including some lawyers, on theory that letter abandoning their client's laboratory constituted illegal disposal of hazardous wastes).
96. *See, e.g.,* Togstad v. Vesely, Otto, Miller & Keefe, 291 N.W.2d 686 (Minn. 1980) (holding lawyer liable for malpractice when he did not meet the minimum standard of care).

22   ISSUES OF LEGAL ETHICS IN THE PRACTICE OF ENVIRONMENTAL LAW

matically in recent years.[97] "The very real threat of malpractice lawsuits is sending practitioners around the country running to in-house legal advisors and state and local ethics committees for advice on interpreting the ethics rules."[98] Additionally, courts now recognize a cause of action in limited circumstances by nonclients against lawyers[99] and other professionals[100] for harm suffered as a result of the negligence or intentional misconduct of the lawyer.[101]

Other professionals also face the risk of malpractice actions both for errors in judgment and omissions such as failure to heed a "red flag" or to follow up on issues that should alert the professional to problems. In the case of *Easton v. Strassburger*, a real estate broker was held liable for a failure to require a soil report for the sale of a residence.[102] The claim arose from the sale of a home in California that was built on a landfill. Settling of the soil and erosion caused damage to the house. Even though the case against the broker did not establish actual knowledge on the part of the broker, the court held that the uneven floor in the house should have alerted the broker to the need for a soil report.[103] Receptive to evidence of "red flags" indicating soil problems, the court found that the broker was on notice of potential soils problems.

Section 552 of the Restatement (Second) of Torts sets forth the elements for recovery under a tort theory of negligent misrepresentation.[104] Traditionally, the bar of privity protected lawyers and other professionals from suits by nonclients. In recent years, however, many jurisdictions have rejected the doctrine, at least in some contexts, creating a complicated system of exceptions to the rule.[105] In a recent book, Jay M. Feinman documents a pattern of

---

97. *See, e.g.*, RONALD E. MALLEN & JEFFREY M. SMTIH, LEGAL MALPRACTICE, 18–25 (3d ed. 1989) [hereinafter MALLEN & SMITH] (stating that there may be as much as a 155% increase in legal malpractice cases in the '90s).

98. Whitney A. McCaslin, *Ethics & Conflicts of Interest*, 9 GEO. J. LEGAL ETHICS 959 (1996).

99. *See* McCamish, Martin, Brown & Loeffler v. F. E. Appling Interests, 991 S.W.2d 787 (Tex. 1999) (holding that lawyers could be sued by third parties for negligent misrepresentation).

100. *See* Marcus Bros. Textiles, Inc. v. Price Waterhouse LP, 350 N.C. 214 (N.C. 1999) (holding that an accounting firm can be sued by a third party for negligent misrepresentation if the firm materially misrepresents a client's financial condition during an audit and knows that a third party is going to rely on the audit).

101. *See* MALLEN & SMITH, *supra* note 97, at 9–17.

102. 199 Cal. Rptr. 383 (Ct. App. 1984).

103. *Id.* at 391.

104. *See* RESTATEMENT (SECOND) OF TORTS 552 (1977) (outlining the tort of negligent misrepresentation).

105. *See* Geoffrey C. Hazard, Jr., *The Privity Requirement Reconsidered*, 37 S. TEX. L. REV. 967 (1996) (arguing that the privity requirement is an unworkable legal concept); JAY M. FEINMAN, PROFESSIONAL LIABILITY TO THIRD PARTIES 76 (2000).

Chapter 1: Regulation of Lawyers   23

protection of third parties by courts[106] to establish the thesis that economic negligence should be analyzed and applied as a separate field of law.[107] Professor Feinman notes that the rule of privity no longer protects lawyers in most jurisdictions as a categorical matter. "Courts take diverse approaches to the issue of the liability of a lawyer to a nonclient, but despite the diversity, one point is clear: The traditional rule, that a lawyer owes no duty to a nonclient with whom the lawyer is not in privity, is no longer the law in most jurisdictions."[108] Cases involving environmental hazards present an even stronger case for protection than threats of economic injury because of the potential for loss of life or other physical injury.[109]

In a legal malpractice action, a plaintiff must establish that the lawyer failed to act with reasonable diligence, skill, or competence, and that plaintiff's loss or damages were proximately caused by the malpractice of the lawyer.[110] Although the Model Rules seek to bar the use of the rules in malpractice actions against lawyers, courts may consider any relevant evidence in deciding the issue of standard of care. In the malpractice context, the question is whether the lawyer performed in a non-negligent manner. Part of the issue is thus whether the standard of care was met. Showing breach of the disciplinary rules, thus, goes a long way toward establishing that a lawyer failed to meet the standard of care set by the disciplinary rules that apply to all lawyers. Accordingly, showing a violation of ethics rules is relevant and persuasive evidence in a malpractice claim.[111]

As a practical matter, when an expert is examined as to the standard of care, the basis of his or her opinion will be explored. A

---

106. *See generally* Jay M. Feinman, Professional Liability to Third Parties (2000).

107. *See id.* at 5–8; *see also* Jay M. Feinman, *Attorney Liability to Nonclients*, 31 Tort & Ins. L.J. 735 (1996).

108. Jay M. Feinman, Professional Liability to Third Parties 76 (2000); *see also* Jay M. Feinman, Economic Negligence: Liability of Professionals and Businesses to Third Parties for Economic Loss (1995).

109. The interest of the third party can outweigh that of the client. "A number of the cases in which a lawyer is held to owe a duty of reasonable care to the third party to or for whom it issues a legal opinion rest on the dependence of the third party rather than on the intent of the lawyer and the client." *Id.* at 325–26.

110. *See* Edmunds v. Superior Court, 29 Cal. Rptr. 2d 281 (Ct. App. 1994) (recognizing the possibility of liability but denying recovery based on plaintiff's failure to establish both tortious conduct of and the nexus between defendant's conduct and damage to plaintiff).

111. *See, e.g., In re* Faucheux, 818 So. 2d 734 (La. 2002) (suspending lawyer from practice for one year for improperly aggregating two clients' settlements).

24 ISSUES OF LEGAL ETHICS IN THE PRACTICE OF ENVIRONMENTAL LAW

> good expert will cite, among other things, the disciplinary rules to show what the standard is. The long and short of it is . . . [that] committees writing rules affects us, no matter what protestations to the contrary are put into the rules.[112]

Generally, a plaintiff suing a lawyer for legal malpractice must establish that the lawyer-client relationship existed between the two regarding the subject matter of the suit. Typically, the relationship is shown by the express terms of a contract of employment. This is not always the case, however. In addition to an express or implied contract based on the facts of an undertaking by the lawyer, courts have found a lawyer-client relationship based on a showing that plaintiff relied reasonably on the lawyer to handle the matter.[113] Moreover, the fact that no lawyer-client relationship exists between two parties may not cut off the risk of liability on the part of the lawyer. The Restatement (Third) of the Law Governing Lawyers notes that even in the absence of a client-lawyer relationship, a lawyer may be liable for a failure to use reasonable care in giving advice.[114] Advice given to a prospective client may give rise to liability on the part of a lawyer who gives advice that violates a reasonableness standard of care.[115] Even a nonclient who was never a prospective client may have an actionable claim against the lawyer in the unlikely event that the lawyer invited that nonclient to rely on an opinion issued by the lawyer.[116]

> Lawyers issue opinion letters in different circumstances, but a typical case is that of a lawyer who renders an opinion to a third party in anticipation of a business transaction between the third party and the lawyer's client. The third party completes the transaction partly in reliance on the opinion. If the lawyer has made an unreasonable legal judgment in the course of preparing the opinion, failed to discover some facts that render the opinion inaccurate, or, having discovered such facts, negligently failed to reveal them to the third party, the third party suffers a loss when the client is unable to fulfill its obligations.[117]

---

112. E-mail from Jett Hanna, Senior Vice President, Texas Lawyers' Insurance Exchange (July 14, 2001) (on file with author).

113. *See* WOLFRAM. *supra* note 1, at 210–11.

114. RESTATEMENT (THIRD) OF THE LAW GOVERNING LAWYERS 51 (2000).

115. RESTATEMENT (THIRD) OF THE LAW GOVERNING LAWYERS 51, cmt. e (2000).

116. *See* RESTATEMENT (SECOND) OF TORTS 552; RESTATEMENT (THIRD) OF THE LAW GOVERNING LAWYERS 52; *see also* William L. Siegel, *Attorney Liability: Is This the New Twilight Zone?*, 27 U. MEM. L. REV. 13 (1996).

117. JAY M. FEINMAN, PROFESSIONAL LIABILITY TO THIRD PARTIES 99 (2000).

To minimize the risk of liability to nonclients, a lawyer can include limiting language in an opinion letter or other product, expressly stating that the lawyer's opinion is intended for the benefit of the client only and that use of the information or analysis by other parties must be at their own risk. "A lawyer may avoid liability to nonclients . . . by making clear that an opinion or representation is directed only to a client and should not be relied on by others."[118] The risk to the lawyer issuing an opinion letter can be dramatic in the environmental context, considering the risks to the client and the nonclient. The drafters of the ABA Model Rules noted the duty of lawyers and the legal profession to serve the public interest, cautioning against allowing self-interest to influence the drafting of ethics rules.[119] Implicit in the ABA's assessment of its responsibility is the fact lawyers cannot escape the reach of the common law by virtue of rules of ethics. "The operation of law external to the law of lawyering—other law—will sometimes 'force' further exceptions, regardless of what a disciplinary code might say."[120]

Malpractice: Limiting Liability (2002 Revision)

The 2002 revision to Model Rule 1.8 also clarifies the ability of a lawyer to enter an agreement that limits his liability for malpractice. Limiting liability by means of an agreement before a representation begins may be especially useful for environmental practitioners, because they often represent sophisticated corporate clients. When the client is knowledgeable about environmental hazards, such as obligations fixed by statute for environmental discharges, or the risk of environmental damage in a particular matter, an agreement limiting the potential liability of a lawyer may be held to be a proper subject of fair bargaining and risk allocation in the event the agreement is later challenged. In such a case a court is likely to respect the right of the parties to bargain vis-á-vis potential liability.

Rule 1.8(h) prohibits lawyers from entering "an agreement prospectively limiting the lawyer's liability to a client for malpractice unless the client is independently represented in making the agreement."[121] Likewise, the revised rule gives guidance regarding former clients and unrepresented persons, prohibiting lawyers from settling "a claim or potential claim for such liability with an unrepresented client or former client unless that person is advised in

---

118. *See* RESTATEMENT (THIRD) OF THE LAW GOVERNING LAWYERS 51, cmt. e (2000).
119. MODEL RULES OF PROFESSIONAL CONDUCT Preamble, ¶ 11.
120. *See* 1 GEOFFREY C. HAZARD, JR., & W. WILLIAM HODES, THE LAW OF LAWYERING: A HANDBOOK ON THE MODEL RULES OF PROFESSIONAL CONDUCT 1.6:109, at 168.1–.2 (1998).
121. REVISED MODEL RULE 1.8(h) (2002).

writing of the desirability of seeking and is given a reasonable opportunity to seek the advice of independent legal counsel in connection therewith."[122]

Comment 14 to Revised Model Rule 1.8 declares the effect of the provision: "Agreements prospectively limiting a lawyer's liability for malpractice are prohibited unless the client is independently represented in making the agreement because they are likely to undermine competent and diligent representation."[123] This comment also indicates the ABA's rationale for scrutinizing limitations on malpractice actions: "many clients are unable to evaluate the desirability of making such an agreement."[124] On the other hand, the comment notes that the rule does not necessarily prohibit arbitration agreements as long as the agreements are enforceable in the jurisdiction in which the agreement is entered and the client is fully informed about the effect of the agreement.

Environmental Context

Courts have found lawyers liable for malpractice in the environmental context. For example, in the case of *Dixon Ticonderoga Co. v. Estate of O'Connor*,[125] the seller of industrial land (Dixon) sued both the lawyer (O'Connor) and the firm representing it in the sale, and another lawyer (Friedman) who represented it in a subsequent malpractice suit. The basis of the suit was that the original lawyer failed to inform Dixon of the enactment of the New Jersey Environmental Cleanup Responsibility Act (ECRA), which created an obligation on the part of the seller to clean up contaminated property before selling the property. After the sale, Venture, the buyer, sued the seller for the cleanup costs associated with the land under ECRA. In addition, Dixon sued Friedman, the lawyer whom the seller had hired to represent it against O'Connor, based on a claim that he committed malpractice because he failed to file suit before the statute of limitations barred the claim. The court upheld a motion to dismiss in favor of O'Connor and his firm on the ground that the statute of limitations had expired two years prior to the suit. The court held that the statute began to run when Dixon's lawyer sent a letter to Venture's counsel responding to demands for money to pay for the cleanup required under ECRA.[126] The court reversed the summary judgment that the district court had granted in favor of Friedman, the lawyer in the litigation, on the ground that issues of material fact were presented regarding whether an attorney-client relationship existed between Dixon and Friedman, and, if so, whether Fried-

---

122. *Id.*
123. REVISED MODEL RULE 1.8 cmt. 14 (2002).
124. *Id.*
125. Dixon Ticonderoga Co. v. Estate of O'Connor, 248 F.3d 151 (3d Cir. 2001).
126. *Id.* at 168.

man breached his professional duties to the client.[127] The court refused to grant summary judgment for either party on the claim against Friedman and remanded the case for further findings.[128]

In the case of *Keywell Corporation v. Piper & Marbury, L.L.P.,*[129] the court denied the defendant law firm's motion for summary judgment, holding that plaintiff could proceed to trial for malpractice upon a showing that it would not have purchased a steel-recycling plant had it known of the environmental problems. Keywell Corp. (Keywell), a company in the business of recycling steel, sued a law firm, Piper & Marbury (Piper), for malpractice in connection with its representation of Keywell in a multimillion-dollar acquisition of industrial sites from Vac Air Alloys Corporation (Vac Air). Keywell alleged that it incurred approximately $6 million in environmental cleanup costs as a result of Piper's malpractice in its 1987 purchase of Vac Air's steel-recycling facility. Prior to the purchase, Piper, with Keywell's approval, hired an environmental consulting firm (CRA) to perform an environmental audit of the Vac Air site.[130] Piper was to assist in the investigation and draft the purchase agreement between Keywell and Vac Air.

According to the CRA employee who did the on-site interview, Piper authorized him to speak with only one Vac Air official concerning Vac Air's history of environmental practices at the site. That official lied to CRA, stating that Vac Air had not engaged in any on-site disposal of toxic wastes. In fact, Vac Air employees had routinely dumped waste on site, creating significant environmental contamination. CRA's report stated that environmental remediation costs at the site could reach $4.8 million, with the cost of treating the groundwater reaching approximately $1 million. Keywell alleged that Piper reported to it only the $1 million potential cleanup cost. The Piper lawyer stated that the audit was free of "red flags."[131] After losing an action against Vac Air for contribution under CERCLA, Keywell filed suit against Piper for legal malpractice. In the malpractice action, the court granted Piper's motion for summary judgment with respect to the 1989 release but held that the defendant law firm was not entitled to summary judgment on the malpractice claim.[132]

---

127. *Id.* at 171.
128. *Id.* at 174–75.
129. 1999 WL 66700 (W.D.N.Y. Feb. 11, 1999); 2000 WL 743970 (W.D.N.Y.).
130. *Id.*
131. *Id.* at *3.
132. *Id.* at *11.

Lawyer Conduct Subject to Regulation

Tasks performed by lawyers can sometimes be delegated to nonlawyer assistants such as paralegals, student law clerks, and secretaries. Environmental lawyers sometimes find it necessary to delegate tasks to biologists, toxicologists, and other scientists. Lawyers who delegate work to these assistants must supervise the work of each assistant in a diligent and responsible manner.[133] Moreover, the lawyer should not delegate the function of giving advice about the law to nonlawyer assistants. The fact that lawyers properly delegate some tasks while others cannot be delegated could have led to a rule that some tasks undertaken by a lawyer (such as those that are appropriately delegated) are not the practice of law. That is, any task that could be properly delegated arguably is not the practice of law even when performed by a lawyer. The weight of authority seems to be to the contrary, however. Tasks relating to providing legal advice to clients undertaken by a lawyer are part of the practice of law and, accordingly, subject to regulation without regard to whether or not the task could be delegated.[134] Thus, all of the tasks undertaken by a lawyer related to the ultimate goal of providing legal advice are within the scope of regulated lawyer conduct. The fact that complex scientific judgments and difficult factual issues relating to scientific evidence are often at issue in environmental law does not release the lawyer from responsibility from making legal judgments.

Likewise, lawyers often delegate work or refer clients to other professionals. Whether to advise a client to retain an expert can be a difficult judgment for a lawyer. A report issued by the Federal Judiciary Center studied the use of expert testimony from 1991 to 1998. It found that the most common problems cited by judges regarding expert evidence were the use of experts who were not objective and the excessive expense of expert testimony.[135] In general, judges' assessments of problems with expert testimony did not differ greatly from 1991 to 1998.[136] In the event the lawyer does recommend that a client retain an expert, Rule 5.7 imposes a duty on lawyers to explain the distinction between professionals to the client. It requires a lawyer to "take reasonable steps to assure that a person obtaining law-related services knows that the services of the separate entity are not legal services and that the pro-

---

133. *See* Kathleen Maher, *No Substitutes: Legal Aides Are Crucial, but Some Tasks Lawyers Should Not Delegate,* A.B.A.J. 66 (October 2001).

134. *See* MODEL RULE 5.7.

135. *Expert Testimony in Federal Civil Trials: A Preliminary Analysis, available at* www.fjc.gov (last visited Mar. 22, 2003).

136. *Id.*

tections of the lawyer-client relationship do not exist."[137] In explaining this provision, the comment includes environmental consulting as an example of "law-related services."[138]

Nonlegal Services Provided by a Lawyer

The fact that a lawyer provides some services that are not legal in nature does not necessarily exempt the lawyer from ethics rules with regard to those services. Model Rule 5.7 declares that a lawyer is subject to ethical rules with regard to "law related services as well as legal services" in certain circumstances.[139] The rule indicates that such circumstances exist when the lawyer provides the law-related services "in circumstances not distinct from the lawyer's provision of legal services." Additionally, the lawyer is subject to the rules when the services are provided by an "entity controlled by the lawyer individually or with others if the lawyer fails to take reasonable measures to assure that a person obtaining the law-related services knows that the services of the separate entity are not legal services and that the protections of the client-lawyer relationship do not exist."[140] Rule 5.7 defines the term "law-related services" as services "that might reasonably be performed in conjunction with and in substance are related to the provision of legal services, and that are not prohibited as unauthorized practice of law when provided by a nonlawyer."[141] Assuming that a lawyer reasonably believes that it is in his client's interest to provide both legal and nonlegal services, he must comply with the rules of ethics in all his services.[142]

The California Ethics Committee received an inquiry from a lawyer who intended to render nonlegal investment advice but also planned to provide some legal services, such as reviewing legal documents drafted by other lawyers.[143] The lawyer had referred to her legal credentials in marketing her services. The Ethics Committee noted that prospective clients who retain the lawyer

---

137. MODEL RULE 5.7.
138. MODEL RULE 5.7 cmt. 9.
139. Model Rule 5.7(a).
140. MODEL RULE 5.7(a)(2).
141. MODEL RULE 5.7(b).
142. *See Indiana Panel Gives Guarded Approval to Attorney's 'Dual Practice' Proposal*, 70 U.S.L.W. 2789 (June 18, 2002) (Indiana State Bar Ass'n Legal Ethics Comm., Op. 1 of 2002) (opining that while lawyer may operate 'dual practice' offering both legal and financial services, lawyer must comply with the ethical rule regulating business transactions with clients).
143. California State Bar Standing Committee on Professional Responsibility and Conduct, Formal Op. 1999-154 (Aug. 27, 1999).

30   ISSUES OF LEGAL ETHICS IN THE PRACTICE OF ENVIRONMENTAL LAW

might reasonably believe that they were contracting for legal services in addition to financial services.[144] The committee advised that both legal and nonlegal services performed by a lawyer fall within the constraints of the professional conduct rules, including the rules on conflicts and confidentiality.[145]

The California opinion on nonlegal services is relevant to lawyers who wish to practice primarily as environmental advisers rather than in a legal capacity. The intermingling of legal and scientific judgments in the environmental area is similar to the legal and nonlegal considerations in investment advising. Additionally, clients are likely to hire such a lawyer because of their legal expertise as well as their scientific or technical expertise. No principled distinction seems to exist between a practice that blends financial and legal services and one that blends legal services and environmental expertise. Thus, the best practice for a lawyer intending to practice as an environmental adviser is to assume that all of his professional endeavors are subject to the rules of professional conduct of his jurisdiction.

Moral Judgment

In some cases, the lawyer is called upon to exercise moral judgment as part of his service to a client.[146] The Preamble to the Model Rules acknowledges that lawyers must draw upon their own moral judgment in resolving ethics issues. "Within the framework of these rules, many difficult issues of professional discretion can arise. Such issues must be resolved through the exercise of sensitive professional and moral judgment guided by the basic principles underlying the rules."[147] Likewise, the Scope section of the Model Rules notes that the rules do not "exhaust the moral and ethical considerations that should inform a lawyer," noting that "no worthwhile human activity can be completely defined by legal rules."[148] Comment 2 to Model Rule 1.2 notes that

---

144. *Id.* at *3.
145. *Id.* at *2. Similarly, some states prohibit lawyers from engaging in some sorts of financial services. *See, e.g., Ohio Lawyers May Not, Even With Consent, Market Annuities to Estate Planning Clients,* 70 U.S.L.W. 2144 (Sept. 11, 2001).
146. Robert R. Kuehn, *Shooting the Messenger: The Ethics of Attacks on Environmental Representation,* 26 HARV. ENVTL. L. REV. 417, 421 (2002) (rejecting the idea "that only explicit codes of professional conduct define ethical attorney behavior").
147. *See* MODEL RULES Scope.
148. MODEL RULE 2.1; *See also In re* Marriage of Foran, 834 P.2d 1081, 1089 n.14 (Wash. Ct. App. 1992) (noting a lawyer representing either party to a prenuptial may consider moral and social factors; an unenforceable, unfair contract does not promote marital tranquility); Friedman v. Comm'r of Pub. Safety, 473 N.W.2d 828 (Minn. 1991), 834, *citing* MINN. R. PROF. CONDUCT 2.1 (determining that if the underlying goal of DWI laws is to deter drinking and driving and promote sobriety, a lawyer can play a crucial role).

"purely technical legal advice can sometimes be inadequate." Accordingly, the comment notes, "[i]t is proper for a lawyer to refer to relevant moral and ethical considerations in giving advice. Although a lawyer is not a moral advisor as such, moral and ethical considerations impinge upon most legal questions and may decisively influence how the law will be applied."[149] Similarly, Rule 2.1 authorizes the lawyer to "refer not only to law but to other considerations such as moral, economic, social and political factors" in advising clients.[150]

Application of Rules to Lawyers Acting in Nonprofessional Capacity (2002 Revision)

The revised Model Rules make clear that a lawyer cannot escape the duties of the profession. To some extent, the duties imposed by the rules reach the lawyer's conduct in his personal as well as his professional life. Paragraph three of the Preamble states:

> [T]here are rules that apply to lawyers who are not active in the practice of law or to practicing lawyers even when they are acting in a nonprofessional capacity. For example, a lawyer who commits fraud in the conduct of a business is subject to discipline for engaging in conduct involving dishonesty, fraud, deceit or misrepresentation. See Rule 8.4.[151]

Forum and Laboratory Shopping

Among the ethical problems not discussed in the Model Rules is the issue of forum shopping. Is forum shopping an ethical practice? Many practitioners use all available means in many cases undertaken in environmental or other matters both to learn about past holdings of a particular judge or court and to secure a hearing in as favorable a forum as possible. In the environmental arena, lawyers sometimes engage in a similar practice—shopping for a laboratory based on a desired outcome.[152] A lawyer who represents a buyer may

---

149. Choices lawyers make in practice, like choices made in life generally, carry possible or likely consequences. When these consequences are bad—in this context, this means likely to result in lawyer liability or a violation of the rules of ethics—this book labels the potential consequences as "pitfalls."

150. MODEL RULE 2.1.

151. MODEL RULE Preamble ¶ 3.

152. See Marla B. Rubin, *The Mine Field: Ethics and "Science,"* 19 N.Y. ENVTL. LAW. 46 (Spring 1999).

try to acquire property at a lower price by hiring a laboratory that has new equipment and an ability to quantify low-level contamination.[153] A lawyer representing a seller or another client seeking to exonerate a site from a charge of contamination might seek a laboratory with older equipment that could produce a nondetect level.[154] Such practices present a type of gaming of the system that seems out of step with professional conduct. They do not seem to fall within a particular prohibition of the Model Rules, however, and such attempts to gain an advantage for a client are commonplace in practice.

Taking Advantage of an Opponent's Mistakes

Another area not spoken to specifically in the rules of ethics but provoking intense debate among ethics scholars[155] is the issue of taking advantage of the mistakes of opponents.[156] Opportunities for mistakes and misconceptions in environmental law are legion. Accordingly, there is significant likelihood in environmental law that a lawyer will make a misstep. When the opponent lawyer identifies the misstep, he will either remain silent and profit from the mistake or help the less informed lawyer fix the mistake and proceed on with the substance of the transaction or controversy. The propriety of the lawyer's decision turns on the facts of the case, including whether the lawyer added to the misconception and whether the lawyer's silence was the equivalent of a misrepresentation.[157]

For example, different jurisdictions have adopted different meanings for the term "disposal" under CERCLA. In *United States v. CDMG Realty Co.*, the U.S. Court of Appeals for the Third Circuit held that a thorough investigation requiring drilling and possibly causing movement of contaminants may constitute disposal for purposes of CERCLA.[158] Other courts have held that passive disposal that occurs simply by virtue of the migration of the contaminant itself can constitute "disposal" under CERCLA.[159]

---

153. *Id.*

154. *Id.*

155. Listserv Archive at legalethics@lists.washlaw.edu.

156. While lawyers are sometimes referred to as "opponents," this title seems out of place in the transactional context.

157. *See, e.g.,* Nathan M. Crystal, *The Lawyer's Duty to Disclose Material Facts in Contract or Settlement Negotiations*, 87 Ky. L.J. 1055 (1998–99).

158. 96 F.3d 706 (3d Cir. 1996).

159. *See, e.g.,* Carson Harbor Village Ltd. v. Unocal Corp., 227 F.3d 1196 (9th Cir. 2000). The Fourth and Ninth Circuits have held that the term "disposal" as used in CERCLA includes passive as well as active disposal or movement of hazardous waste. The Second, Third, and Sixth Circuits have held that only active disposal comes within CERCLA.

Chapter 1: Regulation of Lawyers 33

Suppose that in negotiating an indemnification in a sale of property, it became apparent to you that the other lawyer is unaware of the meaning of "disposal" adopted in your jurisdiction. This lack of knowledge may prevent the other lawyer from effectively protecting his client's interest. Whether the lack of knowledge on the part of an opponent means that a knowledgeable lawyer should bring this point to the attention of the less knowledgeable lawyer is an open question of ethics. While there is an obligation on the part of lawyers to inform a tribunal of authority contrary to the lawyer's argument,[160] the Model Rules include no clear-cut requirement that a lawyer give information to an opponent when bargaining. The absence of a rule leaves the lawyer to his own conscience in deciding whether to be fully candid in bargaining.

A similar problem may arise in negotiating an indemnification agreement. Suppose you represent a seller of property that is contaminated. While the severity of the problem is unclear, your client has reduced the sales price because of the results of the environmental audit that revealed some level of contamination. Your client has offered to indemnify the buyer for all past contamination, and the buyer, who received a copy of the environmental audit, is considering going forward with the deal despite the contamination. While CERCLA allows indemnification by potentially responsible parties,[161] such agreements do not extinguish liability of the indemnified party vis-á-vis a CERCLA action by the government.[162] Moreover, courts are likely to construe an indemnification strictly against the party seeking to enforce the indemnification[163] and may refuse to enforce an indemnification provision requiring payment of Superfund cleanup costs unless the contract expressly indicates the possibility of environmental contamination.[164] Suppose you know the statutory provision on indemnification and its limitations and you are certain that the lawyer representing the buyer is unaware of this statutory limitation on the indemnification power just explained. Do you have an ethi-

---

160. *See* MODEL RULE 3.3.

161. *See* CERCLA 107(e), 42 U.S.C. § 9607(e); *see also* Daniel R. Avery, *Enforcing Environmental Indemnification Against a Settling Party Under CERCLA*, 23 SETON HALL L. REV. 872 (1993).

162. *Id.*

163. *See* Advanced Technology Corp. v. Eliskim, Inc., 87 F. Supp. 2d 780 (N.D. Ohio 2000) (holding settlement agreement applies only to indemnification for cleanups taking place after the agreement); Servco Pacific Inc. v. Dods, 106 F. Supp. 2d 1034 (D. Haw. 2000).

164. *See, e.g.,* Servco Pacific Inc. v. Dods, 106 F. Supp. 2d 1034 (D. Haw. 2000) (finding lease provision not to require defendant to indemnify plaintiff for cleanup of a property, reasoning that indemnification provisions are strictly construed absent express reference to environmental problems).

34   ISSUES OF LEGAL ETHICS IN THE PRACTICE OF ENVIRONMENTAL LAW

cal responsibility to explain the limit to him? While at least one court has held that a party who seeks to enforce an indemnification agreement under CERCLA must show that it disclosed the possibility of future liability under CERCLA,[165] no clear-cut authority requires the lawyer to make a disclosure relating to the parameters of the law as opposed to the physical state of the property. State rather than federal law determines whether a provision effectively creates a right of indemnification as a matter of contract law. Accordingly, the legal knowledge necessary to advise a client on the efficacy of an indemnification is multilayered.[166] The lawyer who refrained from educating the lawyer representing the other side of a sales transaction may use this point as a justification for his action. The multilayered effect is an example of the phenomenon of indeterminacy in law. The next section explores this topic in greater depth.

Indeterminacy in the Law

Perhaps all areas of human study involve indeterminacy. Both law and science present significant uncertainty. The two fields of law and science combine in environmental law to exacerbate the indeterminacy problem.[167] Because of the fact of indeterminacy, lawyers often advise clients facing issues that are not well settled to recognize the risk presented by some interpretations of the law and to conduct business in a way that minimizes that risk.

Just as zero risk is not a realistic goal in the world of environmental policy, zero risk is hardly attainable in the practice of law. Avoiding pitfalls and fostering habits of prudent practice minimize the risk of disciplinary actions and help the lawyer make a choice that he can look back on without regret. In a sense, ethical precepts present a system for risk assessment. The risks being assessed by lawyers include the risks of liability, suspension[168] or disbarment, and the potential for loss of clients, of reputation, of self-confidence and self-respect.

---

165. *See* Fina, Inc. v. Arco, 200 F.3d 266 (5th Cir., Jan. 4, 2000).

166. *See* Diversified Services, Inc. v. Simkins Indus., 974 F. Supp. 1448 (S.D. Fla. 1997).

167. Eileen Gay Jones, *Risky Assessments: Uncertainties in Science and the Human Dimension of Environmental Decisionmaking*, 22 WM. & MARY ENVTL. L. & POL'Y REV. 1 (1997).

168. *See* Oklahoma *ex rel* Oklahoma Bar Ass'n v. Watson, 897 P.2d 246 (Okla. 1994) (suspending lawyer who accepted settlement without consent of each of his clients, collected excessive fees, mishandled client's funds, and accepted compensation from someone other than the client).

Indeterminacy in Lawyering

Lawyers must assess law, opinions, and rules of ethics as a whole to get a sense of the possible pitfalls in practice. Like other areas of law, uncertainty attaches to the application of the rules of legal ethics. Not surprisingly, courts and boards of professional responsibility often are not unanimous in their decisions resolving ethical issues. Additionally, boards of professional responsibility often will not comment or make holdings regarding substantive law.[169] Some boards also have a policy against "opin[ing] on the ethical conduct of anyone other than the inquiring attorney."[170] For example, the Pennsylvania Bar Committee included the following caveat in its opinion:

> Caveat: the foregoing opinion is advisory only and is not binding of the disciplinary board of the supreme court of Pennsylvania or any court. It carries only such weight as an appropriate reviewing authority may choose to give it.[171]

Accordingly, lawyers, like businesses and people in general, want to take steps to minimize the risks. Another example of indeterminacy comes from the area of conflicts of interest. Some courts have held that the conflicts of a corporate affiliate (a parent or subsidiary) of an existing client are conflicts of that client's firm.[172] Other courts reject this bright-line test and focus instead on the relationship of the entities.[173] The ABA Standing Committee on Ethics and Professional Responsibility has held that the fact that a lawyer represents a parent corporation does not necessarily mean that he represents a subsidiary of the parent.[174]

Similarly, the question of who is a client can present problems in the seemingly simple area of representation of individuals. Courts have held that a

---

169. *See, e.g.*, Pennsylvania Bar Association Legal Ethics and Prof'l Responsibility Comm., Informal Op. No. 98-98, 1998 WL 1286249 (Oct. 12, 1998).

170. Pennsylvania Bar Association Legal Ethics and Prof'l Responsibility Comm., Informal Op. No. 99-10 (Mar. 25, 1999).

171. *See supra* note 169.

172. *See* Gould, Inc. v. Mitsui Mining and Smelting Co., 738 F. Supp. 1121 (N.D. Ohio 1990); Strategim Development Corp. v. Heron, 1991 U.S. Dist. LEXIS 1474 (S.D.N.Y. 1991).

173. *See* Apex Oil Co. v. Wickind Oil Co., 1995 U.S. Dist. LEXIS 6398 (N.D. Cal. 1995); Meehan v. Hopps, 301 P.2d 10 (Calif. 1956); *see also* ABA Comm. on Ethics and Prof'l Responsibility, Formal Op. 95-390 (holding that lawyer is not necessarily barred from representing a client in a matter adverse to a corporate affiliate of lawyer's existing client in unrelated matter).

174. *See* ABA Comm. on Ethics and Prof'l Responsibility, Formal Op. 95-390.

lawyer-client relationship exists between parties despite the absence of a contract and the absence of any payment or agreement to pay legal fees. For example, in the case of *Togstad v. Vesely, Otto, Miller & Keafe*,[175] the Minnesota Supreme Court affirmed a judgment in plaintiffs' favor based on the jury determination that Jerre Miller, a lawyer, was negligent in his representation of plaintiffs (John and Joan Togstad). The Togstads sued Miller for legal malpractice based on conversations Joan Togstad held with Miller concerning injuries her husband sustained as a result of treatment for an aneurysm. The treatment had left John Togstad severely paralyzed and unable to speak. Fourteen months after his hospitalization began, Joan met with Miller (the lawyer) for approximately 45 minutes and discussed her husband's claim. The plaintiffs and Miller did not discuss fee arrangements for legal services, nor did Miller seek or receive medical authorizations. Miller did not bill the Togstads for the consultation. At the conclusion of the meeting, Miller told Ms. Togstad that he did not think the couple had a case, but he said he would discuss the claim with his partner. Because Miller never made contact again, Ms. Togstad assumed that she and her husband had no actionable claim. The primary rationale for the court's holding of liability was the fact that Miller neither informed the plaintiffs of the existence of a statute of limitations nor referred them to another lawyer. In their suit for legal malpractice, plaintiffs bore the burden of establishing the existence of a lawyer-client relationship. The court found that plaintiffs met this burden and that the evidence established that a lawyer-client relationship arose when Miller provided legal advice at Mrs. Togstad's request. Moreover, the court relied on the fact that Miller should have foreseen that Mrs. Togstad would be injured if the advice were negligently given.

Indeterminacy: Environmental Example

The risk of liability as a result of casual judgments is at least as pronounced in the environmental area. Points of uncertainty plague most of the environmental statutes. Even in cases when a lawyer considers a cause of action to be hopeless, she should be careful to make this judgment after thorough research. Because of the difficulty in making legal judgment with certainty, lawyers generally should indicate their reasoning and the basis for declining to represent the client on a matter and should, additionally, indicate to the potential client the statute of limitations that would be likely to apply to the claim. Of course, uncertainties may also attach to the issue of the statute of limitations. In the case of environmental statutes, the statute of limitation issue can be a complicated one. For example, difficulties sometimes arise under CERCLA in determining whether the six-year statute of limitations for remediation

---

175. 291 N.W.2d 686 (Minn. 1980).

Chapter 1: Regulation of Lawyers 37

actions applies or the three-year statute of limitation for legal actions controls.[176] Determining which limitation applies to a given case can be difficult and dicey. "Somewhat confusing on its face, the [CERCLA] limitation statute becomes bewildering when applied to an actual response. . . . A party undertaking the response can easily classify an action differently than the court does, and therefore apply the wrong statute of limitations."[177] Moreover, different statutes may apply to different actions within a particular case.[178] When such a statute of limitations problem is present, the lawyer should advise the client of the risk that a court may hold that the running of the earlier statute concludes the party's opportunity to seek redress in the courts. Indicating to the client that other lawyers might take a different view or might be willing to represent the client is also appropriate in most cases.

Indeterminacy: Example of Endocrine Disrupters

An example of indeterminacy in both science and the law is found in the developing area referred to as the Endocrine Disruption Hypothesis. This hypothesis presents the case that some chemical substances that imitate human hormones can cause birth defects, cancer, infertility, and immunity problems.[179] The hypothesis has received widespread review in scientific studies. A growing body of scientific investigation suggests that the hypothesis has a basis in reality and that endocrine disrupters create a significant public health risk.[180] As a result, EPA is currently screening over 87,000 chemicals to determine whether these chemicals pose serious threats of disruption of the endocrine system.[181] Programs and initiatives of different federal agencies are directed at understanding and controlling endocrine disrupters.[182] Such programs do not, for the most part, mandate reporting by industry.[183]

---

176. *See* 42 U.S.C. § 9613 (g) (2) (A)–(B) (2002).

177. Jerry L. Anderson, *Removal or Remedial? The Myth of CERCLA's Two-Response System*, 18 COLUM. J. ENVTL. L. 103, 118 (1993).

178. "Even if an action can be properly categorized, the statute does not indicate whether the limitations period runs as to each individual action or only once with respect to all action in a particular category." *Id.*

179. *See* THEO CORLBORN ET AL., OUR STOLEN FUTURE: ARE WE THREATENING OUR FERTILITY, INTELLIGENCE, AND SURVIVAL—A SCIENTIFIC DETECTIVE STORY (Penguin 1996).

180. *See generally* www.epa.gov/oscpmont/oscpendo/history/endo4_2.htm (last visited Mar. 22, 2003).

181. *See* www.epa.gov/endocrine (last visited Mar. 22, 2003).

182. The Occupational Health and Safety Administration has also moved to attempt to control risks in the workplace posed by endocrine disrupters. For example, a pesticide known as DCBP is the subject of an OSHA guidance document. *See* ENVTL. NEWS, Nov. 1, 1998, at 484A-485.

183. *See* Stanley H. Abramson & Rachel G. Lattimore, *Kids' Risk: Expanding Health and*

38 ISSUES OF LEGAL ETHICS IN THE PRACTICE OF ENVIRONMENTAL LAW

Assume that your client proposes to dump a significant quantity of chemicals into a waterway. Although the plant has a permit, the permit does not speak to the chemical that is, according to the scientists advising you, a known endocrine disrupter. Arguably, your client is not violating its permit. since the substance is not yet the subject of environmental regulation. Nonetheless, the lawyer who has information from scientists indicating a significant public health risk is justified in counseling against this conduct and remonstrating if the client persists in its intention. This situation presents a difficult and unresolved ethics issue, particularly if the threatened conduct is likely to result in death or substantial bodily harm. Some jurisdictions require that the lawyer disclose the client information necessary to avert the harm if the conduct constitutes a crime.[184] In such jurisdictions, however, unless a legislature has addressed the danger involved and criminalized the conduct, the requirement of a crime is not met. Accordingly, state ethics rules do not speak to the situation. In cases in which a client intends to create peril for another, scientists may have a duty to disclose this information. Moreover, if harm comes to individuals as result of the client's action, the injured parties may bring a claim against the client and perhaps even the lawyer based on the unreasonable risk of harm created by the conduct.

Genetically engineered foods, including vegetables, fish, and animals, raise additional concerns about the relatively unknown technological revolution.[185] In the fall of 2000, manufacturers of taco shells and other food products were forced to recall products that contained genetically engineered corn that had not been approved for human consumption.[186] Some scientists are concerned about the release of genetically altered salmon into the environment because of the lack of knowledge about how the genetically altered species will interact with other fish, especially the already depleted Pacific salmon.[187]

The uncertainty attached to scientific judgments on topics such as these has repercussions for legal decisions as well as for business practices. Envi-

---

Safety Protection for Infants and Children, 14 NAT. RESOURCES & ENV'T 227, 230 (Spring 2000).

184. *See* Fla. State Bar Rule 4-1.6 (Confidentiality of Information); Va. S. Ct. Rule 1.6(c) (requiring that lawyers "promptly reveal intention of client to commit crime" after advising client of the obligation).

185. *See* Mark Koffman, *Biotech Fish Ready, But Not Approved*, THE COMMERCIAL APPEAL, Oct, 22, 2000, at 16.

186. *See* Philip Brasher, *EPA Asked to OK Genetic Corn as Food*, THE COMMERCIAL APPEAL, OCT. 26, 2000, at 68.

187. *See supra* note 185.

Chapter 1: Regulation of Lawyers   39

ronmental law is particularly susceptible to this problem of indeterminacy because of its close connection to public safety and the basis for risk assessments for regulating public health and safety. The tension between the duty of lawyers to serve the public good and to advocate for the interests of individual clients presents a complicated calculus, challenging lawyers to maintain professional independence as well as zealous advocacy.[188] In the arena of environmental law the tension between these competing demands is even greater. "Environmental law cannot protect society unless environmental lawyers ensure that it does so."[189] Moreover, the skepticism that the public holds for lawyers in general may be heightened in environmental law because the safety of the public can be placed at risk by the client's business regulated by environmental laws.

The task of assessing risks in a setting of indeterminacy has another dimension, relating to the level of subjectivity that a lawyer employs in advising clients. In the absence of a request for a subjective legal judgment, how should the lawyer regard his duty to give legal advice? Should a lawyer merely deliver all the relevant information about the law on a particular issue to the client or, instead, reveal his own bottom-line judgment on the legal issue at hand? Some physicians personalize their medical judgments: "If it were my wife, I would counsel her to have the surgery." This personalized advice may come in response to a patient's request for an explanation of the doctor's views of the best course, or the doctor may volunteer the personal view as a way of making his judgment as clear as possible to the patient. Many legal judgments, like medical judgments, include significant uncertainty. Should she give her personal judgment or simply an overview of legal risks and benefits, leaving the decision of what to do with the information to the client? A factor that further complicates this area of consideration is the fact that the lawyer's own risk assessment may push her toward merely giving objective assessments, leaving the decision firmly in the client's purview. This is because, all other things being equal, a client is less able to assert that he followed and relied on the lawyer's decision making if the lawyer's communications consistently underscore that she is giving legal information and the risks and benefits of different courses of conduct rather than advocating a particular course to the client.

---

188. *See* Douglas R. Williams, *Loyalty, Independence, and Social Responsibility in the Practice of Environmental Law*, 44 St. Louis U.L.J. 1061 (2000).

189. William Futrell, *Environmental Ethics, Legal Ethics, and Codes of Professional Responsibility*, 27 Loy. L. A. L. Rev. 825, 837–38 (1994).

CHAPTER 2

The Duty of Competence and the Lawyer's Duty of Diligence

Model Rule 1.1

The first rule of ethics is the duty of competence. The importance of this duty of competence is clear from its place in the Model Rules. It is set forth in Rule 1.1, the first substantive rule of the Model Rules.[1] Model Rule 1.1 states its requirement simply: "A lawyer shall provide competent representation to a client. Competent representation requires the legal knowledge, skill, thoroughness and preparation reasonably necessary for the representation."[2] Inherent in this duty is the requirement that the lawyer develop competence in the areas in which she accepts employment. This duty is of particular importance in the lawyer's area of specialty or focus. The lawyer must spend the requisite time and attention needed to serve client interests in the areas relating to the representation.[3]

Environmental Context

This rule has special importance in highly technical areas of practice such as environmental law. In general, the learning curve for any environmental representation is so great that as a practical matter only lawyers who specialize in

---

1. MODEL RULE 1.1 states: "A lawyer shall provide competent representation to a client. Competent representation requires legal knowledge, skill, thoroughness and preparation reasonably necessary for the representation."
2. MODEL RULE 1.1.
3. The Model Code recognizes this duty. *See, e.g.,* DR 6-101(A)(3) (forbidding neglect); DR 6-101(A)(2) (requiring adequate preparation).

41

environmental law should undertake a representation that involves complicated environmental issues. Most major law firms now have a department of lawyers who devote all or substantially all of their time to environmental matters. The intricacies of the legal questions presented in environmental legislation and common law make it essentially impossible for a general practitioner to accept environmental representations in light of the duty of competency. For this reason, most general practitioners who are asked to represent a party in a matter that will involve environmental issues will either refer the case to an environmental lawyer or associate an environmental lawyer on the particular matter.

Lawyer's Duty of Diligence

Common sense dictates that lawyers owe their clients diligence in all matters undertaken. It is not enough to be competent; lawyers must focus their energies and competence on behalf of their clients. It does the client no good if a lawyer is competent but not concerned with the client's case or problem. Accordingly, the lawyer's duty of diligence is of paramount importance. In environmental law, diligence seems more important than ever because of the wide range of indeterminacy on many issues and the complexity of the factual and scientific judgments required in those cases. The duty of diligence may require that the environmental lawyer take extra time to learn the meaning of all those acronyms and the substance of the difference between requirements that vary based on context and categories. For example, TMDL (total maximum daily load) requirements create a separate requirement for clients who may be discharging into waterways where TMDLs have been set. The duty of diligence is another way of stating the duty of loyalty. In most references, loyalty is presented as a passive virtue, a state of mind or attitude that strives to prevent any other interest to sidetrack the underlying service to a client. The duty of diligence makes the obligation of loyalty active, requiring the lawyer to move forward to serve the client's interests "despite opposition, obstruction or personal inconvenience to the lawyer."[4]

The Limits of Diligence

Prohibited Conduct

The term often used to describe the commitment of the lawyer to her clients is "zealousness." This term points to high level of diligence and commitment on the part of the lawyer. Of course, there are limits to this zealousness. Lawyers

---

4. MODEL RULE 1.3 cmt. 1.

Chapter 2: The Duty of Competence and the Lawyer's Duty of Diligence   43

are not entitled to assist clients in undertakings that are criminal or fraudulent or to gain advantages through deceit or trickery.

Model Rule 1.3 imposes the duty of diligence on lawyers. It states in full: "A lawyer shall act with reasonable diligence and promptness in representing a client." When a lawyer accepts a representation, she should represent the client with "commitment and dedication."[5] She binds herself to serve the client's interests "with zeal in advocacy"[6] and without unreasonable delay.[7] A comment to Model Rule 1.3 notes that after accepting a representation, the lawyer "should carry through to conclusion all matters undertaken for any client."[8]

Comments to Rule 1.3 focus the lawyer's attention on the paramount importance of acting in the client's best interest. The comments to Model Rule 1.3 emphasize "commitment and dedication to the interests of the client," as well as "zeal in advocacy."[9] A comment to the rule notes that diligence is not an absolute. A lawyer is "not bound to press for every advantage."[10] Indeed, offensive conduct by a lawyer may be sanctioned even though the lawyer believes that his conduct furthers the client's cause.[11] The comment also notes that the lawyer has "discretion in determining the means" of pursuing the client's case.[12] The active nature of the duty of diligence is emphasized by the comment's criticism of procrastination. The comment singles out procrastination as a "widely resented professional shortcoming," noting that delay can "destroy" the client's legal position in some cases. Even when no substantive harm is done, procrastination and delay can result in "needless anxiety."[13]

Choice of Clients

Generally, a lawyer is not forced to accept every client that offers to retain him. Although lawyers are sometimes appointed by courts to undertake a representation, such appointments are infrequent, considering the universe of legal representation; and it is rare for a lawyer to be required to accept the appointment against his will. This is especially true when the lawyer indicates to the court that he has strong personal feelings about subject matter or allega-

---

5. *Id.*
6. *Id.*
7. MODEL RULE 1.3 cmt. 2.
8. MODEL RULE 1.3 cmt. 3.
9. MODEL RULE 1.3 cmt. 1.
10. MODEL RULE 1.3 cmt. 2.
11. *In re* First City Bancorporation, 282 F.3d 864 (5th Cir. 2002) (sanctioning lawyer for rudeness despite lawyer's argument that his conduct is in the best interest of his clients).
12. *Id.*
13. *Id.*

44 ISSUES OF LEGAL ETHICS IN THE PRACTICE OF ENVIRONMENTAL LAW

tions that could compromise the representation. Certainly, environmental lawyers are entitled to strong personal feelings about the environment. After all, the topic has provoked major divisions among the people and has sparked dramatic protests in society in recent years.

The scholarship of professional responsibility includes some dramatic and florid statements of the duty of lawyers to accept any client.[14] In practice, however, lawyers may reject a prospective representation on a variety of grounds, including lack of available time or lack of expertise in an area. A simple belief that the prospective representation is not one in which the lawyer would do a good job or is one in which the client's position is repugnant to the lawyer also should be regarded as a legitimate basis for declining a proffered representation.[15]

Duration of Representation

The duty of diligence applies to a representation as long as the representation lasts. If the lawyer is uncertain whether or not the representation has ended, she must take the initiative to clarify the existence or termination of the representation. The question of whether the representation has terminated may present many factual difficulties. Such a question of whether the representation currently exists often arises when a significant period of time has passed in which there has been no contact between the lawyer and the client. Additionally, the question of whether the representation still exists often arises when the client has failed to pay for past services despite billings and requests for payment. In these circumstances, a lawyer may believe that the relationship is over or may have a serious doubt about whether the client remains a client. Model Rule 1.3 makes clear that the lawyer rather than the client has the responsibility to determine whether the representation continues.[16]

> Doubt about whether a client-lawyer relationship still exists should be clarified by the lawyer, preferably in writing, so that the client will not mistakenly suppose the lawyer is looking after the client's affairs when the lawyer has ceased to do so. For example, if a lawyer has handled a judicial or administrative proceeding that produced a result adverse to the client but has not been specifically

---

14. *See* MONROE H. FREEDMAN, UNDERSTANDING LAWYER'S ETHICS 67 (1998), and references cited therein.
15. Both the Model Code and the Model Rules note that lawyers may refuse a representation. *See* MODEL CODE, ETHICAL CONSIDERATION 2-26; MODEL RULE 6.2 cmt. 2.
16. *Compare* MODEL RULE 1.16 and MODEL CODE DR 2-110(A).

Chapter 2: The Duty of Competence and the Lawyer's Duty of Diligence   45

instructed concerning pursuit of an appeal, the lawyer should advise the client of the possibility of appeal before relinquishing responsibility for the matter.[17]

Comment 3 reinforces the need for the lawyer to take the initiative and resolve questions about whether the representation has ended. The lawyer must keep in touch with the client and continue to represent the client actively until the relationship is clearly terminated. Additionally, transferring a client to other counsel does not necessarily end the client-lawyer relationship.[18]

When the client fails to make agreed payments for legal services and the representation was not intended to be pro bono, the lawyer may want to terminate the representation. The most prudent practice for the lawyer is to anticipate this issue and address it at the outset in the representation agreement. The lawyer's retention letter for compensated representation should state the obligation and timing of payment for legal services and the events that justify or constitute termination.[19] In the event of failure to pay, the lawyer should write the client stating that termination is imminent.[20] This notice should state the date upon which the representation will terminate if the client fails to remit payment and should reference the provisions of the representation agreement that provide for this result. After the stated time period has passed, the lawyer should write another letter declaring the representation terminated. Copies of termination letters should be filed with the court when they relate to pending matters. In the event the representation was created by court appointment, the lawyer must seek leave of the court to terminate the relationship.[21]

Environmental Example

Environmental lawyers, especially those representing large groups of people, face difficult questions relating to whether the representation has terminated. When a claim is delayed for months (or years), a group's consensus may fail or change, making it unclear whether the group wishes to continue to pursue the matter at all or whether it intends to continue to use the lawyer's services. The practices noted above for determining whether a representation continues and for giving a client due notice of imminent or completed termination apply with equal force in the environmental area.

---

17. MODEL RULE 1.3 cmt. 3.
18. *See* Tormo v. Yormark, 398 F. Supp. 1159 (D. N.J. 1975).
19. *See* MODEL RULE 1.16(b)(4).
20. MODEL RULE 1.2.
21. MODEL RULE 1.16 cmt. 3.

46 ISSUES OF LEGAL ETHICS IN THE PRACTICE OF ENVIRONMENTAL LAW

Even in cases where a lawyer is representing an environmental client pro bono (probably a plaintiff group), it may be wise for the lawyer to charge the client some reduced rate for the representation. In a totally pro bono matter, in which a lawyer charges no fees at all, the lawyer may find herself swamped with questions and requests for meetings from the client, even to such an extent that the lawyer's ability to represent the client effectively may be compromised.[22]

---

22. Comments of Charles F. Newman, counsel for a plaintiff in *Citizens to Preserve Overton Park, Inc. v. Volpe*, Presentation to Leo Bearman, Sr., American Inns of Court (Jan. 9, 2001).

CHAPTER 3

The Lawyer-Client Relationship

The lawyer owes each client the duty of unfettered loyalty.[1] Loyalty is "the essential element in the lawyer's relationship to a client."[2] While the relationship between a client and his lawyer is often described as one of agency,[3] the lawyer's obligations to the client go beyond those of ordinary agency,[4] and the concept of agency is not used by courts to limit the application of the rules of ethics or to lessen the lawyer's obligation to his client. General principles of agency law suggest that both the agent and the principal must manifest intent to form a relationship. "An agency relation exists only if there has been a manifestation by the principal to the agent that the agent may act on his account, and consent by the agent so to act."[5] Nevertheless, a court may infer formation of the relationship from conduct. The Restatement (Third) of the Law Governing Lawyers indicates that the attorney-client relationship may result despite lack of assent by the lawyer. It states that the relationship is formed when "a person manifests to a lawyer the person's intent that the lawyer provide legal services for the person; and either (a) the lawyer manifests to the person consent to do so; or (b) the lawyer fails to manifest lack of consent to do so, and the lawyer knows or reasonably should know that the

---

1. *See generally* Eleanor W. Myers, *Examining Independence and Loyalty*, 72 Temp. L. Rev. 857 (1999).
2. Model Rule 1.7 cmt. 1.
3. Brinkley v. Farmers Elevator Mut. Ins. Co., 485 F.2d 1283, 1286 (10th Cir. 1973); Rothman v. Wilson, 121 F.2d 1000, 1006 (9th Cir. 1941).
4. *See* Udall v. Littell, 366 F.2d 668, 675-76 (1966), *cert. denied*, 385 U.S. 1007 (1967).
5. Restatement Second Agency, § 15. Even under the standard set by the Restatement, formal communication of assent is not always necessary. "[I]f the principal requests another to act for him with respect to a matter, and indicates that the other is to act without further communication and the other consents so to act, the relation of principal and agent exists. If, under such circumstances, the other does the requested act, it is inferred that he acts as agent unless he manifests that he does not so intend or unless the circumstances so indicate." *Id. cmt. B.*

48   ISSUES OF LEGAL ETHICS IN THE PRACTICE OF ENVIRONMENTAL LAW

person reasonably relies on the lawyer to provide the services."[6] The Restatement also notes the relationship may arise as a result of appointment by a court, noting the relationship arises when "a tribunal with power to do so appoints the lawyer to provide the services."[7]

Although authority exists to the effect that parties must expressly or impliedly consent to formation of an attorney-client relationship,[8] this view appears to be the minority.[9] At any rate, a risk exists for lawyers that a court may find an attorney-client relationship in cases where the lawyer believed no relationship existed. Courts have so ruled in cases in which the parties did not enter a formal contract and the client neither paid nor agreed to pay legal fees.[10] The basic ethical duties of the lawyer to a client do not vary based on whether the parties entered a formal agreement or the court inferred a representation based on the circumstances.[11] The scope of a representation may limit the role of the lawyer, however. In the event it is necessary to show the limitation of the representation, it is valuable to have a written contract of employment that sets forth the limitation. Additionally, a written contract or clear retention letter can be of great benefit in making the relationship clear to both parties and specifying the extent of the tasks undertaken and the expectations of each party regarding performance and payment for services.[12] Moreover, the Scope section of the Model Rules makes clear that the duty of confidentiality applies to prospective client information, whether or not an attorney-client relationship comes into being. "[S]ome duties, such as that of confidentiality under Rule 1.6 . . . may attach when the lawyer agrees to consider whether a client-lawyer relationship shall be established."[13]

---

6. RESTATEMENT (THIRD) OF THE LAW GOVERNING LAWYERS § 14 (2000).

7. *Id.*

8. *See* Torres v. Divis, 494 N.E.2d 1227, 1231 (1986) (stating that attorney-client relationship is consensual, arising only when both lawyer and client consent to its formation); Comm. on Prof'l Ethics and Grievances v. Johnson, 447 F.2d 169, 174 (3d Cir. 1971).

9. *See* Westinghouse Electric Corp. v. Kerr-McGee Corp., 580 F.2d 1311 (7th Cir. 1978) (reversing district court determination that absence of express contract for lawyer's services prevented formation of attorney-client relationship).

10. *See, e.g.*, Togstad v. Vesely, Otto, Miller & Keefe, 291 N.W.2d 686 (Minn. 1980).

11. *See* Westinghouse Electric Corp. v. Kerr-McGee Corp., 580 F.2d 1311 (7th Cir. 1978).

12. *See generally* DOCUMENTING THE ATTORNEY-CLIENT RELATIONSHIP : LAW FIRM POLICIES ON ENGAGEMENT, TERMINATION, AND DECLINATION (Committee on Law Firms, Section of Business Law, American Bar Association, 1999).

13. MODEL RULES Scope [15].

The Client's Objectives

One of the guiding principles of legal practice is that the client, rather than the lawyer, determines the objectives of the representation. Subject to some exceptions, Model Rule 1.2 requires that lawyers "abide by a client's decisions concerning the objectives of representation."[14] Important safeguards counterbalance this point. Model Rule 1.2(d) prohibits a lawyer from knowingly assisting a client in wrongful or fraudulent activity. It does not require, however, that the lawyer engage in an investigation of the client to determine whether the client is acting unlawfully. The Model Rules empower a lawyer to withdraw from a representation for a variety of reasons, many of which provide substantial discretion to lawyers.[15] For example, the fact that the lawyer considers the client's objectives to be "repugnant or imprudent"[16] provides a basis for withdrawal. The rule also expressly states that lawyers must abide by "a client's decision whether to accept an offer of settlement."[17] Compliance with Rule 1.2 can be difficult in the environmental arena. Potential for disagreement exists whenever a large number of people are involved in legal action. Such a situation often exists in the environmental area, as when an environmental public interest group forms to save a particular resource or geographic feature or to collect damages based on a mass toxic tort. Consider, for example, a toxic tort case in which numerous plaintiffs have varying objectives and interests.[18] Different individuals may seem to speak with authority about the objectives of the group. And they may present differing instructions to the lawyer. Mass tort settlements present a pronounced opportunity for infighting within a represented group and for lawyers to seek to finalize a deal as quickly as possible to minimize the amount of time consumed on a particular matter.

Problems arise in many environmental cases. Cases seeking injunctive relief rather than damages seem to present less potential for differential treat-

---

14. MODEL RULE 1.2. *See also* Lord v. Money Masters, Inc., 435 S.E.2d 247 (Ga. 1993).

15. Similarly, the decision of whether to accept a representation is essentially unlimited. *See* Nathan M. Crystal, *Developing a Philosophy of Lawyering,* 14 NOTRE DAME J. L. ETHICS & PUB. POL'Y 75 (2000).

16. MODEL RULE 1.16(b)(3). *See also* James P. Hemmer, *Resignation of Corporate Counsel: Fulfillment or Abdication of Duty,* 39 HASTINGS L.J. 641 (1988).

17. For a full treatment of the complexities and ethical problems raised in settlement of mass tort actions, see Carrie Menkel-Meadow, *Ethics and the Settlements of Mass Torts: When the Rules Meet the Road,* 80 CORNELL L. REV. 1159 (1995) (arguing that the Model Rules do not contemplate lawyer-client relations of mass torts and do not provide adequate guidance for mass tort settlements).

18. *See* State Bar of Michigan Standing Comm. on Prof'l and Judicial Ethics Op. R-16, 1993 WL 566247.

50 ISSUES OF LEGAL ETHICS IN THE PRACTICE OF ENVIRONMENTAL LAW

ment of plaintiffs and, thus, fewer conflicts among the participants. But individuals within the group or within the leadership may disagree regarding whether accommodations offered by an industrial source are sufficiently protective for a neighborhood group. The exception to the rule that disagreement is inherent in public interest groups is found in the famous case of *Citizens to Preserve Overton Park, Inc. v. Volpe.*[19] According to Charles Newman, lead counsel for the citizens group, the success of the group was due, in part, to the fact that the plaintiff group was a "small and absolutely unified group of about twelve people with about three leaders who made decisions [regarding the litigation]."[20]

While the environmental lawyer may not be able to resolve or control such conflicts, she can reduce conflicts regarding the process of decision making itself by encouraging the group to decide at the outset what percentage of the membership is necessary for a binding decision by the entity and by refusing to "take sides" in such controversies. This does not mean, however, that the lawyer should withhold her legal judgments that relate to the controversy. In some cases, the lawyer may decide to make a clear mandate for action a condition of accepting a particular representation. Taking this step indicates to the members of the group the importance of reaching a consensus (at some predetermined level). When a controversy is spotlighted by the media, as environmental disputes often are, such a condition of employment could protect the lawyer's reputation as well as facilitating agreement in the group and settlement of the controversy. For example, some of the environmental groups formed to save parkland, a beach, a bay, or some other geographical feature can result in stalemate simply because the members of the group cannot reach closure on the settlement. While some believe that mitigating measures to protect the parkland or the geographical feature are sufficient to allow a public project to go forward, others may object that any accommodation is not only inconsistent with the group's goals but even evil. In such a circumstance, all of the legal fees and efforts can be lost and the group may dissolve as a result of the inability to reach consensus. Such a conclusion is counter to the original purposes of the group and the representation.

Limitations of the Client's Objectives

Despite the importance of the principle that the lawyer should "abide by a

---

19. Citizens to Preserve Overton Park, Inc. v. Volpe, 401 U.S. 402 (1971).

20. Comments of Charles Newman at the American Inns of Court of Memphis, Tennessee, Jan. 9, 2001; *see also* Oliver Houck, *Unfinished Stories*, 73 U. Colo. L. Rev. 867 (2002) (noting nucleus of organizers of Citizens to Preserve Overton Park was "never large in number").

Chapter 3: The Lawyer-Client Relationship 51

client's decisions concerning the objectives of representation,"[21] this admonition is not absolute or unfettered by limiting principles. The client may determine the objectives of the representation, but the lawyer has discretion in continuing the representation and duties not to further criminal or fraudulent conduct or to advance a frivolous litigation. Moreover, Rule 11 does require that lawyers engage in some level of inquiry concerning the matter asserted in litigation on behalf of a client.

In recent years, the phenomenon of SLAPP suits has generated significant public interest.[22] The acronym "SLAPP" stands for "Strategic Lawsuit Against Public Participation"[23] and refers to actions instituted for the purpose of retaliating against a person who seeks redress in a public forum.[24] SLAPP suits are not the only method for silencing opposition. Covenants not to sue have also been used to quiet criticism and prevent dissemination of information.[25]

SLAPP actions are lodged against individuals who oppose particular developments and are sometimes brought against lawyers who represent nongovernmental organizations (NGOs) or others in suits against industry or

---

21. MODEL RULE 1.2.

22. *See* Phillip S. Berry, *SLAPP: Strategic Lawsuits Against Public Participation in Government: The "Environmental" SLAPP*, C935 ALI-ABA 61 (Aug. 19, 1994); Jennifer E. Sills, *SLAPP (Strategic Lawsuits Against Public Participation): How Can the Legal System Eliminate Their Appeal?*, 25 CONN. L. REV. 547 (1993); John C. Barker, *Common-Law and Statutory Solutions to the Problem of SLAPP*, 26 LOY. L.A. L. REV. 395 (1993).

23. The acronym was coined by George W. Pring and Penelope Canan. *See* 47 SMU L. REV. 95 n.4.

24. *See* George W. Pring, Penelope Canan, *Strategic Lawsuits Against Public Participation (SLAPP): An Introduction for Bench, Bar and Bystanders*, 12 BRIDGEPORT L. REV. 937 (1993); George (Rock) Pring & Penelope A. Canan, *SLAPP: An Overview of the Practice*, C935 ALI-ABA 1 (co-sponsored by the University of Denver College of Law's Political Litigation Project and California Continuing Education of the Bar) (Aug. 19, 1994). Similar techniques include retaliation for environmental claims, proceedings to impose sanctions against lawyers, and political maneuvers to silence opponents. What follows is a discussion of SLAPP suits from the perspective of legal ethics; other aspects of SLAPP suits are discussed in Chapter 7. *Id.* Carl Tobias, *Environmental Litigation and Rule 11*, 33 WM. & MARY L. REV. 429 (1992) (noting the use of Rule 11 actions to discourage lawyers and the parties they represent from "commencing, or zealously pursuing, legitimate actions").

25. *See, e.g.,* Robert R.M. Verchick, *Free Speech, Toxic Torts, and the Battle of Sugar Creek*, 70 UMKC L. REV. 245 (2001) (exploring use of overly restrictive covenants not to sue to chill speech about toxic torts and related claims and grievances).

52 ISSUES OF LEGAL ETHICS IN THE PRACTICE OF ENVIRONMENTAL LAW

developers.[26] For example, in *Kashian v. Harriman*, a California court dismissed a claim against Harriman based on an anti-SLAPP statute.[27] In this case, Edward Kashian, a businessman who planned to build a for-profit hospital, brought a suit alleging unfair business practices and defamatory statements against Richard L. Harriman, a lawyer representing local advocacy organizations that opposed the hospital development. Harriman wrote the state attorney general, seeking an investigation of the developer's activities. After a newspaper published an article about Harriman's letter, Kashian sued Harriman, accusing him of seeking to extort a settlement by using the advocacy group. Harriman moved to strike the complaint based on California's anti-SLAPP statute. The trial court granted the motion. The appellate court affirmed, finding that filing a lawsuit was an exercise of the organizations' constitutional right of petition. The appellate court noted that Kashian could not avoid the statutory bar by casting his claim as one for injunctive relief. It found that Harriman's letters to other medical providers were protected by the common-interest privilege.

Courts have denounced strongly the use of the judicial process for the purpose of silencing individuals or squelching the individual's exercise of his legal rights.[28] Several states (including California, Delaware, Georgia, Minnesota, Nevada, New York, Rhode Island, and Washington) have passed legislation aimed at protecting citizens from SLAPP suits.[29] Moreover, Federal Rule of Civil Procedure 11 provides sanctions against lawyers who file frivolous suits or pleadings.[30] Rule 11 requires that lawyers sign any pleading or motion filed with a court as a representation that the filing is "warranted by

---

26. Robert R. Kuehn, *Shooting the Messenger: the Ethics of Attacks on Environmental Representation*, 26 HARV. ENVT'L L. REV. 417 (2002) (detailing severe attacks on lawyers who provide environmental representation and demonstrating dangers inherent in representing controversial clients in the environmental arena).

27. Kashian v. Harriman, 98 Cal. App. 4th 892, 120 Cal. Rptr. 2d 576 (2002).

28. "[T]he wholly lawful exercise, by citizens in a community, of the right to petition their local government to follow a certain course of action . . . should be vigorously protected and should not expose individuals to suit by persons unhappy with the results of such petitioning." Westfield Partners, Ltd. v. Hogan, 740 F. Supp. 523 (N.D. Ill. 1990) (dismissing complaint of conspiracy by real estate developer against landowners who had successfully petitioned against development), quoted in Chad Baruch, *"If I Had a Hammer": Defending SLAPP Suits in Texas*, 3 TEX. WESLEYAN L. REV. 55 (1996).

29. *See* Yvette Mendez, *"SLAPP" Attack: Has Public Concern Gone South in Massachusetts?*, 42-MAR BBJ 6, 21 (1998); Edward W. McBride, Jr., *The Empire State SLAPPs Back: New York's Legislative Response to SLAPP Suits*, 17 VT. L. REV. 925 (1990).

30. *See* Elihu Root, Note, *The Dynamics of Rule 11: Preventing Frivolous Litigation by Demanding Professional Responsibility*, 61 N.Y.U. L. REV. 300 (1986).

Chapter 3: The Lawyer-Client Relationship 53

existing law or a good faith argument" for a change in the law and that the document filed is not intended to harass or delay any judicial proceedings or for any improper purpose.[31]

Scholars have debated whether SLAPP suits are unethical per se and whether they amount to malicious prosecution.[32] The question of whether a particular action is a SLAPP suit turns on the issue of the motivation of the person bringing suit. Accordingly, it is difficult to judge whether a suit falls into this category of taking legal action for an improper purpose.

Model Rule 3.1, entitled "Meritorious Claims and Contentions," states: "A lawyer shall not bring or defend a proceeding, or assert or controvert an issue therein, unless there is a basis for doing so that is not frivolous, which includes a good faith argument for an extension, modification or reversal of existing law."[33]

This rule deals with the minimum basis for filing an action. A comment to Rule 3.1 provides a gloss on the meaning of a "frivolous" action, indicating that an action is frivolous if:

> [T]he client desires to have the action taken primarily for the purpose of harassing or maliciously injuring a person, or, if the lawyer is unable either to make a good faith argument on the merits of the action taken or to support the action taken by a good faith argument for an extension, modification or reversal of existing law.[34]

By using the disjunction "or," the comment suggests that the malicious purpose is independently sufficient to take an action outside the definition of "meritorious claim."

A SLAPP suit is, by definition, an action brought for the purpose of discouraging a person or group from engaging in legal action or participation in legal process. This purpose is squarely within the description of Model Rule 3.1 of intending to harass or maliciously injure a person. Thus, the SLAPP suit should be recognized as a nonmeritorious matter. The fact that a

---

31. *See* Fed. R. Civ. P. 11; *see also* Victor H. Kramer, *Viewing Rule 11 as a Tool to Improve Professional Responsibility*, 75 Minn. L. Rev. 793 (1991); Root, *supra* note 30.

32. Marnie Stetson, *Reforming SLAPP Reform: New York's Anti-SLAPP Statute*, 70 N.Y.U. L. Rev. 1324 (1995).

33. Model Rule 3.1. The rule qualifies this statement in the criminal context, noting that in criminal proceedings, the lawyer "may nevertheless so defend the proceeding as to require that every element of the case be established."

34. Model Rule 3.1 cmt. ¶ 2.

54   ISSUES OF LEGAL ETHICS IN THE PRACTICE OF ENVIRONMENTAL LAW

lawyer can articulate an argument for the action does not make it a "good faith argument."

A lawyer often will not know a client's motivation for instructing the lawyer to file suit. In litigation and disciplinary hearings, a lawyer should not assume that a suit is brought in bad faith or for improper purposes. To do so is to prejudge the client who wishes to use legal process. In some cases, however, a lawyer may either know for a certainty or have good evidence of the client's motivation. Statements such as "X will pay for his stand," or "It's time to go after X," give a clear indication that the suit constitutes retaliation and the client's purpose is to misuse legal process. A lawyer who brings an action when he has such knowledge is bringing a nonmeritorious action and is misusing the legal process.

The 2002 revision to Model Rule 3.1 added the language "in law and fact" to describe the basis upon which a lawyer may assert or controvert an issue. The rule as revised provides:

> A lawyer shall not bring or defend a proceeding, or assert or controvert an issue therein, unless there is a basis *in law and fact* for doing so that is not frivolous, which includes a good faith argument for an extension, modification or reversal of existing law.[35]

The revision to Comment 2 to Model Rule 3.1 may have significance with regard to SLAPP suits and other inquiries regarding whether an action is meritorious. Comment 2 to Model Rule 3.1 defines a "frivolous" action. Under the 1983 version, the comment indicated that a claim is frivolous "if the client desires to have the action taken primarily for the purpose of harassing or maliciously injuring a person or if the lawyer is unable either to make a good faith argument on the merits of the action taken or to support the action taken by good faith argument for an extension, modification or reversal of existing law."[36] The revised Comment deletes the language "client desires to have the action taken primarily for the purpose of harassing or maliciously injuring a person," destroying the issue of the client's motivation as a basis for finding a claim to be frivolous. This deletion is significant because it appears to remove from consideration the client's motivation, even though a lawyer may know to a substantial certainty that the client intends to injure or harass another by the use of legal process. Whether this change of a Model Rule Comment will have effect on the law relating to malicious prosecution or to Rule 11 claims is an open question.

---

35. MODEL RULE 3.1 (2002) (italics added to show addition).

36. MODEL RULE 3.1 cmt. ¶ 2 (1983).

Chapter 3: The Lawyer-Client Relationship 55

Limitations of the Client's Objectives (2002 Revision)

The revised rules adopted by the ABA in February 2002 deleted the portion of Comment 2 to Rule 3.1 relied on in the above analysis. As a result of this deletion, the lawyer may have a more difficult analytical task. Additionally, the lawyer may face a dilemma by this change, in the event it is adopted by states, in that it may force the lawyer to violate obligations of professionalism that require that he not bring a claim that he has reason to know is motivated by client animus or a desire to harass or maliciously use the judicial process.

SLAPP Suits in the Environmental Context

Environmental plaintiff groups are particularly susceptible to SLAPP suits. Retaliation against an individual for pursuing a citizen suit or taking a political stand on an environmental issue can discourage the environmental plaintiff from continuing in a matter. Such retaliation distorts the judicial and political processes and discourages political action. If a lawyer knows that her client is bringing a suit for an improper purpose, she should counsel the client against the action and withdraw from the representation if the client persists in its objective of misusing the judicial process.

Often environmental plaintiffs sue polluters or the administrator of EPA or other agencies that have failed to undertake a nondiscretionary duty. For example, in *Equilon Enterprises, LLC v. Consumer Cause, Inc.*,[37] the California Second District Court of Appeal affirmed a trial court's dismissal of the plaintiff oil companies' case because it violated California's SLAPP statute[38] as an impermissible strategic lawsuit against public participation. Prior to the lawsuit by Equilon, the consumer group Consumer Cause, Inc., gave Equilon notice of its intent to sue for alleged violations of the California Safe Drinking Water and Toxic Enforcement Act of 1986,[39] asserting that 78 of Equilon's gas stations had been polluting local groundwater with benzene, lead, and toluene. Rather than seeking clarification of the claims under Proposition 65, Equilon filed a lawsuit seeking an injunction against the enforcement action by Consumer Cause. The trial court dismissed the *Equilon* case as a SLAPP suit on the basis that California's statute prohibits strategic lawsuits and protects the right of the defendant to petition under Proposition 65. Additionally, the court held that declaratory relief was not appropriate because plaintiffs were unlikely to prevail on their claims. The court of appeals affirmed the trial court's judgment, holding that Consumer Cause's notices fell within the

---

37. 85 Cal. App. 4th 654 (Dec. 18, 2000).
38. Cal. Civ. Proc. Code 425.16.
39. This statute is also known as Proposition 65.

type of speech or right to petition protected by the statute and agreeing with the trial court that the oil companies were unlikely to prevail on their claims. Moreover, the appellate court held that the consumer group was clearly privileged to bring a claim under the water act.

The Lawyer's Role as Advisor

Lawyers have traditionally served a counseling role in their relationship with clients. This role is often broader than advising a client on the state of the law or legal consequences. Model Rule 2.1 notes that the scope of the lawyer's role is not limited to purely legal or technical considerations. The rule provides: "In representing a client, a lawyer shall exercise independent professional judgment and render candid advice. In rendering advice, a lawyer may refer not only to law but to other considerations such as moral, economic, social and political factors, that may be relevant to the client's situation."[40]

Model Rule 2.1 is evidence of the ABA's recognition of the breadth of practice for many lawyers and the confidence of the ABA in the ability of lawyers to provide clients with helpful advice beyond the technical considerations of legal rules. It specifically endorses the right of the lawyer to speak to moral questions and to considerations of economics and social and political factors that so often interact with legal issues. The rule thus encourages lawyers to take a wholistic and practical approach to assessing the client's interests in consultation with the client. The wide range of matters in which lawyers serve as advisors makes it difficult to contextualize fully the significance of the role of the lawyer as advisor. This rule merely hints at the reality of the breadth of the lawyer's role beyond the adversary system. The lawyer's role in serving the ends of a client is not limited to representing the client in court or administrative proceedings or to rendering merely technical legal advice. Often lawyers use methods for resolving disputes outside the traditional juridical or administrative system. They properly act outside the judicial system (and sometimes at the direction of the court), using alternative dispute resolution (ADR) techniques such as negotiation, mediation, arbitration and sample trials. Lawyers also further the interests of their clients by explaining law and policy and providing advice on the most prudent course for a client to take in day-to-day operations as well as in litigation and business transactions.[41]

Lawyers act as negotiators and advisors to clients on a wide range of

---

40. MODEL RULE 2.1.
41. *See generally* Andrea Kupfer Schneider, *Building a Pedagogy of Problem-Solving: Learning to Choose Among ADR Processes*, 5 HARV. NEGOT. L. REV. 113 (2000) (presenting model for providing counseling throughout ADR process).

issues and interests. Individuals seek counsel both as a matter of routine and as a response to a crisis. They sometimes seek moral assessments of different courses of action as well as the lawyer's opinion of legal obligations. In the corporate setting particularly, lawyers often become trusted advisors not only for their legal knowledge but also for the practical wisdom that draws on legal, economic, and political factors. Lawyers often do and should use both their technical expertise and their good judgment. The lawyer whose attitude communicates that her role is to aid the client in complying with the law rather than trying to escape from the penalties or hide noncompliance is likely to have fewer problems with client conduct. In serving in the broader role of advisor, the lawyer must carefully judge his own motivations and abilities to speak to issues beyond the strictly legal sphere, applying practical judgment to determine what type of advice goes beyond the sphere of the lawyer's expertise.

Although circumstances dictate exceptions, some general assessments of the role of lawyers are possible. The best practice seems to be for lawyers to share unstintingly their candid judgments and the bases for those judgments. Part of the lawyer's responsibility as advisor is to explain to the client the reasons for the advice given. The lawyer should identify which considerations are legal in nature and which are based on moral, economic, political, or other factors. Such identification of the background reasons for the lawyer's views puts the advice given into perspective for the client and prevents the client from regarding everything the lawyer says as having a legal mandate attached to it. Such explanations also lead naturally to advice by the lawyer that it may be in the client's best interest to seek further information or analysis from other professionals such as psychiatrists, financial specialists, accounting specialists, toxicologists, or environmental consultants.[42]

Environmental Practice

Examples of the broad role of lawyers serving as advisors abound in environmental practice. For example, a lawyer representing a landowner in a sale of real property is justified in pointing to moral as well as legal considerations mandating disclosure of dangerous conditions. A lawyer advising a company to reduce its waste stream of hazardous substances is justified in noting economic advantages of the reduction. Under the Clean Air Act, the lawyer may assess for the client the potential for trading emission limits of nitrous oxide and sulfur dioxide as well as the legal requirement of limiting air pollution. In advising a governmental entity, the lawyer may explain his views that pursuing litigation may have financial benefits but political detriments or that the

---

42. *See* MODEL RULE 1 cmt. 4.

policy at issue does not comport with general principles of good government. In this regard, it is important for the government lawyer to remember that courts as well as commentators often impose a higher duty of candor and ethics on government lawyers without reference to a specific rule of legal ethics.

The complexity of environmental laws today makes it crucial that clients (both corporate clients and individuals) have access to legal advisors. The Clean Air Act is only one example of the level of complexity present in many areas of environmental law.

> With the 1990 amendments to the federal Clean Air Act running over 300 pages, and other environmental statutes that courts find "mind-numbing" and capable of understanding by very few people even within the U.S. Environmental Protection Agency (EPA), no regulated entity could competently participate in any important environmental proceeding without highly trained lawyers. Citizens who attempt to participate without legal assistance in the maze of environmental agency rule-making or permitting proceedings, much less sophisticated court cases, find themselves at a significant and usually insurmountable disadvantage.[43]

Rule 2.1 presents an example of the Model Rules' respect for lawyers as decision makers. Rather than constraining lawyers to give only legal advice, it respects the ability of lawyers to speak to the broader range of human affairs and, implicitly, to explain the reasons for the advice to the client. Environmental practice, perhaps more than any other area, presents opportunities for lawyers to advise clients on the long-term impact of their actions and to identify for clients the benefits of innovative solutions to difficult problems.

Client Status

The question of client status is of threshold importance in every lawyer-client relationship. For environmental lawyers, the issue can be clouded for a number of reasons. For example, a lawyer attending a meeting of an environmental nonprofit organization may give advice casually without thinking that he is entering a lawyer-client relationship. Because the existence of the relationship does not depend on compensation or on a formal understanding that a relationship has been formed, the lawyer may later be held to have been giving legal advice as the lawyer for the organization. On the other hand, courts have

---

43. Robert R. Kuehn, *Shooting the Messenger: The Ethics of Attacks on Environmental Representation,* 26 HARV. ENVTL. L. REV. 417, 418 (2002).

held that no professional attorney-client relationship arises when an individual consults a lawyer in some other capacity.[44] Thus, if the individual calls an environmental lawyer to obtain biological information rather than legal advice, it is arguable that an attorney-client relationship is not created for purposes of the attorney-client privilege or other issues.

When client status is disputed in a case, the court decides whether an individual is a client of a particular lawyer, applying the substantive law of the jurisdiction. A "client" is defined as a "person who employs or retains an attorney, or counselor, to appear for him in courts, advise, assist, and defend him in legal proceedings, and to act for him in any legal business."[45] The Scope section of the rules states that: "for purposes of determining the lawyer's authority and responsibility, principles of substantive law external to these rules determine whether a client-lawyer relationship exists."[46] As with any important fact question, the risk that a court may deem the attorney-client relation to exist (or not to exist) can have dramatic effects in terms of the rights and responsibilities (and potential liability) of the parties. Thus, the cautious lawyer will clarify situations of uncertainty to resolve the question of representation. Because the duties of the lawyer spring from the lawyer-client relationship, client status presents an important threshold ethical issue. It determines whether the lawyer owes the individual competent services and loyalty as well as a host of other issues such as the attorney-client privilege, the work product doctrine, and confidentiality.

Typically, a lawyer and client will enter an express agreement concerning legal services. A written agreement is desirable because it can provide certainty about the representation. A written agreement often details the scope of the representation and the tasks the lawyer has agreed to undertake on behalf of the client, such as representing the client in a lawsuit or in a particular business transaction. The best practice is for the lawyer and client to enter a written agreement that clearly states the scope and duration of the representation, the duties of each party, and events that will result in termination of the representation. Requiring a written agreement seems not to be problematic in most environmental litigation or transactions involving sophisticated clients such as corporate clients that often hire environmental lawyers. When the environmental lawyer represents an individual, however, it often may be important to explain the need for an agreement in writing as well as the risks and benefits of each step in the transaction or litigation.

---

44. McCormick on Evidence 88, 179–80 (2d ed. 1972).

45. Black's Law Dictionary.

46. *See* Model Rule 1.2 cmt. ¶¶ 4 & 5.

60   ISSUES OF LEGAL ETHICS IN THE PRACTICE OF ENVIRONMENTAL LAW

Some jurisdictions require a written agreement for certain types of representation.[47] For example, Illinois requires that when a lawyer enters an agreement to represent a client in seeking settlement of a personal injury within five days "after the occurrence which gave rise to the claim," the lawyer must provide the client with a copy of the agreement of representation and a copy of the act creating the requirements. Additionally, the act provides that the client has the power to void the agreement "within a 10 day period after the occurrence."[48] The lawyer must provide the client with the address to which the notice terminating the agreement may be sent and must "obtain written acknowledgment of receipt of such from the party represented."[49] Illinois also requires a writing for an agreement to provide legal representation in a claim for fire damage. Guam goes further, requiring that lawyers enter a written fee agreement signed by the client in any matter in which the fee is contingent or the contemplated fee is in excess of $500, or if an appearance by the attorney before a court or agency is contemplated.[50] When an agreement is required under the Guam statute, the contract must be presented in "clear and concise language" and "clearly spell out the general nature of the work to be done by the attorney and the financial obligation of the client."[51]

The fact that a lawyer does not enter a written agreement or an express oral agreement with a potential client does not prevent a court from finding a contractual relationship between them. An attorney-client relationship may be implied from conduct of the parties—even without any payment of a fee.[52] Whether a client-lawyer relationship exists between two individuals can be a difficult question. Courts have held that the question of whether an attorney-client relationship has arisen should be determined by considering whether the putative client had a reasonable belief that he was consulting with the lawyer as a legal advisor.[53]

The fact that no written or express contract exists between the parties and the fact that the putative client paid no legal fees is not always sufficient to

---

47. *See, e.g.*, 815 ILL. COMP. STAT. 640/1 (1998).
48. *Id.*
49. *Id.*
50. 7 GUAM CODE ANN. 9216 (1999).
51. *Id.*
52. *See* Westinghouse Electric Corp. v. Kerr-McGee Corp., 580 F.2d 1311 (7th Cir. 1978); Tormo v. Tormark, 398 F. Supp. 1159 (D.N.J. 1975) (imposing client-lawyer relationship duties upon a lawyer who gave legal advice and counsel without expectation of payment).
53. *See, e.g.,* Bridge Products, Inc. v. Quantum Chemical Corp., 1990 WL 70857, N.D. Ill., 1990.

defeat the claim of an attorney-client relationship. For example, in the case of *Togstad v. Vesely, Otto, Miller & Keafe*,[54] discussed in Chapter 1, the Minnesota Supreme Court affirmed a holding that a lawyer was negligent in his representation of plaintiffs even though the plaintiffs did not discuss fee arrangements for legal services with the lawyer or enter a clear contract.

In *Arpadi v. First MSP Corp.*,[55] the court held that a lawyer for a partnership also represented all the partners to the partnership individually.[56] The court held that a lawyer owed a duty of care to limited partners by virtue of his representation of a general partner, reasoning that general partners owe a fiduciary duty to limited partners in an enterprise.[57] By contrast, in *State v. Hansen*, the Supreme Court of Washington held that a phone conversation between a defendant and a lawyer did not create a lawyer-client relationship.[58] The court held that a lawyer had a duty to reveal threats made by a defendant while attempting to retain him as counsel because the harm threatened related to a judge.[59] A Washington criminal statute prohibits intimidation or threats against a judge as a result of a ruling or decision.[60] The court held that no attorney-client relationship arose as a result of the phone conversation between the lawyer and the defendant. In that conversation the defendant uttered threats against the judge and others. The court reasoned, arguendo, that if an attorney-client relationship existed, the client's remarks would not be protected because they related to a future crime.[61]

Representing Governmental Entities

Potential also exists for problems relating to client status for lawyers who work for governmental entities. Many environmental lawyers are employed by governmental agencies, from the federal through the local level. Moreover, a private lawyer may also be retained to represent a government entity in a particular matter. Lawyers who work for a governmental entity face a challenge at times in determining who should be regarded as the client for purposes of setting objectives of the agency and determining the litigation or

---

54. 291 N.W.2d 686 (Minn. 1980).

55. 628 N.E.2d 1335 (Ohio 1994).

56. *See also* Ronson v. Superior Court, 29 Cal. Rptr. 2d 281 (Ct. App. 1994).

57. *See Arpadi*, 628 N.E.2d 1335 (Ohio 1994).

58. 862 P.2d 117, 118–19 (Wash. 1993).

59. *Id.* at 118.

60. RCW 9A.72.160 (Intimidating a Judge).

61. *Id.* (relying on Model Rule 1.6, the court held that the attorney-client privilege did not protect the information).

62   ISSUES OF LEGAL ETHICS IN THE PRACTICE OF ENVIRONMENTAL LAW

regulatory agenda. The lawyer may disagree with a particular decision or even believe that a particular decision is contrary to the law. Does he have an obligation to go forward with his supervisor's charge or may he question the charge as contrary to the public interest?[62] Who at the agency is empowered to set the objectives that the lawyer will seek to fulfill? The Restatement (Third) of the Law Governing Lawyers notes the issue:

> No universal definition of the client of a governmental lawyer is possible. For example, it has been asserted that government lawyers represent the public, or the public interest. However, determining what individual or individuals personify the government requires reference to the need to sustain political and organizational responsibility of governmental officials, as well as the organizational arrangements structured by law within which governmental lawyers work. Those who speak for the governmental client may differ from one representation to another. The identity of the client may also vary depending on the purpose for which the question of identity is posed. . . . A lawyer who represents a governmental official in the person's public capacity must conduct the representation to advance public interests as determined by appropriate governmental officers and not, if different, the personal interests of the occupant of the office.[63]

This comment indicates that difficulty may inhere in determining the appropriate role for a lawyer employed by the government. In situations of concern, the lawyer may need to seek documentation on the question of who is empowered to decide a particular question.

Prospective Client

The lawyer owes some duties to the prospective client, even when the relationship between the two does not mature into a lawyer-client relationship. The most significant duties created by consulting with an individual who may become a client relate to conflicts and confidentiality. These are discussed in the Chapters 4–6.

---

62. *See, e.g.,* Robert P. Lawry, *Who Is the Client of the Federal Government Lawyer? An Analysis of the Wrong Question,* FED. B.J. (Fall 1978); Harold R. Tyler, Jr., *The Attorney General of the United States—Counsel to the President or to the Government?,* 45 ALB. L. REV. 1 (1980).

63. RESTATEMENT (THIRD) OF THE LAW GOVERNING LAWYERS 97 cmt. c, f (2000).

Chapter 3: The Lawyer-Client Relationship   63

Prospective Client (2002 Revision)

In February 2002, the ABA House of Delegates adopted a new rule relating to prospective clients. This new rule, Rule 1.18, was drafted "in response to the Commission's concern that important events occur in the period during which a lawyer and prospective client are considering whether to form a client-lawyer relationship."[64] The Reporter's Explanation noted that the 1983 version of the Model Rules did not address the preretention period or the rights of prospective clients.

The 2002 revision to the Model Rules clarifies the duties of a lawyer to a prospective client, in the new Model Rule 1.18 indicating that the prospective client is entitled to protection of client information. A comment to Model Rule 1.18 states: "prospective clients should receive some but not all of the protection afforded clients."[65] The new rule indicates that the rules on conflicts apply when the lawyer has received information from a prospective client that could be "significantly harmful to that person in the matter" if revealed. Additionally, when the lawyer who conferred with a prospective client and received qualified information is prohibited by the rules from representing a client based on this conflict, others associated with that lawyer may undertake a representation if the lawyer "took reasonable measures to avoid exposure to more disqualifying information than was reasonably necessary to determine whether to represent the prospective client."[66] Additionally, in order to go forward with a representation that is a conflict with a prospective client of a lawyer, the firm must timely screen the disqualified lawyer from participation in the matter and "apportion no part of the fee" from that matter to the lawyer who received disqualifying information and, additionally, must give written notice to the prospective client of the conflict.[67]

The 2002 revision to the Model Rules makes clear in its comment to the new Model Rule 1.18 that a prospective waiver of a conflict may be effective for both conflict and confidentiality purposes. Comment 5 to Model Rule 1.18 provides: "A lawyer may condition conversations with a prospective client on the person's informed consent that no information disclosed during the consultation will prohibit the lawyer from representing a different client in the matter. . . . If the agreement expressly so provides, the prospective client

---

64. MODEL RULE 1.18 Reporter's Explanation of Changes.
65. MODEL RULE 1.18 cmt. 1 (2002).
66. MODEL RULE 1.18(d)(2) (2002).
67. *Id.*

ISSUES OF LEGAL ETHICS IN THE PRACTICE OF ENVIRONMENTAL LAW

may also consent to the lawyer's subsequent use of information received from the prospective client."[68]

Former Clients

A lawyer continues to owe duties to a former client, including the duty of confidentiality and the duty not to take representations that conflict with a former client. The lawyer's duty of confidentiality continues after the termination of the client-lawyer relationship, whatever the basis for that termination.[69] Lawyers have a duty not to reveal client information relating to a former client[70] and not to use information of a former client to the disadvantage of the former client.[71] Additionally, the duty to refrain from conflicting representations protects former clients. Rule 1.9 specifically prohibits lawyers from accepting an offer to represent a client if the representation will be materially adverse to a former client. It states:

> A lawyer who has formerly represented a client in a matter shall not thereafter represent another person in the same or a substantially related matter in which that person's interests are materially adverse to the interests of the former client unless the former client gives informed consent, confirmed in writing.[72]

Likewise, Revised Model Rule 1.7 prohibits a lawyer from representing a party if "there is a significant risk that the representation of one or more clients will be materially limited by the lawyer's responsibilities to another," including a former client.[73]

Former Clients (2002 Revision)

The 2002 revision to Model Rule 1.9 left the text of the rule intact with the exception of adding the informed consent standard that is applied throughout the new rules. The revision emphasizes that if a representation involving a conflict is to go forward, the client formerly represented by a lawyer must consent to the new representation.[74]

---

68. MODEL RULE 1.18 cmt. 5.
69. *See* RULE 1.9(c)(2).
70. *See id.*
71. *See* RULE 1.9(c)(1).
72. *See* RULE 1.9(a)(1).
73. *See* RULE 1.7(a)(2).
74. REVISED MODEL RULE 1.9(a) (2002).

The Environmental Context

Environmental matters present significant risks for lawyers. Lawyers should not assume that they will not be held to have entered an attorney-client relationship except when such a relationship is intended. A court may find an attorney-client relationship from conduct of the parties.[75] Courts have looked to the putative client's belief that he was consulting with the lawyer as a legal advisor in deciding whether an attorney-client relationship existed. The case of *Bridge Products, Inc. v. Quantum Chemical Corp.*[76] involved an environmental cleanup that Bridge had paid for and sought reimbursement from Quantum of some expenses under Comprehensive Environmental Response, Compensation, and Liability Act (CERCLA). The court found that the client disclosure of confidential information to the lawyers gave rise to an implied attorney-client relationship because Bridge Products disclosed the information "with a reasonable belief that the lawyer was acting as the party's attorney."[77] Although the parties did not dispute that the firm and the corporation did not enter a formal attorney-client relationship, the court held that "an implicit attorney/client relationship . . . derived from the nature of the parties' interview,"[78] because Bridge Products showed that it "submitted confidential information to a lawyer" and held a "reasonable belief that the lawyer was acting as the party's attorney."[79]

This distinction between individual and group clients is significant for a variety of reasons, including the appropriate way to proceed in settling claims and the ability of group representatives to instruct the lawyer in what decisions the group has made about management of the case. A rule of reason approach suggests that the group must make a decision regarding settlement as a group. The best practice in such a setting may be to set forth in the retainer agreement the percentage of members required for a quorum and the percentage of voting members required to approve a settlement or other group decision. By contrast, in the case of separate claims, each individual client retains the power to accept or reject a settlement offer.

---

75. *See* Westinghouse Electric Corp. v. Kerr-McGee Corp., 580 F.2d 1311 (7th Cir. 1978); Tormo v. Yormark, 398 F. Supp. 1159 (D.N.J. 1975) (imposing client-lawyer relationship duties upon a lawyer who gave legal advice and counsel without expectation of payment).

76. Bridge Products, Inc. v. Quantum Chemical Corp., 1990 WL 70857, N.D. Ill.,1990.

77. *Id.* at *2.

78. *Id.*

79. *Id.* at *3, *quoting* DCA Food Indust. v. Tasty Foods, Inc., 626 F. Supp. 54, 59–60 (W.D. Wis. 1985).

Any issues that could arise in relation to client identity should be dealt with straightforwardly in the written representation agreement or letter of representation.[80] In the case of joint representation, great care should be taken to explain any potential conflicts and to set forth clearly the objectives of the representation.[81] A related issue may arise in bellwether actions when the plaintiff group chooses representative plaintiffs with the assistance of the lawyer. A bellwether trial is one intended to resolve claims or issues common to a large number of claimants while leaving related matters for determination in individual cases.[82] The purpose of such a trial is to establish causation or liability or to resolve other issues common to the group.[83] These benefits cannot be secured, however, if the named plaintiffs are not representative of the group.[84]

Environmental Matters (2002 Revision)

In explaining the concept of a "substantially related matter," a new comment to Model Rule 1.9 uses an environmental example.

> [A] lawyer who has previously represented a client in securing environmental permits to build a shopping center would be precluded from representing neighbors seeking to oppose rezoning of the property on the basis of environmental considerations; however, the lawyer would not be precluded, on the grounds of substantial relationship, from defending a tenant of the completed

---

80. *In re* Chevron U.S.A., Inc., 109 F.3d 1016, 1019 (5th Cir. 1997), *citing* MANUAL FOR COMPLEX LITIGATION 33.27–.28 (3d ed. 1995).

81. The Joint Defense Doctrine (sometimes called the "Pooled Information" Doctrine) allows parties to share information without waiving the attorney-client privilege when those parties have a common interest in defending against a common adversary.

82. If a representative group of claimants are tried to verdict, the results of such trials can be beneficial for litigants who desire to settle such claims by providing information on the value of the cases as reflected by the jury verdicts. Common issues or even general liability may also be resolved in a bellwether context in appropriate cases. *In re* Chevron U.S.A., Inc., 109 F.3d 1016, 1019 (5th Cir. 1997) (granting defendant's request for mandamus and holding that the trial had no preclusive effect on the ground that trial court's method of selecting "bellwether" cases failed to represent the core claims of all plaintiffs adequately).

83. *See* CHARLES ALAN WRIGHT et al. FEDERAL PRACTICE AND PROCEDURE, FEDERAL RULES OF CIVIL PROCEDURE 23 (1782); *see also* James W. Elrod, Comment, *The Use of Federal Class Actions in Mass Toxic Pollution Torts*, 56 TENN. L. REV. 243 (1988) (arguing that pollution cases should be tried under Rule 23); Rob Harrison, *It Only Counts If It's Clear: To Be Effective Class Action Settlement Notices to Be Easily Understood*, A.B.A. J. 76 (June 2000).

84. *See* MODEL RULE 1.13(d).

shopping center in resisting eviction for nonpayment of rent. Information that has been disclosed to the public or to other parties adverse to the former client ordinarily will not be disqualifying.[85]

Additionally, Revised Model Rule 1.9 indicates that lawyers are prohibited from representing one side of a controversy in disputes arising out of multiple representations, a common phenomenon in environmental matters. A comment to Rule 1.9 as revised notes that "a lawyer who has represented multiple clients in a matter" must not "represent one of the clients against the others in the same or a substantially related matter after a dispute arose among the clients in that matter, unless all affected clients give informed consent."[86]

Attorney-Client Privilege

One of the primary vehicles for protecting clients from required disclosure of information and documents sought in discovery is the attorney-client privilege.[87] The issue is one the environmental lawyer should be sure to take into consideration. Since environmental litigation often involves scientific documents, such as reports relating to the environmental condition of property or the level of discharges from factories or other facilities, discovery disputes relating to documents are to be expected in environmental litigation.

The privilege protects a client by exempting testimony in a court or other tribunal about a communication with his lawyer. All jurisdictions within the United States apply the attorney-client privilege.[88] The policy supporting the privilege is the same as the policy supporting confidentiality generally: to encourage full disclosure of information from a client to a lawyer. The scope of the privilege does not extend to work done by a lawyer in a nonlegal capacity, however. The determination of whether the privilege for lawyer-client communications should protect particular information from discovery or admission "hinges upon the client's belief that he is consulting a lawyer in that capacity and his manifested intention to seek professional legal advice."[89] In making the decision to grant the privilege, courts consider "what the prospective client thought when he made the disclosure, not what the lawyer thought."[90]

---

85. MODEL RULE 1.9 cmt. 3 (2002).

86. MODEL RULE 1.9 cmt. 1 (2002).

87. For a full discussion of each element of the privilege and the doctrine, *see* EDNA SELAN EPSTEIN, THE ATTORNEY-CLIENT PRIVILEGE AND THE WORK-PRODUCT DOCTRINE (4th ed. 2001).

88. *See* WOLFRAM, *supra* note at 6.3.1.

89. *See* MCCORMICK ON EVIDENCE 88, 179 (2d ed. 1972).

90. R. WISE, LEGAL ETHICS 284 (1970).

68 ISSUES OF LEGAL ETHICS IN THE PRACTICE OF ENVIRONMENTAL LAW

The privilege does not protect client communications with a lawyer as a result of nonlegal services such as serving as a courier or conduit for the client's funds,[91] as a scrivener,[92] a lobbyist,[93] or a business advisor.[94] The attorney-client privilege does not apply to facts as opposed to documents or communications. Lawyers must provide truthful answers in response to interrogatories and other discovery requests. Likewise, the privilege does not allow the client to refuse to answer interrogatories based on the fact that he had shared information about the subject matter of the interrogatories with his lawyer.[95] The privilege does not protect from disclosure communications between the lawyer and client that further an ongoing criminal enterprise.[96]

In *United States v. Horvath*,[97] the Court of Appeals for the Eighth Circuit reviewed a case in which a criminal defendant challenged the admission of testimony from his lawyer at trial. During the process of the trial, the district court had conducted an in camera hearing and found that "the alleged privileged communications were made in furtherance of the conspiracy charged in the indictment."[98] Accordingly, the court held that the communications were not privileged.[99] The reviewing court affirmed the ruling, holding that it could not conclude that the trial court abused its discretion in admitting the lawyer's testimony, noting that the lawyer admitted that he "functioned primarily as a courier" in setting up accounts, transferring funds. The court reasoned that the attorney-client privilege does not protect these actions by the lawyer.[100] The court found "that the primary purpose of the [defendants'] relationship with [their lawyer] was to conceal from the government the extent of their finan-

---

91. *See* Morgan v. United States, 380 F.2d 686, 693 (9th Cir. 1967), *cert. denied,* 390 U.S. 962, 88 S. Ct. 1064, 19 L. Ed. 2d 1160 (1968).

92. *See* Canaday v. United States, 354 F.2d 849, 857 (8th Cir. 1966).

93. *See In re* Grand Jury Subpoenas Dated March 9, 2001, 179 F. Supp. 2d 270 (S.D.N.Y. 2001) (holding attorney-client privilege inapplicable to lawyers who acted as lobbyists in seeking presidential pardons for clients); *see also* United States Postal Service v. Phelps Dodge Refining Corp. 852 F. Supp. 156 (E.D.N.Y. 1994) (holding that letter from in-house counsel lobbyist lawyer was not privileged).

94. *See* Colton v. United States, 306 F.2d 633, 638 (2d Cir. 1962), *cert. denied,* 371 U.S. 951, 83 S. Ct. 505, 9 L. Ed. 2d 499 (1963).

95. *See* MODEL RULES 1.2(d) and 3.3(a)(2).

96. *See* United States v. Horvath, 731 F.2d 557 (1984) (distinguishing between attorney-client privilege for past criminal acts and the crime-fraud exception to privilege for an ongoing criminal enterprise).

97. 731 F.2d 557 (1984).

98. *Id.* at 561.

99. *Id.*

100. *Id.*

Chapter 3: The Lawyer-Client Relationship   69

cial holdings and their sources of income, thus facilitating an ongoing criminal conspiracy."[101] Therefore, the crime-fraud exception to the privilege applied and the attorney's testimony was properly allowed. The court also noted that a lawyer's ignorance of the client's wrongful purpose is irrelevant. According to Professor Wolfram, the privilege applies when:

> (1) a person (client) who seeks legal advice or assistance (2) from a lawyer acting in behalf of the client, (3) for an indefinite time may invoke, and the lawyer must invoke in the client's behalf, an unqualified privilege not to testify (4) concerning the contents of a client communication (5) that was made by the client or by the client's communicative agent (6) in confidence (7) to the lawyer or the lawyer's confidential agent, (8) unless the client expressly or by implication waives the privilege.[102]

The privilege is based on the client's right to privacy, right to counsel, and the autonomy of the individual. "[F]rom a moral point of view, confidentiality is also supportable on the grounds that a person should have some control over the spread of personal information and that others should respect relationships of confidentiality based on the bonds of shared information between lawyer and client."[103] In situations in which the attorney-client privilege applies, a court will grant a protective order barring omission of a communication between the lawyer and client.

Some scholars have suggested that the effect of attorney-client privilege doctrine may extend beyond its legitimate purposes.[104] In applying the attorney-client privilege rule, courts must determine whether the communication in dispute was advice from a lawyer to that lawyer's client. The analysis of what constitutes legal practice varies depending on the reason for raising the question. In the context of discovery, the court in *American Cyanamid Co. v. Hercules Powder Co.*[105] addressed the issue, holding that documents and letters were not protected by the attorney-client privilege and, accordingly, were

---

101.   *Id.* at 562.

102.   *See id.*

103.   CHARLES W. WOLFRAM, MODERN LEGAL ETHICS 245 (1986).

104.   *See* Geoffrey C. Hazard, Jr., *An Historical Perspective on the Attorney-Client Privilege*, 66 CAL. L. REV. 1061 (1978) (suggesting that the scope of the privilege should be limited to litigation).

105.   211 F. Supp. 85 (D. Del. 1962); *see also In re* Fisher, 51 F.2d 424 (S.D.N.Y 1931) (holding that there is no "accountant-client privilege" though accountant is also the client's attorney).

70   ISSUES OF LEGAL ETHICS IN THE PRACTICE OF ENVIRONMENTAL LAW

discoverable. The plaintiff sought documents in a patent infringement suit and the defendant resisted discovery on the basis of the attorney-client privilege. The court defined the issue as a clash between confidentiality and the philosophy of the Federal rules that "'mutual knowledge of all the relevant facts . . . is essential to proper litigation'"[106] and held that although the documents sought were written by a lawyer who worked in the patent department of the company, discovery of the documents should be allowed because the lawyer was not acting in a legal capacity when he created the documents. The court noted that its task in the discovery dispute made it necessary to determine whether the employee was acting as a lawyer or as a businessman.[107] Moreover, it noted that the client's conversation with the lawyer concerning technical (as opposed to legal) aspects of a patent did not entitle the information to protection from discovery. According to this authority, protection under the attorney-client privilege is conditioned on a communication occurring within the context-legal advice or services.

In the case of *State v. Olwell*,[108] the Supreme Court of Washington held that both information and objects (knives) are privileged within the meaning of the Washington statute when delivered by the client to his lawyer after committing a crime. The court interpreted a Washington statute that codified the attorney-client privilege, including lawyers in a group of persons disqualified from testifying. The statute stated that: "An attorney or counselor shall not, without the consent of his client, be examined as to any communication made by the client to him, or his advice given thereon in the course of professional employment."[109] Although the statute does not expressly refer to objects, the court applied it to protect physical objects as well as communications. The court noted that, to come within the privilege, the client must have delivered the items or made the communication to the lawyer. It excluded from the privilege information or objects the lawyer obtained while acting as the client's lawyer but that were not delivered by the client to the lawyer.[110]

Environmental Context

The attorney-client privilege may protect communications between the lawyer and her client even though nonclients may know or have access to the information. For example, communications between a lawyer and the lawyer's

---

106. *American Cyanamid*, 211 F. Supp. at 87, *quoting* Hickman v. Taylor, 329 U.S. 495, 507, 67 S. Ct. 385, 91 L. Ed. 451 (1947).
107. *Id.* at 88–89.
108. 394 P.2d 681 (Wash. 1964) (holding lawyer's refusal to testify at inquest was not contemptuous because subpoena violated attorney-client privilege).
109. *Id.* at 683, *quoting* WASH. REV. CODE § 60.060.
110. 394 P. 2d 681, 684 (Wash. 1964).

Chapter 3: The Lawyer-Client Relationship   71

agent or between the client's agent and the lawyer may come within the protection of the privilege.[111] Concerns that sharing information with a nonlawyer professional could result in loss of the attorney-client privilege has resulted in opposition to approval of multidisciplinary practice. Because of the interplay of scientific and legal judgment in some environmental matters, it may be necessary to share information with nonlawyers such as toxicologists, biologists, or environmental accountants. One court has held that the privilege may protect reports from an environmental consulting firm retained by a lawyer to do work for a particular client.[112] In the case of *Olson v. Accessory Controls and Equipment Corp.*,[113] the Connecticut Supreme Court affirmed a trial court's grant of both a protective order and a motion in limine barring the introduction of evidence about a report by an environmental consulting firm that was prepared in anticipation of litigation.

Crime-Fraud Exception

All states recognize an exception to the attorney-client privilege that allows admission of evidence when the communication was intended to further a crime or fraud by the client.[114] The crime-fraud exception to the attorney-client privilege is a significant limitation on the attorney-client privilege that is generally recognized as a matter of common law. The crime-fraud exception to the attorney-client privilege denies the protection of the privilege to communications between a client and his lawyer when the lawyer's services are used to further a crime or fraud even if the lawyer did not know the client was engaged in a crime or fraud.[115] The exception applies to both the attorney-client privilege and the work product rule.

In *United States v. Costanzo*,[116] the Third Circuit Court of Appeals remanded a matter to the trial court for an evidentiary hearing to determine

---

111. *See* WOLFRAM, *supra* note 88 at 267.

112. *See, e.g.*, Olsen v. Accessory Controls and Equip. Corp., 757 A.2d 14 (Conn. 2000).

113. 254 Conn. 145, 757 A.2d 14 (Conn. 2000).

114. *See, e.g.*, *In re* Sealed Case, 107 F.3d 46 (D.C. Cir. 1997) (requiring showing of ongoing or imminent crime or fraud for exception to apply); Olsen v. Accessory Controls and Equip. Corp., 757 A.2d 14 (Conn. 2000) (adopting civil fraud exception to attorney-client privilege, holding standard is satisfied by showing of probable cause to believe communication was made with intent to defraud, but finding exception not met on facts of case); Supplee v. Hall, 52 A. 407 (Conn. 1902) (recognizing exception to the attorney-client privilege when communication was in furtherance of a crime).

115. *In re* Grand Jury Proceedings, 680 F.2d 1026 (5th Cir. 1982) (holding that lawyer's ignorance of intended crime does not affect applicability of exception).

116. 625 F.2d 465 (3d Cir. 1980).

72   ISSUES OF LEGAL ETHICS IN THE PRACTICE OF ENVIRONMENTAL LAW

whether the conviction of an accused must be set aside because it was based on evidence that should have been excluded under the attorney-client privilege. In this case, Anthony Costanzo discussed his case with a lawyer he had hired in the past on both civil and criminal matters. Costanzo did not hire the lawyer, Frank Paglianite, for this case, however, because the lawyer told Costanzo that he (Paglianite) had a conflict that prevented him from accepting the representation. In seeking to overturn his conviction, Costanzo argued that Paglianite furnished information to FBI agents relating to the case against Costanzo. Noting that the "client-lawyer relationship is not dependent on the payment of a fee nor upon the execution of a formal contract," the Third Circuit held that an evidentiary hearing was necessary to determine whether a confidential relationship existed between the two.[117]

In *State v. Macumber*,[118] the Supreme Court of Arizona affirmed a decision refusing to allow lawyers to testify in the trial of another defendant although their deceased client had admitted to murders. Although the lawyers had obtained permission from the state ethics committee to testify, the court held that the attorney-client privilege prevented the testimony offered.[119] Because the decision of whether particular evidence deserves protection under the privilege can be a difficult one, it may be wise to refrain from accessing the documents at issue until after review of the trial court's decision.[120]

In *Purcell v. District Attorney for the Suffolk District*,[121] the Massachusetts Supreme Judicial Court noted the distinction between the right to disclose information under the state's disciplinary code and the attorney-client privilege for the purpose of admissibility.[122] In *Purcell*, the court held that a lawyer who reported to the police his client's intent to burn down an apartment building acted within his rights under the disciplinary rules. Nevertheless, the court held that the client's communication was inadmissible in his trial on arson because the evidentiary privilege applied, noting that courts "must be cautious in permitting the use of client communications that a lawyer has revealed only because of a threat to others. Lawyers will be reluctant to come forward if

---

117.   *Id.* at 469. *See also* Robinson v. United States 144 F.2d 392, 405 (6th Cir. 1944).

118.   544 P.2d 1084 (Ariz. 1976).

119.   *See* W. William Hodes, *What Ought to Be Done—What Can Be Done—When the Wrong Person Is in Jail or About to be Executed? An Invitation to a Multi-Disciplined Inquiry, and a Detour About Law School Pedagogy*, 29 Loy. L.A. L. Rev. 1547 (1996).

120.   *See In re* Nitla S.A. de C.V., 45 Tex. Sup. Ct. J. 571, 2002 WL 534089 (Tex. Apr. 11, 2002) (holding that trial court erred in finding documents not privileged but overruling appellate court's disqualification of lawyers who reviewed disputed documents).

121.   676 N.E.2d 436 (Mass. 1997).

122.   *Id.* at 438.

they know that the information that they disclose may lead to adverse consequences to their clients."[123]

The Organizational Client

Much of the environmental practitioner's work is undertaken on behalf of corporate clients. The lawyer representing a corporation owes his allegiance to the corporate entity rather than to the individuals who are constituents of the corporation.[124] Model Rule 1.13 deals with the lawyer's relations with organizations, including governmental entities, corporations, and unincorporated entities.[125] It mandates that the lawyer representing an organization client act for the organization rather than for its constituents.[126] Likewise, the Model Code states that "[a] lawyer employed or retained by a corporation or similar entity owes his allegiance to the entity and not to a stockholder, director, officer, employee, representative, or other person connected with the entity."[127]

In representing a corporate client, the lawyer will often seek information from officers, directors, employees, and constituents of the client. Generally, information imparted to the lawyer is subject to the duty of confidentiality and the attorney-client privilege. A comment to Model Rule 1.13 notes the application of the duty of confidentiality to this setting, indicating that the communications of lawyers and the constituents of an organization are protected by the lawyer's duty of confidentiality.[128] This point is discussed more fully in the section on the lawyer's duty of confidentiality.

The economic climate of a post-Enron world may have temporary or even long-lasting effects for the legal profession generally and corporate counsel in particular. Heightened public concern leads to heightened regulation and scrutiny of corporate management and, additionally, the role of legal counsel in serving corporations. An example of the renewed interest and concern relating to corporations is found in the Sarbanes-Oxley Act.[129] The Act, which was passed shortly after the collapse of Enron, addressed corporate practices generally and, additionally, the role of the lawyer in responding to corporate

---

123. *Id.* at 440.

124. *See* Waggoner v. Snow, Becker, Kroll, Klaris & Krauss, 991 F.2d 1501 (9th Cir. 1993).

125. *See* REVISED MODEL RULE 1.13 cmt. 6.

126. "Group claim" in this context means a nondivisible claim advanced by a group of individuals such as a petition to EPA's Office of Civil Rights seeking denial of a permit or other prospectively protective action.

127. *See* ABA MODEL CODE EC 5-18.

128. "This does not mean, however, that constituents of an organizational client are the clients of the lawyer." MODEL RULE 1.13 cmt. 2.

129. 15 U.S.C. § 7245 (2002).

74 ISSUES OF LEGAL ETHICS IN THE PRACTICE OF ENVIRONMENTAL LAW

wrongdoing. Every lawyer should be aware of the provisions of this Act relating to the role of lawyers who represent corporations. In particular, in-house counsel should study the Act, regulations required in its implementation, and the interaction of these laws with the ethical rules of the lawyer's jurisdiction.[130] The mandate of the Act requires the SEC to issue a rule requiring lawyers to report evidence of securities violations "to the chief legal counsel or the chief executive of the company,"[131] and, if necessary, "to the audit committee of the board of directors of the issuer or to another committee of the board of directors comprised solely of directors not employed directly or indirectly by the issuer, or to the board of directors."[132] Section 307 of the Sarbanes-Oxley Act directs SEC to issue a rule:

> (1) requiring an attorney to report evidence of a material violation of securities law or breach of fiduciary duty or similar violation by the company or any agent thereof, to the chief legal counsel or the chief executive officer of the company (or the equivalent thereof); and
>
> (2) if the counsel or officer does not appropriately respond to the evidence (adopting, as necessary, appropriate remedial measures or sanctions with respect to the violation), requiring the attorney to report the evidence to the audit committee of the board of directors of the issuer or to another committee of the board of directors comprised solely of directors not employed directly or indirectly by the issuer, or to the board of directors.[133]

While the requirement that a lawyer report evidence of violations of law to the highest authority within the corporate structure is consistent with Model Rule 1.13, the rule mandated by the Sarbanes-Oxley Act includes specificity that goes beyond that of Rule 1.13 and may create concerns that the constraints of the Act will affect the attorney-client relationship.

The issue of the identity of the client may also arise in situations in which

---

130. See Richard W. Painter, *Game Theoretic and Contractarian Paradigms in the Uneasy Relationship Between Regulators and Regulatory Lawyers*, 65 FORDHAM L. REV. 149, 174–77 (1996) (noting potential for use of disciplinary rules to promote cooperation between agencies and lawyers and concluding that default rules of professional responsibility "could be supplemented by a few new rules imposed by regulators" negotiated by regulators and lawyers).

131. 15 U.S.C. § 7245 (2002).

132. *Id.*

133. *Id.*

Chapter 3: The Lawyer-Client Relationship 75

an employee of a corporation seeks a lawyer's advice. If an employee of a corporation seeks advice from a lawyer who represents the corporation, the lawyer needs to analyze the situation carefully. If the employee has no relationship to the employer-client, the lawyer must analyze the prospective client's case and the representation proffered from the employee like any new potential representation, considering workload, time commitments, the lawyer's competency in the area of concern, and, of course, conflicts issues. If the employee's question relates to his role in the corporation, the employee may be assuming that the lawyer represents him as an individual in addition to the corporation. This mistaken assumption seems most likely to arise in situations in which the employee works closely with a lawyer over a significant period of time and develops a friendly relationship or when the employee lacks sophistication in legal matters. When an employee seeks out the corporation's lawyer, should the lawyer automatically remind the employee of her sole allegiance to the corporation, or may the lawyer hear the information the employee wishes to raise?

A lawyer who works for a corporate client should be particularly cautious when an employee or other constituent seeks her advice. In cases relating to violations of environmental discharge permits, allegations that a supervisor ordered the alleged discharges are likely. If the conversation develops in a way that suggests the individual is assuming that the lawyer protects his or her interests, compliance with Rule 1.13 demands that the lawyer stop the flow of information from the employee and inform him (perhaps again) of the lawyer's duty to the corporation rather than to individuals associated with the corporation.

When the corporation is the only client, the lawyer may need to advise the employee that his representation relates to the corporation, not to the corporation's employees, although the lawyer works closely with the employees. In some circumstances, it is necessary to apprise the employee of this information sooner rather than later to avoid learning information that could disqualify the lawyer from representing the corporation in a particular matter or generally.[134] For example, if the employee who seeks the lawyer's ear is the corporate official responsible for certifying discharge monitoring reports (sometimes referred to as the "designated felon"), the lawyer may need to provide the caution of his representation earlier than would otherwise be necessary.

Issues relating to client identity should be dealt with straightforwardly in the written representation agreement or letter of representation.[135] In the case of joint representation, great care should be taken to explain any potential

---

134. This issue is dealt with in greater detail in the chapter dealing with conflicts.
135. A sample representation letter is included in Appendix C.

76   ISSUES OF LEGAL ETHICS IN THE PRACTICE OF ENVIRONMENTAL LAW

conflicts and to set forth clearly the objectives of the representation to the extent possible.[136]

Organizational Client (2002 Revision)

The 2002 revision of the Model Rules by the ABA left Model Rule 1.13 substantially the same with the exception of adding functional words and changing the standard for the lawyer's obligation to explain the identity of the lawyer's client from a standard of what is "apparent" to a standard based on what the lawyer "knows or reasonably should know." The new provision states:

> In dealing with an organization's directors, officers, employees, members, shareholders or other constituents, a lawyer shall explain the identity of the client when *the lawyer knows or reasonably should know* that the organization's interests are adverse to those of the constituents with whom the lawyer is dealing.[137]

The Organizational Client (Environmental Context)

Model Rule 1.8 does not speak explicitly to unincorporated or loosely defined groups such as defendants working together on a unified defense or environmental justice plaintiff groups organized to lodge a complaint with the EPA's Office of Civil Rights (OCR). The force of the rule may be applied by analogy to such clients, however. The lawyer who represents a group in an environmental action may face difficult questions of who commands his primary allegiance—the group or the individuals named as plaintiffs. The lawyer's representation should be clearly defined in a detailed joint representation agreement. This agreement should specify not only the existence and scope of the representation but also the governance structure of the group and the methods for achieving agreement on important issues such as settlement. The lawyer, organizations, and individuals (if some are represented individually) should all sign as the parties to the agreement.[138]

The situation described above involving a constituent can arise in a variety of ways. If an employee seeking advice from the corporation's lawyer is the corporate official responsible for certifying discharge monitoring reports, the lawyer may need to stop the employee's narrative to advise or remind him

---

136. *See* MODEL RULE 1.7.

137. MODEL RULE 1.13(d) (2002) (italics added to show new language).

138. It may also be advisable for the environmental group to form a nonprofit corporation to seek tax-exempt status from the Internal Revenue Service. Fund-raising for the group is often enhanced when supporters can deduct their contributions to the organization.

Chapter 3: The Lawyer-Client Relationship 77

of the lawyer's role as representative of the corporation rather than for its employees. For example, an employee who has been involved in a discharge that violates reporting requirements or other environmental requirements may want to unburden himself of this knowledge to the lawyer and to seek the advice of the lawyer. The lawyer should avoid learning information about the incident from the employee because such information could jeopardize the lawyer's representation of the existing client. The lawyer should inform the employee of the role and duty to the corporate client rather than simply listening to the individual's story. Failure to cut off the disclosures made by the individual can result in disqualification of the lawyer from representing a corporate client in a matter in which the employee or other constituent is involved. The corporate employees who interact with the lawyer are likely to be involved in reviewing her work and judgment, including the questions of the lawyer's role, whether the lawyer's relations with the company should extend to representing officers or employees and the lawyer's elevation of issues up the chain of command because of a judgment of imminent wrongdoing.[139] Obviously, the lawyer should approach all such issues with diplomacy as well as good legal judgment and analysis.

An argument exists that unless the lawyer has reason to know that the employee of the corporate client is confiding information that creates a conflict, the lawyer may listen to problems or other information from the employee to represent the corporate client fully. Arguably, the lawyer's duty to the corporate client requires the lawyer to listen and learn of problems that could affect the client as long as the information gathering does not mislead another or prejudice the rights of another. From this perspective, a lawyer may talk with the corporation's employee without advising the employee specifically about the lawyer's role, particularly when the lawyer has advised the employee of his role when the representation or working relationship began. The information a lawyer will learn from an employee is likely to vary dramatically depending on which model of interaction the lawyer uses with the employee wishing to confer about job issues.

Communicating with the Client (Environmental Context)

When an organization is a client, the lawyer will have contact and communicate with the membership through the officers of the organization. Comment 3 to Model Rule 1.4 notes that "ordinarily, the lawyer should address communications to the appropriate officials of the organization." An environmental group that wants to maintain a high degree of group control may include

---

139. MODEL RULE 7.2. The Model Code provision differs significantly. *Compare* MODEL RULE 7.2 with DR 2-101.

provisions in its bylaws to ensure group involvement and to preserve mechanisms for communication and consensus. For example, a representation agreement could indicate that the lawyer will communicate with specified officers and that the officers will communicate with the members of the group. The agreement may also indicate the methods by which these communications will be accomplished. The prudent lawyer will include in the agreement the specifics of how the organization will determine the objectives of representation in the future. For example, if the environmental group seeks an injunction against a discharge under the Clean Air Act or Clean Water Act, the representation agreement should indicate what percentage of voting members will determine whether the organization will take significant steps including filing an action, offering a settlement, or rejecting a settlement offer. Some groups may decide that a simple majority should control the organization's decisions. Others may choose a super majority for important decisions such as whether to accept a settlement. The agreement should also expressly state that neither the lawyer nor the officers are authorized to settle a group claim absent the required vote by the membership.[140]

Compliance

The lawyer's attitude about compliance with law is likely to have significant impact on the way the organization goes about its business. Indeed, efforts of lawyers to educate clients regarding the seriousness of environmental violations have been influential in shifting the attitude of corporate clients regarding environmental compliance. The attitude of two decades ago on the part of some corporations could be summarized as "everyone does it," or "these regulations are not realistic. They cannot be serious." Within the professional lifetime of many lawyers who are practicing today, a dramatic shift has occurred regarding environmental laws and compliance with environmental laws. Environmental lawyers have succeeded to a great extent in convincing clients of the seriousness of environmental hazards and of environmental laws. Moreover, the fact that criminal liability applies to some conduct in this area has also focused the attention of corporation officers on the level of care needed to control environmental hazards and to comply with environmental laws.

When a violation occurs, particularly one involving public safety issues, the lawyer's duty is to urge compliance with the law.[141] In the case of repre-

---

140. MODEL RULE 1.13(b)(1)–(3).

141. *See* MODEL RULE 1.13(b) (noting lawyer's obligation to seek reconsideration of course of action and consideration at a higher level in the organization to protect the interests of the clients); MODEL RULE 1.16 (noting obligation of lawyer to decline representation likely to result in a violation of law).

Chapter 3: The Lawyer-Client Relationship 79

sentation of an organization, the lawyer has the right and obligation to elevate a matter involving a client's improper conduct to higher authorities within the organization.[142] Given both the general desire of corporations and other organizations to comply with law and the existence of significant criminal sanctions against corporations and their designated officials for failure to report environmental hazards, such elevation or notice by the lawyer that he will elevate the matter will result in compliance in most cases.

Reporting Violations of Law

The lawyers representing corporate clients face other problems. Model Rule 1.13 makes clear that the lawyer's duty runs to the corporate entity rather than to individuals in the company. Model Rule 1.13 explains the need to act to protect the corporate entity. The lawyer representing an organization must take action to protect it when he learns that someone associated with the organization intends to violate a law or a legal obligation to the organization. The lawyer's response depends on the seriousness of the situation. In such a situation, the lawyer has several options, including "asking reconsideration" of an issue, advising the client to seek "a separate legal opinion," and "referring the matter to higher authority in the organization."[143] In some circumstances, the lawyer has a duty to bring the violation to the attention of the board of directors or other authority in the corporation. The rule states that the lawyer should refer the issue to the "highest authority that can act on behalf of the organization" when "warranted by the seriousness of the matter."[144] This provision requires the lawyer to judge whether a particular problem warrants this action.[145]

Both Model Rule 1.13 and public policy indicate a lawyer should report to a corporation's board of directors information about illegal conduct of

---

142. *See* MODEL RULE 1.13.

143. MODEL RULE 1.13(b)(3).

144. The current position of the Office of Thrift Savings (OTS) seems to be that, while the lawyer may have a duty to report misconduct to the directors of a financial institution, this duty does not extend to reporting to the regulators absent special circumstances. However, the regulators have argued that Model Rule 1.13 requires the lawyer to attempt to change the offending conduct by talking to the perpetrator and disclosing the problem up the chain of command to the directors, if necessary, to remedy the misconduct. Both the RTC and the OTS have taken the position that a lawyer's failure to inform the directors of misdeeds that are occurring may be the basis for lawyer liability.

    Brian W. Smith & M. Lindsay Childress, *Avoiding Lawyer Liability in the Wake of Kaye, Scholer*, 8 ST. JOHN'S J. LEGAL COMMENT 392 (1993).

145. There is, of course, the potential for disciplinary boards to later judge the decision of the lawyer.

80   ISSUES OF LEGAL ETHICS IN THE PRACTICE OF ENVIRONMENTAL LAW

employees of the corporation when senior management refuses to act to correct or to rectify the violations.[146] If the lawyer's efforts to advise the client on compliance are not successful and the client indicates that it will go forward with a course of action that will violate the law, the lawyer should disaffiliate herself from the client.[147]

When a lawyer elevates an issue to higher authority within an organization, it is likely that other corporate employees who know and interact with the lawyer may resent her decision to report the permit violation to higher authorities—even when she makes the report to corporate officials rather than outside authorities. They are likely to regard this move as disloyalty to the client or to them individually. In the case of outside counsel, employees of the corporation may see the decision to consult higher authorities as "going over the head" of the in-house counsel. Nevertheless, Rule 1.13 requires the lawyer to make a judgment in such a case and to communicate the problem to a corporate employee or officer with authority to remedy the violation.

Courts regard the ethical obligations of corporate (in-house) and private (outside) lawyers as substantially the same for purposes of ethics rules, particularly the attorney-client privilege.[148] Lawyers who serve as in-house counsel for a corporate entity sometimes face more difficult decisions than outside counsel for a variety of reasons. For example, because corporate counsel wears many hats, it is important for the in-house lawyer to be continuously aware of the role he or she is playing in a particular meeting or project undertaken for the corporation. The attorney-client privilege applies only to communications with corporate counsel when the person seeking input from corporate counsel reasonably believes he is seeking legal advice as opposed to advice relating to financial, business, or management issues.[149] Accordingly, it is important for corporate counsel to know which role she is fulfilling at any given time. It is of equal importance for corporate counsel to document the role she is serving.

The lawyer who serves as in-house counsel is obviously economically dependent on his single client to a much greater degree than a practicing lawyer representing numerous clients. In *General Dynamics v. Superior Court*,[150]

---

146.   Directors also have a duty to report illegal conduct to the corporation's board of directors. *See In re* Caremark International, Inc. Derivative Securities Litigation, 698 A.2d 959 (Del. Ch. 1996).

147.   *See* MODEL RULE 1.13(c) (noting the lawyer "may resign in accordance with Rule 1.16").

148.   *See* United States v. Rowe, 96 F.3d 1294 (9th Cir. 1996).

149.   *See, e.g.,* Financial Technologies Int'l Inc. v. Smith, 2000 WL 1855131 (S.D.N.Y. 2000) (finding no privilege where in-house counsel was not licensed lawyer).

150.   7 Cal. 4th 1164, 1165–66 (Cal. 1994).

Chapter 3: The Lawyer-Client Relationship 81

the California Supreme Court noted that the in-house counsel is tied to one client and, thus, may experience greater pressure to bend the rules for his only client.[151]

> More than with outside counsel, corporate in-house counsel may be faced with a moral dilemma between ethical norms and the client's interest, since in-house counsel is dependent on one employer to provide his or her livelihood and career success. Therefore, an in-house attorney faced with a choice between the demands of an employer and the requirements of an ethical code has an even greater claim to judicial protection than a non-attorney employee.[152]

Similarly, in *Parker v. M & T Chemicals, Inc.,*[153] a New Jersey court rejected the argument that the duty of confidentiality required a lawyer to remain silent about a client's misdeeds. The New Jersey court refused to limit an in-house lawyer's right to seek damages from his former employer for retaliatory discharge when the lawyer refused to join in the employer's fraudulent scheme.[154]

Many companies want a company officer to oversee litigation, contracting, and other matters of legal significance. Unless the officer is also a lawyer, this role of overseeing litigation is extremely difficult. Although the rules of ethics do not prohibit such a dual role for lawyers, this situation carries risks. One such risk is that the lawyer may face conflicts as a result of his joint roles of legal counsel and officer or board member.

Whether discussions between corporate officials and the lawyer serving as in-house counsel are protected by the attorney-client privilege depends on a variety of factors. In the course of day-to-day operations of the company, in-house counsel is routinely consulted regarding personnel and management matters. Whether the lawyer's role in these discussions is that of a legal advisor or simply another corporate officer can be difficult to ascertain. An officer who seeks legal advice from corporate counsel without entering a joint defense agreement with the corporation may not be protected by the attorney-client privilege.[155]

---

151. This case is discussed in detail in the section on confidentiality.
152. *Id.* at 1165–66.
153. 566 A.2d 215 (N.J. Super. 1989).
154. Parker v. M & T Chemicals, Inc., 566 A.2d 215 (N.J. Super. Ct. 1989).
155. *See* Grand Jury Proceedings v. United States, 156 F.3d 1038 (10th Cir. 1998). The Joint Defense Doctrine (sometimes called the "Pooled Information" Doctrine) allows parties to

82 ISSUES OF LEGAL ETHICS IN THE PRACTICE OF ENVIRONMENTAL LAW

Additionally, the joint defense privilege seems to be applicable only when litigation is actually under way or nearly filed. In *In re Santa Fe Int'l Corp.*,[156] the Fifth Circuit held that "a communication qualifies for protection under the common legal interest, or 'joint defense,' doctrine only if there is a 'palpable threat of litigation' at the time of the communication rather than a mere awareness that litigation may one day ensue."[157] The dispute arose from communication during discovery in a class-action suit. Plaintiffs' counsel sought a ruling to require defendants to turn over documents relating to communications relevant to antitrust issues in the case. Defense counsel argued the documents were privileged under the doctrine of common legal defense. The court disagreed, holding that the common legal interest privilege protects communications only when they occur between codefendants and their counsel in litigation or when litigation is likely.[158] The court limited the joint defense doctrine to situations in which an actual threat of litigation is present.

Reporting Violations of Law (Environmental Context)

Because of the numerous laws and regulations relating to reporting discharges of hazardous substances under the Clean Air Act and the Clean Water Act and other environmental statutes and regulations, the potential need to elevate discussion of a problem up the corporate ladder is very real. For example, if the lawyer learns that the employee in charge of reporting discharge amounts is misrepresenting the quantities on a required discharge monitoring report or lab employees are falsifying test results, the lawyer would have a duty to report the information to higher authorities within the corporation. If the violation creates a risk of death or substantial bodily harm, the lawyer may have a duty under her jurisdiction's rule on confidentiality to disclose the information to authorities outside the corporation. Because of the high risks in the environmental field, it seems particularly appropriate for a lawyer to discuss both the laws relating to monitoring and reporting requirements and the requirements of Model Rule 1.13 with officers, directors, and employees with whom the lawyer works before a problem arises.

---

share information without waiving the attorney-client privilege when those parties have a common interest in defending against a common adversary. *See* CHARLES W. WOLFRAM, MODERN LEGAL Ethics 276–77 (1986).

156. 5th Cir. No. 01-40421 (Nov. 7, 2001).

157. *Common Interest Privilege Does Not Apply When Recipients Weren't Yet Co-Defendants*, 70 U.S. LAW W. 1308 (Nov. 27, 2001).

158. *Id.*

Corporate Clients: Environmental Example

As environmental laws have grown in scope and significance,[159] enforcement actions have increased at both the state and federal levels.[160] Environmental matters have come to the fore in corporate decision making. Corporations must consider environmental laws in issues of management, planning, permitting, and compliance. Accordingly, corporations rely on lawyers to explain what is required to comply with the complexities of environmental laws. In the case of *Georgia-Pacific v. GAF Roofing Manufacturing*,[161] GAF Roofing resisted a motion to compel answers about environmental provisions of a contract on the basis that the negotiator of the contract served as GAF Roofing's in-house counsel for environmental issues. The court rejected this argument because the negotiation of the contract was not undertaken in anticipation of litigation as required by the attorney-client privilege.

Paying for Employee's Representation

When a corporation or its employees are prosecuted under an environmental criminal statute, the corporation may consider paying for the defense of the employee, either in conjunction with or separate from the hiring of its own counsel. The practice of an organizational client compensating a lawyer for providing services for a constituent of the organization or corporation is not unusual. Model Rule 1.8(f) indicates that this practice is acceptable in some circumstances. The 1983 version of the rule, which provides the basis for most state rules, states:

> A lawyer shall not accept compensation for representing a client from one other than the client unless:
> (1) the client consents after consultation;

---

159. *See, e.g.,* United States v. Brittain, 931 F.2d 1413, 1414 (10th Cir. 1991) (upholding 18-count conviction of director of utility company who submitted false information); United States v. Gordon Stafford, Inc., 952 F. Supp. 337, 337 (N.D. W. Va. 1997) (finding president of company personally liable for improper waste disposal); DOJ, EPA Enforcement Officials Outline Plans to Bolster Actions Against Corporate Polluters, [May 1989—April 1990 File Binder] 20 Env't Rep. (BNA) No. 52, at 2012 (Apr. 27, 1990) (quoting Joseph G. Block, Chief of Environmental Crimes Unit of Department of Justice).

160. *See, e.g.,* Martin Harrell, *Why Eight Plus Six Means Prison for Environmental Criminals,* 14 Tul. Envtl. L.J. 197 (2000) (describing the potential sentencing enhancement under the Federal Sentencing Guidelines applicable in environmental criminal prosecutions).

161. 1996 WL 29392 (S.D.N.Y. 1996).

84   ISSUES OF LEGAL ETHICS IN THE PRACTICE OF ENVIRONMENTAL LAW

(2) there is no interference with the lawyer's independence of professional judgment or with the client-lawyer relationship; and
(3) information relating to representation of a client is protected as
required by Rule 1.6.[162]

In addition to obtaining informed consent from the client, this rule imposes
additional obligations on the lawyer, including determining that the representation will not result in "interference with the lawyer's independent professional judgment" and will not compromise the lawyer's duty of confidentiality.[163]

Paying for Employee's Representation (2002 Revision)

The revisions to the Model Rules adopted by the ABA in February 2002
continue to acknowledge the practice of corporate employers paying for representation for employees in certain circumstances. "Lawyers are frequently
asked to represent a client under circumstances in which a third person will
compensate the lawyer, in whole or in part."[164] Revised Model Rule 1.8(f)
declares that payment by someone other than the client is permissible as long
as specified conditions are met. It retained the language of the 1983 rule with
the exception of changing the standard for client consent to "informed consent."[165]

Comment 11 to Model Rule 1.8 explains the reasons for special protections in this context:

Because third-party payers frequently have interests that differ from
those of the client, including interests in minimizing the amount
spent on the representation and in learning how the representation
is progressing, lawyers are prohibited from accepting or continuing such representations unless the lawyer determines that there
will be no interference with the lawyer's independent professional
judgment and there is informed consent from the client.[166]

Termination and Retaliatory Discharge

In-house counsel who are employed under an employment contract that provides for termination based on good cause or just cause may bring a cause of
action for breach of that contract duty if discharged or demoted as a result of

---

162. MODEL RULE 1.8(f).
163. *Id.*
164. REVISED MODEL RULE 1.8 cmt. 11 (2002).
165. REVISED MODEL RULE 1.8(f) (2002).
166. *Id.*

Chapter 3: The Lawyer-Client Relationship 85

the lawyer's refusal to engage in conduct in violation of rules of legal ethics.[167] Additionally, lawyers who receive discriminatory treatment as a result of their refusal to violate the rules of professional ethics may have recourse against their employers based on statutory law as well as the common law of wrongful or retaliatory discharge.[168] Specifically, lawyers may have a right to sue for retaliatory discharge based on impermissible discrimination against the lawyer.[169] In some states, the right of in-house counsel to sue former employers for wrongful termination appears to be essentially similar to the right of other nonlawyer employees.[170]

Nevertheless, in some jurisdictions the ability of corporate counsel to sue for wrongful termination of employment is more limited than that of other employees because of the lawyer's duty of confidentiality to the employer-client. Courts have dismissed actions by in-house counsel to allege retaliatory discharge on the basis that plaintiff failed to identify a violation of public policy that resulted from the discharge.[171] In *Balla v. Gambro, Inc.,*[172] the Illinois Supreme Court overturned a favorable ruling for plaintiff in his claim

---

167. *See* Mourad v. Automobile Club Ins. Ass'n, 465 N.W.2d 395 (Mich. Ct. App.), *appeal denied,* 478 N.W.2d 443 (Mich. 1991) (holding lawyer may maintain action for retaliatory demotion resulting from lawyer's refusal to act in a way that would violate rules of professional ethics).

168. *See* X Corp. v. Doe, 816 F. Supp. 1086 (E.D. Va. 1993) (rejecting retaliatory discharge claim by in-house lawyer by noting plaintiff's right to bring whistleblower action under Federal False Claims Act); *see also* Parker v. M & T Chems., Inc., 566 A.2d 215 (N.J. Super. App. Div. 1989) (holding discharged lawyer may have a right to damages from employer under Conscientious Employee Protection Act for wrongful treatment based on lawyer's refusal to conspire to defraud competitor); Hoskins v. Droke, 1995 WL 318817 (N.D. Ill. 1995) (recognizing former general counsel suit for retaliatory discharge under Title VII).

169. *See* Stinneford v. Spiegel Inc., 845 F. Supp. 1243 (N.D. Ill. 1994) (recognizing action for retaliatory discharge under Federal Age Discrimination in Employment Act); Kachmar v. SunGard Data Sys., Inc., 109 F.3d 173 (3d Cir. 1997) (allowing claim for discharge by in-house counsel on the basis of sex discrimination); Golightly-Howell v. Oil, Chem. & Atomic Workers Int'l Union, 806 F. Supp. 921 (D. Colo. 1992) (holding in-house counsel may sue employer based on discrimination that violates Title VII).

170. *See, e.g.,* General Dynamics Corp. v. Superior Court, 876 P.2d 487 (Cal. 1994); Burkhart v. Semitool, 5 P.3d 1031, 1041 (Mont. 2000).

171. Crews v. Buckman Laboratories Int'l, 2001 WL 687137 (Tenn. Ct. App. 2001) (dismissing former in-house lawyer's action for retaliatory discharge for failure to state claim of discharge in violation of state public policy); Considine v. Compass Group USA, 2001 WL 880531 (Ct. Appeal N.C. 2001) (dismissing suit based on plaintiff's failure to allege specific conduct by defendant violating public policy).

172. 584 N.E. 2d 104 (Ill. 1991).

for retaliatory discharge, holding that a lawyer has no claim for retaliatory discharge against his former employer and, additionally, that the plaintiff-lawyer in the case was acting as counsel rather than in a "layman" capacity in controversy.[173] The case involved an in-house lawyer for Gambro, a distributor of kidney dialysis equipment manufactured by its affiliate, Gambro Germany. The lawyer, Balla, opposed his employer's violation of a food and drug agency regulation and ultimately reported the violation to the FDA. Based on Balla's advice to reject the dialyzers as not complying with FDA regulations, the president of Gambro originally notified Gambro Germany that it was rejecting the machines. Later, however, the president informed Gambro Germany that it would accept the machines.[174] In compliance with the ethics rules of Illinois, Balla reported his employer's violation of law to the FDA. The FDA seized the imported machines, and the employer, Gambro, discharged Balla from its employment as in-house counsel. The trial court rejected Balla's claim and granted the employer's motion for summary judgment. The court of appeals overturned the summary judgment, holding that "an attorney is not barred as a matter of law from bringing an action for retaliatory discharge."[175] The Illinois Supreme Court overruled the court of appeals, rejecting Balla's claim and reinstating the summary judgment. The supreme court emphasized that corporations would not engage in full and frank discussions with their in-house counsel if they knew the lawyer might later make them subject to claims of retaliatory discharge. "[T]he danger exists that if in-house counsel are granted a right to sue their employers in tort for retaliatory discharge, employers might further limit their communication with their in-house counsel."[176]

Other courts have reached divergent results on the issue of whether in-house counsel may sue his former employer for retaliatory discharge.[177] For example, in the case of *Crews v. Buckman Laboratories Int'l Inc.*, the Tennessee Supreme Court held that a lawyer serving as in-house counsel has a right to maintain an action for retaliatory discharge when a substantial factor influ-

---

173. *Id.* at 111.

174. *Id.* at 106.

175. *Id.* at 107.

176. *Id.* at 109.

177. *See, e.g.*, Jacobson v. Knepper & Moga, P.C., 706 N.E.2d 491 (Ill. 1998) (holding lawyer-plaintiff was obligated to report client's unethical conduct under Illinois law and deeming expansion of tort law of retaliatory discharge to reach in-house counsel unnecessary); Volberg v. Pataki, 917 F. Supp. 909 (N.D. N.Y.), *aff'd*, 112 F.3d 507 (2d Cir. 1996), *cert. denied*, 520 U.S. 1119 (1997) (dismissing claim for a retaliatory discharge by former general counsel for New York State Department of Environment and Conservation). *But see* General Dynamics Corp. v. Super. Ct., 876 P.2d 487 (Cal. 1994); Burkhart v. Semitool, 5 P.3d 1031, 1041 (Mont. 2000).

Chapter 3: The Lawyer-Client Relationship 87

encing the employer's decision to discharge the lawyer was the employee's exercise of a protected right or compliance with clear public policy.[178] The holding permits lawyer-employees to divulge client secrets when the disclosure is necessary to support a claim of wrongful discharge.[179]

The rationale of these and other cases considering the issue of termination of in-house counsel is considered further in the section on the lawyer self-defense exception of Model Rule 1.6 (see pages 122–24). Commentators on legal ethics have noted the "bizarre" result of the case, leaving "a lawyer employee, who has affirmative duties concerning the administration of justice" without "redress for discharge resulting from trying to carry out those very duties."[180]

---

178. Crews v. Buckman Laboratories Intt'l. Inc., 2002 WL 1050247 (Tenn. 2002).
179. *Id.*
180. 1 G.C. HAZARD & W.W. HODES, LAW OF LAWYERING § 1.16:206, at 477 (Supp. 1994).

CHAPTER 4

Confidentiality

Confidentiality is a time-honored principle of many professions, including the legal profession. From an environmental lawyer's perspective, it is likely to create the greatest concerns if environmental contamination or other environmental hazards create a risk of harm to individuals or the public. The intent of the rules is to protect all clients (including existing, former, and prospective clients) and their interests in information they share with lawyers. Even general knowledge of the policies or practices of a former client may constitute a basis for disqualification in some cases.[1]

> Clergymen are aware that the narrow and formalistic "priest-penitent" privilege has broadened into a more general privilege that applies whenever confidences are lodged with a spiritual adviser. Psychotherapists are conscious that the traditional, narrow doctor-patient privilege for treating physicians has broadened into a privilege that encompasses a wide range of counseling activities.[2]

Many professionals are obligated to maintain client confidences.[3] Like any agent, the lawyer cannot use client information (even without disclosing

---

1. *See* LaSalle National Bank v. Lake County, 703 F.2d 252 (7th Cir. 1983).
2. W. William Hodes, *What Ought to Be Done—What Can Be Done—When the Wrong Person Is in Jail or About to be Executed? Invitation to a Multi-Disciplined Inquiry, and a Detour About Law School Pedagogy*, 29 Loy. L.A. L. Rev. 1547 (1996).
3. From doctors to lawyers and priests to massage therapists, the professional who receives client confidences is ordinarily bound by a professional code or norm to hold them confidential. *See* Massage Therapist Code at http://www.amtamassage.org/about/codeofethics.htm (last visited Mar. 25, 2003); *see also* http://www.ama-assn.org/ama/pub/category/4256.html (last visited Mar. 23, 2003); Hodes, *supra* note 2 (comparing the roles of a lawyer, a religious counselor, and a psychotherapist who receive the confession of person who committed a crime); Clark, *Confidential Communications in a Professional Context: Attorney, Physician and Social Worker*, 24 J. Legal Prof. 79 (2000).

89

90 ISSUES OF LEGAL ETHICS IN THE PRACTICE OF ENVIRONMENTAL LAW

it) for his own benefit.[4] The prohibition against use of client information for a lawyer's self-interest applies without regard to whether the client will suffer loss as a result of the self-dealing.[5] It seems beyond dispute that, of the duties imposed on lawyers, the duty of confidentiality is one of the most important. Confidentiality is one of the oldest tenets of the legal profession,[6] and it is undoubtedly the most well-known obligation of lawyers in terms of the general public's knowledge. Both lawyers and clients regard the duty of confidentiality as crucial to the lawyer's duty of loyalty to the client.[7] Confidentiality has been called the "central moral tradition of the profession"[8] and is the bedrock of legal ethics.[9] The often-noted purpose of the duty is to encourage the free flow of information between clients and the professionals they consult.[10] An additional purpose is to ensure that a lawyer serves the client's interests.

The duty of confidentiality has never been viewed, however, as an absolute.[11] Nor does the rule justify assisting a client in a fraud or crime.[12] "Counsel's duty of loyalty to, and advocacy of, the defendant's cause is limited to legitimate, lawful conduct compatible with the very nature of a trial as a search for truth."[13]

---

4. *See* David Welch Co. v. Erskine & Tulley, 250 Cal. Rptr. 339 (Cal. Ct. App. 1988). In this case, the court held a law firm liable for using information about a client's debt collection business to set up a computing business.

5. *See, e.g., In re* Guidone, 653 A.2d 1127 (N.J. 1994) (sanctioning lawyer for purchasing an interest in client's property without client's knowledge even though the client suffered no damage as a result of the acquisition).

6. CHARLES W. WOLFRAM, MODERN LEGAL ETHICS 2.2.1, at 242–44 (1986).

7. *The Duty of Confidentiality Is a Corollary of the More General Duty of Loyalty, in* GEOFFREY C. HAZARD ET AL., THE LAW AND ETHICS OF LAWYERING 269 (3d ed. 1999).

8. *See* Robert P. Lawry, *The Central Moral Tradition of Lawyering*, 19 HOFSTRA L. REV. 311 (1990).

9. Professor Daniel R. Fischel begins his argument with declaration that: "Confidentiality is the bedrock principle of legal ethics." Daniel R. Fischel, *Lawyers and Confidentiality*, 65 U. CHI. L. REV. 1 (1998).

10. *See* WOLFRAM, *supra* note 6, at 296–300 (1986); Harry I. Subin, *The Lawyer as Superego: Disclosure of Client Confidences to Prevent Harm*, 70 IOWA L. REV. 1091, 1096 (1985).

11. *See* State v. Whiteside, 272 N.W.2d 468 (Iowa 1978). "Counsel owes a client charged with a crime honest, loyal, and faithful representation. However, this duty extends only to the use of fair and honorable means. A lawyer may never assist in the perpetration of a crime or countenance any other dishonest act." *Id*. at 470.

12. *See* Nix v. Whiteside, 475 U.S. 157 (1986); State v. Metcalf, 540 P.2d 459, 465 (Wash. Ct. App. 1975) (holding advice sought in furtherance of crime or fraud is not protected from discovery).

13. *See Nix*, 475 U.S. at 158.

Society's Interest in Disclosure of Dangerous Conditions

A competing interest that a lawyer must consider in the environmental area is the interest of society in avoiding or minimizing dangers to the public and individuals. This interest can arise in a variety of settings. For example, the confidentiality of settlements can affect the incentives of parties considering settling. In considering rules relating to settlement, the societal interest in encouraging settlements must be balanced with the public interest in knowing about hazards that continue to exist in the world. Clearly, rules on settlement can significantly affect the resolution of environmental disputes and the balance of party interests in the settlement process. For example, some courts are considering rules that would limit the time a settlement would be secret.[14]

In one sense, such a rule seems eminently reasonable. It seems axiomatic in our open society that the public should be able to obtain information about a site that created a risk to the environment or residents in the area—especially if that risk included contamination. It may be that this information could prevent future harm. Take, for example, the situation in which parties involved in a Superfund site or some other situation in which parties must determine the appropriate share of costs each will bear to pay for a cleanup of environmental contamination (whether this is at a Superfund site, an undergound storage tank site, or some other location involving environmental dangers). The information contained in the settlement could prevent others in the community from entering the property at issue or purchasing the property at issue, because they would have more information about the risk of harm associated with the property.

On the other hand, if a party wishes to keep the terms of the settlement from entering the public domain (and perhaps influencing the way the public views that party), the decision to make that settlement public (now or in the future) could result in a decision not to settle. If the information that would become public as a result of the settlement would provide information useful for future plaintiffs, the issue of making the information public could defeat the company's interest in settling. Thus, a rule that allows the settlement to become public may reduce the likelihood that some parties will settle (without regard to the cost of the settlement).

---

14. See Adam Liptak, *Judges Seek to Ban Secret Settlements in South Carolina*, N.Y. TIMES, Sept. 2, 2002, *available at* http://www.nytimes.com/2002/09/02/national/02JUDG.html.

92 ISSUES OF LEGAL ETHICS IN THE PRACTICE OF ENVIRONMENTAL LAW

Background Principles

Conflicts: Environmental Example

Because of the need to protect client information, knowledge about the way a former client operates can result in a conflict of interest in some cases. In the environmental case of *LaSalle National Bank v. Lake County*,[15] for example, the U.S. Court of Appeals for the Seventh Circuit granted a motion by Lake County to disqualify plaintiff's law firm in an action in which plaintiff challenged the court's denial of access to the county sewer system. The court based its decision on the fact that plaintiff's law firm had represented the county not on the particular access petition at issue but, rather, on similar sewage agreements. Additionally, the court noted that the lawyer had participated in formulating legal strategies concerning litigation involving the agreements generally. The court found that the lawyer possessed confidential information regarding the practices of the county that could be used against the county in the instant lawsuit. It reasoned that the lawyer had knowledge of the county's policies relating to sewer services as a result of the firm's representations.

History of Confidentiality

Like so many things about the duty of confidentiality, its history is the subject of controversy.[16] Because of the continuing controversy surrounding Model Rule 1.6, the history of confidentiality within the legal profession is of great significance. For this reason, this work explores the history in detail. The conventional wisdom is that the concept of confidentiality is ancient.[17] Some believe aspects of the duty of confidentiality reach back to Roman times,[18] or at least to the early English common law.[19] The recent history of confidentiality in American rules of ethics has been a story of an expanding duty for lawyers. Canon 37, which was based on the common-law attorney-client privilege and similar common-law rules in the ethics setting, spoke only to confidences of a client.[20] The 1969 Code reformulated the statement of the duty of confidentiality, expressly including "secrets" as well as "confidences" within the scope of the lawyer's

---

15. 703 F.2d 252 (7th Cir. 1983).

16. *See* WOLFRAM, *supra* note 6, at 242–44 (1986).

17. *Id.*

18. *Id.*, *citing* Radin, *The Privilege of Confidential Communication between Lawyer and Client*, 16 CAL. L. REV. 487 (1982).

19. *Id.*

20. *See* ABA Comm. on Prof'l Ethics and Grievances, Formal Op. 202 (May 25, 1940).

Chapter 4: Confidentiality   93

obligation. In 1983, the ABA adopted the Model Rules of Professional Conduct, expanding the universe of the duty to its logical extreme of "all information relating to the representation whatever its source."[21]

Canon 37

Despite its importance to ethics rules, the ABA's first formal statement of a confidentiality rule apparently did not emerge with the first version of the Canons of Professional Ethics in 1908. The ABA issued its official statement on confidentiality in 1928 along with 12 other new canons.[22] The ABA amended Canon 37 in 1937, declaring "the duty of a lawyer to preserve his client's confidences."[23] The Canon's allusion to client "confidences" derived from common law-rules such as the attorney-client privilege and the work product doctrine. Like these common-law rules, the Canon excluded a client's intended crime from the definition of confidences.[24] "The announced intention of a client to commit a crime is not included within the confidences which [a lawyer] is bound to respect."[25] This rule expressly authorized disclosure of client confidences to prevent criminal acts by clients.

Model Code

The Model Code of Professional Responsibility, adopted by the ABA in 1969, superseded the ABA Canons. The Code prohibits lawyers from revealing cli-

---

21. MODEL RULE 1.6 cmt. 5.
22. ABA COMPENDIUM OF PROF'L RESPONSIBILITY Rules and Standards 311 (1997).
23. Canon 37 provided:

> It is the duty of a lawyer to preserve his client's confidences. This duty outlasts the lawyer's employment, and extends as well to his employees; and neither of them should accept employment which involves or may involve the disclosure or use of these confidences, either for the private advantage of the lawyer or his employees or to the disadvantage of the client, without his knowledge and consent, and even though there are other available sources of such information. A lawyer should not continue employment when he discovers that this obligation prevents the performance of his full duty to his former or to his new client.

> If a lawyer is accused by his client, he is not precluded from disclosing the truth in respect to the accusation. The announced intention of a client to commit a crime is not included within the confidences which he is bound to respect. He may properly make such disclosures as may be necessary to prevent the act or protect those against whom it is threatened.

> Canon 37 as amended September 30, 1937.

24. *Id.*
25. Canon 37.

94 ISSUES OF LEGAL ETHICS IN THE PRACTICE OF ENVIRONMENTAL LAW

ent confidences and secrets.[26] The Code allows disclosures permitted by the Disciplinary Rules, or required by law or court order, and also permits a lawyer to reveal "the intention of his client to commit a crime and the information necessary to prevent the crime."[27]

The Kutak Rule

In 1977 the president of the ABA appointed Robert J. Kutak as chair of a commission to study and revise the Model Code. This commission, which came to be known as "the Kutak Commission" in honor of its chair,[28] drafted the Proposed Rules, which the ABA House of Delegates of the Association debated and ultimately adopted with modifications on August 2, 1983.[29] Model Rule 1.6 was the most debated of the proposed rules before the ABA House of Delegates.[30] It also was the rule most changed by states in the process of adopting the Model Rules as the law of the jurisdiction. The proposed Rule 1.6, drafted by the Kutak Commission, allowed a lawyer to reveal client information to the extent the lawyer reasonably believes necessary, not only to prevent crimes and frauds, but also to rectify harm caused by crimes and frauds created by a client by using a lawyer's services.[31]

The Kutak Proposed Rule did not survive attacks led by the American Trial Lawyers Association in the debates on the floor of the House of Delegates. The ABA adopted the rule after amending it to delete all but two of the exceptions proposed by the Commission. The exceptions are discussed below. These include both the exceptions adopted in 1983 and the additional exceptions finally adopted in 2002.

---

26. *See* MODEL CODE OF PROFESSIONAL RESPONSIBILITY DR 4-101 (1980). Disciplinary Rule 4-101 of the Code defines client confidences and secrets and prohibits lawyers from disclosing either except in specified instances. It defines "confidences" as "information protected by the attorney-client privilege under applicable law" and "secret" as "other information gained in the professional relationship that the client has requested be held inviolate or the disclosure of which would likely be embarrassing or detrimental to the client." *See* MODEL CODE OF PROFESSIONAL RESPONSIBILITY DR 4-101(A).

27. MODEL CODE OF PROFESSIONAL RESPONSIBILITY DR 4-101(C)(3). The provision does not qualify the type of crime justifying disclosure.

28. *See* STEPHEN GILLERS & ROY D. SIMON, JR., REGULATION OF LAWYERS: STATUTES AND STANDARDS ix (1995).

29. *Id.*

30. *See* 1 GEOFFREY C. HAZARD, JR. & W. WILLIAM HODES, THE LAW OF LAWYERING: A HANDBOOK ON THE MODEL RULES OF PROFESSIONAL CONDUCT § 1.6:101, at 127 (1997).

31. *See* Center for Prof'l Responsibility, American Bar Assn., *The Legislative History of the Rules of Professional Conduct: Their Development in the ABA House of Delegates* 12 (1987); MODEL CODE OF PROFESSIONAL RESPONSIBILITY, at 47–48 (1983).

Chapter 4: Confidentiality   95

Model Rule 1.6

The Model Rules, adopted by the ABA House of Delegates in 1983, provided the basis for the rules of ethics currently in force in the majority of states.[32] Model Rule 1.6 departed dramatically from the previous statement of the duty of confidentiality set forth in the ABA Code, and from the statement proposed by the Kutak Commission. The final rule approved by the ABA deleted acknowledgment of other law, protection of the financial and property interests of third parties, and the right of lawyers to disclose information to rectify the harm flowing from a client's crime or fraud.

Current Law

Model Rule 1.6

Model Rule 1.6 establishes the lawyer's duty to protect client information and the ability of the lawyer to reveal such confidences in limited circumstances.[33] The current Model Rule has drawn sustained and heated criticism.[34] While nearly all states have adopted the ABA Model Rules of Professional Conduct, only six states retained Model Rule 1.6 as written.[35] Most states moderated the force of the general prohibition of Model Rule1.6 by adopting additional or broader exceptions than those presented in the model.

The Model Code

The Model Code of Professional Responsibility continues to provide the basis for the legal ethics rules in a few states.[36] The Model Code provides greater

---

32. All but a few states have now adopted rules based on the 1983 Model Rules. The vast majority rejected the 1983 version of Model Rule 1.6. The revised rules adopted by the ABA in February 2002 present the current articulation of the ethical obligations of lawyers by the leading professional association for lawyers in the United States.

33. Legal scholars have criticized the rule and the ABA Standing Committee on Ethics and Professional Responsibility proposed amending the rule. *See generally* Geoffrey C. Hazard, Jr., *Lawyers and Client Fraud: They Still Don't Get It*, 6 Geo. J. Legal Ethics 701, 721–24 (1993).

34. *See* Deborah L. Rhode, In the Interests of Justice: Reforming the Legal Profession, at 109 (2000); 1 Hazard & Hodes, *supra* note 30, at 130.2; *see generally* Irma Russell, *Unreasonable Risk: Model Rule 1.6, Environmental Hazards, and Positive Law*, 55 Wash. & Lee L. Rev. 117 (1998).

35. *See* Russell, *supra* note 34, at 172 (1998).

36. Approximately six of the jurisdictions of the United States base their ethics rules on the Model Code. *See* Ga. State Bar Rules and Regulations, Rule 4-101 (2001); Ia. Code of

96 ISSUES OF LEGAL ETHICS IN THE PRACTICE OF ENVIRONMENTAL LAW

discretion to lawyers considering disclosures under the rule on confidentiality. This wider discretion is the result of several differences in the provisions. First, the scope of information protected from disclosure under the Model Code approach is narrower than that recognized by the Model Rules. The duty of confidentiality, as defined by the Model Code, applies to client "confidences and secrets,"[37] while the duty defined by the Model Rules extends to all "client information." Additionally, the Code allows disclosure of such client secrets or confidences when permitted under the Disciplinary Rules.[38] It also expressly allows disclosure when required by law or by a court order.[39] Under the Code, a lawyer may reveal "the intention of his client to commit a crime and the information necessary to prevent the crime."[40] The provision does not specify the type of crime, but a rule of reason approach suggests that some serious consequence is needed to justify disclosure.[41] For example, a client's statement that he will "speed to the bank" to make a deposit would not seem sufficient to trigger the disclosure requirement.

The Restatement Approach

The American Law Institute (ALI) has also articulated standards for judging lawyer conduct, including standards on the lawyer's duty of confidentiality.[42] In the Restatement (Third) of the Law Governing Lawyers (Restatement), the ALI creates the same framework of a general prohibition and limited exceptions to articulate its standard for the lawyer's obligation of confidentiality. The Restatement defines the scope of the duty of confidentiality by reference to the attorney-client relationship. Section 59 states the definition of confidential information: "Confidential client information consists of information relating to representation of a client, other than information that is generally known."[43] This definition is narrower than the definition set forth in the Model

---

PROF'L RESPONSIBILITY DR 4-101 (1996); NEB. CODE OF PROF'L RESPONSIBILITY DR 4-101 (1998); N.Y. CODE OF PROF'L RESPONSIBILITY DR 4-101 (1995); OHIO CODE OF PROF'L RESPONSIBILITY DR 4-101 (Banks-Baldwin 1996); OR. CODE OF PROF'L RESPONSIBILITY DR 4-101(1995); TENN. CODE OF PROF'L RESPONSIBILITY DR 4-101 (1995).

37. *See* MODEL CODE OF PROFESSIONAL RESPONSIBILITY DR 4-101 [hereinafter Model Code DR].
38. *See* DR 4-101(C)(2).
39. *See id.*
40. MODEL CODE DR 4-101.
41. Some jurisdictions require disclosure without regard to the type of crime contemplated by a client. *See, e.g.,* Fla. St. Bar Rule 4-1.6; Va. S. Ct. Rule 1.6.
42. RESTATEMENT (THIRD) OF THE LAW GOVERNING LAWYERS § 60 (2000).
43. *Id.* at § 59.

Rules, since it excludes "generally known" information from its protection. Nevertheless, this definition is sufficiently broad to protect client interests.

The Restatement states a general duty to safeguard client information and prohibits the use of confidential client information when "there is a reasonable prospect that doing so will adversely affect a material interest of the client or if the client has instructed the lawyer not to use or disclose such information."[44] It validates using or disclosing confidential client information in seven defined situations:

(1) to advance client interests;
(2) with client consent;
(3) when required by law;
(4) to enable the lawyer to defend against a charge that the lawyer acted wrongfully in the course of a representation;
(5) in a compensation dispute;
(6) to prevent death or serious bodily harm; and
(7) to prevent, rectify, or mitigate substantial financial loss.[45]

The Restatement provides exceptions to the duty similar to those of the current Model Rule 1.6. Like the Model Rule, it validates disclosure to prevent the loss of life or substantial bodily injury, allowing disclosure to prevent "reasonably certain death or serious bodily harm to a person."

The Restatement also presents some marked differences from Model Rule 1. It is similar to the rules instituted by many of the states that changed the language of Model Rule 1.6, relating to the risk of death justifying disclosure.[46] The Restatement requires that death be reasonably certain before a lawyer has the discretion to reveal confidential client information to prevent harm.[47] It commits the issue to the discretion of the lawyer.[48] The Restatement makes clear

---

44. RESTATEMENT (THIRD) OF THE LAW GOVERNING LAWYERS § 60 (2000). Section 60 of the Restatement states as follows:

> Lawyer's Duty To Safeguard Confidential Client Information. (1) Except as provided in §§ 61–67, during and after representation of a client: (a) the lawyer may not use or disclose confidential client information as defined in § 59. . . . (b) the lawyer must take steps reasonable in the circumstances to protect confidential client information against impermissible use or disclosure by the lawyer's associates or agents that may adversely affect a material interest of the client or otherwise than as instructed by the client.

45. *Id.* at §§ 61–67.

46. *Id.*

47. RESTATEMENT (THIRD) OF THE LAW GOVERNING LAWYERS § 66 (2000).

48. Each section stating the exceptions to the prohibition against disclosure is stated in the permissive form, stating the lawyer "*may* use or disclose" the information. *See* §§ 61–67.

that disclosure may be permissible because of a risk to life or bodily integrity created by nonclient action as well as client action. "Threats to life or body encompassed within this section may be the product of an act of the client or a nonclient and may be created by wrongful acts, by accident, or by circumstances."[49] The timing element of the Restatement provision on prevention of death or bodily injury turns not on whether the action that creates the threat of harm is past or future but on whether the harm has not yet occurred and, thus, can be prevented. "If a crime or fraud described in Subsection (1) has already occurred, a lawyer may use or disclose confidential client information when the lawyer reasonably believes its use or disclosure is necessary to prevent, rectify, or mitigate the loss."[50] By contrast, the timing of a loss has some bearing on the issue of disclosure in the context of a crime or fraud that threatens a financial loss. Section 67 allows disclosure to prevent "a crime or fraud" only when important qualifiers are met: The crime or fraud threatens "substantial financial loss" that has not yet occurred, the lawyer's client "intends to commit" the harmful act personally or through a third party, and, finally, the client used the lawyer's services in the matter in which he intends to commit the crime or fraud.[51]

Moreover, the Restatement qualifies the right to disclose information, even in the case of risks to life or body, by imposing a duty on the lawyer to make a good faith effort to dissuade the client from the dangerous course of action.

> Before using or disclosing information under this section, the lawyer must, if feasible, make a good faith effort to persuade the client not to act. If the client or another person has already acted, the lawyer must, if feasible, advise the client to warn the victim or to take other action to prevent the harm and advise the client of the lawyer's ability to use or disclose information as provided in this Section and the consequences thereof.[52]

The exception found in Section 67 of the Restatement, allowing a lawyer to disclose information to prevent, rectify, or mitigate substantial financial loss, is controversial in the minds of some lawyers.[53] The provision gives a basis for disclosure of some cases of fraud in transactions. Because the loss involved is not as significant as a physical injury or loss of life, some lawyers believe that the financial interest should not trump the duty of confidentiality.

---

49. RESTATEMENT (THIRD) OF THE LAW GOVERNING LAWYERS § 66 cmt. b (2000).

50. RESTATEMENT (THIRD) OF THE LAW GOVERNING LAWYERS § 67(2) (2000).

51. RESTATEMENT (THIRD) OF THE LAW GOVERNING LAWYERS § 67 (2000).

52. RESTATEMENT (THIRD) OF THE LAW GOVERNING LAWYERS § 66(2) (2000).

53. *Id.* at § 67(2).

Section 67 validates disclosure only when narrow requirements are met, however. First, the client creating a threat of financial loss is engaging in a crime or fraud. Second, and of great importance, the disclosure is permitted only when the client has used the services of the lawyer in the matter in which the crime or fraud is committed. Third, the right to disclose is limited to situations in which the lawyer made "a good faith effort to persuade the client not to act" in a harmful way.[54] Thus, the permissive disclosure under this exception is allowed only as "a last resort."[55]

The self-defense exception is closely related to the crime-fraud exception.[56] A comment to the Restatement notes this relationship between the two exceptions:

> [W]hen a client charges a lawyer with wrongdoing in the course of a representation, the client thereby waives the attorney-client privilege by putting the lawyer's services into issue. . . . Some charges against a lawyer brought by nonclients involve the course of conduct in which the lawyer's client is implicated in crime or fraud. In such situations the crime-fraud exception to the attorney-client privilege may independently permit the lawyer to defend based on otherwise confidential client information.[57]

Model Rule 1.6

The reach of the current Model Rule 1.6 is broad, covering all client information within its prohibition against disclosure by a lawyer and allowing disclosure only in the rare circumstance of a client who intends to commit a crime that will imperil the life of another or create substantial bodily harm.

> The ABA's Model Rules demand confidentiality in all contexts regarding information from all sources if it relates to client representation and does not involve physically dangerous criminal activity. Although state ethical codes generally incorporate more

---

54. *Id.* at § 67(3).

55. RESTATEMENT (THIRD) OF THE LAW GOVERNING LAWYERS § 67 cmt. j (2000).

56. *See, e.g.,* Stirum v. Whalen, 811 F. Supp. 78 (N.D.N.Y. 1993). In this case, the court allowed a protective order allowing a lawyer to disclose confidential client information to defend against a charge of assisting the client in a fraud. In the case of *In re* Friend, 411 F. Supp.776 (S.D.N.Y. 1975), the court allowed a lawyer to disclose client information to a grand jury, which was investigating charges of criminal activity by the lawyer and the client.

57. RESTATEMENT (THIRD) OF THE LAW GOVERNING LAWYERS 64 cmt. b (2000).

100 ISSUES OF LEGAL ETHICS IN THE PRACTICE OF ENVIRONMENTAL LAW

exceptions to confidentiality requirements than the Model Rules, these exceptions still are strikingly limited.[58]

The Text of Model Rule 1.6

The Model Rules set the scope of the duty of confidentiality as client "information," thus prohibiting a lawyer from revealing anything within the inclusive category of "information relating to representation of a client."[59] By this definition, the rule includes essentially all conceivable data about a client regardless of its source or significance.

Model Rule 1.6 provides:

> Confidentiality of Information.
> (a) A lawyer shall not reveal information relating to representation of a client unless the client consents after consultation, except for disclosures that are impliedly authorized in order to carry out the representation, and except as stated in paragraph (b).
> (b) A lawyer may reveal such information to the extent the lawyer reasonably believes necessary:
> (1) to prevent the client from committing a criminal act that the lawyer believes is likely to result in imminent death or substantial bodily harm; or
> (2) to establish a claim or defense on behalf of the lawyer in a controversy between the lawyer and the client, to establish a defense to a criminal charge or civil claim against the lawyer based upon conduct in which the client was involved, or to respond to allegations in any proceeding concerning the lawyer's representation of the client.[60]

Model Rule 1.6 sets forth a strong prohibition against lawyers revealing client information. It creates two exceptions, allowing lawyers to disclose information (1) to prevent the client from committing a crime that is likely to result in "imminent death or substantial bodily harm," and (2) to protect the lawyer's interests (sometimes referred to as the "self-defense exception").[61]

---

58. DEBORAH L. RHODE, IN THE INTERESTS OF JUSTICE: REFORMING THE LEGAL PROFESSION 109–10 (2000).

59. MODEL RULE 1.6(a).

60. MODEL RULE 1.6(b)(1) (1983).

61. MODEL RULE 1.6(b)(2).

Each of the exceptions is permissive. The exception set forth in subsection (b) is not controversial among lawyers.[62] It liberally allows disclosure to protect the interests of lawyers, including allowing disclosure by a lawyer when he reasonably believes it is necessary to establish a claim or defense for the lawyer's benefit. This exception applies in a suit by the lawyer, a client, or a third party. Subsection (a), by contrast, is a narrow exception, met only when two conditions are present: (1) a client intends to commit a crime, and (2) that crime is likely to result in a terrible consequence (imminent death or substantial bodily harm). The Model Rules require disclosure of confidential information only to prevent fraud on a tribunal.[63] The rules do not permit disclosure to prevent noncriminal but life-threatening acts. They do not permit disclosure to avert economic injuries, no matter how dramatic the injuries may be. Lawyers may advise clients to rectify their conduct and to comply with law, but they have no recourse in most cases if the clients choose to ignore this advice.

ABA Ethics 2000 Commission Proposals

At the 2001 Annual Meeting in Chicago, the 532-member ABA House of Delegates debated the proposals of the ABA Ethics 2000 Commission. With a majority of 51 percent (a six-vote margin), the House voted to approve the Commission's proposal to amend 1.6(b)(1) to permit disclosure of client confidences to prevent reasonably certain death or substantial bodily harm, broadening the grounds for disclosure under the Model Rule. The House voted by a wide margin to defeat the Commission's proposed 1.6(b)(2), which would have permitted lawyers to disclose client confidences to prevent future crimes or frauds that threaten substantial financial loss when the lawyer's services had been used to perpetrate the crime or fraud. The argument that 41 jurisdictions currently have a rule like that proposed in 1.6(b)(2) was not persuasive. In light of the delegates' votes on this proposal, the Commission withdrew the proposed 1.6(b)(3), which would have permitted disclosure to prevent or mitigate future harms from crimes or frauds involving the lawyer's services.[64] The

---

62. *But see* MONROE H. FREEDMAN, UNDERSTANDING LAWYERS' ETHICS 102–03 (1990) (noting the incongruous comparison of the two exceptions and deeming the exceptions a "mockery" of the sacred trust of the lawyer).

63. *See* MODEL RULE 3.3.

64. Proposed Rule 1.6 from March 23, 1999, prohibits disclosure of "information relating to the representation of a client or a former client" unless the client consents to the disclosure or one of the exceptions noted below applies. The proposed rule would have allowed a lawyer to reveal client information "to the extent the lawyer reasonably believes necessary" in specified circumstances:

102 ISSUES OF LEGAL ETHICS IN THE PRACTICE OF ENVIRONMENTAL LAW

exception defeated at the House of Delegates would have also authorized lawyers to disclose information when the lawyer reasonably believes it is necessary to prevent, mitigate, or rectify "substantial injury to the financial interests or property of another" when the client has used the lawyer's services in the furtherance of a crime or fraud.

2002 Revisions

In February 2002, the American Bar Association House of Delegates adopted amendments to Model Rule 1.6, making significant remedial changes to the rule. "The Commission addressed head-on one of the most frequently criticized aspects of the Model Rules—their narrow exceptions to the duty of confidentiality."[65] The revised rule authorizes permissive disclosure when necessary to prevent "reasonably certain death or substantial bodily harm,"[66] to "secure legal advice" about compliance with the Model Rules, and to comply with "other law or a court order." The House also retained the provision of the rule that allows lawyers to disclose client information "to establish a claim or defense on behalf of the lawyer." The revised rule states:

(a) A lawyer shall not reveal information relating to the representation of a client unless the client gives informed consent, the disclosure is impliedly authorized in order to carry out the representation or the disclosure is permitted by paragraph (b).

(b) A lawyer may reveal information relating to the representation

---

(1) to prevent reasonably certain death or substantial bodily harm;

(2) to prevent the client from committing a crime or fraud that is reasonably certain to result in substantial injury to the financial interests or property of another and in furtherance of which the client has used or is using the lawyer's services;

(3) to prevent, mitigate or rectify substantial injury to the financial interests or property of another that is reasonably certain to result or has resulted from the client's commission of a crime or fraud in furtherance of which the client has used the lawyer's services;

(4) to secure legal advice about the lawyer's compliance with these Rules;

(5) to establish a claim or defense on behalf of the lawyer in a controversy between the lawyer and the client, to establish a defense to a criminal charge or civil claim against the lawyer based upon conduct in which the client was involved, or to respond to allegations in any proceeding concerning the lawyer's representation of the client; or

(6) to comply with other law or a court order.

65. David W. Raack, *The Ethics 2000 Commission's Proposed Revision of the Model Rules: Substantive Change or Just a Makeover?*, 27 OHIO N. U. L. REV. 233, 237 (2001).

66. REVISED MODEL RULE 1.6(b)(1).

of a client to the extent the lawyer reasonably believes necessary:
(1) to prevent reasonably certain death or substantial bodily harm;
(2) to secure legal advice about the lawyer's compliance with these rules;
(3) to establish a claim or defense on behalf of the lawyer in a controversy between the lawyer and the client, to establish a defense to a criminal charge or civil claim against the lawyer based upon conduct in which the client was involved, or to respond to allegations in any proceeding concerning the lawyer's representation of the client; or
(4) to comply with other law or a court order.[67]

A new comment to Revised Model Rule 1.6 acknowledged the fact that lawyers in the same firm often share information. The comment endorses this practice as ordinary and acceptable under the duty of confidentiality unless the client instructs the lawyer against engaging in the common practice. "Except to the extent that the client's instructions or special circumstances limit that authority, a lawyer is impliedly authorized to make disclosures about a client when appropriate."[68] The comment also provides guidance on the issue of sharing client information among the lawyers of the firm in any given case. "Lawyers in a firm may, in the course of the firm's practice, disclose to each other information relating to a client of the firm, unless the client has instructed that particular information be confined to specified lawyers."[69]

A new comment to Model Rule 1.6 cautions lawyers that disclosures that may not reveal protected information may still violate Model Rule 1.6 if such a disclosure "could reasonably lead to the discovery of such information by a third person."[70]

These changes are a significant improvement over the 1983 version of the rule. By amending Rule 1.6 to allow lawyers to disclose client information to prevent reasonably certain death or substantial bodily harm, the House cured the most severe proportionality problem raised by the confidentiality rule. Under the revised rule, a lawyer who reasonably believes that a statute or the common law requires that he disclose a danger should not be seen as violating the rule by reporting the danger.

The revised Model Rule 1.6 is likely to increase uniformity among jurisdictions. Currently, most state rules, the Restatement of the Law Governing

---

67. REVISED MODEL RULE 1.6.
68. MODEL RULE 1.6 cmt. 5 (2002).
69. *Id.*
70. MODEL RULE 1.6 cmt. 4 (2002).

Lawyers, and the ethical codes of other professions allow disclosures to protect the public and third parties in some situations.[71] The revised rule protects lawyers by providing leeway to disclose information when necessary to protect third parties. Absent such an exception, a lawyer could be caught between the rock of the law and the hard place of the rule.

> It is the exceptional case in which the client refuses or fails to act to abate the danger. In those cases, the lawyer and engineer are faced with the vexing dilemma of how to reconcile conflicting obligations. The professional is bound on the one hand by the duty of confidentiality to honor the client's confidences and secrets. Breach of the duty may be actionable under tort law and may subject the lawyer or engineer to professional disciplinary action. In seeming opposition to that duty are three others: the ethical duty to refrain from assisting a client in the commission of acts that are criminal or fraudulent; a possible statutory duty to report unsafe environmental conditions; and the moral duty to protect fellow human beings and the environment from avoidable and possibly irreversible injury. Breach of any of those duties may, in a given set of circumstances, expose the professional adviser to civil or criminal penalties, to tort liability to third parties, or to professional discipline.[72]

The House also rejected some important and beneficial changes proposed by the Commission. The House's rejection of limited exceptions to protect third parties and the public in regard to financial interests raises serious questions of proportionality and the lawyer's role in society, however. The Commission's proposed subsection (b)(2) would have permitted the disclosure of client information by lawyers "to prevent the client from committing a crime or fraud that is reasonably certain to result in substantial injury to the financial interest or property of another" when the client used the lawyer's services to further the crime or fraud. After the defeat of subsection (b)(2), the Commission withdrew proposed subsection (b)(3), which would have permitted lawyers to disclose client information to "mitigate, or rectify substantial injury" in the same circumstances of a client's use of lawyer services to further the crime or fraud.

---

71. Of the states that adopted the Model Rules, only six (Alaska, Delaware, Louisiana, Missouri, Montana, and Rhode Island) accepted Rule 1.6 as written.

72. David Richman & Donald B. Bauer, *Responsibilities of Lawyers and Engineers to Report Environmental Hazards and Maintain Client Confidences: Duties in Conflict*, 5 Toxics L. Rptr. 1458 (Apr. 17, 1991).

The current exceptions allow lawyers to speak to protect their own interests, to "establish a claim or defense," without regard to the strength of the interest. In other words, the claim or defense asserted by the lawyer need not be of any particular value. A claim for a $500,000, $5,000, or $5 all trigger the exception, allowing disclosure without regard to the value of the lawyer's claim. This exception for lawyer self-interest is in sharp contrast to the House's rejection of the limited protection for third parties and the public,[73] even where the interests at stake are substantial. The deletion of proposed subsections (2) and (3) left third parties and the public at risk to significant harm from a lawyer's client if states were to adopt the rule adopted by the ABA. The final rule leaves lawyers without discretion to reveal information to prevent substantial financial harm that would flow from a crime or fraud in which the client used the lawyer's services. The same analysis that led the House of Delegates to empower lawyers in the situations of peril to life and bodily harm also argues for empowering lawyers in situations when the interests of third parties clearly outweigh the interests of a client who misuses the lawyer's services to commit a crime or fraud resulting in substantial financial injury to others.

The 2002 Revised Model Rule 1.6 clarifies the right of the lawyer to disclose information necessary to defend against a claim. Comment 8 states: "Such a charge can arise in a civil, criminal, disciplinary, or other proceeding and can be based on a wrong allegedly committed by the lawyer against the client or on a wrong alleged by a third person, for example, a person claiming to have been defrauded by the lawyer and client acting together."[74]

Remonstrating with a Client (2002 Revision)

A new comment to Model Rule 1.6 adopted by the ABA in 2002 reminds lawyers that, before making disclosures, they should consult with the client when practicable, seeking to "persuade the client to take suitable action to obviate the need for disclosure."[75]

Disclosure of Confidential Client Information

The ABA Standing Committee on Ethics and Professional Responsibility has

---

73. Proposed subsection (b)(5) carries forward verbatim (b)(2) from the former rule, empowering lawyers to protect their own interests. Although this exception is sometimes called the "Attorney Self-Defense Exception," it allows lawyers to use client information to establish a claim as well as a defense. *See, e.g.*, Nathan M. Crystal, *Core Values: False and True*, 70 FORDHAM L. REV. 747, 774 n.73 (2001).

74. MODEL RULE 1.6 cmt. 8 (2002).

75. MODEL RULE 1.6 cmt. 12 (2002).

76. ABA Formal Op. 98-411 (1998).

106   ISSUES OF LEGAL ETHICS IN THE PRACTICE OF ENVIRONMENTAL LAW

cautioned against identifying clients when consulting with another lawyer about a client matter. The Committee favored "hypothetical or anonymous consultations" so that the identity of the client is protected and client information is not associated with the actual client. The Committee also made clear that consulting with another lawyer does not create a "client-lawyer relationship between the consulting lawyer's client and the consulted lawyer."[76]

Environmental Example of Disclosure

Section 66 to the Restatement includes an illustration in the environmental context.

> As the result of confidential disclosures at a meeting with engineers employed by Client Corporation, Lawyer reasonably believes that one of the engineers released a toxic substance into a city's water-supply system. Lawyer reasonably believes that the discharge will cause reasonably certain death or serious bodily harm to elderly or ill persons within a short period and that Lawyer's disclosure of the discharge is necessary to permit authorities to remove that threat or lessen the number of its victims. Lawyer's efforts to persuade responsible Client Corporation personnel to take corrective action have been unavailing. Although the act creating the threat has already occurred, Lawyer has discretion to disclose under Subsection (1) for the purpose of preventing the consequences of the act.[77]

Revised Model Rule 1.6 includes a similar example.

> Paragraph (b)(1) recognizes the overriding value of life and physical integrity and permits disclosure reasonably necessary to prevent reasonably certain death or substantial bodily harm. Such harm is reasonably certain to occur if it will be suffered imminently or if there is a present and substantial threat that a person will suffer such harm at a later date if the lawyer fails to take action necessary to eliminate the threat. Thus, a lawyer who knows that a client has accidentally discharged toxic waste into a town's water supply may reveal this information to the authorities if there is a present and substantial risk that a person who drinks the water will contract a life-threatening or debilitating disease and the lawyer's disclosure is necessary to eliminate the threat or reduce the number of victims.[78]

---

77. RESTATEMENT (THIRD) OF THE LAW GOVERNING LAWYERS § 66, Ill. 3.

78. REVISED MODEL RULE 1.6 cmt. 6.

Both the 1983 rule and the revised rule specifically allow disclosure when necessary to prevent death or substantial bodily harm. The 1983 rule makes it unlikely that lawyers will disclose such information, however, by allowing disclosure only when the client's conduct creating the risk constitutes a crime that threatens "imminent death" or "substantial bodily harm." The revised rule eliminates the requirement that the intended act be a crime, stating a straightforward exception that allows disclosure "to prevent reasonably certain death or substantial bodily harm." Another new exception allows the lawyer to reveal client information "to secure legal advice about the lawyer's compliance" with the rules. Both approaches allow lawyer discretion for judgments about reasonably certain death or harm. Under the 1983 rule, the lawyer's judgment is hedged in by the requirement that the threatened harm result from criminal conduct and the "imminent death" standard.

Conflicts Issues

The need for confidentiality is an underlying reason for the rule against conflicting representation.[79] The lawyer's duty to maintain confidences of clients is an important factor in analyzing questions of conflicts of interest.[80] The rule that a lawyer may be disqualified from representing a party whose interests are in conflict with those of an existing client protects against violations of the principle of confidentiality. When a lawyer is considering taking a new client or moving to a new law firm, considerations of confidentiality of that lawyer's clients are paramount. The lawyer considering a new representation must confer with existing clients to make sure that conflicts issues are not implicated or, if they are, to ensure against problems relating to the confidences of either client and to secure the consent of the clients to the representations.[81]

Disclosure Necessary to Obtain Consent (2002 Revision)

A new comment to the 2002 Revised Model Rule 1.7 makes the point that a lawyer cannot ask a client to consent without providing information regarding the effect of the consent. Moreover, in some circumstances, the lawyer may not make such a disclosure because of the confidentiality concern of the client

---

79. *The Duty of Confidentiality Is a Corollary of the More General Duty of Loyalty.* in GEOFFREY C. HAZARD, ET AL., THE LAW AND ETHICS OF LAWYERING 269 (3d ed. 1999).

80. *See* Amoco Chemicals Corp. v. MacArthur, 568 F. Supp. 42 (D.C. Ga. 1983) (granting motion to disqualify lawyer representing third-party defendant in wrongful termination case on basis that subject was identical to lawyer's prior representation of third-party plaintiff).

81. See Chapter 5.

ISSUES OF LEGAL ETHICS IN THE PRACTICE OF ENVIRONMENTAL LAW

whose information is protected. Accordingly, the comment concludes "it may be impossible to make the disclosure necessary to obtain consent."[82]

Organizational Clients

In cases involving organizational clients, lawyers may need to refer matters involving serious legal violations to the highest authority in the organization. However, if the client refuses to take corrective action, the lawyer's only recourse is to withdraw from representation, at the same time disavowing her own prior statements or work product to put third parties on notice that something is amiss with the representation.

The lawyer's duty of confidentiality owed to the organizational client extends to information received from constituents of the organization, bringing all information that a lawyer receives from a constituent within the scope of the protection of the duty of confidentiality. In this way, the client organization is protected. The individual who gave the information receives no protection unless he justifiably believed that he was consulting the lawyer as his legal advisor.

> When one of the constituents of an organizational client communicates with the organization's lawyer in that person's organizational capacity as an agent of the organization, the communication is protected by Rule 1.6. Thus, by way of example, if an organizational client requests its lawyer to investigate allegations of wrongdoing, interviews made in the course of that investigation between the lawyer and the client's employees or other constituents are covered by Rule 1.6. This does not mean, however, that constituents of an organizational client are the clients of the lawyer.[83]

The reasonable expectations of the parties seems to justify this distinction. In such a situation, the individual constituent of the organization is not ordinarily the client of the lawyer, and the lawyer is not empowered to share confidential information of the organizational client with the individual.[84]

Client Wrongdoing: 1983 Version of Model Rule 1.6

The 1983 version of Model Rule 1.6 does not require disclosure in any situation, nor does it encourage disclosure in any situation. Although the Model

---

82. Model Rule 1.7 cmt. 19 (2002).
83. MODEL RULE 1.13 cmt. 2.
84. *Id.* Nevertheless, some cases have found an attorney-client relationship arises based on the expectations of the individual who sought the lawyer's counsel. *See* Togstad v. Vesely, Otto, Miller & Keafe, 291 N.W.2d 686 (Minn. 1980).

Rules prohibit lawyers from aiding a client's crime or fraud,[85] they do not encourage lawyers to take any action to counter client wrongdoing.[86] Withdrawing from a representation is the most active measure the rules endorse in the face of client wrongdoing. ABA Formal Ethics Opinion 92-366 requires a lawyer to withdraw from a representation if a client is using the lawyer's services to further a fraud or crime.[87] The opinion also establishes that a lawyer may disaffirm documents prepared in the course of the representation in certain circumstances.[88] The lawyer has a right to disaffirm his work product by notifying anyone who relies on it that the lawyer no longer stands behind the opinion or other documents even though such a "noisy" withdrawal and disaffirmance of work product "may have the collateral effect of inferentially revealing client confidences."[89] The comments recognize that a client may harm others and that the lawyer may not always be successful in convincing the client to abandon his plans for harm.[90] Nevertheless, the rules do not encourage a lawyer to disclose client information in such circumstances. Indeed, the 1983 version of Model Rule 1.6 forbids disclosure even when harm is likely to result from client conduct unless the two elements (a crime and extreme consequences of death or significant injury) are established. This approach of harm to third parties is clarified in Model Rule 1.2. A comment to the rule indicates that dangers to third parties are outside the scope of the lawyer's task. "The lawyer should assume responsibility for technical and legal tactical issues, but should defer to the client regarding such questions as the expense to be incurred and concern for third persons who might be adversely affected."[91] This view seems more understandable in the litigation context than in the transactional setting. The comment does not distinguish between the type of practice involved, however, nor does it note a distinction between litigation and transactional work.

Although the text of the 1983 Model Rule 1.6 presents the familiar structure of a general rule and exceptions, the rule and its comments advocate lawyer silence in almost all circumstances. While the general rule is a clear and powerful prohibition against disclosure, the exceptions are permissive. The exception for harm to third parties is also difficult to apply. It requires

---

85. *See* MODEL RULE 3.3; *see also* Geoffrey C. Hazard, Jr., *Lawyer Liability in Third-Party Situations: The Meaning of the Kaye Scholer Case*, 26 AKRON L. REV. 395, 399 (1993).
86. *See* 1 HAZARD & HODES, *supra* note 30, at 168.49.
87. *See* ABA Formal Ethics Op. 92-366 (1992).
88. *Id.*
89. *Id.*
90. *See* MODEL RULE 1.6 cmt. 9.
91. *See* MODEL RULE 1.2 cmt. 1.

110 ISSUES OF LEGAL ETHICS IN THE PRACTICE OF ENVIRONMENTAL LAW

application of imponderable elements, such as uncertain future acts and whether a crime will result in "imminent death."[92] The purpose of the rule's broad prohibition is to "encourage fuller and franker communication between a lawyer and client,"[93] and to encourage people to seek advice from lawyers.

> In becoming privy to information about a client, a lawyer may foresee that the client intends serious harm to another person. However, to the extent a lawyer is required or permitted to disclose a client's purposes, the client will be inhibited from revealing facts which would enable the lawyer to counsel against a wrongful course of action. The public is better protected if full and open communication by the client is encouraged than if it is inhibited.[94]

The 1983 Rule justifies its constraints with generalities. "Based upon experience, lawyers know that almost all clients follow the advice given, and the law is upheld."[95] The commentary answers concerns about wrongful conduct of clients by minimizing the risk.[96] It simply notes that the problem is rare: "almost all" clients conform to the law, harming no one. The comment does not provide empirical evidence for this assertion. Nor does it address the rare circumstances of an unworthy client who goes against the law. It simply notes the rarity of such situations, suggesting that low likelihood answers any problem. The rule's prohibition applies in all cases. Model Rule 1.6 makes no mention and gives no examples of cases in which the law requires a lawyer to disclose client information. Thus, the rule leaves for lawyers the difficult issue of balancing the Rule with other law. Silence on this important point could mislead lawyers who seek guidance in difficult cases. For example, a lawyer who consults the Model Rule upon learning that a client is using his services to further a crime or a fraud finds little guidance.

Recognition of Other Law

The Preamble to the Model Rules acknowledges other law. It states: "A lawyer should keep in confidence information relating to representation of a client

---

92. *See* MODEL RULE 1.6 cmt. 13.

93. CENTER FOR PROF'L RESPONSIBILITY, AM. BAR ASS'N, THE LEGISLATIVE HISTORY OF THE MODEL RULES OF PROFESSIONAL CONDUCT: THEIR DEVELOPMENT IN THE ABA HOUSE OF DELEGATES 13 (1987) [hereinafter LEGISLATIVE HISTORY].

94. MODEL RULE 1.6 cmt. 9.

95. MODEL RULE 1.6 cmt. 3.

96. *Id.*

Chapter 4: Confidentiality 111

except so far as disclosure is required or permitted by the Rules of Professional Conduct or other law."[97] This statement acknowledges the lawyer's duty to obey the law. The 1983 version of Model Rule 1.6 that currently provides the basis for most state rules[98] does not, however, acknowledge or refer to an exception to comply with law. Numerous judicial and board opinions recognize the need to allow or require lawyer disclosure of client information in some situations. For example, many states require or allow lawyers to disclose client information in order to prevent a crime or a fraud. The American Academy of Matrimonial Lawyers endorses disclosure of client information to protect a child from conduct by the client that, though not criminal, is severely detrimental to the well-being of the child.[99] The Academy notes that when a matrimonial lawyer is convinced that "the client or a person with whom the client has a relationship has abused one of the children," the lawyer should act to protect a child who is at a substantial risk of abuse.

> Notwithstanding the importance of the attorney-client privilege, the obligation of the matrimonial lawyer to consider the welfare of children, coupled with the client's lack of any legitimate interest in preventing his attorney from revealing information to protect the children from likely physical abuse, requires disclosure of a substantial risk of abuse and the information necessary to prevent it. If the client insists on seeking custody or unsupervised visitation, even without the attorney's assistance, the attorney should report specific knowledge of child abuse to the authorities for the protection of the child.[100]

Similarly, the American College of Trust and Estate Counsel recognizes "a reasonable degree of discretion in determining how to respond to any particular case" when one client opposes disclosure of information to another joint client. "In such cases the lawyer should have a reasonable degree of discretion in determining how to respond to any particular case."[101] New York's State Bar Committee on Professional Ethics has opined that a lawyer repre-

---

97. LEGISLATIVE HISTORY, *supra* note at 12.
98. While many states have moderated the prohibition of MODEL RULE 1.6, the 1983 version of the rule is important because it provided and continues to provide the basic template for regulation by the states.
99. *See* AMERICAN ACADEMY OF MATRIMONIAL LAWYERS, GOALS FOR FAMILY LAWYERS, comments on MR 1.6.
100. *Id.*
101. AMERICAN COLLEGE OF TRUST AND ESTATE COUNSEL, COMMENTARIES ON THE MODEL RULES OF PROFESSIONAL CONDUCT (3d ed. 1999).

senting an executor should disclose the executor's breach of trust in some circumstances.[102]

The Effect of Deletion of References to Other Law

Because the 1983 version of Model Rule 1.6 makes no mention of other law, it is likely that a lawyer facing an ethical question and seeking guidance from this rule will fail to analyze the effect of other law on his decision of whether or not to disclose information. This is particularly interesting, since other Model Rules refer to other law.[103] The silence of Rule 1.6 regarding other law seems to suggest that there is nothing to talk about on this point and, thus, that the full inquiry on confidentiality is accomplished within the confines of the rule. Nevertheless, other law continues to exist and continues to have force. Professor Hazard rejected the literal meaning of Rule 1.6 and advocated recognition of an exception "in practice" for disclosure of a client's fraud.

> [The] peril to the innocent lawyer is so obvious as to impugn the seriousness of the notion that competent lawyers can take care of themselves under a confidentiality rule that does not have an exception concerning client fraud. In pondering the rhetoric in favor of such a rule, I indeed conclude that [Model Rule 1.6] is not intended to be taken seriously. Instead, the idea is that the confidentiality rule should state no qualifications concerning client fraud, but should be understood as having an exception "in practice."[104]

Rather than salvaging a workable rule, Professor Hazard's observation points up the deficiency of the rule as written. This deficiency is corrected to a degree by the revised rule adopted by the ABA in February 2002. Comment 8 to Revised Model Rule 1.6 notes the right of a lawyer to reveal client information to protect herself from charges of wrongdoing (without regard to

---

102. N.Y. Op. No. 649 (1993) (opining that "although retained by the executors, [a lawyer] has a duty not only to represent them individually, but also to serve the best interest of the estate to which they, in turn, owe their fiduciary responsibilities."

103. *See, e.g.,* The MODEL RULES Preamble (noting the "larger legal context" that shapes the lawyer's role); MODEL RULE 3.4(b) (stating that lawyers shall not offer an inducement to a witness when it is prohibited by law); MODEL RULE 3.5 (indicating that lawyers must not communicate with judges or jurors except as permitted by law); MODEL RULE 4.2 (indicating that a lawyer may communicate with a person as authorized by law).

104. *See* Geoffrey C. Hazard, Jr., *Rectification of Client Fraud: Death and Revival of a Professional Norm,* 33 EMORY L.J. 271, 284–85 (1984).

Chapter 4: Confidentiality 113

whether the disclosure relates to a current or former client). The comment notes the ability of the lawyer to answer charges of wrongdoing notwithstanding the duty of confidentiality. "Where a legal claim or disciplinary charge alleges complicity of the lawyer in a client's conduct or other misconduct of the lawyer involving representation of the client, the lawyer may respond to the extent the lawyer reasonably believes necessary to establish a defense."[105] Although the comment notes that a lawyer need not "await the commencement of an action or proceeding"[106] that states charges against the lawyer in order to respond to a claim that the lawyer was complicit with client wrongdoing, the comment seems implicitly to reject Professor Hazard's approach, which would allow prospective disclosure for the lawyer's self-defense: "The lawyer's right to respond arises when an assertion of such complicity has been made."[107]

Lawyers face a difficult choice when the law appears to require disclosure. The lawyer facing the dilemma of whether disclosure is appropriate can hardly be expected to recognize the unspoken exception of other law—especially in a situation of urgency. The exposure of lawyers to common law and statutory liability should encourage the bar to recognize the force of other law in a meaningful way to allow lawyers to respond within the law to situations as they arise. The Restatement (Third) of the Law Governing Lawyers and the revisions to the Model Rules both acknowledge the right of lawyers to disclose confidential client information to comply with law.[108]

The Tension With Other Law: Environmental Examples

In light of the real potential for negative consequences to lawyers, including liability, disbarment, and even criminal penalties, Model Rule 1.6 as revised provides better protection than existed under the old rule, perhaps especially for environmental lawyers, where the potential for harm may be greatest. The protection is better not only for the public and third parties but also for lawyers. The duty of confidentiality has a clear purpose of protecting clients and encouraging the use of lawyers to resolve disputes. Nevertheless, as with many legal doctrines, other needs and policies must be taken into consideration. Thus, the policy reasons for the duty of confidentiality are in competition with laws and norms that require candor and disclosure in certain settings. The duty of confidentiality exists in tension with laws that require disclosure

---

105. MODEL RULE 1.6 cmt. 8 (2002).

106. *Id.*

107. *Id.*

108. *See* RESTATEMENT (THIRD) OF THE LAW GOVERNING LAWYERS § 63, REVISED MODEL RULE 1.6 (4).

of client information and rules of ethics that require candor to the tribunal and limit the assistance a lawyer may provide to a client.

Model Rule 1.6 is based on an assumption that clients will not inform their lawyers of all relevant information absent a strong rule in favor of confidentiality. Environmental hazards and the laws created to minimize the risks that arise from these hazards challenge the unfettered use of such an assumption. Because environmental hazards present special dangers to the public at large as well as to individuals, it makes sense to consider the public's paramount interest in a safe environment in relation to professional responsibility in the arena of environmental law. J. William Futrell, president of the Environmental Law Institute, has argued forcefully that the environmental laws demand more open disclosure rather than the technique of "stonewalling" the government to avoid revealing information.[109]

> Current codes of attorney conduct do not directly address the heightened duties of environmental lawyers to assist their clients in implementing the new self-reporting schemes of the regulatory state. The current codes are based on a tradition of advising the client to offer as little information as possible in order to avoid self-incrimination. Under such codes discreet silence—not open disclosure—is the norm. This approach runs counter to the operation of our environmental laws.[110]

Significant dangers to the public or to individuals, such as those created by environmental hazards, call for protection despite the tradition of lawyer silence. Such protection can be achieved by creating effective exceptions recognizing a duty to warn or disclose information in defined situations or by legislation dealing directly with lawyer obligations.

The Tension With the Lawyer's Duty of Candor

Model Rule 3.3 imposes a duty on lawyers not to mislead a tribunal. The rule creates clear and significant prohibitions. For example, it prohibits lawyers from offering evidence "that the lawyer knows to be false"[111] and from making a "false statement of material fact or law to a tribunal."[112] This duty can

---

109. William Futrell, *Environmental Ethics, Legal Ethics, and Codes of Professional Responsibility*, 27 Loy. L.A. L. Rev. 825, 835 (1994).

110. *Id.*

111. Model Rule 3.3(a)(4).

112. *Id.* at (a)(1).

Chapter 4: Confidentiality   115

present the environmental lawyer with practical problems regarding truth and falsity. For example, is a property assessment that describes accurately contamination documented by soil and water samples truth or falsity? What if no additional testing has been done but circumstances lead the lawyer to believe that other areas not yet tested may be contaminated with hazardous substances? The rule goes further, creating an affirmative obligation to disclose legal authority. It prohibits lawyers from failing to disclose legal authority when the authority is known to the lawyer "to be directly adverse to the position of the client" and opposing counsel does not report the authority.[113] Most important, Rule 3.3 prohibits a lawyer from failing to disclose a material fact "when disclosure is necessary to avoid assisting a criminal or fraudulent act by the client."[114]

The duty of candor set forth in Model Rule 3.3 creates significant duties of disclosure in formal proceedings before a tribunal.[115] Model Rule 3.3 provides the strongest limitation on the duty of confidentiality of Model Rule 1.6,[116] expressly noting that the duties of candor stated in the rule "apply even if compliance requires disclosure of information otherwise protected by Rule 1.6."[117]

The rule does not, however, create an affirmative duty on the lawyer to police the conduct of his clients or monitor or certify statements of the client to a court or to a government agency. Moreover, its mandate does not reach the transactional legal sphere operating without the oversight of a court or administrative body.

---

113. *Id.* at (a)(3).

114. *Id.* at (a)(2).

115. *See* People v. DePallo, 2001 WL 735739 (N.Y. July 2, 2001) (holding that a lawyer confronted at trial with knowledge of his client's perjury has a duty to reveal that information to the court); Fox Searchlight Pictures, Inc. v. Paladino, 106 Cal. Rptr. 2d 906 (2001) (holding in-house counsel who sued former employer may disclose relevant facts to her lawyer, including privileged communications and client confidences).

116. The only other rule that speaks to a situation in which disclosure may be necessary despite the prohibition of MODEL RULE 1.6 is MODEL RULE 2.3 concerning evaluation for use by third persons. It provides that a lawyer may "undertake an evaluation of a matter affecting a client" for the use of a third party when the client consents to the evaluation and the lawyer "reasonably believes that making the evaluation is compatible with other aspects of the lawyer's relationship with the client." The rule notes the preeminence of confidentiality in this context by its statement that: "[e]xcept as disclosure is required in connection with a report of an evaluation, information relating to the evaluation is otherwise protected by Rule 1.6." This formulation allows disclosure despite MODEL RULE 1.6 but it does so in the setting of prior client consent to the evaluation.

117. MODEL RULE 3.3(b).

Government Lawyers

The duty of confidentiality applies to government lawyers as well as other lawyers. Much of the information in the hands of the government is subject to the Freedom of Information Act (FOIA), however, and must be disclosed when sought under that Act unless a statutory exception prevents disclosure. Nevertheless, the lawyer who works for the government must maintain confidentiality of the client's information as steadfastly as other lawyers except when the requirements of FOIA or some other law trumps the duty of confidentiality. She must not take the duty of confidentiality lightly simply because avenues exist for compelling production of information. Additionally, she must not use information gained while working for the government to the disadvantage of the government.

> The government lawyer's duty of confidentiality differs from that of a lawyer in private practice in two significant ways. First, pervasive regulations govern much of the information with which a government lawyer must necessarily deal. A large portion of the information in the hands of the federal government consists of public records or information available upon request to the public. Recent legislation, in particular the Freedom of Information Act, provides citizens with access to a wide range of government documents. . . . Second, the government lawyer functions within a complex federal system based on the principle of separation of powers. It is an untidy structure of incredible complexity in which the President provides the principal focus of cohesion and unity while Congress, responding to interest groups, tends to further the centrifugal tendencies of a pluralistic society.[118]

In *Jacobs v. Schiffer*,[119] the court considered a related question: whether "a government lawyer 'reveals' his client's confidences and secrets when he discloses them to his personal attorney"[120] to allow the lawyer to evaluate potential claims and give advice. In this case, Daniel S. Jacobs, a Justice Department lawyer in the Environmental and Natural Resources Division, Environmental Enforcement Section became concerned about the strategies of the section.[121]

---

118. Roger C. Cramton, *The Lawyer as Whistleblower: Confidentiality and the Government Lawyer*, 5 Geo. J. Legal Ethics 291, 294 (1991).

119. 47 F. Supp. 2d 16 (D.C. Cir. 1999).

120. *Id.*

121. *Id.* at 18.

Jacobs consulted a private lawyer on the question of whether the division was acting illegally and, additionally, whether his reassignment and reduced performance rating was improper retaliation by his employer. The court held that Jacobs' disclosure of nonpublic government information to his own lawyer was not a violation of rules of professional conduct. In the same case, however, the court approved a restriction by the Department of Justice, barring the release of information by a lawyer that would disclose information relating to his case against the government to unidentified lawyers for public interest groups.[122] The 2002 revision to Model Rule 1.6 makes this right clear.[123]

Government Lawyers (2002 Revision)

The ABA revisions to the Model Rules adopted in February 2002 underscored the need for confidentiality of government information known to both former and current government lawyers. In addition to setting forth conflicts rules regarding involvement of government lawyers in representations, Model Rule 1.11 also provides for disqualification of lawyers based on confidential information. Rule 1.11 originally created a bar to representation based on confidential information. It states that a lawyer may not represent a private client when the lawyer knows "confidential government information about a person acquired when the lawyer was a public officer or employee, whose interests are adverse" to the potential client when the confidential "information could be used to the material disadvantage of that person." Revised Rule 1.11 clarified the meaning of "confidential government information," defining it to mean, for purposes of the rule, "information that has been obtained under governmental authority and which, at the time this rule is applied, the government is prohibited by law from disclosing to the public or has a legal privilege not to disclose and which is not otherwise available to the public."[124] Conflicts based on this part of the Model Rule 1.11 are discussed more fully in the section of this work on conflicts (see Chapters 5 and 6).

Duty of Candor

The Government Lawyers' Dilemma

The case of *United States v. Shaffer Equipment Company* recognized the importance of the government lawyer's duty of candor.[125] In this case, the court held that government lawyers breached the duty of candor to the court by

---

122. *Id.*
123. MODEL RULE 1.6(b)(2).
124. MODEL RULE 1.11(c) (2002).
125. 11 F.3d 450 (4th Cir. 1993).

failing to reveal that EPA's on-scene coordinator for a cleanup had misrepresented his academic credentials in both a pending and other cases. After EPA undertook activities to clean up leaking drums of transformer fluid at the hazardous waste facility costing over five million dollars, it commenced a CERCLA cost-recovery action against Shaffer. Before trial, the Assistant U.S. Attorney filed a motion for stay of the proceedings while an investigation was undertaken into Robert Caron, the on-scene coordinator. The court ultimately found that Caron had falsified his academic credentials, placing in doubt the work he had done on the site. The district court dismissed the action on the basis that the government violated its duty of candor and obstructed the defendants' efforts to uncover Caron's misrepresentations. On appeal, the government claimed that the fraud of the EPA employee was not a material fact of the case. The court of appeals agreed that the government lawyers breached the duty of candor to the court. It also noted that the trial court possessed inherent power to vacate a judgment obtained by fraud. Nevertheless, the court reversed the dismissal of the action, holding that a less dramatic sanction is sufficient to deter fraudulent conduct. The court remanded the case to the trial court.[126]

Government Counsel: Whistleblowing

State statutes protect whistleblowers in some circumstances of risk to the public. These statutes may apply to lawyers. Special protection may be necessary for government lawyers who take a stand against the policies of the government entity that employs them. Recent laws giving protection to whistleblowing government employees may pose an ethical dilemma for the government lawyer who, in the course of litigating or otherwise representing an agency, finds evidence of fraud, waste, or abuse in government processes or expenditures. The government lawyer then faces the issue of whether his duty of confidentiality to his client outweighs his duty to reveal fraudulent activities under a whistleblower statute. A government lawyer's duty of confidentiality already differs from other lawyers in that much of the information they deal with is regulated by the government and they exist within the complex system of separation of powers. The dilemma faced by government lawyers also involves the public interest, and whether the lawyer's duty to serve the public interest overrides the decisions of the lawyer's governmental client. The question may come down to whether the disclosure of evidence of government misconduct is prohibited by law. One scholar has noted that "since no statute directly addresses the issue of public disclosures on the part of lawyers employed by the federal government, agency regulations requiring lawyer confi-

---

126. *Id.* at 463.

Chapter 4: Confidentiality 119

dentiality appear to be overridden by the whistleblower protection provisions."[127]

Environmental Context

A great deal of the work of environmental lawyers is not within the context of a judicial proceeding. Rule 3.3 uses the term "tribunal" rather than "court," creating a wider sphere of operation than if it had merely referred to a court, and including within its mandate administrative law judges and possibly other adjudicative bodies of agencies. Whether the rule imposes an obligation on a lawyer not to make a false statement to an administrative agency acting as a regulator is unclear, however. Does it apply to discharge monitoring reports required under the CWA and CAA, for example? An agency does not seem to fit squarely within the category of "tribunals," although agencies serve quasi-judicial functions necessary under environmental law and other areas. For example, state and local water authorities grant water allocations, the U.S. Army Corps of Engineers makes wetlands determinations, state agencies approve implementation plans for discharging hazardous waste, and EPA and state authorities issue discharge permits. There is no certainty regarding whether any of these official actions by governmental authorities bring the agency within the term "tribunal" as used by Model Rule 3.3.[128] Although the client has a clear duty under the regulations to report truthfully and fully, whether the lawyer has a duty of candor remains unclear in many of these settings.

The Environmental Lawyer's Nightmare

Perhaps the most troubling issue of confidentiality for environmental lawyers is the problem of a client who refuses to disclose information required by law and necessary to prevent harm to another. This problem can arise because of a client's active fraudulent concealment or simply because the client remains silent in the face of significant dangers to others. The transfer of contaminated property that creates a risk of substantial bodily harm is a dramatic example of the environmental lawyer's nightmare. Although some state laws require disclosure of releases of chemicals that result in environmental contamination, such statutes typically impose an obligation on the transferor of real property (the client) or the owner or operator of the facility rather than on the lawyer for these entities. The duty of candor, as stated in Model Rule 3.3, will not necessarily arise in land transfers. The rule provides no exemption for land

---

127. Cramton, *supra* note 117, at 312.
128. *See* WOLFRAM, *supra* note 6, at 674.

120 ISSUES OF LEGAL ETHICS IN THE PRACTICE OF ENVIRONMENTAL LAW

transfers or other particular types of matters. Nevertheless, a land transfer simply may not be within the jurisdiction of a tribunal. Unless a lawyer filed a false document of title with a court, or in some other way presented a false assertion to a tribunal, the duty does not seem to come into play. Although courts sometimes refuse to impose liability for damages resulting from bare nondisclosure,[129] a court may impose liability when it determines that a party created a misleading situation or had a duty to reveal a dangerous latent condition.[130]

An owner of contaminated property may wish to transfer the property without revealing the contaminated state of the property. This scenario provides a clear example of the type of problems lawyers face in seeking to comply with both the environmental laws and the ethical duty of confidentiality. The situation is by no means the only type of dilemma faced by lawyers practicing environmental law, however.

Suppose you represent a company that is selling a parcel of property that has been used for industrial purposes. You have seen reports from an environmental consultant indicating that significant hazardous wastes have been stored, deposited, and released on the property, and you know the consultant has concluded that the property presents serious risks and should be cleaned up under the Comprehensive Environmental Response, Compensation, and Liability Act (CERCLA). You also know that the buyer has no information about the contamination and that your client has made statements indicating there are no environmental problems present on the property. The client instructs you to keep all damaging information about the site confidential. Although you want to reveal the danger, the 1983 version of Model Rule 1.6 prohibits any disclosure unless the jurisdiction of the sale makes the seller's conduct a crime and the lawyer reasonably believes that the sale is likely to result in serious bodily injury or imminent death.

A lawyer faced with this dilemma may minimize the risk of disciplinary action in his own mind, believing that the state's disciplinary board would decline to impose discipline in a case where his moral intuition is strong. This may or may not prove to be the case, however. Disciplinary boards are re-

---

129. *See, e.g.*, Swinton v. Whintonsville Sav. Bank, 42 N.E.2d 808 (Mass. 1942) (refusing to award damages for seller's failure to disclose the existence of termite infestation in residential property subject to contract).

130. *See, e.g.*, Smith v. Coldwell Banker, 122 F. Supp. 2d 267 (D. Conn. 2000) (holding that real estate agent and broker violated Residential Lead-Based Paint Hazards Reduction Act by failing to provide purchasers with copy of lead paint report prior to closing and that this failure was not excused when purchasers were informed of lead paint at property and of existence of lead paint report).

Chapter 4: Confidentiality   121

quired to apply the ethics rules adopted by the state. For example, an opinion by the Delaware Professional Ethics Committee responded to a request by a lawyer who inquired regarding whether he has a duty to warn a woman living with his client that the client is infected with the AIDS virus.[131] The lawyer indicated that the client requested that the lawyer tell no one about his medical condition and also informed the lawyer that he had not told the woman living with him about his condition. The Ethics Committee concluded that the lawyer has no duty to warn the nonclient of the danger to her. It stated that a "literal reading" of the rule on the lawyer's duty of confidentiality prevents him from warning the client's girlfriend of the client's condition. The opinion noted, however, that the lawyer should advise the client of his duty to warn his girlfriend of danger to her and of possible civil or criminal liability for a failure to warn of this danger. Finally, the Committee noted that, if the lawyer chooses civil disobedience by warning the woman despite his professional duty, he should be prepared to accept discipline if the authority does not accept a "moral compulsion" exception to the rule of confidentiality.[132]

In another case, a Washington lawyer was disciplined for revealing a judge's misconduct.[133] The judge was removed from the bench for defrauding a client's estate while he was a lawyer. The Washington State Bar Association held that the lawyer's disclosure violated Rule 1.6(a) and recommended that the lawyer be suspended from practice for one year. Other cases deal with conflicts between the intuition of individual lawyers and the rules of that lawyer's jurisdiction of practice. A Colorado lawyer currently faces discipline for engaging in a deception that he was a public defender to coax a triple murderer into surrendering to police.[134] After murdering three women and raping another, William Neal was caught in a standoff with police. He held three hostages, including the woman he had raped. When Neal asked to speak with a public defender, Mark Pautler, a Colorado lawyer, spoke with him for approximately seven minutes, misrepresenting himself as a public defender. Pautler convinced Neal to give himself up to police. Later Neal pleaded guilty to three charges of first-degree murder. Although Mark Pautler may have saved the lives of the hostages, his conduct included misrepresenting himself as a public defender.[135] Because his conduct violated Colorado's ethics prohib-

---

131. Delaware Ethics Op. 88-2, *available at* http://www.dsba.org/ethics1988.htm.

132. *Id.*

133. *In Hot Water for Exposing Injustice*, SEATTLE TIMES, Aug. 5, 1999, *available at* http:// archives.seattletimes.nwsource.com/cgi-bin/texis/web/vortexdisplay?slug=brod&date= 19990805.

134. *See* Stephen Tarnoff, *Hard Line on a White Lie: Colorado Panel Disciplines Prosecutor Who Helped Coax Triple Murderer into Surrendering*, 87 A.B.A. J. 32 (June 2001).

135. *Id.*

122 ISSUES OF LEGAL ETHICS IN THE PRACTICE OF ENVIRONMENTAL LAW

iting dishonest conduct by lawyers, the Colorado disciplinary board imposed sanctions on Pautler, recommending a three-month suspension of his license to practice law.

Lawyer's Dilemma in Environmental Context

Whether an individual client has a duty to disclose information depends on a variety of factors and circumstances. Similarly, whether a lawyer has an independent duty to disclose information held secret by a client depends on a number of considerations. Lawyers facing such a difficult issue should consider the tension between the duty of confidentiality and other duties imposed on the lawyer by other laws, including statutory environmental laws and the requirements of common law.

The duty of confidentiality stated in the 1983 version of Model Rule 1.6 cautions against disclosure. It prohibits disclosure in all but the most perilous situations. On the other hand, Model Rule 1.2 emphatically prohibits a lawyer from counseling or assisting a client in "conduct that the lawyer knows is criminal or fraudulent."[136] Additionally, the lawyer self-defense exception in Model Rule 1.6 provides a basis for disclosing information if the failure to reveal the information would subject the lawyer to liability.[137] Procedural common-law rules such as the attorney-client privilege, the coclient rule, and the work product doctrine also play a role in a court's determination of whether evidence may be discovered and used at trial.

The following sections of this chapter take up some of the laws implicated in this difficult situation as examples of the applicable laws. The intersection of the duty of confidentiality and other laws is, in large measure, uncertain and indeterminate. Few cases have addressed the issue, and the determination is likely to turn on the facts of a given situation.

Preemptive Self-Defense

A comment to Model Rule 1.6 notes that a lawyer may respond to a legal claim or disciplinary charge that alleges that the lawyer has been complicit

---

136. MODEL RULE 1.2(d). The Rule allows the lawyer to "discuss the legal consequences of any proposed course of conduct with a client and may counsel or assist a client to make a good faith effort to determine the validity, scope, meaning or application of the law."

137. A lawyer is entitled to introduce evidence necessary to defend himself against accusations of wrongful conduct. *See In re* Nat'l Mortgage Equity Corp. Mortgage Pool Sec. Litig, 120 F.R.D. 687, 692 (C.D. Cal. 1988); *see also* MODEL CODE OF PROF'L RESPONSIBILITY DR 4-101(c)(4); MODEL RULE 1.6(b)(2).

regarding misconduct of a client or former client "to the extent the lawyer reasonably believes necessary to establish a defense."[138] The comment also indicates that the lawyer need not await a legal proceeding to respond to such charges. "The lawyer's right to respond arises when an assertion of such complicity has been made. Paragraph (b)(2) does not require the lawyer to await the commencement of an action or proceeding that charges such complicity, so that the defense may be established by responding directly to a third party who has made such an assertion."[139] Of course, this exception does not provide a blanket provision for disclosure. "Disclosure should be no greater than the lawyer reasonably believes is necessary to vindicate innocence."[140] Hazard and Hodes discuss the right of "preemptive self-defense," arguing that lawyers should be entitled to disclose information when actions of the client are likely to result in a cause of action against the lawyer at a later time.[141] The preemptive self-defense rationale rests on the language of Model Rule 1.6 that allows the lawyer to disclose client information "to establish a claim or defense on behalf of the lawyer." In the situation in which a client is engaged in wrongful conduct, the lawyer in an enterprise later held to be wrongful may also be sued by the victim of the scheme. Noting that the "self-defense" exception to the prohibition against disclosure is "not controversial," Hazard and Hodes point to commentary to Rule 1.6 that suggests that it may be "proper in a 'preemptive' mode" as well.[142] "[A] lawyer aware that plausible charges are being drawn up need not 'await the commencement of an action or proceeding,' but may establish a defense by responding directly to a third party who has made such an assertion."[143] This analysis suggests a lawyer may claim the defense to act before a controversy or claim has arisen.

Hazard and Hodes note the realities of lawyers faced with possible future charges of wrongdoing.

> [T]he lawyer might legitimately fear criminal or civil prosecution or feel a moral obligation to right the wrong. Papers innocently drafted by the lawyer might work their fraudulent effect even after the lawyer had withdrawn, for example, or a misrepresentation might remain uncorrected. Furthermore, to wait to achieve vindication until after charges are filed (or even publicly asserted) may

---

138. MODEL RULE 1.6 cmt. 18.
139. *Id.*
140. *Id.*
141. GEOFFREY HAZARD & W. WILLIAM HODES, THE LAW OF LAWYERING (3d ed. 2001).
142. *Id.*
143. *Id.* at § 9.27.

be too late, in terms of reputation and simply the cost of defense. In these situations, therefore, a lawyer may be morally justified in engaging in especially early preemptive self-defense. But in almost all such cases the effect of disclosure will be to warn the intended third-party victim and thus achieve prevention—or at least mitigation or rectification—of the harm. For this practical reason, it may be said that a broad reading of Rule 1.6(b)(2) restores the deleted exception.[144]

Under the preemptive self-defense, a lawyer who is "fearful that possible charges could be asserted"[145] against him may disclose client information as "early self-defense" to avert charges altogether.[146]

[T]he exception [of pre-emptive self-defense] will not only help extricate lawyers from dangers presented by abusive clients (which is obviously a major point of ordinary self-defense), but it will also serve the interests of third-party victims of the same clients' wrongdoing. This reading of the self-defense exception to confidentiality will therefore put it on firmer moral ground, free of the objection that it is a self-serving rule designed by lawyers for the use of lawyers only.[147]

Reporting Obligations: Environmental Examples

The prevalence of environmental risks in the modern world and the federal and state statutes and regulations enacted to control those risks create potential conflicts for lawyers between the duty to disclose hazardous environmental conditions and the duty of confidentiality owed the client. In response to concern about environmental risks, Congress and state legislatures have passed numerous acts protective of the environment. Some of these statutes include requirements that owners and operators of hazardous sites report discharges to EPA or other authorities.[148] From 1964 to 1980, Congress responded to grow-

---

144. *Id.* at § 9-97-98. *See also In re* Bryan, 61 P.3d 641 (Kan. 2003).
145. Hazard & Hodes, The Law of Lawyering (3d ed. 2001), at § 9.27. *See also* Restatement (Third) of the Law Governing Lawyers 66(1) (2000).
146. *Id.*
147. *Id.*
148. *See* Michael B. Gerrard, Whose Backyard, Whose Risk: Fear and Fairness in Toxic and Nuclear Waste Siting 12 (1995).

ing public concern by enacting sweeping environmental protections.[149] Since 1980, Congress has continued to scrutinize environmental problems, amending the major statutes and attempting to form a comprehensive framework of environmental protection.[150] Some statutes signal the dramatic need for public protection from environmental hazards. For example, the text of CERCLA indicates the preeminence of environmental concerns represented by this legislation in declaring its sanctions "[n]otwithstanding any other provision or rule of law."[151] Other statutes have as their motivating purpose to clean up hazardous substances or to encourage waste reduction to reduce the risks created by hazardous substances in the environment.[152]

One way federal and state statutes seek to minimize risks from environmental hazards is by compiling a body of information about the manufacture, storage, use, and disposal of toxic and hazardous substances. Both state and federal laws require extensive reporting of hazardous substances and industrial processes that result in hazardous waste.[153] Additionally, many environmental statutes enhance the likelihood of enforcement by empowering citizens to bring actions against polluters for violations of the laws, including the failure to meet the reporting requirements imposed by the statutes.[154] Federal laws require that persons report hazardous releases and environmental con-

---

149. *See* Robert V. Percival, *Environmental Federalism: Historical Roots and Contemporary Models*, 54 Md. L. Rev. 1141, 1160–61 (1995); Irma S. Russell, *The Role of Public Opinion, Public Interest Groups, and Political Parties in Creating and Implementing Environmental Policy*, 23 Env'l. L. Rep. 10,665 (1993).

150. *See, e.g.*, Clean Water Act (CWA), 33 U.S.C. §§ 1251–1387 (1994); the Clean Air Act (CAA), 42 U.S.C. §§ 7401–7671q (1994); SWDA, 42 U.S.C. §§ 6901–6992k (1994); and CERCLA, 42 U.S.C. §§ 9601–9675 (1994); the Toxic Substance Control Act (TSCA), 15 U.S.C. §§ 2601–2692 (1994); the Oil Pollution Act, 33 U.S.C. §§ 2701–2761 (1994); CERCLA, 42 U.S.C. §§ 9601–9675. The Forest and Rangeland Renewable Resources Acts, 16 U.S.C. §§ 1600–1687 (1994); the Multiple-Use Sustained-Yield Act (MUSYA), 16 U.S.C. §§ 528–531 (1994); the Endangered Species Act (ESA), 16 U.S.C. §§ 1531–1544 (1994).

151. CERCLA 107(a), 42 U.S.C. § 9607(a) (1994).

152. *See, e.g.*, the Resource Conservation and Recovery Act (RCRA), 42 U.S.C. § 6901–6992k (1995); CAA 42 U.S.C. §§ 7401–7671q (1995); CWA 33 U.S.C. §§ 1251–1387 (1986); TSCA 15 U.S.C. §§ 2601–2692 (1997). For a discussion of statutes that require reporting of hazardous substances, *see* David W. Case, *Legal Considerations in Voluntary Corporate Environmental Reporting*, 30 E.L.R. 10375 (2000).

153. The common law also creates duties to protect the public and individuals from environmental hazards.

154. *See, e.g.*, CWA 505(g), 33 U.S.C. § 1365(g) (1986); CERCLA 310, 42 U.S.C. § 9659 (1995); RCRA 7002, 42 U.S.C. § 6972 (1995); CAA 304, 42 U.S.C. § 7604 (1995).

126 ISSUES OF LEGAL ETHICS IN THE PRACTICE OF ENVIRONMENTAL LAW

tamination within prescribed time limits.[155] CERCLA prescribes technology and standards required for the cleanup of contaminated property. Some states require sellers to disclose information to purchasers about known or suspected contamination. For example, under the Residential Lead-Based Hazard Reduction Act, sellers or lessors of residential property must disclose "the presence of any known lead-based paint" on their property.[156]

State and federal environmental statutes provide both civil and criminal sanctions, including imprisonment for knowing violations.[157] For example, under the Resource Conservation and Recovery Act (RCRA), knowingly transporting a hazardous waste to a facility that lacks a permit to store or dispose of such waste without a permit is a felony.[158] Punishment includes up to five years' imprisonment and fines of up to $50,000 per day.[159] A subsequent similar violation by one convicted of an earlier violation can result in a prison term of up to 10 years and fines that are twice the maximum for first-time offenders.[160] CERCLA also imposes criminal sanctions for failure to notify the EPA of a release into the environment of a "reportable quantity" of hazardous substances.[161] The penalty for violation of this provision includes fines up to $25,000 per day and imprisonment up to three years (or not more than five years in the case of a second conviction).[162] The Emergency Planning and

---

155. See CERCLA 103(a), 42 U.S.C. § 9603(a) (1994) (requiring any person in charge of vessel or facility to report release of hazardous substance "as soon as he has knowledge of any release" in specified quantities); Pollution Prevention Act of 1990 (PPA) 6607(b)(1), (3), (7), 42 U.S.C. § 13,106(b)(1), (3), (7) (1994) (requiring annual report of chemicals discharged into environment).

156. Pub. L. No. 102-550 (1992).

157. See, e.g., United States v. Laughlin, 10 F.3d 961, 962 (2d Cir. 1993) (upholding sentence for knowingly disposing of hazardous waste without permit and knowingly failing to report release of hazardous substance); United States v. Johnson & Towers, Inc., 741 F.2d 662 (3d Cir. 1984) (noting that courts may hold employees criminally liable for illegal disposal even when made at direction of superior). *Air Pollution: New Civil Penalty Policy Will Boost Fines, Speed Processing of Cases, EPA Attorney Says*, 22 ENV'T REP. (BNA) No. 41, at 2327 (Feb. 7, 1992); *Enforcement: Corporations Face Increased Penalties Under Revised RCRA Civil Enforcement Policy*, 21 ENV'T REP. (BNA) No. 27, at 1245 (Nov. 2, 1990).

158. See SWDA 3008(d), 42 U.S.C. § 6928(d) (1994); *see also* Sidney M. Wolf, *Finding an Environmental Felon Under the Corporate Veil: The Responsible Corporate Officer Doctrine and RCRA*, 9 J. LAND USE & ENVTL. L. 1, 24 (1993) (noting relaxation of scienter requirement in environmental statutes).

159. See SWDA 3008(d), 42 U.S.C. § 6928(d).

160. See id.

161. 42 U.S.C. § 9603(b).

162. Id.

Chapter 4: Confidentiality 127

Community Right to Know Act (EPCRA) imposes criminal penalties of up to $25,000 per day and imprisonment for up to five years for failure to report releases of "extremely hazardous substances."[163] Federal statutes such as CAA and CWA also regulate discharges of hazardous substances into the air and water and impose criminal sanctions for violations of these laws.[164] State statutes set both civil and criminal penalties for violations. For example, the Tennessee statute dealing with hazardous wastes, like most statutes of this sort, classifies some violations of environmental law as a felony and provides for both civil and criminal penalties for these violations.[165] Like many states, the Tennessee statute indicates that each day constitutes a separate offense.[166]

Although violations of environmental statutes are sometimes regarded as regulatory in nature, such violations can result in catastrophes.[167] Legislatures have revealed a strong policy of protection through the imposition of criminal penalties. Some statutes impose criminal penalties for negligent conduct such as the negligent discharge of pollutants into the waters of the United States.[168] Additionally, many statutes declare that a violation that persists in the environment constitutes a new (punishable) offense for each day it continues.[169] Enforcement of environmental statutes has also risen in recent years.[170] The agency plans to continue its enforcement actions in the future.[171] Prosecutors seek to hold responsible the highest corporate official connected with an environmental crime because "[i]ncarceration is the one cost of business that you can't pass on to the consumer."[172]

---

163. 42 U.S.C. § 11,004.

164. *See* CAA, 42 U.S.C. § 7401 et seq. (1986); CWA, 33 U.S.C. §§ 1251–1376 (1994).

165. Tenn. Code Ann. 68-212-114 (1999).

166. *Id.*

167. *See, e.g.*, Ethan H. Jessup, *Environmental Crimes and Corporate Liability: The Evolution of the Prosecution of "Green" Crimes by Corporate Entities*, 33 New Eng. L. Rev. 721 (1999).

168. *See* CWA, 309(c)(1), 33 U.S.C. § 1319(c)(1) (1994) (classifying enumerated negligent violations as criminal and providing significant terms of imprisonment).

169. *See id.* (enacting fine of $2,500 to $25,000 "per day of violation").

170. *See* Daniel Riesel, *Criminal Prosecution and Defense of Environmental Wrongs*, 15 Envtl. L. Rep. 10,065 (Mar. 1985) (discussing the disappearance of prosecutor reluctance to prosecute violators of environmental statutes).

171. *See EPA Fiscal 2001 Plan for Compliance, Creating Credible Deterrent to Pollution*, BNA Daily Env't Rep., at E-1 (Feb. 25, 2000).

172. *See* John F. Cooney et al., Criminal Enforcement of Environmental Laws, 25 Envtl. L. Rep. (Envtl. L. Inst.) 10,459, 10,462 (1995) (citing Memorandum from Peggy Hutchins, paralegal, to Ronald A. Sarachan, Chief, Environmental Crimes Section, Environmental Criminal Statistics FY 1983 Through FY 1994 (Apr. 7, 1995)) at 10,469 (noting Justice

128 ISSUES OF LEGAL ETHICS IN THE PRACTICE OF ENVIRONMENTAL LAW

Protection of Confidential Business Information

The duty of confidentiality to one's client is well known and often in the lawyer's consciousness. Interestingly, the confidentiality of business information of opponents can also create obligations and problems for lawyers. Caution should be used in dealing with proprietary business information no matter whom that information belongs to. This issue may be of heightened concern in the environmental area because of the industry processes that are employed by corporate clients and the potential for significant financial harm in the event such that competitors are able to obtain the information relating to the corporation's process. A dramatic example of this issue is found in the case of *National Wildlife Federation v. EPA.*[173] In the *National Wildlife Federation* case, the D.C. Court of Appeals noted the conduct of an environmental lawyer who used confidential information in his brief. EPA had disclosed some of this information erroneously in response to a motion by the National Wildlife Federation (NWF). The court of appeals held that privilege is preserved if the holder of the privilege has made reasonable efforts to protect and preserve the privilege. The court found that EPA had made reasonable attempts to protect its confidential business information by opposing a previous motion to compel made by the NWF requesting the same information they received in error. Accordingly, the court referred the matter to the D.C. Committee on Admissions and Grievances for consideration of the ethics issue of this disclosure.

Some environmental laws protect trade secrets from disclosure to the public.[174] For example, the Clean Water Act states that records and other information submitted to EPA or the state under the Act will be made available to the public, except "upon a showing satisfactory to the Administrator" that the information (other than effluent data) "would divulge methods or processes entitled to protection as trade secrets" of the submitter.[175] Additionally, the FOIA exempts "trade secrets and commercial or financial information obtained from a person and privileged or confidential"[176] from the types of in-

---

Department's unpublished policy to this effect). Commentators in other areas such as antitrust have made the point that incarceration provides a strong deterrent by preventing penalty shifting. *See* Amanda Kay Esquibel, Note, *Protecting Competition: The Role of Compensation and Deterrence for Improved Antitrust Enforcement*, 41 FLA. L. REV. 153, 172, 174 (1989).

173. 286 F.3d 554 (D.C. Cir. No. 99-1452, Apr. 19, 2002).
174. *See, e.g.*, FIFRA, 7 U.S.C. § 136h(b), 136f, 136g; TSCA, 15 U.S.C. § 2613(b) (B) and (c).
175. 33 U.S.C. § 1318(b).
176. 5 U.S.C. § 552(b)(4).

Chapter 4: Confidentiality 129

formation that an agency must provide to individuals who make a request for information within the agency's control.[177]

Interpretation and Enforcement of Environmental Statutes

Enforcement of environmental laws has increased over the last decade, with greater interaction and cooperation between local, state, and federal agencies and organizations as well as increased use of criminal sanctions.[178] Moreover, courts frequently interpret environmental statutes liberally. For example, in *Mid-Atlantic National Bank v. New Jersey Department of Environmental Protection,* the United States Supreme Court held that a bankruptcy trustee could not abandon property listed as a facility under CERCLA when the abandonment would endanger the public.[179] Similarly, in *Superior Air Products Co. v. NL Industries, Inc.,*[180] the New Jersey Superior Court held that, because of the threat posed by pollution, the New Jersey Environmental Rights Act allowed interested citizens the right to sue polluters without having to prove special injury. The court also held that a liberal construction of the statute is mandatory.[181]

Owner/Operator Liability

Environmental statutes and regulations often create a legal obligation on the part of an owner of property or the owner or operator of a facility to disclose information relating to environmental hazards. These laws undercut the confidentiality interest of property owners, requiring owners to abandon secrecy with respect to such hazards. For example, under the CAA Amendments of 1990, facilities that produce, handle, or store extremely hazardous substances

---

177. *See* Brian Gregg, *Setting Priorities for Phase Three of the Toxic Release Inventory: Trade Secrets or Community Right-to-Know,* 4 ENVTL. L. 943 (1998).

178. *See, e.g.,* Steve Cook, *FY 2000 Fines Total $224.6 Million in EPA Criminal, Civil Actions,* 32 ENVTL RPTR 191 (Jan. 26, 2001) (noting that EPA enforcement in 2000 amounts to the third largest total in the 30 years EPA has been in existence); Daniel Riesel, *Criminal Prosecution and Defense of Environmental Wrongs,* 15 ENVTL. L. REP. 10,065 (Mar. 1985).

179. 474 U.S. 494 (1986); *see also* One Wheeler Road Assoc. v. Foxboro Co., 843 F. Supp. 792, 795 (D. Mass. 1994) (noting CERCLA should be given "a broad and liberal construction" rather than a narrow interpretation that would "frustrate the government's ability to respond promptly, or to limit the liability of those responsible for cleanup costs beyond the limits expressly provided"); United States v. United Nuclear Corp., 814 F. Supp. 1552 (D. N.M. 1992) (applying a liberal interpretation to CERCLA's statute of limitations).

180. 522 A.2d 1025 (N.J. Ct. App. 1987).

181. *Id.*

130   ISSUES OF LEGAL ETHICS IN THE PRACTICE OF ENVIRONMENTAL LAW

must assess the dangers of such substances.[182] The Amendments require that operators of facilities of the targeted chemicals draft a Risk Management Plan, outlining and evaluating the potential for release and establishing the effects of the release.[183] In other words, companies that store or use extremely hazardous substances must now tell the government and citizens what would happen to people in the vicinity of the facility in the event of an accident. An EPA guidance statement clarified the requirements of the Risk Management Program and announced plans to audit Risk Management Plans submitted by companies.[184] A knowing failure or refusal to comply with reporting requirements is a crime under federal and state environmental statutes.[185]

"Any Person" Liability

While many environmental statutes create a duty only on the owner or operator of a site, some statutes state a duty to report a dangerous environmental condition and impose that duty on "any person" having knowledge of the condition.[186] Both the CAA and the CWA provide for criminal penalties for "any person" who knowingly violates specific requirements of the acts. For example, the CAA imposes criminal penalties on anyone who makes a false statement regarding information required under the Act.[187] Such provisions do not state an exception for lawyers.

Some environmental statutes hold owners and operators liable for failure to report the release of hazardous substances and hold "any person" liable for knowingly making "any false statement, representation, or certification in any application, record, report, plan, or other document filed or required to be maintained under this chapter."[188] Florida law presents a typical example of such a state statute.[189] It recognizes a violation by "any person who owns or

---

182. *See* CAA 112(r), 42 U.S.C. § 412(r) (1994).

183. *Id.*

184. This guidance document is available on the Internet. *See* Guidance for Auditing Risk Management Programs under Clean Air Act § 112 Cr, *at* http://www.epa.gov/ceppo/pubs/audit_gd.pdf. (visited Mar. 26, 2003).

185. *See, e.g.,* CAA §§ 113(c)(2), 42 U.S.C. § 7413(c)(2) (1994).

186. *See* N.J. STAT. ANN. 58:10A-21 to -37 (West 1992). The New Jersey Administrative Code, which implements the Act, provides that "any person including but not limited to the owner or operator of an underground storage tank system" shall report the release after confirming its existence to the local health agency. N.J. ADMIN. CODE tit. 7, 14B-7.3(a) (1990).

187. 42 U.S.C. § 7413 (1994) (authorizing imprisonment of up to two years for a first offense).

188. *See, e.g.,* FLA. STAT. ANN. § 403.161 (1998).

189. *Id.*

Chapter 4: Confidentiality 131

operates a facility to fail to report . . . within one working day of discovery of a release that must be reported under CERCLA."[190] The statute also makes it a violation for "any person" who causes pollution that harms "human health or welfare, animal, plant, or aquatic life or property" to fail to obtain a required permit, or who "knowingly make[s] any false statement" on required documents.[191] Similarly, some state statutes create a duty on any person with knowledge of a spill of a hazardous substance to report the spill to environmental authorities.[192] For example, New York creates a duty on "any person with knowledge" to report a petroleum leak or spill. Section 613.8 provides:

> Any person with knowledge of a spill, leak or discharge of petroleum must report the incident to the department within two hours of discovery. The results of any inventory record, test or inspection which shows a facility is leaking must be reported to the department within two hours of the discovery. Notification must be made by calling the telephone hotline (518) 457-7362.[193]

Other statutes use language similar to "any person shall report . . . " to impose requirements for reporting hazardous releases. For example, Delaware law declares that "No person shall knowingly allow a release from an underground storage tank to continue without taking immediate steps to report the release to the Department."[194] In the Delaware case of *Clark v. Sun Refining & Mktg. Co.*,[195] the court construed the statutory language to support the state's claim of damages it incurred in cleaning up a contaminated site.

Statutes such as these raise the interpretive question of whether a lawyer is within the definition of "any person" under the statute. Courts may need to resolve this interpretive question in the environmental context. In the administrative context, the New York State Department of Environmental Conservation (DEC) explained the reach of the New York statute quoted above, applying it to an environmental consultant and suggesting that statutory liability in the environmental area may have a greater reach than lawyers may assume.[196] The

---

190. FLA. STAT. ANN. § 403.161(d) (1998).

191. FLA. STAT. ANN. § 403.161(a)–(c) (1998).

192. *See, e.g.*, N.J. STAT. ANN. §§ 58:10A-21 to -37 (West 1990) (New Jersey Underground Storage Tank Act).

193. N.Y. COMP. CODES R. & REGS. tit. 6, § 613.8.

194. DEL. CODE ANN. tit. 7, § 7406(a).

195. 1990 WL 91072 (Del. Super. 1990) (construing DEL. CODE ANN. tit. 7, § 7406(a)).

196. *See* Michael B. Gerrard, *Duty of Consultants, Lawyers to Report Contamination*, N.Y. L. J. (Mar, 26, 1999).

132   ISSUES OF LEGAL ETHICS IN THE PRACTICE OF ENVIRONMENTAL LAW

DEC applied the reporting requirement under the New York law regulating underground storage tanks to an environmental consultant, Donald J. Middleton. Jr., the vice president of Middleton, Kontokosta Associates Ltd., an environmental consulting firm.[197] Based on a finding that "any person" was limited to owners or operators, an administrative law judge dismissed the action against Middleton.[198] The Commissioner of the DEC reviewed the case and overruled the administrative law judge, finding that the term "any person" in the statute applied to "all other persons with knowledge of a spill, leak or discharge in order to implement the remedial and preventive purposes of the Petroleum Bulk Storage Code, of which 613.8 is a part." The Commissioner's opinion noted that the lawyer's duty of confidentiality was not involved in the case and that the case did not reach the question of whether the law would trump the lawyer's duty of confidentiality.

> Mr. Middleton is not a professional engineer. . . . Nor is Mr. Middleton an attorney, and therefore the attorney-client privilege could not be asserted as a basis for his non-disclosure. This case therefore raises the question of the duty of a non-engineer, non-lawyer who is not the facility owner or operator to report under 613.8, and what sanction should be imposed in cases where a timely report is not given.[199]

Lawyers may take some satisfaction in the Commissioner's dicta that notes that the case did not involve a lawyer or a claim of attorney-client privilege. Nevertheless, the opinion makes clear that the term "any person" is not limited to owners and operators. The opinion does not provide analysis regarding the question of whether the result would change if the person failing to report the release had been the lawyer for the person who caused the release.

Complying With Law

Implied Authorizations

Model Rule 1.6(a) also refers to the right of a lawyer to disclose information when the disclosure is "impliedly authorized in order to carry out the representation."[200] This provision seems to set forth a common-sense exception. It may provide justification for a disclosure required by law but not expressly

---

197. *Id.*
198. 1998 WL 939495 (N.Y. Dept. Env. Conserv.).
199. *Id.*
200. MODEL RULE 1.6(a).

Chapter 4: Confidentiality 133

authorized by the client. The statement suggests that, in cases where a disclosure is required by law and the client is silent about the need to report, the lawyer is justified in making a report to comply with the law. If a lawyer is asked to undertake an action that is subject to interpretation, the lawyer is justified in interpreting the request to authorize only legal acts. Thus, the need to comply with law arguably may create an implied authorization in some situations.[201]

Court Orders

Courts may require individuals, including lawyers, to report information. For example, if a court issues a subpoena to a lawyer or otherwise orders a lawyer to reveal information, the lawyer must reveal any information not covered by the attorney-client privilege or the work product rule.[202] When information may be deemed privileged as a result of the attorney-client privilege, lawyers are required to reveal any evidence the court finds falls within the crime-fraud exception to the privilege.[203] For example, a court applying the "required by law" exception ordered a criminal defense lawyer to turn over a letter in his possession in which his client threatened a third party.[204] Similarly, a court responded to allegations that defense counsel had made secret recordings of telephone conversations with plaintiff's witnesses by requiring the lawyer to turn over the tape recordings.[205] The court rejected the lawyer's assertions that the tapes were protected by the work product doctrine because surreptitious taping violated the local court rules.[206]

Comment 20 to the 1983 version of Model Rule 1.6 notes the lawyer's duty to comply with law in response to final orders of a court or other tribunal.[207] The statement endorses limited disclosure but stops short of creating an exception to comply with statutory laws. As a practical matter, the fact that this point appears in the comment rather than the rule diminishes its significance. The comments to the Model Rules "do not add obligation to the rules."[208]

---

201. Professor Hazard advocated recognition of an exception "in practice" for disclosure of a client's fraud. *See* Geoffrey C. Hazard, Jr., *Rectification of Client Fraud: Death and Revival of a Professional Norm*, 33 EMORY L.J. 271, 285 (1984).
202. *See* United States v. Nixon, 418 U.S. 683, 709 (1974).
203. *See* Upjohn Co. v. United States, 449 U.S. 383 (1981).
204. *See In re* Original Grand Jury Investigation, 733 N.E.2d 1135 (Ohio 2000) (applying DR 4-101).
205. *See* Anderson v. Hale, 2001 WL 417991 (N.D. Ill. Apr. 23, 2001).
206. *Id.*
207. MODEL RULE 1.6 cmt. 20.
208. MODEL RULE Scope.

134   ISSUES OF LEGAL ETHICS IN THE PRACTICE OF ENVIRONMENTAL LAW

Additionally, comment 20 to Rule 1.6 authorizes disclosure only in the case of a court order. It does not expressly authorize compliance with law established by statutes or judicial decisions. Comment 21 to Model Rule 1.6 also refers to other law outside the ethics rules. It states:

> The Rules of Professional Conduct in various circumstances permit or require a lawyer to disclose information relating to the representation. See Rules 2.2, 2.3, 3.3 and 4.1. In addition to those provisions, a lawyer may be obligated or permitted by other provisions of law to give information about a client. Whether another provision of law supersedes Rule 1.6 is a matter of interpretation beyond the scope of these rules, but a presumption should exist against such a supersession.[209]

While comment 21 acknowledges the existence of other law and, additionally, the possibility of a need to disclose information based on other rules, it broadens disclosure very little. With the sole exception of Rule 3.3, none of the rules listed calls for disclosure in situations that do not meet the requirements of Rule 1.6. The usual deference of other rules to the prohibition of Rule 1.6 is clear from the treatment of the disclosure inquiry under Model Rule 4.1. Model Rule 4.1 deals with the obligation of the lawyer to disclose a "material fact to a third person." It states that disclosure must be made, but limits the obligation by the exception "unless disclosure is prohibited by Rule 1.6." This treatment incorporates the broad prohibition of Rule 1.6 at the same time it seems to suggest a duty to disclose. The net effect is lawyer discretion to disclose client information only when the client consents or when the difficult analysis of Rule 1.6 would allow disclosure.

It is doubtful that either of these bases produces a disclosure not otherwise allowed under Rule 1.6. Model Rule 2.2 and 2.3 expressly require client consent. The other rules listed give way to Model Rule 1.6 in all but the narrow case of Model Rule 3.3 requiring candor to a tribunal. Model Rule 3.3 has the distinction of trumping Model Rule 1.6, stating that the duties of the provision "apply even if compliance requires disclosure of information otherwise protected by Rule 1.6."[210] It operates only in the context of an action heard "by a tribunal," leaving untouched the many transactional matters. For example, the sale of real property is a transactional matter typically accomplished without judicial oversight. The sale of real property presents significant dangers if it is contaminated with hazardous substances. Nevertheless, Model Rule 3.3

---

209. MODEL RULE 1.6 cmt. 21.
210. MODEL RULE 3.3(b).

does not require disclosure of such contamination—no matter how grave the danger—except in the rare case when the sale occurs under the guidance or auspices of a court.

Two important limitations on this concept should be noted. First, Model Rule 1.2, which is not listed in comment 20 to Model Rule 1.6, is of significance in this area. Model Rule 1.2 establishes the requirement that, subject to stated exceptions, the lawyer must "abide by a client's decisions concerning the objectives of representation."[211] In setting forth the exceptions to this general rule, the rule declares clearly that a lawyer "shall not counsel a client to engage, or assist a client, in conduct that the lawyer knows is criminal or fraudulent."[212] Model Rule 1.2(d) provides an important limitation on the actions of the lawyer. Additionally, a broad reading of the lawyer self-defense exception under Rule 1.6 allows a lawyer to reveal information to obviate a risk that he will be charged with violating the law or injuring a third party by his acquiescence or assistance in a client's course of conduct.

In environmental practice, the rule requires that a lawyer refrain from helping a client respond to requests for information in an incomplete or misleading manner. For example, under a CERCLA § 104 request or a discharge monitoring report under the CWA, a client might wish to misrepresent the true nature of the quantity or quality of a discharge. A transporter of hazardous substances may wish to minimize its involvement in choosing a disposal site for depositing hazardous substances because one basis for liability under CERCLA is that a transporter chose the disposal site.[213] The lawyer must not assist in such conduct and, additionally, must "consult with the client regarding the relevant limitations on the lawyer's conduct" when the lawyer knows the client expects prohibited assistance.[214] The rule also requires that a lawyer avoid any involvement in criminal conduct. A lawyer who alters documentary evidence such as a discharge monitoring report or a report showing hazardous contamination as a result of underground storage tanks would be in violation of this rule. Moreover, altering or destroying physical evidence relevant to a judicial proceeding is a crime.[215]

---

211. MODEL RULE 1.2(a).

212. MODEL RULE 1.2(d). The Rule tempers this prohibition by expressly allowing the lawyer to "discuss the legal consequences of any proposed course of conduct with a client and may counsel or assist a client to make a good faith effort to determine the validity, scope, meaning or application of the law." *Id.*

213. 42 U.S.C. § 9607.

214. MODEL RULE 1.2(e).

215. *See, e.g.,* 18 U.S.C. § 1505 (1994).

ISSUES OF LEGAL ETHICS IN THE PRACTICE OF ENVIRONMENTAL LAW

Misprision

Although rarely prosecuted, the crime of misprision also has relevance to questions of required disclosure under environmental statutes. Misprision involves "concealment or nondisclosure of a serious crime by one who did not participate in the crime."[216] Some state and federal statutes, read literally, require any person to disclose information he knows about a crime. Courts have applied the statute to lawyers, notwithstanding the duty of confidentiality. For example, an Ohio statute provides as follows: "No person, knowing that a felony has been or is being committed, shall knowingly fail to report such information to law enforcement authorities."[217] Similarly, the United States Code provides: "Whoever, having knowledge of the actual commission of a felony cognizable by a court of the United States, conceals and does not as soon as possible make known the same to some judge or other person in civil or military authority under the United States, shall be fined under this title or imprisoned not more than three years, or both."[218]

Two different consequences should be noted with regard to the felony of misprision: (1) penalties including fines and imprisonment; and (2) suspension from the practice of law. In the *Matter of Morris,*[219] the Supreme Court of Arizona took up the question of the length of time a lawyer should be suspended from practicing law as a result of his conviction under the federal misprision statute. In this case, Richard Morris, the lawyer of a person convicted of tax fraud, was charged as an alleged conspirator to defraud the United States by impeding the work of the IRS.[220] The court noted that the prosecutor made no charges of overt fraud against Morris and that the indictment against him alleged only a failure to reveal a crime to the government, the client's tax fraud.[221] The State Bar Hearing Committee imposed a one-year suspension on Morris. The Arizona Disciplinary Commission recommended that the one-year suspension be reduced to six months. The court adopted the recommendation to reduce the suspension, reasoning that the lawyer had not engaged in dishonest conduct in the circumstances of his conviction for misprision under the federal statute.[222] The Arizona lawyer suffered a suspension of his license, although he won a reduction of the period of time the suspen-

---

216. BLACK'S LAW DICTIONARY (7th ed. 1999).
217. OHIO REV. CODE ANN. § 2921.22 (West 1997); *see also* State v. Flynn, 217 A.2d 432 (R.I. 1966).
218. 18 U.S.C. § 4 (misprision of felony).
219. 793 P.2d 544 (Ariz. 1990).
220. *Id.* at 545.
221. *Id.*
222. *Id.* at 547.

sion was effective. This case makes clear that the offense of misprision may apply to lawyers even though they have a duty of confidentiality.

The case of *Duncan v. Board of Disciplinary Appeals*[223] addressed the issue of whether a Texas lawyer who had pleaded guilty to misprision under the federal statute should be suspended from practicing law during the period of his probation.[224] The Texas Disciplinary Rule at issue in the case requires that the state disciplinary counsel initiate a disciplinary proceeding against a lawyer convicted of an intentional crime.[225] The rule defines the term "intentional crime" as a "serious crime" and includes within this definition "any felony involving moral turpitude."[226] In the *Duncan* case, a federal court placed James Duncan on probation for a term of four years and ordered him to pay restitution of $156,753 and a fine of $30,000 as punishment for misprision. In a subsequent decision, the Disciplinary Board suspended Duncan's license, holding that the felony of misprision constitutes moral turpitude per se. It did not discuss the facts of the concealment charged. The court reversed the board's holding. Contrasting the violation to that of perjury, the court noted that, unlike perjury, the crime of misprision can be committed by mere silence, and held that violation of the misprision statute did not constitute a crime of moral turpitude per se. As a result of this holding, the court remanded the case to the Texas Disciplinary Board for consideration of the conduct of the lawyer to determine whether he should be suspended from practice.[227]

State Environmental Laws: Mandatory Sanctions

Some states provide for mandatory minimum fines in certain cases of violations of environmental statutes. California provides an example. In its Water Code, California incorporates protections of the Federal Water Pollution Control Act, including requirements imposed by pretreatment programs. In addition to specifying penalties "for each day in which the violation occurs," the Act states: "a mandatory minimum penalty of three thousand dollars ($3,000) shall be assessed for the first serious violation and each additional serious violation in any period of six consecutive months. . . ."[228]

---

223. 898 S.W.2d 759 (Tex. 1995).

224. *Id.* at 760.

225. Tx. St. Rules Disc. P. 8.01.

226. 898 S.W.2d 760.

227. *Id.* at 762.

228. Cal. Water Code § 13385(h)(i) (West Supp. 2003). The statute also creates an exception to allow a state or regional board to require the discharger to spend an amount equal to the penalty for a supplemental environmental project in accordance with the enforcement policy of the state board and any applicable guidance document. *See id.*

Environmental Audits

Some state statutes promise immunity for companies that report and correct problems identified in voluntary environmental audits.[229] The security afforded by such statutes for both clients and lawyers may be less certain than it appears at first blush, however, because EPA allows the mitigation or forgiveness of penalties but does not provide for immunity or an evidentiary privilege for such audits.[230]

Securities Act Requirements

Securities laws require that publicly traded companies routinely disclose potential liabilities (including environmental liabilities). Many companies must manage environmental concerns and liabilities as part of their underlying business. Additionally, they must report discharges and other environmental issues to the EPA. Publicly traded companies must also report environmental liabilities and contingent claims or other information relevant to the financial status of the company to the SEC when the information is called for under the rules and regulations of the SEC. Under the 1990 Remedies Act,[231] the SEC has the power, after affording a person notice and an opportunity to be heard, to order a person to cease and desist conduct that it finds will result in a violation of securities law, including a provision of the Code or a rule or regulation.[232] The Commission may publish its findings relating to the cease-and-desist order.[233] The SEC also has the power to disbar or suspend lawyers who violate securities laws.[234] Future legislation requiring the disclosure of additional information seems likely following the Enron and WorldCom scandals. Courts have

---

229. *See, e.g.*, Ohio Rev. Code Ann. § 3745.72 (2000) (promising immunity from "administrative and civil penalties" except where "disclosed violation resulted in significant economic benefit to the owner or operator"). *See also* David R. Erickson & Sarah D. Mathews, *Environmental Compliance Audits: Analysis of Current Law, Policy, and Practical Considerations to Best Protect Their Confidentiality*, 63 UMKC L. Rev. 491 (Summer 1995).

230. *See* 60 Fed. Reg. 66,706 (*Incentives for Self-Policing: Discovery, Disclosure, Correction, and Prevention of Violations*); s*ee also EPA's Audit Policy Spells Success for Corporate Users, EPA, the Public, and Most Importantly, the Environment*, 29 Envtl. L. Rep. 10,705 (Nov. 1999). The Environmental Protection Partnership Act introduced by Sen. Hutchinson was referred to the Judiciary Committee on Sept. 29, 1999. *See Bills Introduced*, 29 Envtl. L. Rep. 10,789.

231. 15 U.S.C. § 77h-1 (1996).

232. *Id.*

233. *Id.*

234. *See* S.E.C. Rule 102(e).

Chapter 4: Confidentiality 139

recognized that the antifraud provisions of the Securities Exchange Act of 1934[235] apply to lawyers as well as corporate executives.[236] The SEC regulates lawyers who appear before it. Even considering the U.S. Supreme Court's recognition that the Commerce Clause is not unlimited,[237] the federal government's ability to regulate the conduct of lawyers practicing before an agency is not controversial, particularly when the subject matter of the regulation involves national interests such as the economic effects of publicly held companies.

Under Rule 2(e) of the SEC's Rules of Practice, the SEC may suspend or disbar any person from appearing before the Commission if it finds that the person has engaged in unethical conduct. Rule 2(e) provides:

> (e) Suspension and disbarment. (1) The Commission may deny, temporarily or permanently, the privilege of appearing or practicing before it in any way to any person who is found by the Commission after notice of and opportunity for hearing in the matter (i) not to possess the requisite qualifications to represent others, or (ii) to be lacking in character or integrity or to have engaged in unethical or improper professional conduct, or (iii) to have willfully violated, or willfully aided and abetted the violation of, any provision of the Federal securities laws (15 U.S.C. §§ 77a to 80b-20), or the rules and regulations thereunder.[238]

In 2002, Congress passed the Sarbanes-Oxley Act, attempting to address problems of corporate fraud and the resulting impacts on the economy. The Act requires the SEC to issue a rule requiring lawyers to report evidence of securities violations "to the chief legal counsel or the chief executive of the company,"[239] and, if necessary, "to the audit committee of the board of directors of the issuer or to another committee of the board of directors comprised solely of directors not employed directly or indirectly by the issuer, or to the board of directors."[240] The Act deals with fraudulent filings with the SEC by an issuer (corporation) and wrongdoing of corporate officers or directors generally and with the role of the lawyer in responding to corporate wrongdoing.

---

235. 15 U.S.C. § 78j (1988).

236. *See, e.g.,* Ahern v. Gaussoin, 611 F. Supp. 1465, 1488 (D. Or. 1985).

237. United States v. Lopez, 115 S. Ct. 1624 (1995) (holding Gun-Free School Zones Act, which criminalized the knowing possession of firearms in a place that defendant knows is a school zone, exceeded Congress's Commerce Clause authority); Solid Waste Agency of Northern Cook County v. U.S. Army Corps of Engineers, 121 S. Ct. 675, 683 (2001) (noting that Commerce Clause authority of Congress is "not unlimited").

238. 15 U.S.C.A. following section 78u (1998).

239. 15 U.S.C. § 7245 (2002).

240. *Id.*

140 ISSUES OF LEGAL ETHICS IN THE PRACTICE OF ENVIRONMENTAL LAW

Lawyers are vulnerable to charges of cooperating with a dishonest client to violate securities law, although it may not be clear what information the lawyer's client provided to him.[241] In one of the cases generated by the failure of the Lincoln Savings and Loan, Judge Stanley Sporkin asked in essence: Where were the lawyers when the clients were engaging in fraudulent conduct? Judge Sporkin wrote:

> The questions that must be asked are: Where were these professionals, a number of whom are now asserting their rights under the Fifth Amendment, when these clearly improper transactions were being consummated? Why didn't any of them speak up or disassociate themselves from the transactions? Where also were the outside accountants and attorneys when these transactions were effectuated? What is difficult to understand is that with all the professional talent involved (both accounting and legal), why at least one professional would not have blown the whistle to stop the overreaching that took place in this case.[242]

In this highly publicized case, the New York law firm of Kaye, Scholer, Fierman, Hays & Handler paid $41 million to settle an action brought by the Office of Thrift Supervision (OTS), in which the OTS alleged that the law firm knowingly misrepresented information about the failed Lincoln Savings and Loan Association to federal authorities.[243] The case was not resolved by judicial decision. Nevertheless, the Kaye Scholer case presents a dramatic example of the potential for lawyer liability under Securities laws. The law firm paid the amount as settlement rather than as a result of a judgment against the firm.[244]

---

241. *See generally* Richard W. Painter & Jennifer E. Duggan, *Lawyer Disclosure of Corporate Fraud: Establishing a Firm Foundation*, 50 SMU L. REV. 225–26 (1996) (noting the risks created by securities lawyers who deal with dishonest clients and the protracted and unpredictable nature of the SEC disciplinary and enforcement proceedings).

242. Lincoln Sav. & Loan Ass'n v. Wall, 743 F. Supp. 901, 920 (D.D.C. 1990).

243. *See* H. Lowell Brown, *The Dilemma of Corporate Counsel Faced with Client Misconduct: Disclosure of Client Confidences or Constructive Discharge*, 44 BUFF. L. REV. 777, 848 (1996).

244. *See* Geoffrey C. Hazard, Jr., *Lawyer Liability in Third Party Situations: The Meaning of the Kaye Scholer Case*, 26 AKRON L. REV. 395, 399 (1993). "A lawyer can be held liable under criminal law for aiding or abetting a crime, including the crime of fraud." *Id.*

Regulations S-K and S-X

Securities Regulations S-K and S-X require disclosure of facts material to the value of securities. Although the regulations are not aimed specifically at environmental disclosures, they include environmental disclosures that come within the mandates of these sections. Thus, when a publicly traded company faces liability or potential liability as a result of environmental contamination, it has an obligation to comply with the disclosure requirements of regulations S-K and S-X.

Staff Accounting Bulletin 92

SEC Staff Accounting Bulletin No. 92 (SAB 92) specifically targets environmental disclosure. The bulletin is the result of a perception on the part of the Securities and Exchange Commission that companies fail to make the required disclosure of information in a significant number of cases. SAB 92 states that companies reporting to the SEC may not offset a claim for recovery against another party to reduce a probable contingent liability under CERCLA or other environmental statutes. It indicates that liability and potential recoveries should be reported separately. The separate reporting requirement is not favorable to companies because it requires disclosure to the public of full probable liabilities and, accordingly, may present a less favorable financial report for the company. Nevertheless, because all publicly traded companies are required to disclose this information, the regulation creates equal treatment among companies. Accordingly, the investing public has the ability to compare such information about publicly traded companies. In response to SAB 92, the Accounting Standards Executive Committee issued Statement of Position 96-1, which provides detailed guidance on reporting requirements in a variety of situations relating to environmental liabilities. The American Institute of Certified Public Accountants has also made available statements of position relating to SEC Staff Accounting Bulletins and interpretations of the SEC's regulations relating to reporting environmental remediation.[245]

Rule 10b-5

The antifraud provision of SEC Rule 10b-5 provides shareholders as well as regulators with a cause of action against corporations that make false statements or material omissions in filings with the SEC. Great uncertainty at-

---

245. *See* AICPA Technical Practice Aids, Statement of Positions, ACC § 10, 680 (October 10, 1996).

taches to the issue of environmental disclosures under Section 10(b) of the Securities Act of 1934[246] and SEC Rule 10b-5.[247] The antifraud provision found in SEC Rule 10b-5 applies to any information misstated or omitted if "a reasonable shareholder would consider [the information] important in deciding how to vote."[248] The provision includes environmental matters as well as other information. Under Rule 10b-5, a plaintiff claims injury based on a misstatement or omission of material fact by defendant "in connection with the purchase or sale of a security."[249] Pursuant to an informal agreement between the EPA and the SEC, EPA trains SEC staff to understand environmental liabilities to help the SEC staff members understand the scope of environmental liabilities and to identify inconsistencies in reports filed by regulated companies relating to environmental liabilities. Additionally, the EPA provides the SEC with lists of companies that have been named as potentially responsible parties under CERCLA.

The intent of Section 10(b) of the Securities Act is to prevent material misrepresentations and omissions by corporations to investors through essentially any medium, including press releases as well as more formal documents.[250] In an action based on Rule 10b-5, a plaintiff must prove scienter by showing defendant's knowledge of the material omission or misstatement or establishing that the defendant acted recklessly by making the statement or omission.[251] A plaintiff must also show that the misstatement or omission made by the defendant injured the plaintiff.[252] With respect to this causation requirement, courts employ a relaxed showing referred to as the "fraud-on-the-market" standard.[253] In addressing the issue of causation under Rule 10b-5, the Supreme Court accepted a rebuttable presumption of the fraud-on-the-market theory in cases involving an efficient market, reasoning that publicly available information is reflected in the market price, and, thus,

---

246. 15 U.S.C. § 78j(b) (1988).

247. 17 C.F.R. § 240.106-5.

248. TSC Indus., Inc. v. Northway, Inc., 426 U.S. 438, 449 (1976).

249. *See* 17 C.F.R. § 240.10b-5 (1997).

250. *See* John W. Bagby, *How Green Was My Balance Sheet?: Corporation Liability in Environmental Disclosure*, 14. VA. ENVT'L L.J. 225, 314 (1995).

251. *See In re* Software Tool Works, Inc., 50 F.3d 615, 628 (9th Cir. 1994) (holding that failure to follow generally accepted accounting principles may not constitute scienter absent egregious violation); Marksman Partners, L.P. v. Chantal Pharmaceutical Corp., 927 F. Supp. 1297, 1313 (C.D. Cal. 1996) (relying on GAAP violation in combination with overstatement of revenues to establish scienter requirements).

252. *See* Basic, Inc. v. Levinson, 485 U.S. 224, 243 (1988).

253. *See* Affiliated Ute Citizens of Utah v. U.S., 406 U.S. 128, 153–54 (1978).

Chapter 4: Confidentiality   143

an investor's act of purchasing stock is an act of reliance on representations, misrepresentations, or omissions that influence the price.[254] Accordingly, a misleading statement is actionable "even if the purchasers do not directly rely on the misstatements."[255]

Securities Act Requirements: Environmental Disclosures

In his article "Legal Considerations in Voluntary Corporate Environmental Reporting," David W. Case notes the need for companies to be sure that all corporate environmental reports are consistent with the information provided in filings made to the SEC or EPA.[256]

> If brought to the attention of government authorities, such inconsistency would be, at best, embarrassing and require explanation satisfactory to the regulatory authority. At worst, such inconsistency may be a potential basis for fines, sanctions, or other liability for inaccurate or insufficient compliance with statutory disclosure obligations, including liability under federal securities antifraud laws as discussed below. To avoid inconsistencies in reporting, those responsible for preparation of the company's formal corporate environmental report should be aware of all relevant environmental disclosure obligations of the company.[257]

Confidentiality and the Common Law: Environmental Issues

Despite the passage of significant environmental statutes, common-law rights and responsibilities continue to operate in the environmental area.[258] The com-

---

254. *See* Basic, Inc. v. Levinson, 485 U.S. 224, 243 (1988).

255. *Id.* at 242, *quoting* Peil v. Speiser, 806 F.2d 1154, 1160–61 (3d Cir. 1986).

256. David W. Case, *Legal Considerations in Voluntary Corporate Environmental Reporting,* 30 E.L.R. 10,375 (May 2000).

257. *Id.* at 10,378.

258. *See, e.g.,* Davis v. Sun Ref. & Mktg. Co., 671 N.E.2d 1049, 1056 (Ohio Ct. App. 1996) (concluding that the fact that plaintiff had no right to bring action under Ohio Underground Storage Tank Act did not preclude common-law action for petroleum contamination); *see also Appeals Court Allows Common-Law Recovery for UST Contamination at Former Gas Station,* 10 Toxics L. Rep. (BNA) 1032 (Feb. 14, 1996); Tom Kuhnle, Note, *The Rebirth of Common Law Actions for Redressing Hazardous Waste Contamination,* 15 Stan. Envtl. L.J. 187, 210-14 (1996); Randall G. Vickery & Robert M. Baratta, Jr., *Back to the Legal Future: Environmental Claims Come Full Circle as Plaintiffs Return to the Common Law for Relief,* Nat'l L.J., June 10, 1996, at C1.

mon law can raise difficult questions regarding the obligations of lawyers to clients and to third parties, particularly regarding the duty of confidentiality. "[G]iven the nature of the common law system, the lawyer cannot be sure when the courts will treat the breach of an ethical duty as the breach of a legal duty."[259]

Since the major federal environmental statutes do not abrogate common-law actions, one who suffers harm as a result of environmental hazards may have recourse via the common law. Thus, traditional common-law remedies have importance in environmental cases. One who suffers harm as a result of environmental hazards may have recourse via common-law actions.[260] Indeed, the "toxic torts" area has become increasingly important in environmental law. Generally, federal environmental statutes provide no compensation for individuals who suffer injuries as a result of a defendant's violation of the statute.[261] Individuals who suffer injuries as a result of a violation of environmental law committed by a company or an individual, such as an unpermitted release of hazardous pollutants, may seek compensation under the common law. Additionally, some state statutes afford individuals injured by the release of hazardous chemicals a cause of action.[262]

Unlike criminal statutes, which require fair notice, courts may impose common-law liability without clear notice to a defendant prior to the action complained of.[263] Because of the expansion of tort liability and the abrogation of the bar of privity, some lawyers have concerns that they may be held liable

---

259. RAY L. PATTERSON, LEGAL ETHICS: THE LAW OF PROFESSIONAL RESPONSIBILITY § 3.02, at 12 (2d ed. 1984); *see also* Gomez v. Hawkins Concrete Constr. Co., 623 F. Supp. 194, 198–200 (N.D. Fla. 1985) (concluding that lawyer is liable to client for breach of fiduciary duty and negligence for failing to make full disclosure regarding company receiving loan from client when lawyer had financial interest in borrower).

260. *See* Davis v. Sun Ref. & Mktg. Co., *supra* note 256.

261. *See, e.g.*, Lutz v. Chromateux, 725 F. Supp. 258 (M.D. Pa. 1989).

262. *See, e.g.*, CAL. HEALTH & SAFETY CODE § 25359.7 (2001) (in sale of nonresidential land context); CONN. GEN. STAT. ANN. § 52-577c (1991) (setting two-year limitation "to recover damages for personal injury or property damage caused by exposure to a hazardous chemical substance"); N.J. STAT. ANN. § 58:10-23.11g (1992) (declaring liability for person who causes release of hazardous substances and designating state funds for cleanup of hazardous substance and limited consequential damages); MINN. STAT. ANN. § 115B.05 (1997) (specifying damages recoverable against person responsible for the release of hazardous substances).

263. The *Tarasoff* case, discussed *infra*, provides an example of imposition of liability based on a case of first impression of the duty to warn. 551 P.2d 334 (Cal. 1976). *See also* Lee A. Pizzimenti, *The Lawyer's Duty to Warn Clients About Limits on Confidentiality*, 39 CATH. U. L. REV. 441 (1990).

Chapter 4: Confidentiality   145

to third parties injured by the conduct of their clients if the lawyer knows that the client is creating the risk of harm to a third party. In some situations, judicial recognition of a duty to warn may allow individuals injured by client conduct to bring a claim against a professional counselor who knew of the intended harm.[264] While mixed results are to be expected in litigation, the environmental lawyers share realistic concerns that courts may be more willing to impose liability when environmental dangers are presented in a case. The following sections discuss these common-law developments.

Risks attach to the professional's services, including liability for negligent disclosure or for negligent failure to disclose. "[P]rofessionals cannot ignore the possibility that giving advice that backfires, or wrongfully revealing confidential material, may lead to malpractice liability."[265] Traditionally, although it is clear that a lawyer may be required to forfeit fees because of a violation of disciplinary rules, the drafters of the Model Rules have sought to restrict the use of ethics rules to the context of disciplinary action only. The Model Rules note that the rules should not be used to establish malpractice liability.

> Violation of a Rule should not give rise to a cause of action nor should it create any presumption that a legal duty has been breached. The Rules are designed to provide guidance to lawyers and to provide a structure for regulating conduct through disciplinary agencies. They are not designed to be a basis for civil liability. Furthermore, the purpose of the Rules can be subverted when they are invoked by opposing parties as procedural weapons. . . . [N]othing in the Rules should be deemed to augment any substantive legal duty of lawyers or the extra-disciplinary consequences of violating such a duty.[266]

Nevertheless, the concept of lawyer liability seems to be firmly established in the law.[267] Once standards for competence, care, or other professional norms exist, courts may rely on them in determining issues before them, including issues of malpractice.[268]

---

264. *See* Tarasoff v. Regents of University of California, 551 P.2d 334 (Cal. 1976).

265. Hodes, *supra* note 2, at 1549.

266. MODEL RULES Preamble ¶ 18.

267. *See* Collins v. Reynard, 607 N.E.2d 1185, 1186 (Ill. 1992) (ruling that complaint against lawyer for professional malpractice may be couched in either contract or tort).

268. *See* Susan Koniak, *The Law Between the Bar and the State,* 70 N.C. L. REV. 1389, 1412 (1992) (noting that courts are bound to treat the ethics rules as binding precepts only in disciplinary proceedings).

Even though environmental statutes do not provide for relief for the party injured by a toxic or hazardous substance, they benefit the injured party by providing information that is helpful to an environmental plaintiff. For example, the statutes require research and reporting of scientific data on the causal relationship between different chemical substances and harm to humans. They also may provide a basis for preventing future harm to individuals by authorizing a plaintiff to secure an injunction when the plaintiff can establish that future harm will come as a result of a breach of a legal duty imposed by an environmental statute. A plaintiff harmed by environmental discharges or other hazards may bring a common-law claim under one or more of the traditional actions of nuisance, negligence, fraud, and deceit. Additionally, courts have imposed common-law liability for environmental harms on a strict liability basis.[269]

Judicial decision making under the traditional theories is based on judgments about the reasonableness of individual action by the plaintiff and defendant and is subject to great uncertainty. For example, in the case of *Folmar v. Elliot Coal Mining Co.*, the plaintiffs purchased homes in 1931 and 1959.[270] Although the defendant had operated an industrial plant in the area since 1948,[271] and the plaintiffs knew at the time they purchased the homes that the area had been used for coal mining and other industrial purposes, they sued for damages to their property resulting from air pollution from the defendant's coal-cleaning plant.[272] Because of complaints of residents, the defendant installed pollution control devices in 1962, but the problem of coal dust continued. Accordingly, the plaintiffs received no damages.[273] At the time of the decision, the defendant had agreed to install modern pollution devices or to abandon its industrial use if it could not add the devices. Additionally, the defendant was not in default with respect to then-applicable air pollution statutes or regulations in the operation of its business. The reviewing court noted that the plaintiffs could revisit the issue of damages if the defendant did not fulfill his stated plan to install pollution devices or discontinue operations at the plant. "Because the verdict was based in part on an expectation, however, the judgment thereon is not to be considered Res judicata as to any damage subsequent to the date of the verdict in the event the appellee has not subsequently fulfilled that expectation or discontinued what otherwise might be

---

269. *See* Sterling v. Velsicol Chemical Corp., 647 F. Supp. 303, 316 (W.D. Tenn. 1986), *aff'd*, 855 F.2d 1188, 1192 (6th Cir. 1988).

270. 272 A.2d 910, 911 (1971).

271. *Id.*

272. *Id.*

273. *Id.* at 913.

Chapter 4: Confidentiality   147

considered an unreasonable invasion of the appellants' property."[274] Based on all these factors, the court held that the injury was a result of the defendant's coal-cleaning plant but that the invasion of theplaintiff's property by air pollution from the operation of the plant was nontrespassory and not unreasonable.

Relevant Common-Law Developments

A duty of confidentiality can be created in a variety of ways. In addition to the lawyer's general duty of confidentiality, a duty may be created by a fiduciary relationship of parties or by contract obligation. Nevertheless, a court may consider public policy in determining the scope of a duty of confidentiality and in determining whether to enforce a confidentiality agreement. In *Lachman v. Sperry-Sun Well Surveying Co.*,[275] for example, the court refused to honor a nondisclosure agreement on the ground of public policy. The agreement would have resulted in harm to third parties by allowing one of the parties of the agreement to "take advantage of the adjoining owners"[276] by depleting gas from tracts of land adjoining the defendant's land. Articulating the public policy of "Oklahoma and everywhere to encourage the disclosure of criminal activity,"[277] the court held that enforcing the nondisclosure agreement would frustrate this public policy.

Although both federal and state laws require disclosure of environmental hazards by the owner or operator of a site,[278] the 1983 version of Model Rule 1.6 does not require or permit a lawyer to disclose dangers created by a violation of these laws unless the violation is a crime likely to result in death or serious bodily harm.

Lawyer Liability to Nonclients

Environmental lawyers sometimes find themselves in a difficult position with regard to supplying information to third parties because of the rigors of the duty of confidentiality to their clients. Nevertheless, courts hold that the law-

---

274. *Id.*
275. 457 F.2d 850, 852–53 (10th Cir. 1972).
276. Lachman v. Sperry-Sun Well Surveying Co., 457 F.2d 850, 853-54 (10th Cir. 1972).
277. *Id.* at 853.
278. *See, e.g.*, Solid Waste Disposal Act (SWDA) (as amended by the Resource Conservation and Recovery Act of 1976 (RCRA)) 3008(d)(3), 42 U.S.C. § 6928(d)(3) (1994) (knowing omission of material information or falsely filing required RCRA report subject to criminal penalties); SWDA 3008(d)(4), 42 U.S.C. § 6928(d)(4) (1994) (knowing failure to file record or report or document required under SWDA subject to criminal penalties).

yer must avoid negligently misrepresenting facts to others as well as protecting client confidentiality.[279] The area of environmental law puts lawyers in the hot seat because courts may be more willing to impose liability on a person who serves as a conduit for information when the information provided or withheld creates significant dangers such as is possible in environmental matters.

> In general, when a lawyer renders an opinion in circumstances in which the lawyer knows or should know that an identifiable person or persons are likely to rely on it in a particular kind of transaction, the lawyer owes to the third party a duty of reasonable care. This rule has been followed by numerous courts applying different doctrines.[280]

The American public is noted for being litigious in general and, more specifically, in the environmental field, and the risk of malpractice action against a lawyer has increased in recent years.[281] "Throughout the United States, there appears to be a rising tide of cases brought by opposing parties or nonclients against attorneys based on fraud, negligent misrepresentation, conspiracy, aiding and abetting, negligence, and conversion."[282] The increase in legal malpractice claims has resulted from expansion of the concept of what constitutes legally cognizable harm and, additionally, from the widening circle of who can be held responsible for such harm. The possibility of common-law liability has created legitimate concern among lawyers about potential tort liability to both clients and nonclients.[283]

Environmental professionals seem particularly susceptible to judicial scrutiny. Developers, real estate brokers, and professionals involved with environ-

---

279. Jay M. Feinman, Professional Liability to Third Parties 99 (A.B.A. 2000).

280. *Id.*

281. *See* J. Randolph Evans & Ida Patterson Dorvee, *Attorney Liability for Assisting Clients with Wrongful Conduct: Established and Emerging Bases of Liability*, 45 S.C. L. Rev. 803 (1994); *Hazardous Advice: Lawyer, Firm Prosecuted for Telling Client Not to Clean Up Waste*, A.B.A. J. (Sept. 1991) (discussing felony charges filed against eight lawyers on theory that letter abandoning their client's laboratory constituted illegal disposal of hazardous wastes).

282. William L. Siegel, *Attorney Liability: Is This the New Twilight Zone?* 27 U. Mem. L. Rev. 13, 14 (1996).

283. *See generally* Davalene Cooper, *The Ethical Rules Lack Ethics: Tort Liability When a Lawyer Fails to Warn a Third Party of a Client's Threat to Cause Serious Physical Harm or Death*, 36 Idaho L. Rev. 479 (2000) (arguing that individual interest in life should give rise to a duty to warn enforceable in tort).

Chapter 4: Confidentiality 149

mental issues have all incurred liability for environmental hazards.[284] *Caldwell v. Bechtel*[285] presents a case of liability based on tenuous relationships. Caldwell, a heavy-equipment operator working on a Washington Metropolitan Area Transit Authority construction project, sued Bechtel, alleging that Bechtel's negligence caused his lung disease.[286] Bechtel had no contractual relationship with the plaintiff or his employer. Rather, Bechtel had contracted with the Transit Authority to provide "safety engineering services" on the project.[287] The court held Bechtel liable on the ground that Bechtel had a responsibility to inform the plaintiff about known health risks.

Environmental lawyers are often called upon to provide information to a nonclient, particularly in the transactional setting. Lawyers may be involved in providing a buyer of a business or property with the environmental information necessary to satisfy the buyer's standards of due diligence. The worst-case scenarios for lawyers may be found in cases imposing liability for negligent misrepresentation despite a lack of privity with the plaintiff.[288] In *Mehaffy, Rider, Windholz & Wilson v. Central Bank Denver, N.A.*, the Colorado Supreme Court recognized an action for negligent misrepresentation against lawyers by a nonclient.[289] The case was remanded for trial on this issue, but,

---

284. *See* Easton v. Strassburger, 199 Cal. Rptr. 383, 391–92 (Ct. App. 1984) (finding realtor liable for failure to discover fact that property sold had been used as landfill); Haberstick v. Gordon A. Gundaker Real Estate Co., 921 S.W.2d 104, 108 (Mo. Ct. App. 1996) (finding developers liable for failure to disclose presence of nearby hazardous waste site); Strawn v. Canuso, 657 A.2d 420, 429 (N.J. 1995) (finding developer liable when it marketed housing development as "peaceful, bucolic setting with an abundance of fresh air and clean lake waters," and failed to disclose to buyers of single-family residences that their homes were located within one-half mile of toxic waste dump); *see also In re* TMI, 67 F.3d 1103, 1118 (3d Cir. 1995) (holding operators of Three Mile Island nuclear power plant liable for violating their duty of care).

285. 631 F.2d 989 (D.C. Cir. 1980).

286. *Id.*

287. *Id.* at 992.

288. *See, e.g.,* McCamish, Martin, Brown & Loeffler v. F. E. Appling Interests, 991 S.W.2d 787 (Tex. 1999) (holding that action for negligent misrepresentation exists in client or nonclient relationship when lawyer supplies false information to third party, knowing third party will rely on information); *but see* McCamish, Lynwood Lesikar & Harriet Lewis Lesikar v. Rappeport, 2000 WL 1281164 (Tex. App. 2000) (finding that plaintiff's action for negligent misrepresentation failed for lack of proof of justifiable reliance on defendant-lawyer's misrepresentation).

289. Mehaffy, Rider, Windholz & Wilson v. Central Bank Denver, N.A., 892 P.2d 230 (Colo. 1995) (holding that a lawyer may be liable to nonclient for negligent misrepresentation).

because the statute of limitations had expired, the action was dismissed.[290] In *McCamish, Martin, Brown, & Loeffler v. F. E. Appling Interests*, the court held that a lawyer may be liable to a nonclient for a negligent misrepresentation, noting the greater likelihood that an action for negligent misrepresentation will arise in the transactional setting rather than in the litigation context.[291] In support of this holding, the court relied on the Restatement (Second) of Torts § 552 entitled "Information Negligently Supplied for the Guidance of Others."[292] This Restatement states:

> (1) One who, in the course of his business, profession or employment, or in any other transaction in which he has a pecuniary interest, supplies false information for the guidance of others in their business transactions, is subject to liability for pecuniary loss caused to them by their justifiable reliance upon the information, if he fails to exercise reasonable care or competence in obtaining or communicating the information.[293]

The provision limits liability to persons who are harmed as a result of their reliance on information supplied by a professional and who were within "a limited group of persons for whose benefit and guidance [the professional] intends to supply the information or knows that the recipient intends to supply it."[294]

Some jurisdictions employ a standard that can result in wider liability than is approved by the Restatement. In *Kirkland Construction Company v. James*,[295] for example, the Massachusetts Court of Appeals reversed a dismissal for failure to state a claim against a lawyer for negligent misrepresentation by a nonclient. The court noted that the standard for liability in Massachusetts for negligently supplying information is "less demanding" than the Restatement.[296]

Courts historically have been reluctant to impose a duty on a lawyer for the purpose of protecting the client's adversaries. "[T]he legal duty owed to adversaries is merely the duty encompassed in the common-law actions of malicious prosecution and abuse of process, and any statutory adaptations thereof. While it is desirable that litigation attorneys exercise every consider-

---

290. *McCamish*, *supra* note 286, 991 S.W.2d at 791.
291. *See, generally McCamish*, *supra* note 286.
292. *Id.*
293. RESTATEMENT (SECOND) OF TORTS § 552.
294. *Id.*
295. Kirkland Const. Co. v. James, 39 Mass. App. Ct. 559, 658 N.E.2d 699 (1995) (applying rule in the transactional setting).
296. *Id.* at 701, n.6, *citing* DaRosa v. Arter, 416 Mass. 377, 622 N.E.2d 604 (1993).

Chapter 4: Confidentiality 151

ation to avoid causing needless pain to opposing parties, the law recognizes no legal duty to exercise care for the interests of opposing parties."[297] Despite this reluctance, courts have now found lawyers liable to plaintiffs who lack the status of a client on a wide variety of common-law actions. This discussion considers the claim of negligent representation as an example of a common-law claim that can create a risk of liability for lawyers practicing in the environmental field.

The fact that a client is guilty of a fraud or failure to provide information to another does not pose a bar to an additional suit against the lawyer who represents the tortfeasor.[298] A lawyer, in addition to the client, can be held liable for failure to provide information.[299]

Despite the requirements of Model Rule 1.6, a court may hold a lawyer in contempt of court[300] or find a lawyer liable for failing to disclose information in some circumstances.[301] For example, a lawyer's failure to reveal known and dangerous contamination may create a basis for liability for the seller when the condition constitutes a material defect unknown to the buyer. Even a failure to disclose information can create a basis for liability.[302] In the environmental area, for example, courts have allowed recovery for reasonable fear of cancer (cancer phobia).[303]

---

297. Bates v. Law Firm of Dysart, Taylor, Penner, Lay, Lewandowski, 844 S.W.2d 1, 5 (Mo. Ct. App. 1992); *see also* Collins v. Binkley, 750 S.W.2d 737, 739 (Tenn. 1988) (finding no duty to nonclients unless the lawyer knows that the nonclient will rely on the lawyer's work, and the work falls below the standard of care required of a lawyer performing that work).

298. *See* Geoffrey C. Hazard, *An Historical Perspective on the Attorney-Client Privilege*, 66 CAL. L. REV. 1061, 1090–91 (1978).

299. *See* Davin, LLC v. Daham, 746 A.2d 1034 (N.J. Sup. Ct. 2000) (holding landlord's lawyer had obligation to be fair and candid with the tenants though not representing tenants).

300. *See In re* Original Grand Jury Investigation, 733 N.E.2d 1135 (Ohio 2000) (holding "required by law" exception required criminal defense lawyer to turn over letter in his possession written by his client and threatening a third party).

301. Consider, for example, the hypothetical of a farmer who contracts cancer as a result of purchasing and living on contaminated property that the lawyer knew was contaminated.

302. *See* Binette v. Dyer Library Ass'n, 688 A.2d 898, 904 (Me. 1996); *Maine High Court Says Seller of Property Had Absolute Duty to Disclose Leaky Tank*, 11 TOXICS L. REP. (BNA) 838, 838–39 (Jan. 10, 1997) (discussing case in which seller of land breached "absolute" statutory duty to inform buyers of 3,000-gallon underground oil storage tank on the property).

303. *See, e.g.*, Boughton v. Cotter Corp., 65 F.3d 823, 834 (10th Cir. 1995); Sterling v. Velsicol Chem. Corp., 855 F.2d 1188, 1206 (6th Cir. 1988); Herber v. Johns-Manville Corp., 785

152 ISSUES OF LEGAL ETHICS IN THE PRACTICE OF ENVIRONMENTAL LAW

Traditionally, only clients could sue a lawyer for damages resulting from the lawyer's malpractice; lack of privity precluded a nonclient from suing a lawyer for acts or omissions in his professional capacity.[304] Today, many jurisdictions have abrogated privity in some circumstances, such as negligent drafting of a will.[305] Professor Hazard has suggested that because of its numerous exceptions, the doctrine of privity has become unworkable.[306] Courts have held lawyers liable to both clients and nonclients on several different theories, including third-party beneficiary analysis,[307] negligence,[308] fraud,[309] negligent misrepresentation,[310] and breach of fiduciary or agency duties,[311] including

---

F.2d 79, 85 (3d Cir. 1986); Hagerty v. L & L Marine Servs., Inc., 788 F.2d 315, 319–21 (5th Cir. 1986).

304. *See* Buckley v. Gray, 42 P. 900 (Cal. 1895). The bar did not, however, immunize the lawyer from claims of malicious acts, evil intent, or fraudulent purpose. *Id.* at 901.

305. *See* Scott Peterson, *Extending Legal Malpractice Liability to Nonclients—The Washington Supreme Court Considers the Privity Requirement, Bowman v. John Doe Two, 704 P.2d 140 (1985),* 61 Wash. L. Rev. 761, 765 (1986); *but see* Brooks v. Zebre, 792 P.2d 196, 197 (Wyo. 1990) (finding lawyer not liable to prospective lessors of ranch for damages arising out of lease because of nonclient status of plaintiffs and failure to allege specific misrepresentations by lawyer).

306. *See* Geoffrey C. Hazard, Jr., *The Privity Requirement Reconsidered,* 37 S. Tex. L. Rev. 967 (1996) (arguing that the privity requirement is an unworkable legal concept).

307. *See* Heyer v. Flaig, 449 P.2d, 161, 163 (Cal. 1969); Ogle v. Fuiten, 466 N.E.2d 224, 227 (Ill. 1984); York v. Stiefel, 458 N.E.2d 488, 492 (Ill. 1983); Flaherty v. Weinberg, 492 A.2d 618, 625, 626 (Md. 1983) (allowing actions for negligent injury to third parties under third-party beneficiary theory).

308. *See Heyer,* 449 P.2d at 163–65 (finding lawyer liable for negligently failing to fulfill testamentary directions of client); Glanzer v. Shepard, 135 N.E. 275, 276–77 (N.Y. 1922) (reasoning that weigher of beans who certified incorrect weight knew purpose of his certificate was for buyer of beans and, thus, bean weigher owed duty of care to buyer despite lack of privity); Auric v. Cont'l Cas. Co., 331 N.W.2d 325, 327 (Wis. 1983) (finding lawyer liable to nonclient beneficiary when lawyer failed to have will properly executed).

309. *See In re* U.S. Oil & Gas Litig., No. 83-1702-A1-CIV, 1988 WL 28544, at *12 (S.D. Fla. Feb. 8, 1988) (stating that lack of fiduciary or formal relationship between knowing participant in fraud and injured party is not barrier to liability).

310. *See* Greycas, Inc. v. Proud, 826 F.2d 1560, 1565–66 (7th Cir. 1987) (holding lawyer liable for negligently misrepresenting to bank that his client's farm equipment was not subject to prior security interests).

311. *See* Granewich v. Harding, 985 P.2d 788 (Or. 1999) (reversing dismissal of claim based on allegations that lawyers knew of and participated in scheme to "squeeze out" minority shareholder, which resulted in breach of fiduciary duties of controlling shareholders and lawyers for joint liability); Stewart v. Sbarro, 362 A.2d 581, 588

Chapter 4: Confidentiality 153

special duties imposed by statutes.[312] Courts have imposed liability even though the danger created by a client did not relate to an identifiable person.[313] They have even imposed liability on lawyers whose negligence resulted in economic loss to a nonclient.[314]

The Restatement (Second) of Torts Section 552 seems to support imposition of liability against a lawyer in some cases.[315] Section 552 recognizes a professional's duty to supply accurate information and suggests liability for negligently supplied information and for breach of a duty to provide information.[316] The section speaks to one who "supplies false information for the guidance of others" or who "fails to exercise reasonable care" in "communicating the information."[317] In a broader context, the Restatement of Torts recognizes the right of a person to report another who "intends to kill or rob or commit some other serious crime against a third person."[318]

The Professional's Duty to Warn

Generally, the lawyer has no duty of care toward an opponent or nonclient.

> [I]t is to be assumed that the legal duty owed to adversaries is merely the duty encompassed in the common-law actions of mali-

---

(N.J. Super. Ct. App. Div. 1976) (stating that lawyer has fiduciary duty to nonclients who reasonably rely on lawyer's services); McEvoy v. Helikson, 562 P.2d 540, 543–44 (Or. 1977).

312. For example, Section 10(b) and Rule 10b-5 of the Securities Exchange Act of 1934 requires disclosure of information. *See* Securities Exchange Act of 1934, ch. 404 10(b), 15 U.S.C. § 78j(b) (1994); 17 C.F.R. § 240.10b-5 (1997); *see also* Walco Invs., Inc. v. Thenen, 881 F. Supp. 1576, 1583 (S.D. Fla. 1995).

313. *See generally* Susan Lorde Martin, *If Privity Is Dead, Let's Resurrect It: Liability of Professionals to Third Parties for Economic Injury Caused by Negligent Misrepresentation*, 28 Am. Bus. L.J. 649 (1991).

314. *See, e.g.*, Roberts v. Ball, Hunt, Hart, Brown & Baerwitz, 57 Cal. App. 3d 104, 110–11 (Cal. Ct. App. 1976); Collins v. Binkley, 750 S.W.2d 737, 739 (Tenn. 1988); Stinson v. Brand, 738 S.W.2d 186, 191 (Tenn. 1987).

315. *See* Restatement (Second) of Torts § 552 (1976).

316. *See id.*; Tartera v. Palumbo, 453 S.W.2d 780, 784 (Tenn. 1970) (finding surveyor liable to nonclient for negligence); Cook Consultants, Inc. v. Larson, 700 S.W.2d 231, 234 (Tex. App. 1985, *writ ref'd n.r.e.*) (holding surveyor liable to third party); *see also* Blue Bell, Inc. v. Peat, Marwick, Mitchell & Co., 715 S.W.2d 408, 413 (Tex. App. 1986, *writ ref'd n.r.e.*) (doubting "the wisdom of continuing to apply different standards for determining the liability of different professionals to third parties").

317. Restatement (Second) of Torts § 552 (1976).

318. Restatement (Second) of Torts § 595 cmt. g (1977).

154   ISSUES OF LEGAL ETHICS IN THE PRACTICE OF ENVIRONMENTAL LAW

cious prosecution and abuse of process, and any statutory adaptations thereof. While it is desirable that litigation attorneys exercise every consideration to avoid causing needless pain to opposing parties, the law recognizes no legal duty to exercise care for the interests of opposing parties.[319]

In *Tarasoff v. Regents of University of California*,[320] the California Supreme Court recognized the professional's duty to warn a nonclient of danger threatened by a client is a situation of clear peril.[321] In *Tarasoff*, a patient, Prosenjit Poddar, murdered Tarasoff a short time after he confided his intention to his psychologist.[322] The parents of the murder victim sued the psychologist and others for failing to warn their daughter of the patient's stated intention to kill her.[323] Psychiatrists, like lawyers, are bound by a duty of confidentiality to their clients.[324] Nevertheless, the California Supreme Court held that the plaintiffs stated a cause of action by showing a psychologist's "failure to warn Tatiana or others likely to apprise her of her danger."[325] The court allowed the victim's parents to amend their complaint to allege that the therapist breached the duty to exercise reasonable care by failing to warn Tarasoff of the danger.[326]

While recognizing the important public policy in the privacy of mental health patients,[327] the California Supreme Court held that the public policy pro-

---

319. Bates v. Law Firm of Dysart, Taylor, Penner, Lay, Lewandowski, 844 S.W.2d 1, 5 (Mo. Ct. App. 1992); *see also* Collins v. Binkley, 750 S.W.2d 737, 739 (Tenn. 1988).

320. 551 P.2d 334 (Cal. 1976).

321. *See id.* at 346–47 (concluding that health care professionals have duty to warn nonclient of threats of violence made by patient); *see also* People v. Poddar, 518 P.2d 342 (Cal. 1974) (involving criminal prosecution of patient in *Tarasoff*, Prosenjit Poddar); *see also* Marin v. United States, 814 F. Supp. 1468, 1485–86 (E.D. Wash. 1992) (holding that government agents had duty to warn known victim that she was target of released informant, and failure of agents to warn victim or authorities or to apprehend felon constituted a proximate cause of victim's murder by the informant).

322. *See Tarasoff*, 551 P.2d at 339; *see also Poddar*, 518 P.2d at 344–45.

323. *See Tasaroff*, 551 P.2d at 341.

324. All 50 states respect the confidential nature of psychotherapy by recognizing an evidentiary privilege for communications between patients and psychotherapists. *See* Jaffee v. Redmond, 116 S. Ct. 1923, 1928–29 (1996).

325. *Tarasoff*, 551 P.2d at 340, 342.

326. *See id.* at 340–42.

327. *See id.* at 346. The U.S. Supreme Court has recognized the strong public interest in confidentiality of information revealed to mental health professionals. *See Jaffee*, 116 S. Ct. at 1928–29 (discussing confidentiality in context of psychotherapist privilege). The

Chapter 4: Confidentiality 155

tecting patient confidence "must yield to the extent to which disclosure is essential to avert danger to others."[328] In summary, the court held that "[t]he protective privilege ends where the public peril begins."[329] The *Tarasoff* court did not analyze the doctrine of privity but focused instead on the theory of duty to warn a stranger, which naturally erodes privity. Whether the approach of the *Tarasoff* case should apply to lawyers has been the subject of significant debate.[330] While no reported judicial decision has applied the *Tarasoff* case to lawyers, none has exempted lawyers from potential application of the principles enunciated in the case. The Model Rules do not protect lawyers from such tort liability, since the rules of ethics do not (and could not) abrogate common-law judicial power. While it would be possible for courts to limit the rule to situations in which a mandatory disclosure is necessary, no court has taken that step.

The case of *Durflinger v. Artiles*[331] recognized the duty of physicians to guard against dangers created by their patients' dangerous mental conditions in less definite circumstances than those of the *Tarasoff* case.[332] Bradley Durflinger murdered his mother and one brother after he was released from the Larned State Hospital in April of 1974. Bradley's father brought a wrongful death action against five physicians who participated in the decision to discharge his son from custody. Although Durflinger had articulated no intent to kill particular people, one physician admitted that he regarded the patient as dangerous. The court ruled that the physicians failed to exercise reasonable care in determining whether the patient should be discharged.[333]

In the more recent case of *In re Goebel*,[334] the Indiana Supreme Court imposed sanctions on a lawyer who gave (erroneous) information to his client about a guardianship client of another partner in his firm. William A. Goebel,

---

Court specifically noted that it did not address the scope of the privilege and made no suggestion that the privilege should prevent liability imposed in cases of harm to third parties such as the *Tarasoff* case. *Id.* at 1932.

328. *Tarasoff*, 551 P.2d at 347. It should be noted that the peril at issue in this case was not "public peril" in the sense of dangers to the public at large. The "public" aspect of the peril came from the cumulative interest of all persons in receiving the benefit of a warning in such circumstances.

329. *Id.*

330. *See, e.g.*, Spaulding v. Zimmerman, 116 N.W.2d 704 (Minn. 1962); *see also* Shelly Stucky Watson, *Keeping Secrets that Harm Others: Medical Standards Illuminate Lawyer's Dilemma*, 71 NEB. L. REV. 1123 (1992).

331. 563 F. Supp. 322 (D. Kan. 1981).

332. *See id.* at 332–34.

333. *See id.* at 332–35.

334. 703 N.E.2d 1045 (Ind. 1998).

156   ISSUES OF LEGAL ETHICS IN THE PRACTICE OF ENVIRONMENTAL LAW

the lawyer sanctioned in the case, represented a client in a criminal matter. This client revealed to Goebel his intention to kill a guardianship client of the law firm and her husband because the husband intended to serve as a witness against him in the criminal matter. Goebel's client knew the firm represented the guardianship client, and he demanded that Goebel give him information about the guardianship client. Goebel refused. Later, however, when the criminal client demanded that Goebel reveal the address of the guardianship client, Goebel showed him an envelope that had been mailed from the firm to the guardianship client at a certain address and that had been returned with the notation "No Such Street." The client copied the erroneous address and used it to find the home of the guardianship client at a similar address. He murdered the husband of the guardianship client. The criminal client was later convicted of the murder.[335] In holding the lawyer guilty of misconduct and reversing the hearing officer assigned to the case, the court acknowledged that the lawyer owes a duty of confidentiality to clients of the firm as well as to clients he is representing directly. The Indiana Supreme Court sanctioned Goebel with a public reprimand for revealing the address despite the hearing officer's finding that Goebel showed the client the envelope with an incorrect address "to thwart" his efforts.[336] The court reviewed the case de novo, holding that Goebel revealed the incorrect address because he feared the firm's client.[337]

The *Goebel* decision rests on the duty of confidentiality as applied to firm clients as well as the clients of the individual lawyer. The case does not recognize an obligation on the part of a lawyer to warn a client of dangers posed by other clients. In other words, it was the act of providing information to the murderous client, that resulted in discipline, not the failure to reveal information of a threat by a client according to the court's analysis. The facts of the *Goebel* case suggest collateral questions. Would the lawyer have been guilty of misconduct if, in the situation described, he had revealed the fact of the threats to the firm's guardianship client, possibly preventing the murder? Would such conduct be a sanctionable violation if the party threatened was not a client? If the lawyer had a duty to the firm's guardianship client not to reveal information, did he also have a duty to warn her of a reasonable likelihood of danger posed by the other client? Some scholars have suggested such a duty exists.[338] One difficulty in assessing such a situation is that when harm is

---

335. *Id.* at 1047.

336. *Id.* at 1048.

337. *Id.*

338. *See, e.g.*, Forest J. Bowman, *Lawyer Liability to Nonclients*, 97 Dick. L. Rev. 267 (1993); Marc L. Sands, *The Attorney's Affirmative Duty to Warn Foreseeable Victims of a Client's Intended Violent Assault*, 21 Tort & Ins. L.J. 355 (1986).

Chapter 4: Confidentiality 157

prevented, it is unknowable whether the harm would have occurred but for the revelation of the danger. Arguably, the lawyer's duty to a client does not include the duty to respond to requests for information not relevant to the representation or to provide the client with confidential information about a nonclient. The general duty of care should make lawyers (and everyone) want to avoid foreseeable risks of physical harm to others.

A new comment to Model Rule 1.6 cautions lawyers that disclosures that may not reveal protected information may still violate Model Rule 1.6 if such a disclosure "could reasonably lead to the discovery of such information by a third person."[339] This comment would have bearing on any future case raising issues similar to those in *Goebel.*

In *Hawkins v. King County,*[340] Michael Hawkins and his mother sued Hawkins' lawyer for injuries Hawkins suffered when he "attempted suicide by jumping off a bridge"[341] after assaulting his mother. The client argued that the defense lawyer appointed for Michael Hawkins was negligent and committed malpractice by failing to divulge information regarding his client's mental state at a bail hearing. The Court of Appeals of Washington affirmed the trial court's rejection of the claim, refusing to find that the lawyer had a duty to warn the client's mother or sister of Hawkins' condition because the mother "was already fully cognizant" of her son's dangerous nature.[342] The court enunciated the common-law duty of lawyers. "We are of the opinion that the obligation to warn, when confidentiality would be compromised to the client's detriment, must be permissive at most, unless it appears beyond a reasonable doubt that the client has formed a firm intention to inflict serious personal injuries on an unknowing third person."[343] By accepting the test advanced by the amicus, the court adopted a general principle of confidentiality and an exception to the general rule created by the "unless" clause. The court stated that the obligation to warn "must be permissive" except when "the client has formed a firm intention to inflict serious personal injuries on an unknowing third person." The plain implication is that when the stated elements are present (that is, the client clearly has formed a firm intent to inflict serious harm on another), the step of warning a third party is obligatory rather than permissive. In denying liability, the court recognized a lawyer's common-law duty to warn third parties. "The difficulty lies in framing a rule that will balance properly 'the public interest in safety from violent attack' against the public

---

339. MODEL RULE 1.6 cmt. 4 (2002).

340. *See* Hawkins v. King County, 602 P.2d 361 (Wash. Ct. App. 1979).

341. *Id.* at 363.

342. *Id.*

343. *Id.* at 365.

158 ISSUES OF LEGAL ETHICS IN THE PRACTICE OF ENVIRONMENTAL LAW

interest in securing proper resolution of legal disputes without compromising a defendant's right to a loyal and zealous defense."[344]

State v. Hansen[345] presents the rare case of a court imposing a duty to reveal a threat. The Supreme Court of Washington held that a lawyer had a duty to reveal threats made by a defendant while attempting to retain him as counsel because the threat related to a judge.[346] A Washington criminal statute prohibits intimidation or threats against a judge as a result of a ruling or decision.[347] The court presented its reasoning on two separate bases. First, it found that no attorney-client relationship arose as a result of the phone conversation. Second, it reasoned, arguendo, that even if an attorney-client relationship existed, the client's remarks would not be protected because they related to a future crime. "The attorney-client privilege is not applicable to a client's remarks concerning the furtherance of a crime, fraud, or to conversations regarding the contemplation of a future crime."[348]

In most cases, the scope of the lawyer's duty to warn is uncertain. Courts are reluctant to impose liability on lawyers as a general matter, particularly in favor of a nonclient.[349] Fearing that liability would dilute the ability of lawyers to provide full representation, courts have held lawyers not liable for injury to third parties even when it is foreseeable that the nonclients will rely on the lawyer's representation.[350] While authority for imposing a duty to warn

---

344. *Id.*

345. *See* State v. Hansen, 862 P.2d 117 (Wash. 1993).

346. *See id.* at 118.

347. *See id.* at 122.

348. *See id.* at 121.

349. *See, e.g.*, Rubin v. Schottenstein, Zot & Dunn, 110 F.3d 1247, 1255–56 (6th Cir. 1997) (lawyer not liable to creditor for misrepresentation concerning client's finances); Abell v. Potomac Ins. Co., 858 F.2d 1104, 1125,1131–33 (5th Cir. 1988) (overturning jury verdict against lawyer and holding that third-party suits for legal malpractice are allowed "only if the lawyer prepares an opinion for the nonclient on which he knows the nonclient will rely"); Bowman v. Two, 704 P.2d 140, 143 (Wash. 1985) (noting that lawyer may have duty to nonclient but finding that defendant lawyer in this case was not liable to his minor client's mother despite lawyer's failure to follow state procedures relating to alternative residential placement of child).

350. *See* Clagett v. Dacy, 420 A.2d 1285, 1289–90 (Md. Ct. Spec. App. 1980) (providing that high bidders in foreclosure sale had no action for damages against seller's lawyer because there existed no direct privity nor was bidder "intended to be the beneficiary of the lawyer's undertaking"). To infer that a relationship existed would mean in effect that the lawyer represented both the mortgagee and the bidder, whose interests likely would conflict. *See id.*; *see also* Friedman v. Dozorc, 312 N.W.2d 585, 588, 591–92 (Mich. 1981) (finding that physician who had successfully defended medical malpractice action brought by deceased patient's family had "no actionable claim on a theory of negligence

Chapter 4: Confidentiality 159

seems strongest against health professionals[351] and accountants,[352] it is doubtful that lawyers have immunity from claims based on a duty to warn without regard for the circumstances.

The rule that accountants must report client information to the public[353] is in contrast to the general rule that the lawyer serves his clients to the exclusion of all others. Health care professionals (in particular, mental health care professionals) arguably should be subject to a higher standard of care (including a duty to warn) because (unlike lawyers) they have the training and expertise necessary to make judgments regarding the mental state of a client and the seriousness of his threat. Nevertheless, it may not be prudent to assume that lawyers are free from any duty to warn nonclients on the basis that the role of lawyer can be distinguishable from that of mental health care professionals. Although the policies favoring silence by lawyers are strong, it is far from certain that lawyers are free of the risk of liability for a failure to warn a third party of danger posed by a client. The analysis of the *Tarasoff* court suggests it could have imposed liability on the defendants for failure to warn even if they had been lawyers rather than psychiatrists. Thus, no bright-line rule against lawyer liability has been established, and the risk exists that a court may impose liability on a lawyer for a failure to speak in a case of clear danger.

Attorney-Client Privilege

The strong public policy favoring confidentiality is evidenced by the attorney-client privilege. All states and the federal government recognize the attorney-client privilege.[354] The privilege bars introduction of evidence of

---

[against family's lawyers] because a lawyer owes no duty of care to an adverse party in litigation").

351. The Court in *Jaffee v. Redmond* noted that psychotherapy serves the public's interest in addition to the private individual's interest and thus recognized a privilege protecting confidential communications between a patient and a psychotherapist. *See* Jaffee v. Redmond, 116 S. Ct. 1923, 1929 (1996).

352. *See* Brumley v. Touche, Ross & Co., 463 N.E.2d 195, 199 (Ill. App. Ct. 1984).

353. *See* Michael M. Neltner, Comment, *Government Scapegoating, Duty to Disclose, and the S&L Crisis: Can Lawyers and Accountants Avoid Liability in the Savings and Loan Wilderness?*, 62 U. Cin. L. Rev. 655, 680 (1993); Richard W. Painter & Jennifer E. Duggan, *Lawyer Disclosure of Corporate Fraud: Establishing a Firm Foundation*, 50 SMU L. Rev. 225, 235 (1996).

354. *See* Wolfram, *supra* n.6, at 6.3.1; *see also* Fed. R. Evid. 501, 29 C.F.R. § 18.501 (2002) (ALJ rule on privilege); Jaffee v. Redmond, 518 U.S. 1, 11 (1996) (noting Fed. R. Evid. 501 encourages full and frank disclosures to lawyers).

communications between a client and his lawyer.[355] Like the duty of confidentiality, the privilege predates ethics codes.[356] In discussing the development of the attorney-client privilege, Professor Fischel explains that the rule originated to encourage the employment of lawyers in the early English common law.

> [A]s parties were not then obliged to testify in their own cases, and could not be compelled to disclose facts known only to themselves, they would hesitate to employ professional men and make the necessary disclosures to them, if the facts thus communicated were thus within the reach of their opponent. To encourage the employment of attorneys, therefore, it became indispensable to extend to them the immunity enjoyed by the party.[357]

Although the attorney-client privilege is narrower than confidentiality, it is often confused with confidentiality.[358]

> [E]thical rules shield far more compromising information than the laws of evidence concerning the attorney-client privilege. The privilege only exempts lawyers from testifying in court concerning communications that come directly from clients and that do not involve future crimes or frauds. The ABA's Model Rules demand confidentiality in all contexts regarding information from all sources if it relates to client representation and does not involve physically dangerous criminal activity.[359]

---

355. *See* Gerrits v. Brannen Banks of Florida, Inc., 138 F.R.D. 574 (D. Col. 1991) (holding that in shareholders' securities fraud action, attorney-client privilege barred discovery of corporate lawyer's communications with corporation about merger, tender offer, and legal advice).

356. "While legal codes of ethics are relatively recent . . . the attorney-client privilege has existed for hundreds of years. Initially, the privilege was based on 'the oath and the honor of the attorney,' who needed to be spared from the unseemly task of having to testify in court." Daniel R. Fischel, *Lawyers and Confidentiality*, 65 U. CHI. L. REV. 1 (1998).

357. *Id.*

358. *See* Fred C. Zacharias, *Harmonizing Privilege and Confidentiality*, 41 S. TEX. L. REV. 69 (1999).

359. DEBORAH L. RHODE, IN THE INTERESTS OF JUSTICE: REFORMING THE LEGAL PROFESSION at 109–10 (2000).

The Model Rules note the importance of the privilege to the protection of confidentiality. A comment to Model Rule 1.6 states that confidentiality "is given effect in two related bodies of law, the attorney-client privilege (which includes the work product doctrine) in the law of evidence and the rule of confidentiality established in professional ethics."[360] The modern form of the attorney-client privilege applies when:

> (1) a person (client) who seeks legal advice or assistance (2) from a lawyer acting in behalf of the client, (3) for an indefinite time may invoke, and the lawyer must invoke in the client's behalf, an unqualified privilege not to testify (4) concerning the contents of a client communication (5) that was made by the client or by the client's communicative agent (6) in confidence (7) to the lawyer or the lawyer's confidential agent, (8) unless the client expressly or by implication waives the privilege.[361]

In *United States v. United Shoe Machinery Corp.*,[362] the court considered whether the attorney-client privilege barred the introduction of exhibits in a civil antitrust action against United Shoe Machinery Corporation. The court held that some of the exhibits were within the attorney-client privilege. It noted that the privilege applies only when:

> (1) the asserted holder of the privilege is or sought to become a client; (2) the person to whom the communication was made (a) is a member of the bar of a court, or his subordinate and (b) in connection with this communication is acting as a lawyer; (3) the communication relates to a fact of which the attorney was informed (a) by his client (b) without the presence of strangers (c) for the purpose of securing primarily either (i) an opinion on law or (ii) legal services or (iii) assistance in some legal proceeding, and not (d) for the purpose of committing a crime or tort; and (4) the privilege has been (a) claimed and (b) not waived by the client.[363]

Like the ethical duty of confidentiality, the attorney-client privilege is based on the need for clients to disclose all information about a case to the

---

360. MODEL RULE 1.6 cmt. 5.
361. WOLFRAM, *supra* note 6, at 6.3.1.
362. 89 F. Supp. 357 (D. Mass. 1950).
363. *Id.* at 358–59.

lawyer.[364] Both communications from the client to the lawyer for the purpose of enabling the lawyer to form a legal opinion and from the lawyer to the client for the purpose of communicating the lawyer's advice are privileged. Evidence that is acquired in breach of privilege is inadmissible at trial.[365]

> The attorney-client privilege exists to protect confidential communications, to assure the client that any statements he makes in seeking legal advice will be kept strictly confidential between him and his attorney; in effect, to protect the attorney-client relationship.[366]

Although there are exceptions to the attorney-client privilege,[367] its thrust is to empower both lawyers and clients to refuse to testify regarding a communication despite significant interests in disclosing the information. The attorney-client privilege "shield[s] communications to others when the purpose of the communication is to assist the attorney in rendering advice to the client."[368] The attorney-client privilege applies to evidence acquired or created as a result of consulting a lawyer for legal advice.[369] The reasons for hiring a lawyer and the nature of the services provided are significant in determining the capacity in which a person is engaged.[370] Accordingly, a "consultant" who is a lawyer may or may not be within the privilege, depending on a variety of factors, including whether the client sought his services as a legal advisor or served as an employee of the client.[371]

The attorney-client privilege applies to corporations as well as individu-

---

364. *See* Upjohn Co. v. United States, 449 U.S. 383 (1981); Fisher v. United States, 425 U.S. 391 (1976).

365. United States v. Sindona, 636 F.2d 792 (2d Cir. 1980).

366. Permian Corp. v. United States, 665 F.2d 1214, 1219 (D.C. Cir. 1981), *citing* United States v. AT&T, 642 F.2d 1285, 1299 (D.C. Cir. 1980).

367. *See* discussion of the crime-fraud exception at 165–66, *infra*.

368. United States v. Adlman, 68 F.3d 1495, 1499 (2d Cir. 1995).

369. The privilege may extend to documents revealed to third parties helping the lawyer provide legal advice. In Cavallaro v. United States, 284 F.3d 236 (1st Cir. 2002), the court of appeals held that the privilege was waived for documents provided to an accounting firm when the accountants were not hired to help the lawyer provide legal advice.

370. Montgomery County v. MicroVote Corp., 175 F.3d 296 (3d Cir. 1999).

371. *See, e.g., In re* Bieter Co., 16 F.3d 929 (8th Cir. 1994) (holding attorney-client privilege applied to communications between consultant and client's lawyers based on finding that consultant intimately involved in client's business and sole representative at meetings with potential tenants and local officials was the functional equivalent of an employee).

Chapter 4: Confidentiality 163

als.[372] In *Upjohn v. United States*, the Internal Revenue Service demanded production of documents that a pharmaceutical company produced after its general counsel learned that one of the company's foreign subsidiaries had made payments to a foreign government to secure business. In *Upjohn*, the leading case on the attorney-client privilege, the U.S. Supreme Court held that the attorney-client privilege applied to questionnaires and memoranda of lawyers, noting that the privilege applies both to professional advice from a lawyer and to information provided to the lawyer by the client.[373] The Supreme Court noted that the corporation's lawyers needed the information produced by the corporation in order to provide legal advice. Noting that a narrow reading of the attorney-client privilege unduly limits "the valuable efforts of corporate counsel to insure their client's compliance with law,"[374] the Court rejected the "control group test," which would have excluded from the privilege communications by officers and agents "not responsible for directing [petitioner's] actions in response to legal advice."[375]

Limitations of Attorney-Client Privilege

The attorney-client privilege is not absolute, and it is the subject of sharp disagreement and debate.[376] The privilege does not protect all information arising from the attorney-client relationship. For example, the identity of the client and information about the fee charged generally are not protected by the attorney-client privilege.[377] Courts often interpret the attorney-client privi-

---

372. *See Upjohn*, 449 U.S. 383 (1981); Niesig v. Team I, 76 N.Y.2d 363 (1990) (interpreting attorney-client privilege to prohibit contact with employees with authority to commit the corporation regarding the matter at issue).

373. *See Upjohn*, 449 U.S. at 384. Professor Wolfram has criticized the *Upjohn* decision as "a remarkable example of the one-sided discussion" of the confidentiality principle. WOLFRAM, *supra* note 6, 6.1.4 at 247.

374. *Id.* at 684.

375. *Id.* at 383.

376. *See, e.g.*, Paul R. Rice, *Attorney-Client Privilege: The Eroding Concept of Confidentiality Should Be Abolished*, 47 DUKE L.J. 853 (1998). "None of [the] privacy justifications, separately or together, justifies an unqualified privilege." WOLFRAM, *supra* note 6, at 6.1.4 at 245. Professor Hazard suggests that the appropriate scope of the attorney-client privilege is litigation. *See* Geoffrey C. Hazard, Jr., *An Historical Perspective on the Attorney-Client Privilege*, 66 CAL. L. REV. 1061 (1978).

377. Gerald B. Lefcourt, P.C. v. United States, 125 F.3d 79, 86 (2d Cir. 1997), *cert. denied*, 118 S. Ct. 2314 (1998); United States v. Ellis, 90 F.3d 447, 450 (11th Cir. 1996); *see also* ABA Informal Op. 1141 (Aug. 9, 1970) (holding lawyer should advise military deserter who seeks legal advice to turn himself in and that lawyer will reveal his whereabouts if he refuses to turn himself in). *But see* Dean v. Dean, 607 So. 2d 494 (Fla. App. 4th Dist.,

164   ISSUES OF LEGAL ETHICS IN THE PRACTICE OF ENVIRONMENTAL LAW

lege narrowly, limiting it to the litigation setting and to communications by and to the client. "Privilege is designed to protect confidences in the narrowest possible way that will ensure client candor without interfering overly with the discovery of facts."[378] Courts have held that the privilege does not apply to information created by a third party.[379] Sometimes confidential information must be revealed as a result of a court order despite the attorney-client privilege.[380]

> Because privilege applies only when one client attempts to prevent the other side's access to potentially probative evidence in litigation, courts implementing privilege are cognizant of secrecy's negative attributes. . . . Attorney-client privilege has numerous exceptions, which courts apply liberally. Much of what would be confidential ultimately proves to be subject to discovery or production in court.[381]

The privilege may be waived if the client has shown the documents at issue to a third party not within the lawyer-client relationship.[382] For example, in the case of *Permian Corp. v. U.S.*,[383] the court held that the client waived protection of attorney-client privilege for documents turned over to the Securities and Exchange Commission. The court stated that "[a]ny voluntary disclosure by the holder of such a privilege is inconsistent with the confidential relationship and thus waives the privilege."[384] In *In re Colum-*

1992) (holding lawyer could refuse to reveal client's whereabouts). State statutes requiring the release of information relevant to child abuse have withstood challenges that the statutes infringe the rights protected by the attorney-client privilege.

378. *See In re* Grand Jury Proceeding, 680 F.2d 1026, 1027 (5th Cir. 1982); Fred C. Zacharias, *Harmonizing Privilege and Confidentiality*, 41 S. Tex. L. Rev. 69, 89–90 (1999).

379. *See, e.g.*, Occidental Chemical Corp. v. OHM Remediation Services Corp., 175 F.R.D. 431 (W.D.N.Y. 1997) (holding that documents pertaining to an environmental cleanup prepared by a third-party consultant were not protected by attorney-client privilege or the work product doctrine).

380. *See In re* Marriage of Decker, 606 N.E.2d 1094, 1107 (Ill. 1992) (validating principle that lawyer must comply with final court order to disclose client confidences but reversing contempt citation for lawyer's refusal to disclose information about client's intent to abduct child from custodial parent because of trial court errors in proceeding).

381. Zacharias, *supra* note 376, at 74–75 (citations omitted).

382. *See Party That Discloses Papers to Government Waives Attorney-Client Privilege as to Others*, 70 U.S. L.Wk. 1772 (June 25, 2002).

383. 665 F.2d 1214 (D.C. Cir. 1981).

384. *Id.* at 1219.

bia/HCA Healthcare Corp., the Court of Appeals for the Sixth Circuit affirmed the trial court's ruling that defendant health care provider could not successfully assert the attorney-client privilege to withhold documents it had provided to the DOJ in a settlement negotiation.[385] The court held that, by providing the documents to DOJ, the defendant waived the attorney-privilege, even though the documents were the subject of "stringent confidentiality provisions" of an agreement with DOJ.[386] The court rejected the concept of selective waiver of the privilege.[387]

The application of rules of evidence may require disclosure despite a strong rule against disclosure of client information. For example, while California firmly prohibits disclosure of client information under its rules of legal ethics, the California Evidence Code requires disclosure in litigation "if the lawyer reasonably believes that disclosure of any confidential communication relating to the representation of a client is necessary to prevent the client from committing a criminal act that the lawyer believes is likely to result in death or substantial bodily harm."[388]

The law of attorney-client privilege presents a significant limitation on the ethics rule of confidentiality. The privilege does not protect client information from disclosure in court when the information sought falls into the crime-fraud exception to the privilege. Thus, clients who undertake wrongful conduct have no reasonable expectation that the information at issue will be protected.

Crime-Fraud Exception

The most significant limitation on the attorney-client privilege is the crime-fraud exception.[389] The crime-fraud exception to the attorney-client privilege is recognized as a matter of common law. "Even in jurisdictions whose statutory formulations of the attorney-client privilege do not mention such an exception, courts construe their statutes to include the exception because of its solid application at common law."[390] The party seeking to pierce the attorney-client privilege has the burden of showing reasonable cause to believe that the attorney's advice was sought to further illegal or fraudulent conduct and that the work product sought to be discovered or introduced at

---

385. 293 F.3d 289 (6th Cir. 2002).
386. *Id.* at 292.
387. *Id.* at 295.
388. CAL. EVID. CODE 956.5 (West Supp. 1998).
389. *See, e.g.*, Olson v. Accessory Controls & Equipment Corp., 757 A.2d 14 (Conn. 2000).
390. WOLFRAM, *supra* note 6, at 6.4.10, *citing* State *ex rel* North Pac. Lumber Co. v. UNIS, 579 P.2d 1291, 1294–95 (Or. 1978).

166 ISSUES OF LEGAL ETHICS IN THE PRACTICE OF ENVIRONMENTAL LAW

trial was created in furtherance of the crime or fraud.[391] The court's determination of whether the exception applies turns on whether that conduct is illegal or fraudulent.[392] The lawyer's lack of knowledge of the crime or fraud and his innocence are irrelevant to discovery or use of the evidence.

The crime-fraud exception to the attorney-client privilege denies the protection of the privilege to communications between a client and his lawyer when the lawyer's services are used to further a crime or fraud.[393] The exception applies to both the attorney-client privilege and the work product rule[394] and is notoriously difficult to apply. The party urging disclosure has the burden of making a prima facie showing of criminal or fraudulent conduct to demand an in camera review of evidence.[395] In the context of the attorney-client privilege, the United States Supreme Court has held that a court may review communications in camera to determine whether the crime-fraud exception to the privilege applies.[396]

The exception to the attorney-client privilege presents a significant limitation on the ethics rule of confidentiality, requiring disclosure of the conduct of clients that will constitute a crime or a fraud. Thus, clients who use the lawyer's services to further a crime or a fraud have no reasonable expectation that the information at issue will be protected. The exception means that the attorney-client privilege will not protect client information from ultimate disclosure in court.

Attorney-Client Privilege: Environmental Example

The need for protection for documents is common in environmental practice in a wide range of contexts.[397] For example, lawyers advise clients regarding the regulatory requirements of environmental law in general and the elements of a claim that might be brought against a company based on environmental contamination under statutes or the common law. Because scientific data and

---

391. *See In re* In-Store Advertising Secs. Litig., 163 F.R.D. 452, 459 (S.D.N.Y. 1995).

392. United States v. Chen, 99 F.3d 1495, 1504 (1996).

393. *In re* Grand Jury Proceedings, 680 F.2d 1026 (5th Cir. 1982) (holding that lawyer's ignorance of intended crime does not affect applicability of exception).

394. *See In re* Sealed Case, 676 F.2d 793 (D.C. Cir. 1982); *see also* WOLFRAM, *supra* note 6, at 6.4.10.

395. *See* Romo v. Southern Pacific Transp. Co., 139 Cal. Rptr. 787, 795 (1987).

396. U.S. v. Zolin, 491 U.S. 554, 565–66 (1989).

397. *See* Mark D. Coldiron & Connie M. Bryan, *Use of Experts in Environmental Litigation and Enforcement Matters*, 11 NAT. RESOURCES & ENV'T 13 (1996) (noting that environmental matters "almost always require" the lawyer to enlist the assistance of experts).

Chapter 4: Confidentiality 167

informed scientific judgment are crucial ingredients of many legal decisions required in the environmental area, lawyers often work with experts and often authorize or rely on reports generated by those experts. For example, documents produced by a consulting firm may detail the environmental condition of property for purposes of complying with regulations or to defend a lawsuit. In the case of *In re Grand Jury Matter*,[398] the court held that documents prepared by an environmental consultant were not protected by either the attorney-client or work product privileges even though the consultant was paid by the client's lawyer. The court found that the 76 documents for which the privilege was sought were not made for the purpose of providing legal advice to the company but, rather, solely to prepare a waste management plan to comply with regulations of the client's waste disposal practices.[399] The court did not consider that the underlying reason for compliance with the regulations is to meet legal responsibilities.

In *Olson v. Accessory Controls and Equipment Corp.*,[400] a Connecticut trial court granted a protective order to a defendant-employer in a wrongful termination case regarding privileged information from an environmental consulting firm. The Connecticut Supreme Court affirmed the trial court's decision, granting both a protective order and a motion in limine, to bar the introduction of evidence of communications between the defendant's lawyer and an environmental consulting firm retained by the defendant's lawyer. After an on-site inspection of defendant's plant by the state department of environmental protection (department), the defendant company retained a lawyer for advice on how to proceed. The company anticipated a lawsuit against it by the department. The lawyer met with the environmental consultant and authorized an inspection. After its inspection, the environmental consultant issued a report, referred to by the court as "the Diaz report." This report from the environmental consultant dealt with waste contamination identified by the department and, additionally, information about improper storage and disposal of hazardous wastes in other areas at the site. The plaintiff reviewed these reports in his capacity as plant manager. Shortly after the report was issued, a French company acquired an ownership interest in the defendant company. The plant manager (the plaintiff) disclosed information about the improper storage and disposal of toxic and hazardous waste that he had learned from the Diaz report to the French company.

In his wrongful termination claim, plaintiff alleged that the defendant-employer retaliated against him for disclosing this information to the French

---

398. 147 F.R.D. 82 (E.D. Pa. 1992).

399. *Id.* at 85.

400. 757 A.2d 14 (Conn. 2000).

168 ISSUES OF LEGAL ETHICS IN THE PRACTICE OF ENVIRONMENTAL LAW

purchasing company and, ultimately, discharged him because of the disclosure.[401] Before the trial on plaintiff's wrongful termination claim, the defendant company moved for a protective order and filed a motion in limine to prevent admission of the evidence about the Diaz report. The court prohibited use of the Diaz report, and the defendant successfully moved to dismiss the action.[402]

The Supreme Court of Connecticut upheld the rulings of the trial court and the intermediate appellate court that found the Diaz report was within the attorney-client privilege even though the communication at issue was one from the environmental consulting firm rather than from the client or the lawyer. The court expressly declined to base its analysis on the work product doctrine, applying the attorney-client privilege to both the communication and the consultant's report.[403] In this opinion, the Connecticut Supreme Court announced its adoption of a civil fraud exception to the attorney-client privilege, allowing admission of otherwise privileged information at trial when the evidence relates to a civil fraud. The court held, however, that the plaintiff failed to meet the burden of establishing that the defendant engaged in civil fraud relating to the privileged information. Accordingly, it barred the evidence.

Another environmental case, *United States Postal Service v. Phelps Dodge Refining Corp.*,[404] involved a claim of privilege relating to the documents of a consultant hired in connection with the removal of toxic wastes from property. The court held that the attorney-client privilege did not protect documents produced by the scientific consultant who conducted environmental soil studies, oversaw remedial work, and developed the supplementary remedial program despite the fact that the documents contained handwritten comments of in-house counsel. The court reasoned that "the fact the document is sent to a third party ordinarily removes the cloak of confidentiality necessary for protection under the attorney-client privilege."[405]

Although the court noted that the privilege covers some communications made to agents of lawyers who assist in rendering legal services, it held that the consulting firm was not an agent of the lawyer.[406] The court found one document privileged because it was a note from the client indicating it was

---

401. *Id.* at 20.
402. *Id.* at 17.
403. *Id.* at 28.
404. 852 F. Supp. 156 (E.D.N.Y. 1994).
405. *Id.* at 162.
406. *Id.* at 161.

confidential and noting changes to be made in the final document, which was apparently not shared with the consultant. [407]

The court also held that the underlying factual data is not protected by attorney-client privilege. "[T]hese consultants based their opinions on factual and scientific evidence they generated through studies and collected through observation of the physical condition of the Property, information that did not come through client confidences. Such underlying factual data can never be protected by the attorney-client privilege and neither can the resulting opinions and recommendations."[408] The court's explanation of its reasoning suggests the difficulty of obtaining protection of consultant reports. "There are few, if any, conceivable circumstances where a scientist or engineer employed to gather data should be considered an agent within the scope of the privilege since the information collected will generally be factual, obtained from sources other than the client."[409]

Corporate Lawyers

Comment 35 to Revised Rule 1.7 gives additional guidance to lawyers who serve on boards of corporations or other organizations. The new comment cautions lawyers to advise clients and members of the board of directors "that in some circumstances matters discussed at board meetings while the lawyer is present in the capacity of a director might not be protected by the attorney-client privilege."[410] The comment also notes that lawyers may need to advise clients that the lawyer should recuse himself as a director in some circumstances because of conflict of interest considerations.[411]

Government Lawyers

In *In re Lindsey*, the Court of Appeals for the District of Columbia held that a government lawyer could not invoke the attorney-client privilege to refuse to testify before a grand jury inquiry relating to a federal crime.[412] The court recognized that the attorney-client privilege applies to the clients of government lawyers in some settings. It held, nevertheless, that the privilege does not extend to federal grand jury inquiries relating to criminal matters because

---

407. *Id.* at 163.
408. *Id.* at 162.
409. *Id.*
410. MODEL RULE 1.7 cmt. 35 (2002).
411. *Id.*
412. *In re* Bruce R. Lindsey, 158 F.3d 1263 (D.C. Cir. 1998).

170 ISSUES OF LEGAL ETHICS IN THE PRACTICE OF ENVIRONMENTAL LAW

the public's interest in uncovering government illegality outweighs the interest of the lawyers and clients in confidentiality.[413]

In *Lindsey,* the court faced the issue in the context of the highest government office, that of the President of the United States. Bruce Lindsey, a government lawyer in the office of President Clinton, claimed the privilege in response to a grand jury investigation involving the President and the Whitewater investigation. Lindsey refused to answer certain questions, asserting that the attorney-client privilege protected his communications with the President from disclosure. In denying the protection of the attorney-client privilege to Lindsey, the court drew a sharp distinction between government and private lawyers. It reasoned that government lawyers owe special duties to the public that can limit the attorney-client privilege in the context of a grand jury criminal investigation.[414] The court noted that government lawyers have a duty to the public and must comply with statutory law. The court found that government lawyers have a statutory duty to report to the Attorney General evidence of a violation of the federal criminal code.[415] The *Lindsey* court concluded that this duty prevents government lawyers from asserting attorney-client privilege in federal grand jury criminal investigations. The court analogized government lawyer duties to the public to a corporate officer's fiduciary duties to stockholders of a corporation.

The court drew an important distinction between government lawyers and private lawyers, noting that officials who consult with private lawyers receive broader protection under the attorney-client privilege.[416] Accordingly, the President and other government officials may consult a private lawyer to secure legal advice concerning possible criminal misconduct without losing the attorney-client privilege.

A later case, *Herman v. Crescent Publ. Group,* recognized the attorney-client privilege in a case involving a government lawyer.[417] In *Herman,* the Secretary of Labor successfully argued that the attorney-client privilege protected documents in the possession of a government lawyer from discovery. Relying on *In re Lindsey,* the U.S. District Court for the Southern District of

---

413. *Id.* at 1283.

414. *Id.* at 1274.

415. *Id.* at 1275, *citing* 28 U.S.C. § 535(b) (1994) (stating, subject to exceptions, that "any information, allegation, or complaint received in a department or agency of the executive branch of the Government relating to violations of Title 18 involving Government officers and employees shall be expeditiously reported to the Attorney General by the head of the department or agency").

416. *Id.*

417. Herman v. Crescent Publ. Group, 2000 U.S. Dist. LEXIS 13738, at *3 (S.D.N.Y. 2000).

Chapter 4: Confidentiality 171

New York noted that the attorney-client privilege is limited in some contexts involving government lawyers. "Courts, commentators, and government lawyers have long recognized a government attorney-client privilege in several contexts."[418] In *Herman*, the Secretary of Labor brought an action against the defendant employer (Crescent) to redress an alleged discriminatory firing. Crescent terminated its employee shortly after the employee accused it of OSHA violations. The Secretary moved for a protective order to preclude disclosure of documents on the basis of the work product doctrine and the attorney-client privilege. The document was a 1999 memorandum from the OSHA regional administrator to the OSHA regional solicitor that included a final investigative report with communications from a government client to a government lawyer, considering whether to bring a civil suit for retaliatory discharge. The court held this communication was protected by the government attorney-client privilege.[419]

On a related point, the Court of Appeals for the First Circuit has held that the fact that a lawyer represents a corporate official as an individual client does not prevent the corporation that employs the official from waiving the attorney-client privilege as it relates to communications between the lawyer and the officer acting in a corporate capacity. Although the officer signed a joint defense agreement and was represented individually by the lawyer also representing the company, the company's waiver of the attorney-client privilege was effective. The joint defense agreement does not restrict a grand jury's investigation of the company. [420]

Work Product Rule

Because of the need for documentation of environmental findings, the potential for use of the work product rule in environmental cases is great. The work product rule prevents the discovery and use of documents prepared in anticipation of litigation or intended to help the client or the lawyer prepare for litigation.[421] The rule in force in most states extends to documents prepared by or for a representative or agent of a party. In considering a claim for protection under the work product doctrine, courts determine "whether, in light of the nature of the documents and the factual situation in a particular case, the document can be fairly said to have been prepared or obtained because of the prospect of litiga-

---

418. *Id.* at 5.
419. *Id.* at 11 (holding also that report was protected by work product and government informant privilege).
420. *In re* Grand Jury Subpoena, Newparent Inc., No. 01-1975 (1st Cir., Dec. 8, 2001).
421. *See* Hickman v. Taylor, 329 U.S. 495 (1947).

172 ISSUES OF LEGAL ETHICS IN THE PRACTICE OF ENVIRONMENTAL LAW

tion."[422] Although the work product doctrine applies to corporations as well as individuals, it does not protect all documents about all corporate or board meetings simply because a lawyer is a member of the board.[423]

Work Product Rule: Environmental Example

Application of the work product doctrine in the environmental context turns on the reason for production of the material at issue. Material prepared in anticipation of litigation is generally protected.[424] In the case of *Occidental Chemical Corporation v. OHM Remediation Services Corp.*,[425] Occidental Chemical Corporation (OCC) sued OHM for damages for remediation services based on an alleged breach of contract for environmental cleanup of a hazardous waste disposal site. During the contract, OCC hired Rust Environment and Infrastructure, Inc. (Rust) as its consulting engineer on the cleanup project. OCC later sued OHM for breach of contract for the cleanup of hazardous waste. OCC sought to defeat OHM's discovery of documents prepared by Rust on the basis of the work product doctrine. The court rejected OCC's claim to protection of the documents, finding that OCC "failed to establish . . . that Rust was hired for the project to assist its counsel in providing legal advice, or that any of the documents were generated for that purpose."[426] Although the Court acknowledged the application of the privilege to communications by a lawyer's agent,[427] it found that the plaintiff failed to establish that Rust was a representative or agent of the lawyer.[428] Thus, the court deemed the disputed documents subject to admission at trial.

In *State ex rel. Corbin v. Ybarra*,[429] the court held that the work product doctrine protected a hazardous chemical report prepared by an expert when defense counsel had hired the expert to investigate and produce a report on the technical aspects of specific litigation. In such circumstances, the court found that the expert was part of the lawyer's investigative staff for purposes of the

---

422. Litton Industries, Inc. v. Lehman Bros. Kuhn Loeb Inc., 125 F.R.D. 51, 54 (S.D.N.Y. 1989).

423. *See* Great Plains Mutual Ins. v. Mutual Reinsurance Bureau, 150 F.R.D. 193 (D. Kan. 1993).

424. Briggs & Stratton Corp. v. Concrete Sales and Services, Inc., 174 F.R.D. 506 (M.D. Ga. 1997) (holding documents generated in response to an EPA cleanup order were generated in anticipation of litigation and therefore protected as lawyer work product).

425. 175 F.R.D. 431 (W.D.N.Y. 1997).

426. *Id.* at 435.

427. *Id.* at 436, *citing* United States v. Schwimmer, 892 F.2d 237, 243 (2d Cir. 1989), *cert. denied*, 502 U.S. 810, 112 S. Ct. 55, 116 L. Ed. 2d 31 (1991).

428. *Id.* at 437.

429. 777 P.2d 686 (Ariz. 1989).

work product rule. The court also held, however, that the work product doctrine would not protect the document if the defense called the expert to testify in the case. "The work product doctrine is not absolute. Like any qualified privilege, a defendant may waive all or part of the protection by electing to present the expert as a witness."[430]

In the *Olson* case discussed in the above discussion of the attorney-client privilege,[431] the court applied the attorney-client privilege to reject submission of an environmental consulting report that showed contamination of real property. The court expressly declined to consider the work product doctrine or to determine whether the crime-fraud exception should apply to documents subject to the work product doctrine, however.[432] Testing or consulting reports are frequently an issue in environmental matters. When the testing is conducted in the normal course of business, the report generated to present the results of testing ordinarily will not be protected by the doctrine even if a law firm commissioned the material.[433] When testing is conducted as a result of a filed or anticipated lawsuit, any report of the testing likely merits protection from admission at trial.

Federal Rule of Civil Procedure 26

Federal Rule of Civil Procedure 26 also provides protection against disclosure of the lawyer's work product.[434] The scope of this doctrine is broader than the attorney-client privilege.[435] It protects not only materials prepared by a lawyer or agents of the lawyer in anticipation of litigation,[436] but also statements of the lawyer's opinions, conclusions, mental impressions, and legal theories set forth in a document.[437] Perhaps because of concern about the proprietary na-

---

430. *Id.* at 691.

431. Olson v. Accessory Controls & Equipment Corp., 757 A.2d 14 (Conn. 2000).

432. *Id.* at 28.

433. *In re* Grand Jury Matter, 147 F.R.D. 82 (E.D. Pa. 1992) (holding work of expert environmental consultant was not protected by the work product privilege although paid by law firm from client's escrow account); Horan v. Sun Co., Inc., 152 F.R.D. 437 (D. R.I. 1993) (holding that environmental test results are not protected by the work product privilege).

434. FED. R. CIV. P. 26(b)(5).

435. United States v. Nobles, 422 U.S. 225 (1975).

436. *Id.* at 238–39 (1975); Hickman v. Taylor, 329 U.S. 495 (1947).

437. *See, e.g.*, United States v. Weisman, 1995 WL 244522, at *5 (S.D.N.Y. Apr. 26, 1995). FED. R. CIV. P. 26(b) states that "the court shall protect against disclosure of the mental impressions, conclusions, opinions, or legal theories of an attorney or other representative of a party concerning the litigation." FED. R. CIV. P. 26(b)(3). The rule in the criminal context is FED. R. CRIM. P. 16(a)(2) and (b)(2).

ture of the thought processes of a lawyer, documents setting forth legal opinions are often held to deserve more protection than other types of documents.[438] The documents for which the work product privilege is sought need not be produced for the "sole purpose" of litigation.[439] The scope of the protection includes documents that may have been prepared for multiple purposes, as long as the purposes include use in anticipated litigation.

Sharing a document with another lawyer does not necessarily waive the work product privilege, as long as the parties anticipate litigation against a common adversary and have "strong common interests in sharing the fruit of trial preparation efforts."[440] However, sharing a document or information with a public relations firm may waive the attorney-client privilege and the work product doctrine.[441] Distinguishing the work product privilege from the attorney-client privilege, the Court of Appeals for the D.C. Circuit stated:

> [T]he work product privilege does not exist to protect a confidential relationship, but rather to promote the adversary system by safeguarding the fruits of an attorney's trial preparations from the discovery attempts of the opponent. . . . A disclosure made in the pursuit of such trial preparation, and not inconsistent with maintaining secrecy against opponents, should be allowed without waiver of the privilege. We conclude, then, that while the mere showing of a voluntary disclosure to a third person will generally suffice to show waiver of the attorney-client privilege, it should not suffice in itself for waiver of the work product privilege.[442]

The court's reasoning suggests that the argument of waiver may have more power in the context of the attorney-client privilege than in seeking to overcome the work product doctrine. Like the duty of confidentiality, the privilege flowing from the work product doctrine is not an absolute, how-

---

438. *In re* Murphy, 560 F.2d 326, 336 (8th Cir. 1977).

439. *Id.* at 510.

440. *See* Permian Corp. v. United States, 665 F.2d 1214 (D.C. Cir. 1981) (holding 29 of 36 documents protected by work product privilege but rejecting corporation's claim of attorney-client privilege as basis for refusing to provide documents to Energy Department based on fact that corporation provided documents to Securities and Exchange Commission, waiving protection); Niagara Mohawk Power Corp. v. Stone & Webster Engineering Corp., 125 F.R.D. 578, 587 (N.D.N.Y. 1989).

441. *See* Calvin Klein Trademark Trust v. Wachner, 198 F.R.D. 53 (S.D.N.Y. 2000).

442. Permian Corp. v. United States, 665 F.2d 1214, 1219 (D.C. Cir. 1981), *citing* United States v. AT&T, 642 F.2d 1285, 1299 (D.C. Cir. 1980).

Chapter 4: Confidentiality 175

ever.[443] Limited exceptions narrow the scope of the work product rule. The most important of these is the crime-fraud exception.[444] The rule relates to the document itself, rather than the information set forth in the document. Accordingly, the doctrine does not prevent questions about the subject matter contained in a protected document.[445]

Inadvertent Disclosure of Client Information

The pace of modern life has affected the practice of law. Like many advancements, the efficiency of high-tech communication brings some unintended consequences, including a heightened risk of inadvertent disclosure of client information for unwary or unlucky lawyers. The danger of inadvertent disclosure should be a particular concern to environmental lawyers, because environmental assessment reports and scientific documents can be the pivotal point in many environmental cases. Mistaken disclosure of client information can occur in a variety of ways, including a misdirected letter, fax, or e-mail. Not surprisingly, disclosure of confidential matters is more common in large-scale litigation or negotiations, such as Superfund matters. The lawyer who fails to check and double-check transmission lists and any other method used to send communications to clients, consultants, experts, and others endangers the attorney-client privilege for her client.

The ABA Standing Committee on Ethics and Professional Responsibility has considered the issue of inadvertent disclosure of client information in several different opinions.[446] In an Informal Opinion, entitled "Notice to Opposing Counsel of Inadvertent Omission of Contract Provision," the Committee concluded that a lawyer does not violate ethics rules by informing an opponent of a drafting mistake without obtaining the permission of his client.[447] The lawyer who posed the question to the Committee received a document that was intended to set forth the agreement of the lawyer's client and another party to a commercial contract. The opposing party to the contract had insisted on a contract term, and the lawyer's client had acquiesced in the term to close the deal. The lawyer for the party who insisted on the term

---

443. *See* United States v. Nobles, 422 U.S. 225, 239 (1975).
444. *See, e.g., In re* Richard Roe, Inc., 68 F.3d 38, 39–40 (2d Cir. 1995).
445. *See* Ward v. Maritz Inc., 156 F.R.D. 592, 599 (D.N.J. 1994).
446. *See, e.g.,* ABA Formal Op. 99-413 (1999) (Protecting the Confidentiality of Unencrypted E-mail); ABA Formal Op. 94-382 (1994) (Unsolicited Receipt of Privileged or Confidential Materials); ABA Formal Op. 92-368 (1992) (Inadvertent Disclosure of Confidential Materials).
447. ABA Informal Op. 86-1518 (1986).

176   ISSUES OF LEGAL ETHICS IN THE PRACTICE OF ENVIRONMENTAL LAW

drafted the contract document, mistakenly omitting the material term that the parties had agreed to. The inquiring lawyer noticed the error and informed opposing counsel. Noting that the case involved a "scrivener's error," the Committee concluded that the lawyer had no duty to consult with his client before advising the opposing counsel of the error. The Committee reasoned that, while the lawyer has a duty to fulfill "reasonable client expectations for information"[448] about his case, the client in this situation had no right to exercise his decision making since he had already entered the contract. Additionally, the Committee indicated that Rule 1.2 allocates to the lawyer the choice of "technical" means to carry out client objectives without the need to consult with the client. The Committee also noted that the client had no right "to take unfair advantage of the error"[449] or to expect counsel to assist the client in fraudulent conduct. Analysis in this area could turn either on issues of mistake in contract law or on issues of deceit and fraud in both the tort and contracts areas.

Attempting to take advantage of an error of an opponent may not achieve the desired result. For example, in *Stare v. Tate*,[450] a California appellate court affirmed an order of reformation of a divorce settlement agreement because the document contained a mathematical error that was made by the wife's lawyer and known to the husband's lawyer. The court held that the wife was entitled to reformation of the agreement even though the husband did not affirmatively assent to the property valuation set forth in the agreement, noting that the husband did not contest that he was "bound by his attorney's knowledge and actions."[451] After negotiations that stretched over several years, the divorcing parties agreed to even division of the community property of the marriage. The parties disagreed, however, on the value of some of the items of property and, additionally, on whether some stocks that were held in the husband's name were community property. The wife's lawyer prepared a document that proposed a settlement that was approximately $50,000 lower than it should have been because he made two math errors. The husband's accountant noted the error and called it to the attention of the husband's lawyer. The husband's counteroffer accepting the property figure proposed by the wife was designed to make it unlikely that the wife or her lawyer would notice the earlier mistake. The husband called the mistake to his former wife's attention after the divorce was final, with evident satisfaction.[452] Noting that the

---

448. *Id.*
449. *Id.*
450. 98 Cal. Rptr. 264 (1971).
451. *Id.* at 267.
452. *Id.* at 266.

Chapter 4: Confidentiality 177

parties had settled their claims by contract rather than submitting them for a court's determination and that the husband's lawyer swept the mistake or error in the proposal "under the rug," the court reformed the agreement to express the wife's intent "which was known to [the husband] who also knew, through his attorney, that the instrument did not express it."[453]

In a 1992 opinion, the ABA Committee on Ethics and Professional Responsibility considered a similar question: the lawyer's ethical responsibilities upon receiving materials that appear to be confidential and, additionally, appear not to be intended for the lawyer who received them. The opinion concludes that a lawyer who receives such materials should stop reviewing them as soon as he is aware of their confidential nature, notify the lawyer who sent the materials of the problem, and follow his directions.[454] Stressing "the vital importance society places upon the 'full, free and frank' exchange between lawyer and client," the Committee decided that the priority placed on attorney-client confidentiality is best protected when the receiving lawyer cannot take advantage of material accidentally sent to him.[455] A receiving lawyer has an obligation to maximize advantages for his client, but the Committee said this obligation is outweighed by the need to maintain lawyer-client confidences. For this reason, a receiving lawyer may not utilize information gained from the inadvertent disclosure to gain advantage over the sending party. The opinion analogized this situation to a bailment, noting that the lawyer who mistakenly sent the materials terminates the bailment when he becomes aware of the mistake and requests the return of the materials. The opinion also noted that a court may respond harshly to a lawyer's action of retaining or using the materials that were mistakenly sent.

Two years later, the ABA Committee took up a related topic in Opinion 94-382, focusing on the ethical duties of a lawyer who receives materials from a person not authorized to send them.[456] This situation differs from that discussed in Opinion 92-368 in that the transmittal is intentional but wrongful in this case. The ABA Committee concluded that the receiving party should not use confidential material sent intentionally but without authorization unless the receiving party follows the specific guidelines set forth in the opinion. The Committee advised lawyers who receive privileged or confidential materials to satisfy professional responsibility by "(a) refraining from reviewing materials which are probably privileged or confidential, any further than is necessary to determine how appropriately to proceed; (b) notifying the ad-

---

453. *Id.*
454. ABA Comm. on Ethics and Prof'l Responsibility, Formal Op. 92-368 (1992).
455. *Id.*
456. ABA Comm. on Ethics and Prof'l Responsibility, Formal Op. 94-382 (1994).

verse party or the party's lawyer that the receiving lawyer possesses such documents; (c) following the instructions of the adverse party's lawyer; or (d), in the case of a dispute, refraining from using the materials until a definitive resolution of the proper disposition of the materials is obtained from a court." [457] The Committee noted that the lawyer who follows these guidelines will be giving the adverse party "a reasonable and timely opportunity to resort to judicial remedies to determine legal rights and allow the receiving lawyer, under appropriate circumstances, to use relevant materials in the prosecution or defense of an action on behalf of her client."[458] It also noted that several state ethics committees have reached a different conclusion in this setting. The Maryland, Michigan, and Virginia Bar Associations have all opined that lawyer may use unauthorized copies sent to them but must return original documents.[459] While the ABA Committee opinion was that a lawyer has responsibilities upon receiving the confidential matter and may not make unlimited use of such materials, situations exist in which a receiving lawyer may use unauthorized materials. The opinion carved out an exception to requirement (b) in the criminal context, dispensing with the requirement that the lawyer give notice to the opposing counsel when "the documents appear to disclose criminal activity likely to result in imminent death or substantial bodily harm."[460] The opinion also noted that judicial concern about the appearance of impropriety and a desire to preserve the attorney-client privilege may result in a court decision to grant a motion to disqualify a lawyer even though he had complied with the recommended procedures.[461]

Of course, different jurisdictions reach different results in balancing the goals of protecting confidential information and allowing use of all relevant information in a trial.

> When a lawyer conducts a public records search prior to litigation and through no wrongdoing obtains a copy of an inadvertently disclosed memorandum that either on its face or upon closer examination appears to contain information subject to the attorney-client privilege, there is no ethical duty to refrain from reading the memorandum or to refrain from revealing the contents to the cli-

---

457. *Id.*

458. *Id.*

459. *Id.*, *citing* Maryland Bar Ass'n, Op. 89-53 (1989), Virginia Bar Ass'n, Op. 1076 (1988), and Michigan Bar Ass'n, Op. CI-970 (1983).

460. *Id.*

461. *Id.*

ent; however, the attorney does have an ethical duty to notify the source and to return a copy of the memorandum upon request.[462]

Inadvertent Disclosure of Client Information (2002 Revision)

The ABA House of Delegates adopted a revision that requires lawyers who receive documents that they know were sent inadvertently to promptly notify the sender. The 2002 revision to Model Rule 4.4 adopted the view of the ABA Standing Committee by including an additional provision expressly indicating that a lawyer must "promptly notify the sender" when the lawyer "receives a document relating to the representation of the lawyer's client and knows or reasonably should know the document was inadvertently sent."[463] The revised rule serves as a brake on the lawyer's zeal of representation, ensuring basic protections to third parties. It does not speak to what additional steps a lawyer should take in this situation. Nor does it deal with the question of what a lawyer should do if he receives a document that he believes has been wrongfully obtained.

Termination of In-House Counsel

The Lawyer Self-Defense Provision

A significant number of environmental lawyers practice exclusively for one client as that client's in-house counsel. The law relating to termination of employees has particular import for these lawyers. The ethics rules of all jurisdictions include an exception to the duty of confidentiality to allow a lawyer to establish a claim or defense on his behalf. Model Rule 1.6 allows a lawyer to disclose client information

> to the extent the lawyer reasonably believes necessary . . . to establish a claim or defense on behalf of the lawyer in a controversy between the lawyer and the client, to establish a defense to a criminal charge or civil claim against the lawyer based upon conduct in which the client was involved, or to respond to allegations in any proceeding concerning the lawyer's representation of the client.[464]

The cases in this area relate both to confidentiality and to the issue of termination of in-house counsel. Some of the cases discussed in this section are also discussed in the section on the in-house lawyer's relationship with his orporate client (see pages 179–91).

---

462. Ohio Advisory Op. 93-11.
463. MODEL RULE 4.4(b) (2002).
464. MODEL RULE 1.6(b)(2) (2002).

180   ISSUES OF LEGAL ETHICS IN THE PRACTICE OF ENVIRONMENTAL LAW

In *Balla v. Gambro, Inc.*, the Illinois Supreme Court considered an in-house lawyer's claim for retaliatory discharge in light of the duty of confidentiality and overturned a judgment in favor of the lawyer.[465] The case involved an in-house lawyer (Balla) who opposed the company's violation of a food and drug agency regulation and who, in compliance with the ethics rules of Illinois, later reported the violation to the FDA. The company (Gambro) ordered importation of a kidney dialysis machine that failed to meet FDA standards. After the lawyer reported the violation, the FDA seized the machine. Additionally, Gambro discharged Balla. The trial court entered summary judgment in favor of the employer. On appeal, the appellate court[466] reversed the summary judgment and remanded the case to the trial court for further proceedings. The Illinois Supreme Court rejected Balla's claim, holding that lawyers do not have cause of action against their employers for retaliatory discharge. The court rejected Balla's claim for retaliatory discharge, and rejected the court of appeals holding that lawyers are not barred from bringing such claims as a matter of law. The *Balla* court emphasized the need for confidentiality between in-house lawyers and their employers, reasoning that corporations would not engage in full and frank discussions with the in-house counsel if they knew a lawyer could later make them subject to claims of retaliatory discharge.

The Illinois ethics rule on confidentiality requires that lawyers reveal client information "to the extent it appears necessary to prevent the client from committing an act that would result in death or serious bodily injury."[467] It permits the disclosure of client confidences when such disclosure is "necessary to establish or collect the lawyer's fee or to defend the lawyer or the lawyer's employees or associates against an accusation of wrongful conduct."[468] The court found this exception inapplicable to the case, however, and refused to see the exception to defend against accusations of wrongdoing as applicable. The court also noted its view that allowing an action for retaliatory discharge when the client has broken the law is "inappropriate" because it forces the "employer/client to bear the economic costs and burdens of their in-house counsel's adhering to their ethical obligations under the Rules of Professional Conduct."[469]

---

465.   584 N.E.2d 104 (Ill. 1991). Additional information on this case is provided in the section on termination of in-house counsel (pages 179–91).

466.   560 N.E.2d 1043 (Ill. App. Ct. 1990).

467.   134 Ill. 2d R. 1.6(b).

468.   134 Ill. 2d R. 1.6(c).

469.   *Balla*, 584 N.E.2d at 110. The Tennessee Supreme Court case of *Crews v. Buckman Laboratories Int'l. Inc.* expressly rejected the analysis from the *Balla* court to the effect that such an action improperly shifts the costs of compliance with ethics rules from the lawyer to the employer. Crews v. Buckman Laboratories Int'l Inc., 2002 WL 1050247 (TN 2002). "The very purpose of permitting a claim for retaliatory discharge in violation

Chapter 4: Confidentiality 181

In dealing with the issue of danger to the public from the company's violation of federal law, the court noted the strong policy in favor of protection of life. "There is no public policy more important or more fundamental than the one favoring the effective protection of the lives and property of citizens."[470] Moreover, the court agreed that Balla had an obligation to report Gambro's intended crime under Illinois Rule 1.6(b), which makes disclosure of intended crimes mandatory. The court disagreed, however, with the argument that lawyers deserve protection from clients in this situation. It relied on the special duty of lawyers to deny Balla's claim. The court based its decision on both "the nature and purpose of the tort of retaliatory discharge"[471] and, additionally, "on the effect on the attorney-client relationship that extending the tort would have,"[472] asserting that public policy is adequately protected without recognizing the right of an action by lawyers for retaliatory discharge. "In this case, the public policy to be protected, that of protecting the lives and property of citizens, is adequately safeguarded without extending the tort of retaliatory discharge to in-house counsel."[473] The court rejected the argument that the lawyer faced a "difficult decision of choosing between whether to file a workers' compensation claim and risk being fired, or retaining their jobs and losing their right to a remedy"[474] because, unlike other employees, lawyers have a duty to disclose the client information when necessary to prevent a client's act that would result in death or seriously bodily harm. Thus, the court reasoned that the lawyer was not put to a Hobson's choice between protecting his job and protecting the public because, under the Illinois ethics rule, the lawyer had no choice. In effect, this view forces the lawyer to take the punishment of discharge without recourse when his client is engaged in acts that must be disclosed under the ethics rule.[475]

The dissent noted that protection of the public argues in favor of creating

---

of public policy is to encourage employers to refrain from conduct that is injurious to the public interest. Because retaliatory discharge actions recognize that it is the employer who is attempting to circumvent clear expressions of public policy, basic principles of equity all but demand that the costs associated with such conduct also be borne by the employer." *Id.* at 8.

470. *Id.* at 108.
471. *Id.* at 108–09.
472. *Id.*
473. *Id*
474. *Id.* at 109.
475. *See also Herbster*, 501 N.E.2d 343 (Ill. 1986) (finding no right to claim of retaliatory discharge by lawyer who revealed client's request that the lawyer destroy or remove discovery information requested pending lawsuits).

incentives for lawyers to reveal wrongful conduct by clients. "[T]his court must take whatever steps it can, within the bounds of the law, to give lawyers incentives to abide by their ethical obligations, beyond the satisfaction inherent in their doing so."[476] Although the Illinois ethics rule arguably lacked precise language relating to the right of a lawyer to reveal client confidences when necessary to bring a claim against the client other than a fee claim, the court's interpretation appears to put the lawyer in a Catch-22 situation.

In a similar case, *General Dynamics v. Superior Court*, the California Supreme Court afforded protection to lawyers who wish to bring a wrongful discharge action against a former employer.[477] The court held that a client's right to dismiss a lawyer-employee does not prevent a former in-house counsel from suing for wrongful discharge.[478] The court also held, however, that evidence of the wrongful discharge is inadmissible if it violates client confidentiality. In this case, a former in-house counsel claimed that he was terminated because he spearheaded an investigation into employee drug use, protested the company's failure to investigate the bugging of an office, and advised General Dynamics that the company's salary policy could be in violation of the Fair Labor Standards Act. The court held that while the company could discharge the lawyer at any time, this fact did not bar the lawyer from bringing a contract action for wrongful discharge. "We conclude that, because so-called 'just cause' contractual claims are unlikely to implicate values central to the attorney-client relationship, there is no valid reason why an in-house attorney should not be permitted to pursue such a contract claim in the same way as the non-attorney employee."[479] The *General Dynamics* court also cautioned, however, against allowing lawyers to exploit or breach the attorney-client privilege when bringing a case against a former employer. While the court's focus on protection of client information limits the lawyer's suit, it is more than a pyrrhic victory for in-house lawyers. In each case of wrongful termination brought by a lawyer against an employer, the lawyer-plaintiff will need to establish wrongful conduct on the part of the defendant-employer. The *General Dynamics* court, unlike the *Balla* court, recognized the right of a lawyer to bring a retaliatory action against the lawyer's former employer.[480] Although the court noted that the in-house lawyer must be careful not to breach the duty of confidentiality to the client, it gave lawyers in

---

476. *Balla*, 584 N.E.2d at 113.

477. General Dynamics Corp. v. Superior Court, 876 P.2d 487 (Cal. 1994).

478. *Id*. at 495.

479. *Id*. at 490.

480. *Id*. at 503; *contra* Balla v. Gambro Inc., 584 N.E.2d at 108 (holding generally that in-house counsel have no claim for retaliatory discharge).

Chapter 4: Confidentiality 183

this setting some leeway, noting that the court can protect client information by the use of sealed orders, limited admissibility, and in camera proceedings.[481] The opinion limits but does not completely frustrate a lawyer's claim to recover damages against a former client.

In *Fox Searchlight Pictures, Inc. v. Paladino,* a California court held that an in-house counsel suing her former employer could disclose facts relevant to her wrongful termination suit to her lawyers, including privileged and confidential communications.[482] The court reasoned that, while the in-house counsel has the general duty not to disclose confidential and privileged communications, in-house counsel is also "an employee and entitled to the same legal protections afforded all employees."[483] It noted that, if it accepted Fox's view, the disqualification rules would effectively ban any litigation by a former in-house counsel against the employer as well as bar in-house counsel from defending actions brought by the employer.[484] In this case, the employer (Fox) brought suit, alleging disclosure of confidential matter before the lawyer's retaliatory suit was filed. Fox moved to have Paladino's lawyers disqualified because Paladino had disclosed confidential matters to them.

The lawyer's difficult choice in these cases is analogous to problems of environmental violation. An environmental lawyer who learns that his client will violate an environmental standard is in essentially the same situation as the lawyers in the cases discussed above. Other courts have reached a variety of results on the question of an action by a lawyer for retaliatory discharge, often as a result of differing versions of the duty of confidentiality adopted by the jurisdiction.[485] The Supreme Court of Montana reached a different result from that of the *Balla* and *General Dynamics* cases. In *Burkhart v. Semitool,* Montana's highest court ruled that an in-house lawyer has a right to bring a retaliatory suit against a former employer and may disclose confidential information necessary to prove the claim brought against the employer.[486] The Montana Supreme Court considered both the state ethics rule on confidentiality and ABA Model Rule 1.6. To interpret the rule, it considered the history of the Model Rule, noting the language change the drafters made from the older ABA Model Code to the ABA Model Rule.[487] The language of Model Rule 1.6

---

481. *General Dynamics Corp.*, 876 P.2d 487, at 504.
482. Fox Searchlight Pictures, Inc. v. Paladino, 89 Cal. App. 4th 294, 314 (Cal. Ct. App. 2001).
483. *Id.* at 309.
484. *Id.* at 304.
485. *See, e.g.,* Jacobson v. Knepper & Moga, P.C., 706 N.E.2d 491 (Ill. 1998) (holding lawyer could not maintain action against law firm for retaliatory discharge).
486. Burkhart v. Semitool, 5 P.3d 1031, 1041 (Mont. 2000).
487. *Id.* at 1040.

184   ISSUES OF LEGAL ETHICS IN THE PRACTICE OF ENVIRONMENTAL LAW

had the effect of broadening the reach of the exception that allows lawyers to disclose client information in specified situations. The narrow exception of the Model Code allowed lawyers to reveal client information only when necessary to defend against claims or to establish the lawyer's right to a fee. The broader language of the second exception of Model Rule 1.6 states that lawyers may reveal client information "to assert a claim or defense" in any "controversy between the lawyer and the client."[488] The court based its reasoning on the "plain language" of Montana's confidentiality rule, which is based on Model Rule 1.6. The court concluded that Montana's rule "contemplates that a lawyer may reveal confidential attorney-client information, to the extent the lawyer reasonably believes necessary, to establish an employment-related claim against an employer who is also a client."[489] The court noted that a lawyer "does not forfeit his rights simply because to prove them he must utilize confidential information. Nor does the client gain the right to cheat the lawyer by imparting confidences to him."[490]

The *Burkhart* decision was a dramatic rejection of the notion that the attorney-client privilege prevented the in-house lawyer from filing a retaliatory action where confidential matters might be disclosed. The Illinois Supreme Court decision in *Balla* interpreted a different formulation of Rule 1.6. The Montana Professional Conduct Rule 1.6 (b)(2) incorporates the language of the Model Rule verbatim. By contrast, the Illinois rule on confidentiality did not adopt the precise language of Model Rule 1.6. The Illinois ethics rule on confidentiality requires that lawyers reveal client information "to the extent it appears necessary to prevent the client from committing an act that would result in death or serious bodily injury."[491] The Illinois rule makes permissive disclosures of client confidences when the disclosure is "necessary to establish or collect the lawyer's fee or to defend the lawyer or the lawyer's employees or associates against an accusation of wrongful conduct."[492] Thus, the Illinois court narrowed the exception for lawyer self-defense claims for retaliatory discharge within the rule allowing disclosure.

The ABA rule allows disclosure of client information when necessary "to establish a claim or defense on behalf of the lawyer in a controversy between the lawyer and the client, to establish a defense to a criminal charge or civil claim against the lawyer based upon conduct in which the client was involved, or to respond to allegations in any proceeding concerning the lawyer's repre-

---

488. *Id.*
489. *Id.* at 1041.
490. *Id.*
491. 134 Ill. 2d R. 1.6(b).
492. 134 Ill. 2d R. 1.6(c).

sentation of the client."[493] Jurisdictions that have adopted the ABA rule on confidentiality provide the lawyer a better basis for arguing that the rule allows the use of client information to establish a retaliatory discharge claim. Revised Model Rule 1.6 retains the language of the 1969 rule on self-defense, providing that the lawyer may disclose client information "to establish a claim or defense on behalf of the lawyer in a controversy between the lawyer and the client, to establish a defense to a criminal charge or civil claim against the lawyer based upon conduct in which the client was involved, or to respond to allegations in any proceeding concerning the lawyer's representation of the client."[494]

In *Crews v. Buckman Laboratories Int'l Inc.*, the Tennessee Supreme Court recognized the right of corporate counsel to sue his employer (client) for retaliatory or wrongful discharge resulting from the lawyer's compliance with the Tennessee rules of legal ethics.[495] The plaintiff alleged that she was discharged as a result of her report to the Board of Law Examiners that the general counsel of the corporation engaged in the unauthorized practice of law. The court noted that the context of a claim for retaliatory discharge is significant and, additionally, that lawyers owe clients the duty of confidentiality. It read the exception to the duty of confidentiality more broadly than the *Balla* or *General Dynamics* courts, however, relying on its inherent authority to regulate lawyers in the state and adopting a rule that "permit[s] in-house counsel to reveal the confidences and secrets of a client when the lawyer reasonably believes that such information is necessary to establish a claim or defense on behalf of the lawyer in a controversy between the lawyer and the client."[496]

In 2001 the ABA Standing Committee on Ethics and Professional Responsibility issued an opinion on the ethical considerations involved when a former in-house lawyer sues her former employer (which is also her former client) for retaliatory or wrongful discharge.[497] The opinion emphasizes that the Model Rules "do not prevent an in-house lawyer from pursuing a suit for retaliatory discharge when a lawyer was discharged for complying with her ethical obligations." The Committee reiterated that the lawyer "must take reasonable affirmative steps, however, to avoid unnecessary disclosure and limit the information revealed."[498] The Committee noted that its opinion did not

---

493. MODEL RULE OF PROF'L CONDUCT 1.6(b)(2).
494. REV. ABA MODEL RULE 1.6(b)(3).
495. Crews v. Buckman Laboratories Int'l Inc., 2002 WL 1050247 (TN 2002).
496. *Id.* at *9.
497. ABA Comm. on Ethics and Prof'l Responsibility, Formal Op. 01-424 (2001).
498. *Id.*

address the substantive legal question of whether discharge gives rise to an enforceable claim by a lawyer. Rather, the Committee addressed only the ethical considerations as within the ambit of the Committee's expertise. The Committee opined that nothing in the Model Rules "precludes a lawyer from suing" a former client, and, additionally, that the Rules contemplate such actions.[499] The opinion focused on the primary obligations of lawyers to maintain the confidentiality of client information of former clients and to avoid using or revealing "information relating to the representation to the disadvantage of the former client" except as Rule 1.6 or Rule 3.3 allows disclosure.

Noting that the Model Rules do not define the term "claim," the Committee determined the meaning of the term under the Model Rules by comparing the approach of the Model Rules to that of the earlier Model Code. It concluded that "a retaliatory discharge or similar claim by an in-house lawyer against her employer is a 'claim' under Rule 1.6(b)(2)."[500] The force of this determination is that it justifies disclosure under the Model Rules provision. The Model Code provision allowed disclosure of client information only within a narrow exception for disclosure "necessary to establish or collect his fee or to defend himself or his employees or associates against an accusation of wrongful conduct."[501]

The current approach of Model Rule 1.6 broadened this exception to the prohibition against disclosure, allowing disclosure related to other claims. The Committee relied on *Burkhart v. Semitool*, the case discussed previously in which the Montana Supreme Court held that the Montana rule on confidentiality allowed a lawyer to use and disclose information to bring a retaliatory discharge claim against her former employer.[502] The Montana Supreme Court's interpretation of the rule has important application because the Montana rule was adopted verbatim from the ABA Model Rule. Based on both its own reasoning and that of the Montana court, the Committee reached its determination that the exception to Rule 1.6 allows disclosures of client information necessary for a lawyer to pursue a suit for retaliatory discharge against a former employer who discharged the lawyer for complying with ethical obligations.

Even in a situation of litigation for retaliatory discharge, lawyers have a duty to maintain the confidentiality of client information to the greatest extent possible. The Committee noted this duty and also stated that measures such as in camera review at a pretrial evidentiary hearing should be used to minimize

---

499. *Id.*

500. *Id.*

501. MODEL CODE OF PROF'L RESPONSIBILITY, DR 4-101(C).

502. ABA 01-424 (2001), *citing* 5 P.3d 1031 (Mont. 2000).

the disclosure of client information.[503] The lawyer's difficult choice in the *Balla* case is analogous to problems of environmental violations. An environmental lawyer who learns that his client will violate an environmental standard is in essentially the same situation as *Balla*.

Termination of In-House Counsel: Environmental Example

In *Willy v. Coastal States Management Co., Inc.*,[504] the termination issue arose in the environmental context. Donald Willy, a former in-house lawyer for Coastal States Management Company, brought a wrongful termination suit against his former employer, contending that he was discharged because he refused to falsify environmental reports and refused to engage in criminal concealment of the company's violations of state and federal environmental laws. Willy received a jury award of more than $900,000, which the trial judge reduced, disallowing prejudgment interest, to just over $400,000.[505] Coastal successfully appealed the verdict on the basis that, in proving his claim, Willy breached the attorney-client privilege.[506]

In reversing the trial court decision, the Texas Court of Appeals held that the lawyer could pursue the wrongful discharge action but that he could not reveal the illegal acts that the employer allegedly demanded of Willy. Thus, the court ruled that the lawyer's status as in-house counsel did not preclude an action for wrongful termination but that it prevented the use of evidence that would violate the lawyer's obligation to maintain client confidences. In this case, the court held that Willy could not accomplish the necessary proof without breaching his ethical obligations to his former employer. Accordingly, the court of appeals barred the action.

While other cases note that the duty of confidentiality survives the termination of a representation, this case presents a particularly dramatic example of the point. It presents the duty of confidentiality in a contest with the duty of candor. In essence, the court of appeals held that the duty of confidentiality trumps the right of an employee to bring a wrongful termination claim and provide evidence necessary to litigate that claim.[507] The ruling recognizes the lawyer's cause of action for wrongful termination and defeats it simultaneously. It notes that the lawyer should be treated like other employees and, thus, allows such suits. It also seems to ensure defeat for the lawyer, however, by prohibiting the use of information damaging to the client though it is neces-

---

503. *Id.*
504. 939 S.W.2d 193 (Tex. App. 1996).
505. *Id.* at 194.
506. *Id.* at 200.
507. *Id.*

188   ISSUES OF LEGAL ETHICS IN THE PRACTICE OF ENVIRONMENTAL LAW

sary to the lawyer's case. Based on the duty of confidentiality, the holding deprives environmental lawyers of the right to sue for wrongful discharge, since any action by a discharged lawyer would involve information damaging to the client. In every case for wrongful termination, the discharged lawyer who served as in-house counsel and an employee of the client will need to disclose client information to prove his case of wrongful termination by the employer-client. The defendant employer will always oppose such disclosure, and the rule of the *Willy* case seems to present a general bar to the use of evidence necessary to such cases.

The Texas disciplinary rule the court considered in the *Willy* case is based on the Model Code of Professional Responsibility.[508] The court noted that the disciplinary rule exception for self-defense of the lawyer did not allow a lawyer to "reveal client confidences and secrets when necessary to prove a claim against the client."[509] Although the rule provided that a lawyer may reveal confidential information "[t]o the extent necessary to enforce a claim or establish a defense on behalf of the lawyer in a controversy between the lawyer and the client,"[510] the court limited the self-defense provision to "situations in which a lawyer is attempting to collect a fee."[511] The court refused to recognize the lawyer self-defense provision of the ethical rule as a basis for disclosure in the wrongful termination context. "Willy has provided no authority, and we can find none, to support his assertion that he is entitled to reveal confidential information in order to prove his claim of wrongful termination."[512] The Supreme Court of Texas granted Willy's application for a writ of error, but after oral arguments, it withdrew the order and denied the application.[513]

Termination of Government Counsel: Environmental Example

Statutes protecting whistleblowers generally apply to lawyers as well as other employees of government entities and corporations. Special protection may be necessary for government lawyers who take a stand against the policies of the government entity that employs them. For example, the California legislature passed a new law that protects government lawyers who disclose client confidences of the governmental entity to protect the public. The safe harbor created by the California legislation protects a lawyer from discipline when

---

508.   *Id.* n.5. (When Willy initiated suit, the disclosure of a client's secrets and confidences was governed by the Texas Code of Professional Responsibility DR 4-101.)

509.   *Id.* n.6.

510.   *Id., citing* TEX. DISCIPLINARY R. PROF'L. CONDUCT 1.05(c)(5).

511.   *Id.*

512.   *Id.* at 200.

513.   977 S.W.2d 566 (Tex. 1998).

the lawyer discloses information based on a good faith belief that the governmental activity was wrongful.[514]

While the duty of loyalty clearly applies to government lawyers as well as lawyers working for private clients, the risk of harm to individuals in the public is great when individuals working in the government engage in wrongdoing. Special protection of whistleblowing lawyers may be necessary to counterbalance this risk. The best course of action for a lawyer, whether the lawyer is an employee of a governmental entity or a corporation, is to work on the inside to try to convince the client to reconsider the wrongdoing that would affect the public interest. If such remonstrance is not successful, some lawyers will become whistleblowers.

In *Jacobs v. Schiffer*,[515] the court considered whether "a government lawyer 'reveals' his client's confidences and secrets when he discloses them to his personal attorney"[516] to allow the lawyer to evaluate potential claims and give advice. The court held that such a disclosure of nonpublic government information by a government lawyer to his own lawyer was not a violation of rules of professional conduct. Moreover, the court concluded that the department's requirement of advance approval before the government lawyer could reveal the information to his own lawyer "violates the right to free speech guaranteed Mr. Jacobs by the First Amendment."[517] The court validated the Department's restriction, however, as it related to disclosures to unidentified lawyers for public interest groups.[518]

Daniel S. Jacobs, a lawyer employed in the Environmental and Natural Resources Division, Environmental Enforcement Section, of DOJ, became concerned about the "propriety of certain strategies and tactics"[519] he saw in his section. He addressed these concerns to Ms. Schiffer, the assistant attorney general in charge of the division. After his communication of concerns to Ms. Schiffer, evaluators lowered Jacobs' performance rating and transferred him to another division against his wishes. Jacobs consulted a private lawyer to determine whether the conduct that concerned him was illegal and, additionally, whether his reassignment and reduced performance rating amounted to improper retaliation by his employer. The court noted that Jacobs sought legal advice on his "rights and obligations, personally and professionally, and as a

---

514. *See California Legislature Passes New Law for Whistle Blowing Government Attorneys*, 71 U.S. L. Wk. 2171.
515. 47 F. Supp. 2d 16 (D.C. Cir. 1999).
516. *Id.*
517. *Id.* at 24.
518. *Id.*
519. *Id.* at 18.

190 ISSUES OF LEGAL ETHICS IN THE PRACTICE OF ENVIRONMENTAL LAW

potential whistleblower."[520] In pursuing the potential claim, Jacobs asked his lawyer whether he could lawfully make public disclosures of division information relating to his issues of concern under the Whistleblower's Protection Act. Jacobs' lawyer contacted Schiffer and requested documents needed to evaluate Jacobs' claim. In response, Schiffer indicated that Jacobs would be required to make a formal request to the department to receive permission to disclose any nonpublic information (information not subject to disclosure under the FOIA.

Among other things, Jacobs argued that the predisclosure clearance requirement set by Shiffer violated his First Amendment rights. Because Jacobs obtained the information sought while representing EPA as the agency's lawyer rather than a lay employee, Shiffer argued that Jacobs' disclosure would violate the ethics rule against revealing client confidences or secrets.[521] Shiffer relied on Comment 10 to Rule 1.6, which states that lawyers should neither associate another lawyer "in the handling of a matter" nor consult with another lawyer if "there is a reasonable possibility that the identity of the client or the client's confidences or secrets would be revealed to such lawyer."[522] The court rejected Shiffer's argument that Rule 1.6 requires client consent for the disclosures at issue, noting that Jacobs did not seek "advice on how to handle his representation of the EPA," but rather advice on his own rights.[523] The court also agreed with Jacobs that his lawyer could not answer the questions posed by the representation without reviewing the documents relating to the claims.[524]

In reaching its decision that the First Amendment protects a lawyer's right to share nonpublic information with his own lawyer for the purpose of securing representation, the court regarded such sharing of information with a personal lawyer as essentially no disclosure at all but, rather, providing information to "a learned *alter ego* of the government lawyer . . . equally dutybound to treat the confidences and secrets of the government lawyer's client as his own."[525] The court reasoned that any other interpretation "would effectively deny Mr. Jacobs the ability to obtain legal advice" and place the confidentiality rule of ethics in "tension with the Fifth Amendment's guarantee of due process."[526] This analysis is similar to the rationale for the provision of

---

520. *Id.*

521. *Id.* at 20, *citing* the D.C. RULE OF PROF'L CONDUCT 1.6 (which states "a lawyer shall not knowingly . . . [r]eveal a confidence or secret of the lawyer's client."

522. *Id.* at 20, *quoting* cmt. 10 to D.C. RULE OF PROF'L CONDUCT 1.6.

523. *Id.* at 20.

524. *Id.* at 18.

525. *Id.* at 21.

526. *Id., citing* Martin v. Lauer, 686 F.2d 24, 32 (D.C. Cir. 1982).

Revised Model Rule 1.6 allowing a lawyer to disclose client information when necessary for the lawyer to obtain legal advice. Additionally, the court reasoned that the department had imposed a prior restraint on Jacobs' use of information. On the other hand, the court held that DOJ was justified in resisting Jacobs' request to disclose nonpublic information to unidentified lawyers of unnamed public interest organizations without prior permission from his agency-employer.[527] In reaching this decision, the court noted that Shiffer's fear that Jacobs would reveal agency information to public interest groups and risk harm to legitimate interests of the agency was "not entirely misplaced."[528] Accordingly, the court held that the predisclosure clearance for any disclosures to other unspecified individuals did not infringe Jacobs' constitutional rights. The court noted that an agency's interests in confidentiality could be protected by a court order that would prohibit an employee and his lawyer from disclosing confidential information.

Other Common Issues

Prospective Clients

When a lawyer confers with a prospective client, the would-be client is ordinarily entitled to an expectation of confidentiality. Absent a warning from the lawyer, a prospective client normally will expect a lawyer to maintain his confidences and to keep the information provided by the prospective client to himself so that he might assess his ability and willingness to accept a representation.

The Restatement of the Law Governing Lawyers provides that information that a lawyer acquired before or during a representation is confidential if not generally known.[529] Likewise, the ABA Commission on Ethics and Professional Responsibility held in Formal Opinion 90-358 that a prospective client who consults a lawyer for the purpose of obtaining legal advice or representation is entitled to an expectation that information revealed to a lawyer will be kept confidential.[530] The Commission's opinion interpreted the reach of Model Rule 1.6 to apply to the prospective client situation, stating: "Information imparted to a lawyer by a would-be client seeking legal representation is protected from revelation or use under Model Rule 1.6 even though

---

527. *Id.* at 24.
528. *Id.* at 23.
529. RESTATEMENT (THIRD) OF THE LAW GOVERNING LAWYERS § 59 cmt. c (including within the protection information that "might be acquired by the lawyer in considering whether to undertake a representation").
530. ABA Formal Op. No. 90-358.

192   ISSUES OF LEGAL ETHICS IN THE PRACTICE OF ENVIRONMENTAL LAW

the lawyer does not undertake representation of or perform legal work for the would-be client."[531] While recognizing the interests of prospective clients, the ABA Commission's opinion also addressed conflict issues, extending protection to the lawyer who "takes adequate measures to limit the information initially imparted by the would-be client," noting that "in most situations the lawyer may continue to represent or to undertake representation of another client in the same or a related matter."[532] The opinion admits the possibility that the protection it creates for the potential client may compromise the lawyer's ability to represent another client. The opinion also recommends measures to guard against lawyer disqualification in this setting. Specifically, it notes that lawyers should undertake procedures to identify conflicts of interest before undertaking a representation and should limit the information received in the interview. The lawyer should control the flow of the interview to avoid receiving confidential information unnecessarily.

> When obtaining the preliminary information before undertaking the representation, the lawyer should obtain from the would-be client only information sufficient to determine whether a conflict or potential conflict of interest exists and whether the new matter is one within the lawyer's capabilities and one in which the lawyer is willing to represent the would-be client.[533]

In this opinion, the Commission endorsed both waivers and screening in some circumstances, noting that the waiver should be memorialized in writing and signed by the client and, additionally, that the lawyer should explain the consequences of the waiver to the client. The related issues of screening, firm disqualification, and imputed disqualification are of great importance to both confidentiality and conflicts questions. They are discussed in depth in the section on conflicts (see Chapters 5 and 6).

Prospective Clients (Ethics 2000 Revision)

The ABA clarified the issue of the lawyer's duty of confidentiality to a prospective client by adopting the new Model Rule 1.18. By adding this rule, the ABA indicated that lawyers have duties to prospective clients, even when no attorney-client relationship arises with the prospective client. The new rule indicates that information provided to a lawyer by a prospective client comes

---

531. ABA Comm. on Ethics and Prof'l Responsibility Formal Op. No. 90-358.

532. *Id.*

533. *Id.*

within the duty of confidentiality. "Even when no client-lawyer relationship ensues, a lawyer who has had discussions with a prospective client shall not use or reveal information learned in the consultation, except as Rule 1.9 would permit with respect to information of a former client."[534]

Prospective Client Waiver (2002 Revision)

The 2002 revision by the ABA of the Model Rules expressly indicates in a comment that a prospective client may waive the duty of confidentiality with regard to information disclosed in an initial consultation. "A lawyer may condition conversations for the prospective client on the person's informed consent that no information disclosed during a consultation will prohibit the lawyer from representing a different client in the matter. . . . If the agreement expressly so provides, the prospective client may also consent to the lawyer's subsequent use of information received from the prospective client."[535]

Former Clients

Clients are entitled to protection of information shared with lawyers even after termination of the attorney-client relationship.[536] The duty to former clients is articulated in Model Rule 1.9, which provides:

> (a) A lawyer who has formerly represented a client in a matter shall not thereafter represent another person in the same or a substantially related matter in which that person's interests are materially adverse to the interests of the former client unless the former client consents after consultation.[537]

The prohibition against representations that are materially adverse to former clients extends to other lawyers in the firm.

Deceased Clients

The attorney-client privilege survives the death of the client. In *Swindler & Berlin v. United States*,[538] the United States Supreme Court considered whether the Office of the Independent Counsel, through a grand jury, had a right to

---

534. Rev. Model Rule 1.18(b).
535. Model Rule 1.18 cmt. 5 (2002), *citing* Rule 1.10(e) regarding "informed consent." This provision is a subject of additional analysis and comment in this work in the chapter on conflicts.
536. Model Rule 1.9.
537. Model Rule 1.9(a).
538. 524 U.S. 399 (1998).

subpoena notes that a lawyer took during a meeting with Deputy White House Counsel Vincent W. Foster, Jr., shortly before his death.[539] Mr. Foster sought legal advice from James Hamilton, a lawyer with Swindler & Berlin, relating to the investigations into the White House Travel Office scandal. The district court denied enforcement of the subpoenas. The court of appeals reversed the trial court decision, creating a balancing test to determine whether notes relating to a deceased client could be revealed. It reasoned that the testamentary exception to the attorney-client privilege should be applied to allow disclosure in the criminal context.[540]

The Supreme Court reversed the court of appeals, holding that the lawyer's notes were protected by the attorney-client privilege. The Court noted that the majority of jurisdictions that have addressed the attorney-client privilege in cases of deceased clients have done so in the context of testamentary law,[541] and that most courts presume that the privilege survives the death of the client. The testamentary disclosure of communications is an exception to the privilege.[542] "[T]he general rule with respect to confidential communications . . . is that such communications are privileged during the testator's lifetime and, also, after the testator's death unless sought to be disclosed in litigation between the testator's heirs."[543]

Multiparty Representation

Many environmental matters involve large numbers of corporate clients. Perhaps the best examples of such representation are Superfund work, including litigation, negotiation, allocation cases, and toxic tort cases. In such representations, lawyers frequently represent more than one client and they sometimes represent a large number of clients at a single site. In such cases, the coclient rule generally applies to hold that communications of joint parties are presumed not to be confidential from the other joint parties, unless the information does not relate to the subject matter of the common representation.[544] In other words, the lawyer may assume that information provided by one of the clients may be shared with all the coclients.

---

539. *See id.* at 401.

540. *See id.* at 400.

541. *See id.* at 404.

542. *Id.* at 404.

543. *Id.*, *quoting* United States v. Osborn, 561 F.2d 1334, 1340 (9th Cir. 1977).

544. *See* Eureka Invest. Corp. v. Chicago Title Ins. Co., 743 F.2d 932, 937–38 (D.C. Cir. 1984) (finding lawyer has duty to preserve confidentiality of communication from co-client when the information does not relate to co-client).

Chapter 4: Confidentiality 195

Sharing of information among the co-clients with respect to the matter involved in the representation is normal and typically expected. . . . Limitation of the attorney-client privilege as applied to communications of co-clients is based on an assumption that each intends that his or her communications with the lawyer will be shared with the other co-clients but otherwise kept in confidence.[545]

To make this result clearer, lawyers should note in agreements for joint representation that client information will be shared among the parties to the agreement.

Requirement of Complying with Discovery Requests

In addition to the requirements of substantive law, lawyers and clients have a duty to comply with the procedural requirements imposed by a statute or court rule such as federal, state, or local court procedural rules, the rules of civil procedure, and orders of a court. Both the Federal Rules of Civil Procedure and decisional law authorize the imposition of sanctions on parties who fail to fully disclose relevant information sought in the discovery process.[546]

Environmental Example

Failure to comply by disclosing required information can result in penalties and sanctions on the client, the lawyer, or both. For example, in the case of *In re Tutu Wells Contamination Litigation*,[547] the District of the Virgin Islands imposed sanctions against an oil company and its former counsel for discovery violations.[548] The sanctions on the lawyers included a bar from practicing before the court for misconduct in failing to respond to discovery requests. The court barred two lawyers from practice before the court for three years and one lawyer for one year.[549] It also granted the opponents damages for costs incurred in their attempts to obtain evidence and for their participation in the sanction proceedings. Finally, the court imposed a sanction of community service by requiring a payment of $1 million toward the Criminal Justice Center of the area. The Court of Appeals for the Third Circuit upheld the monetary sanctions but overruled the order directing payment of money to the

---

545. RESTATEMENT (THIRD) OF THE LAW GOVERNING LAWYERS § 60 cmt. l.
546. *See* Roadway Exp., Inc. v. Piper, 100 S. Ct. 2455 (1980); Chambers v. NASCO, Inc., 501 U.S. 32, 50 111 S. Ct. 2123, 2136 (1991).
547. 120 F.3d 368 (3d Cir. 1997).
548. *Id.* at 371-72.
549. *Id.* at 372.

196　ISSUES OF LEGAL ETHICS IN THE PRACTICE OF ENVIRONMENTAL LAW

Criminal Justice Center, holding that this penalty was outside the scope of the district court's power.[550] The reviewing court also found that the trial court had failed to afford the lawyers particularized notice of the form of sanctions they faced and that this failure violated the lawyers' due process rights.[551]

The *Tutu* case involved the contamination of the Tutu aquifer in the Virgin Islands by gasoline and chlorinated organics. After a well owner in the area reported the smell of gasoline in his well, federal and local environmental agencies investigated, found contamination of the Tutu aquifer, and closed many of the wells in the area. Private individuals filed CERCLA cost recovery actions and common-law claims against several businesses as a result of the contamination, including claims against several related Esso corporate entities. The Goldman, Antonetti law firm represented the Esso companies. After a discovery that spanned several years, the district court lodged three opinions over the space of 13 months in which the court described the violations by Esso and its lawyers and considered motions for sanctions.[552] The trial court found that Esso and its lawyers engaged in bad-faith practices to prevent their opponents in the litigation from obtaining needed information,[553] used legal tactics to delay the litigation, and harassed their opponents. For example, the defendants routinely refused to turn over requested documents until forced to do so by court order. In one particularly egregious example, the court found that Esso and its lawyers intentionally refused to provide a summary memorandum written by a consultant.

The results of soil analysis revealed contamination. Jose Agrelot, the president of the consulting firm, summarized the findings of the soil testing in a memorandum, which he forwarded to the lawyers. ETC, the company that ran the analysis, provided final results of the testing in 1990. Despite discovery requests, the lawyers for Esso refused to produce the document (the Agrelot memo) until ordered to do so in 1993. The court held that this delay was the result of an intentional decision to refuse to produce the document rather than an error in filing, as the defendant claimed. In affirming a sanction of $120,000 against the law firm, based on the firm's misconduct in failing to turn over the Agrelot memo, the appellate court noted that it could not find that the district court abused its discretion in awarding the amount of damages it chose al-

---

550. *Id.* at 384-85, 392.

551. *Id.* at 380-81.

552. *Id.* at 373-77. For greater detail with respect to the factual and procedural underpinnings of the case, *see In re* Tutu Wells Contamination Litig., 166 F.R.D. 331 (D. V.I. 1996). *See also* related case, *In re* Tutu Wells Contamination Litig., 162 F.R.D. 46, *order clarified*, 162 F.R.D. 81 (D. V.I. 1995).

553. *In re* Tutu Wells Contamination Litig., 162 F.R.D. at 75.

though the firm had turned over 800 pages of technical material that the memo summarized.[554]

Even though the lawyers in the *Tutu* case ultimately escaped disbarment, the case presents a cautionary tale. Its moral is that the risk of disbarment or other sanctions for unfair practices is real.

Solutions: 2002 Revision to Model Rule 1.6

The implicit advice of the 1983 version of Model Rule 1.6 is that the silent lawyer will always be in compliance with the Rule 1.6, but the lawyer who reveals client information is likely to violate the rule. When the lawyer reasonably believes that the client intends to commit a criminal act that will result in the dramatic harm of imminent death or substantial bodily harm to a third party, the rule recognizes the need for disclosure. The preference and analytical framework of Model Rule 1.6 fails to take into consideration legislation that attempts to limit environmental risks or modern tort developments that suggest a case-by-case determination of the interests of individuals put at risk by environmental hazards. In fact, there is no clear-cut cautious practice. The 1983 version of Model Rule 1.6 restricts lawyer discretion, however, allowing disclosure only when the client's conduct constitutes an intended crime and the risk threatens "imminent death or substantial bodily harm." The revised rule on confidentiality rejects these limitations in the exception to prevent death or substantial bodily harm. In this exception, the revised rule has no additional element other than that disclosure is necessary "to prevent" the harm described. The other exceptions allow disclosure to prevent less drastic harm only when the client conduct is culpable (a crime or a fraud) and the client has used the lawyer's services in furtherance of the culpable conduct.

Some lawyers fear that the rule as revised might encourage lawyers to disclose client information too readily. States have addressed the issue, deciding overwhelmingly that exceptions to the duty of confidentiality are justified. Most give lawyers discretion to disclose client information to prevent harm in significant, definable circumstances. The changes to Rule 1.6 provide the benefits of greater protection for lawyers, allowing disclosures in circumstances in which the lawyer is at risk of liability for undisclosed dangers. For example, under the revised rule, a lawyer who reasonably believes that a statute or the common law requires that he disclose the contaminated condition of property will not violate the rule by reporting the danger in the face of a continuing refusal by the client to comply with the law. Moreover, the revised rule is almost certain to increase uniformity among the states, since the

---

554. *In re* Tutu Wells Contamination Litig., 120 F.3d 368, 372.

198 ISSUES OF LEGAL ETHICS IN THE PRACTICE OF ENVIRONMENTAL LAW

majority of the states incorporated at least part of the approach adopted in the revised rule. The vast majority of state rules, as well as the Restatement of the Law Governing Lawyers and ethical codes of other professions, allow disclosures to protect the public and third parties.[555]

Whether a lawyer's disclosure or silence creates a risk of sanction or liability depends on the circumstances of each case. The lawyer, like everyone else, must weigh the factors involved in determining the best course of action. The 1983 version of Model Rule 1.6 prefers the risks that accompany silence over risks that accompany disclosure. Based on this preference, the rule encourages lawyer silence. It recognizes harm to others as a basis for disclosing client information only in the rarest of circumstances. As the foregoing discussion illustrates, other laws may have the effect of putting the lawyer in a Catch-22 situation. Revised Model Rule 1.6 allows the lawyer to reveal client information to the extent necessary to avert serious harm. Consequently, it protects not only others who could be subject to that harm but, additionally, lawyers who might be held liable for that harm absent disclosure.

---

555. *See* Final Rule: Implementation of Standards of Professional Conduct for Attorneys, Securities and Exchange Commission, 17 C.F.R. Part 205 [Release Nos. 33-8185; 34-47276; IC-25919; File No. S7-45-02] RIN 3235-AI72, Implementation of Standards of Professional Conduct for Attorneys, Agency: Securities and Exchange Commission, n. 92. *Available at* http://www.sec.tzov/rules/final/33-8185.htm (last visited Mar. 31, 2003) (noting that 37 states permit lawyers to reveal confidential client information in order to prevent the client from committing criminal fraud and citing *Restatement (Third) of the Law Governing Lawyers* (2000) '67, Cmt. f.

CHAPTER 5

Basic Conflicts Concerns

Conflicts of interest occur with significant frequency in environmental matters. Large firms involved in environmental practice have identified conflict of interest problems as their greatest fear.[1] Such issues often arise as a result of representation of multiple parties or because a former client challenges a firm's current representation. The relatively small numbers of lawyers practicing in the environmental area can mean that parties seek out the same lawyer in different matters, particularly in small cities. The extent of the conflict problem fluctuates with the level of enforcement activity relating to environmental violations. For example, when Superfund enforcement was strong, some corporate clients could likely find themselves without experienced counsel in a Superfund case if it construed the conflict rule strictly and refused to consent to any conflict of interest.

The issue of multiple representation has received significant attention because of the common practice of environmental lawyers representing multiple potentially responsible parties (PRPs) in Superfund settlement negotiations and litigation under the Comprehensive Environmental Response, Compensation and Liability Act (CERCLA).[2] Many environmental matters—notably Superfund litigation, toxic tort matters, and challenges to rule making by the Environmental Protection Agency (EPA)—involve large numbers of stakeholders, enhancing the possibility of conflict problems.[3] In part because

---

1. *See* Patrick E. Donovan, *Serving Multiple Masters: Confronting the Conflicting Interests that Arise in Superfund Disputes*, 17 B.C. ENVTL. AFF. L. REV. 371 (1990); *see also* Marla B. Rubin, *The Problems Get Tougher*, THE RECORDER, Sept. 1992, at 16.
2. *See* Carol E. Dinkins & Lewis C. Sutherland, *Ethics in the Environmental and Toxic Tort Practice*, SB 73 ALI-ABA 319, 326 (1997).
3. *See* David Littell, *Consent and Disclosure in Superfund Negotiations: Identifying and Avoiding Conflicts of Interests Arising from Multiple Representation*, 17 HARV. ENVTL. L. REV. 225 (1993).

of the significant numbers of parties involved in CERCLA matters, conflict issues are a particularly compelling example of ethics problems in environmental law. In some cases, joint or multiple representation may equalize the bargaining power of the parties and may even "increase the likelihood that parties can reach an equitable settlement" with the EPA.[4] Plaintiffs may enhance the power of their arguments by forming a group to oppose a work practice or the siting of a hazardous waste facility. In most cases, a group protest is a more effective strategy than protests or suits by separate individuals. This strategy may include using joint legal representation as a way of coordinating legal theories and pooling resources. For example, when an entire district or neighborhood unites to file a claim with the Office of Civil Rights (OCR) of the EPA,[5] or to take other legal action, the complainants are likely to have more effect than if only a few residents filed claims individually. Moreover, united efforts provide moral support for people engaged in a dispute and build a sense of community and common purpose that may be crucial to the continuation of the protest or lawsuit. Additionally, some clients choose an environmental lawyer because of her experience and knowledge in the science and law of a particular area, even though she represents other parties in a particular matter.

Environmental matters frequently involve difficult factual records, lengthy and voluminous discovery, and other time-consuming problems that accompany big litigation or complicated transactional work. In such cases, it is difficult to overstate the severity of the hardship imposed on parties by the loss of counsel because of a conflict of interest. The problem is exacerbated when the lawyer has a significant history (perhaps years) on the case and expertise in the complex factual issues relating to the case. Even when a matter involves a transaction between parties rather than litigation, potential conflicts of interest should be assessed and discussed with clients.[6]

Organization and Terminology

This discussion focuses on conflicts issues that are likely to be pertinent in

---

4. Donovan, *supra* note 1, at 372.
5. While the Office of Civil Rights at the EPA has existed for some time (at least since 1975), EPA has expanded its role to include processing complaints filed under Title VI of the Civil Rights Act. The Office of Civil Rights at the EPA "has traditionally been almost exclusively concerned with personnel issues." Richard J. Lazarus, *Pursuing "Environmental Justice": The Distributional Effects of Environmental Protection*, 87 Nw. U. L. Rev. 787 (1993); Mariaea Ramirez Fisher, *On the Road from Environmental Racism to Environmental Justice*, 5 Vill. Envtl. L.J. 475–76 (1994).
6. *See* Model Rule 1.7 cmt. 7.

Chapter 5: Basic Conflicts Concerns 201

environmental practice and gives background information on the law of conflicts to inform the discussion. This chapter deals with the varied circumstances that present possible conflicts of interest. The organization breaks the discussion of the complicated area of conflicts into two major parts: conflicts relating to (1) private practitioners and (2) government lawyers. Within these categories, the discussion is organized to deal with conflicts relating to current clients, former clients, and prospective clients. The discussion notes the possibility of conflicts of interest as a result of direct adversity of the clients or the possibility that a representation may pose a material limitation on the lawyer's ability to represent another client. The possibility of curing the conflict is addressed in each section.

Courts and scholars refer to conflicts with various adjectives, including joint, multiple, and common representation, as well as simultaneous representation. This discussion refers to the issue of "simultaneous representation" to include all of these types of representations, distinguishing the situation of conflicts in simultaneous representations from conflicts that arise as a result of former or prospective clients. It uses the terms joint, multiple, and common to refer to representations in which the parties share representation in the same matter. The category of simultaneous representation includes these representations as well as representations of current clients in different matters.

The focus of this discussion is the 1983 version of the Model Rules of Professional Conduct because this set of ethical rules is the primary framework for rules of the states of this country. The discussion also notes changes in the 2002 revision of the Model Rules and some variations of the approach of the Model Code and the Restatement of the Law Governing Lawyers. Additional issues such as positional or issue conflicts and special concerns relating to representation of corporate clients appear in the sections on special issues.

Overview and General Principles

Conflicts of interest provide some of the most difficult and troubling issues facing environmental lawyers today. Conflicts issues have been called "probably the most pervasively felt of all of the problems of professional responsibility that might haunt lawyers."[7] The main thrust of the rules against allowing conflicts of interest seems to be based on three foundational needs: (1) loyalty

---

7. CHARLES W. WOLFRAM, MODERN LEGAL ETHICS, § 7.1, at 313 (2d ed 1986) [hereinafter WOLFRAM].

8. *See* MODEL CODE OF PROF'L RESPONSIBILITY Canon 5; *see e.g.,* Matter of Disciplinary Proceedings Against Eisenberg, 344 N.W.2d 169 (1984) (suspending lawyer for six months because of inappropriate representation of defendant and prosecutorial witness).

202   ISSUES OF LEGAL ETHICS IN THE PRACTICE OF ENVIRONMENTAL LAW

to the client, (2) independent professional judgment by the lawyer,[8] and (3) client confidentiality. If one of these foundational needs is impaired because of a conflict, courts and disciplinary boards are likely to disallow the representation and sanction the lawyer who has a conflict.[9] A client's reasonable expectation of loyalty from a lawyer requires that the lawyer owe no allegiance to a party adverse to the client. Such an allegiance would necessarily compromise the lawyer's loyalty to the client.

This rule operates without regard to the transient nature of many representations and the practical need of the lawyer to make a living. It springs from the general obligations of loyalty owed to the client and the lawyer's role as a fiduciary agent to a principal (the client). Courts have held that the challenge to representation is not necessarily determined by the person's status. The rules on conflicts apply to summer clerks, secretaries, and paralegals as well as lawyers, although courts may apply the rules in a more lenient fashion when the conflict arises as a result of contact between a nonlawyer and a client.[10]

Conflicts arise at varying levels of importance in every legal representation and, indeed, perhaps in every human relationship, whether professional or personal. The fact that a client has a dispute is clearly a bad thing for the client. Yet, it is in one sense a good thing for the lawyer. The existence of a dispute is advantageous for the lawyer, since the resolution of the dispute constitutes the lawyer's livelihood. Addressing lawyers, Professor Monroe Freedman notes: "If you charge your client by the hour for conducting litigation, it will be less in your interest than your client's to settle the case at an early stage, because your hourly fee will end with the case."[11] This type of conflict of interest is present in every profession. The professional's livelihood is based on this inherent conflict: the client's problems are the lawyer's bread and butter.

Inherent conflicts are real. Indeed, such conflicts may be a primary motivating factor for the development of codes of ethics for professionals. Such codes seek to quiet the concerns of laypersons who may fear the experience of consulting a professional because of the inherent conflict between the professional and the client and the asymmetry of knowledge that marks the relation-

---

9. *See, e.g.,* Mich. Eth. Op. RI-98, 1991 WL 519877 (Sept. 9, 1991) (holding that lawyer must obtain the consent of the six clients who discharged him to continue representation of the remaining 108 clients in a class-action suit).

10. *See* Allen v. Academic Games Leagues of America, Inc., 831 F. Supp. 785 (C.D. Cal. 1993); Brown v. Eighth Judicial Dist. Court, 14 P.3d 1266 (Nev. 2000) (holding law firm disqualified based on hiring secretary formerly employed by opposing counsel).

11. MONROE H. FREEDMAN, UNDERSTANDING LAWYER'S ETHICS 173 (1990).

ship. The ethics rules, such as the rule requiring reasonable fees and honest billing, seek to neutralize such conflicts. Inherent conflicts are not, however, the type of conflicts that necessitate termination of a representation. Almost no representation could survive such a broad-based restriction. Rather, the scope of the prohibition against conflicting representation relates to avoidable rather than inherent conflicts.

The Duty of Loyalty

The lawyer owes the client unfettered loyalty. The principle of loyalty seems to be the linchpin of the prohibition against representing clients who are adverse to one another or who have materially adverse interests. Comment 1 to Model Rule 1.7 identifies loyalty as "an essential element in the lawyer's relationship to a client."[12] The duty of confidentiality derives from the lawyer's duty of loyalty.

"It is clear that there are two broad principles underlying all conflicts rules for lawyers—the principle of loyalty and the principle of confidentiality."[13] The client's sense of trust and confidence in the lawyer and the need to preserve the independent professional judgment are also central reasons for conflicts rules. The lawyer is the client's agent. Accordingly, the lawyer's loyalty includes the duty to "act solely for the benefit of the principal in all matters connected with his agency."[14] Indeed, some courts and commentators have noted that the lawyer's duty to his client exceeds that of an ordinary agent.[15]

In most cases, clients may consent to a representation that presents a conflict, effectively waiving the conflict. In some cases, the conflict presented is not waivable by the clients. Disputes and other matters arising in the law impinge directly on the client's autonomy. The close relationship of the lawyer and client vis-à-vis the client's business interests, a particular dispute, or criminal charges inevitably results in the sharing of information by the client and advice by the lawyer that the client does not wish to reveal to others. In representing another client, the lawyer will owe loyalty and diligence to that

---

12. MODEL RULE 1.7 cmt. 1.

13. WOLFRAM, *supra* note 7, § 7.1.3, at 316 (2d ed. 1986). "The duty of confidentiality is a corollary of the more general duty of loyalty." GEOFFREY C. HAZARD ET AL., *The Duty of Confidentiality Is a Corollary of the More General Duty of Loyalty, in* THE LAW AND ETHICS OF LAWYERING 269 (3d ed. 1999) [hereinafter HAZARD ET AL].

14. RESTATEMENT (SECOND) OF AGENCY 387 (1957).

15. *See* Halstead v. Murray, 547 A.2d 202 (N.H. 1988) (noting "unity" or special relationship between lawyer and client as justification for holding the Statute of Frauds is satisfied by signature of lawyer); WOLFRAM, *supra* note 7, § 4.1.

client. If the lawyer has information about the first client that would be useful to the second client, she is in a situation of conflict. The lawyer's duty to maintain confidences of the first client is in conflict with her duty to represent the second client fully. Therefore, the need for confidentiality is an underlying reason for the rule against conflicting representation.[16] The rule that a lawyer may be disqualified from representing a party whose interests are in conflict with those of an existing client protects against violations of the principle of confidentiality.

> For an attorney, the danger is that he will be tempted, perhaps unconsciously, to favor the interests of a particularly important client over the adverse or potentially adverse interests of a less favored client. The lawyer's conflicting loyalties might lead him to recommend, for example, that the less favored client appear as a co-defendant or that the former unnecessarily concede a point in a negotiation with the latter.[17]

The 1983 Model Rules Approach

Most jurisdictions model their rules on the 1983 version of the Model Rules. Rather than a single rule on conflicts, the Model Rules present a set of rules relating to the issue. This grouping of concepts is presented in Model Rules 1.7 through 1.11. The provisions include the general rule against representing parties when the representation adversely affects the relationship with another client or materially limits the lawyer's ability to represent a client. They include limitations against lawyers entering business transactions with clients, the bar against representing a client in the same or a substantially related matter in which the lawyer represented a former client, imputed disqualification based on a lawyer's association with other lawyers, and the limitations on successive government and private employment.

The Principal Rule: Model Rule 1.7

Model Rule 1.7 sets forth the ABA's principal rule against conflicting representation of clients. Two distinct types of conflicts should be noted: (1) where the lawyer is asked to represent two different clients in two different matters (the simultaneous or concurrent representation situation);[18] and (2) where the

---

16. HAZARD ET AL., *supra* note 13, at 269.
17. *Developments in the Law: Conflicts of Interest in the Legal Profession*, 94 HARV. L. REV. 1244, 1296 (1981).
18. *See* RONALD D. ROTUNDA, LEGAL ETHICS: THE LAWYER'S DESKBOOK ON PROFESSIONAL RESPONSIBILITY § 8-1.1 (2002–2003) (referring to concurrent representation as "simulta-

Chapter 5: Basic Conflicts Concerns 205

lawyer represents several parties in the same litigation (the coclient or multiple representation situation, also called joint or common representation). Model Rule 1.7 presents standards for judging these representations, though this distinction does not dictate the organization of the rule. The rule speaks to two different types of conflicts: (1) one that is "directly adverse to another [old] client," and (2) one in which the representation of a new client "may be materially limited" by other responsibilities or interests of the lawyer.[19] The first of these situations is concerned with the impact of a proffered representation on interests of another client or clients. The second is concerned with the interests of the new client seeking representation. Model Rule 1.7 protects the interests of current clients under the analysis of the first subsection, inquiring into whether the new representation is "directly adverse" to a current client.[20] A lawyer may represent two parties in unrelated matters even when the interests of the two are adverse in a general (rather than a direct) sense, such as when the two clients have competing economic interests. A comment to Rule 1.7 explains the rationale:

> [A] lawyer ordinarily may not act as advocate against a person the lawyer represents in some other matter, even if it is wholly unrelated. On the other hand, simultaneous representation in unrelated matters of clients whose interests are only *generally* adverse, such as competing economic enterprises, does not require consent of the respective clients.[21]

The principle that a lawyer should not accept a representation that will directly oppose an existing client is clear from this comment. Line drawing is necessary by both lawyers and clients to determine whether a conflict is based on merely generally adverse interests. A new comment to Model Rule 1.7 adopted by the ABA in February 2002 clearly indicates that representation of a client adverse to an affiliate of a corporate client is not a conflict under the Model Rules.[22]

The second subsection protects the new client under the "materially lim-

---

eous" representation in discussion of Rule1.7); ABA Formal Op. 92-367 (Lawyer Examining a Client as an Adverse Witness, or Conducting Third Party Discovery of the Client) (using "simultaneous representation" and "concurrent representation" as synonyms).

19. MODEL RULE 1.7(a)-(b).
20. MODEL RULE 1.7(a).
21. MODEL RULE 1.7 cmt. 3 (emphasis added).
22. Model Rule 1.7 cmt. 34 (2002).

206   ISSUES OF LEGAL ETHICS IN THE PRACTICE OF ENVIRONMENTAL LAW

ited" standard,[23] requiring analysis of the problem if the representation may be materially limited by "the lawyer's responsibility to another client or a third person, or by the lawyer's own interests."[24] The rule creates an exception to its prohibition against representations marked by conflicts when the lawyer believes that the representation will not be adversely affected and all clients consent to the representation.

The Steps of a Decision to Accept Representation

The lawyer facing a choice of representing a client directly adverse to another client must accomplish five tasks under Rule 1.7 (a) to comply with the rules in accepting employment proffered by a new client. After noting the existence of a potential conflict (the first step), the lawyer must gather information about the proffered employment (the second step) and determine whether the representation will adversely affect the current client (step three). If the lawyer's decision in step three is that the representation will not adversely affect the current client, the lawyer must consult (step four) with the current and potential clients, taking care to preserve the confidentiality of each and to adequately inform the clients involved of the potential for adverse consequences from the conflict. Finally, to accept the potential client's representation and retain the current client, the lawyer must obtain the waiver and consent of each of the clients after the consultation (step five). Applying a rule of reasonableness, the consent should meet an "informed consent" standard. Accordingly, the lawyer should disclose all relevant information, including possible adverse consequences of the conflict.[25]

Under Model Rule 1.7(b), the lawyer must accomplish a similar type of sequential analysis to accept a new representation when the lawyer believes that the representation "may be materially limited" by other interests. When a lawyer determines that a material limitation of the lawyer's responsibility is a possibility in the representation (step one), he must assess the limiting factors (step two), including the "lawyer's responsibilities to another client or to a third person, or the lawyer's own interest."[26] The lawyer must also assess (step three) whether he "reasonably believes the representation will not be adversely affected."[27] When the lawyer's analysis favors representation, the lawyer must consult with the client, providing full information necessary for the client to make an informed decision in the matter (step four).

---

23. MODEL RULE 1.7(b).

24. *Id.*

25. The requirement of informed consent is made explicit by the 2002 revision. *See* MODEL RULE 1.7, 1.0(e)(2002).

26. MODEL RULE 1.7(b).

27. MODEL RULE 1.7(b)(1).

Chapter 5: Basic Conflicts Concerns   207

Under the inquiries of both subsections to Model Rule 1.7, the lawyer applies the standard "of a disinterested lawyer."[28] The rule varies slightly from the description of the lawyer's belief in each of the two circumstances. In the "directly adverse" case, the rule focuses on the relationship of the lawyer and the original client. It permits the representation if the client gives informed consent and the lawyer "reasonably believes the representation will not adversely affect the relationship with the other client."[29] In the case of a "materially limited" representation, the rule focuses the test on the representation rather than the relationship. It permits the representation if the lawyer "reasonably believes the representation will not be adversely affected" by the conflict and the client gives informed consent.[30]

Reasonable Reading of the Rule

The rules on conflicts and the curative measures in the area seem circuitous and counterintuitive. At first blush, the elements seem contradictory, as though they assert both "x" and "not x." Under the first situation discussed, Model Rule 1.7(a), a conflict is presented when a representation of a new client "will be directly adverse to another client [the old client]." In the second situation, the conflict problem arises if the representation may be "materially limited." In either case, accepting or continuing the representation does not violate the rule when two curative elements are present: (1) the client or clients consent to the representation after consultation; and (2) the lawyer reasonably believes that the representation will not adversely affect an existing client or the new client.[31] The first element presents the objective test of client consent after consultation. The second element adds a subjective test: the lawyer's belief regarding the effect of the representation. The curative elements in the exception create a possible defense to a conflicts charge even when the representation seems to present a problem.

The rule stops short of a clear prohibition, leaving room for lawyer judgment and defense. The apparent contradiction lies in the fact that the lawyer who has identified the representation as "directly adverse" may, nevertheless, go forward with it if he "reasonably believes" that the representation will

---

28. MODEL RULE 1.7 cmt. 5.
29. MODEL RULE 1.7(a)(1).
30. MODEL RULE 1.7(b).
31. The MODEL CODE presents a similar structure to that of the MODEL RULES for resolving conflicts issues except for variation in the standard of the lawyer's judgment. The MODEL CODE permits representation despite the existence of representation of another party with differing interests when "it is obvious that [the lawyer] can adequately represent the interest of each [client]."

not adversely affect his relationship with his old client. One might ask how it is possible that a directly adverse relationship could go forward without an adverse effect on the relationship. Likewise, under subsection(s) of Model Rule 1.7, one might ask how a lawyer who notes that a representation "may be materially limited" by a lawyer's responsibilities to others or his own interests could reasonably conclude that the representation "will not be adversely affected." Nevertheless, the rules acknowledge both possibilities, juxtaposing the general concept of adversity of the representation with the specific belief of the lawyer regarding the future of the particular case. Close cases are to be expected.[32]

As a matter of sequence, a lawyer should address his conscience first regarding whether a disinterested lawyer would see multiple representation as appropriate (i.e., that the lawyer can adequately represent all the clients). It is important to ask this question prior to seeking consent of the clients, because the consent will be ineffective unless the lawyer can reasonably conclude from the perspective of a disinterested lawyer that he can adequately represent all the clients involved.[33]

Model Rule 1.7 (2002 Revision)

The Ethics 2000 Commission recommended important clarifications and stylistic changes rather than dramatic substantive changes to Model Rule 1.7. The revision requires that the client consent to conflicts be "confirmed in writing," though it does not require that the client produce or sign the writing. The ABA revision to Model Rule 1.7 recasts the entire rule rather than making piecemeal or phrasing changes. While the overall effect of the rule is substantially similar to that of the 1983 version, the approach of the 2002 Rule seems more straightforward and easier to apply. The prohibition of the new rule is set forth in Model Rule 1.7(a):

> Except as provided in paragraph (b), a lawyer shall not represent a client if the representation involves a concurrent conflict of interest. A concurrent conflict of interest exists if:
> (1) the representation of one client will be directly adverse to another client; or
> (2) there is a significant risk that the representation of one or

---

32. *See, e.g.,* Commonwealth Ins. Co. v. Stone Container Corp., 178 F. Supp. 2d 938 (N.D. 2001) (finding no inappropriate conflict when lawyer's role as a testifying expert in insurance litigation was unrelated to the firm's limited representation of corporation).

33. *See* Kansas Bar Assoc. Ethics Advisory Services Comm., Op. 95-11 (1995).

more clients will be materially limited by the lawyer's responsibilities to another client, a former client or a third person or by a personal interest of the lawyer.[34]

Revised Rule 1.7 retains the reasonable belief standard from the 1983 version regarding the lawyer's belief that the representation will be adequate. What the lawyer must believe varies between the two rules, however. The 1983 version required that the lawyer have a reasonable belief that "the representation will not adversely affect"[35] the other client and "will not be adversely affected"[36] by the conflict. The 2002 version requires that the lawyer reasonably believe that he or she will be able to provide competent and diligent representation"[37] to each client. It also adds a requirement that the representation not be "prohibited by law."[38] The rule also expressly prohibits a representation of clients who are adverse to one another in "the same litigation or other proceeding before a tribunal."[39] The new rule requires that the informed consent of the client be confirmed in writing.[40] The rule appears to allow the lawyer to produce the writing that serves as the necessary confirmation.

Current Clients

Model Rule 1.7 prohibits a lawyer from bringing a suit against a current client. It is axiomatic that a lawsuit directly against a person is an adverse effect and would adversely affect the representation of the client sued. Although a court has the power to find that exceptional circumstances justify such a representation, such a finding appears to be highly unlikely.[41] Courts disqualify lawyers from representations against a current client based on either the direct adversity test or the material limitation test. The revised rule makes this point more clearly by including the prohibition against suing a current client as one of the enumerated points that disallows the repre-

---

34. MODEL RULE 1.7(a) (2002).
35. MODEL RULE 1.7(a)(1).
36. MODEL RULE 1.7(a) (2).
37. MODEL RULE 1.7(b)(1) (2002).
38. MODEL RULE 1.7(b)(2) (2002).
39. MODEL RULE 1.7(b)(3) (2002).
40. MODEL RULE 1.7(b)(4) (2002).
41. *See In re* Dresser Industries, Inc., 972 F.2d 540 (5th Cir. 1992) (holding no exceptional circumstances existed to justify firm's representation of plaintiffs in class action against firm's current client).

210   ISSUES OF LEGAL ETHICS IN THE PRACTICE OF ENVIRONMENTAL LAW

sentation. In addition to the informed consent of the clients and a reasonable belief by the lawyer that the representation will not be adversely affected by a conflict, the revised rule requires a showing that "the representation does not involve the assertion of a claim by one client against another client represented by the lawyer in the same litigation or other proceeding before a tribunal."[42]

Direct Adversity

Perhaps the clearest rule of conflicts is that a lawyer must not represent one client against another client. Such a case presents direct adversity in terms of the language of Model Rule 1.7. "Because of the duty of loyalty, almost without exception, a lawyer may not represent adverse parties in the same litigation."[43] Even when the representation of the first client is "wholly unrelated"[44] to the suit by another client, the representation presents a conflict. In cases of simultaneous representation, a per se prohibition applies to representations that would result in the lawyer suing a current client or a past client when the lawyer terminated the representation to take the case against the (now former) client.[45] "If a lawyer is on general retainer for a client, even if no active matters are being handled, the stricter simultaneous representation rules will generally apply."[46] This rule forms a bedrock principle, relating directly to the principle of loyalty rather than to instrumental problems such as confidentiality.

---

42. MODEL RULE 1.7(b)(3) (2002).
43. WOLFRAM, *supra* note 7, at 350.
44. *See* MODEL RULE 1.7 cmt. 3.
45. *See* Glueck v. Jonathan Logan, Inc., 512 F. Supp. 223, 227 (S.D.N.Y.), *aff'd,* 653 F.2d 746 (2d Cir. 1981) (lawyer prohibited from representing trade association and, simultaneously, plaintiff suing one of the corporations in the association). Similarly, in cases of actual conflict, courts react strongly against dual representation. In dicta, in *Klemm v. Superior Court,* the California Court of Appeal noted the distinction between actual and potential conflicts and demonstrated a strong conviction against allowing joint representation in cases of actual conflict.

> As a matter of law a purported consent to dual representation of litigants with adverse interests at a contested hearing would be neither intelligent nor informed. Such representation would be per se inconsistent with the adversary position of an attorney in litigation, and common sense dictates that it would be unthinkable to permit an attorney to assume a position at a trial or hearing where he could not advocate the interests of one client without adversely injuring those of the other.

Klemm v. Superior Court, 142 Cal. Rptr. 509, 512, 75 Cal. App. 3d 893 (1977).
46. WOLFRAM, *supra* note 7, at 359.

Something seems radically out of place if a lawyer sues one of the lawyer's own present clients in behalf of another client. Even if the representations have nothing to do with each other, so that no confidential information is apparently jeopardized, the client who is sued can obviously claim that the lawyer's sense of loyalty is askew.[47]

Who Is a Client?

An example of the difficult factual determinations encompassed in conflicts decisions is provided in the case of *Westinghouse Electric Corp. v. Kerr-McGee Corp.*[48] In this case, a uranium supplier brought an antitrust action against oil companies and others. Defendants sought to disqualify the law firm of Kirkland & Ellis from representing the plaintiff (Westinghouse) on several grounds. A lawyer at Kirkland & Ellis, a large, multicity law firm, had written and issued a report on the uranium industry on behalf of a trade association of oil companies at the same time it filed the lawsuit representing Westinghouse against the oil companies, alleging an illegal conspiracy in the uranium industry. The defendant argued and the trial court held that, in writing the report on the uranium industry, the firm represented the oil companies as an expert rather than as a lawyer. The reviewing court disagreed, finding that the district court erred in concluding that the attorney-client relationship arises only with consent: "[I]t is obvious why an attorney-client relationship does not arise only in the agency manner such as when the parties expressly or impliedly consent to its formation."[49] The reviewing court suggested that an attorney-client relationship can arise when the lay party submits confidential information to the lawyer believing that the lawyer is acting in his behalf,[50] and noted that the professional relationship "hinges upon the client's belief that he is consulting a lawyer in that capacity and his manifested intention to seek professional legal advice."[51] Thus, it is possible to become a lawyer for a client even though the lawyer does not intend that an attorney-client relationship be formed.

Hot Potato Rule

The "Hot Potato Rule" prohibits a lawyer or a law firm from dropping a client

---

47. WOLFRAM, *supra* note 7, § 7.3.2, at 350.
48. 580 F.2d 1311 (7th Cir. 1978).
49. *Id.*
50. *Id.* at 1317.
51. *Id.* at 1319, *citing* McCORMICK ON EVIDENCE, § 88, at 179 (2d ed. 1972).

"like a hot potato" to accept representation with another client.[52] Professor Charles Wolfram noted the universal opprobrium that courts have expressed against lawyers who withdraw from representing one client to represent a new client in a matter adverse to the first client.[53]

> Courts, obviously motivated by concern over the lawyer's disloyalty, have spoken with one voice. The now widely accepted rule is that a lawyer who withdraws—whether otherwise in conformity with the lawyer code rules or not—from representing a current client for the purpose of proceeding adversely to the client on behalf of another client does not thereby convert the representation into that of a former client.[54]

Courts sometimes apply a presumption favoring disqualification,[55] reasoning that the public will disfavor lawyers if they believe they drop one client to take a more lucrative client.[56] Professor Ronald D. Rotunda explained the rationale of the Hot Potato Rule in terms of the lawyer's role as a fiduciary, noting that:

> A fiduciary should not be able to profit from its breach of the fiduciary obligation of loyalty. . . [A] law firm may not drop a client like a hot potato simply to take on another, more favored client. If a law firm has created a conflict, it will not be allowed to automatically shift resolution of a conflicts issue . . . by the simple expedient of dropping one client to take on a more favored one.[57]

The Hot Potato Rule may create an incentive for undertaking representation on a case-by-case basis rather than on a continuing basis. This rule may

---

52. *See, e.g.,* Ronald D. Rotunda, *Conflicts Problems When Representing Members of Corporate Families,* 72 Notre Dame L. Rev. 655, 663 (1997) [hereinafter Rotunda, *Conflicts Problems*]; John A. Edginton, *Managing Lawyers' Risks at the Millennium,* 73 Tul. L. Rev. 1987, 2021 (1999) [hereinafter Edginton, *Managing Lawyers' Risks*].
53. Charles W. Wolfram, *Former-Client Conflict,* 10 Geo. J. Legal Ethics 677, 708–09 (1997).
54. *Id.*
55. *See, e.g.,* Pickard Int'l v. Varion Assocs., 670 F. Supp. 1363 (1987).
56. *Id., but see* Unified Sewerage Agency v. Jelco Inc., 646 F.2d 1339 (9th Cir. 1981) (refusing to disqualify lawyer based on representation in unrelated matters of clients with adverse interests).
57. Rotunda, *Conflicts Problems, supra* note 51, at 664.

Chapter 5: Basic Conflicts Concerns 213

be the reason that some law firms now evaluate annual billings and terminate representations when annual payments do not justify retaining a client in light of possible future actions against the former client.[58] Such a termination seems especially likely when it is probable that competitors will sue a client and seek representation from the firm. As another means of controlling risks associated with the Hot Potato Rule, some firms include in their representation agreements a clause waiving conflicts for future litigation against the new client.[59] The ABA Commission on Ethics and Professional Responsibility validated such a waiver of a future conflict, noting that such a representation must meet the "requirements of a waiver of a contemporaneous conflict of interest,"[60] and must contemplate the particular conflict with enough clarity that the client's consent "can reasonably be viewed as having been fully informed when it was given."[61]

Disqualification

Courts will disqualify a lawyer from a representation if they determine that the lawyer dropped a current client to take a different client in an action against the first client. When a lawyer opposes a motion for disqualification that is based on a current or prior representation, she is likely to argue that the party asserting a conflict should be viewed as a former client rather than as a current client and that the subject matter of her representation is not substantially related to any prior representation she engaged in. The distinction between current and former representation is important, because the test for a conflict varies based on whether the party at issue (and often the party seeking the disqualification of the lawyer) is a former client or a current client. In the case of the current client or ongoing representation, the per se rule is that a lawyer may not represent a party adverse to an existing client.[62] The court considering a disqualification motion in the current client situation looks to the propriety of the conduct of the lawyer "measured not so much against the similarities in litigation, as against the duty of undivided loyalty which a lawyer owes to each of his clients."[63] By contrast, when a court judges a motion seeking to disqualify a lawyer based on a former representation, it

---

58. Blake Biles, Comments at panel for ABA Administrative Law Section, in New York, N.Y. (July 7, 2000),

59. *See* Richard W. Painter, *Advance Wavier of Conflicts*, 13 GEO. J. LEGAL ETHICS 289 (2000).

60. ABA Formal Op. 93-372 (1993).

61. *Id.*

62. *See* MODEL RULE 1.7 and discussion at 203–13.

63. Cinema 5, Ltd. v. Cinerama, Inc., 528 F.2d 1384, 1386 (2d Cir. 1976).

214   ISSUES OF LEGAL ETHICS IN THE PRACTICE OF ENVIRONMENTAL LAW

generally will disqualify a lawyer only if it determines that the current representation and the earlier matter are substantially related.[64]

In the *Strategem* case,[65] the court disqualified the plaintiff's lawyer on the ground that the lawyer was representing the defendant at the time it filed suit on behalf of the plaintiff. The court held that the lawyer's obligation to Strategem (the client that the lawyer sought to continue representing) did not trump the duty it owed to FSC (the opponent), even if the lawyer's relationship with Strategem predated the relationship with FSC.[66] Further, the court stated that the lawyer "may not undertake to represent two potentially adverse clients and then when the potential conflict becomes actuality, pick and choose between them."[67] The court emphasized that a lawyer may not "seek consent for dual representation and, when such is not forthcoming, jettison the uncooperative client."[68]

Environmental Example

The hot potato scenario is particularly likely to arise in environmental matters. For example, many corporate clients are involved in numerous Superfund actions, and many corporations are involved in each Superfund cleanup action and each cost recovery action based on prior cleanups. The likelihood that these corporations may wish to sue other major corporations for cost recovery is high. The problem is also likely to arise in real estate and asset transfers. For example, assume you are an environmental lawyer in private practice. One of your clients is a large, diversified company involved in a variety of production processes. Although this client is a large company, you are not the only lawyer working for the company, and the amount of work that comes to your practice is not significant. This corporate client parcels out work to many lawyers at other firms. Your billings to this client have decreased over the years. The annual billings to the client are now so low that your law firm might hesitate to accept the company as a new client if it knew that the annual billing would continue at this level. Another production company calls a partner in your firm and discusses in detail with her the possibility of bringing a cause of action based on your client's violations of its permit under the Clean Water Act. Your partner and the representative of the firm seeking representa-

---

64. *See* Silver Chrysler Plymouth, Inc. v. Chrysler Motors Corp., 518 F.2d 751 (2d Cir. 1975).

65. Strategem Dev. Corp. v. Heron, 756 F. Supp. 789, 794 (S.D.N.Y. (1991) (granting defendant's motion for disqualification of plaintiff's counsel on basis that plaintiff's counsel began preparations for suing defendant while it represented defendant).

66. *Id.*

67. *Id.* at 788.

68. *Id.*

tion discuss the basis for the cause of action, the discharge monitoring reports that the prospective client believes shows the client's violation and unfair trade practices. The prospective client conveys confidential information and strategy choices for the litigation. When your partner undertakes a conflicts check, he learns of your representation of the original client. While both you and your partner may wish to drop the original client and sue on behalf of the prospective client, such a choice is unethical on its face. It is an example of the hot potato scenario.[69]

Determining Adversity Standard (2002 Revision)

The 2002 revision to Model Rule 1.7 clarifies the standard for determining whether parties are sufficiently adverse to create a conflict of interest for a lawyer representing the parties. Comment 6 to Model Rule 1.7 substitutes the term "economically" for the term "generally," making clear that two parties who are merely economic competitors do not present a conflict under the rule based on this attribute.[70] As revised, comment 6 states:

> simultaneous representation in unrelated matters of clients whose interests are only economically adverse, such as representation of competing economic enterprises in unrelated litigation, does not ordinarily constitute a conflict of interest and thus may not require consent of the respective clients.[71]

Generally Adverse Interests: Environmental Example

Suppose, for example, a lawyer who currently represents an environmental consulting firm that works on Superfund sites is asked to undertake representation of another environmental consulting firm that does the same type of work. Model Rule 1.7 does not proscribe a representation when the clients are "only generally adverse" to each other. Unless the two companies have a dispute with each other, the fact that they are engaged in ordinary competition against each other does not appear to require the disqualification of the lawyer from representing both companies separately.[72] In an advisory opinion, the Philadelphia Bar Association's Professional Guidance Committee held that a lawyer may represent an insurance company and insureds of that company in

---

69. The scenario is drawn from materials for the ABA Administrative Law Section Meeting in New York (July 7, 2000).

70. MODEL RULE 1.7 cmt. 6 (2002).

71. MODEL RULE 1.7 cmt. 6 (2002).

72. Conflicts that arise in the organizational context are spoken to in greater depth in the discussion of MODEL RULE 1.13.

216 ISSUES OF LEGAL ETHICS IN THE PRACTICE OF ENVIRONMENTAL LAW

different lawsuits involving environmental insurance coverage.[73] Although the Committee held that the firm could go forward with the representation, it also emphasized that lawyers must disclose the representation to each client and obtain the consent of each. The Committee conditioned its holding on the assumption that the insureds and the insurer are not adverse in a specific lawsuit handled by the firm and that the clients consented to the representation in writing. Additionally, the Committee noted that a law firm representing these clients must screen lawyers in the firm from communicating client information in the cases. In reaching its decision, the Committee assumed that although the policy provisions of the insured may be identical, the parties are not connected by a contract of insurance.

The Model Code Approach

The Model Code appears to create a more difficult test for lawyers wishing to accept a representation. Under DR 5-105, the Code prohibits conflicting representations when a lawyer's judgment "in behalf of a client will be or is likely to be adversely affected by the employment or if the employment would be likely to involve him in representing differing interests."[74] The Code's formulation requires a lawyer to decline employment or to discontinue employment when a conflict occurs except as allowed under Section (C). The exception in Section (C) requires client consent and also requires that it be "obvious that [the lawyer] can adequately represent the interests of each client." This text, by its terms, seems to require lawyers to decline representation in a greater number of cases than is necessary under Model Rule 1.7. It creates an objective standard of "obviousness" that is not stated in terms of the lawyer's own subjective judgment. The Model Code provision has a contradictory ring. If the test for when a lawyer may accept a representation (in addition to client consent) is that it is "obvious" that the lawyer can adequately represent both clients, it is unclear why there is a conflict in this representation to begin with.[75] While the "obviousness" standard seems to set a higher hurdle than the "reasonable belief" standard of Model Rule 1.7, scholars have suggested that the two are essentially the same.[76]

---

73. Philadelphia Bar Ass'n Prof'l Guid. Comm. Guid. Op. 89-27, Mar. 1990 (1990 WL 303938).

74. MODEL CODE DR 5-105.

75. Professor Freedman argues that the standard of obviousness creates internal inconsistency that necessitates reading the "and" of DR 5-105 as "or" to allow two independent grounds for the representation going forward. MONROE H. FREEDMAN, UNDERSTANDING LAWYER'S ETHICS 173 (1990).

76. *See id.*, at 187–88.

Chapter 5: Basic Conflicts Concerns 217

The Restatement Approach

Like the Model Rules, the Restatement (Third) of Law Governing Lawyers treats conflicts in several separate provisions. Sections 128 through 135 provide applications of the principles of conflicts to various contexts. The Restatement unifies the analysis by merging the "materially affected" and "adversely affected" standards. Section 121 of the Restatement defines a conflict. "A conflict of interest is involved if there is a substantial risk that the lawyer's representation of the client would be materially and adversely affected by the lawyer's own interests or by the lawyer's duties to another current client, a former client, or a third person."[77] The basic prohibition against representing a client when a conflict of interest exists appears in Section 121 of the Restatement.[78] "Unless all affected clients and other necessary persons consent to the representation under the limitations and conditions provided in section 122, a lawyer may not represent a client if the representation would involve a conflict of interest."[79]

The Restatement generally gives effect to a client waiver or consent, allowing representations to go forward despite conflicts, except in the defined circumstances of nonwaivable conflicts.[80] Section 122 of the Restatement provides that a lawyer may not represent a client when the representation is prohibited by law, the representation would involve litigation of one client against another, or when it is "not reasonably likely that the lawyer will be able to provide adequate representation to one or more of the clients."[81] The Restatement relies on client autonomy as a justification for client consent despite a conflict. It draws the line against consent, however, where "joint representation would be objectively inadequate despite a client's voluntary and informed consent."[82] Professor Zacharias noted the conceptual difficulty of the standard: "If the adequacy of the representation is to be considered in deciding whether honoring client choice enhances autonomy, then the Restatement drafters must be saying that the autonomy in question is a 'good thing' only if it benefits, or might benefit, the client."[83]

---

77. *See* RESTATEMENT (THIRD) OF THE LAW GOVERNING LAWYERS § 121 (2000).
78. *Id.*
79. *Id.*
80. *Id.* at 122.
81. *Id.* at 122(2)(c).
82. *Id.* at 122 cmt. g(iv).
83. Fred C. Zacharias, *Waiving Conflicts of Interest*, 108 YALE L.J. 407, 413 (1998).

218 ISSUES OF LEGAL ETHICS IN THE PRACTICE OF ENVIRONMENTAL LAW

Multiple Representation

Environmental Matters

Multiple representation is common in environmental matters—especially in Superfund cases and toxic tort cases. Representing multiple parties can be an effective way to decrease costs and share information among parties with a common purpose.[84] The Comprehensive Environmental Response, Compensation and Liability Act (CERCLA) requires the cleanup of hazardous contamination in soils and water. In administering the Act, EPA sometimes names hundreds of companies and individuals as Potentially Responsible Parties (PRPs) for a given Superfund (CERCLA) site. These entities can be charged under the Act on the basis that they are or were owners or operators.[85] Additionally, they can be charged on the ground that they were transporters, and generators, or "arrangers," who contributed to the contamination at the site or are current owners or operators of the site.[86]

When EPA or a PRP names a large number of PRPs and calls upon them to pay for the cleanup, the stage is set for conflict problems. When these companies and individuals seek legal representation, they often contact lawyers who represent other PRPs at the site. Indeed, simply because of the high numbers of clients and the fairly limited number of lawyers qualified to conduct Superfund representations, conflict problems seem inevitable. This phenomenon is a matter of supply and demand: there are fewer environmental lawyers than PRPs. Accordingly, lawyers and clients must deal with the problem of conflicts in this area or some clients will be forced to go through negotiations and even litigation without legal representation. In Superfund negotiations, PRPs have significant interests in common, particularly during the early stages of the CERCLA process.

> The initial phases of a Superfund site cleanup generally provide the greatest unity of interest among the various PRPs. During this period, someone, either EPA, a state, or one or more of the PRPs, conducts a Remedial Investigation and Feasibility Study ("RIFS") to determine the nature and extent of the contamination, evaluate the risk to the public and environment, and identify potential methods to clean up or adequately manage the contamination. . . . Dur-

---

84. For a full treatment of conflicts at Superfund sites, *see* Andrew Kenefick et al., *Assessing Conflicts of Interest at Multi-party Superfund Sites: From First Involvement to Litigation,* 4 ENVTL. L. 721 (1998).

85. *See* 42 U.S.C. § 9607.

86. *Id.*

Chapter 5: Basic Conflicts Concerns 219

ing the investigation and initial cleanup phases the common interests of the PRP group usually outweigh any disputes among the individual parties.[87]

This fact argues for allowing multiple representation absent circumstances that indicate predominant adverse interests. Because of the principle of joint and several liability under CERCLA, PRPs are virtually always adverse to one another in the sense that the decrease in contribution by one PRP necessarily produces an increase in liability for other PRPs. Such adversity does not always result in a nonwaivable conflict, however. In some cases, the interest of all PRPs in reducing legal fees and sharing information and costs may outweigh the general adverseness of PRPs. When the parties are in different categories of contributors, it is unlikely that the parties' interest in reducing fees and sharing information will outweigh the adverse nature of the relationship of the parties, however. In other words, it is generally not advisable for a de minimis PRP and other full-fledged PRPs to share a lawyer.

Because each of the PRPs has similar interests in minimizing the costs and insuring the adequacy of any remedial action, there are often substantial economies of scale associated with the single law firm representing multiple clients in certain phases of the site investigation and remediation process. Nevertheless, the different PRPs also have antagonistic interests for some matters.[88]

At least one state bar committee has found it is permissible for lawyers in the same firm to represent separate parties who are seeking cost recovery from other PRPs in a Superfund cost recovery action.[89] Applying the standard of the disinterested lawyer, the Michigan Standing Committee on Professional and Judicial Ethics held that a lawyer may not represent clients from different PRP groups at a Superfund site. Settlements with the EPA in Superfund matters often include different levels or tiers to classify PRPs by how much of the percentage of cleanup costs the particular PRPs should contribute to the site. According to the Michigan Standing Committee, PRPs who are contributing at different levels on a formula for funding a remediation plan[90] have an

---

87. *See* Carol E. Dinkins & Lewis C. Sutherland, *Ethics in the Environmental and Toxic Tort Practice*, SB 73 ALI-ABA 319, 323 (1997) [hereinafter Dinkins & Sutherland].
88. *Id.* at 320.
89. State Bar of Michigan Standing Comm. on Prof'l and Judicial Ethics, Op. R-16, 1993 WL 566247 (Nov. 19, 1993).
90. *Id.*, at *6.

220   ISSUES OF LEGAL ETHICS IN THE PRACTICE OF ENVIRONMENTAL LAW

inherent conflict of interest.[91] The Committee noted, however, that in some circumstances PRPs may have antagonistic interests that will preclude joint representation, and it held that a law firm is barred from representing de minimis and other PRPs at the same site based on the law of conflicts.[92] In some circumstances, conflicts can disqualify a lawyer from representing one or more clients even though the clients consent to the representation.[93] For example, lawyers from the same firm may not represent clients who are opposed to each other in the same litigation even when the clients consent.

Because the EPA often names many corporate clients as PRPs in Superfund matters, the potential for conflicts is great. The number of corporations named in a letter calling PRPs to meet and discuss a Superfund site can reach into the hundreds. Even after a lawyer negotiates with named PRPs, obtaining consent or referring some prospective clients to other lawyers, a significant potential exists for discovering additional clients at the site during investigations. Searching for other corporations or individuals who may have liability at a site is a task many lawyers undertake early in a site investigation.[94] Lawyers who do factual investigations for other PRPs may be successful at uncovering other PRPs to share in the costs of a site. Such success can also produce new conflict problems for the lawyers representing the PRPs, however.

All PRPs liable under Section 107 of CERCLA for a particular site have the potential to be adverse parties even though one of them has agreed to perform the complete cleanup. Because the risk of Superfund liability persists even after a client has entered a consent decree with the government, the risk of a conflict relating to newly discovered PRPs also persists. In *United States v. Occidental Chemical Corp.*,[95] the Third Circuit held that EPA may issue a CERCLA Section 106 order requiring that a company participate in a cleanup despite the fact that the government has entered a consent decree with other PRPs to perform the full cleanup. Additionally, after completing a cleanup, a PRP has a right of contribution justifying a cost-recovery action against all other PRPs who have not secured contribution protection by settling with EPA.[96]

A lawyer faces a risk throughout a multiple representation situation that a party will become dissatisfied with the representation or with the results of a

---

91. *See supra* note 87.
92. *Id.*
93. Cinema 5, Ltd. v. Cinerama, Inc., 528 F.2d 1384, 1386–87 (2d Cir. 1976) (holding that where law firm of plaintiff's counsel was also representing defendant in a separate antitrust suit, counsel and partners must be disqualified).
94. *See* Dinkins & Sutherland, *supra* note 85, at 326.
95. 200 F.3d 143 (3d Cir. 1999).
96. *See* 42 U.S.C. § 9613.

settlement and challenge the ethics of the lawyer who provided the representation. While there are good reasons for joint representation from the perspectives of both plaintiffs and defendants, lawyers who represent more than one party in a case may face conflict problems. Accordingly, the best practice is to analyze and fulfill the requirements of the applicable rules on conflicts in a careful and deliberate fashion before accepting representation and before learning important confidential information about the potential clients.

Confidentiality

Generally, clients who are represented jointly (multiple representation) do not expect that the lawyer will keep the facts relevant to the common representation secret from either client.[97] The common law recognizes this point in the coclient rule.[98] Nevertheless, the cautious lawyer will set forth this understanding in a representation letter describing the joint representation. The letter or agreement should expressly state that communications made to the lawyer will not be kept secret from the coclient. Because of the problems of confidentiality, many lawyers now require that clients expressly consent in writing to a joint representation and to sharing all information relevant to the subject matter of the representation with other jointly represented parties.[99]

Preserving Client Confidentiality

In consulting with clients about conflicts, the lawyer must preserve the confidentiality of each of the clients, whether the client information at risk is that of a current, former, or prospective client. It may be impossible to give a client the disclosure necessary to allow him to make an informed judgment regarding whether a conflict is significant. In such a circumstance, the lawyer cannot reveal the confidential information unless the client whose confidences are involved consents to the disclosure for the purpose of allowing the other potential client to assess the possibility of a conflict of interest. If the client does not consent to the disclosure, the lawyer must not reveal the information to the potential client. If the prospective client needs to know this information to make an informed judgment, then informed consent is impossible; and, accordingly, because the lawyer cannot obtain informed consent of the potential client without violating the duty of confidentiality to the other client, the

---

97. *See* WOLFRAM, *supra* note 7, § 6.4.8, at 274.

98. *Id.*

99. *See generally* Christopher Q. King, *A Checklist for the Compliance Officer or In-house Counsel Managing Customer-Broker Arbitration and Litigation, in* SECURITIES ARBITRATION 1997, 377, 380 (PLI Corporate Law and Practice Course Handbook Series No. B4-7195, 1997).

222 ISSUES OF LEGAL ETHICS IN THE PRACTICE OF ENVIRONMENTAL LAW

lawyer must decline the proffered representation. In such a case, the lawyer's representation is impossible because one representation poses a material limitation on the lawyer's ability to represent the other client's interests.

The Use of a Conflict to Seek Disqualification

Although the Model Rules expressly state that they do not intend to create or increase "any substantive legal duty of lawyers or the extra-disciplinary consequences of violating such duty,"[100] lawyers increasingly use the conflict rules substantively as a basis for a motion to disqualify opposing counsel.[101] Some commentators have suggested that lawyers are using disqualification motions abusively.[102] Because assessment of the possibility of future conflicts is often difficult, the most cautious course for the lawyer considering representation involving a possible conflict is to decline the proffered representation or withdraw from representing both clients, particularly if he has learned confidential information about either client relating to the representation that cannot be revealed to the other.[103] It is understandable that lawyers generally want to accept a proffered representation. The desire of the lawyer in the vast majority of cases is to analyze the conflict rules and find no conflict or a waivable conflict because the lawyer needs additional clients to maintain a viable practice. The counterbalance in this analysis is the standard of the disinterested lawyer that the lawyer must apply as well as the possibility of disqualification and consequent forfeiture of fees in the event that a court later finds a conflict. The opposing party may move for disqualification of the lawyer who refuses to withdraw from a case involving a conflict of interest.[104] When a lawyer is ordered to withdraw from a case, it is unlikely that he will be able to collect any fees related to the representa-

---

100. MODEL RULES Scope note.

101. FREEDMAN, *supra* note 73, at 183.

102. *See e.g.*, Dorothy M. Gibbons-White, *Migratory Lawyers in Private Practice: Should California Approve the Use of Ethical Walls?*, 33 LOY. L.A. L. REV. 161 (1999).

103. *See* MODEL RULE 1.16(a)(1). A representation will result in a conflict when it will, in the terms of MODEL RULE 1.16(a)(1), "result in violation of the Rules of Professional Conduct." Accepting a representation that results in a conflict of interest violates MODEL RULE 1.7 or MODEL RULE 1.9.

104. In *Brennan's, Inc. v. Brennan's Restaurants, Inc.*, applying the MODEL CODE OF PROF'L RESPONSIBILITY Canon 4, EC4-4, EC4-5, the Court of Appeals for the Fifth Circuit held that a lawyer was properly barred from representing a corporate defendant on the ground of conflict of interest when the lawyer had represented both plaintiff and defendant on earlier matters substantially related to the action. Brennan's, Inc. v. Brennan's Rests., Inc., 590 F.2d 168 (5th Cir. 1979).

tion. Indeed, the court may expressly order the disqualified lawyer to refund fees paid in the course of the representation.

Consequences and Sanctions

Lawyers sometimes use the offensive measure of motions to disqualify opposing counsel based on a conflict. Additionally, former clients may sue for malpractice, charging that the lawyer's conflict of interest resulted in malpractice and injury to the plaintiff.[105] Malpractice settlements and awards have risen dramatically in recent years, often involving claims of conflicts of interest.[106] The Attorneys' Liability Assurance Society, Inc. (ALAS) identifies "alleged representation of multiple parties" as "the most common conflict problem in business transactions."[107] According to ALAS, it has paid hundreds of millions of dollars to settle conflict of interest claims in its capacity as the insurer of lawyers charged with malpractice.[108]

The seriousness of knowingly representing a client despite a conflict should be apparent from the above discussion. Further evidence of the seriousness of conflicts is found in the ABA Standards for Imposing Lawyer Sanctions, which recommend disbarment for such conduct.[109] The strength of this sanction underscores the importance of the principle against representing adverse parties. Numerous adverse consequences flow from violations of the prohibition against representing clients in the face of a conflict of interest. Possible consequences include disqualification from a particular representation, suspension, disbarment, delay for the client's case, disgorgement of fees, malpractice liability for breach of a fiduciary duty, and the imposition of fees and expenses in favor of the opponent.[110] Courts may also reverse a case in which a lawyer represented a client despite a conflict.[111] Indeed, some courts have

---

105. Roy Simon, *Conflicts of Interests and Legal Malpractice*, Pract. Law Inst. PLI Order No. H0-003Q [hereinafter Simon].

106. *See* www.capitalconsultantsllc.com (visited Mar. 28, 2003) for listing of multimillion-dollar awards in a case involving malpractice claims against several large law firms.

107. Brian J. Redding, Conflicts of Interest in Business Transactions: A Serious Problem That Is Getting Worse, ABA Section of Environment, Energy, and Resources, 8th Section Fall Meeting (Sept. 20–24, 2000).

108. *Id.*

109. *See* ABA Standards for Imposing Lawyer Sanctions § 4.3.

110. *See* Simon, *supra* note 103, at 17.

111. *See* U.S. v. Tatum, 943 F.2d 370 (4th Cir. 1991) (holding that lawyer who assists at trial and represents the client, the client's partner, and his own partner in the law firm is ineffective counsel for the client, resulting in a reversal and remand of the case).

224 ISSUES OF LEGAL ETHICS IN THE PRACTICE OF ENVIRONMENTAL LAW

awarded damages for emotional distress as part of an award for malpractice against lawyers.[112]

Avoiding Conflicts

Given the broad sweep of the rule, it seems inevitable that, over time, conflicts will arise for most lawyers. Lawyers and firms generate defensive measures to guard against conflicts. Firms employ computer programs to compare new client names and adverse party names to lists of existing and former clients. Such computer searches are merely the first step of the time-consuming process of conflicts checks. Firms undertake a case-by-case review of the parties identified by the computer search. This task can require a significant amount of time on the part of employees and lawyers. After identifying a conflict, lawyers either decline the proffered employment or seek a waiver from the existing client to allow the representation of the new client.

Curative Measures

Client Consent

Representation of multiple parties in environmental matters is often appropriate and consensual.[113] For example, a New Jersey Supreme Court Advisory Committee on Professional Ethics considered and validated a defense representation for multiple municipal clients in a case in which the plaintiffs named 450 defendants in the environmental tort suit. Plaintiffs alleged that waste from an area landfill migrated, causing personal injury and property damage to the numerous plaintiffs. The lawyer who sought an opinion from the Committee was a member of a firm that had received requests for representation from insurance carriers and several uninsured cities named as defendants.[114] The New Jersey Committee viewed joint representation of clients with potentially differing interests as permissible if the clients present a "substantial identity of interests" between the clients represented "in terms of defending

---

112. *See, e.g.,* Wagenmann v. Adams, 829 F.2d 196 (1st Cir. 1987) (allowing damages for emotional distress in circumstances in which client was forced to spend a night in a mental hospital as a result of the lawyer's malpractice); Lawson v. Nugent, 702 F. Supp. 91 (D.N.J. 1988) (basing ruling on client's loss of liberty resulting from malpractice).

113. *See, e.g.,* New Jersey Supreme Court Advisory Comm. on Prof'l Ethics, Conduct of Interest: Multiple Representation of Public Entities in Environmental Damage Suit, Op. 588 (July 24, 1986) *available at* 1986 WL 175254.

114. *Id.*

Chapter 5: Basic Conflicts Concerns 225

claims brought against all defendants."[115] The court also required that "elements of mutuality must preponderate over the elements of incompatibility to justify the representation."[116]

Often, the existence of a conflict may be cured by the consent of the clients involved. In such cases, the representation is allowed notwithstanding the conflict. As the discussion of Model Rule 1.7 indicates, the rule often allows a lawyer to go forward with a representation despite an apparent conflict. Client consent cures a conflict under Rule 1.7 when the lawyer reasonably believes that the new representation will not adversely affect an existing representation and that the new representation will not be adversely limited.[117] The lawyer should get this consent from all clients in a signed writing. The representation should be barred despite consent only when a conflict is so pronounced that it is not reasonable to believe that the lawyer can adequately represent the interests of the clients involved. Ethics rules allowing clients to consent to conflicts evince respect for the autonomy and free will of clients.[118] Professor Hazard notes that strong policies favor client selection of counsel. "Although courts are quick to disapprove 'unconsented' concurrent representation, they are reluctant to overrule client consent to the representation of conflicting interests. Respect for client consent recognizes the importance of a client's right to select counsel of her own choosing."[119] Moreover, the concept of consent is consistent with other areas of the law in which waivers are given legal effect despite potentially adverse consequences to the party waiving the right. The Restatement approach gives effect to client consent as a cure to a conflict of interest in most cases. The Model Code approach also requires client consent but seems to limit the scope of representations subject to cure by the requirement that it be obvious the lawyer can represent all clients adequately.

The Model Rules allow a representation to go forward when the clients consent and the lawyer reasonably believes that the potential for conflict will not be a disadvantage to either client.[120] The lawyer's belief is judged by the

---

115. *Id.*, In the Matter of Petition for Review of Op. 552 of Advisory Comm. on Prof'l Ethics, 507 A.2d 233, 238 (N.J. 1986).

116. *Id.*

117. *See* MODEL RULE 1.7.

118. MONROE H. FREEDMAN & ABBE SMITH, UNDERSTANDING LAWYERS' ETHICS 267 (2d ed. 2002).

119. HAZARD ET AL., THE LAW AND ETHICS OF LAWYERING at 580–81 (citing In the Matter of Op. 552 of Advisory Comm. on Prof'l Ethics, 507 A.2d 233, 239 n.3 (N.J. 1986)).

120. *See, e.g., Vermont Committee Changes Course, Allows Representation of Lender, Borrower*, 71 U.S. L. WK. 2038 (July 16, 2002) (Vermont Bar Ass'n Comm. on Prof'l

standard of a "disinterested lawyer."[121] Thus, a representation should not go forward according to the Model Rules if "the lawyer concludes that the consent is tactically unwise."[122] The inquiry under the Model Rules concerning the belief of the lawyer varies depending on the interest protected. In the first case considered (in which the representation of a new client "will be directly adverse to another client"), the curative belief required of the lawyer is that the new representation "will not adversely affect the relationship" with the old client.[123] Considering the case in which the lawyer must decline or withdraw makes the statement more straightforward. If the lawyer sees that the representation will "adversely affect" her relationship with another client, she must not accept the representation. Similarly, Model Rule 1.7(b) allows a representation to go forward that "may be materially limited" when the lawyer reasonably believes that "the representation with the [new] client will not be adversely affected." Stating the case in the negative, the lawyer must not accept the new representation if she believes or should believe that the new representation will be "adversely affected"[124] by other interests.

Client Consent (2002 Revision)

The ABA Revised Model Rules adopted in February 2002 incorporate the standard of informed consent.[125] In doing so, the revised rules rejected the 1983 standard of "consent after consultation."[126] The 2002 Revision notes the protections afforded by the concept of consent to a conflict of interest. "Consentability is typically determined by considering whether the interests of the clients will be adequately protected if the clients are permitted to give their informed consent to representation burdened by a conflict of interest. Thus, under paragraph (b)(1) [to Model Rule 1.7], representation is prohib-

---

Responsibility, Op. 2001-02) (rejecting previous standard that precluded simultaneous representation of lender and borrower-buyer involved in the same transaction, but conditioning representation on client consent to the representation and reasonable belief by lawyer that such representation will not adversely affect the client).

121. *See* MODEL RULE 1.7 cmt. 5; *see also* Clay v. Doherty, 608 F. Supp. 295, 302 (N.D. Ill. 1985); WOLFRAM, *supra* note 7, at § 7.2.3.

122. Fred C. Zacharias, *Waiving Conflicts of Interest*, 108 YALE L.J. 407, 410 (1998) hereinafter Zacharias].

123. *See* MODEL RULE 1.7(a). MODEL RULE 1.7(a) allows a directly adverse representation when "the lawyer reasonably believes the [new] representation will not adversely affect the relationship with the other [old] client."

124. Zacharias, *supra* note 120, at 411.

125. MODEL RULE 1.0(e) (2002).

126. *See, e.g.,* MODEL RULE 1.6(a), MODEL RULE 1.7(a)(2).

Chapter 5: Basic Conflicts Concerns   227

ited if in the circumstances the lawyer cannot reasonably conclude that the lawyer will be able to provide competent and diligent representation."[127]

The revision requires that the client's consent to conflicts be "confirmed in writing." This language does not, however, require that the client produce or sign the writing. It is apparently permissible for the lawyer to create the writing confirming the consent to a conflict. The terminology section defines "confirmed in writing" as "used in reference to the informed consent of a person, denotes informed consent that is given in writing by the person or a writing that a lawyer promptly transmits to the person confirming an oral informed consent."[128] Additionally, the Commission substituted the term "informed consent" for the term "consent after consultation" used in the consent provision in the 1983 rules.[129] The terminology section defines informed consent as "agreement by a person to a proposed course of conduct after the lawyer has communicated adequate information and explanation about the material risks of and reasonably available alternatives to the proposed course of conduct."[130] The informed consent standard presents an improvement in the statement of the rule, since it is a well-established legal principle. The revision also dispenses with a possible argument that the standard of "consent after consultation" presents a timing standard rather than requiring adequate communication for client understanding of possible adverse effects of the representation.

Although some conflicts rules require a writing confirming the client's consent or representation, most do not require that the client sign the writing. An exception to this approach is found in the rule on undertaking a business transaction with a client and settlement. Revised Model Rule 1.8(a) creates an exception to the prohibition against a lawyer entering a business transaction with a client. To come within the exception, a lawyer must show that the transaction involved is fair and reasonable, fully disclosed in a writing that is reasonably understandable.[131] The rule requires that the lawyer advise the client in writing of the desirability of obtaining advice of independent legal counsel concerning the transaction[132] it also requires the lawyer to obtain informed consent of a client in a writing "signed by the client."[133] Similarly, Model Rule 1.8(g), as revised, requires that the lawyer obtain

---

127. MODEL RULE 1.7 cmt. 15 (2002), *citing* RULE 1.1 (competence) and RULE 1.3 (diligence).

128. REV. MODEL RULE 1.0(b).

129. *See* http://www.abanet.org/cpr/ethics2k.html (visited Mar. 28, 2003).

130. REV. MODEL RULE 1.0(e).

131. MODEL RULE 1.8(a)(1) (2002).

132. *Id*. at 1.8(a)(2).

133. MODEL RULE 1.8(a)(3) (2002).

228 ISSUES OF LEGAL ETHICS IN THE PRACTICE OF ENVIRONMENTAL LAW

informed consent "in a writing signed by the client" in making an aggregate settlement.[134]

Revoking Consent (2002 Revision)

A comment to the 2002 revision of Model Rule 1.7 makes clear that a client may revoke consent to allow representation that would constitute a conflict.[135] Comment 21 to Revised Rule 1.7 provides:

> A client who has given consent to a conflict may revoke the consent and, like any other client, may terminate the lawyer's representation at any time. Whether revoking consent to the client's own representation precludes the lawyer from continuing to represent other clients depends on the circumstances, including the nature of the conflict, whether the client revoked consent because of a material change in circumstances, the reasonable expectations of the other client and whether material detriment to the other clients or the lawyer would result.[136]

Close Cases and Consent: Environmental Example

In a 1986 opinion allowing representation of multiple entities by a lawyer, the Supreme Court of New Jersey noted that "the appropriate rule for dealing with potential conflicts of interest . . . must be grounded upon common sense, experience and realism."[137] The court embraced a rule allowing "joint representation of clients with potentially differing interests" as long as there is a "substantial identity of interests between them in terms of defending claims that have been brought against all defendants."[138] The New Jersey Supreme Court Advisory Committee on Professional Ethics addressed this issue in a case in which plaintiffs brought suit against hundreds of defendants on the basis that waste from a landfill used by defendants "migrated and caused personal and property damage" to the plaintiffs.[139] The Advisory Committee relied on the New Jersey Supreme Court opinion to decide that a lawyer's

---

134. MODEL RULE 1.8 (g) (2002).
135. MODEL RULE 1.7 cmt. 21 (2002).
136. *Id.*
137. *See supra* note 111, *available at* 1986 WL 175254, *quoting* N.J. S.C. Op. 552.
138. *Id.*
139. *Supra* note 111.

Chapter 5: Basic Conflicts Concerns   229

representation of several municipalities in a multiparty environmental tort suit did not offend the conflict of interest rules.[140]

Nonwaivable Conflicts

The client and lawyer can cure many conflict problems if the client fully understands the situation and consents to the representation despite the conflict.[141] At least one scholar argues that client consent should be sufficient to cure any conflict, provided that the consent is voluntarily given and based on full information about the conflict at issue.[142] Others contend for an objective standard limiting the client's power to waive a conflict.[143]

In most cases, clients may consent to a representation that presents a conflict, effectively waiving the conflict. In some circumstances, however, a representation should not proceed even when the affected clients consent. In such cases, the conflict presented is not waivable by the clients. For example, in *Richards v. Commission for Lawyer Discipline*, the court held that the lawyer violated professional ethics rules in representing both the husband and wife in divorce proceedings.[144] Commentators sometimes speak of "nonconsentable" or "nonwaivable" conflicts,[145] meaning that the lawyer should decline an offer of representation despite the fact that all the clients concerned consent to the representation. A comment to Model Rule 1.7 recognizes the power of a client "to consent to representation notwithstanding a conflict."[146] However, the comment also notes that when a "disinterested lawyer would conclude that the client should not agree to the representation under the circumstances, the lawyer involved cannot properly ask for such agreement or provide representation on the basis of the client's consent."[147] Thus, the Model Rules regard some conflicts as nonwaivable or nonconsentable. The Restatement (Third) of the

---

140. *Id.*
141. MODEL RULE 1.7(a) and (b). *See also* Unified Sewerage Agency v. Jelco Inc., 646 F.2d 1339, 1350 (9th Cir. 1981) (holding that conflict was nonconsentable). *In re* Mercer, 652 P.2d 130 (1982) (holding that lawyer could not continue in blatant conflict situation despite alleged fully informed and free consent of the client).
142. FREEDMAN, *supra* note 73, at 182–83.
143. Zacharias, *supra* note 120, at 412–14.
144. 35 S.W.3d 243 (Tex. App. 2000).
145. *See* WOLFRAM, *supra* note 7, § 7.2.3. *See also* Unified Sewerage Agency v. Jelco Inc., 646 F.2d 1339 (9th Cir. 1981) (refusing to disqualify lawyer and holding that Code of Professional Responsibility does not create per se rule against dual representation in unrelated matters of clients with adverse interests).
146. *See* MODEL RULE 1.7 cmt. 5.
147. *Id.*

230   ISSUES OF LEGAL ETHICS IN THE PRACTICE OF ENVIRONMENTAL LAW

Law Governing Lawyers allows the affected clients to give informed consent that waives a conflict of interest in a broader set of circumstances.[148] Additionally, the Restatement gives more substance to "informed consent" by explaining that the concept requires that the client "have reasonably adequate information about the material risks of such representation to that client or former client."[149] Even assuming informed consent, however, the provision prohibits representation if a "client will assert a claim against the other in the same litigation" or circumstances make it "not reasonably likely that the lawyer will be able to provide adequate representation" to any client.[150] The circumstances that may compel this result are far from clear. For example, in the case of *In re Mercer*,[151] the court disbarred a lawyer because he entered into a business transaction with a client that proved unfavorable to the client. Despite the fact that the client consented and was allegedly fully informed of the risks, the court found the conflict to be so blatant that the consent of the client was insufficient to cure the conflict and disbarred the lawyer for his conduct.[152]

The case of *In re Thayer* presents an extreme example of a nonwaivable conflict.[153] In this case, the Indiana Supreme Court suspended a lawyer's license based on a finding that the lawyer violated ethics rules of the jurisdiction. The lawyer involved in this case was arrested after his girlfriend accused him of battering her. Two days after his release, he was contacted by an officer trying to speak with the girlfriend. The respondent told the officer that he and another lawyer were her counsel and that she refused to speak. The Indiana Supreme Court agreed with the trial court's holding that the lawyer's conduct violated Indiana Rule 1.7(b).[154] The court found that this phone conversation evidenced an implied attorney-client relationship between the respondent and the girlfriend.[155] Furthermore, the court held that because the client had lodged criminal charges against the lawyer, a representation of this client was an impermissible conflict of interest.[156] Less dramatic fact situations may also present conflicts that cannot be cured by waiver.

---

148. *See* RESTATEMENT (THIRD) OF THE LAW GOVERNING LAWYERS § 122 (2000).
149. *See* RESTATEMENT (THIRD) OF THE LAW GOVERNING LAWYERS § 122(1) (2000).
150. *See* RESTATEMENT (THIRD) OF THE LAW GOVERNING LAWYERS § 122(2) (2000).
151. *In re* Mercer, 652 P.2d 130 (Ariz. 1982) (holding that lawyer could not function in a blatant conflict of interest situation despite the alleged fully informed and free consent of the client).
152. *Id.*
153. 745 N.E.2d 207 (Ind. 2001).
154. *Id.* at 210.
155. *Id.*
156. *Id.*

Chapter 5: Basic Conflicts Concerns 231

In *Abbott v. Kidder Peabody & Co.*[157] the district court held that a law firm was disqualified from representing a large group of plaintiffs in a securities lawsuit brought by over 200 individual investors. The representation agreement between the plaintiffs and the firm allowed the representation and settlement to be guided by a "steering committee" rather than the individual clients. The client group consisted of 200 separate clients, each with an individual suit against the defendant. The defendant attempted to settle with the clients in small groups and then individually, but the plaintiffs refused to settle individually. The court disqualified the firm on the basis that it gave a minority of the clients the ability to direct the case and decide settlement in violation of Model Rule 1.7.[158]

Some jurisdictions have adopted a more laissez-faire system. For example, California created a bright-line rule that recognizes the absolute right of clients to waive conflicts as long as the waiver is informed and freely given.[159] Even in jurisdictions having a bright-line rule, courts have the inherent power to overturn a contractual provision giving client consent when the court finds the provision contravenes public policy.

Nonwaivable Conflicts (2002 Revision)

Both the text of the 2002 Revised Model Rule 1.7 and new comments to the rule make clear that some conflicts cannot be waived by the clients, either because the representation is prohibited by law or such a representation is contrary to institutional interests of the profession.[160] The text of the rule provides:

> Notwithstanding the existence of a concurrent conflict of interest under paragraph (a), a lawyer may represent a client if:
> (1) the lawyer reasonably believes that the lawyer will be able to provide competent and diligent representation to each affected client;
> (2) the representation is not prohibited by law;
> (3) the representation does not involve the assertion of a claim by one client against another client represented by the lawyer in the same litigation or other proceeding before a tribunal; and
> (4) each affected client gives informed consent, confirmed in writing.[161]

---

157. Abbott v. Kidder Peabody & Co., Inc., 42 F. Supp. 2d 1046 (D. Colo. 1999).
158. *Id.*
159. CAL. RULES OF PROF'L CONDUCT R. 3-310(C) (1992).
160. MODEL RULE 1.7 cmt. 16, 17 (2002).
161. MODEL RULE 1.7(b) (2002).

The permission to represent clients despite a concurrent conflict rests on meeting all four of the requirements noted. The first of these requirements sets forth the reasonable belief standard relating to the lawyer's assessment of the situation and his ability to represent each client fully. The second requirement relates to conflicts that are not waivable as a matter of law. The third requirement notes the prohibition against representing clients that are opponents in the same litigation based on the institutional interests of the profession and the justice system. Finally, the fourth requirement indicates the need for client consent. Unless each of these four tests is met, the conflicting representation is prohibited.

Comment 14 to Revised Model Rule 1.7 notes the nonconsentable nature of some conflicts. "Ordinarily, clients may consent to representation notwithstanding a conflict. However, some conflicts are nonconsentable, meaning that the lawyer involved cannot properly ask for such agreement or provide representation on the basis of the client's consent. When the lawyer is representing more than one client, the question of consentability must be resolved as to each client."[162] Comment 23 to Revised Model Rule 1.7 notes that conflicts are often waivable in the context of civil litigation. "[C]ommon representation of persons having similar interests in civil litigation is proper if the requirements of paragraph (b) are met."[163] It also makes the point that representing opponents in the same matter is a nonconsentable conflict.[164]

Comment 19 to Model Rule 1.7 addresses the situation in which one client refuses to consent to disclosure of information relating to his case to another potential client. The comment concludes that "the lawyer cannot properly ask" a prospective client to consent to a representation when a client in a related matter "refuses to consent to the disclosure" that is necessary for the prospective client to provide informed consent.[165]

Curative Measures

Declining Representation

When an unresolved or nonconsentable conflict arises, a lawyer who is representing multiple parties must withdraw from representing any of the clients unless otherwise agreed. For this reason, the prudent practice for a lawyer

---

162. MODEL RULE 1.7 cmt. 14 (2002). Comment 6 to MODEL RULE 1.10 makes this point with regard to imputed conflicts.
163. MODEL RULE 1.7 cmt. 23 (2002).
164. *See* MODEL RULE 1.7 cmt. 23 (2002). ("Paragraph (b)(3) prohibits representation of opposing parties in the same litigation, regardless of the clients' consent.")
165. MODEL RULE 1.7 cmt. 19 (2002).

who is uncertain about whether a representation is appropriate under Rule 1.7 is to decline the representation. In many circumstances, a lawyer may be confident that a new representation does not ethically require client consent because he believes that the representation "will not adversely affect" the clients or materially limit the representation of either an old or new client. Even when a lawyer reasonably believes that a representation "will not adversely affect" another client or the new client, it may be advisable to obtain the consent of clients with any relationship to the new client. Obtaining client consent may be wise for a variety of reasons.[166] For example, the lawyer should recognize that even if she is confident in her judgment, other reasonable minds could draw a different conclusion. Obtaining client consent in cases in which the consent arguably is not required by the rule serves as insurance against a difference of opinion on this point by others, maximizing the chance that the lawyer would be able to withstand a motion to disqualify him from the representation. Model Rule 1.4 seems to provide an independent reason for reporting a new representation to a client. This rule requires lawyers to communicate with clients to keep them "reasonably informed about the status of a matter," to "comply with reasonable requests for information," and to explain the matter sufficiently to allow the client "to make informed decisions regarding the representation."[167]

The 2002 revision to Model Rule 1.4 added detail to the obligation to keep a client informed about the status of a matter. It added five specific points relating to this duty, including informing a client of any decision or circumstance that relates to the client's informed consent, consulting with a client about the means to achieve the objectives of the representation, keeping the client informed, complying with reasonable requests for information, and consulting about relevant limitations when the lawyer "knows that the client expects assistance not permitted by the Rules of Professional Conduct or the law."[168] The 2002 Revised ABA Model Rules provide the example of a negotiation for settlement as a way of explaining the lawyer's duty to provide sufficient information to his client.[169]

Similarly, the Restatement (Second) of Agency notes that agents are obligated to communicate relevant information to their principals. Lawyers, as agents of their clients, are subject to the rule. Section 381 states that: "Unless

---

166. *See* ABA Formal Op. 95-390 (noting lawyer not barred from representing party adverse to client's corporate affiliates unless affiliate is client or understanding between lawyer and client excludes such representation).

167. MODEL RULE 1.4(a).

168. REV. MODEL RULE 1.4 (a)(1)-(5) (2002).

169. MODEL RULE 1.4 cmt. 5.

234 ISSUES OF LEGAL ETHICS IN THE PRACTICE OF ENVIRONMENTAL LAW

otherwise agreed, an agent is subject to a duty to use reasonable efforts to give his principal information which is relevant to affairs entrusted to him and which, as the agent has notice, the principal would desire to have and which can be communicated without violating a superior duty to a third person."[170] Arguably, accepting a new client who has some relationship to the old client is information that the lawyer should report to the old client under both of these standards.

Additionally, an important real-world consideration is the fact that failing to consult an existing client about a prospective representation may offend the existing client. Such a circumstance may affect or destroy the good will of the existing client. In the case of joint representation in a transaction, a client who is later dissatisfied with the deal may sue the lawyer as well as his business partner, alleging malpractice and ethics violations and pointing to the lawyer's failure to obtain his consent as evidence of wrongdoing.

The Consultation Requirement

The 1983 version of Model Rule 1.7 is the basis for most state rules. The language of this rule qualifies client consent with the phrase "after consultation."[171] The terminology section of the Model Rules defines "consultation" as "communication of information reasonably sufficient to permit the client to appreciate the significance of the matter in question."[172] A reasonable reading of "consultation" in the context of adverse representation requires that the lawyer provide the client with information necessary to make an informed judgment about the representation and its risks to the client. In other words, the consent of clients required under Model Rule 1.7 should comport with the concept of "informed consent."[173] Reading the language "after consultation" to require consultation without considering the substance of the consultation would render the requirement meaningless. The cautious lawyer will ensure a meaningful consultation with the client by fully disclosing actual and potential conflicts and possible consequences to the client.[174]

Environmental Matters: Need for Meaningful Disclosure

A client may want to hire a particular lawyer because of her experience and

---

170. RESTATEMENT (SECOND) OF AGENCY § 381 (1957).

171. MODEL RULE 1.7(a)(2).

172. MODEL RULES Terminology ¶ 2.

173. The 2002 revision clarifies this point by using the term "informed consent." *See* http://www.abanet.org/cpr/ethics2k.html (visited Mar. 28, 2003).

174. *See* Patrick E. Donovan, *Serving Multiple Masters: Confronting the Conflicting Interests That Arise in Superfund Disputes*, 17 B.C. ENVTL. AFF. L. REV. 371 (1990).

Chapter 5: Basic Conflicts Concerns 235

knowledge, even though she represents other parties in a particular matter. The emphasis or "spin" that some lawyers put on the option of multiple representation may, however, cloud the issue facing clients and may mislead some clients who are deciding whether to consent to a conflict. For example, in Superfund cases, some lawyers circulate to potential clients (or brag about) the fact that they have been retained by other PRPs at a site, using the existing representations as evidence of the lawyer's skills in the area. Rather than identifying and discussing the possibility of conflicts as a problem, the lawyer using this tactic presents the representation of other parties as a reason the new client should hire him. While this practice discloses the existence of other representations in the same matter, it is questionable whether this disclosure fulfills the mandate of Model Rule 1.7. Far from focusing the client's attention on the problematic nature of the issue at hand or analyzing the potential adverse effect of the multiple representation on the client, the lawyer engaging in this practice seeks to enhance his reputation and to bolster his apparent competence in this area of law. While the lawyer may encounter success in attracting new clients with this tactic, the new clients come with a risk. The lawyer is vulnerable to a claim of conflict of interest. Additionally, the lawyer is vulnerable to claims of malpractice for failure to represent the client fully if an active conflict develops between the clients.

Written Disclosure

Disclosing any conflict and its potential consequences to the client is a valuable cautionary measure. Providing full information about a conflict to all concerned potential or current clients and discussing the potential consequences of the conflict will minimize the potential for a client to raise a conflict issue later. Of course, it is still possible for opposing counsel to raise this issue in a disqualification motion. The 2002 revision to Model Rule 1.7 requires that client consent be confirmed in writing. It does not require that the client sign the writing, however. Accordingly, a letter or other document created by the lawyer and transmitted to the client may be sufficient evidence to meet the standard.

Written Consent

Most state rules and the Model Rules on conflicts do not require that clients sign a written document to memorialize their consent to a representation that presents a conflict or potential conflict. Cautious lawyers obtain a writing memorializing the client's consent. Having a signed writing gives the lawyer a record and creates evidence of the scope and terms of the agreement as well as evidence that the lawyer gave full disclosure of the conflict to the client and that the client consented to the representation despite the conflict.

Terminating Clients

Some firms (including some well known for environmental expertise) routinely cull their client list to terminate representations that do not involve current legal work. Whether such a practice is ethical is open to debate. The measure seems contrary to the general duty of loyalty because it conditions loyalty on continued expenditures for legal fees and smacks of loyalty based on the economic bottom line.[175] On the other hand, law firms have a legitimate interest in being able to represent new clients to sustain a practice. Moreover, terminating a representation that has accomplished the particular purpose it was undertaken to achieve does not offend ethics rules. In a representation for a single purpose, the representation terminates when that purpose is accomplished. Finding it unethical for firms to terminate representations would seem to allow large clients effectively to limit or foreclose expert representation to opponents by parceling out its work to all or most of the law firms qualified in a given area of law. A lawyer who would cut his ties with existing clients on the chance that a future client may wish to sue that client might act strategically in other ways.[176] Arguably, the requirement of Model Rule 1.9(a) that a lawyer obtain consent from former clients adequately protects against such strategic action.

Withdrawal from Representation

The typical cure for a conflict of interest is withdrawal by the lawyer when the clients do not consent to the representation after receiving full information about the scope and possible consequences of the conflict. The 2002 revision to Model Rule 1.7 makes clear that withdrawal is the ordinary remedy for a conflict that arises after a representation has been established. "If a conflict arises after representation has been undertaken, the lawyer *ordinarily must* withdraw from the representation, *unless the lawyer has obtained the informed consent of the client under the conditions of paragraph (b).*"[177]

---

175. A similar problem arises when a lawyer determines he or she must withdraw from some representations because of lack of time to provide service to all his or her clients. Professor Tuchler questions the effectiveness of the MODEL RULES regarding withdrawal. *See* Dennis J. Tuchler, *Unavoidable Conflicts of Interest and the Duty of Loyalty*, 44 St. Louis U. L.J. 1025 (arguing withdrawal from representation on the basis of too much work violates the duty of loyalty to the client referred to another under MODEL RULE 1.7 "since decision to stop work on one matter for the benefit of others (and help the client find new counsel) could be seen as a betrayal of the client whose matter is dismissed").

176. *See generally* WOLFRAM, *supra* note 7, at 361–63.

177. MODEL RULE 1.7 cmt. 4 (2002) (italics added to indicate new language).

Chapter 5: Basic Conflicts Concerns 237

Limiting Representation

In some cases, a limitation of the lawyer's representation may alleviate a conflict between a current and a former client by clarifying the role of the lawyer and excluding from the representation the tasks or interactions that raise the conflict problem. Ordinarily, however, such a limitation does not justify representation when a conflict exists between current clients.

> As a general proposition, loyalty to a client prohibits undertaking representation directly adverse to that client without that client's consent. Paragraph (a) expresses that general rule. Thus, a lawyer ordinarily may not act as advocate against a person the lawyer represents in some other matter, even if it is wholly unrelated. On the other hand, simultaneous representation in unrelated matters of clients whose interests are only generally adverse, such as competing economic enterprises, does not require consent of the respective clients.[178]

While Model Rule 1.2 establishes that, subject to stated exceptions, the lawyer must "abide by a client's decisions concerning the objectives of representation,"[179] it also notes that the lawyer "may limit the objectives of the representation if the client consents [to the limitation] after consultation."[180] The Restatement also recognizes the right of a client and lawyer to limit the duties owed by the lawyer. "Subject to other requirements stated in this Restatement, a client and lawyer may agree to limit a duty that a lawyer would otherwise owe to the client if: (a) the client is adequately informed and consents; and (b) the terms of the limitation are reasonable in the circumstances."[181] This limitation may constrain the scope of the representation. A comment to Section 19 articulates the right of clients and lawyers to "define in reasonable ways the services a lawyer is to provide."[182] The comment also indicates safeguards that apply to limited representations and gives examples of appropriate types of limitations, including a lawyer handling a trial but expressly not handling any appeal of the same matter and "counsel[ing] a client on the tax aspects of a transaction but not other aspects."[183] The comment explains that such limitations on representation "are not waivers of a client's right to more extensive services but a definition of the services to be performed."[184]

---

178. MODEL RULE 1.7 cmt. 3.
179. MODEL RULE 1.2(a).
180. MODEL RULE 1.2(c).
181. *See* RESTATEMENT (THIRD) OF THE LAW GOVERNING LAWYERS 19(1) (2000).
182. *See* RESTATEMENT (THIRD) OF THE LAW GOVERNING LAWYERS 19(1) cmt. c (2000).
183. *Id.*
184. *Id.*

Prospective Clients

The 1983 Model Rules do not speak directly to the duties of lawyers to prospective clients. The ABA Commission on Ethics and Professional Responsibility has held that a lawyer has a duty of confidentiality to a prospective client who consults her to obtain legal advice or to choose a lawyer.[185] In Formal Opinion 90-358, the Committee noted that the duty of confidentiality exists without regard to whether the prospective client retains the lawyer as a result of the consultation.[186] Recognizing that the lawyer owes a duty of confidentiality to a prospective client as well as to actual clients can result in difficult conflicts problems. Such recognition of the interests of prospective clients means that consulting with a prospective client may compromise a lawyer's representation of an existing client. The opinion also notes the possibility that conferring with a potential client may put a lawyer in a situation in which he will be required to decline a representation or withdraw from an existing representation. "When the information imparted by the would-be client is critical to the representation of an existing or new client in the same or related matter . . . the lawyer must withdraw or decline the representation unless a waiver of confidentiality has been obtained from the would-be client."[187]

The ABA opinion gives some comfort to lawyers regarding this risk, noting that if the lawyer "takes adequate measures to limit the information initially imparted by the would-be client, in most situations the lawyer may continue to represent or to undertake representation of another client in the same or a related matter."[188] The opinion recommends measures to guard against disqualification as a result of information revealed by a prospective client. Specifically, the opinion notes that lawyers should undertake procedures to identify conflicts of interest before undertaking a representation. A records check of existing clients and actions may convince a lawyer to decline a meeting with a party seeking to interview the lawyer. Additionally, when the lawyer meets with a prospective client, the lawyer should limit the information provided by the prospective client. In other words, the lawyer should take control of the interview rather than simply asking an open-ended question or inviting a narrative in which the prospective client will spill out his account of the problem that brings him to the lawyer.

---

185. ABA Comm. on Ethics and Prof'l Responsibility Formal Op. 90-358.

186. This Opinion's explanation of confidentiality issues is considered in the section on confidentiality.

187. *Id.*

188. *Id.*

Chapter 5: Basic Conflicts Concerns   239

When obtaining the preliminary information before undertaking the representation, the lawyer should obtain from the would-be client only information sufficient to determine whether a conflict or potential conflict of interest exists and whether the new matter is one within the lawyer's capabilities and one in which the lawyer is willing to represent the would-be client.[189]

The opinion notes that the lawyer should caution the prospective client "not to volunteer information pertaining to the matter until after the lawyer has had an opportunity to determine whether a conflict of interest exists and whether the lawyer is capable and willing to undertake the representation,"[190] if the client offers to retain the lawyer. The opinion endorses both waivers and screening lawyers with a conflict from others in a firm in some circumstances. Moreover, it notes the ability of a lawyer to seek an agreement from the prospective client that information the prospective client provides in the initial interview is not subject to the lawyer's duty of confidentiality.

It also would be proper, in the Committee's opinion, for the lawyer to advise the would-be client that, because of the need to obtain information from which to determine whether a conflict of interest or a potential conflict exists, the information divulged preliminarily for this purpose will not be confidential, and that the lawyer or firm would not be barred as a result of receiving the information from representing another client if a conflict of interest or potential conflict is found to exist or if for other reasons no representation is undertaken.[191]

The opinion notes that the waiver should be memorialized in a writing signed by the client and should explain the consequences of the waiver (in other words, that the lawyer could represent another client against the prospective client in the event the prospective client does not become a client of the lawyer). Some courts favor existing clients over prospective clients, however. For example, in the case of *Flatt v. Daniel*,[192] the Supreme Court of California held that the lawyer's duty to a prospective client may be limited by the lawyer's duty to an existing client. In the *Flatt* case, a client brought a legal malpractice action against a lawyer who had consulted with the client con-

---

189. *Id.*
190. *Id.*
191. *Id.*
192. Flatt v. Daniel, 3 U.S.L.W. 2417, No. S031687 (Cal. 1994).

cerning possible litigation but who did not go forward with the litigation. The lawyer severed the relationship with the prospective client when he learned that this client wished to sue one of his existing clients. The court held that a lawyer's duty of undivided loyalty to an existing client negated any duty on the part of the lawyer to inform a prospective client of the applicable statute of limitations relating to the lawsuit that the prospective client had proposed. Further, the court held that the duty of loyalty obviated any requirement that the lawyer advise the prospective client that it would be advisable to seek another lawyer in the matter.

Initial Consultation

Ordinarily, the initial consultation undertaken by lawyers and clients to determine whether or not to enter a contract for legal representation should not constitute a basis for forcing a lawyer to withdraw from representing another client.[193] Even if the prospective client shares confidential information with the lawyer, this information may not disqualify the lawyer from representing an existing client as long as the shared information was relevant to determining whether or not to undertake the representation.[194]

A frequent example of the problem arises when real estate developers come to a lawyer after they have negotiated a deal. The parties to the deal ask the lawyer to "paper the deal," meaning that the lawyer will draw up the necessary transfer documents, corporate minutes, and resolutions. If members of the investment group later have a disagreement or some of the parties suffer economic harm, the dissatisfied members sometimes sue the lawyer as well as the partner or shareholder with whom they entered the agreement, alleging that the lawyer represented the entire group and failed to fairly represent the plaintiffs' interests. An alternative scenario arises when a client or former client of a lawyer enters a business transaction with another client of the lawyer. If the deal turns out badly, the old client may sue the lawyer, alleging that the lawyer aided the new client in wrongdoing and breached a fiduciary obligation to the old client. This argument is possible even though the old client retained separate counsel in the transaction. If the lawyer did not obtain the consent of the old client in undertaking this new deal, the old client is likely to argue that the lawyer violated the ethics rules on conflicts.[195] Model Rule 1.7 permits representation of multiple clients when the tests of Model Rule 1.7 (a) and (b) are met. The rule states that the lawyer must explain to

---

193. *See* WOLFRAM, *supra* note 7, at 327.

194. *Id.*

195. *Id.* at 2.

the clients "the implications of the common representation and the advantages and risks involved" in the multiple representation.[196]

Consent/Advance Waiver

In some instances, it may be advisable for a lawyer to obtain an "advance waiver" or "prospective waiver" from a new client. Such a waiver, also called an "advance consent," may serve as the consent required under Model Rule 1.7 in some circumstances. In Formal Opinion 93-372, the ABA Committee on Ethics and Professional Responsibility held that such a waiver of a future conflict of interest may be permissible provided it meets the requirements of a waiver of a contemporaneous conflict of interest and contemplates the type of conflict that later arises with sufficient clarity.[197] Thus, only after a future conflict has arisen can the lawyer (or a disciplinary board) determine whether the earlier waiver is sufficient. The written waiver must have set forth the particular conflict with enough clarity that the client's consent "can reasonably be viewed as having been fully informed when it was given."[198] The opinion expressed doubt that a client can fully appreciate the consequences of such a waiver unless it identifies the potential party or type of conflict that is likely to arise.[199] Moreover, the opinion noted that such a waiver does not permit disclosure of confidential information relating to the representation of the waiving client unless that result is expressly provided for in the waiver. The opinion indicated that generally lawyers must revisit the issue of the waiver prior to undertaking a representation adverse to the client. At that time, the lawyer should know the particulars of "the representation the lawyer wishes to undertake pursuant to the prospective waiver."[200] The Committee noted the need for the later consideration of the conflicts issue, concluding that the lawyer must revisit the issue before accepting an adverse representation even when he has obtained the signed waiver. It stated:

> Even though one might think that the very purpose of a prospective waiver is to eliminate the need to return to the client to secure a 'present' second waiver when what was once an inchoate matter

---

196. MODEL RULE 1.7(b)(2).

197. ABA Formal Op. 93-372 (1993); *see also* N.Y. County Lawyers Ass'n Comm. on Prof'l Ethics, Op. 724 (1998) (approving of use of prospective waiver when lawyer's disclosure of potential conflicts is adequate).

198. *Id.*

199. *Id.*

200. *Id.*

ripens into an immediate conflict, there is no doubt that in many cases that is what will be ethically required.[201]

Revisiting the analysis and consulting with the client when the lawyer is considering undertaking a second (conflicting) representation is necessary to keep the client fully informed of the conflict. The fact that the client waived future conflicts does not mean that he or she waived the right to be apprised of developments relevant to its case (including conflicts) or the right to terminate the representation. Accordingly, the lawyer must reveal a conflicting representation when it arises.

Prospective Clients (2002 Revision)

In response to concerns that "important events occur in the period during which a lawyer and prospective client are considering whether to form a client-lawyer relationship"[202] the ABA House of Delegates adopted a new rule relating to prospective clients. The new rule set forth in Rule 1.18 incorporates the conflicts rule into the prospective client context, prohibiting a representation when the lawyer represents a client with interests materially adverse to the prospective client in the "same or substantially related matter."[203]

By adding Model Rule 1.18, the ABA indicated that lawyers have duties to prospective clients, even when no attorney-client relationship arises with the prospective client. A comment to Model Rule 1.18 states: "prospective clients should receive some but not all of the protection afforded clients."[204] The new rule incorporates the conflicts rule, prohibiting a representation when the lawyer represents a client with interests materially adverse to the prospective client in the "same or substantially related matter."[205] The rule calls for imputation of conflicts based on information gained from prospective clients.[206] An exception to this prohibition against representation also applies, allowing representation if both affected clients give informed consent and the lawyer "took reasonable measures to avoid disclosure to more disqualifying information than was reasonably necessary to determine whether to represent the prospective client."[207]

---

201. *See* ABA Formal Op. 90-358. Similarly, some firms and lawyers also seek a waiver of the duty of confidentiality before meeting with a prospective client to determine whether a lawyer-client relationship will be formed.

202. Model Rule 1.18 Reporter's Explanation of Changes.

203. REV. MODEL RULE 1.18(c).

204. MODEL RULE 1.18 cmt. 1 (2002).

205. MODEL RULE 1.18(c) (2002).

206. *Id.*

207. MODEL RULE 1.18(d) (2002).

Chapter 5: Basic Conflicts Concerns   243

As with former clients, the new Model Rule allows the prospective client to cure a conflict by giving informed consent "confirmed in writing."[208] Additionally, when the lawyer who conferred with a prospective client and received qualified information is prohibited by the rules from representing a client based on this conflict, others associated with that lawyer may undertake a representation if the lawyer "took reasonable measures to avoid exposure to more disqualifying information than was reasonably necessary to determine whether to represent the prospective client."[209] To go forward with a representation that is a conflict with a prospective client of a lawyer, the firm must timely screen the disqualified lawyer from participation in the matter and "apportion no part of the fee" from that matter to the lawyer who received disqualifying information and, additionally, must give written notice to the prospective client of the conflict.[210]

Limiting Representation (2002 Revision)

The 2002 Revised Model Rule 1.2 makes clear that limiting a representation by contract "does not exempt a lawyer from the duty to provide competent representation."[211] A comment to the revised rule indicates that the lawyer may need to consult substantive law in resolving disagreements between the lawyer and the client regarding the representation.

> Because of the varied nature of the matters about which a lawyer and client might disagree and because the actions in question may implicate the interests of a tribunal or other persons, this Rule does not prescribe how such disagreements are to be resolved. Other law, however, may be applicable and should be consulted by the lawyer. The lawyer should also consult with the client and seek a mutually acceptable resolution of the disagreement.[212]

Consent/Advance Waiver (2002 Revision)

Comment 22 to Revised Model Rule 1.7 refers to circumstances in which a lawyer may request a waiver and a client may give a waiver relating to future conflicts.[213] Comment 22 thus acknowledges the possibility that a client may

---

208. MODEL RULE 1.18(d)(1).
209. MODEL RULE 1.18(d)(2) (2002).
210. *Id.*
211. REV. MODEL RULE 1.2 cmt. 7 (2002).
212. MODEL RULE 1.2 cmt. 2 (2002).
213. *See* http://www.abanet.org/cpr/ethics2k.html (visited Mar. 28, 2003). For a thorough discussion of the appropriateness of advance waivers, see Richard W. Painter, *Advance Waiver of Conflicts*, 13 GEO. J. LEGAL ETHICS 289 (2000).

be able to waive a future conflict appropriately in some circumstances.[214] Comment 22 makes clear that future conflicts are within the scope of Model Rule 1.7 as revised. "Whether a lawyer may properly request a client to waive conflicts that might arise in the future is subject to the test of paragraph (b)."[215] The comment indicates that the effectiveness of advance waivers depends on whether the client reasonably understands the material risks that the waiver entails. The comment also notes that explanations "of the types of future representations that might arise and the actual and reasonably foreseeable adverse consequences of those representations" make the waiver more likely to be enforceable.[216]

> [I]f the client agrees to consent to a particular type of conflict with which the client is already familiar, then the consent ordinarily will be effective with regard to that type of conflict. If the consent is general and open-ended, then the consent ordinarily will be ineffective, because it is not reasonably likely that the client will have understood the material risks involved.[217]

Comment 22 provides significant detail regarding the factors that relate to whether such a waiver should be given effect. It notes the need for comprehensive and detailed explanations to clients who may consider agreeing to a prospective waiver of future conflicts. Implicit in the discussion of the comment is the possibility that a court or other authority may find a waiver to be ineffective after it is made, even though it may have been freely bargained for. The factors focus on the sophistication and understanding of the client and the specificity of the lawyer's explanation of the waiver.

> The effectiveness of such waivers is generally determined by the extent to which the client reasonably understands the material risks that the waiver entails. . . . [I]f the client is an experienced user of the legal services involved and is reasonably informed regarding the risk that a conflict may arise, such consent is more likely to be effective, particularly if, e.g., the client is independently represented by other counsel in giving consent and the consent is limited to future conflicts unrelated to the subject of the representation.[218]

---

214. MODEL RULE 1.7 cmt. 22 (2002).
215. *See id.*
216. *Id.*
217. *Id.*
218. *Id.*

Chapter 5: Basic Conflicts Concerns 245

The comment also notes the limitation of prospective waivers to matters that are reasonably foreseeable. The comment notes that describing the particular type of conflict to the client is important. "[If the client agrees to a particular type of conflict with which the client is already familiar, then the consent ordinarily will be effective with regard to that type of conflict."[219] Thus, "general and open-ended" waivers are ordinarily ineffective.[220] It makes clear, nevertheless, that the lawyer cannot guarantee that an advance consent will be effective. Circumstances may develop that make the waiver nonconsentable. "In any case, advance consent cannot be effective if the circumstances that materialize in the future are such as would make the conflict nonconsentable under paragraph (b)."[221]

The Consultation Requirement: Limiting an Interview (2002 Revision)

Comment 4 to the new Model Rule 1.18 indicates that lawyers should be in control of the interview process. "In order to avoid acquiring disqualifying information from a prospective client, a lawyer considering whether or not to undertake a new matter should limit the initial interview to only such information as reasonably appears necessary for that purpose."[222]

Former Clients

Overview

The lawyer owes a duty to refrain from engaging in representations that create conflicts of interest with respect to former clients. In part because of the significant numbers of lawyers who move from firm to firm and in part because of the large number of corporations involved in CERCLA matters and other environmental cases, former client conflicts are particularly problematic in environmental practice. The fact that a lawyer or client has terminated a representation does not mean that all the lawyer's duties to the client have ended. For example, the lawyer continues to owe the client the duty of confidentiality. The lawyer cannot reveal any information about the client that he could not have revealed during the representation itself.[223] Nor can a lawyer use former client information to the disadvantage of the former client.[224]

---

219. *Id.*
220. *Id.*
221. *Id.*
222. MODEL RULE 1.18 cmt. 4 (2002).
223. *See* MODEL RULE 1.9.
224. *See* MODEL RULE 1.9(c).

246   ISSUES OF LEGAL ETHICS IN THE PRACTICE OF ENVIRONMENTAL LAW

Moreover, clients are entitled to protection from conflicts of interest of lawyers after termination of the attorney-client relationship.[225]

> [A]s a general rule, a duty is owed on the part of an attorney to a former client to avoid representation if either (a) there is a potential that confidential information may be revealed or (b) the subject matters are substantially related and the attorney is taking a position directly adverse to the client's position in the former representation.[226]

The substantial relationship test as a basis for disqualification of a lawyer had its genesis in the case of *T.C. Theatre Corp. v. Warner Bros. Pictures*,[227] which involved a private antitrust action. Two defendant movie companies moved to disqualify several of the plaintiffs' lawyers, arguing that the plaintiffs' lead counsel had represented defendants in a nearly identical antitrust action brought by the government. The court held that where "it can reasonably be said that in the course of the former representation the attorney might have acquired information related to the subject of his subsequent representation . . . then the relationship between the two matters is sufficiently close to bring the later representation within the prohibition" against the representation.[228]

Disqualification Motions

Former client conflicts are often the basis of disqualification motions. Courts consider a variety of factors in determining whether a representation by a lawyer or his firm requires disqualification of the lawyer or firm from representing another client. In such motions, an opponent argues that the lawyer's former representation makes the current representation improper and disadvantages the former client. Additionally, an opposing party may have standing to move for disqualification of a lawyer when the interests of the public are implicated or an apparent conflict of interest may tend to undermine the validity of the proceedings.[229]

Model Rule 1.9

The 1983 version of Model Rule 1.9 prohibits representations against former clients in matters that are substantially related to the earlier representation if

---

225. MODEL RULE 1.9.

226. Griffith v. Taylor, 937 P.2d 297, 303 (Ala. 1997).

227. 113 F. Supp. 265 (S.D.N.Y. 1953).

228. *Id.* at 269.

229. *See* Abbott v. Kidder Peabody & Co., Inc., 42 F. Supp. 2d 1046 (D. Colo. 1999).

the representation will be materially adverse to a former client.[230] It states:

> (a) A lawyer who has formerly represented a client in a matter shall not thereafter represent another person in the same or a substantially related matter in which that person's interests are materially adverse to the interests of the former client unless the former client consents after consultation.[231]

The test of Rule 1.9 is similar but not identical to Model Rule 1.7. Model Rule 1.7 uses the dual standard of "directly adverse" representation and "materially limited" representation. If a representation is directly adverse to another client or may be materially limited by another representation, Rule 1.7 allows the lawyer to accept the representation only when the clients consent and the lawyer has a reasonable belief that neither of the representations will be adversely affected.

The standard of Rule 1.9 gives somewhat more leeway to lawyers, creating a narrower universe within the prohibition than Rule 1.7. It prohibits a representation by a lawyer who represented a former client in the same matter or in a matter substantially related to the new matter if the interests of the new client are materially adverse to those of the former client. The conflict can be cured by consent of the clients. Model Rule 1.9 does not include an express requirement of a judgment that neither representation will be adversely affected. Rule 1.9 also imputes conflicts to lawyers on a retrospective basis, prohibiting a lawyer from representing a person in a matter when "a firm with which the lawyer formerly was associated had previously represented a client"[232] if that former client's interests are "materially adverse" to the representation and the lawyer acquired confidential information about the client "material to the matter."[233] The rule also prohibits use or disclosure of confidential information about the former client. Comment 8 to Revised Model Rule 1.6 notes the ability of the lawyer to reveal client information about a former client when necessary to answer a claim that the lawyer engaged in wrongdoing. "Where a legal claim or disciplinary charge alleges complicity

---

230. Model Rule 1.9.
231. Model Rule 1.9(a).
232. "A lawyer who has formerly represented a client in a matter or whose present or former firm has formerly represented a client in a matter shall not thereafter: (1) use information relating to the representation to the disadvantage of the former client except as Rule 1.6 or Rule 3.3 would permit or require with respect to a client, or when the information has become generally known; or (2) reveal information relating to the representation except as Rule 1.6 or Rule 3.3 would permit or require with respect to a client." MODEL RULE 1.9(c).
233. MODEL RULE 1.9.

of the lawyer in a client's conduct or other misconduct of the lawyer involving representation of the client, the lawyer may respond to the extent the lawyer reasonably believes necessary to establish a defense."[234]

Model Rule 1.9 (2002 Revision)

The 2002 version of Model Rule 1.9 also prohibits representations against former clients in matters that are substantially related to the earlier representation if the representation will be materially adverse to a former client.[235] The revision adds the standard of informed consent and requires a writing confirming the consent.

> A lawyer who has formerly represented a client in a matter shall not thereafter represent another person in the same or a substantially related matter in which that person's interests are materially adverse to the interests of the former client unless the former client gives informed consent, confirmed in writing.[236]

The Restatement Approach

The Restatement (Third) of the Law Governing Lawyers presents a rule on former client conflicts that is similar to the Model Rules approach. Section 132 of the Restatement indicates that a lawyer continues to owe some duties to former clients and that the lawyer must avoid conflicts of interest with regard to the interests of both current and former clients.[237] Like the Model Rule, the Restatement rule prohibits a lawyer from representing a new client in "the same or a substantially related matter" with interests "materially adverse" to a former client unless both clients consent to the representation.[238] Additionally, the Restatement addresses the background issue of confidentiality head-on, stating that a lawyer must not serve in an unrelated matter if there is a "substantial risk" that the representation would involve the use of client information not generally known.[239] The Restatement expressly notes that a client injured by a lawyer's breach of the duty to avoid creating conflicts has the right to malpractice damages.[240]

---

234. MODEL RULE 1.6 cmt. 8 (2002).
235. MODEL RULE 1.9(a) (2002).
236. *See* RULE 1.9(a).
237. RESTATEMENT OF THE LAW GOVERNING LAWYERS 132 (2000).
238. *Id.*
239. *Id.*
240. RESTATEMENT OF THE LAW GOVERNING LAWYERS 121 cmt. f (2000); *see also* RESTATEMENT OF THE LAW GOVERNING LAWYERS 48 (2000).

Environmental Examples

Chrispens v. Coastal Refining & Marketing, Inc. involved environmental litigation by a landowner against a pipeline owner, alleging injury as a result of substances that leaked from the pipeline.[241] The defendant (pipeline owner) moved to disqualify plaintiff's counsel. The trial court denied the motion. The reviewing court reversed, granting the disqualification motion and holding that plaintiff's lawyer had formerly represented the pipeline owner in cases that were "substantially related" to the case at issue and that the owner's interests were materially adverse to those of the plaintiff in the action. Moreover, the court held that the lawyer had acquired material and confidential information during the course of his employment with his former firm. The court held that the party against whom imputed disqualification is alleged bears the burden of proof. The court noted that an irrebuttable presumption arises that a lawyer acquired confidential information in a former representation once the party moving for disqualification of a lawyer establishes that the challenged lawyer formerly represented the adverse client and now represents another client in the same or a substantially related matter in which that client's interests are materially adverse to interests of former client.

In *Texaco, Inc. v. Garcia*,[242] the Texas Supreme Court held in an action for environmental contamination that the plaintiffs' lawyer, Ronald Secrest, should be disqualified from further representation and that the trial court abused its discretion in denying Texaco's motion to disqualify the lawyer. The plaintiffs sought to recover economic and environmental damages as a result of contamination of plaintiffs' property by petroleum products from a Texaco service station. Texaco filed a motion to disqualify the plaintiffs' lawyer on the basis that the lawyer had practiced with a firm that had served as a lawyer for Texaco for seven years in at least 106 different matters. Nine of these cases dealt with the environmental issues of contamination and property damages. Secrest had participated in defending Texaco in an environmental contamination lawsuit, which involved allegations similar to those in the case under consideration, such as an allegation that Texaco had improperly disposed of petroleum by-products and hazardous wastes. In reaching its decision, the Texas Supreme Court also noted the extensive involvement of Secrest in the preparation of Texaco's case in another environmental contamination matter, which involved "similar liability issues, similar scientific issues, and similar defenses and strategies"[243] as the case at bar. Based on Secrest's disqualifica-

---

241. 897 P.2d 104 (Kan. 1995).
242. 891 S.W.2d 255 (Tex. 1995).
243. *Id.* at 257.

250   ISSUES OF LEGAL ETHICS IN THE PRACTICE OF ENVIRONMENTAL LAW

tion, the Texas Supreme Court disqualified the entire firm from representing the plaintiff against Texaco.

An example of the difficult issues related to former clients is found in the case of *City of Kalamazoo v. Michigan Disposal Service Corp.*[244] In this case, the court granted defendant's motion to disqualify plaintiffs' counsel in a contribution action under CERCLA. The defendant, Brunswick, moved to disqualify plaintiffs' counsel based on an allegation that the lawyer, Dykema Gossett, had represented Brunswick as common counsel for it and other PRPs in an earlier, related CERCLA cost recovery action. The analysis of the *Kalamazoo* court suggests that all common counsel in Superfund groups are vulnerable to disqualification challenges. Any member of such a group may later challenge the representation of a lawyer who served as common counsel for their group on related matters. Whether an express waiver of conflicts arising from the group representation would be effective is an unresolved question.

The lawsuit arose from remediation orders by EPA concerning the Cork Street Landfill in Kalamazoo, Michigan. The plaintiffs sought contribution under CERCLA. In an earlier CERCLA lawsuit, plaintiffs had sought response costs incurred due to the release of hazardous substances from a different landfill site in Kalamazoo County, the West KL Avenue landfill. Defendants in that action (including the plaintiff in the instant action) formed a common defense group to engage in activities such as hiring experts and mounting a common defense.[245] In considering the challenge to Gossett's representation, the court applied a three-part test on the issue of disqualification: "(1) a past attorney-client relationship existed between the party seeking disqualification and the attorney it seeks to disqualify; (2) the subject matter of those relationships was substantially related; and (3) the attorney acquired confidential information from the party seeking disqualification."[246]

Gossett represented General Motors, a member of the common defense group in the earlier action, but did not represent Brunswick individually. Brunswick was, however, a member of the defense group. The joint defense agreement for the PRP group provided that a lawyer's service on group committees was not intended to create attorney-client relationships with other members of the defense group. Gossett acknowledged that she performed several assignments as common counsel of the defense group, including taking depositions, drafting motions, and conducting research. She also received payment from the common defense trust fund. The court held that because of the roles she played as common counsel for the joint defense

---

244.   125 F. Supp. 2d 219 (W.D. Mich. 2000).

245.   *Id*. at 224.

246.   *Id*. at 222.

Chapter 5: Basic Conflicts Concerns 251

group, Gossett had a direct attorney-client relationship with Brunswick in the West KL landfill lawsuit.[247] The court noted that while the provisions of the joint defense agreement negated an implication that the attorney-client relationship arose from participation by counsel in committee work, it did not extend that protection to common counsel.[248] Thus, the agreement was evidence of a representation by Gossett of all members of the defense group.

The court also found that the two matters involved were substantially related and that the plaintiffs' interests in the case were materially adverse to the interests of Gossett's former clients in the West KL Avenue site. The cost recovery action in the lawsuit at issue in the case concerned the Cork Street Landfill, the predecessor to the West KL Avenue landfill. The two landfills accepted waste from virtually the same companies, including Brunswick. The West KL landfill opened for business immediately after the Cork Street Landfill closed. In deciding whether the matters involved met the substantial relationship test, the court noted that two different tests are applied by courts to determine the issue: the "transactional analysis" or an "issue analysis."[249] The transactional analysis finds a substantial relationship when the "prior representation and the subsequent representation involved interconnected (but not the same) events which could reveal a pattern of client conduct; this is done on the theory that relevant confidences could have been acquired by the lawyer in question."[250] The issue analysis approach finds a substantial relationship when the issues involved in the two cases or transactions are more or less identical.[251] The court concluded that Gossett's representation in the two cases was substantially related under either test. Finally, the court held that Gossett acquired confidential information from the party seeking disqualification. Noting that courts "are most likely to impose an unrebuttable presumption where, as here, the attorney has 'switched sides,'" the court ruled that Gossett failed to rebut the presumption with regard to her representation as common counsel.[252] The court also found that Brunswick did not consent to or waive the conflict of interest.[253]

Imputed Conflicts

The prohibition against representations that are materially adverse to former clients extends to lawyers who have left a firm. When a lawyer acquired

---

247. *Id.* at 231.
248. *Id.* at 234.
249. *Id.* at 240.
250. *Id.* at 239.
251. *Id.*
252. *Id.*
253. *Id.* at 244.

knowledge about the firm's former clients, Model Rule 1.9 imputes a conflict to a lawyer formerly associated with a firm. It prohibits a lawyer from representing a person "in the same or a substantially related matter in which a firm with which the lawyer formerly was associated had previously represented a client" when the former client's interests are materially adverse to the prospective client and the lawyer "had acquired information protected by Rules 1.6 and 1.9(c) that is material to the matter."[254] The former client has the power to consent to the representation, however.[255]

Disqualification Motions

Some jurisdictions allow the lawyer to represent clients adverse to a client of her former firm when she shows that she did not work directly on matters for the client and gained no confidential information. When a lawyer did not work directly on a matter and has departed from a firm, the inference that he obtained confidential client information while at that firm is rebuttable.[256] If a lawyer worked on the case or a related case for the client seeking the disqualification, even though briefly, he will be unable to rebut the presumption of acquisition of confidential information. Other jurisdictions apply a conclusive presumption that a lawyer who had a substantial relationship with a client received confidences from the client and, thus, should be disqualified from a representation adverse to that client.[257]

Appearance of Impropriety

Concerns about the appearance of impropriety are a factor in some decisions.[258] Such concerns are particularly strong in jurisdictions that use the Model Code of Professional Responsibility as the basis for their rules of legal ethics because Canon 9 of the Code states that "a lawyer should avoid even the appear-

---

254. MODEL RULE 1.9(b).
255. *See* MODEL RULE 1.9(b).
256. *See* Silver Chrysler Plymouth, Inc. v. Chrysler Motors Corp., 518 F.2d 751 (2d Cir. 1975); Adams v. Aerojet—Gen. Corp., 104 Cal. Rptr. 2d 116 (Cal. App. 2001) (holding lawyer not automatically disqualified from representation against a client of his former firm when he did not represent the client in a substantially related matter).
257. *See, e.g.,* Flatt v. Superior Court, 9 Cal. 4th 275, 283 (Cal. 1994); Global Van Lines, Inc. v. Superior Court, 144 Cal. App. 3d 483, 192 Cal. Rptr. 609 (1983).
258. *See* Kala v. Aluminum Smelting & Refining Co., Inc., 688 N.E.2d 258 (Ohio 1998) (disqualifying entire firm despite extensive screening based on appearance of impropriety); *In re* Inquiry to Advisory Comm., 616 A.2d 1290 (N.J. 1992) (holding that law firm whose associate is full-time police officer is disqualified from representing private clients in criminal matters in township because of appearance of impropriety).

Chapter 5: Basic Conflicts Concerns   253

ance of impropriety." In *First American Carriers, Inc. v. Kroger Co.*, the court disqualified a firm based on the appearance of impropriety despite the fact that it found that the disqualified firm had received no confidential information from the former client.[259] The court noted that the fact that it had adopted the Model Rules of Professional Conduct, which do not include the language of Canon 9 of the Model Code cautioning lawyers to "avoid even the appearance of impropriety," did not alleviate the need for lawyers to avoid the appearance of impropriety.[260]

Some courts have noted that screening will not cure a clear appearance of impropriety.[261] When a lawyer is disqualified from representing a client at the new firm because of her involvement in a substantially related matter at her old firm, the lawyer's conflict may be imputed to the other lawyers in the firm.[262] In *Clinard v. Blackwood,*[263] Maclin P. Davis, Jr., a partner in the Waller firm, represented the Blackwoods. Davis left the Waller firm in 1988 and joined the Baker firm. He continued to represent the Blackwoods. John and Edward Clinard sued the Blackwoods, and the Blackwoods retained Davis to represent them in the suit. Davis ultimately withdrew from this representation after determining that the Baker firm represented a third-party defendant in the case. In June 1997, Davis left the Baker firm and returned to the Waller firm. Subsequently the Clinards retained the Waller firm to represent them. Because of Davis's past association with the case, the Waller firm implemented its "Conflict of Interest Screening Procedure" to shield Davis from information about the Blackwoods' case. The Blackwoods filed a motion to disqualify the Waller firm from continuing to represent the Clinards. The trial court denied the motion. The court of appeals reversed and the Tennessee Supreme Court affirmed the judgment of the appellate court, holding that Disciplinary Rule 5-105(D) of the Tennessee Code of Professional Responsi-

---

259. 787 S.W.2d 669 (Ark. 1990).
260. *Id.* at 671.
261. *See, e.g.*, Clinard v. Blackwood, 46 S.W.3d 177 (Tenn. 2001); Petroleum Wholesale, Inc. v. Marshall, 751 S.W.2d 295 (Tex. App. 1988) (affirming disqualification of lawyer and firm when lawyer had actual knowledge of confidences of former clients in particular case and noting use of Chinese wall would not cure appearance of impropriety).
262. *See e.g.*, Henriksen v. Great American Sav. & Loan, 11 Cal. App. 4th 109, 114 (Cal. App. 1 Dist. 1992) (disqualifying firm based on involvement of one lawyer); Gipson v. Brown, 706 S.W.2d 369 (1986) (disqualifying lawyer who represented church in its incorporation from representing party seeking financial data and business information concerning the church).
263. 46 S.W.3d 177 (Tenn. 2001).

bility required disqualification of the firm and the lawyer.[264] The court affirmed the disqualification, despite its finding that the Waller firm implemented an adequate screening procedure, basing its decision on the appearance of impropriety and the fact that Davis had worked on the case at issue.

In *First American Carriers, Inc. v. Kroger Co.*, the court disqualified a firm based on the appearance of impropriety, despite the fact that it found that the disqualified firm had received no confidential information from the former client.[265] The court noted that the fact that the Model Rules of Professional Conduct did not include the language of Canon 9 of the Model Code cautioning lawyers to "avoid even the appearance of impropriety" did not result in lawyers having no need to avoid the appearance of impropriety.[266]

Similarly, in Ohio, another state that bases its ethics rules on the Model Code,[267] the reviewing court affirmed a disqualification of lawyers based on the appearance of impropriety when a lawyer switched sides in a case.

> At the heart of every "side-switching attorney" case is the suspicion that by changing sides, the attorney has breached a duty of fidelity and loyalty to a former client, a client who had freely shared with the attorney secrets and confidences with the expectation that they would be disclosed to no one else. It is for this reason that the "appearance of impropriety doctrine" was adopted to protect the public, our profession, and those it serves.[268]

Ethics 2000 Proposal

The Ethics 2000 Commission proposed that firms be allowed to screen a lateral hire despite the fact that the new lawyer is disqualified from a representation when the lawyer associating with the firm receives no part of any fee generated by the conflicted representation, and that written notice of the association of the lawyer be provided to the former client to allow that client to test the compliance of the firm with the rule. The House of Delegates rejected this proposal despite the strong arguments of scholars and commenters that the imputed disqualification rule should be moderated by a screen for lateral hires. The Commission's proposal included the following language:

---

264. *Id.* at 183.

265. 787 S.W.2d 669 (Ark. 1990).

266. *Id.* at 671.

267. Kala v. Aluminum Smelting & Ref. Co., 688 N.E.2d 258 (Ohio 1998).

268. Cardona v. General Motors Corp., 942 F. Supp. 968, 975 (D.N.J. 1996), *cited in* Kala v. Aluminum Smelting & Ref. Co., *supra* note 265.

Chapter 5: Basic Conflicts Concerns 255

c) When a lawyer becomes associated with a firm, no lawyer associated in the firm shall knowingly represent a person in a matter in which that lawyer is disqualified under Rule 1.9 unless:
(1) the personally disqualified lawyer is timely screened from any participation in the matter and is apportioned no part of the fee therefrom; and
(2) written notice is promptly given to any affected former client to enable it to ascertain compliance with the provisions of this Rule.

The ABA House of Delegates rejected this standard for private lawyers but approved screening of government lawyers to provide for screening of former clients.

Former Clients Conflicts (2002 Revision)

Revised Model Rule 1.9 indicates that lawyers are prohibited from representing one side of a controversy in disputes arising out of multiple representations, a common phenomenon in environmental matters. Comment 1 to Rule 1.9 as revised notes that "a lawyer who has represented multiple clients in a matter" must not "represent one of the clients against the others in the same or a substantially related matter after a dispute arose among the clients in that matter, unless all affected clients give informed consent."[269] Some types of conflicts are not imputed to other members of the firm under the revised rules. For example, personal matters, such as financial interests in an opposing party or a personal relationship with opposing counsel, are not imputed to members of the lawyer's firm.

Environmental Matters (2002 Revision)

In explaining the concept of a "substantially related matter," a new comment to Model Rule 1.9 uses an environmental example.

[A] lawyer who has previously represented a client in securing environmental permits to build a shopping center would be precluded from representing neighbors seeking to oppose rezoning of the property on the basis of environmental considerations; however, the lawyer would not be precluded, on the grounds of substantial relationship, from defending a tenant of the completed shopping center in resisting eviction for nonpayment of rent. Information that has been disclosed to the public or to other parties adverse to the former client ordinarily will not be disqualifying.[270]

---

269. MODEL RULE 1.9 cmt. 1 (2002).
270. MODEL RULE 1.9 cmt. 3 (2002).

Close Calls and Factual Difficulties

Ethics Committee decisions also reflect the difficult factual issues that give rise to conflicts problems in the environmental context involving a former client. In an advisory opinion, the Pennsylvania Bar Association Committee on Legal Ethics and Professional Responsibility considered the former client standard in a question regarding a law firm's representation of a husband and wife on financial matters.[271] The couple had consulted the firm regarding preparation of wills for both the husband and wife. The firm also represented a corporate client that provided environmental services. The corporate client delivered fuel oil to an underground storage tank (UST) at the residence of the individual clients. A few days after the delivery, the corporate client disarmed the heating unit located within the individual clients' residence. After the shutdown of the heating unit, the unit caught fire, causing extensive damage to the residence. The Pennsylvania Committee found that the firm's representation of the corporate client without the consent of the former individual clients would not violate the ethical rule, since the litigation relating to the fuel oil fire was not "the same or a substantially related matter."

In this case, the firm had represented the husband in the past in the purchase of a parcel of land from his father's estate. A lawyer in the firm also had met with the individual clients about the preparation of a will. No documents had been prepared because the clients needed to make decisions about care for minor children and other matters. Before the individual clients contacted the lawyer again, the fire erupted at their home. Because the facts were not clear regarding when the firm terminated the representation, the Committee assumed for purposes of its decision that a letter from the firm terminating the representation on the will occurred before the individual client contacted the firm about the fire.[272] The Committee applied the former client standard to the case. It allowed the lawyer to continue the representation of the corporate client unless the firm had obtained information about the individual clients that could be used to their detriment—for example, knowledge of the individual clients' financial condition that could help determine if they would settle.

> If you determine that there is a possibility that any such information which is not "generally known" or other confidential information may be used to the detriment of the client, you should avoid the representation of the Corporate Client in this matter.[273]

---

271. Pennsylvania Bar Ass'n Comm. on Legal Ethics and Prof'l Responsibility Informal Op. 98-98 Inquiry No. 98-98, 1998 WL 1286249.

272. *Id.*

273. *Id.*

The important judgment call in this case was the decision that the individual clients were former clients rather than current clients. Because the Committee classified the individuals as former clients, it applied the more lenient standard of Model Rule 1.9 to prohibit the representation only if the representation of the other (corporate) client was the same or substantially related to the representation of the individual clients. If the Committee had viewed the individual clients as current clients, the representation would have fallen within the per se prohibition, preventing the lawyer or members of his firm from representing the corporate client in an action defending against a claim by the individual client. Moreover, terminating the relationship with the individual client would not enable the lawyer to go forward in representing the corporate client, since the Hot Potato Rule prohibits dropping one client to represent another.[274] Conflicts involving former clients can present challenging fact questions. For example, in Texas Ethics Opinion 527, the Supreme Court of Texas Professional Ethics Committee dealt with the following question under the Texas ethics rules:

> Are the members of Law Firm 2 disqualified from representing Corporation D by virtue of their prior personal representation of Corporation P or vicariously by the prior representation of Corporation P by other members of Law Firm 1 while the members of Law Firm 2 were members of Law Firm 1?[275]

After considering the Texas general rule relating to conflicts of interest and related rules, the Committee decided that such representation may be appropriate in limited circumstances.[276] The Committee's analysis focused on confidentiality concerns. Under the facts of the case, the lawyers had "no relevant confidential information from the former client."[277] The Committee relied on this fact and, additionally, the fact that the lawyers now with Firm 2 who had represented the opponent did no work on the lawsuit at issue and no work on any matter similar to the present lawsuit. The Committee concluded that the fact that lawyers were members of a firm at the time that firm represented a client that is now an opponent to their clients did "not necessarily disqualify" the lawyers from representing the new client.

---

274. *See infra* note 276.
275. *Id.*
276. Tex. Prof'l Ethics Comm., 1 Op. 527 (Tex. 1998).
277. *Id.*

258   ISSUES OF LEGAL ETHICS IN THE PRACTICE OF ENVIRONMENTAL LAW

Hot Potato Rule

The "Hot Potato Rule" prevents a lawyer or a law firm from accepting a new representation by terminating a representation with a current client that presents a conflict.[278] Thus, even though the client terminated is no longer a current client, courts analyze the issue as though the "fired" client remained a current client. For example, a lawyer who sought to drop a client involved in a Superfund action to represent another client at the same site is likely to be disqualified from the second representation. When a lawyer opposes a motion for disqualification that is based on a current or prior representation, she is likely to argue that the party asserting a conflict should be viewed as a former client rather than as a current client. Courts disqualify lawyers, however, rejecting the distinction between current and former clients when the lawyer dropped one client to take a case against that client.[279]

Curative Measures

Consent

The analysis relating to client consent in the context of former clients is essentially the same as the analysis relating to consent by current clients. In most cases, clients may waive a conflict by giving consent to the representation under question. Only in extreme cases is the conflict presented not waivable by the clients.

Screening

A few states recognize and validate measures to screen lawyers from each other vis-à-vis a particular representation.[280]

Screening (Ethics 2000)

The Ethics 2000 Commission proposal to permit screening to remove imputed disqualification in the case of former clients was defeated at the ABA House of Delegates.

Termination of Representation

Some large firms have begun monitoring their client files and terminating representations that are not active because the standard for accepting represen-

---

278. *See, e.g.,* Ronald D. Rotunda, *Conflicts Problems, supra* note 51, at 663; John A. Edginton, *Managing Lawyers' Risks,* at *supra* note 51, at 2021.

279. *See* Strategem Dev. Corp. v. Heron, 756 F. Supp. 789, 794 (S.D.N.Y. 1991) (granting defendant's motion for disqualification of plaintiff's counsel on basis that plaintiff's counsel began preparations for suing defendant while it represented defendant).

280. *See, e.g.,* Tennessee Formal Op. 89-F-118.

tation is more difficult in cases of simultaneous representation as compared with a former client situation. Thus, it may be to the law firm's advantage to turn current clients into former clients except when the clients generate a significant volume of legal work for the firm. This perception has not always operated in lawyer-client relations. In the past, many firms would nurture long-term relations with a client even though the client required no legal services for long periods of time. Both the lawyer and the client assumed that the client would return to the firm when it required additional legal services and that the firm would carry the client on the firm's records as a current client. In today's legal world, however, some firms believe that the potential loss of future clients as a result of conflicts outweighs the benefits of long-term but quiescent representations.

Like their counterparts in private practice, these lawyers must deal with issues that arise as a result of direct adversity or material limitation of the representation and problems that relate to current, former, or prospective clients.[281] The analysis relating to current or prospective clients of government lawyers is largely consistent with the analysis discussed in relation to private lawyers. The problems of determining conflicts of interest of government and former government arise most often in relation to former representations (both government and private), probably because the question of representing multiple current clients or prospective clients is determined as a matter of policy by the governmental entity that employs the lawyer.

---

281. REV. MODEL RULE 1.11 makes clear that MODEL RULES 1.7 and 1.9 apply to government lawyers.

CHAPTER 6

Special Conflicts Concerns

Imputed Conflicts

The potential for problems for environmental lawyers from imputed conflicts are significant, since so much of the practice involves multiple corporate clients who may be represented by a number of different firms on different types of matters. According to the imputed conflict principle, no lawyer may accept representation when any lawyer associated with the firm in which he practices would be prohibited from accepting the representation under the conflict of interest rules. Ethics rules impute conflicts to members of a firm whether the lawyer involved is in private practice or government work.[1] Imputed conflicts can arise with regard to current, prospective, and former conflicts.

Suppose you represent Corporation A in environmental matters, including environmental compliance. As a result of this work, you know that Corporation A recently discovered environmental contamination at one of its plants. Meanwhile, Corporation B meets with one of your partners for the purpose of engaging her to represent Corporation B in negotiations with Corporation A to purchase one of A's plants. Corporation B shares with your partner the (high) ultimate price it will pay for the property in addition to its opening bid and other strategies of the purchase. When your partner runs a conflicts check, she discovers that you represent Corporation A.[2] Rule 1.10 prohibits her representation of Corporation B, since the representation would be directly adverse to your representation of Corporation A. Model Rule 1.10 imputes the conflict of interest from her to you and other members of the firm. Moreover, your representation

---

1. The issue of imputed conflicts for government lawyers is discussed in the section *infra,* on government lawyers.
2. This fact pattern is drawn from a hypothetical created by Blake Biles for the ABA Section Administrative Law Annual Meeting, in Washington, D.C. (Oct. 17, 2002).

of A in the negotiations with Corporation B may be imperiled because of your partner's knowledge regarding Corporation B's negotiation strategy.[3]

Both the Model Code and the Model Rules impute conflicts to members of a firm of a lawyer who is disqualified from a representation by an ethics rule.[4] The imputed disqualification rule of the Model Code states no exceptions and acknowledges no power for a client to consent to the conflict. Courts have allowed client consent to waive such conflicts or screening to cure such conflicts in some cases, however.[5]

Imputed disqualification creates a secondary effect of conflicts, resulting in disqualification of an entire law firm based on the conflict of one lawyer. The rule that lawyers practicing together share each other's conflicts by imputation is based on an assumption that lawyers talk about their cases with others in their firm. "Imputed, or 'vicarious,' disqualification is based on the day-to-day realities of how lawyers who are associated together practice law."[6] The rule operates by an automatic presumption of conflict. Accordingly, no special factual allegation is necessary in a motion to disqualify lawyers in a firm with a lawyer who represented an opponent in the past. Generally, lawyers in a firm need to talk with each other. This need is part of the reason that the practice of law is built on a structure of law firms, allowing lawyers to share ideas, strategy, and expertise. The notion that lawyers in the same firm generally share information is noted in comment 5 to Revised Model Rule 1.6, acknowledging the fact of shared information and accepting it as appropriate under the duty of confidentiality unless the client instructs the lawyer against engaging in the common practice. "Except to the extent that the client's instructions or special circumstances limit that authority, a lawyer is impliedly authorized to make disclosures about a client when appropriate."[7] It provides the example of the assumption that lawyers share information to generate ideas about the best way to proceed in any given case. "Lawyers in a firm may, in the course of the firm's practice, disclose to each other information relating to a client of the firm, unless the client has instructed that particular information be confined to specified lawyers."[8]

---

3. The need for disqualification is clearer in the case of a dispute between parties rather than a transaction such as a purchase agreement. *See, e.g.,* Bridge Products, Inc. v. Quantum Chemical Corp., 58 U.S.L.W. 2733, 20 ENVTL. L. REP. 20,940 (N.D. Ill. Apr. 27, 1990).

4. *See* MODEL RULE §1.10 DR 5-105(D) of the MODEL CODE.

5. *See* CHARLES W. WOLFRAM, MODERN LEGAL ETHICS 394 (2d ed. 1986) [hereinafter WOLFRAM] and cases cited therein.

6. MODEL RULE 1.10 Legal Background.

7. MODEL RULE 1.6 cmt. 5 (2002).

8. *Id.*

Chapter 6: Special Conflicts Concerns 263

In addition to discussing the law as it relates to cases within the firm, partners also discuss ways of attracting new clients, retaining existing clients, and expanding the amount and type of work that the firm does. They discuss the effect of legal developments on cases in the office and on the business of significant clients. If a law firm sought to avoid conflict problems by prohibiting all discussion among lawyers concerning cases, it would destroy one of the primary reasons for doing business as a firm. The presumption that lawyers freely discuss cases in firm meetings and on an individual basis within firms may be justified in many cases, including those in the environmental context. The technical nature of environmental law makes it virtually impossible for lawyers to specialize confidently in multiple environmental areas without relying on trusted advisors from time to time. The lawyer with Superfund expertise may be inexperienced in water allocations or discharge requirements under the Clean Water Act. The energy lawyer may know as little about endangered species law as one who practices estate planning. The fact that environmental law is subject to frequent change exacerbates this situation, making it unlikely that a lawyer who has not practiced in Clean Water Act or Clean Air Act matters for any significant period of time can confidently make a judgment without seeking guidance from other lawyers in the firm.

Private Lawyers

Model Rule 1.10 imputes conflicts from a lawyer associated in a firm to all members of the firm. The revised rule creates an exception for lawyers who are disqualified from a representation as a result of a personal interest that does not create a significant risk that the representation by another member of the firm will be materially limited. Courts assess conflicts of a lawyer who has changed firms in a variety of ways. Courts consider the substantial relationship between matters in determining whether disqualification is necessary,[9] and often presume that a lawyer has obtained confidential information by working for a former client.[10] Testimony regarding the present recollection of members of a firm is not ordinarily sufficient to rebut the presumption that the lawyer received confidential information.[11] The facts relating to the lawyer's move to the challenged law firm are also important. In *Van Jackson v. Check 'N Go of Illinois, Inc.,*[12] for example, the court noted with disapproval that the

---

9. Rosenfeld Const. Co., Inc. v. Superior Court (Sivas), 286 CAL. RPTR. 609 (Cal. App. 5 Dist. 1991).

10. *See* Solow v. W.R. Grace & Co., 632 N.E.2d 437 (N.Y. 1994).

11. *Id.*

12. 114 F. Supp. 2d 731 (N.D. Ill. 2000).

firm it held disqualified made the "personnel decision to recruit [the challenged lawyer] away from its courtroom adversary in the midst of this case."[13] Similarly, the Tennessee Supreme Court indicated its disapproval of continuing representations after a lawyer has switched firms. In affirming the disqualification of a lawyer and his firm despite finding that the challenged firm implemented an adequate screening procedure, the court stated: "To analogize to baseball, Mr. Davis has not only switched teams, he has switched teams in the middle of the game after learning the signals. That Mr. Davis has been benched by his new team does little to ameliorate the public perception of an unfair game."[14]

The Mobile Lawyer

Large, multi-city law firms handle a significant portion of environmental representation. One scholar has suggested that the best way to avoid conflicts problems in Superfund practice is to become "a sole practitioner whose only vocation is Superfund common counsel positions."[15] When a lawyer wishes to move to a new firm, she must provide information to that firm to determine whether hiring her will create conflicts for the firm. Some states expressly require such conflict checks in their rules of ethics.[16] The lawyer seeking to join a firm should provide the identity of clients for the conflicts check. The joining lawyer must be careful, however, not to disclose confidences of the prior clients. If the new firm seeks additional information about prior or current clients of the lawyer who wishes to join the firm, the joining lawyer should seek the consent of that client before releasing information.[17] Most large firms have computer programs to facilitate conflicts checks. Because the lawyer must not reveal confidential information of a client or a prospective client, the disclosure necessary to satisfy Model Rule 1.7 can be a complicated endeavor. The duty of confidentiality may prevent a lawyer from revealing relevant information to the new firm. If a client refuses to allow the lawyer to reveal client information to the firm, the lawyer is barred from revealing the information by the duty of confidentiality.

---

13. *Id.* at 734.

14. 46 S.W.3d 177, 188 (Tenn. 2001).

15. *See* MARLA B. RUBIN, UNCOMMON ETHICS PROBLEMS: SUPERFUND COMMON COUNSEL, ENVIRONMENTAL COMPLIANCE & LITIGATION STRATEGY (May 1995). Conflict issues can arise for common counsel as well, however. *See* City of Kalamazoo v. Michigan Disposal Services, 125 F. Supp. 2d 219 (W.D. Mich. 2000).

16. *See, e.g.*, NEW YORK CODE OF PROF'L RESPONSIBILITY DR5-105(E).

17. *See* New York State Bar Ass'n Comm. on Prof'l Ethics, Op. 720 (1999).

Chapter 6: Special Conflicts Concerns 265

Although the Model Rules do not forbid a lawyer from pursuing employment with a firm that is adverse to a current client, the rules require lawyers to withdraw or obtain client consent to the adverse job negotiations when the negotiations materially limit the representation of the client. In a formal opinion, the ABA Committee on Ethics and Professional Responsibility decided that Rule 1.7(b) requires lawyers to obtain the consent of a client before participating in substantive employment discussions with a firm that represents a party adverse to the client.[18] The opinion also noted that a lawyer need not obtain client consent to engage in nonsubstantive discussions with a potential employer, to search classified job ads, or to engage in general discussions about other firms with colleagues.[19] The extent of the lawyer's involvement with the client is the basis for deciding whether the lawyer must seek the client's consent to his contact with the adverse firm. Additionally, the relationship of the lawyer to the client should be considered. For example, the lawyer serving as lead counsel should seek consent before engaging in any negotiations with an adverse firm. On the other hand, a lawyer who plays only a minor role or who has little client contact has more flexibility to pursue employment with an adverse firm. The lawyer who has little client contact should disclose his desire to pursue other employment to his supervising partner. The supervisor may seek client consent or may remove the lawyer from working on the matter.[20]

The lawyer has some leeway in this situation. For example, she may choose to withdraw rather than seeking client consent. This avenue of dealing with the desire to seek other employment is restricted, however. If the lawyer chooses to withdraw, she should do so before undertaking substantive discussions with the adverse firm. This restriction makes withdrawal less feasible, since the lawyer would be giving up employment without any clear ability to obtain a new position.

The ABA Committee noted that Rule 1.7(b) conflicts that arise from adverse job negotiations should not be imputed to the entire firm through Rule 1.10.[21] Thus, such a conflict will not disqualify other lawyers in the firm from working with the client due to one lawyer's desire to explore other job possibilities. The Committee opinion recommended that firms discuss with the client the lawyer's withdrawal. The Committee also noted that clients deserve notice and information about the flip side of this situation. When a

---

18. ABA Comm. on Ethics and Prof'l Responsibility, Formal Op. 96-400 (1996).
19. *Id.*
20. *Id.*
21. *Id.*

law firm wishes to pursue an association with a lawyer who is adverse in a pending matter, the firm should consult with the client and obtain its consent before proceeding with discussions with the lawyer.[22]

In Ethics Opinion 99-414, the ABA Standing Committee on Ethics and Professional Responsibility dealt with the related question of "Ethical Obligations When a Lawyer Changes Firms." The opinion details important duties of the lawyer who changes firms, including informing the firm and clients of her departure in a timely fashion, insuring against conflicts of interest for the new firm, protecting the confidentiality of client information and making sure that "no client matters are adversely affected as a result of her withdrawal," avoiding misconduct, and fulfilling fiduciary duties to clients and the firm.[23] When a departing lawyer is responsible for representing the client or plays a significant role in providing legal services to that client, the departing lawyer must give the client timely notice of his departure.[24] The lawyer should inform the client whether he can continue to represent the client at the new firm, making clear that the client has the right to choose to be represented by the firm the lawyer is leaving, the departing lawyer, or some other lawyer.[25] Additionally, the departing lawyer must provide relevant information requested by the client.[26]

The Committee noted that in some circumstances, the departing lawyer has the right to give notice of her departure to clients in person or over the telephone before notifying the firm of her withdrawal from the firm. This right is limited to cases in which the lawyer has a family or sufficient prior professional relationship with the client. The fact that the lawyer has worked for the client does not establish a sufficient prior professional relationship if the lawyer has had little or no direct contact with the client.[27] After the lawyer has left the firm, she may send written notice of her new affiliation to any firm clients without showing a family or professional relationships with the clients contacted.[28] The lawyer's duty of confidentiality continues after departure whether or not the client elected to retain the lawyer as counsel. A lawyer's obligation to protect client information and property does not terminate when the lawyer changes firms.[29] The lawyer should ensure that client files are pro-

---

22. *Id.*
23. ABA Comm. on Ethics and Prof'l Responsibility, Formal Op. 99-414 (1999).
24. *Id.*
25. *Id.*
26. *Id.*
27. *Id.*
28. *Id.*
29. *See* MODEL RULE 1.9.

tected and that client matters are not adversely affected by the withdrawal. The lawyer must avoid conflicts of interest regarding matters at both firms.[30] The lawyer must also adhere to ethical and fiduciary duties regarding both firms.

The Committee noted that the departing lawyer must adhere to the Model Rules and other laws, including laws relating to agency, partnership, property, contracts, and unfair competition when departing from a law firm. For example, in giving notice of his departure to the client, the lawyer must not disparage the former firm or attempt to lure clients to his new firm. To avoid liability for unfair competition or appropriation of trade secrets, the attorney should not use firm client lists or other proprietary information. The departing lawyer may retain files relating to his representation of former clients, to the extent the documents were prepared by the lawyer and are considered the lawyer's property or are in the public domain.[31]

Disease Metaphors

Disease is the metaphor often used in describing imputed conflicts. The opinions dealing with imputed disqualification often speak in terms of "contamination." They point to an "infected" lawyer who carries the germ or taint of the conflict into the firm, where it spreads to others. The infected lawyer has been characterized as "typhoid Mary."[32]

Disqualification: Model Rules Provision

The imputed disqualification rule of the ABA Model Rules is set forth in Model Rule 1.10. Model Rule 1.10 prohibits a lawyer "associated in a firm" from knowingly representing a client that any firm member would be prohibited from representing under Rules 1.7, 1.8(c), 1.9 or 2.2 if he were "practicing alone."[33] Disqualification may be necessary because of prior contacts by a nonlawyer employee as well as lawyer contacts.[34] The rule does not prevent a representation by a firm member, however, of a person with "interests materially adverse to those of a client" represented by a lawyer formerly associated with the firm when that client is "not currently represented by the firm."[35]

---

30. ABA Comm. on Ethics and Prof'l Responsibility, Formal Op. 99-414 (1999).

31. *Id.*

32. *See, e.g.*, Armstrong v. McAlpin, 625 F.2d 433 (2d Cir. 1980), *vacated on other grounds*, 449 U.S. 1106 (1981).

33. MODEL RULE 1.10(a).

34. *See* ABA Comm. on Ethics and Prof'l Responsibility, Informal Op. 88-1526 (1988).

35. MODEL RULE 1.10(a).

This exception is also subject to an exception, however. Even though the challenged lawyer departs from the firm, a conflict may be imputed to the firm if the representation is "the same or substantially related" to the matter in which the former lawyer represented the client and client information is in the hands of a firm member.[36] Like Rule 1.7, this rule allows waiver by the client affected.[37]

Imputed Conflicts (2002 Revision)

The 2002 revision to Model Rule 1.10 made clear that conflicts are imputed to all members of a firm during the association. Lawyers are prohibited from knowingly representing a client when any of the lawyers in the firm is prohibited from representing the client.

Exceptions (2002 Revision)

The 2002 revision to Model Rule 1.10 made clear that conflicts are not imputed to a firm in all cases. An addition to the text of the rule excluded matters that involve a conflict based on a "personal interest of the prohibited lawyer" from the operation of the imputation rule. Additionally, the revised rule indicates that if a lawyer associated with the prohibited lawyer intends to go forward with the representation, the matter must "not present a significant risk of materially limiting the representation." A lawyer associated with the prohibited lawyer may not accept the representation unless the matter does "not present a significant risk of materially limiting the representation." A comment to Rule 1.10 explains that the imputation of conflicts is not applicable "where neither questions of client loyalty nor protection of confidential information are presented."[38] Another new comment indicates that conflicts created as a result of the involvement of an employee who is not a lawyer at the time of the contact with the client, such as a law student, a paralegal, or legal secretary, do not result in a prohibition of representation by other lawyers in the firm as long as the person involved in the conflict is "screened from any personal participation in the matter to avoid communication to others in firm of confidential information."[39]

Firm Size

Conflicts rules apply to all lawyers and all firms, large and small alike. As one

---

36. *Id.*
37. *Id.*
38. Model Rule 1.10 cmt. 3 (2002).
39. Model Rule 1.10 cmt. 4 (2002).

Chapter 6: Special Conflicts Concerns   269

court noted, there is "no basis for creating separate disqualification rules for large firms even though the burden of complying with ethical considerations will naturally fall more heavily upon their shoulders."[40] Practical differences exist between big and small firms for the purposes of conflicts, however. Large firms may generate more conflicts because of the larger number of clients they serve. Nevertheless, they also may be more successful in asserting that a lawyer can be screened to cure a conflict—especially if the infected lawyer is in a different office or department from those connected with the challenged representation. It seems more likely that partners in a small firm (with, say, only six or eight partners) would be aware of a particular client and its disputes. Likewise, it seems more difficult to screen particular lawyers effectively in the small firm setting.

While large firms generally have more opportunities for conflicts based on sheer numbers of clients, small firms may have more trouble resisting a motion to disqualify based on screening, whether the context is prospective clients, former government lawyers or a newly hired associate. The small firm may be less likely to convince a court that the presumption of an imputed conflict is rebutted by the facts of the case because the contact and discussion of client information between lawyers is likely in this setting. Professor Wolfram notes the significance of the size of the partnership in this context.

> If a lawyer moves from one small partnership to another it is natural to assume that the lawyer is extensively acquainted with information about clients of both firms, thus requiring imputed disqualification of the second firm based on every secondary disqualification that the lawyer acquired while a member of the first firm.[41]

The firm or lawyer seeking to rebut the presumption of shared confidences must present clear and effective proof that it did not obtain or have access to a client's confidential information while employed by a firm.[42] This task may be easier to accomplish in a large firm in which different departments and offices in different locations operate largely independently of each other. When the challenged lawyer has left a large firm and did not work for the client who is now adverse to her current client, it seems more likely that the lawyer has no knowledge of the client or the client's affairs. Additionally,

---

40. Westinghouse Electric Corp. v. Kerr-McGee Corp., 580 F.2d 1311, 1321 (7th Cir. 1978).

41. WOLFRAM, *supra* note 5, at 398.

42. Schiessle v. Stephens, 717 F.2d 417, 420 (7th Cir. 1983).

when a lawyer moves to another large firm, the ability of the firm to screen her effectively from the lawyers involved in matters adverse to her old firm's client also seems more of a realistic possibility than when her new firm is composed of only a few lawyers. In *INA Underwriters Insurance Company v. Rubin*, the court denied a motion to disqualify the plaintiff's lawyers, finding that the law firm's effective screening of a partner who had conferred with the opponent rebutted presumption imputing the knowledge of one lawyer to others in his firm.[43] The court noted: "If ever a screening mechanism can be effective, this is the case. Wolf Block is a very large law firm, and only one of its members, Magarity, needs to be screened. Magarity's involvement in Rubin's case is not an ongoing affair: it consisted of one meeting with Rubin only."[44] This commentary suggests that the court considered the size of the firm in making its decision.

Environmental Matters

Environmental lawyers often practice in the large firm setting, for a variety of reasons. Environmental practice frequently seems to require substantial support staff and a core group of lawyers. In the context of Superfund representation, multiple representation of clients is commonplace.[45] In Superfund representations, many clients choose large firms for representation because the matter requires a team of lawyers and support staff to respond in a timely manner to EPA requests for information and to fulfill other necessary tasks. Finally, because Superfund enforcement actions have decreased in recent years, many lawyers who once routinely undertook Superfund matters have retooled and refocused their practice on different areas. As a result, the pool of lawyers with expertise and inclination to accept Superfund representation has decreased, making it more likely that a client will retain a lawyer who represents other potentially responsible parties (PRPs) at a particular Superfund site. The complex nature of the factual and scientific information involved in Superfund matters, and in environmental law generally, is a factor that reduces the pool of lawyers available to provide legal services in this area.

Arguably, factors such as the availability of separate counsel and the custom of lawyers in the particular legal area should have a bearing on a court's judgment regarding whether a representation should be allowed despite an argument that a conflict exists in a given case. Of course, the context of the

---

43. INA Underwriters Ins. Co. v. Rubin, 635 F. Supp. 1 (E.D. Pa. 1983).

44. *Id.* at 5.

45. *See* David Littell, *Consent and Disclosure in Superfund Negotiations: Identifying and Avoiding Conflicts of Interests Arising from Multiple Representation*, 17 HARV. ENVTL. L. REV. 225 (1993).

Chapter 6: Special Conflicts Concerns   271

representation and the facts of each case make a difference in terms of the lawyer's decision whether to accept representation of multiple parties.

> Where this scope is restricted to representation of the PRP group before EPA, there is much less likelihood of later arising material conflicts. In contrast, where allocation is an element of the representation and there are no prior agreements regarding division of responsibility, there is a much greater likelihood of material conflict. Under these circumstances, if a lawyer does decide to represent multiple parties, it may be necessary to confine the representation to parties with aligned interests, such as only de minimis PRPs, or only generators, or only transporters, or only the owner of the site.[46]

In many cases, the practice of representing multiple clients in Superfund cases or other environmental matters provides more economical legal services because lawyers divide their billing time among the clients. Thus, the time the lawyer spends in attending PRP meetings, doing legal research, and seeking information and negotiating with the EPA is shared among the parties represented.

Environmental Example

Environmental lawyers often affiliate with firms, in part because of a need to offer clients expertise in a variety of environmental areas. The changeable nature of environmental law also heightens the need for affiliation with other environmental lawyers. The relationship of the lawyer to the firm is central to the inquiry of conflicts. For example, in *Solow v. W.R. Grace & Co.,*[47] the court held that a large, departmentalized firm was not disqualified from working for a plaintiff in asbestos litigation although a former partner in the firm had represented the asbestos manufacturer in a related litigation, preparing an expert witness to testify. In this case, the partner had left the firm several years before the firm undertook representation of the current plaintiff. Additionally, the lawyers who remained at the law firm had only limited contact with the previous litigation, and the firm did not appear to have access to confidential information of the defendant.

When the moving party establishes the lawyer's employment during the

---

46. *See* Carol E. Dinkins & Lewis C. Sutherland, *Ethics in the Environmental and Toxic Tort Practice*, SB 73 ALI-ABA 319, 324 (1997) [hereinafter Dinkins & Sutherland].

47. *Id.*

time of the representation, the challenged lawyer has the burden of showing that she had no access to client information. Ordinarily, such access comes as a result of working directly for the client on the matter.[48] Courts also consider the relationship between matters in determining whether disqualification is necessary.[49] In the *Solow* case discussed above, the court stated that a "party seeking to disqualify an attorney or a law firm, must establish (1) the existence of a prior attorney-client relationship and (2) that the former and current representations are both adverse and substantially related."[50] In the case of *Adams v. Aerojet–Gen. Corp.*,[51] the court held that a lawyer was not automatically disqualified from representation against a client of his former firm. The *Aerojet* case involved claims by neighbors and occupants of an area surrounding the Aerojet hazardous waste disposal site stating claims based on negligence, strict liability, and violations related to the alleged release and disposal of toxic chemicals resulting in contamination of groundwater and surrounding soils.[52] The trial court disqualified the plaintiffs' lawyer and his firm on the basis of "imputed knowledge" from representation of the defendant by the former firm of the plaintiff. The court of appeals reversed and remanded, reasoning that a lawyer who changes firms is "not automatically disqualified" on the basis of imputed knowledge.[53]

Curative Measures

Client Consent

Consent to a representation by an informed and knowledgeable client can cure imputed disqualification in most cases.[54] The analysis of this area echoes that of informed consent to a conflict generally.

---

48. *See* Solow v. W.R. Grace & Co., 632 N.E.2d 437 (N.Y. 1994) (holding that large, departmentalized firm was not disqualified from representing plaintiff in asbestos litigation based solely on fact that former partner was retained by asbestos manufacturer in related litigation to prepare expert witness for testimony when partner left firm several years before current representation and law firm did not have access to confidential information of former client).
49. Rosenfeld Const. Co., Inc. v. Superior Court (Sivas), 286 Cal. Rptr. 609 (Cal. App. 5 Dist. 1991).
50. 632 N.E.2d 437 (N.Y. 1994).
51. 104 Cal. Rptr. 2d 116, 119 (Cal. App. 2001).
52. *Id.*
53. *Id.*
54. *See* MODEL RULE 1.10(c).

Referrals

In some cases, a lawyer who is conflicted out of a representation may recommend another firm or lawyer to the client. When a firm makes a referral to a second firm because the first firm has been disqualified on an imputed basis, courts have refused to disqualify the second firm unless the party moving for disqualification can show that the second firm received confidential information from the first firm.[55]

Affidavits of Lawyers

Courts have recognized affidavits of lawyers in the new firm of a challenged lawyer stating that the challenged lawyer provided no confidential information to the firm or firm members.[56] In such cases, the claim is that the lawyer formerly employed by the opponent's firm contaminates the firm he is now working for and, accordingly, the entire firm should be disqualified from the representation on the basis of imputed conflict.[57] After the movant establishes an employment relationship that suggests a conflict, the challenged lawyer bears the burden of establishing affirmatively that he did not gain knowledge or confidential information relating to the opponent. The challenged lawyer may seek to rebut the motion by his own affidavit, stating that he did not work on the matter and did not obtain confidential information about the opponent during his earlier employment.[58] The purpose of the affidavit is to shift the burden of proof back to the firm moving to disqualify. The movant firm meets this burden if it produces billing records or other documents to show the challenged lawyer in fact worked on the matter at issue. It can also proffer affidavits by lawyers in the firm declaring their personal knowledge about the challenged lawyer's involvement. Screening is not an issue in such cases, since the lawyer's basis for arguing against the disqualification is that he did not obtain confidential information that would make him subject to screening.

An affidavit by the challenged lawyer seems particularly effective in the case of a lawyer who worked as an associate rather than as a partner for the firm that is now seeking disqualification. This distinction flows from a general belief that partners freely share information about cases in the office among themselves but share less information with their associates. Neverthe-

---

55. *See, e.g., In re* Airport Car Rental Antitrust Litig., 470 F. Supp. 495 (N.D. Cal. 1979), *cited in* WOLFRAM, *supra* note 5, at 398.

56. *Id.*

57. *See* MODEL RULE 1.10.

58. *See* Silver Chrysler Plymouth, Inc. v. Chrysler Motors Corp., 518 F.2d 751, 756 (2d Cir. 1975) (noting affidavit by challenged lawyer detailing his responsibilities in matters for Chrysler).

274   ISSUES OF LEGAL ETHICS IN THE PRACTICE OF ENVIRONMENTAL LAW

less, contact by associates and even summer associates (also known as law clerks) and paralegals has provided a basis for successful disqualification motions.[59] In assessing a conflict in a screening device, courts consider the role of the challenged lawyer. A lawyer who was a partner at the old and new firms (as opposed to an associate) is generally regarded as having access to information.

Screening for Private Lawyers

The opportunity to cure a conflict by screening is available under the Model Rules only for government lawyers. Screening is mentioned as a curative device only in Model Rule 1.11. This distinction is maintained in the Revised Model Rules. Nevertheless, some states have allowed screening in relation to private sector lawyers, principally in states that base their conflicts rules on the 1969 Model Code of Professional Responsibility and those that amended the rule on conflicts to expressly provide for screening when they adopted rules based on the ABA Model Rules of Professional Conduct.

The ABA has noted with favor the use of screening in cases involving private practice lawyers rather than a former government lawyer in the context of prospective clients. In Ethics Opinion 90-358, the ABA Commission on Ethics and Professional Responsibility advised lawyers to use the screening device as early in a case as possible. Speaking in the imperative voice, the comment suggests damage control measures.

> As soon as a conflict of interest is identified or the would-be client's representation not undertaken for another reason, screen the lawyer with information relating to the proposed representation from disclosing it within the law firm. . . . In litigated matters where the information disclosed by the would-be client is not extensive or sensitive, this mechanism may avoid disqualification of other lawyers in the firm from representing another client in whose representation the information might prove useful.[60]

When screening is allowed, the firm's rules on screening should include a requirement of locks on computer files that make the files accessible only with the use of passwords not provided to the challenged lawyer. Additionally, hard copies of files and documents should be kept in locked cabinets or files that are physically separated from the working area of the challenged lawyer. In large firms, it may be feasible to have a check-out system for files whereby

---

59. *See, e.g.,* Actel Corp. v. Quicklogic Corp., 1996 WL 297045 (N.D. Cal. 1996).

60. ABA Comm. on Ethics and Prof'l Responsibility Formal Op. No. 90-358.

Chapter 6: Special Conflicts Concerns 275

a staff person rather than a lawyer enters the filing area, retrieves files, and provides the files to authorized personnel. In such a system, lists and file labels can be used to give the file clerk explicit instructions to keep the files from designated lawyers or to allow lawyers to retrieve files only on a need-to-know basis. To have an effective screen (and to rebut the presumption that knowledge of one lawyer in a law firm has been shared with other lawyers in the firm), the "firewall" or screening arrangement should be in place when the disqualified lawyer joined the firm or when the firm accepted a case presenting a conflict because of one lawyer's past representation.[61]

Court Decisions

Some courts have allowed screening in the nongovernmental lawyer context, validating screening as a curative measure in cases that involve private lawyers moving from one firm to another.[62] In the case of *Nemours Foundation v. Gilbane*, the court refused to disqualify a firm in litigation although a new lawyer in the firm had represented an opponent to the law firm's client prior to joining the firm.[63] Although the new lawyer was disqualified from working on the case, the court held that the "shielding mechanism used by the lawyer and firm made it unnecessary to disqualify the entire law firm."[64] The court in *INA Underwriters Insurance Co. v. Rubin* suggested that the analysis for allowing screening in the case of former government lawyers should also be applied to former private lawyers.[65] Courts consider a variety of factors in assessing the efficacy of a "screen" or "ethical wall."[66] These factors include the firm's efforts relating to continuing education on professional responsibility, particularly regarding confidentiality and conflicts. The factors also include the physical, geographic, and departmental separation of lawyers in a

---

61. *See* Gerald v. Trunock Plumbing, Heating and Cooling, L.L.C., 768 N.E.2d 498 (Ind. Ct. App. 2002).

62. *See* Nemours Found. v. Gilbane, 632 F. Supp. 418 (D. Del. 1986); INA Underwriters Ins. Co. v. Rubin, 635 F. Supp. 1 (E.D. Pa. 1983) (holding that, if former government lawyers can be screened effectively, former private lawyers are also capable of being screened effectively); Lemaire v. Texaco, Inc., 496 F. Supp. 1308 (E.D. Tex. 1980) (allowing firm to continue representation of client after finding that lawyer with conflict had been screened effectively). *But see* Atasi Corp. v. Seagate Tech., 847 F.2d 826, 831–32 (Fed. Cir. 1988) (interpreting 9th Circuit law and holding that neither a Chinese Wall nor a cone of silence could allow the firm to proceed).

63. Nemours Found. v. Gilbane, 632 F. Supp. 418 (D. Del. 1986).

64. *Id.*

65. 635 F. Supp. 1 (E.D. Pa. 1983).

66. In the past, courts and scholars referred to such a screen as a "Chinese wall." *See* WOLFRAM, MODERN LEGAL ETHICS *supra* note 5, § 7.6.4 at 401.

firm, the firm's procedures for preventing affected or "infected" lawyers from accessing files or sharing in profits from the challenged representation, and the sanctions the firm has in place for violations of firm rules prohibiting discussions of confidential matters.[67] In the case of *Manning v. James, Sklar, and Allen*,[68] for example, the court held that objective and verifiable evidence of screening procedures to prevent transfer of information between lawyers can satisfy ethics rules against conflicts and disputed conflicts.

In *Hughes v. PaineWebber, Jackson & Curtis, Inc.*,[69] the court held that screening cured an asserted conflict of interest in a case involving a private lawyer rather than a former government lawyer. The court denied a motion to disqualify the lawyers representing plaintiffs despite the fact that two of the lawyers learned confidential information by interviewing the defendants. The screening mechanism was intended to prevent the passing of information about the defendant from being communicated to the lawyers representing the plaintiff. This case involved a prospective client, although the court analyzed the issue assuming that an attorney-client relationship arose as a result of the consultation.

In *INA Underwriters Insurance Company v. Rubin*, the court denied a motion to disqualify INA's lawyers because it found that the law firm had effectively screened a partner who had conferred with Rubin prior to undertaking the action for the plaintiff insurance company.[70] A partner in the firm had spoken with the defendant regarding possible representation on a related criminal investigation. Even though the partner had received confidences in the interview that were relevant to the civil suit, the court allowed the representation based on its finding that the firm effectively screened the partner from divulging those confidences to others in the firm and would continue to screen the partner.[71] The court relied on uncontroverted affidavits from lawyers in the firm, in which the lawyers swore that they never discussed the content of the meeting with the partner who met with Rubin.[72]

---

67. *See, e.g.*, Henriksen v. Great American Sav. & Loan, 14 Cal. Rptr. 2d 184 (Cal. App. 1 Dist. 1992).

68. 849 F.2d 222, 225 (6th Cir. 1988).

69. 565 F. Supp. 663 (N.D. Ill. 1983) (relying on screening mechanism under ABA CODE rule to prevent flow of information about the defendant to the lawyers representing plaintiff and denying a motion to disqualify). *Cf.* Bridge Prods., Inc. v. Quantum Chem. Corp., 1990 U.S. Dist. LEXIS 5019 (N.D. Ill. 1990) (lawyers disqualified from representing new client because of prior conferences with adverse party in lawsuit).

70. INA Underwriters Ins. Co. v. Rubin, 635 F. Supp. 1 (E.D. Pa. 1983).

71. *Id.* at 5.

72. *Id.* at 12.

Chapter 6: Special Conflicts Concerns 277

By contrast, in *Bridge Products, Inc. v. Quantum Chemical Corp.,*[73] the U.S. District Court for the Northern District of Illinois granted a disqualification motion against the firm of Sidley & Austin on the basis that the information it learned from an opponent during an interview for possible representation created a conflict of interest. At trial the parties agreed that no formal attorney-client relationship existed between the plaintiff and Sidley & Austin as a result of the interviews.[74] The Sidley firm argued that the interviewing process represented by the phone conference and in-person meeting with two Sidley & Austin lawyers was merely a "beauty contest," meaning the client was interviewing and evaluating law firms for the purpose of selecting counsel.[75] Although the court accepted the contention that the interview was a "beauty contest," it granted the motion to disqualify the Sidley & Austin firm from representing the defendant, holding that an "implicit attorney-client relationship" arose as a result of the meeting. The court noted that the fact that Bridge Products disclosed the same information to the other lawyers it interviewed did not destroy the confidential nature of the disclosures.[76] Based on the scope of the representation, the sharing of confidential information, and relevance of the information to the issues of the litigation, the court also found that a substantial relationship existed between this brief representation and the subsequent litigation in which Sidley & Austin appeared as counsel for Bridge's opponent, Quantum.[77] The court rejected the argument by Sidley & Austin that it had cured any conflict by use of a screen, in part because the screen was imposed after the firm learned of the challenge to the representation. It noted that the lawyer screened was not a new lawyer arriving at the firm after the contact that created the conflict problem. "The Seventh Circuit . . . has explicitly rejected the concept of a Chinese Wall where the infected attorney is not an associate who has come from another firm or government service, but is simply another lawyer within the firm in question."[78] The fact that the disqualified lawyers obtained confidential information during the interview was a significant factor in the court's analysis.[79] The court recognized the expanded Chinese Wall exception relied on in *Hughes v. PaineWebber,*[80]

---

73. Bridge Products, Inc. v. Quantum Chemical Corp., 1990 WL 70857 (N.D. Ill. 1990).
74. *Id.* at *2.
75. *Id.*
76. *Id.* at *3.
77. *Id.*
78. *Id.* at *6.
79. *Id.*
80. *Id., citing* Hughes v. PaineWebber, Jackson & Curtis, Inc., 565 F. Supp. 663 (N.D. Ill. 1983).

278   ISSUES OF LEGAL ETHICS IN THE PRACTICE OF ENVIRONMENTAL LAW

but declined to apply the approach in the case because of the failure of the law firm to put the prospective clients "on notice that there [was] no attorney/client relationship"[81] in the preliminary interview situation.

Government Lawyers

Overview

Government lawyers face many difficult conflict problems, owing in part to the special responsibilities of governmental lawyers, the variety of roles they play, and the complex nature of representing government agencies, sometimes in cooperation with other governmental entities or even in common representation with private individuals. The Model Rules apply generally to government lawyers.[82] The fact that government lawyers are also subject to conflict of interest statutes heightens the need for careful study of the applicable rules.[83] Courts have held that lawyers are not necessarily conflicted out of a nongovernmental representation merely by virtue of their employment by a governmental agency.[84]

The Revolving Door

Because many environmental lawyers work for government agencies at the federal, state, or local government, the ethics rules on conflicts have great impact in the area. The phenomenon sometimes referred to as the "revolving door" in government practice describes the situation of government lawyers who leave public employment to work in the private sphere. The term "revolving door" may seem to be a misnomer, since the great majority of the lawyers involved are going out the door to take up private practice after gaining experience working in a governmental agency. While some lawyers enter government service after engaging in private practice, few revolve back in the

---

81. *Id.*
82. Comment 4 to MODEL RULE 1.10, as amended February 17, 1987, notes the applicability of the MODEL RULES to government lawyers. It states: "The individual lawyer involved [moving between government and private practice] is bound by the rules generally, including in Rules 1.6, 1.7, and 1.9."
83. Such statutes create criminal penalties for some violations of conflicts of interest. See the final sections of this part (pages 292–94) for discussion of the statutes.
84. *See, e.g.,* State v. Jones (*In re* Banks), 726 S.W.2d 515 (Tenn. 1987) (affirming finding of contempt against lawyer who refused to act as counsel for indigent and holding that county attorneys are not per se disqualified from representing criminal defendants); ABA Informal Op. 1285 (1974) (opining that municipal attorneys with no responsibility for state prosecutions may represent criminal defendants in a county criminal court in matters involving charges of state law violations).

Chapter 6: Special Conflicts Concerns 279

door as a matter of professional affiliation once they leave government work. Nevertheless, many return or wish to return to the agency for the purpose of representing companies in the industry the agency regulates. They often appear before an agency board or other regulatory tribunal. Many private environmental lawyers worked for governmental agencies before entering private practice. Additionally, some government lawyers for EPA, the U.S. Army Corps of Engineers, and other agencies practiced privately before accepting employment with the government agency. Some lawyers represent both governmental and private entities jointly.[85] Many environmental statutes include citizen suit provisions, allowing individuals to enforce the acts as private attorneys general. This fact may enhance the likelihood that former government lawyers may represent private clients after leaving government employment on matters that have been prosecuted by the government. Model Rule 1.11 is of crucial importance for any lawyer in any of these situations. It is important in environmental practice because of the significant and increasing number of lawyers who leave governmental agencies in the environmental sphere to work in the private sector, often representing industrial clients.[86] Generally, lawyers who worked for the government continue in the same legal field as that of the agency that formerly employed them. Continuity of practice area is the norm rather than the exception in environmental law.

As a practical matter, a government lawyer who is considering leaving the government for private practice should talk with the ethics officer of the agency regarding the scope of work undertaken by the lawyer while in the employ of the government and guidelines for what would be off-limits in private practice. One lawyer suggests confirming this conference in a letter to the ethics officer.[87]

Rationale

The conflict rules presented in both the original Model Rules and the Revised Model Rules as well as statutes relating to government lawyers seek to strike a balance that protects the government from undue influence and yet allows lawyers to move from government employment to the private sector and vice versa.

---

85. Comment 9 to the REV. MODEL RULE 1.11 indicates that conflicts rules do not necessarily prohibit joint representation of government and private clients.
86. *See Developments in the Law: Conflicts of Interest in the Legal Profession*, 94 HARV. L. REV. 1244, 1428 (1981).
87. Agencies engage in this sort of prospective advice to lawyers leaving government employ. Telephone conference with David Novello (Sept. 17, 2002).

280 ISSUES OF LEGAL ETHICS IN THE PRACTICE OF ENVIRONMENTAL LAW

> [T]he rules governing lawyers presently or formerly employed by a government agency should not be so restrictive as to inhibit transfer of employment to and from the government. The government has a legitimate need to attract qualified lawyers as well as to maintain high ethical standards.[88]

Ethics rules and statutes seek to avoid an unfair advantage for lawyers (and the clients of lawyers) as a result of a lawyer's former association with a governmental agency.[89]

> [I]t is a premise of basic fairness that a lawyer who has gained intimate knowledge about a party during representation either as a government or private lawyer should not use that knowledge against the same party if the lawyer "switches." Using private client information gathered under the auspices of governmental authority would erode faith in the government.[90]

An inflexible rule prohibiting lawyers from representing private individuals after the lawyers have worked for a government agency would not only penalize the lawyers involved, it would also discourage many qualified lawyers from entering government service at all, potentially resulting in reduction of the quality of representation for government agencies. The rule also seeks to prevent a lawyer from unfairly using information or connections gained as the result of the lawyer's work for the government. Rule 1.11 also seeks to neutralize the potential for abuse of the lawyer's public position or access to personal contacts made at the agency. A comment to the rule makes this point.

> Where the successive clients are a public agency and a private client, the risk exists that power or discretion vested in public

---

88. MODEL RULE 1.11 cmt. 4 (2002).
89. *See* Matter of Petition for Review of Op. 569 of Advisory Comm. on Prof'l Ethics, 511 A.2d 119 (N.J. 1986) (holding former deputy attorneys general barred for six months from appearing before agencies they represented in state service in connection with representation of private party subject to disciplinary proceeding before state agency when investigation began during employment of deputy attorney general by that agency); Forti v. New York State Ethics Comm'n, 555 N.Y.S.2d 235 (N.Y. 1990) (holding state law constitutional that imposed expanded restrictions on professional activities of former government employees following separation from state).
90. Grant Dawson, *Working Guidelines for Successive Conflicts of Interest Involving Government and Private Employment*, 11 GEO. J. LEGAL ETHICS 329, 330–31 (1998).

Chapter 6: Special Conflicts Concerns 281

authority might be used for the special benefit of a private client. A lawyer should not be in a position where benefit to a private client might affect performance of the lawyer's professional functions on behalf of public authority.[91]

Current Clients

Environmental lawyers often work for governmental agencies. Some work for more than one governmental unit. Such a representation is not automatically prohibited by the ethics rules of many states.[92] Comment 9 to Revised Rule 1.11 states that the provisions "do not prohibit a lawyer from jointly representing a private party and a government agency when doing so is permitted by Rule 1.7 and is not otherwise prohibited by law."[93] The Pennsylvania Bar Association Committee on Legal Ethics and Professional Responsibility considered an environmental case and provided an example of one way to handle a potential concurrent conflict of interest.[94] In this case, the inquirer served as special counsel for governmental matters for both the city and the county. The lawyer advised both clients of the possibility of conflict in a written notification to both clients. The lawyer also advised both clients that in the event a conflict developed, he would withdraw from both representations.

In response to the lawyer's request for written acknowledgment of the clients' consent, the county responded with its consent but the city declined to consent, justifying its decision by the fact that there was no present conflict. The Pennsylvania Committee approved of the lawyer's handling of the matter, noting that the lawyer complied with the Pennsylvania Rule on conflicts by fully informing the clients of the potential for conflict and receiving their consent. The Bar also noted that the lawyer's advice to the clients that he would withdraw in the event of conflict obviated any problem of adverse

---

91. MODEL RULE 1.11 cmt. 3.
92. *See, e.g., Illinois Panel Advises When Firm's Lawyers May Represent Related Government Units*, 70 U.S.L.W. 2758 (June 4, 2002) (Illinois State Bar Ass'n Comm. on Prof'l Ethics, Op. 01-07, Apr. 2002, opining that lawyers in the same firm may represent related government units whose interests may conflict as long as there is no current, direct adversity between clients).
93. MODEL RULE 1.11 cmt. 9 (2002).
94. Informal Op. 95-37, 1995 WL 937830 (Mar. 31, 1995); *but see In re* Inquiry to Advisory Comm., 616 A.2d 1290 (N.J. 1992) (holding that law firm whose associate is full-time police officer is disqualified from representing private clients in criminal matters arising in township, regardless of screening; court applied because of appearance of impropriety).

282 ISSUES OF LEGAL ETHICS IN THE PRACTICE OF ENVIRONMENTAL LAW

effect on his relationship with either client. A more difficult case is presented when a lawyer's representation agreement indicates that in the event a conflict arises, the lawyer will terminate the relationship with one client and continue as lawyer for the other client. Such advance agreements have been upheld. Nevertheless, a court could regard the arrangement as one that suggests the lawyer is ranking the clients and has accepted a higher order of allegiance to one client (the one that the agreement designates for continuing representation). Thus, the agreement may be evidence that the representation of the other client is materially limited and, thus, not appropriate.

Former Clients

Courts have disqualified former government lawyers who leave the government and use knowledge gained in government service to bring a civil action on behalf of a private party against the same defendant they had prosecuted while employed by a government agency.[95] Moreover, general knowledge of the defendant's policies can constitute a basis for disqualification of a former government lawyer. In *LaSalle National Bank v. Lake County*,[96] the court granted a motion by Lake County to disqualify the plaintiff's law firm in an action in which the plaintiff challenged the county's denial of access to the county sewer system.

A former government lawyer who had worked for the county of Lake County, Illinois, went into private practice with a large law firm. When he accepted a representation in which his clients challenged the county's denial of access to the sewer system, the county filed a motion to disqualify. The district court granted the motion, disqualifying both the lawyer and the firm on the basis that the past association of the lawyer created an appearance of impropriety. The court of appeals affirmed, noting that it was unnecessary for the defendant to prove that the lawyer actually received confidential information relevant to the matter at issue. The court based its decision on the fact that the plaintiff's law firm had represented the county on similar sewage agreements. Even though the representation did not relate to the particular access

---

95. *See, e.g.*, Allied Realty of St. Paul v. Exchange Nat'l Bank of Chicago, 283 F. Supp. 464 (D. Minn. 1968), *aff'd*, 408 F.2d 1099 (8th Cir. 1969) (granting a motion to disqualify a lawyer who represented the government in a criminal fraud action against a bank and later represented a private party against the same bank in a civil fraud action for the same conduct); Helo Meadows Co. v. Learner Co., 258 F. Supp. 23 (D. Haw. 1966) (disqualifying a lawyer who had represented Department of Justice and, later, in private practice brought a private antitrust suit against the company it had prosecuted while in government service).

96. 703 F.2d 252 (7th Cir. 1983).

Chapter 6: Special Conflicts Concerns 283

petition at issue, the court reasoned that the lawyer had knowledge of the county's policies relating to sewer services as a result of the firm's representations. The challenged lawyer had been employed in the office of the state attorney in Lake County as the principal lawyer for all civil matters, leading an office of six lawyers. The division of the state attorney's office had handled the formulation and the strategy behind the agreement upon which the claim was based.[97]

The court held that the former representation was substantially related to the current representation and, accordingly, the court applied a rebuttable presumption that the "attorney might have acquired information related to the subject matter of the subsequent representation."[98] The court concluded that the present litigation fell within the scope of the prior representation and that it was reasonable to infer that confidential information would have been given to the lawyer who was the chief of the civil division.[99] The court imputed the conflict to the other lawyers in the disqualified lawyer's firm. Although the court recognized that other circuits "either explicitly or implicitly . . . approve the use of screening as a means to avoid disqualification of an entire law firm by 'infection,'"[100] it found that the firm had failed to establish a formalized screening process.[101] The court noted the problem presented by disqualification of lawyers based on former practice with the government. "If past employment in government results in the disqualification of future employers from representing some of their long-term clients, it seems clearly possible that government attorneys will be regarded as 'Typhoid Marys.'"[102] Although the lawyer involved submitted an affidavit that he did not disclose information about the case or the county's strategy, the court noted that the firm did not have specific screening mechanisms in place to prevent sharing of information. The court also noted the concern that the "reputation of the bar as a whole is implicated" in the case.[103]

Model Rules

The Model Rules include specific conflicts rules relating to government lawyers, former government lawyers, and lawyers who serve as public officers. Model Rule 1.11 speaks directly to the issue of government lawyers who have left the employ of the government for private practice. Other Model Rules

---

97. *Id.* at 256.
98. *Id.* at 255.
99. *Id.* at 256.
100. *Id.*
101. *Id.* at 259.
102. *Id.* at 258.
103. *Id.* at 259.

284 ISSUES OF LEGAL ETHICS IN THE PRACTICE OF ENVIRONMENTAL LAW

apply generally to lawyers in government practice even when they do not mention government practice specifically. Model Rule 1.11 prohibits a lawyer from representing a private client "in a matter in which the lawyer participated personally and substantially as a public officer or employee" unless the lawyer obtains the consent of the agency involved after consultation.[104] Model Rule 1.11 also prohibits lawyers from using "confidential government information about a person acquired when the lawyer was a public officer or employee,"[105] prohibiting lawyers from representing a person whose interests are adverse to a person about whom the lawyer acquired information while working for the government.[106] The rule defines confidential government information as any information obtained under government authority that the law protects from disclosure or that the lawyer has a privilege not to disclose.[107]

The rule also imputes such a conflict to the firm with which such a lawyer is associated unless the lawyer is screened from any participation or fee relating to the matter.[108] Model Rule 1.11 includes a provision prohibiting a current government lawyer from participating in a matter when he "participated personally and substantially" while in private practice, essentially presenting a mirror-image of the rule for former government lawyers, except when no other government representative can act in "the lawyer's stead."[109] In the setting of former private lawyers now representing a governmental entity, the rule also prohibits lawyers from negotiating for private employment during their tenure with the government except in defined settings, such as judicial law clerks who have a limited tenure in the ordinary course of the position.[110] Courts impute disqualification to lawyers associated with lawyers who have conflicts as a result of prior government representation.[111] The opportunity to cure a conflict by screening is available for former government lawyers.[112]

2002 Revision

The 2002 revision to Model Rule 1.11 retained the basic approach of the original rule, making minimal changes to the conflict rules relating to government lawyers. The 2002 revision makes clear that the conflicts rules apply to

---

104. MODEL RULE 1.11(a) (as amended 1987).
105. MODEL RULE 1.11(b) (as amended 1987).
106. *Id.*
107. *Id.*
108. *Id.*
109. MODEL RULE 1.11(c) (as amended 1987).
110. *Id.*
111. *See, e.g.,* Chambers v. Superior Court, 121 Cal. App. 3d 893 (1981).
112. This practice is sometimes referred to as erecting a "Chinese Wall" between lawyers. *See, e.g.,* Tennessee's Formal Op. 89-F-118.

current and former government lawyers as well as to lawyers in the private sector. Revised Model Rule 1.11 expressly states that Model Rule 1.9(c), which protects information of former clients, is applicable to lawyers who formerly were employed by government agencies.[113] The revised rule also states lawyers currently serving as government employees or public officers are subject to Model Rules 1.7 and 1.9 relating to current and former clients.[114] As with former government lawyers, a lawyer who currently represents a governmental entity is prohibited from participating in a representation that the lawyer participated in "personally and substantially while in private practice."[115] The revised rule changed the standard for consent from "consent after consultation" to "informed consent,"[116] acknowledging a cure of such conflicts by the informed consent of the "appropriate government agency" when the consent is "confirmed in writing."[117]

Like the original rule, Revised Model Rule 1.11 prohibits a lawyer from representing a person adverse to one about whom the lawyer acquired "confidential government information" during the lawyer's employment with the government.[118] The rule defines confidential government information as any information obtained under government authority that the law protects from disclosure.[119] The revised rule retained the mirror-image of the rule applicable to former government lawyers. The revised rule prohibits a current government lawyer from participating in a matter when he "participated personally and substantially" in that matter in private practice. The rule did not echo the language of the original rule allowing a representation of the government when no other lawyer could act in "the lawyer's stead," leaving this situation to be resolved by the consent of the government agency.[120]

Because Revised Rule 1.11 expressly applies Model Rule 1.7 to current government lawyers, it is necessary for such lawyers to obtain the consent of former clients they represented in private practice when the test of Rule 1.7 applies. Accordingly, a government lawyer also has the obligation to decline a representation when it "will be directly adverse to another client" or when a significant risk exists that one of the representations will be "materially limited" by the lawyer's responsibilities to another person or client or by interests

---

113. Model Rule 1.11(a)(1) and (d)(1) (2002).

114. Model Rule 1.11(d)(1) (2002).

115. Model Rule 1.11(d)(2)(i) (2002).

116. Model Rule 1.11(a)(2) and (d)(2)(i) (2002).

117. *Id.*

118. Model Rule 1.11(c) (2002).

119. *Id.*

120. Model Rule 1.11(d) (2002) and Reporter's Explanation of Changes ¶ 11.

of the lawyer herself.[121] When the informed consent of a client (either the government agency or the private client) is required, it must be "confirmed in writing."[122]

The revised rule imputes conflicts to the firm with which the lawyer is associated by incorporation of Model Rules 1.7 and 1.9. Conflicts imputed to others by virtue of Revised Model Rule 1.11 may be cured by timely screening of the disqualified lawyer from participation in the matter and notice to the appropriate government agency. Additionally, as applied to former government lawyers, the rule requires that the disqualified lawyer must receive no part of fees from the matter. A comment to the revised rule makes clear that "matter" as used by the rule is broader than may appear at first reading. Comment 10 notes that a matter under the rule "may continue in another form."[123]

Environmental Examples

Assume that a lawyer who worked for EPA as a project manager for Superfund sites leaves government practice to accept a position in the legal department of an energy company. The energy company is a PRP at one of the sites the lawyer managed while employed by EPA. Suppose further that the company assigns the lawyer to the work group that represents the energy company at the Superfund site because she was involved personally and substantially in the matter. Although the lawyer need not obtain the consent of EPA to accept a position as an in-house lawyer for the energy company, Model Rule 1.11 requires that she obtain the agency's consent to represent the client at this particular site. This is because a court or disciplinary board is likely to regard the Superfund site as the same matter on which she worked while employed as a lawyer for the EPA. Obtaining the consent of the agency that formerly employed her is necessary to comply with Model Rule 1.11. The same problem arises, of course, if the former government lawyer wishes to represent an environmental public interest group rather than an industrial client if the lawyer worked on the matter while a government lawyer. Additionally, if the lawyer comes within the definition of "senior employee," the applicable federal statute obligates her to decline to represent the company.[124]

---

121. Model RULE 1.7 (2002).

122. Model RULE 1.11(a)(2) (2002).

123. Model RULE 1.11 cmt. 10 (2002) (noting that in determining "whether two particular matters are the same, the lawyer should consider the extent to which the matters involve the same basic facts, the same or related parties, and the time elapsed").

124. The statute is discussed in detail below.

ABA Opinions

ABA Formal Opinion 342 affirmed the practice of screening government lawyers when they enter law firms. The opinion recognized the need to prevent conflicts from depriving the firm of clients who had contact with the lawyer while he was in government service and to prevent a situation in which government lawyers cannot move on to work in the private sphere. It noted that such a rule would create a disincentive to lawyers entering government practice at all.[125] The opinion indicated that screening and waiver by the governmental agency helps "prevent the disqualification rule from imposing too severe a deterrent against entering public service."[126]

In ABA Formal Opinion 97-409, entitled "Conflicts of Interest: Successive Government and Private Employment," the ABA Standing Committee on Ethics and Professional Responsibility addressed an inquiry from a lawyer regarding whether she may "represent private claimants before her old agency in connection with the same general kinds of claims she handled while in government service."[127] The ABA Committee determined that the primary rules relating to government lawyers who terminate employment with the government and accept employment or representation of private clients are Model Rule 1.11 and Rule 1.9(c). The Committee noted that Model Rule 1.11 deals directly with the topic of inquiry: "Successive Government and Private Employment."

Formal Opinion 97-409 indicates that Model Rule 1.11 disqualifies a former government lawyer from representing a private client when the lawyer "participated personally and substantially as a public officer or employee" in the "particular matter" at issue in the subsequent representation.[128] The opinion expressly notes that the resulting disqualification does not depend on the private representation being adverse to the former government client. It indicates that a former government lawyer may represent a private party if the lawyer did not personally participate in the matter during employment with the government and gained no confidential government information about an adverse third party. The lawyer "is not forbidden from representing private parties in matters in which she did not so participate, or in any matters not involving 'a discrete and isolatable transaction or set of transactions between identifiable parties,' except where she has obtained 'confidential government information' about an adverse third party."[129]

---

125. ABA Formal Op. 342 (1976).
126. *Id.*
127. ABA Formal Op. 97-409 (1997).
128. *Id.*
129. *Id., citing* MODEL RULE 1.11(a) and (b) and ABA Formal Op. 342.

Disqualification under Rule 1.11 occurs only when the former government lawyer personally handled the matter during service with the government or gained confidential information about the matter at issue. The Committee indicated that Rule 1.9(c) ("Conflict of Interest. Former Client") also applies to the use of information relating to a former representation of a government client. The Committee concluded that Rule 1.9(a) and (b) do not apply to a former government lawyer. It found Rule 1.9(c) applicable to bar a former government lawyer from representing a private client when that representation would require the use or disclosure of information relating to her representation of the government. The Rule prohibits the former government lawyer from using information to the disadvantage of the government when it is not generally known. Thus, when a lawyer has been involved in developing generally applicable agency rules, the lawyer may represent a private party challenging those rules unless prohibited from the representation by Rule 1.9(c), which relates to "information relating to her representation of the government that has not become generally known." The opinion also makes clear that other ethics rules, such as Model Rule 1.6 on the duty of confidentiality and Model Rule 3.3 on the lawyer's duty of candor to tribunals, continue to have full application to former government lawyers. It also indicates that firms may use screening to allow other lawyers in a firm to represent a private client, even though one of the firm's lawyers is personally disqualified from representing the private client by virtue of earlier involvement in the matter on behalf of the government.

Ethics Opinions

Bar associations and disciplinary boards have addressed the issue of a conflict based on prior government work. For example, the Pennsylvania Bar Association Committee on Legal Ethics and Professional Responsibility held that a conflict prevented a lawyer from representing a company because the lawyer had been involved in investigating and prosecuting that same company while employed by the Department of Justice (DOJ).[130] Although the lawyer noted that she "did not recall receiving any 'confidential information' on this matter while working for the DOJ," her failure to obtain consent from the DOJ was fatal to her representation. The opinion did not bar the lawyer's firm from undertaking the representation, however, as long as the firm screened the lawyer from discussions of the matter and allocated no part of its fee to the former government lawyer.[131]

---

130. Pennsylvania Bar Ass'n Comm. on Legal Ethics and Prof'l Responsibility Informal Op. 94-132 (1994), 1994 WL 928083.

131. *Id.*

Chapter 6: Special Conflicts Concerns   289

In some circumstances, even consent of the agency might fail to neutralize the conflict problem sufficiently. For example, an advisory opinion by the New Jersey Supreme Court Advisory Committee on Professional Ethics held that a former government lawyer could not accept later employment that would involve attacking rules he helped draft while he worked for the government.[132]

The Model Rules do not expressly address the issue of whether a lawyer entering government practice could be conflicted out of some representations. The District of Columbia Bar Legal Ethics Committee has noted an obligation on the part of such lawyers to refrain from using client information to the detriment of former clients in this setting.[133] The Committee also noted that lawyers may be conflicted out of projects based on the substantial relationship of a project to work performed for a private client.[134]

Curative Measures

Consent

The informed consent of the government agency concerned cures the type of conflict described in Model Rule 1.11(a). Revised Rule 1.11 also makes clear that the former government lawyer must also comply with the general rule on former client conflicts, Rule 1.9, and the current government lawyer must also comply with Rules 1.7 and 1.9, relating to representations that may be directly adverse or materially limited. The rule appears to apply to lawyers who served as a governmental officer or employee whether or not they were lawyers at the time. A lawyer who leaves a government agency for private practice could be involved personally in a representation despite her involvement in the case while working at the agency if she obtains the informed consent of the agency to represent a client in a matter against the government. Consent by an agency should be effective in most conceivable cases, since an agency would normally be presumed to be sophisticated and knowledgeable about the area of law involved. Nevertheless, the possibility that a conflict is not consentable cannot be disregarded.

---

132. New Jersey Supreme Court Advisory Comm. on Prof'l Ethics Op. 379 (1977) (holding that a former government lawyer could not accept later employment appealing rules on the Coastal Areas Facilities Review Act that he helped draft while working as a government lawyer).

133. *See* District of Columbia Bar Legal Ethics Comm. Op. 308 (June 26, 2001) (cautioning lawyers leaving private practice for government work must not use client information to disadvantage client and using example of unethical conduct of using information gained while working for a manufacturer of automobiles to amend environmental regulations in a way that is unfavorable to the former client).

134. *Id.*

Screening

In *Kesselhaut v. United States*,[135] the court refused to disqualify a firm, finding that a screening device was effective to insulate a former government lawyer and holding that imputation of the conflict was unwarranted under the circumstances. Screening was first validated in cases involving government lawyers who leave government work for private practice. In 1976, the ABA gave credence to the practice of screening as a curative measure to allow former government lawyers to join a firm despite a conflict when the lawyer can be screened effectively. The ABA Ethics Committee Opinion 342 limited the use of screening to situations in which the government agency that formerly employed the lawyer consented to the arrangement.[136]

Original Model Rule 1.11 imputed conflicts to other private lawyers associated with a former government lawyer who had participated personally and substantially on a matter while a public employee. The rule allowed cure of the conflict for the associated lawyers by screening the lawyer from participation and fees and giving prompt notice to the government agency involved.[137] The only references to screening in the original Model Rules are found in Rule 1.11, dealing with the movement of lawyers between government and private practice, and Rule 1.12, relating to former judges or arbitrators.[138] Model Rule 1.11 notes that a conflict is imputed from a lawyer to his firm when a lawyer participates unless a disqualified lawyer is "screened from any participation in the matter" and receives no part of the fee generated in the matter.[139]

The net result of this distinction is that the law firm with proper screening measures in place has a better chance of accepting and maintaining representation compared with a firm that lacks appropriate screening measures.[140] The Model Code incorporates essentially the same standard for restricting government lawyers who enter private practice.[141] The fact that a lawyer

---

135. 555 F.2d 791, 792–94 (Cl. Ct. 1977).

136. WOLFRAM, *supra* note 5, § 7 .6.4, at 403.

137. MODEL RULE 1.11(a).

138. *See* MODEL RULE 1.11 cmt. 3 (noting that provisions allowing screening and waiver "are necessary to prevent the disqualification rule from imposing too severe a deterrent against entering public service").

139. MODEL RULE 1.11(a)(1).

140. *See In re* Del-Val Fin. Corp. Sec. Litig., 158 F.R.D. 270 (S.D.N.Y. 1994) (denying motion to disqualify lawyers for nonsettling defendant relying on early institution of screening procedures).

141. *See* MODEL CODE DR 9-101.

Chapter 6: Special Conflicts Concerns   291

formerly worked for the government does not ensure that screening will successfully eliminate a conflict problem.[142]

Screening (2002 Revision)

The 2002 revision to Model Rules imputes to other firm members the conflict resulting from a lawyer's former representation of a government agency. The conflict of a former government lawyer is imputed to other lawyers in his firm unless the firm screened the lawyer in a timely manner and provided the government agency with written notice of the representation to enable the agency to determine whether it agrees the rule of ethics is met.[143] The 2002 Model Rules define "screened" as "the isolation of a lawyer from any participation in a matter through the timely imposition of procedures within a firm that are reasonably adequate under the circumstances to protect information that the isolated lawyer is obligated to protect under these Rules or other law."[144] Whether a lawyer who is a new employee comes from government practice or from another firm, it is critical for firms to have methodical and routine screening measures in place to assert the curative measure of an ethical screen successfully.

Screening Devices

Screening devices should include locks on computer files that make the files accessible only with the use of passwords not provided to the challenged lawyer. Hard copies of files and documents should be kept in locked cabinets or files that are physically separated from the working area of the challenged lawyer. In large firms, it may be feasible to have a checkout system for files whereby a staff person rather than a lawyer enters the filing area, retrieves files, and provides the files to authorized personnel. In such a system, the file clerk can be given lists of restricted files and instructions to provide the files only to designated lawyers. Likewise, lists and file labels can be used to give the file clerk explicit instructions to keep the files from designated lawyers. In fact, some firms use a system in which the default understanding is that lawyers do not have access to files generally and receive access to files only on a need-to-know basis. Additionally, firms should have policies and a serious culture about discussion of client matters. Part of a screening plan should be for lawyers to know not to casually discuss client matters without noting who

---

142. *See generally* Grant Dawson, *Working Guidelines for Successive Conflicts of Interest Involving Government and Private Employment*, 11 GEO. J. LEGAL ETHICS 329 (1998) [hereinafter Dawson].

143. MODEL RULE 1.11(b) (2002).

144. REV. MODEL RULE 1.0(k).

292   ISSUES OF LEGAL ETHICS IN THE PRACTICE OF ENVIRONMENTAL LAW

is included in a conversation and refraining from mentioning any point in the presence of a screened lawyer. Each of these measures adds another layer of protection against sharing of information with lawyers who may present a conflict problem.

Federal Statute

In addition to the ethics rule on this point, a federal statute, the Ethics in Government Act, prohibits former government employees (including lawyers) from working on matters in which they participated while in government service.[145] This provision, entitled "Restrictions on Former Officers, Employees, and Elected Officials of the Executive and Legislative Branches," is lengthy (109 pages on Westlaw). The statute limits contact between the employee and the agency for which he worked and prohibits representation of a client in matters on which the former employee worked.

Section 207(a)(1) of the Ethics in Government Act[146] prohibits former federal employees (including lawyers) from appearing before an agency to represent a private party when the lawyer participated personally and substantially in the matter while employed by the government. Section 207(a)(2) prohibits a former government employee from attempting to influence a federal agency or court in relation to any matter before an agency until two years after the employee exited public service.[147] Additionally, the Act empowers each agency to issue Supplemental Standards of Ethical Conduct.[148] The Act's lifetime prohibition applies to all federal officers and employees and prohibits any attempt to influence the government in a case in which the officer or employee "participated personally and substantially" while working for the government.[149] The Act provides penalties for violation of its provisions, including suspension from practice before the agency,[150] and criminal penalties, including fines and imprisonment.[151] The section defines the prohibited conduct broadly, including any conduct by a person who "knowingly makes, with the intent to influence, any

---

145. *See* 18 U.S.C. § 207 (2000).
146. *Id.*
147. In 1996, Congress amended the Act to allow senior officials to communicate with the agencies that once employed them with the intent to influence official action on behalf of political candidates and organizations. *See* § 207(c)–(e), Office of Government Ethics Authorization Act of 1996, Pub. L. No. 104-179 (1996).
148. Dawson, *supra* note 142, at 343 (citing memoranda of the Office of Government Ethics to designated agency ethics officials (Aug. 21, 1996)).
149. *See* 18 U.S.C. § 207 (2000).
150. *Id.*
151. *See id., citing* 18 U.S.C. § 216 (2000).

communication to or appearance before any officer or employee of any department, agency, court," or other governmental body.[152]

Federal regulations also include a one-year prohibition on departing lawyers who are senior government employees.[153] This rule includes lawyers employed by a government agency who were "senior employees while employed by the government."[154] This prohibition is also broad, including any "communication to or appearance before an employee of a department or agency."[155] Likewise, the regulation is broad in terms of what triggers the prohibition, including service "in any capacity with while working for the agency."[156] Such regulations impose a duty on lawyers that is independent of the rules of ethics.

> For one year after service in a "senior" position terminates, no former "senior" employee may knowingly make, with the intent to influence, any communication to or appearance before an employee of a department or agency in which he served in any capacity during the one-year period prior to termination from "senior" service, if that communication or appearance is made on behalf of

---

152. *See* 18 U.S.C. § 207(a) (2000).

153. *See* 5 C.F.R. § 2641.201 (2001).

154. According to the regulations, a "senior employee" is determined by reference to rank and pay schedules. "Senior employee means an employee, other than a very senior employee, who is:

(1) Employed in a position for which the rate of pay is specified in or fixed according to 5 U.S.C. §§ 5311–5318 (the Executive Schedule);

(2) Employed in a position for which the basic rate of pay, exclusive of any locality-based pay adjustment under 5 U.S.C. § 5304 (or any comparable adjustment pursuant to interim authority of the President) is equal to or greater than the rate of basic pay payable for Level V of the Executive Schedule (including any such position in the Senior Executive Service or other SES-type systems, e.g., the Senior Foreign Service);

(3) Appointed by the President to a position under 3 U.S.C. § 105(a)(2)(B);

(4) Appointed by the Vice President to a position under 3 U.S.C. § 106(a)(1)(B);

(5) Employed in a position which is held by an active duty commissioned officer of the uniformed services who is serving in a grade or rank for which the pay grade (as specified in 37 U.S.C. § 201) is pay grade O-7 or above; or

(6) Detailed to any such position."

155. 5 C.F.R. § 2641.101.

156. 5 C.F.R. § 2641.201 (1998) (prohibiting senior employees from seeking to influence an employee of a department or agency in which he or she was employed for one year following his or her departure).

any other person (except the United States) in connection with any matter on which he seeks official action by any employee.[157]

State Laws

States also limit or prohibit state government lawyers from representing private clients after they leave government employ when they participated in an official capacity in the matter.[158] The provisions vary from state to state. Based on their general rulemaking authority or specific statutory grants, many state agencies have promulgated prohibitions against practice before the agency by former employees.[159]

Corporate Clients

Model Rule 1.13 adopts the rules relating to conflicts in the context of representation of a corporation. It allows representation of a corporation and its directors, officers, employees, members, shareholders, or other constituents under the condition that the lawyer receive the consent of the client as required by Model Rule 1.7. Model Rule 1.13 expressly requires that, in the corporate setting, the consent mandated by Rule 1.7 "be given by an appropriate official of the organization other than the individual who is to be represented, or by the shareholders."[160]

Environmental Examples

The opportunity for conflicts between a corporate client and its employee or

---

157. 5 C.F.R. § 2641.201 (2001).
158. *See, e.g.,* Midboe v. Commission on Ethics for Public Employees, 646 So. 2d 351 (La. 1994) (upholding constitutionality of ethics provision that limited the employment a lawyer can accept for two years following his or her service as a government lawyer); *see also* Rachel E. Boehm, *Caught in the Revolving Door: A State Lawyer's Guide to Post-Employment Restrictions,* 15 Rev. Litig. 525 (1996).
159. *See, e.g.,* Matter of Petition for Rev. of Op. No. 569 of Advisory Comm. on Prof'l Ethics, 511 A.2d 119 (N.J. 1986) (holding that former deputy attorneys general are barred for six months from appearing before agencies they represented while in state service in connection with representation of private party subject of disciplinary proceeding before state agency that deputy attorney general represented and investigation of which party began during employment of deputy attorney general by that agency); Forti v. New York State Ethics Comm'n, 555 N.Y.S.2d 235 (N.Y. 1990) (holding that state law that imposed new and expanded restrictions on the business and professional activities of certain former government employees following their separation from state service was not an unconstitutional ex post facto law as applied to former state officers or employees who left state service before the Act's effective date).
160. *See* Model Rule 1.13(e).

Chapter 6: Special Conflicts Concerns   295

other constituent in environmental matters is acute. Many regulated entities are corporations. The conduct of the corporate entity regulated by environmental laws is, like all corporate activity, accomplished by the acts of human individuals. Such conduct may include discharges of hazardous and regulated substances into the nation's waterways and air from manufacturing facilities and other regulated businesses. Both the corporate entity and the individuals who act for the entity are subject to environmental laws. Both can be subject to sanctions, including criminal penalties, for violations of those laws. Although a corporate entity cannot serve time in prison, it can be sanctioned by criminal monetary penalties. Accordingly, it is understandable that disputes sometimes arise between the corporation and an employee regarding whether the individual employee's actions (such as discharging hazardous substances in excess of permitted amounts) was at the direction of the corporation. Moreover, employees charged with engaging in illegal discharge activity may sometimes implicate corporate officers and directors in the environmental crimes they are charged with.

Assume that you represent a corporate client that operates several manufacturing plants subject to permits issued by EPA pursuant to the Clean Water Act (CWA) and the Clean Air Act (CAA). An employee who is registered as the corporation's designated responsible official[161] seeks your advice in circumstances that indicate he is under stress. He asks to speak with you privately and is visibly agitated. In the private discussion, he begins to relate problems with the discharge monitoring reporting system or other issues relating to discharges. As the lawyer for the corporation, you want to know anything that is happening that may raise legal concerns for your client. Nevertheless, you should consider conflict problems before continuing the discussion with the employee. Similarly, assume that an employee's job involves the actual discharge of waste materials under a permit. If the employee allowed discharges that are in violation of permit requirements, he may come to the corporation's lawyer for advice, assuming incorrectly that the corporation's lawyer is there to protect his individual interests.

In such a situation, the lawyer should be on guard against learning confidential information that could create a conflict in the event the corporation and the employee become adverse parties. The lawyer should be prepared to cut off an employee's narrative of facts if it appears to involve confidential information or prejudicial information. If the employee's question or problem relates to his role in the corporation, the employee may be have an expectation that the lawyer represents him as well as the corporation. A failure by

---

161. A designated responsible corporate official is the official chosen by the company to endorse or certify environmental reports.

ISSUES OF LEGAL ETHICS IN THE PRACTICE OF ENVIRONMENTAL LAW

the lawyer to warn the employee that he does not represent the employee could result in a conflict that could disqualify the lawyer from representing his original corporate client in a matter involving the employee.

On the other hand, unless the lawyer has reason to know that the employee of the corporate client is confiding information that will create a conflict, the lawyer arguably acts responsibly in listening to problems or other information from employees. The lawyer may take the view that his duty to the corporate client requires him to listen and learn of any problems that might affect the corporate client's interests. Under this line of reasoning, the lawyer may be justified in talking with the corporation's employee about his job or concerns arising from his employment. In either case, if the lawyer learns information that a conflict may exist between the employee and the corporation (such as a claim that the corporation ordered discharge of hazardous substances in excess of a permitted level), the lawyer should inform the employee of the lawyer's representation of the employer and terminate the meeting unless the employee chooses to continue the conversation.

Representation of Employees or Constituents

Model Rule 1.13 speaks directly to the issue of representing a corporation and an employee or other constituent of that corporation. The rule indicates that such a representation is subject to the rules on conflicts. Model Rule 1.13 states:

> A lawyer representing an organization may also represent any of its directors, officers, employees, members, shareholders or other constituents, subject to the provisions of Rule 1.7. If the organization's consent to the dual representation is required by Rule 1.7, the consent shall be given by an appropriate official of the organization other than the individual who is to be represented, or by the shareholders.[162]

Whether a lawyer may represent both a corporate client and an employee of the corporate client depends on application of the general conflict rule set forth in Model Rule 1.7. In some cases, a joint defense may be reasonable. Additionally, corporations sometimes pay for both representations, providing a cost savings for the employee.

A significant problem arises, however, if the two parties become adverse during the representation. In such a case, the corporation may want to continue the representation, with the lawyer terminating his services for the em-

---

162. MODEL RULE 1.13(e).

Chapter 6: Special Conflicts Concerns   297

ploee. The representation agreement between the corporate client and the employee may state the consequences if a later conflict develops. For example, the agreement may provide that the lawyer will cease his representation of the employee but continue as the lawyer for the corporation.[163] In the case of *In re Rite Aid Securities Litigation*,[164] a federal trial court held that a law firm could continue to represent a corporate client after the firm withdrew from representing the CEO of the company after a conflict between the company and the CEO developed. The court's opinion emphasized the fact that the retention letter specified that the firm would continue to represent the company in the event such a conflict developed. The firm's letter accepting the representation stated:

> At the present time, we do not see any conflict that would prevent the firm from representing both the Corporation and Mr. Grass. It is possible, however, that such a conflict may arise or become apparent in the future, in which case it is understood that Mr. Grass would retain separate counsel and that the firm would continue to represent the Corporation.[165]

The court relied on the retention letter in its decision and noted that during numerous pretrial hearings and for approximately 14 months after Grass stepped down as CEO, he did not object to the firm's continued representation of Rite Aid. The court also explained that this case was not an example of a "hot potato" case.[166]

Representation of a Corporation's Employee

Payment

Comment 10 to Model Rule 1.7 indicates that a corporation may pay a lawyer to represent its employee, even when the corporation and the employee are both parties to a suit, as long as receiving payment from the corporation does not impair the lawyer's duty of loyalty to the employee-client. It states:

> A lawyer may be paid from a source other than the client, if the

---

163. *See* Los Angeles County Bar Ass'n Prof'l Responsibility and Ethics Comm., Op. 471 (1992) (approving advance written consent by employee allows lawyer to withdraw from employee's representation and to continue in representation of corporation if corporation asserts claim against employee).

164. *In re* Rite Aid Sec. Litig., 139 F. Supp. 2d 649 (E.D. Pa. 2001).

165. *Id.*

166. *Id.* at n.15.

client is informed of that fact and consents and the arrangement does not compromise the lawyer's duty of loyalty to the client. See Rule 1.8(f). For example, . . . when a corporation and its directors or employees are involved in a controversy in which they have conflicting interests, the corporation may provide funds for separate legal representation of the directors or employees, if the clients consent after consultation and the arrangement ensures the lawyer's professional independence.

Payment (2002 Revision)

Comment 13 to the 2002 Revised Model Rule 1.7 considers whether it is appropriate for a lawyer to receive payment for legal services from someone other than the client. Revised comment 13 indicates that a lawyer may receive payment from a client (presumably including corporate clients) to provide services to another client (presumably including its employee) in some cases. Although the comment no longer refers directly to a "corporation" on this point, it notes that a lawyer may be paid from a source other than the client, including a co-client. Revised comment 13 states: "A lawyer may be paid from a source other than the client, including a co-client, if the client is informed of that fact and consents and the arrangement does not compromise the lawyer's duty of loyalty or independent judgment to a client."[167] This comment is a revision of comment 10 from the 1983 version of the Model Rules. Although the revised comment deleted the specific reference to a corporation, its intent seems to be to generalize the language rather than to exclude the corporate client from the scope of the comment.

Even when it is permissible to represent both a corporation and its employee under the rules of legal ethics, the prudent lawyer should give serious thought to such an arrangement, particularly when allegations of misconduct are involved in the case. This point is considered further in the environmental context in the next section.

Environmental Examples: Nonlegal Services

Lawyers who are not, strictly speaking, representing parties in a legal capacity may face conflicts issues. Even a lawyer who works in the environmental arena in a nonlegal capacity should consider conflicts questions. An opinion of the Connecticut Bar Association Committee on Professional Ethics addressed the question of whether a lawyer may accept representation of clients with legal environmental claims when he also works in a nonlegal capacity as

---

167. MODEL RULE 1.7 cmt. 10 (1983).

Chapter 6: Special Conflicts Concerns   299

a sales marketing and business development manager for a company engaged in environmental cleanups.[168] Quoting an earlier comment, the Committee noted that the potential "conflict does not itself preclude the representation."[169] The Committee decided that a lawyer may accept representation although he continues in the employment of the environmental cleanup company if he reasonably believes that his representation of the client will not be adversely affected and obtains the client's consent after consulting with the client and explaining the advantages and risks involved. In its decision entitled "Conflicts of Interest Associated with 'Private Rights of Action Under Connecticut General Statutes (environmental protection) § 22A-452,'" the Committee considered a lawyer's work on environmental causes of action brought either by parties or "governmentally mandated as a result of Sec. 22a-452 actions."[170] The Committee noted that lawyers may serve in a dual capacity, providing legal services to different parties, as long as the lawyer complies with all rules of professional ethics. The opinion indicated that in the case at hand, the lawyer would need to comply with the conflicts rules by obtaining each party's consent after consultation. The Committee noted that in the situation addressed the lawyer is not serving in a dual legal capacity, since he is not representing the parties as a lawyer. The Committee analogized the situation to that in the dual representation problem, however, noting that the lawyer can represent both parties only if he "reasonably believes the representation will not be adversely affected."[171] If the lawyer consults with clients and obtains their consent, the consultation must include an explanation of the advantages and risks involved.

Corporate Clients: Representation Affecting Corporate Affiliates

In some circumstances, the fact that a lawyer's firm represents an affiliate of the adverse corporation may be sufficient to justify disqualification. Courts addressing the issue of representation of corporate affiliates have reached varying results. In the case of *Gould, Inc. v. Mitsui Mining & Smelting Co.*,[172] the court required a lawyer to withdraw as counsel for either the plaintiff or its subsidiary, noting that a representation that is directly adverse to a corporate affiliate of the subsidiary creates a conflict. In *Pennwalt Corp. v. Plough, Inc.*,[173] the court refused to disqualify plaintiff's counsel in an action charging the defendant with deceptive advertising claims despite the fact that plaintiff's

---

168. Conn. Bar Assoc. Comm. on Prof'l Ethics, Informal Op. 99-12 (1999).
169. *Id.*
170. *Id.*
171. MODEL RULE 1.7.
172. 738 F. Supp. 1121 (N.D. Ohio 1990).
173. 85 F.R.D. 264 (D.C. Del. 1980).

counsel had represented the defendant's sister corporation in a separate antitrust suit. The court found that plaintiff's counsel had received no confidential information from the sister corporation that was relevant to the matter at hand. Additionally, the court found that, at the date of the lawyer's withdrawal from representation of the sister corporation, there had been no conflict, and no reasonable possibility of improper professional conduct existed.

In 1995, the ABA Committee on Ethics and Professional Responsibility held that "a lawyer who represents a corporate client may undertake a representation that is adverse to a corporate client affiliate of the client in an unrelated matter, without obtaining the client's consent."[174] The approach adopted by the ABA Model Code of Professional Responsibility gives less leeway for representation of a wholly owned subsidiary of an opponent. "A conflict of interest arising from plaintiff counsel's representation of defendant's wholly owned subsidiary in matters which had no connection to action plaintiff brought against defendant required counsel to withdraw as counsel for either plaintiff or the subsidiary."[175]

Assume that a lawyer who represents Corporation A is presented with the possibility of representing a subsidiary of Corporation B. Corporation B is a competitor of A. Should the lawyer be allowed to undertake the representation without seeking the consent of its client, Corporation A? In Formal Opinion 95-390, the ABA Committee on Ethics and Professional Responsibility dealt with this issue and held that a lawyer representing a corporate client may in some circumstances represent a client adverse to a corporate affiliate of the client without obtaining the consent of the corporate client. The opinion noted that such representation is not appropriate if the lawyer and the corporate client have an understanding that the lawyer will avoid representations adverse to the client's corporate affiliates.

> The fact of corporate affiliation, without more, does not make all of a corporate client's affiliates into clients as well. Nonetheless, the circumstances of a particular representation may be such that the corporate client has a reasonable expectation that the affiliates will be treated as clients, either generally or for purposes of avoidance of conflicts, and the lawyer is aware of the expectation.[176]

Additionally, the opinion notes that the "onus is squarely on the lawyer to anticipate and resolve conflicts of interest involving corporate affiliates."[177]

---

174. ABA Formal Op. 95-390 (1995).

175. ABA Code of Prof'l Responsibility DR 5-105(C).

176. ABA Formal Op. 95-390 (1995).

177. *Id.* (citing Pennwalt Corp. v. Plough, Inc., 85 F.R.D. 264, 273 (D. Del. 1980).

The situation of potential conflict between the existing client and a sister corporation of a competitor seems to be a remote conflict that could be waived by the client, allowing the lawyer to represent both clients without adverse effect on either. Of course, the particulars of the case could render even this apparently benign conflict objectionable if the new representation could compromise the loyalty of the lawyer to the existing client.

Corporate Affiliates

Generally Adverse Interests

A lawyer may represent two parties in unrelated matters even when the interests of the two are adverse in some general sense, such as when the two clients have competing economic interests. Although the principle that a lawyer should not accept a representation that will directly oppose an existing client is clear, line drawing is necessary to determine whether a conflict is based on merely generally adverse interests. The question of whether a lawyer may represent a corporate client while representing an adverse corporate client depends on the level of adversity between the parties and on the closeness of the corporate entities.[178]

Corporate Affiliates (2002 Revision)

A new comment to Model Rule 1.7 adopted by the ABA in February 2002 clearly indicates that representation of a client adverse to an affiliate of a corporate client is not a conflict under the Model Rules. Comment 34 provides:

> A lawyer who represents a corporation or other organization does not, by virtue of that representation, necessarily represent any constituent or affiliated organization, such as a parent or subsidiary. See Rule 1.13(a). Thus, the lawyer for an organization is not barred from accepting representation adverse to an affiliate in an unrelated matter, unless the circumstances are such that the affiliate should also be considered a client of the lawyer, there is an understanding between the lawyer and the organizational client that the lawyer will avoid representation adverse to the client's affiliates, or the lawyer's obligations to either the organizational client or the new client are likely to limit materially the lawyer's representation of the other client.[179]

---

178. *See* Travelers Indem. Co. v. Gerling Global Reinsurance Corp., 2000 WL 1159260 (S.D.N.Y. 2000) (distinguishing Strategem Dev. Corp. v. Heron, 756 F. Supp. 789 (S.D.N.Y. (1991)).

179. Model RULE 1.7 cmt. 34 (2002).

302 ISSUES OF LEGAL ETHICS IN THE PRACTICE OF ENVIRONMENTAL LAW

Criminal Defendants

Although the Sixth Amendment's protection of right to counsel includes a presumption favoring a defendant's choice of his own lawyer,[180] trial courts have substantial latitude in accepting or declining waivers of conflicts of interests.[181] Comment 16 to Revised Model Rule 1.7 notes that some states prohibit lawyers from representing more than one defendant in a capital case without regard to client consent.[182] Additionally, comment 23 to Revised Model Rule 1.7 emphasizes the high risk attached to defending more than one criminal defendant in a matter. "The potential for conflict of interest in representing multiple defendants in a criminal case is so grave that ordinarily a lawyer should decline to represent more than one codefendant."[183]

Similarly, Federal Rule of Criminal Procedure 44(c) cautions against joint representation of criminal codefendants. It states that "[u]nless there is good cause to believe no conflict of interest is likely to arise, the court shall take such measures as may be appropriate to protect each defendant's right to counsel."[184]

In *Wheat v. United States*,[185] the United States Supreme Court held that a trial court did not violate the defendant's Sixth Amendment rights when it refused to permit the defendant to substitute in place of his original counsel a lawyer representing a codefendant in a complex drug distribution scheme.[186] The Supreme Court emphasized that a trial court may decline a proffer of waiver of conflict and require that defendants be separately represented. In this case, the defendant sought to substitute the lawyer of codefendants for his lawyer the day before trial. The Court explained some of the difficulties in deciding this representation question:

---

180. Holloway v. Arkansas, 435 U.S. 475 (1978) (holding that lawyer forced to represent codefendants whose interests conflict cannot provide the adequate legal assistance required by Sixth Amendment); Lollar v. United States, 376 F.2d 243 (D.C. Cir. 1967) (holding that doubts as to potential conflict should be resolved in favor of separate counsel); State v. Bush, 493 P.2d 1205 (Ariz. 1972) (holding doubts should be resolved in favor of separate counsel); Fleming v. State, 270 S.E.2d 185 (Ga. 1980) (imposing per se ban on a lawyer representing more than one defendant in capital cases even where both defendants want same lawyer, because of risk of later assertion of prejudice).

181. *See, e.g.*, Wheat v. United States, 486 U.S. 153 (1988).

182. REV. MODEL RULE 1.7 cmt. 16.

183. MODEL RULE 1.7 cmt. 23 (2002).

184. FED. R. CRIM. P. 44(c).

185. 486 U.S. 153 (1988).

186. *Id*. at 163.

Chapter 6: Special Conflicts Concerns   303

> [The] district court must pass on the issue whether or not to allow a waiver of a conflict of interest by a criminal defendant not with the wisdom of hindsight after the trial has taken place, but in the murkier pre-trial context when relationships between parties are seen through a glass, darkly. The likelihood and dimensions of nascent conflicts of interest are notoriously hard to predict, even for those thoroughly familiar with criminal trials.[187]

The court's explanation indicates that in most cases, the waiver by a defendant is ill-advised. "It is a rare attorney who will be fortunate enough to learn the entire truth from his own client, much less be fully apprised before trial of what each of the Government's witnesses will say on the stand."[188]

Similarly, in *United States v. Edwards,*[189] the district court granted a motion to disqualify a lawyer and his law firm from representing a defendant in proceedings in which his former clients pled guilty and agreed to be witnesses for the government. The court held that an attorney-client relationship existed between the lawyer and codefendants, who were the owners of corporations represented by the lawyer. The court found an actual conflict of interests and, additionally, serious potential conflicts resulting from the lawyer's prior representation of government witnesses in a substantially related matter. Accordingly, the court refused to accept a waiver by the client and disqualified the lawyer.

Environmental Examples

Prosecution of environmental crimes has increased in recent years,[190] enhancing the likelihood of prosecution of individuals involved in discharges in violation of environmental law and the likelihood of prosecution of multiple defendants.

> Whatever the reasons for past reluctance to prosecute violators of pollution control statutes, that reluctance has disappeared, perhaps reflecting a decision that the statutes have been around long enough

---

187. *Id.* at 163–64.

188. *Id.*

189. 39 F. Supp. 2d 716, 744 (M.D. La. 1999).

190. *See* Daniel Riesel, *Criminal Prosecution and Defense of Environmental Wrongs,* 15 ENVTL. L. REP. 10,065 (Mar. 1985) (discussing the disappearance of prosecutor reluctance to prosecute violators of environmental statutes) [hereinafter Riesel]; Raymond C. Marshall, *Conducting Internal Investigations: What to Do and What Not to Do,* 30 ENVTL. L. REP. 10,901 (Sept. 2000).

304   ISSUES OF LEGAL ETHICS IN THE PRACTICE OF ENVIRONMENTAL LAW

to be familiar to all in the regulated community, making knowing violations truly criminal in nature. . . . [F]ederal and state governments are beginning to devote substantial energy to the prosecution of environmental crimes, and there has been some strengthening of both federal and state agencies' ability to conduct criminal prosecutions.[191]

Many environmental laws require extensive reporting of conduct that impacts the environment and even include criminal penalties for knowing violations of the laws.[192] Indeed, some environmental laws provide criminal sanctions for negligent acts that create the risk of significant harm, such as the discharge of hazardous substances.[193] The potential benefit of blaming "the other guy" for environmental violations is always present and, thus, the potential for a conflict to arise is significant. In *United States v. Weitzenhoff*,[194] two managers of a sewage treatment plant were convicted of felony violations of the CWA for discharging waste-activated sludge directly into the Pacific Ocean without treating the waste as required by the plant's permit. The evidence indicated that the two defendants instructed other employees at the plant to dispose of waste on a regular basis by pumping it directly into the ocean. The court of appeals affirmed the conviction. It issued an amended opinion,[195] adopting a theory of general intent and holding that the CWA provision imposing a felony conviction for knowingly violating a permit condition does not require that the prosecution establish that the defendant knew the require-

---

191. Riesel, *supra* note 190.

192. *See, e.g.*, Solid Waste Disposal Act (SWDA) (as amended by the Resource Conservation and Recovery Act of 1976 (RCRA)) § 3008(d)(3), 42 U.S.C. § 6928(d)(3) (1994) (providing criminal penalties for knowing omission of material information); SWDA § 3008(d)(4), 42 U.S.C. § 6928(d)(4) (1994) (providing criminal penalties for knowing failure to file record or report required under SWDA); Clean Air Act (CAA) § 113(c)(2), 42 U.S.C. § 7413(c)(2) (1994) (setting criminal penalties for knowing omission of information or failure to make required report of release); Comprehensive Environmental Response, Compensation and Liability Act (CERCLA) § 103(b), 42 U.S.C. § 9603(b) (1994) (creating criminal penalties for knowing failure to report release subject to CERCLA notification requirements); Oil Pollution Act § 6, 33 U.S.C. § 1005 (1982) (authorizing criminal penalties for intentional discharge of oil from ship).

193. *See, e.g.*, CAA § 113(c)(2)–(5), 42 U.S.C. § 7413(c)(2)–(5) (1994) (setting criminal penalties for negligent or knowing release of hazardous air pollutant or extremely hazardous pollutant).

194. 1 F.3d 1523 (9th Cir. 1993).

195. 35 F.3d 1275 (9th Cir. 1993).

ments of the permit. A knowing violation under the Act is established upon a showing that the defendant knowingly engaged in the conduct that resulted in a permit violation. The court held that the defendants' authorization of illegal discharges established the required intent.[196]

In the *Weitzenhoff* case, the two defendants were represented separately and by different lawyers. No claim of conflict arose. Nonetheless, the case provides an example of the kind of facts that should convince a lawyer that representing joint defendants is not prudent and is likely to violate ethics rules relating to the conflicts—even if the defendants wish to consent to the representation and waive a conflict. One of the defendants was found guilty of perjury, and the conviction of that defendant was enhanced.[197] If a lawyer had represented the defendants jointly, perjury relating to the acts of a codefendant could create a nonwaivable conflict. If the problem arose during trial, it could cause significant delay and prejudice to the case of one or both of the defendants. Because the "blame game" is an ever-present possibility of great significance in the criminal context, multiple representation should not be undertaken lightly.[198]

> In a criminal prosecution, the corporation's defense may attempt to portray certain employees as primarily responsible for violations of company policy that led to the alleged criminal violations. Similarly, individual employees may seek to avoid prosecution or conviction by invoking their reasonable reliance on directions from corporate management. Furthermore, individuals may seek to avoid prosecution by plea bargain agreements that include adverse testimony against the company or company managers.[199]

Lawyers should assess as early as possible the problem of conflicts in environmental matters, especially when criminal charges are a possibility. In the context of representing a corporation and employees or officers of the corporation, for example, the risks of multiple representation may lead the corporation to pay for separate lawyers to represent employees or officers.

> [I]n spite of the costs of additional counsel for employees, it is essential for the company's lawyer to evaluate early in an investi-

---

196. *Id.*
197. *Id.* at 1292.
198. *See generally* Ellen Y. Suni, *Who Stole the Cookie from the Cookie Jar? The Law and Ethics of Shifting Blame in Criminal Cases*, 68 FORDHAM L. REV. 1643 (2000).
199. *See* Dinkins & Sutherland, *supra* note 46, at 328.

306   ISSUES OF LEGAL ETHICS IN THE PRACTICE OF ENVIRONMENTAL LAW

gation whether there are employees of the company who have realistic exposure to criminal liability. Individuals who are determined to have exposure should have separate counsel before being placed in a situation where they need legal advice. . . . Disqualification of the company's lawyer could ultimately be more costly than the up-front expense of separate counsel.[200]

Positional or Issue Conflicts

A positional conflict, also called an issue conflict, presents the question whether a lawyer can ethically take differing positions on a legal issue on behalf of different clients. The legal profession has traditionally condemned the practice of entering a representation that creates an issue conflict. The ABA canons prohibited issue conflicts. "Within the meaning of this canon [prohibiting conflicts] a lawyer represents conflicting interests when, in behalf of one client, it is his duty to contend for that which duty to another client requires him to oppose."[201] The problem of issue conflicts arises when a lawyer "contends for a legal result that, if accepted, would operate against the interest of another client in a pending suit."[202] Thus, positional or issue conflicts can create problems even though the lawyer represents different companies in entirely different cases. Indeed, some authorities recognize a positional conflict in representations that compromise a former client's interests as well as the interests of a current client.[203] Professor Freedman explained the concept, hypothesizing a situation in which a lawyer who has drafted an exculpatory clause for a lessor is asked to argue for a tenant in another lessor's property that the same wording in a lease creates an unconscionable clause.[204] A comment to Model Rule 1.7 presents the analysis of issue conflicts presented in the 1983 Model Rules:

> A lawyer may represent parties having antagonistic positions on a legal question that has arisen in different cases, unless representation of either client would be adversely affected. Thus, it is ordinarily not improper to assert such positions in cases pending in

---

200. *Id.* at 327–28.

201. ABA Canons of Professional Ethics Canon 6 (1908).

202. Wolfram, *supra* note 5, § 7.3.3 at 355.

203. *See* John S. Dzienkowski, *Positional Conflicts of Interest,* 71 Tex. L. Rev. 457 (1993) [hereinafrer Dzienkowski] (classifying positional conflicts as litigational, lobbying, and transactional).

204. Monroe H. Freedman, Understanding Lawyers' Ethics, 179–80 (1990).

Chapter 6: Special Conflicts Concerns 307

different trial courts, but it may be improper to do so in cases pending at the same time in an appellate court.[205]

This guidance from the Model Rules comment is far from exhaustive on the issue of positional conflicts. It suggests that the representation is generally acceptable despite positional conflicts at the trial court level. Bars and disciplinary boards have now begun to address this issue.[206] Recent scholarship addresses some of the difficult issues that arise when a representation presents a possible issue conflict.[207] An ABA formal opinion suggests that issue conflicts may often be impermissible. It draws into question the distinction between trial and appellate work made in comment 9 to the rule.[208] In Formal Opinion 93-377, the ABA Committee on Ethics and Professional Responsibility held that lawyers should refuse to accept a representation if a substantial risk exists that the case will create a legal precedent likely to materially undercut the legal position of another client.[209] The ABA Committee opined that such a risk is likely when the issue conflict arises in the same jurisdiction. It indicated that lawyers should avoid the representation except when each client gives informed consent to the representation. This holding suggests that representation in different jurisdictions is likely to be permissible, since the decision resolving one case would not have precedential effect in the other jurisdiction. The possibility of the persuasive effect from one case to another case in another jurisdiction appears to be an insufficient basis for a finding of positional conflict.

The standard is difficult to apply in some circumstances, however. For example, a lawyer cannot know with certainty whether a court will choose to publish the opinion that resolves a controversy. If the court does choose to publish the opinion, it will create precedent within the jurisdiction. Thus, arguably, every case has the potential to create precedent within the jurisdiction that hears the case. Whether a court or a Board of Professional Responsibility would see this potential for precedent as sufficient to require that a

---

205. Model Rule 1.7 cmt. 9.
206. Calif. Standing Comm. on Prof'l Responsibility and Conduct, Op. 1989-108; Phila. (Pa.) Bar Ass'n, Prof'l Guidance Comm., Op. 89-27 (1990).
207. For a comprehensive exploration of the problems that can arise as a result of issue conflicts and a suggested rule to regulate the area, *see* Dzienkowski, *supra* note 203 (suggesting changes in the Model Rules to clarify lawyer responsibility relating to positional conflicts). *See also* Norman W. Spaulding, *The Prophet and the Bureaucrat: Positional Conflicts in Service Pro Bono Publico*, 50 Stan. L. Rev. 1395 (1998).
208. ABA Comm. on Ethics and Prof'l Responsibility, Op. 93-377 (1993).
209. *Id.*

ISSUES OF LEGAL ETHICS IN THE PRACTICE OF ENVIRONMENTAL LAW

lawyer decline a representation or withdraw from a representation is unclear.

Positional or Issue Conflicts: Ethics 2000

The Ethics 2000 Commission did not dispel entirely the uncertainty surrounding the question of issue or positional conflicts. In an article in the *Michigan Bar Journal,* Noreen L. Slank noted that the Ethics 2000 reporter gave "an informal definition of 'positional conflicts'" as the situation that arises when a lawyer "takes inconsistent positions in different tribunals on behalf of different clients," indicating that a positional conflict may create a material limitation of a representation in some circumstances.[210] The Ethics 2000 Commission did not identify the circumstances in which such a conflict would be material.

As compared with the 1983 version of Rule 1.7, comment 24 to Revised Rule 1.7 seems to move toward a more favorable view of representations that could be seen as positional conflicts. It allows the lawyer to make the judgment regarding whether or not such a conflict will "materially limit the lawyer's effectiveness in representing another client in a different case."[211] Perhaps the most important point of the comment is its statement of the typical case in issue conflicts: "Ordinarily a lawyer may take inconsistent legal positions in different tribunals at different times on behalf of different clients."[212] The new comment also rejects the single test of potentially adverse precedent as a basis for finding a conflict based on legal positions taken by a lawyer: "The mere fact that advocating a legal position on behalf of one client might create precedent adverse to the interests of a client represented by the lawyer in an unrelated matter does not create a conflict of interest."[213] Rather, the comment brings the positional conflict test in line with the general test for conflicts by instructing the lawyer to consider whether "there is a significant risk that a lawyer's action on behalf of one client will materially limit the lawyer's effectiveness in representing another client in a different case."[214] Comment 24 adopts an approach that reaches a result regarding whether a positional conflict is present by assessing several factors, essentially creating a test of the totality of the circumstances facing the lawyer. "Factors relevant in determin-

---

210. Noreen L. Slank, *Positional Conflicts: Is It Ethical to Simultaneously Represent Clients with Opposing Legal Positions?*, Mich. B. J. (May 2002).

211. Model Rule 1.7 cmt. 24 (2002).

212. *Id.*

213. *Id.*

214. *Id.*

Chapter 6: Special Conflicts Concerns   309

ing whether the clients need to be advised of the risk include: where the cases are pending, whether the issue is substantive or procedural, the temporal relationship between the matters, the significance of the issue to the immediate and long-term interests of the clients involved and the clients' reasonable expectations in retaining the lawyer."[215] The rule prohibits representations that create a significant risk of material limitation unless the clients give informed consent to the representations.

Issue Conflicts (Environmental Context)

The opportunities for issue conflicts in the environmental context are possibly as great as the potential for conventional conflicts. Expertise in environmental law can be used to represent either plaintiffs or defendants. Although one might suppose that an environmental lawyer generally would work for one side in a particular type of dispute, this is not necessarily the case. Individuals as well as corporate clients seek representation by environmental lawyers. Some disputes involve individual clients on both sides of the matter. Lawyers may develop a clientele of both defendants and plaintiffs.

Accordingly, it is not surprising that a lawyer may be called on to argue different positions and to take opposing positions on behalf of different clients. For example, one client might wish to retain a lawyer to seek a ruling that a substance should not be listed as a hazardous substance in a particular category under the Resources Conservation and Recovery Act (RCRA). The lawyer he wishes to hire once worked for EPA and was involved in drafting an agency guidance document that classified waste as within the category of RCRA hazardous waste. Or, similarly, another client may instruct the lawyer to argue that the substance is a hazardous waste and should be listed under RCRA. Similarly, suppose a lawyer is asked to represent a client in a Superfund cost recovery action against a former owner of the property in a Superfund site and to argue that an indemnification provision in favor of the seller is overbroad. If this lawyer has drafted similar provisions in other transactions, his position in this case may be directly contrary to his position on behalf of other sellers that he has represented or continues to represent. A lawyer asked to seek insurance coverage by a landowner who incurred liability under CERCLA may need to argue that the insurance coverage for "sudden and accidental" events includes releases of hazardous substances that happened over a long period of time.[216] If this lawyer also represents insurance compa-

---

215. *Id.*

216. *See* Employers Ins. of Wausau v. Amcast Indus. Corp., 709 N.E.2d 932 (Ohio Ct. App. 1998) (holding that trial court erred in granting summary judgment on issue of whether insurers had duty to indemnify Amcast because the policies cover a series of sudden

310   ISSUES OF LEGAL ETHICS IN THE PRACTICE OF ENVIRONMENTAL LAW

nies, he may have argued the opposite side of this question in past cases or he may need to make such an argument in future cases.

In the context of government lawyers who enter private practice, significant questions of issue conflicts can arise. Assume, for example, that a government lawyer worked on legislation establishing procedures and limits for discharges to waters of the United States. Later, the lawyer enters private practice and, on behalf of a discharger, argues that the legislation is unconstitutional. Such a representation raises questions of positional conflicts. It also raises the question of whether the representation itself presents a conflict under Model Rule 1.11.[217]

Business Dealings with a Client

Current Clients

Model Rule 1.8(a) states the rule for when a lawyer may enter a business transaction with a client or acquire an interest adverse to a client. It prohibits such a transaction except when stated conditions are met. Moreover, the material limitation standard of Model Rule 1.7 is implicated in the question of entering business with a client. The dual role of the lawyer in a business with a client can create significant problems for the attorney-client relationship.[218] The conditions set forth in the rule require that the "transaction and terms on which the lawyer acquires the interest are fair and reasonable to the client."[219] It also requires the lawyer to "fully disclose the terms and transmit the terms in writing to the client." The rule requires that the lawyer provide the client with "a reasonable opportunity to seek the advice of independent counsel" concerning the representation.[220] To comply with the rule, the lawyer must obtain the client's consent to the transaction in a writing signed by the client.[221]

---

releases); Cello-Foil Products, Inc. v. Michigan Mut. Liability Co., 1995 WL 854728 (Mich., Aug. 15, 1995) (holding that for insured to overcome the hurdle posed by pollution exclusion there must be no genuine issue of material fact regarding whether the release was "sudden and accidental"); United Technologies Corp. v. Liberty Mut. Inc., 1994 WL 879545 (Mass., June, 9 1994) (holding insured was entitled to coverage only if it could establish that the pollution exclusion clause was inapplicable).

217. *See* LaSalle National Bank v. Lake County, 703 F.2d 252 (7th Cir. 1983).

218. *See generally* LAWYERS DOING BUSINESS WITH THEIR CLIENTS, IDENTIFYING AND AVOIDING LEGAL AND ETHICAL DANGERS: A REPORT OF THE TASK FORCE ON THE INDEPENDENT LAWYER (American Bar Association 2001).

219. *See* MODEL RULE 1.8(a)(1).

220. *See id.* at 1.8(a)(2).

221. *See id.* at 1.8(a)(3); *see also* MODEL RULE 1.8 cmt. 1.

Chapter 6: Special Conflicts Concerns   311

Business Dealings with a Client (2002 Revision)

Revised Model Rule 1.8(a) retains the prohibition against entering business transactions with a client. It changes the rule to require a writing advising the client of the desirability of seeking independent legal advice. It changes the reference to consent to make it clear that the standard to be applied is informed consent. Additionally, the revised rule requires that the consent be memorialized by a writing "signed by the client." This is a higher standard for consent than the writing standard required by most of the 2002 Revised Rules because it requires that the client sign the writing. This mechanism of requiring the client's signature seems to ensure to a greater extent that the client's attention will be focused on this issue at the time of the agreement to enter the transaction. The writing bearing the client's signature must contain the essential terms of the transaction and must state the lawyer's role in the transaction. This statement of the lawyer's role must indicate that the lawyer is representing the client in the transaction if that is the case.[222]

The ABA Standing Committee on Ethics and Professional Responsibility has opined that it is permissible for lawyers to accept stock or an ownership interest in a client's business as payment for legal services in some circumstances.[223] The Committee cautioned, however, that a lawyer who accepts such a payment must follow the requirements of Model Rule 1.8(a). The Committee also reminded lawyers that Model Rule 1.5(a) applies in all cases, requiring that all legal fees charged by the lawyer must be reasonable. Additionally, the Committee warned that a lawyer accepting such payment must consider conflicts as they arise and must exercise independent judgment in advising the client without allowing the business interest to influence her judgment.

Business Dealings with a Client: Environmental Examples

The business of environmental services and consulting has grown along with the proliferation of environmental laws. Many new environmental companies came into existence in the last two decades. Others are currently in the start-up stages. Some have not survived. Both new and old companies need legal representation, which ranges from drafting corporate documents to negotiating services to litigation. Some of these companies would prefer to pay for legal services with stock. Accordingly, some environmental lawyers have the opportunity to receive an interest in the company-client in lieu of cash payment for legal services. Indeed, sometimes a start-up company may lack the cash

---

222. Model RULE 1.8(a) (2002).
223. ABA Standing Comm. on Ethics and Prof'l Responsibility, Formal Op. 00-418 (July 7, 2000).

312 ISSUES OF LEGAL ETHICS IN THE PRACTICE OF ENVIRONMENTAL LAW

necessary to pay billings when due. Sometimes the lawyer will prefer stock in a company because she believes the company offers a good investment opportunity. Of course, the potential for loss of the amount paid accompanies such an investment. Moreover, the lawyer must be aware of the dangers of a business affiliation with a client. She must maintain the ability to make independent legal judgments free from interference based on her relationship with the client and free from her own self-interest as an investor in the company. She should advise the client of the requirement that her role as a lawyer must not be affected by the business interest.

Settlements

Settlement proposals can raise difficult conflict issues. For example, when a lawyer represents several individuals in a plaintiff or defense group, some of those represented may wish to accept a settlement while others are dissatisfied with the offer presented by the opponent. A lawyer who fails to inform all clients of a settlement offer and to obtain the consent of each violates Rule 1.8(g).[224] Similarly, part of the group may have devised an offer to the opponent while others in the group are opposed to making the offer. In *Hayes v. Eagle-Picher Industries, Inc.*,[225] the Tenth Circuit held that attorney-client agreements that allow a case to be settled without the approval of an individual client are "opposed to the basic fundamentals of the attorney-client relationship."[226] In *Quintero v. Jim Walter Homes, Inc.*,[227] the court overturned a settlement on the basis that the lawyer had failed to inform his clients "of the nature and settlement amounts of the claims involved."[228] The settlement at issue involved nearly 350 claims of misrepresentation against a builder. The lawyer had failed to inform the parties that they had won a separate judgment against the opponent prior to consenting to a significantly smaller settlement.

In *Abbott v. Kidder Peabody & Co.*,[229] the district court held that a law firm was disqualified from representing a large group of plaintiffs in a securities lawsuit brought by over 200 individual investors. The representation agreement between the plaintiffs and the firm allowed the representation and settlement to be guided by a "steering committee" rather than the individual

---

224. *See, e.g., In re* Faucheux, 818 So. 2d 734 (La. 2002) (suspending lawyer from practice for one year for improperly aggregating two clients' settlements).
225. 513 F.2d 892, 894 (10th Cir. 1975).
226. *Id.* at 894.
227. 709 S.W.2d 225 (Tex. App. 1985).
228. *Id.* at 229.
229. Abbott v. Kidder Peabody & Co., Inc., 42 F. Supp. 2d 1046 (D. Colo. 1999).

clients. The client group consisted of 200 separate clients, each with an individual suit against the defendant. The defendant attempted to settle with the clients in small groups and then individually, but the plaintiffs refused to settle individually. The court disqualified the firm on the basis that it gave a minority of the clients the ability to direct the case and decide settlement in violation of Model Rule 1.7. The court held that the client could not consent to giving up so much control over the suit.[230]

> The Representation Contract gives counsel the ability to negotiate settlement for each plaintiff without providing him or her with personalized advisement and without obtaining individual authority to enter into a settlement arrangement. Colorado law states that any provision of an attorney-client agreement which deprives a client of the right to control their case is void as against public policy.[231]

Model Rule 1.8 offers guidance, albeit no easy answers. Rule 1.8(g) prohibits a lawyer from participating in settlement negotiations that would result in an aggregate settlement if she represents more than one client unless each client consents to her participation. Moreover, the rule makes clear that the consent of the client is only effective if the lawyer has disclosed to the client all of the relevant information relating to the settlement (that is, the nature of the claims or pleas and the identity of all settling parties). Subsection (g) of Model Rule 1.8 provides:

> A lawyer who represents two or more clients shall not participate in making an aggregate settlement of the claims of or against the clients . . . unless each client consents after consultation, including disclosure of the existence and nature of all the claims or pleas involved and of the participation of each person in the settlement.[232]

In the case of a joint action seeking damages for individual harms suffered by group members, Rule 1.8(g) applies to protect each plaintiff by requiring the lawyer to obtain the consent of each client or refrain from entering a settlement that compromises that client's claim. Fundamental fairness toward each client requires that a lawyer representing a group of clients obtain informed consent of each client before entering an aggregate settlement for

---

230. *Id.*
231. *Id.*
232. MODEL RULE 1.8(g).

314 ISSUES OF LEGAL ETHICS IN THE PRACTICE OF ENVIRONMENTAL LAW

the group. This requirement of Model Rule 1.8(g) prohibits lawyers from sacrificing some group members for the interests of the group as a whole or for individuals in the group. Model Rule 1.8 also protects a client against the lawyer entering a settlement based on his own self-interest. Such a situation could arise when a lawyer is influenced to finalize a settlement to limit the time he spends in negotiating a settlement to meet the needs of each client.[233] Similarly, Rule 1.8(g) prohibits a lawyer from representing two or more clients in a criminal matter except when each client has received full information regarding the claims and pleas and the participation of others involved in the settlement.

Rule 1.8(g) relates to settlements that resolve the claims of all clients entering the settlement. It does not speak to the situation of clients whose claims will not be resolved. Nor does it deal with settlement of a single claim brought by a group of individuals. Ordinarily, a claim for injunctive relief against a future harm is unitary (presenting a single claim) rather than aggregate (presenting a group of claims). Whether Model Rule 1.8 applies to this situation is an open question. Thus, Model Rule 1.8(g) should not be interpreted to create a veto power in each individual represented as part of an organizational party.

It would be possible (though perhaps not advisable) for a group to vest such veto power in individual members via bylaws provisions. For example, a provision could expressly allow settlement only upon unanimous approval or could empower the president or other officers to veto proffering or accepting a settlement offer.

Aggregate Settlement (2002 Revision)

It is worth emphasizing that lawyers must be careful to comply with both Model 1.7 and the special requirements of Model Rule 1.8(g) on aggregate settlements. In its revision of the Model Rules of 2002, the ABA clarified the duty of a lawyer negotiating an aggregate settlement. The revisions to Model Rule 1.8(g) retain the central thrust of the 1983 rule but add the standard of informed consent for the 1983 standard of consent after consultation. It provides:

> A lawyer who represents two or more clients shall not participate in making an aggregate settlement of the claims of or against the clients, or in a criminal case an aggregated agreement as to guilty or nolo contendere pleas, unless each client gives informed con-

---

233. *See* ABA/BNA LAWYERS' MANUAL ON PROFESSIONAL CONDUCT 51:378.

Chapter 6: Special Conflicts Concerns   315

sent, in a writing signed by the client. The lawyer's disclosure shall include the existence and nature of all the claims or pleas involved and of the participation of each person in the settlement.[234]

Additionally, comment 13 to Model Rule 1.8 as revised gives additional analysis of the reason for the protection of clients in the aggregate settlement context. It notes:

> Differences in willingness to make or accept an offer of settlement are among the risks of common representation of multiple clients by a single lawyer. Under Rule 1.7, this is one of the risks that should be discussed before undertaking the representation, as part of the process of obtaining the clients' informed consent.[235]

The same comment links the protections achieved by Model Rule 1.8 with those of Model Rule 1.2, emphasizing the right of each client to make the ultimate decision regarding settlement as it relates to his claim.

> In addition, Rule 1.2(a) protects each client's right to have the final say in deciding whether to accept or reject an offer of settlement and in deciding whether to enter a guilty or nolo contendere plea in a criminal case. The rule stated in this paragraph is a corollary of both these Rules and provides that, before any settlement offer or plea bargain is made or accepted on behalf of multiple clients, the lawyer must inform each of them about all the material terms of the settlement, including what the other clients will receive or pay if the settlement or plea offer is accepted.[236]

Settlements: Environmental Examples

Environmental controversies present both the unitary and the aggregate claim situations of significance in the settlement context. A unitary claim situation arises, for example, when a lawyer represents a group of individuals seeking injunctive relief based on procedural claims under the National Environmental Policy Act (NEPA). Similarly, a group bringing an environmental justice claim that the siting of a hazardous waste facility has a disproportionate impact on minorities states a unitary claim. Model Rule 1.8 appears to allow

---

234. Rev. Model Rule 1.8 (2002).
235. Rev. Model Rule 1.8 cmt. 13 (2002).
236. *Id.*

316   ISSUES OF LEGAL ETHICS IN THE PRACTICE OF ENVIRONMENTAL LAW

negotiation on such a unitary claim based on the consent of the group.

By contrast, persons jointly seeking damages for harm suffered individually generally present aggregate claims. Toxic tort actions often present such claims. The harm suffered may vary from individual to individual. In such cases of aggregate claims, the lawyer should obtain the consent of each client for negotiations on their individual claims. Individual plaintiffs in a toxic tort action have suffered different physical injuries, such as cancer or heart disease. In such a case, the lawyer must provide each client with information about all of the claims involved in the aggregate settlement and the decision of other plaintiffs in the group regarding settlement. The lawyer's representation agreement should indicate the lawyer's obligation to provide information to all clients both for informational purposes and to avoid any misunderstanding concerning the duty of confidentiality in this context. Only if a client consents after receiving the relevant information may the lawyer go forward with the aggregate settlement under Model Rule 1.8. Thus, each plaintiff has the power to consent to an aggregate settlement or reject its application to his claim.

The issue of settlement also arises in the criminal context in environmental matters. Many environmental laws include criminal penalties for knowing (and in some cases negligent) violations of the laws. Thus, Model Rule 1.8 can have enormous impact in environmental litigation if a prosecutor decides to seek the imposition of criminal liability on more than one client represented by a lawyer.

The Lawyer Who Knew Too Much

Perhaps the worst-conflicts scenario from a practice standpoint is the possibility that a lawyer learns information about a potential client who later turns out to be an opponent. Such a scenario can result in loss of an existing client. The fact that a lawyer is prohibited from disclosing the information about the potential client because of the duty of confidentiality may present a material limitation on the ability of a lawyer to represent the existing client.[237] In a formal opinion, the ABA Committee on Ethics and Professional Responsibility made clear that the duty of confidentiality applies to information confided in a lawyer by a prospective client.[238] This duty does not automatically disqualify a lawyer from representing another client in the same matter. The opinion expressly indicates, however, that the lawyer must withdraw from representing an existing client in the same matter or a substantially related matter unless she obtained the consent of the prospective client to other repre-

---

237. *See* MODEL RULE 1.7(b).

238. *See* ABA Formal Op. 90-358 (holding lawyer has an obligation to protect information imparted by a prospective client).

Chapter 6: Special Conflicts Concerns 317

sentations related to the matter. Even so, if the information learned by the lawyer from the prospective client is critical to the case, it is clear that the lawyer must withdraw from representing another client. One way of guarding against disqualification of a representation is for the client and lawyer to expressly agree that the duty of confidentiality does not attach to the initial consultation. Some lawyers expressly note this protection when conferring with prospective clients.

Client Waivers of Prospective Conflicts

Prospective waivers from clients can allow a lawyer to go forward with a representation that would present a disqualifying conflict absent the waiver. Prospective waivers are possible from all three types of clients: current, former, and prospective. Some lawyers favor a waiver of prospective suit before conferring with a prospective client in order to get the most protection from the waiver. The ABA Standing Committee on Ethics and Professional Responsibility validated the use of such waivers in limited circumstances.[239]

Collective Action

Joint Defense Groups

Companies sometimes create joint defense groups, pooling their resources and sharing information about disputed practices or plans of an industry group. Forming a joint defense allows the companies to share information and to secure the privilege of confidentiality for intragroup communications.[240] Sharing counsel and information can expand the attorney-client privilege and work product rule as well as minimizing legal expenses. The joint defense doctrine (sometimes called the "pooled information" doctrine) allows parties to share information without waiving the attorney-client privilege when those parties have a common interest in defending against a common adversary.[241] Not all sharing of information between codefendants qualifies for the joint defense doctrine, however. Only communications that serve a common purpose qualify for protection under the doctrine. Moreover, the doctrine is the subject of

---

239. ABA Formal Op. 93-372 (1993) (allowing prospective waivers if lawyer determines there will be no adverse effect and fully informed client consents).

240. *See* Patrick E. Bradley & David R. King, *Cooperation Among Defendants: Pros and Cons of Joint Defense Agreements: Do You Know Who Your Friends Are?*, 8 Prod. Liab. L. & Strategy 1 (2000) (exploring the risks and benefits of joint defense agreements in the product liability context).

241. *See* Wolfram, *supra* note 5, § 6.4.9, at 276–77.

318 ISSUES OF LEGAL ETHICS IN THE PRACTICE OF ENVIRONMENTAL LAW

significant criticism and is not followed by all jurisdictions.[242] A party who claims the privilege by virtue of a joint defense arrangement has the burden of establishing the relationship of a joint defense and proving that documents for which protection is sought were intended to further the effort of the defendants. "[T]o establish a joint-defense privilege, the Intervenor [is] required to demonstrate (1) the documents were made in the course of a joint-defense effort; and (2) the documents were designed to further that effort."[243]

The attorney-client privilege provides a basis for refusing to disclose a communication in a judicial proceeding when the communication occurred between the client and the lawyer in the course of a representation.[244] With regard to information shared between lawyers representing codefendants, courts generally hold that the attorney-client privilege is not waived.[245] Nevertheless, caution dictates against sharing information unless it is clearly necessary for the joint defense.

> The protection of the joint defense exception extends to protection against disclosure of communication between various codefendants and their attorneys in civil proceedings. Even if such allies later become estranged, they could nonetheless argue entitlement to jointly invoke the attorney-client privilege to protect shared communications from disclosure at the request of a third party.[246]

Joint Plaintiff Groups

Plaintiffs sometimes also combine forces to bring environmental cases, such as opposition to destruction of a natural feature of an area or to development of a particular site, such as a recycling facility or a hazardous waste facility.

---

242. Professor Wolfram has questioned whether the pooled information doctrine is efficient or ethical, noting that the doctrine "permits co-conspirators to continue to conspire at a common defense, now with the privileged assistance of teams of lawyers." *Id.* at 278.

243. *In re* Grand Jury Proceedings, 156 F.3d 1038, 1042 (10th Cir. 1998).

244. FED. R. OF EVID. 503.

245. Leybold-Heraeus Technologies, Inc. v. Midwest Instrument Co., Inc., 118 F.R.D. 609, 613 (E.D. Wis. 1987) (noting that "[d]isclosure of privileged information by a lawyer to actual or potential co-defendants or to their counsel in the course of a joint defense does not constitute a waiver of the attorney-client privilege"); United States v. McPartlin, 595 F.2d 1321, 1336 (7th Cir.), *cert. denied*, 444 U.S. 833, 100 S. Ct. 65, 62 L. Ed. 2d 43 (1979) (noting protection of joint defense exception extends to disclosure of communication between various codefendants and their lawyers in civil proceedings).

246. United States v. McPartlin, 595 F.2d 1321, 1336 (7th Cir.), *cert. denied*, 444 U.S. 833, 100 S. Ct. 65, 62 L. Ed. 2d 43 (1979).

Chapter 6: Special Conflicts Concerns   319

The group may retain common counsel or enter joint agreements legal representation as a way of coordinating legal theories and pooling resources. Such agreements procure essentially the same benefits discussed above for joint defense groups.

The Lawyer Witness

Lawyers who practice environmental law are often called upon to negotiate for and advise clients in a nonlitigation setting as well as to litigate cases. Thus, the risk of disqualification under this rule for environmental lawyers is not trivial. Suppose, for example, that a lawyer confers with a client about compliance with the National Environmental Policy Act (NEPA). Later, he defends the client against a suit alleging the client violated NEPA's requirement to produce an environmental impact statement. The lawyer is at risk to charges by opponents that his testimony is necessary to establish the client's frame of mind in undertaking NEPA procedures and in determining that no Environmental Impact Statement (EIS) was necessary for the project. An overly broad reading of the rule could result in disqualification of lawyers who have served a client in negotiation sessions, in planning sessions, or in advising the client about how to comply with environmental laws. The rule should not empower an opponent to deprive a party of its chosen advocate except when the lawyer's testimony is necessary to the case.[247]

Traditionally, ethics rules have not allowed a lawyer to serve as a witness in a matter where he represents a client, primarily because of the potential for prejudice to the opposing party and the appearance of impropriety. Model Rule 3.7(a) prohibits a lawyer from serving as advocate in a trial "in which the lawyer is likely to be a necessary witness."[248] Exceptions to the rule allow continued representation by the lawyer if the lawyer's testimony would address an uncontested issue or relates to the value of legal services. Additionally, a court may deny a disqualification motion on such a claim when the disqualification would cause substantial hardship for the client.[249] The conflict created by a lawyer's role as a witness generally is not imputed to other members of that lawyer's firm. "A lawyer may act as advocate in a trial in which another lawyer in the lawyer's firm is likely to be called as a witness unless precluded from doing so by Rule 1.7 or Rule 1.9."[250]

A rule of reason is required to prevent misuse of this ethics rule. Lawyers often represent clients in business planning rather than litigation or in addition

---

247. *See* WOLFRAM, *supra* note 5, at 377–78.
248. MODEL RULE 3.7.
249. MODEL RULE 3.7(1)–(3).
250. MODEL RULE 3.7(b).

320   ISSUES OF LEGAL ETHICS IN THE PRACTICE OF ENVIRONMENTAL LAW

to litigation. If knowledge of a planning decision is sufficient to disqualify counsel, governmental entities, corporations, and organizations will be forced to give up their chosen lawyer in litigation or limit the use of the lawyer in the planning process. An opposing counsel should not be allowed to determine unilaterally what testimony is "necessary" under Model Rule 3.7 or the opponent will have a bludgeon to beat away all lawyers knowledgeable about the client's case. The litigant would then need to secure new lawyers whenever litigation ensues, creating significant costs to the client.

Additionally, Model Rule 3.7 contains an important limitation. It applies only to the lawyer's action as an advocate "at a trial." Thus, the prohibition appears not to apply to efforts of the lawyer in relation to the trial as long as the lawyer does not appear as an advocate at the trial. This limitation appears to leave the lawyer free to represent the client in preparation for the trial and even in motions relating to the trial as long as the lawyer's testimony is not implicated in the motions that she argues.[251]

A party may oppose testimony by a lawyer on the basis that the testimony is privileged and inadmissible. Not all conversations with a lawyer are entitled to protection under the attorney-client privilege, however. In the case of *People v. Gionis*,[252] for example, the court held that a lawyer could testify about statements of a criminal defendant made to him after the lawyer declined to represent the defendant because they had a prior social relationship. The court allowed the prosecution to call the lawyer as a witness to reveal the defendant's statements about his intent to harm his former wife. The court reasoned that a person has "no reasonable expectation of being represented by an attorney after the attorney's explicit refusal to undertake representation."[253]

Lawyer as Witness (2002 Revision)

The 2002 ABA revision to the Model Rules added a reference to the tribunal in comment 1, indicating that an additional reason for prohibiting a lawyer from acting as an advocate and as a witness in the same trial is that such a dual role would prejudice the tribunal.[254]

Client Witness

The role of examining a client as an adverse nonparty witness raises a conflict that disqualifies the lawyer's representation in the case unless the client con-

---

251. *See* WOLFRAM, *supra* note 5, at 388.
252. 892 P.2d 1199 (Cal. 1995).
253. *Id.* at 1207.
254. MODEL RULE 3.7 cmt. 1.

sents to the representation.[255] Cross-examining a client creates a problem of direct adversity under Model Rule 1.7 vis-à-vis the current client. It also creates a material limitation as to the client the lawyer represents. In an ABA Formal Opinion, the ABA Ethics Committee held that although the lawyer's representation of Client A is unrelated to the lawyer's representation of Client B, the fact that the lawyer will need to examine Client A as an adverse witness is likely to create a conflict.[256] The opinion suggests that such a conflict may be waived by appropriate consent of the clients. The Committee noted that hazards are inherent in the situation of a lawyer who examines his own client as an adverse witness.

> The Committee believes that as a general matter examining one's own client as an adverse witness on behalf of another client, or conducting third party discovery of one client on behalf of another client, is likely (1) to pit the duty of loyalty to each client against the duty of loyalty to the other; (2) to risk breaching the duty of confidentiality to the client-witness; and (3) to present a tension between the lawyer's own pecuniary interest in continued employment by the client-witness and the lawyer's ability to effectively represent the litigation client.[257]

In the case addressed by the ABA Ethics Committee, a physician-client of the lawyer had agreed to serve as the expert witness in a medical malpractice trial. The Committee ruled the conflict of interest required disqualification of the lawyer absent consent by the client. The Committee also noted that the result would be the same if the client-witness had been a fact witness rather than an expert witness.[258] Likewise, the Committee noted the result would be the same if the examination was in pretrial discovery rather than trial. The Committee noted that, in some cases, a common-sense solution is simply to allow another lawyer to associate with the case for the purpose of examining the client.

In *United States v. Micke*,[259] the court of appeals held that the trial court did not violate the defendant's Sixth Amendment right to counsel by its refusal to permit the defendant's chosen lawyer to conduct defendant's examination as a witness. The requested lawyer had been subpoenaed by the

---

255. *See* ABA Comm. on Ethics and Prof'l Responsibility, Formal Op. 92-367 (1992).
256. *Id.* at 259.
257. *Id.*
258. *Id.*
259. 859 F.2d 473 (7th Cir. 1988).

government as a witness in the case and had previously represented two of the government witnesses in the case in an unrelated civil matter.

In *Alcocer v. Superior Court*,[260] the defendant was prosecuted for lying to a grand jury. The lawyer chosen by the defendant to represent him also represented a confessed drug dealer whom the prosecutor intended to call to testify as a witness. The trial court granted the prosecution's motion to recuse the defense counsel on the basis of conflict of interest because counsel could not adequately cross-examine the drug dealer in the event the prosecution called the lawyer's former client as a witness. The trial court directed the defendant to confer with independent counsel about the conflict. After conferring with independent counsel as directed, the defendant stated that he wished to retain his chosen counsel. On appeal, the court of appeals held that the trial court had abridged the defendant's right to choose his counsel. It set aside the trial court's order recusing defense counsel and ordered a new hearing. The reviewing court noted that, although the case presented the potential for a conflict of interest, the choice of counsel was up to the defendant. It stated that a defendant may waive his right to a conflict-free counsel if he is fully informed of his rights and knowingly and intelligently waives those rights.

The court also stated general guidelines for the trial court to follow when confronted with such a potential conflict.[261] The reviewing court recommended that when a trial court concludes that a lawyer may have a conflict in the case, it must advise the defendant "that his lawyer may not be able to effectively and adequately represent him."[262] It should also advise the accused that he may not receive a fair trial if he continues to retain the lawyer.[263] The court should also appoint counsel to advise the defendant about his rights and the risk of a conflict of interest.[264] If the court determines that the defendant wishes to continue the representation because he has paid the lawyer and cannot afford another lawyer, the court should appoint a new lawyer at government expense. If the defendant wishes to retain the lawyer despite the offer of a replacement at government expense, the court should advise the defendant that waiving his right to a conflict-free representation also waives his right to appeal based on the conflict. The court should also ask the defendant directly whether he agrees to this condition by asking: "Do you specifically give up the right to appeal the issue of incompetence of counsel insofar as it involves the conflict?"[265]

---

260. 254 Cal. Rptr. 72 (Ct. App. 1988).
261. *Id.*
262. *Id.* at 78.
263. *Id.*
264. *Id.*
265. *Id.*

Chapter 6: Special Conflicts Concerns 323

Serving as a Neutral

Intermediary

Representation of multiple clients in a single transaction between them presents risks for the lawyer. Many environmental lawyers include transactional work within their practice, sometimes representing multiple clients in a single transaction between them for development of real estate or other land-use issues. When the lawyer represents parties on both sides of a purchase-sell agreement, significant risks attach. A new comment to Revised Model Rule 1.7 speaks to this situation, suggesting the dangers to the lawyer who goes forward with simultaneous representation of both the buyer and seller in a transaction. "Directly adverse conflicts can also arise in transactional matters. For example, if a lawyer is asked to represent the seller of a business in negotiations with a buyer represented by the lawyer, not in the same transaction but in another, unrelated matter, the lawyer could not undertake the representation without the informed consent of each client."[266]

Like the clear duty of lawyers to refrain from representing clients who are directly adverse to each other, direct adversity arises when one client sues another client. Likewise, a lawyer ordinarily should avoid involvement in a dispute between two clients even when the dispute does not involve litigation. An exception to this rule is found in the function of a lawyer as intermediary. The appropriate context and ground rules for such a representation are set forth in Model Rule 2.2. It provides that "a lawyer may act as intermediary between clients" in certain specified situations.[267] First, the lawyer must consult with each client regarding the "implications of common representation." In such a consultation, the lawyer should discuss both advantages and risks of the arrangement. The lawyer should act as intermediary only when each client consents to the lawyer's involvement as intermediary. Like the principal conflict rule, the rule on serving as intermediary also requires that the lawyer assess the consequences of the representation on other clients. Model Rule 2.2 imposes on the lawyer a reasonable belief standard reminiscent of Model Rule 1.7. The rule accords effect to the consent of the client only when the lawyer reasonably believes that the clients are able "to make adequately informed decisions in the matter."[268] Only in cases where the lawyer reasonably believes that the intermediation "can be undertaken impartially and without improper effect on other responsibilities" can a lawyer ethically seek client consent and, upon receiving it, undertake the intermediary role.

---

266. Rev. Model Rule 1.7 cmt. 7.
267. *Id.*
268. Model Rule 2.2(a)(2).

324   ISSUES OF LEGAL ETHICS IN THE PRACTICE OF ENVIRONMENTAL LAW

Rule 2.2 can be summarized as four steps to appropriately undertaking engagement as an intermediary. The lawyer must analyze the clients' objectives and their relationship to determine whether joint representation is appropriate. Second, the lawyer must objectively analyze his relationship with the clients to determine whether he can act impartially and loyally toward each of the clients. If he determines that he can act with the necessary impartiality and loyalty to each client, the lawyer must confer with each client and disclose all relevant information about the relationship and the potential for conflicts in the future. If the clients give informed consent to the arrangement after the full disclosure, the lawyer may proceed with the representation, being careful to monitor the on-going representation for conflicts that may develop in the future.

Intermediary (Ethics 2000 Revision)

The Commission deleted Model Rule 2.2, leaving the topic of intermediation between clients within the ambit of Model Rule 1.7. Although the ABA deleted the rule on lawyers serving as intermediaries, it added a reference to the role of a lawyer as a third-party neutral. The Preamble to the 2002 Model Rules notes the application of the rules to lawyers serving as third-party neutrals. "In addition to these representational functions, a lawyer may serve as a third-party neutral, a nonrepresentational role helping the parties to resolve a dispute or other matter. Some of these Rules apply directly to lawyers who are or have served as third-party neutrals."[269]

Third-Party Neutrals (2002 Revision)

A rule added to the Model Rules in the 2002 revision raises the types of issues considered in the conflicts area when lawyers serve as third-party neutrals.[270] The term "third-party neutral" refers to services such as arbitration, mediation, or simply assisting in resolving a matter in which the lawyer does not represent the parties to the dispute.[271] The new rule merges treatment of lawyers who have served as judges, arbitrators, mediators, or other third-party neutrals, requiring such lawyers to obtain informed consent from all parties to any proceeding in which that lawyer participated "personally and substantively."[272] The role of a lawyer as a third-party neutral seems to exclude a situation in which the lawyer represents one or both of the clients.

---

269. MODEL RULES, Preamble ¶ 3 (2002).

270. MODEL RULE 2.4 (2002).

271. *See* MODEL RULE 2.4 (2002).

272. MODEL RULE 1.12(a) (2002).

Chapter 6: Special Conflicts Concerns 325

Revised Model Rule 2.4 acknowledges the role of a lawyer serving as a neutral to assist "two or more persons who are not clients" in reaching a "resolution of a dispute or other matter that has arisen between them."[273] The rule includes within its purview of service as a third-party neutral "service as an arbitrator, a mediator or in such other capacity as will enable the lawyer to assist the parties to resolve the matter."[274] Implicit in the rule is the requirement that a third-party neutral must refrain from representing any of the parties to the dispute as a lawyer. Model Rule 2.4 underscores this duty by stating an affirmative duty that the lawyer "explain the difference between the lawyer's role as a third-party neutral and a lawyer's role as one who represents a client" if the lawyer "knows or reasonably should know that a party does not understand the lawyer's role in the matter."[275]

---

273. Model Rule 2.4(a) (2002).
274. *Id.*
275. *Id.*

CHAPTER 7

The Lawyer's Duty of Candor

Although lawyers have an obligation to inform a tribunal of authority contrary to the lawyer's position, no clear authority creates an affirmative duty on a lawyer to volunteer information to an opponent when bargaining or litigating.[1] The environmental lawyer's duty of candor is tested frequently, and the test is not one that the lawyer can "pass" simply by being open and straightforward about everything. This is because the lawyer's duty of confidentiality does not go away by virtue of the competing duty of candor. The lawyer has a duty of candor toward the court or tribunal, toward opposing parties and opposing counsel, and to others.[2] These competing duties are at times contrary to the duty of confidentiality and sometimes directly contrary to each other. Nevertheless, the lawyer must balance these duties with those owed the client on a case-by-case basis. The lawyer's duty to represent the client fully does not nullify the basic duty of candor to tribunals and to other parties.[3] Model Rule 4.1 states:

> In the course of representing a client a lawyer shall not knowingly:
> (a) make a false statement of material fact or law to a third person;
> or (b) fail to disclose a material fact to a third person when disclosure is necessary to avoid assisting a criminal or fraudulent act by a client, unless disclosure is prohibited by Rule 1.6.[4]

---

1. MODEL RULE 3.4 (2002).
2. *See* MODEL RULE 3.3, 3.4, 4.1 (2002).
3. *See* Geoffrey C. Hazard, *The Lawyer's Obligation to Be Trustworthy When Dealing with Opposing Parties*, 33 S.C. L. REV. 181, 194 (1981).
4. MODEL RULE 4.1.

328   ISSUES OF LEGAL ETHICS IN THE PRACTICE OF ENVIRONMENTAL LAW

Although Model Rule 4.1 states an obligation on the part of the lawyer to disclose a "material fact" to a third person, it states that disclosure is limited by the duty of confidentiality to the lawyer's client. The obligation is subject to the exception: "unless disclosure is prohibited by Rule 1.6." This exception essentially destroys the duty to third parties, incorporating the broad prohibition of Rule 1.6. The net effect is lawyer discretion to disclose client information only when the client consents or when Rule 1.6 allows disclosure.

Model Rule 8.4 seems to create a real duty to a nonclient. It identifies misrepresentation as a violation of professional conduct. The rule states: "It is professional misconduct for a lawyer to: (c) engage in conduct involving dishonesty, fraud, deceit or misrepresentation."[5] Courts have recognized the right of a third party to recover against a lawyer for fraud, misrepresentation, or even negligent misrepresentation.[6] For example, in the case of *First National Bank of Durant v. Trans Terra Corporation International*,[7] the plaintiff-bank sued lawyers for negligent misrepresentation, arguing that the bank relied on a faulty title opinion prepared by the lawyers. The plaintiff successfully argued that the lawyers knew (or should have known) that the bank would rely on the faulty title opinion in making a loan to the lawyers' client. The court allowed the suit despite the lack of privity, recognizing an action based on negligent misrepresentation against a lawyer by a nonclient and holding expressly that lack of privity is not a bar to the claim.[8]

A lawyer owes a duty to use care to a nonclient, according to the Restatement, when "(a) the lawyer or (with the lawyer's acquiescence) the lawyer's client invites the nonclient to rely on the lawyer's opinion or provision of other legal services, and the nonclient so relies, and (b) the nonclient is not, under applicable tort law, too remote from the lawyer to be entitled to protection."[9] Lawyers can guard against liability in this setting by "making clear that an opinion or representation is directed only to a client and should not be relied on by others."[10] Additionally, the Restatement suggests that lawyers

---

5. MODEL RULE 8.4(c). Subsection (b) may also be relevant to this point. If the fraudulent conduct involved amounts to criminal fraud, the lawyer would be guilty of professional misconduct under Rule 8.4(b), which states that misconduct includes "engag[ing] in conduct involving dishonesty, fraud, deceit or misrepresentation."
6. *See* McCamish, Martin, Brown & Loeffler v. F. E. Appling Interests, 991 S.W.2d 787 (Tex. 1999) (holding that lawyers could be sued by third parties for negligent misrepresentation).
7. 142 F.3d 802 (5th Cir. 1999) (holding lack of privity not a bar to claim of negligent misrepresentation against a lawyer by a third party).
8. *Id.* at 809.
9. *See* RESTATEMENT (THIRD) OF THE LAW GOVERNING LAWYERS § 73.
10. *See* RESTATEMENT (THIRD) OF THE LAW GOVERNING LAWYERS § 73 cmt. e.

Chapter 7: The Lawyer's Duty of Candor to the Tribunal 329

may minimize liability "by making clear through limiting or disclaiming language in an opinion letter that the lawyer is relying on facts provided by the client without independent investigation by the lawyer (assuming that the lawyer does not know the assumed facts to be false, in which case the lawyer would be liable for misrepresentation)."[11] The Restatement also explains that such a limitation is not a fail-safe measure. "The effectiveness of a limitation or disclaimer depends on whether it was reasonable in the circumstances to conclude that those provided the opinion would receive the limitation or disclaimer and understand its import."[12]

Some recent dramatic examples suggest that lawyers sometimes cross the line into misrepresentation and frivolous arguments that violate the lawyer's duty toward third parties and the court.[13] For example, in her article "Shredding the Truth," Debra Baker notes that lawyers sometimes make arguments that are apparently frivolous.[14]

> Both the ABA Model Rules of Professional Conduct and the ABA Model Code of Professional Responsibility . . . say lawyers must not misrepresent themselves in court or to third parties. Yet, in the criminal context, determining what rises to the level of misrepresentation is unclear.[15]

Similarly, Deborah L. Rhode explored problems of candor in her book, *In the Interests of Justice: Reforming the Legal Profession.* She described a recent case that provides a forceful illustration of the problem of coaching witnesses. The law firm Baron & Budd represented clients who were seeking damages as a result of exposure to asbestos. In 1997 the litigation department provided a summary memorandum to the clients to help prepare them for

---

11. *Id.*
12. *Id.*
13. *See 9th Cir. Questions Ethics of Lawyers in Environmental Cleanup Suit,* ANDREWS INS. INDUS. LITIG, REP. (Nov. 18, 1998) (noting inquiry of Ninth Circuit regarding inaccurate information relating to claims made for releases from underground storage tanks on a claims-made insurance policy issued after the release of the release in the case of Paul Oil v. Federated Mutual, No. 97-16190 (9th Cir., Sept. 8, 1998)).
14. *See* Debra Baker, *Shredding the Truth,* 85 A.B.A. J. 40 (Oct. 2000) (citing frivolous allegations against third parties as part of the defense and noting arguments by Marvyn Kronberg in defense of Justin Volpe in the high-profile case of police brutality against Abner Louima).
15. *Id.* at 41.

330 ISSUES OF LEGAL ETHICS IN THE PRACTICE OF ENVIRONMENTAL LAW

depositions. The firm also mistakenly provided the memorandum in a group of documents sent to the opposing counsel. In part the memo stated:

> When identifying particular asbestos products, "Remember to say you saw [defendant manufacturers'] NAMES on the product or on the containers. Try to remember how close you were. The more often you were around [them], the better for your case. It is important to maintain that you NEVER saw any labels on asbestos products that said WARNING or DANGER."[16]

Additionally, this memo stated that defendants "have NO RECORDS to tell them what products were used on a particular job"[17] and "reminded plaintiffs 'never to mention' the existence of the coaching memo. When the document nonetheless came to light, the firm suffered some embarrassment but no disciplinary or judicial sanctions."[18]

Duty of Candor to Tribunal

Lawyers must inform courts and tribunals of relevant law and fact and must refrain from false statements to a tribunal.[19] Model Rule 3.3 states that a lawyer "shall not knowingly make a false statement of material fact or law to a tribunal."[20] Likewise, Model Rule 3.3 enjoins lawyers against failing to "disclose a material fact to a tribunal when disclosure is necessary to avoid assisting a criminal or fraudulent act by the client."[21] Moreover, the rule requires that lawyers disclose to the tribunal authority contrary to the lawyer's position.[22] Model Rule 3.3 forbids lawyers to "fail to disclose to the tribunal legal authority in the controlling jurisdiction known to the lawyer to be directly adverse to the position of the client and not disclosed by opposing counsel."[23] The rule forbids offering evidence the lawyer knows is false.[24] Given the inherent authority of courts to regulate lawyer conduct,[25] most law-

---

16. DEBORAH L. RHODE, IN THE INTERESTS OF JUSTICE: REFORMING THE LEGAL PROFESSION 97 (2000).
17. *Id.*
18. *Id.*
19. *See generally* MODEL RULE 3.3.
20. MODEL RULE 3.3(a).
21. MODEL RULE 3.3(a)(1).
22. MODEL RULE 3.3(a)(3).
23. *Id.*
24. MODEL RULE 3.3(a)(4).
25. *See* Susan P. Koniak, *The Law Between the Bar and the State*, 70 N.C. L. REV. 1389, 1412 (1992) (noting inherent powers courts as basis of ethics rules).

Chapter 7: The Lawyer's Duty of Candor to the Tribunal   331

yers comply with court rules and pronouncements regarding disclosure of information whether the information sought is contrary authority or client information.

Duty of Candor to Tribunal (2002 Revision)

The 2002 revision of the Model Rules added clarifying language to the Model Rules' statement of the lawyer's duty of candor toward a tribunal. The original Model Rule 3.3 stated that a lawyer "shall not knowingly make a false statement of material fact or law to a tribunal." The revision to this rule deleted the term "material" as a qualifier on statement of fact. This revision broadens the duty of the lawyer, making it a violation of the rule to make a false statement whether it relates to material or immaterial facts. Additionally, the revision added the language "or failed to correct a false statement of material fact or law previously made to the tribunal by the lawyer."[26] This addition to the Model Rule enlarges the duty of the lawyer to create an express duty to correct any statements made if they become false during the pendency of a proceeding.

The 2002 revision of Model Rule 3.3 also added a new section. This new section provides as follows:

> A lawyer who represents a client in an adjudicative proceeding and who knows that a person intends to engage, is engaging or has engaged in criminal or fraudulent conduct related to the proceeding shall take reasonable remedial measures, including, if necessary, disclosure to the tribunal.[27]

This provision makes clear the lawyer's right to act to remedy a crime or fraud of the client. It empowers the lawyer to disclose the criminal or fraudulent conduct to a tribunal if necessary.

Duty of Candor: Environmental Example

In *United States v. Shafer Equipment Co.*,[28] a government cost recovery suit under CERCLA, the district court dismissed the case due to EPA's breach of the duty of candor to the court. The court found that EPA's on-scene coordinator for a CERCLA cleanup action, Robert Caron, misrepresented his credentials in this and other cases and that the government lawyers failed to

---

26. MODEL RULE 3.3(a) (2002).
27. MODEL RULE 3.3(b) (2002).
28. 796 F. Supp. 938 (4th Cir. 1993).

332   ISSUES OF LEGAL ETHICS IN THE PRACTICE OF ENVIRONMENTAL LAW

reveal the misrepresentation and wrongfully obstructed the defendant's efforts to root out the misrepresentation. Caron later resigned from EPA and pled guilty to the criminal charge of making material false declarations.[29] In this case, Caron claimed he received a degree from Rutgers and took classes from other schools. Prior to Caron's deposition, government lawyers learned that Caron's claims were false. Nevertheless, the lawyers allowed Caron to testify that he had this diploma and education. When the deposition resumed two months later, the government lawyer instructed Caron not to answer questions about his credentials and asserted that Caron's credibility was not at issue. When the government lawyer researched the credibility issue and learned it was relevant as a matter of law, he did not supplement the government's response to an interrogatory directed at Caron's credentials and did not withdraw his relevancy objection to discovery.

The district court found the government lawyer "deliberately placed its loyalty and allegiance to its agency client (EPA) and client's servant (Caron) far and above the unending duty of candor to this Court. Such conduct is reprehensible and lies in bad faith."[30] The court dismissed EPA's claim, because of the lawyer's violations of the duty of candor. The Court of Appeals for the Fourth Circuit affirmed the district court's conclusion that the government lawyers violated their duty of candor. Nevertheless, it held that the harm caused by EPA's actions did not warrant dismissal and dismissal would frustrate the resolution on the merits of the case and allow the defendants a release from their obligations under environmental law. Although EPA had expended nearly $6.5 million, the monetary settlement in the consent decree entered in the case was only $725,000.[31] The court sanctioned the two government lawyers $2,000 and $2,500 respectively, specifying the fines must be paid from the lawyer's personal funds rather than from the client.

---

29. *Id.*
30. *Id.* at 951–52.
31. United States v. Shaffer Equip. Co., 158 F.R.D. 80 (S.D. W.Va. 1994).

CHAPTER 8

The Lawyer's Duties to Nonclients

The lawyer's primary duty of loyalty to the client is well known.[1] The lawyer's duties to clients are tempered by duties the lawyer owes to nonclients and the institutions of justice, however. The lawyer's duty to nonclients can be particularly troubling in the environmental area when an environmental condition creates a risk of harm. It is troubling because of the harm itself and, secondarily, because of the potential risk of tort liability to the environmental lawyer if someone is harmed by the client's actions. Candor and truthfulness are the subject of several Model Rules.[2] Moreover, tort law imposes duties on lawyers as well as people generally. Such duties are not completely abrogated by the lawyer's role in the justice system. For example, the common law requires that lawyers refrain from making false statements and that lawyers disclose material facts in some circumstances.[3]

---

1. *See* MODEL RULE 1.1, 1.2, 1.3, 1.4.
2. These include MODEL RULE 2.3, "Evaluation for Use by Third Persons," MODEL RULE 3.3, "Candor toward the Tribunal," and MODEL RULE 4.1, "Truthfulness in Statements to Others." RULE 8.4 defines misconduct to include engaging in conduct that involves "dishonesty, fraud, deceit or misrepresentation," that "is prejudicial to the administration of justice," or that suggests the lawyer has the ability to "influence improperly a government agency or official." The comment to RULE 2.3 acknowledges that a lawyer may owe duties to nonclients. It also notes that these duties spring from law other than the MODEL RULES. "When the evaluation is intended for the information or use of a third person, a legal duty to that person may or may not arise. That legal question is beyond the scope of this RULE." MODEL RULE 2.3 cmt. 4.
3. *See* McCamish, Martin, Brown & Loeffler v. Appling Interests, 991 S.W.2d 787 (Tex. 1999) (holding that lawyers could be sued for negligent misrepresentation).

334 ISSUES OF LEGAL ETHICS IN THE PRACTICE OF ENVIRONMENTAL LAW

Duty of Fairness and Truthfulness

Model Rule 3.4, entitled "Fairness to Opposing Party and Counsel," states broad prohibitions against conduct that would undermine the integrity and functioning of the justice system and, more generally, that would contravene principles of fairness. The speculative nature of causation in environmental matters can create a temptation for the environmental lawyer to save his client by raising the question of whether some other discharger or an employee acting alone may bear the guilt when an environmental crime is charged. The ethical duties set forth in Model Rule 3.4 are those that the environmental lawyer must frequently assess, particularly in cases involving documents that are significant to the determination of environmental violations or environmental hazards and in relation to employees of a client who may be sought out by opposing counsel for statements. Among other things, the rule prohibits unfair conduct by lawyers, including unlawfully obstructing or assisting in obstructing another party's access to evidence or unlawfully altering or concealing a document or item that has "potential evidentiary value,"[4] falsifying or assisting in falsifying evidence,[5] making a frivolous discovery request or failing to use reasonably diligent effort to comply with a proper discovery request,[6] referring in trial to a matter the lawyer "does not reasonably believe is relevant or that will not be supported by admissible evidence," or asserting personal knowledge of facts except when testifying as a witness,[7] or requesting a someone other a client (or a relative, employee, or agent of a client) to refrain from voluntarily giving relevant information to another party.[8] An exception to this prohibition allows the lawyer to ask a person to refrain from giving information about a dispute if the lawyer "reasonably believes that the person's interests will not be adversely affected by refraining from giving such information."[9]

The Ethics 2000 Commission did not recommend changes to Model Rule 3.4. The House of Delegates approved the continuation of the rule as stated in the 1983 rules. It added one point to the commentary, which deals with the ability of a lawyer to take temporary possession of physical evidence in some circumstances.[10]

---

4. MODEL RULE 3.4(a).
5. MODEL RULE 3.4(b).
6. MODEL RULE 3.4(d).
7. MODEL RULE 3.4(e).
8. MODEL RULE 3.4(f).
9. MODEL RULE 3.4(f)(2).
10. MODEL RULE 3.4 cmt. 2.

Chapter 8: The Lawyer's Duties to Nonclients 335

Respect for the Rights of Third Persons

Model Rule 4.4 serves as a limitation on the lawyer's zeal for protecting his client. It provides a common-sense duty to avoid means that unnecessarily embarrass another or delay judicial proceedings. It states: "In representing a client, a lawyer shall not use means that have no substantial purpose other than to embarrass, delay, or burden a third person, or use methods of obtaining evidence that violate the legal rights of such a person."[11] A comment to this rule indicates that a lawyer properly gives his client's interest priority over the interests of others. It also makes clear, however, that the concept of duty to the client does not mean that the lawyer can disregard the rights of others. "Responsibility to a client requires a lawyer to subordinate the interests of others to those of the client, but that responsibility does not imply that a lawyer may disregard the rights of third persons."[12]

Respect for the Rights of Third Persons (2002 Revision)

The ABA House of Delegates adopted a revision to Model Rule 4.4 that requires lawyers who receive documents that they recognize were sent inadvertently to notify the sender promptly. The 2002 revision to Model Rule 4.4 adopted the view of the ABA Standing Committee on this point by including an additional provision expressly indicating that a lawyer must "promptly notify the sender" when the lawyer "receives a document relating to the representation of the lawyer's client and knows or reasonably should know the document was inadvertently sent."[13] The revised rule does not speak to what additional steps a lawyer should take in this situation. Nor does it deal with the question of what a lawyer should do if he receives a document that he believes has been wrongfully obtained.

Also relevant on the issue of duties to nonclients is the lawyer's role in providing evaluations for the use of third persons. This role and the duties that accompany it are discussed below.

Duty of Candor: Environmental Example

In environmental matters, the speculative nature of causation may sometimes tempt lawyers to use any argument to point the finger of liability or guilt away from their clients and toward someone else. The lawyer's duty of truthfulness includes the obligation to use due care in providing information to

---

11. Model Rule 4.4.
12. Model Rule 4.4 cmt. 1.
13. Model Rule 4.4(b) (2002).

336 ISSUES OF LEGAL ETHICS IN THE PRACTICE OF ENVIRONMENTAL LAW

nonclients who will rely on the information.[14] Likewise, lawyers and clients must respond truthfully to discovery requests, such as deposition questions or interrogatories.[15] When a party to a transaction seeks information (such as the environmental condition of property to be conveyed), a misrepresentation can provide a basis for damages or rescission of the contract by a party who relies on a misleading statement.[16] A half-truth can also provide a basis for an action.[17]

Assume that a landowner seeking to sell property provides a factually accurate environmental audit report to prospective buyers. If the seller knows that the report failed to address a portion of the property that has environmental contamination, or if he knows that contamination has occurred on the property after the date of the audit, the technical accuracy of the report may not fully exculpate the seller from failing to provide complete information regarding the condition of the property. The doctrine of latent defect provides a basis for buyer recourse against sellers who fail to reveal significant hidden defects.[18] If a lawyer passes on information that he knows is false, he as well as the client can be held liable to a third party injured by the misrepresentation. Providing incomplete or misleading information relating to discharges of a particular facility may also violate statutes or the common law and result in sanctions or damages.[19]

---

14. *See* Eisenberg v. Gagnon, 766 F.2d 770 (3d Cir. 1985), *cert. denied*, 474 U.S. 946 (1985).

15. FED. R. CIV. P. 26(e) & 26(g).

16. Many states allow avoidance of a contract to purchase property before conveyance when a seller fails to disclose contamination. *See, e.g.*, IDAHO CODE 55-2515, 55-2517 (1994 & Supp. 1997) (providing for rescission); IND. CODE 24-4.6-2-10, 24-4.6-2-13 (1996) (requiring seller disclosure to buyer before acceptance and allowing buyer to nullify contract within two business days of receipt of disclosure); MICH. COMP. LAWS 565.954 (2001) (allowing termination by written notice). *See also* RESTATEMENT (SECOND) OF CONTRACTS § 161 (1979) (when nondiscloser is equivalent to an assertion); RESTATEMENT (SECOND) OF CONTRACTS § 164 (1979) (when misrepresentation makes a contract voidable).

17. When a court avoids a contact on the basis of misrepresentation, a purchaser may be entitled to restitution. *See* RESTATEMENT (SECOND) OF CONTRACTS 376 (restitution when contract is voidable).

18. *See* RESTATEMENT (SECOND) OF TORTS 343.

19. For example, the Clean Water Act requires owners or operators of a facility discharging pollutants to record and report information about discharges into the waters of the United States. *See* Clean Water Act § 308(a), § 502(14), 33 U.S.C. §§ 1318(a), 1362(14) (1994). Similarly, the Clean Air Act requires owners or operators of a source of acid deposition to monitor and report emissions to the state permitting authority. *See* Clean Air Act § 412(a), § 502, 42 U.S.C. §§ 7651k(a), 7661a (1994); 42 U.S.C. §§ 6991a, 6991b (1994); 42

Chapter 8: The Lawyer's Duties to Nonclients 337

Duty to Third Persons

Evaluation for Use of a Third Person

The Model Rules recognize that it is permissible for a lawyer to undertake "an evaluation of a matter affecting a client for the use of someone other than the client."[20] Model Rule 2.3 expressly allows such a task by the lawyer when he "reasonably believes that making the evaluation is compatible with other aspects of the lawyer's relationship with the client."[21] The 1983 version of Model Rule 2.3 also reminds the lawyer that the rule on confidentiality continues to apply except to the extent the client has ordered disclosures.[22] A comment to Model Rule 2.3 acknowledges that other law determines the issue of whether a duty arises to a third party as a result of the lawyer providing information to that party. "When the evaluation is intended for the information or use of a third person, a legal duty to that person may or may not arise. That legal question is beyond the scope of this Rule."[23]

Evaluation for Use of a Third Person (2002 Revision)

The 2002 revision to Model Rule 2.3 clarified the rule rather than changing it in substantive ways. The revision changed the verb describing the action of the lawyer in this setting. It changed the verb "undertake" to "provide," giving a more definite description of the activity of the lawyer in this setting. The revision also created a new provision to the rule on evaluations for use by third parties, creating a common-sense exception to the rule. The revised rule expressly notes that if a lawyer "knows or reasonably should know that the evaluation is likely to affect the client's interests materially and adversely," then the rule prohibits the lawyer from providing the evaluation to the third person "unless the client gives informed consent."[24]

Rescission: Environmental Examples

Courts have recognized the right of a purchaser to rescind a contract that was entered as a result of an intentional or negligent misrepresentation relating to the environmental condition of property. In the case of *Roadmaster Indus-*

U.S.C. § 9603 (1980). *See also* 42 U.S.C. § 7413(c)(2) (classifying knowing failure to make required reports or keep records of compliance required by the Clean Air Act as a felony).

20. Model Rule 2.3 (2002).
21. Model Rule 2.3(a) (2002).
22. Model Rule 2.3(b) (1983).
23. Model Rule 2.3 cmt. 4 (1983); Model Rule 2.3 cmt. 3 (2002).
24. Model Rule 2.3(b) (2002).

338 ISSUES OF LEGAL ETHICS IN THE PRACTICE OF ENVIRONMENTAL LAW

tries, Inc. v. Columbia Manufacturing Company, Inc.,[25] the plaintiff purchased a bicycle factory from the defendant. The defendant failed to disclose the full extent of the contaminated state of the property. The defendant also failed to disclose to the plaintiff that EPA was investigating the site to determine the extent of the contamination. The court allowed the plaintiff to rescind the contract for purchase of the factory.

In *Scruggs v. Roach*,[26] the Tennessee Court of Appeals affirmed a trial court's grant of rescission of two contracts, finding that the defendant made material misrepresentations to plaintiffs to induce the sale.[27] The plaintiffs purchased from the defendant a gasoline station and auto repair shop and, additionally, entered a lease contract for the property on which the business was located. Gasoline sales made up 70 percent of the sales of the business, and the business sold Amoco gas and accepted Amoco credit cards. The plaintiffs did not purchase the Amoco franchise. Rather, it purchased gasoline from the local Amoco franchisee. On the same day the parties entered the contacts, the Tennessee legislature passed new, stricter laws imposing requirements on underground petroleum storage tanks. As a result of the legislation, the supplier removed the old tanks on the property, leaving the plaintiffs with only two tanks, an insufficient number to store and sell the three grades of gasoline required by Amoco. Because they were unable to offer the three grades of Amoco gas, the plaintiffs lost their Amoco certification. For a short time they purchased off-brand gasoline. They lost gasoline sales and ultimately stopped the business.

Before the purchase, the plaintiffs had inspected the premises. Additionally, the lease agreement stated that the plaintiffs accepted the premises "AS IS and WITH ALL FAULTS" and accepted responsibility for the maintenance of the tanks. Nevertheless, the trial court and the court of appeals allowed rescission. The court of appeals held that the defendant made an affirmative misrepresentation by stating that the tanks were "fine" when they had leaks. Moreover, the court held that the defendant knew water had been found in the

---

25. 893 F. Supp. 1162 (D. Mass. 1995) (holding plaintiff company could rescind a purchase contract with defendant company for misrepresentation when defendant failed to disclose extent of toxic contamination at site and existence of ongoing EPA investigation of site).

26. 1993 WL 93362 (Tenn. Ct. App. 1993) (allowing rescission of contract to purchase gas station based on defendant's failure to disclose existence of leaking underground storage tanks at the site when new legislation regulating storage of petroleum in underground tanks would burden the business).

27. The reviewing court rejected the trial court's finding of impossibility as a basis for the rescission but affirmed the rescission on the new ground of misrepresentation. *Id.* at *2.

Chapter 8: The Lawyer's Duties to Nonclients   339

storage tanks. The court held that failing to disclose this fact to the plaintiffs also constituted a material misrepresentation.

Duty of Candor to the Profession

Model Rule 8.3 states an obligation for lawyers to report misconduct of both lawyers and judges. It provides a mandatory reporting duty, stating that a lawyer "shall inform the appropriate professional authority" when he has "knowledge that another lawyer has committed a violation of the Rules of Professional Conduct that raises a substantial question as to that lawyer's honesty, trustworthiness or fitness as a lawyer."[28] The rule uses the same language in describing the obligation of a lawyer to report misconduct of a judge, stating a mandatory duty to report the judge to the appropriate authorities if the lawyer has "knowledge that a judge has committed a violation of applicable rules of judicial conduct that raises a substantial question as to the judge's fitness for office."[29] The provision includes an exception allowing the lawyer to refrain from reporting the conduct when the information that would be disclosed is protected by Rule 1.6.[30] It also excepts information "gained by a lawyer or judge while serving as a member of an approved lawyers assistance program" when it is the type of information that would be protected by the attorney-client privilege.[31]

The general principle that lawyers have an obligation to the public for the integrity of the profession is well established. Lawyers are often reluctant to report wrongdoing by a judge or another lawyer, even when the wrongful conduct is serious. Moreover, the difficulties of indeterminacy related to scientific factual information and, indeed, the indeterminacy of environmental law itself can create situations where an environmental lawyer may sense that there may be something unethical about another lawyer's conduct, though the lawyer lacks the certitude necessary to make a determination of wrongdoing.

Not surprisingly, lawyers who take this step often face criticism and may even suffer attacks on their credibility and integrity. When a law firm is accused of wrongdoing or when an established lawyer in a law firm is accused, the firm may be tempted to respond with accusations against the accuser or with a retaliatory discharge when the one reporting the violations is an employee of the firm. Those who report others in the profession can expect to lose hours to the controversy and suffer anxieties and doubts about the process.

---

28. Model Rule 8.3(a).
29. Model Rule 8.3(b).
30. Model Rule 8.3(c).
31. *Id.*

For example, the case of *Wieder v. Skala*[32] dealt with the problem of retaliation against a lawyer who reported unethical conduct in his firm. The firm discharged the lawyer. Ultimately, the court held that the fact that an associate was an at-will employee did not prevent him from stating a contract claim against the firm for discharging him as a result of his insistence that the firm comply with the ethics rules. The court noted that associates are "independent officers of the court, responsible in a broader public sense for their professional obligations."[33] The court also found an "implied-in-law obligation" that firm members will practice law "in accordance with the ethical standards of the profession."[34]

The case of *Kelly v. Hunton & Williams*[35] extended the *Wieder* rationale to include a cause of action in New York for unadmitted law graduates working as associates, finding implicitly that these employees have a duty to comply with the rules of ethics of the state. The *Kelly* court denied a motion for summary judgment by a law firm, holding that an associate not admitted to the bar nevertheless has a duty to report violations of legal ethics rules and has a right to bring a cause of action for wrongful discharge if he is fired as a result of his insistence that the firm report and correct billing fraud by a partner in the firm.[36]

> It is difficult to conceive of H & W telling its clients what it is now telling me, i.e., that, as far as the firm is concerned, its unadmitted associates are not bound by the disciplinary rules and may knowingly act contrary to them without fear of professional sanction.[37]

Implicit in this holding is the concept that disciplinary boards have the power to sanction both admitted lawyers and associates who are not admitted to the bar for failing to report significant misconduct by a lawyer. "[I]t would be anomalous to permit these associates to ignore unethical behavior that admitted associates are required to report."[38] The court noted that unadmitted associates are common at large New York firms and, further, that both admitted and unadmitted associates "perform generally the same functions at the

---

32. 609 N.E.2d 105 (1992).
33. *Id.* at 108.
34. *Id.*
35. 1999 WL 408416 (E.D. N.Y. 1999).
36. Kelly, *supra* note 35, at *27.
37. *Id.* at *18.
38. *Id.*

Chapter 8: The Lawyer's Duties to Nonclients 341

junior level" in such firms.[39] The *Kelly* court rejected the firm's argument that a firm has a right as a matter of employment law to "fire an associate in retaliation for complaining and threaten to ruin his future with bad references" as long as the firm takes this action before the associate threatens to report violations to the Disciplinary Committee.[40] The court held that the firm's action in retaliating for reports to the Disciplinary Committee was "inherently coercive"[41] and rejected the firm's argument that a report or threat to report a lawyer in the firm to the Disciplinary Committee is "a prerequisite to a successful claim."[42]

Puffery

Perhaps like all businesspeople, lawyers often feel they must impress prospective clients with their abilities, specialized knowledge, experience, and connections in the legal world. Naturally, lawyers hope to attract clients in sufficient numbers to make their practices profitable. Environmental lawyers may feel additional pressure to attract Superfund clients as soon as a letter goes out to potentially responsible parties, for example. Similarly, an environmental lawyer may believe that unless he attracts sufficient numbers of residents as plaintiffs in a toxic tort matter, other lawyers may take the lead in forming a class action. Lawyers expect to be able to support themselves and their families by their work in their chosen profession.

The temptation to emphasize connections with agency personnel is strong in environmental law. The vast majority of environmental matters are disposed of administratively, whether the matter is a dispute, a charge of violation of environmental requirements, or transactional matters such as obtaining a discharge permit. Additionally, many environmental lawyers gain familiarity and a friendly acquaintance with administrators. This context makes it particularly important that the environmental lawyer be careful not to give an impression to a client that the lawyer's relationship with an administrative official is such that the client will be given special consideration or a "break" if the client retains the lawyer's services.

Model Rule 8.4 indicates that a lawyer violates professional standards if he "state[s] or impl[ies] an ability to influence improperly a government agency or official."[43] Although this rule includes the modifying term "improperly," it

---

39. *Id.*
40. *Id.* at *20.
41. *Id.*
42. *Id.* at *21.
43. Model RULE 8.4(e) (defining misconduct to include stating or implying an ability to "influence improperly a government agency or official").

342 ISSUES OF LEGAL ETHICS IN THE PRACTICE OF ENVIRONMENTAL LAW

carries with it a note of caution for the lawyer who might be tempted to emphasize his reputation and connections. Clients may form an impression that a lawyer has "pull" as well as connections. If the client is justified in this understanding, the lawyer may be in violation of Rule 8.4.

Lawyer Misconduct Generally

Model Rule 8.4 summarizes different types of misconduct. Some of these relate to the lawyer's relationship with clients or prospective clients. Other points are broader, relating to clients, nonclients, tribunals, and the public itself. Professional misconduct under Model Rule 8.4 includes violating or attempting to violate the ethics rules.[44] Model Rule 8.4(a) indicates that professional misconduct includes actions a lawyer takes through the acts of another. The rule states: "It is professional misconduct for a lawyer to: (a) violate or attempt to violate the Rules of Professional Conduct, knowingly assist or induce another to do so, or do so through the acts of another."[45]

Misconduct also includes, of course, the commission of a criminal act "that reflects adversely on the lawyer's honesty, trustworthiness or fitness,"[46] and "conduct involving dishonesty, fraud, deceit or misrepresentation."[47] Conduct that is "prejudicial to the administration of justice"[48] is also proscribed by Model Rule 8.4, as is the conduct of stating or implying that the lawyer has the "ability to influence improperly a government agency or official."[49] When a lawyer "knowingly assist[s] a judge or judicial officer in conduct that is a violation of applicable rules of judicial conduct or other law," his actions constitute misconduct within the definition of Model Rule 8.4.[50] As with other areas, context is of significance. For example, a decision of the Utah State Bar Ethics Advisory Committee concluded that Rule 8.4(c), relating to dishonesty, deceit, and misrepresentation, was not meant to prohibit prosecutors or other government lawyers from taking part in covert operations although they do involve deceit.[51]

---

44. MODEL RULE 8.4(a).
45. *Id.*
46. MODEL RULE 8.4(b).
47. MODEL RULE 8.4(c).
48. MODEL RULE 8.4(d).
49. MODEL RULE 8.4(e).
50. MODEL RULE 8.4(f).
51. *Utah Panel Advises That Government Lawyers May Participate in Lawful Covert Operations*, 70 U.S.L.W. 2662 (Apr. 23, 2002) (Utah State Bar Ethics Advisory Opinion Comm., No. 20-05, 3/18/02 determining that Rule 8.4(c) was not meant to prohibit prosecutors or other government attorneys from taking part in covert operations involving deceit).

In *Washington State Physicians Ins. Exch. & Ass'n v. Fisons Corp.*,[52] a court imposed significant monetary sanctions against a well-known law firm for discovery responses that were not candid.

Lawyer Misconduct Generally (2002 Revision)

The 2002 revision to Model Rule 8.4 added the phrase "or to achieve results by means that violate the Rules of Professional Conduct or other laws,"[53] providing a fuller picture of the ways a lawyer may run afoul of the rule. Comment 1 to Rule 8.4 emphasizes that a violation is as much a violation by the lawyer when it is achieved by the acts of another. The comment states that "lawyers are subject to discipline when they violate" the rules, "knowingly assist or induce another to do so or do so through the acts of another."[54]

Disclosures to Protect Third Parties (2002 Revision)

The 2002 Revision to the Model Rules acknowledges that the rights of third parties trump the lawyer's duty of confidentiality when necessary to protect life and bodily integrity. This point is explored in the section on confidentiality.[55]

---

52. 858 P.2d 1054 (Wash. 1993).
53. MODEL RULE 8.4 (e) (2002).
54. MODEL RULE 8.4 cmt. 1 (2002).
55. See pages 99-105.

CHAPTER 9

Alternative Dispute Resolution

ADR in Environmental Matters

The techniques of alternative dispute resolution (ADR) seem to have particular utility in the environmental area, perhaps because of the complex factual and scientific issues implicated in environmental disputes.[1] The use of ADR in our justice system is "one of the most striking changes in the dynamics of law practice" in recent years.[2] When successful, ADR can reduce the cost of resolving problems in many areas.[3] Both the EPA and the Congress have sought to encourage the use of ADR in the environmental context. For example, the Administrative Dispute Resolution Act of 1990 (ADRA) makes ADR available more broadly with the purpose of securing settlements outside the judicial system and, consequentially, reducing the number of cases crowding the federal court system's docket and generally facilitating settlements.[4] The ADRA defines the ADR process as "any procedure that is used to resolve issues in controversy, including, but not limited to, conciliation, facilitation, mediation, factfinding, minitrials, arbitration, and use of ombuds, or any combination thereof."[5] The Act orders that agency or interagency committees be

---

1. *See* Sarah L. Inderbitzin et al., *The Use of Alternative Dispute Resolution in Natural Resource Damage Assessments*, 20 WM. & MARY ENVTL. L. & POL'Y REV. 1 (1995) (outlining various ADR techniques and a key federal statute in that area, the Administrative Dispute Resolution Act (ADRA)); Charlene Stukenborg, *The Proper Role of Alternative Dispute Resolution (ADR) in Environmental Conflicts*, 19 U. DAYTON L. REV. 1305 (1994) (presenting history of ADR in environmental conflicts through case studies and federal statutory framework).
2. Douglas H. Yarn, *Lawyer Ethics in ADR and the Recommendations of Ethics 2000 to Revise the Model Rules of Professional Conduct: Considerations for Adoption and State Application*, 54 ARK. L. REV. 207, 210-11 (2001).
3. *See generally* Douglas H. Yarn, *supra* note 2.
4. 5 U.S.C. § 571 et seq. (2000).
5. 5 U.S.C. § 571 (3) (2003, Supp.).

designated to "encourage and facilitate agency use of alternative means of dispute resolution" and to "develop procedures that permit agencies to obtain the services of neutrals on an expedited basis" when they decide to employ ADR.[6] The Act commits the decision of whether or not to use a dispute resolution process to agency discretion.[7] The Act provides for confidentiality of the ADR process as well as extending immunity to arbitrators.[8] Under the Act, parties are able to reject arbitration awards, opting into the judicial process essentially with no effect from the arbitration. The Act also provides for enforcement of arbitration agreements.[9]

Another federal act, the Negotiated Rulemaking Act, encourages agencies to use ADR techniques in the process of developing regulations necessary to implement federal legislation.[10] This process does not involve a dispute about a particular case. Rather, it seeks to use the process of negotiation to develop regulations that will be less vulnerable to attack both as a matter of substance and as a matter of procedure because the regulated community participated in the development of the regulations. The Act declares that its purpose is to "establish a framework for the conduct of negotiated rulemaking" and "to encourage agencies to use the process when it enhances the informal rulemaking process."[11] The Act also has a general statement of its goal of innovation: "Nothing in this subchapter should be construed as an attempt to limit innovation and experimentation with the negotiated rulemaking process or with other innovative rulemaking procedures otherwise authorized by law."[12] Under this Act, the agencies are empowered to invite stakeholders in a particular issue to be involved in assessing the need for a particular regulation under consideration and to work with the agency toward consensus for the appropriate wording and scope of the regulation.[13] The Act also allows agencies to use the services of a convener to assist in "identifying persons who will be significantly affected by a proposed rule, including residents of rural areas" and "conducting discussions with such persons to identify the issues of concern to such persons, and to ascertain whether the establishment of a negotiated rulemaking committee is feasible and appropriate in the particular rulemaking."[14]

---

6. 5 U.S.C. § 573(c)(1) and (2) (2000).
7. 5 U.S.C. § 581(b) (2000).
8. 5 U.S.C. § 574 (2000).
9. 5 U.S.C. § 576 (2000).
10. 5 U.S.C. §§ 561–570 (2000).
11. 5 U.S.C. § 561 (2000).
12. *Id.*
13. 5 U.S.C. § 563 (2000).
14. *Id.* at § 563(b)(1)(A) and (B) (2000).

One of the most important techniques of ADR is the focus on preventive measures to obviate disputes before they are created. In the development of public projects, for example, such as projects that must comply with the National Environmental Policy Act (NEPA) or a state statute similar to NEPA, governmental agencies should include public participation in the planning process of the project. Giving the public an opportunity to be involved as early as possible can generate useful ideas for the consideration of the agency as well as helping to minimize the disruption caused by the governmental project to local residents who may feel the effects of the project. Such inclusion may also help reduce the likelihood of lawsuits and disputes relating to the project. Public projects should also include processes for involving the public in evaluating the progress of the program at every stage.

The federal system provides special encouragement to environmental litigants to use ADR. For example, the Environmental Policy and Conflict Resolution Act of 1998, passed unanimously by both houses, encouraged the use of ADR in environmental cases by creation of the Institute for Environmental Conflict Resolution.[15] The Act authorizes federal agencies to use the institute for conflicts relating to environmental laws, including public land laws. The Institute, based in Tucson, Arizona, operates under the Morris K. Udall Foundation. It depends on federal funding as well as fees from the parties who use its services.

> Statutory authority specifically permits the EPA to enter into an agreement with any person to perform any response action if the EPA determines that the person will perform the action properly ....EPA must seek settlement whenever it is practicable, providing the following elements are met: (1) settlement is in the public interest, (2) settlement is consistent with the NCP, (3) settlement will expedite remedial action, and (4) settlement will minimize litigation. If the EPA decides not to pursue settlement negotiations for a particular site, it is required to notify PRPs in writing, explaining its decision.[16]

Nevertheless, the use of ADR may not be as effective as possible, because of either the resistance of parties or agencies or inertia.

---

15. 20 U.S.C. § 5602 et seq.

16. Robert A. Shults, *Environmental Disputes, in* ALTERNATIVE DISPUTE RESOLUTION: THE LITIGATOR'S HANDBOOK 220 (Nancy F. Atlas et al. ed., 2000) (citing 42 U.S.C. § 9622).

348 ISSUES OF LEGAL ETHICS IN THE PRACTICE OF ENVIRONMENTAL LAW

At times, governmental agencies unjustifiably fear the employment of ADR techniques for fear of losing control of the enforcement action. This view assumes that the filing of suit or the commencement of other enforcement action allows the agency to maintain a great deal of control over the progress of the proceeding. The existence of this attitude can be verified by virtually any experienced litigator.[17]

The terms of disclosure of settlements raise issues relating to confidentiality and protection of the public. Rules on settlement can significantly affect the resolution of environmental disputes and the balance of party interests in the settlement process. For example, some courts are considering rules that would limit the time a settlement would be secret.[18] A rule requiring disclosure of settlement after a certain period of time seems well designed to protect the public. On the other hand, such a rule may result in decisions not to settle controversies at all. If a party wishes to keep the terms of the settlement from entering the public domain, that party may simply refuse to consider settlement. The party may fear that disclosure of the settlement would provide information useful for future plaintiffs. For example, parties involved in a Superfund site or an undergound storage tank site must determine the appropriate share of costs each will share. A rule allowing settlement to be made public may create a disincentive for these parties to negotiate and settle their dispute. Such a rule could also result in oral settlements, creating additional uncertainty because of the indeterminate nature of agreements that are not documented by a writing.

Third-Party Neutrals

Environmental lawyers have been involved in negotiation and mediation of disputes since the inception of environmental laws in this country—sometimes as a lawyer and other times as a neutral. Factually difficult cases and the scientific dimensions of environmental disputes make arbitration or mediation an attractive alternative to litigation. The role of the lawyer varies somewhat under different laws and in different contexts. For example, considering the role of the lawyer as a counselor or intermediary under Rule 2.2, C. Baird Brown noted in his article *Ethical Considerations in Solid Waste Practice* that

---

17. *Id.*
18. *See* Adam Liptak, *Judges Seek to Ban Secret Settlements in South Carolina,* N.Y. TIMES (Sept. 2, 2002), *available at* http://www.nytimes.com/2002/09/02/national/02JUDG.html.

Chapter 9: Alternative Dispute Resolution **349**

"bringing all disputants in a solid waste disposal matter into a non-adjudicatory forum . . . with the guidance of a neutral mediator" can be difficult in solid waste settings because there may be "no trade-offs that are of interest to opponents of a particular site."[19] He notes, however, that mediation "may be a fruitful course of action that lawyers should encourage."[20] Brown also cautions lawyers to remember that the goals of mediation "are not adjudicatory and treating the process as adversarial will be as damaging as would the commission of fraud in a traditional adversarial process."[21]

Third-Party Neutrals (2002 Revision)

In response to the Ethics 2000 Commission proposal, the ABA adopted a new rule to address the lawyer's role as a third-party neutral when the lawyer "assists two or more persons who are not clients of the lawyer" to resolve a dispute between them.[22] A rule added to the Model Rules in the 2002 revision deals with lawyers who serve as third-party neutrals.[23] The term "third-party neutral" refers to legal services such as arbitration, mediation, or simply assisting in resolving a matter in which the lawyer does not represent the parties to the dispute.[24] The new rule merges treatment of lawyers who have served as judges, arbitrators, mediators, or other third-party neutrals, requiring such lawyers to obtain informed consent from all parties to any proceeding in which that lawyer participated "personally and substantively."[25]

Revised Model Rule 2.4 acknowledges the role of a lawyer serving as a neutral to assist "two or more persons who are not clients" in reaching a "resolution of a dispute or other matter that has arisen between them."[26] The rule includes within its purview of service as a third-party neutral "service as an arbitrator, a mediator or in such other capacity as will enable the lawyer to assist the parties to resolve the matter."[27] The rule applies only to allow the lawyer to function as a neutral when she does not represent any of the parties to the dispute. The rule creates an obligation on the lawyer to "inform unrep-

---

19. C. Baird Brown, *Ethical Considerations in Solid Waste Practice,* C659 ALI-ABA 339, 344 (Jan. 30, 1992).
20. *Id.*
21. *Id.*
22. MODEL RULE 2.4 (2002).
23. *Id.*
24. *See id.*
25. MODEL RULE 1.12(a) (2002).
26. MODEL RULE 2.4(a) (2002).
27. *Id.*

resented parties that the lawyer is not representing them."[28] Model Rule 2.4 underscores this duty by stating an affirmative duty that the lawyer "explain the difference between the lawyer's role as a third-party neutral and a lawyer's role as one who represents a client" if the lawyer "knows or reasonably should know that a party does not understand the lawyer's role in the matter."[29] It also requires that the consent be "confirmed in writing."[30]

In a comment to the new rule, the ABA recognized the importance of ADR in today's legal world, noting that ADR "has become a substantial part of the civil justice system."[31] The comment also recognized the need for lawyers to play the role of neutrals in the context of ADR proceedings in addition to the traditional role of representing parties in ADR. "Aside from representing clients in dispute-resolution processes, lawyers often serve as third-party neutrals."[32] The comment indicates that lawyers may serve in this context as neutrals in a given matter as long as they do not represent a client in the dispute.

---

28. MODEL RULE 2.4(b) (2002).
29. *Id.*
30. *Id.*
31. MODEL RULE 2.4 cmt. 1 (2002).
32. *Id.*

CHAPTER 10

The Anticontact Rule — Represented Persons

For obvious reasons, lawyers are wary of a situation in which an opponent lawyer talks with another lawyer's client without the consent of the lawyer representing that client. Environmental litigation often involves claims that relate to employees or officers of corporate clients. Most environmental lawyers engaged in defending against an action such as an enforcement action by EPA for a discharge alleged to be in violation of a permit would prefer that clients answer EPA's questions in the form of an interrogatory or deposition rather than in the casual and unprotected format of a one-on-one conversation. A lawyer's fear that a client will inadvertently make a statement to opposing counsel that might have legal ramifications unknown to the client is only the tip of the iceberg of concerns lawyers have about client communications with opposing counsel. Undoubtedly, part of what clients bargain for in making the decision to retain a lawyer is to correct the potential disadvantage that the client anticipates could accrue if he represented himself in a dispute or a transaction. The anticontact rule, to a great extent, rests on the realization that the benefits of hiring a lawyer can be lost if opposing counsel is allowed to speak directly with the client without that client's lawyer being present. Generally, disciplinary boards and commentators agree that the client cannot waive the anticontact rule found in Rule 4.2.[1] The rationale for this view may be that it cannot be assumed that a client fully understands what he is giving up by talking to a lawyer who is not his agent. Generally the client's lawyer should make this judgment.

---

1. ABA Comm. on Ethics and Prof'l Responsibility, Formal Op. 95-396 (1995) (committee report that rule 4.2 is not waivable).

352   ISSUES OF LEGAL ETHICS IN THE PRACTICE OF ENVIRONMENTAL LAW

Both the Model Code[2] and the Model Rules[3] prohibit lawyer contact with a represented person. Model Rule 4.2, entitled "Communication with Person Represented by Counsel," prohibits a lawyer from knowingly discussing matters with a represented person concerning the subject matter giving rise to the representation. The purpose of the anticontact rule is to protect individuals who are represented by lawyers from adverse lawyers to reduce the likelihood that the represented person will disclose information harmful to his interests or lose the benefit that he is paying the lawyer to secure (representation).[4] The rule states, as follows:

> In representing a client, a lawyer shall not communicate about the subject of the representation with a person the lawyer knows to be represented by another lawyer in the matter, unless the lawyer has the consent of the other lawyer or is authorized by law to do so.[5]

The *Restatement* recognizes additional situations in which communication with a represented nonclient is appropriate.[6] It states:

> (1) A lawyer representing a client in a matter may not communicate about the subject of the representation with a nonclient whom the lawyer knows to be represented in the matter by another lawyer or with a representative of an organizational nonclient so represented as defined in § 100, unless:
> (a) the communication is with a public officer or agency to the extent stated in [section] 101;
> (b) the lawyer is a party and represents no other client in the matter;
> (c) the communication is authorized by law;
> (d) the communication reasonably responds to an emergency; or
> (e) the other lawyer consents.
> (2) Subsection (1) does not prohibit the lawyer from assisting the client in otherwise proper communication by the lawyer's client with a represented nonclient.

---

2. *See* DR 7-104(A)(1).
3. MODEL RULE 4.2.
4. ABA Comm. on Ethics and Prof'l Responsibility, Formal Op. 95-396 (1995).
5. MODEL RULE 4.2.
6. *See* RESTATEMENT (THIRD) OF THE LAW GOVERNING LAWYERS 99 (2000).

Chapter 10: The Anticontact Rule—Represented Persons 353

Some state rules alter the scope of the anticontact rule, the exceptions to the rule, or both. For example, the California anticontact rule expressly prohibits indirect as well as direct communications.[7] In addition to permitting communications authorized by law, the California rule permits communications with public officers and public boards. It also expressly allows contacts initiated by a party seeking advice or representation from an independent lawyer chosen by that party.[8]

Even when it is determined that a lawyer may ethically contact an individual, this fact does not obligate that individual to talk with the lawyer or to provide the information requested. Some lawyers counsel their clients to advise employees and agents to refuse to talk with opposing counsel whether or not the employee has managerial responsibility or is the type of employee whose act or omission could be imputed to the organization or whose statement could constitute an admission.[9] An employer may want to alert employees to the fact that lawyers representing the government or another party may seek to discuss the case with them. "It is essential that employees understand that while they are free to talk to government investigators, they have no obligation to do so. Employees should also understand that they have a right to consult with an attorney before agreeing to be interviewed by a government investigator."[10] In such cases, the employer should be careful not to create an impression that they are attempting to influence the employees' testimony.

Although some state rules use the term "party"[11] rather than "person," Model Rule 4.2 presents a broader focus. Comment 3 to Model Rule 4.2 makes clear that the prohibition of the rule is not limited to the parties to a proceeding. It states that the rule applies "to communications with any person, whether or not a party to a formal adjudicative proceeding, contract or negotiation, who is represented by counsel concerning the matter to which the communication relates."[12] In 1995, the House of Delegates amended Rule 4.2, changing the term "party" in the rule to "person" to make clear that the rule extends to any person who has retained counsel to represent him in a particular matter. Thus, the ABA broadened the rule in two respects. It extended protection to individuals who are represented by counsel in a matter without

---

7. *See* Calif. Rule of Prof'l Conduct 2-100(A).

8. *Id.*

9. *See* MODEL RULE 4.2 cmt. 4.

10. *See* Carol E. Dinkins & Lewis C. Sutherland, *Ethics in the Environmental and Toxic Tort Practice*, SB 73 ALI-ABA 319, 329 (1997).

11. *See, e.g.,* IL. SUP. CT. R.P.C. RULE 4.2; KY. S. CT. R.P.C. 3.130, 4.2, OH. ST. C.P.R. DR 7-104.

12. MODEL RULE 4.2 cmt. 3.

354   ISSUES OF LEGAL ETHICS IN THE PRACTICE OF ENVIRONMENTAL LAW

regard to whether the person is a party to a formally instituted proceeding. Additionally, this change makes clear that no formally instituted proceeding is necessary to invoke the protection of the rule.

Even state rules that refer to a "party" rather than a person may interpret the term "party" to include more than the named parties in a lawsuit. For example, the Tennessee Supreme Court held that the term "party" in the prohibition[13] includes a witness in a case who is represented by counsel.[14] Thus, the Tennessee Supreme Court sees the prohibition as reaching beyond the plaintiff and defendant in a pending lawsuit to include virtually anyone the lawyer knows is represented by counsel with regard to the case.

At first blush, Rule 4.2 may be taken as simply a straightforward rule that lawyers must not interact with a party to a lawsuit. The breadth of the rule is much larger than the typical case of a represented party, and it is possible for lawyers to stray into a violation of the rule innocently, not appreciating the scope of the prohibition. For example, a decision in the U.S. District Court for the District of Pennsylvania held that the rule prohibits a defense lawyer from informally interviewing potential witnesses in a personal injury action.[15] If the witnesses are also possible plaintiffs in a proposed class action tort suit involving the same conduct, the defense lawyer must have the consent of the class action lawyer. The court reasoned that Rule 4.2 of the Pennsylvania Rules of Professional Conduct applies prior to class certification and extends to all possible members of a class action. "As a practical matter, a court cannot decide the issue of class certification immediately upon the filing of the complaint. . . . Thus, certain benefits must be afforded the putative class members in the interim."[16]

Courts vary in their view of the seriousness of violations of the anticontact rule. In *In re FMC Corp.*, for example, a federal court held that it need not take action to prevent lawyers for the EPA from contacting a corporation's agents and managing employees without obtaining the consent of the corporation's counsel under the anticontact rule.[17] The court noted that the government had been "sensitive to ethical considerations in its conduct of investigation"[18] and that the corporation had time "to notify its employees of investigation and advise them of their right to counsel."[19] Accordingly, the

---

13. DI 7-104 (A)(1).
14. *See* Moncrete v. Board of Prof'l Responsibility, 25 Tenn. Att. Memo. 32-1 (July 27, 2000).
15. Dondore v. NGK Metals Corp., 152 F. Supp. 2d 662 (E.D. Pa. 2001).
16. *Id.* at 666.
17. 430 F. Supp. 1108 (D.C. W.Va. 1977).
18. *Id.*
19. *Id.*

Chapter 10: The Anticontact Rule—Represented Persons 355

court refused to issue a protective order, holding that it was "unnecessary for district court to undertake further control of Government's activities."[20]

In Formal Opinion 95-396, the ABA Committee on Ethics and Professional Responsibility considered the scope of the anticontact rule. It noted that Rule 4.2's bar applies only to communications that are within the scope of the representation. Likewise, the rule does not bar communications with a person unless the inquiring lawyer knows that another lawyer represents the person and that the representation is related to the communication.[21] Although Rule 4.2 does not impose a duty to inquire, a lawyer is deemed to have knowledge of the representation if it can be inferred from the circumstances. The opinion also noted that the rule only limits communications on the particular matter for which the client is being represented; it does not prohibit communications when the lawyer who represents the party allows the communication with that client.[22] Thus, counsel can consent to a communication with his client. and matters outside the scope of the representation do not require counsel's consent. The opinion states that the subject of the representation must "have crystallized between the client and the lawyer."[23] For this reason, a lawyer's general representation of a client seems to lack the required specificity to trigger Rule 4.2.

When a person's representation terminates, the anticontact bar no longer exists with regard to that person. In a situation in which a lawyer believes that a communication is permitted because the representation has terminated, the lawyer should seek reasonable assurance of the termination before proceeding with communications by obtaining evidence of the termination from the person or contacting the representing lawyer to confirm the termination.

The fact that the represented party initiates contact with a lawyer does not remove the Rule 4.2 bar. The represented party cannot waive the Rule 4.2 ethical prohibition.[24] Only the lawyer can waive the anticontact rule to allow another lawyer to discuss a matter with his client. The Rule 4.2 bar applies to both civil and criminal matters, and the committee opined that the rule applies to the conduct of both federal and state prosecutors. The rule also bars vicarious communications (with investigators acting under the lawyer's instructions, for example) by holding the lawyer responsible for communications that would violate the rule if the lawyer directs or orders the investigator to communicate with a represented person with regard to the subject matter of

---

20. *Id.*
21. ABA Comm. on Ethics and Prof'l Responsibility, Formal Op. 95-396 (1995).
22. *Id.*
23. *Id.*
24. *Id.*

the representation. The ABA Committee noted that an exception to Rule 4.2 authorizes communications authorized by law. An "authorized by law" communication is one where a constitutional provision, state, or court rule expressly permits the communication to occur. The committee opined that authorization by a government agency falls within the "authorized by law" exception only when the power to issue that directive is "embodied in formal regulations that have been properly promulgated pursuant to statutory authority that contemplates regulation of the character in question."[25]

The rule does not, of course, purport to impose a duty on any nonlawyer, including the lawyer's client. A comment to Rule 4.2 makes clear that the client is not prohibited from contacting the opponent. "Parties to a matter may communicate directly with each other, and a lawyer is not prohibited from advising a client concerning a communication that the client is legally entitled to make."[26] An ABA Formal Opinion[27] notes that, when a party wishes to communicate a settlement offer directly to an opposing party the lawyer for that party has a duty to discuss with his client the client's freedom to communicate with the opposing party. The resolution of this issue is not clear-cut, however. After all, Model Rule 8.4 indicates that a lawyer violates professional standards when she accomplishes through another what she is prohibited from doing by a rule of ethics. Model Rule 8.4(a) states that professional misconduct includes not only violating a rule but also "knowingly assist[ing] or induc[ing] another to do so, or do[ing] so through the acts of another."[28] Simply using the client as a conduit for the lawyer's arguments seems to circumvent Model Rule 4.2.

The opinion also noted that problems exist with the scenario. "The prohibition of this Rule against a lawyer's violating the Rules through the acts of another raises a number of questions about, inter alia, what a lawyer may or may not say to the lawyer's client, sufficiently broad and complex to require separate attention."[29] The *Restatement* suggests that the lawyer for a client wishing to communicate directly with an adversary "may advise the client regarding legal aspects of the communication, such as whether an intended communication is libelous or would otherwise create risk for the client."[30] The *Restatement* indicates that the lawyer may even "suggest that the client make

---

25. *Id.*
26. *See* MODEL RULE 4.2 cmt. 4.
27. ABA Formal Op., 92-362.
28. MODEL RULE 8.4(a).
29. *Id.*
30. RESTATEMENT (THIRD) OF THE LAW GOVERNING LAWYERS § 99 cmt. k (2000).

Chapter 10: The Anticontact Rule—Represented Persons 357

such a communication."[31] But it notes that the lawyer "must not assist the client inappropriately to seek confidential information."[32]

Anticontact Rule (2002 Revision)

The Revised Model Rule 4.2 prohibits "communications with a constituent of the organization who supervises, directs or regularly consults with the organization's lawyer concerning the matter or has authority to obligate the organization with respect to the matter or whose act or omission in connection with the matter may be imputed to the organization for purposes of civil or criminal liability."[33]

The 2002 revision to Model Rule 4.2 also added specificity to the right of a lawyer to communicate with a person who is represented by another lawyer when authorized by law. The revision includes an exception to the bar against communicating with a person represented by counsel when the lawyer is authorized to speak with the represented person by "a court order."[34] A new comment to the revised rule makes clear that the rule does not bar communications with former employees or officers. "Consent of the organization's lawyer is not required for communication with a former constituent."[35] The comment cautions lawyers against using unfair tactics in interviewing constituents of a corporation. "In communicating with a current or former constituent of an organization, a lawyer must not use methods of obtaining evidence that violate the legal rights of the organization."[36] Additionally, new comment 6 makes clear that lawyers may seek a court order regarding communicating with a represented party.

> A lawyer who is uncertain whether a communication with a represented person is permissible may seek a court order. A lawyer may also seek a court order in exceptional circumstances to authorize a communication that would otherwise be prohibited by this Rule, for example, where communication with a person represented by counsel is necessary to avoid reasonably certain injury.[37] The 2002

---

31. *Id.*
32. *Id.*
33. MODEL RULE 4.2 cmt. 7 (2002).
34. MODEL RULE 4.2 (2002).
35. MODEL RULE 4.2 cmt. 7 (2002).
36. MODEL RULE 4.2 cmt. 7 (2002) *citing* MODEL RULE 4.4.
37. MODEL RULE 4.2 cmt. 6 (2002).

358 ISSUES OF LEGAL ETHICS IN THE PRACTICE OF ENVIRONMENTAL LAW

revision of Model Rule 4.2 makes clear that a lawyer may contact former employees and constituents.[38]

Anticontact Rule: Environmental Examples

To explore some of the problems that can arise in the environmental arena, assume you represent a municipal agency or an agency involved in a road project that must comply with the National Environmental Policy Act (NEPA). The lead agency calls together all stakeholder agencies involved for a scoping meeting. Such a meeting serves both informational and planning functions. In the meeting, the agencies make plans for the entire project, or a major portion of the project. The group schedules major events such as public hearings and allocates responsibilities for the work of compiling the information for the environmental assessment. Suppose that upon receiving a scoping memorandum, you notice that the document gives conflicting dates or other incorrect or confusing statements. Your impulse may be to contact the project manager or governmental official who drafted the memorandum containing the incorrect or inconsistent information. Suppose a meeting summary states that the Federal Highway Administration representative indicated that the "entire area is not a parkland." You know that the Federal Highway officer stated that not all of the area constituted a parkland under applicable federal regulations. This presents an important point that the lawyer may need to check, whether or not it seems to implicate or impact your client directly or relate to a current litigation issue. If the party sending the memo is represented by counsel, however, the text of Rule 4.2 seems to require that the lawyer seek permission of counsel before calling the governmental employee.

Efficiency may advocate encouraging staff members of the governmental agencies to consult with one another directly. Lawyers should beware that they are making a judgment call when they allow apparently trivial inconsistencies to go unchallenged. They are also making a judgment call when they authorize direct contact between other counsel and an agency client.

In these situations, the cautious practice is to contact the lawyer for the lead agency for which the government official works. Contacting the lawyer will inevitably take more time. It also creates additional work for the lawyer contacted and creates the possibility that she may need to serve as the liaison with the employees for her agency. This burden may also influence lawyers to waive the anticontact vis-á-vis employees of an agency when the matter is largely cooperative or the prospect of abuse seems remote. The situation raises a tangential concern relating to public records laws. If the consultant has sent

---

38. MODEL RULE 4.2 cmt.7 (2002).

the document to federal and state agencies, any correction should be in the form of a supplementation to the record rather than a single corrected document.

One possible solution to the anticontact issues in the NEPA scoping example might be for the party who generates meeting summary notes (probably a consultant) to solicit all comments on the meeting summary and circulate those to the group. In this way, the questions regarding accuracy of a statement of one of the persons in a meeting can be brought to the fore without directly contacting a represented person.

Corporate Entities

The anticontact rule presents challenging questions in the corporate context because of factual difficulties relating to who can speak for a corporation and who might bind a corporation. Corporations have special concerns in this area because of the number of employees that might be contacted and the possibility that the employees who are contacted may be unsophisticated about the law or easily influenced by a questioner.

> It is very common in criminal investigations of corporations for trained government investigators to contact employees of the corporation and seek to interview them. Often, these interviews will occur when the employee is away from work, and the investigators will suggest to the employees that they do not need to seek counsel or consult with company representatives before being interviewed. The employee often will be asked to keep the details of the interview secret.[39]

Application to Employees and Agents

The language of Rule 4.2 refers to "a person the lawyer knows to be represented by another lawyer on the matter." Although the rule may appear, on its face, to prohibit communication only with the person or entity who hires a lawyer, as opposed to an employee or agent, comment 1 to the Rule suggests that employees and agents of the represented person are included in the prohibition. It states: "This Rule does not prohibit communication with a represented person, or an employee or agent of such person, concerning matters outside the representation."[40] This comment creates an exception based on the

---

39. *See* Carol E. Dinkins & Lewis C. Sutherland, *Ethics in the Environmental and Toxic Tort Practice*, SB 73 ALI-ABA 319, 329 (1997).

40. MODEL RULE 4.2 cmt. 1.

360 ISSUES OF LEGAL ETHICS IN THE PRACTICE OF ENVIRONMENTAL LAW

nature of the communication, stating the noncontroversial principle that it is appropriate to communicate with parties regarding matters "outside the representation." Because this comment speaks to an exception to the Rule, it must mean that employees and agents of represented persons are within the exception to the anticontact provision. Otherwise, there would be no reason to address them in the exception, since they would never be within the prohibition in the first place. Accordingly, the exception indicates that the rule includes employees and agents when the communication with that person is *inside* the representation. Comment 4 to the rule gives more information about individuals who fall within the anticontact rule prohibition by virtue of their role in an organization. It states:

> In the case of an organization, this Rule prohibits communications by a lawyer for another person or entity concerning the matter in representation with persons having a managerial responsibility on behalf of the organization, and with any other person whose act or omission in connection with that matter may be imputed to the organization for purposes of civil or criminal liability or whose statement may constitute an admission on the part of the organization.[41]

While this comment indicates some employees or agents of a represented party may be included within the prohibition, the decision of whether a particular individual falls inside or outside the prohibition is fraught with uncertainty. Additionally, a comment to the rule recognizes that special needs may exist to communicate with government lawyers or officials.[42] "Communications authorized by law include, for example, the right of a party to a controversy with a government agency to speak with government officials about the matter."[43] Similarly, the rule does not prevent a lawyer from seeking information from an agency via a Freedom of Information Act (FOIA) request.

Former Employees

The 1983 version of Model Rule 4.2 provides limited guidance on whether a lawyer may contact a former employee of a party. Although the text of Model Rule 4.2 makes no mention of employees, whether current or former, Comment 4 to the rule indicates that the prohibition extends to "persons having managerial responsibility on behalf of the organization," persons "whose act or omission in connection with that matter may be imputed to the organiza-

---

41. MODEL RULE 4.2 cmt. 4.
42. *See* Fusco v. Albany, 509 N.Y.S.2d 763 (1986).
43. MODEL RULE 4.2 cmt. 1.

Chapter 10: The Anticontact Rule—Represented Persons 361

tion," and persons "whose statement may constitute an admission on the part of the organization."[44] The bar does not appear to prevent lawyers from contacting former employees of a corporation, however, regardless of whether they were once in one of the prohibited categories. The ABA Committee on Ethics and Professional Responsibility decided that the prohibition of Rule 4.2 does not prohibit contact with former employees of a person represented by a lawyer.[45] In its opinion, entitled "Contact with Former Employee of Adverse Corporate Party," the committee considered the purposes of Model Rule 4.2 and noted that the rule applies to independent contractors "whose relationship with the organization may have placed them in the factual position contemplated by the Comment." The committee considered policy arguments for extending Model Rule 4.2 "to cover some former corporate employers" and some judicial decisions reaching this result,[46] but ultimately decided that a lawyer does not violate Model Rule 4.2 by communicating with an unrepresented former employee of the corporate party without the consent of the corporation's lawyer.[47]

While many courts have held that lawyers may contact former employees of adverse organizations,[48] some courts have held that such contacts violated professional ethics when the acts of the former employees may be imputed to the company.[49] In *Camden v. State of Maryland*,[50] for example, the court relied on Rule 4.2, the Restatement, and the attorney-client privilege in deciding to disqualify a lawyer and suppress evidence on the basis that the lawyer's action of contacting a former employee of the defendant university was inappropriate.[51]

---

44. MODEL RULE 4.2 cmt. 4.

45. *See* ABA Comm. on Ethics and Prof'l Responsibility, Formal Op. 91-359.

46. *Id., citing* Niesig v. Team I et al., 558 N.E.2d 1030 (1990); Wright by Wright v. Group Health Hosp., 691 P.2d 564 (1984).

47. *Id.*

48. *See* Lang v. Reedy Creek Improvement Dist., 888 F. Supp. 1143, 1146 (M.D. Fla. 1995); Aken v. Business Industry Health Group, Inc., 885 F. Supp. 1474, 1477 (D. Kan. 1995); Wright by Wright v. Group Health Hosp., 691 P.2d 564 (1984).

49. *See* Public Service Elec. & Gas Co. v. Associated Elec. & Gas Ins. Servs., Ltd. (AEGIS), 745 F. Supp. 1037 (D.N.J. 1990) *superseded by* regulation Andrews v. Goodyear Tire & Rubber Co., Inc., 191 F.R.D. 59 (D.N.J. Feb.14, 2000); Matter of Opinion 668 of the New Jersey Advisory Committee on Prof'l Ethics, 633 A.2d 959 (N.J. 1993).

50. 910 F. Supp. 1115, 1120 (D. Md. 1996) (lawyer must avoid encouraging disclosure of privileged information by former employee of adversary).

51. New comment 7 clears up the important question by making certain that former employees are not within the scope of the prohibition. "Consent of the organization's lawyer is not required for communication with a former constituent. "REV. MODEL RULE 4.2 cmt. 7.

362 ISSUES OF LEGAL ETHICS IN THE PRACTICE OF ENVIRONMENTAL LAW

Corporate Clients: Environmental Examples

The anticontact rule can have far-reaching consequences in environmental matters, creating a need for care to avoid violating the rule when communicating with representatives of an opposing party. The scope of the prohibition is of particular importance in environmental class actions as well as any environmental matter with numerous parties and numerous professionals. A lawyer engaged in an environmental matter may need to communicate with a professional employed by an opponent. Contact with an employee or consultant of an opponent raises the ethical issues dealt with in the anticontact rule of Model Rule 4.2. For example, environmental plaintiffs may need to learn the state of contamination of a site or the effects of various options for remediation.

The case of *In re Environmental Ins. Declaratory Judgment Actions*[52] provides a good example of a lawyer who proceeded with due caution to interview former employees of a corporate party to a lawsuit in light of varying decisions regarding whether former employees are covered by the prohibition of Rule 4.2.[53] In this case of litigation over insurance coverage for environmental damage, the lawyers for both plaintiffs and defendants sought the guidance of this court on how to conduct such interviews to avoid breaching the rules of professional conduct when they interviewed former employees of the parties. The court held that the lawyers and investigators could properly contact former employees of the insureds, but cautioned that the lawyers and investigators must identify themselves and inform the former employees of the lawsuit.[54]

Because many issues of environmental law involve corporate entities, the question of contacting employees of a corporation arises frequently in environmental litigation and negotiation. Although the rule applies to bar some communications with corporate employees, the fact that a corporation has in-house counsel does not mean that communications are barred with all company employees. Consent of in-house counsel is not needed to contact employees that cannot by act, statement, or omission bind the company regarding the particular matter.[55] The Rule 4.2 bar does apply to employees who manage

---

52. 600 A.2d 165 (N.J. Super. Law Div. 1991).

53. Some courts have granted protective orders prohibiting ex parte contacts with employees. *See, e.g.,* McCallum v. CSX Transp., Inc., 149 F.R.D. 104 (M.D.N.C. 1991). Courts have also proscribed inquiry into matters subject to the attorney-client privilege in questioning of former employees and managers. *See* Strawser v. Exxon Co., U.S.A., a Div. of Exxon Corp., 843 P.2d 613 (Wyo. 1992).

54. *Id.*

55. *Id.*

Chapter 10: The Anticontact Rule—Represented Persons 363

and speak for the company or whose act or omission could be attributed to the corporation for liability purposes with respect to the matter in question.

A frequent issue in environmental practice is whether a lawyer may initiate ex parte contact with an expert witness without opposing counsel's consent if the opposing party has engaged the witness. The Model Rules do not specifically address this issue. In addressing this question, the ABA Committee on Ethics and Professional Responsibility noted that the rules do not make distinctions between fact witnesses and expert witnesses.[56] Taken together, Model Rule 3.4(c) and Federal Rule of Civil Procedure 26(b)(4)(A) suggest that ex parte contacts with an opponent's expert witness are impermissible. Relying on several Model Rules, including Model Rules 3.4(c), 4.1, and 4.2, the ABA Committee on Ethics and Professional Responsibility concluded that such contacts may be impermissible when the matter at issue is pending in federal court or a jurisdiction that patterns its expert-discovery rule on the federal rule.[57] Rule 3.4(c) requires that lawyers adhere to the court rules, including the tribunal's rules of procedure, with regard to any pending matter. The ABA Committee quoted Rule 3.4 (c), which prohibits lawyers from "knowingly disobey[ing] an obligation under the rules of a tribunal except for an open refusal based on an assertion that no valid obligation exists."[58] Federal Rule of Civil Procedure 26(b)(4)(A) requires lawyers to serve written interrogatories for discovery of adverse expert opinions or obtain discovery upon leave of the court. Additionally, the ABA Committee noted that courts have reached the same decision regarding such ex parte contacts,[59] and that some jurisdictions have additional rules restricting contact with particular witnesses.[60]

In the environmental context, the large number of parties involved in a lawsuit, such as a toxic tort or class actions, can create confusion. Superfund negotiations, negotiated rule making, and toxic torts all involve staggering numbers of parties, lawyers, and experts. Additionally, these and many other environmental controversies bring together various agencies (state, local, and federal), as well as representatives of industry, nongovernmental organizations, and other interested parties. These individual entities may wish to share information to facilitate settlement negotiations, to join forces with other groups, or to develop strategies and arguments for litigation. Often the representatives of these entities are lawyers or other persons who are knowledgeable about the

---

56. ABA Formal Op. 93-378 (1993).

57. *Id.*

58. *Id., quoting* MODEL RULE 3.4(c).

59. *Id., citing* Campbell Industries v. M/V Gemini, 619 F.2d 24 (9th Cir. 1980); American Protection Insurance Co. v. MGM Grand Hotel-Las Vegas, 748 F.2d 1293, 1303 (9th Cir. 1984); Heyde v. Xtraman, Inc., 404 S.E.2d 607 (1991).

60. *Id.*

364 ISSUES OF LEGAL ETHICS IN THE PRACTICE OF ENVIRONMENTAL LAW

law. Understandably, a lawyer for a party may want to learn the views of such individuals or to obtain information from them about the project, their actions relating to the project, or their judgments about relevant law. If one of these parties is represented by counsel, Rule 4.2 requires that the lawyer seek permission from the representing lawyer before discussing issues about the matter with the represented party, its agents or employees. This measure should be taken whether or not the matter is the subject of litigation.[61]

Former Employees: Environmental Example

In *Public Service Elec. and Gas Co. v. Associated Elec. & Gas Ins. Services, Ltd.,*[62] the New Jersey Department of Environmental Protection (DEP) brought numerous claims against Public Service Electric and Gas Company (PSE&G) based on environmental contamination at 35 coal gasification sites within the state that were owned or used by PSE&G. As a result, the plaintiff brought a declaratory judgment action against several of its insurance carriers relating to environmental contamination liability. It sought an order declaring that its liability insurance policies required the insurers to indemnify it for property damage claims by third parties. The U.S. magistrate ordered the insurers to inform the plaintiff two days before it initiated ex parte contact with former employees of the utility. The magistrate's order also required the insurance company to send a warning letter to the employee indicating the nature of the lawsuit and the purpose of the interview.

Reasoning that its interpretation should reflect the same caution used by the drafters of the Model Rules, the court held that a former employee's statements could be imputed to a corporation, including PSE&G, "for the purposes of civil or criminal liability." It thus held that Rule 4.2 applies to former employees, making informal contacts impermissible. "Indeed, the prevailing party in this action will be straddled with the enormous liability of funding the cleanup of the various polluted sites at issue. An adjudication of such responsibility is certainly liability within the scope of Model Rule 4.2."[63] The court noted the significant liability that can attach under environmental laws because of the conduct of former employees. "The most obvious example

---

61. Rule 4.2 refers to representation "in the matter." It makes no mention of litigation. Additionally, comment 3 to the rule states: "This Rule also applies to communications with any person, whether or not a party to a formal adjudicative proceeding, contract or negotiation, who is represented by counsel concerning the matter to which the communication relates."

62. 745 F. Supp. 1037 (D.N.J. 1990), *superseded by* regulation Andrews v. Goodyear Tire & Rubber Co., Inc., 191 F.R.D. 59 (D.N.J. Feb.14, 2000).

63. *Id.* at 1040.

would be the former employee who would testify that, at the direction of his superiors, he continually dumped the toxic byproduct of the Coal Gasification process into the ground."[64]

Knowledge of Representation

Comment 5 to Rule 4.2 indicates that the prohibition against communication applies only when the lawyer knows that another lawyer represents the person he wishes to contact in the matter.

> The prohibition on communications with a represented person only applies, however, in circumstances where the lawyer knows that the person is in fact represented in the matter to be discussed. This means that the lawyer has actual knowledge of the fact of the representation; but such actual knowledge may be inferred from the circumstances.[65]

While the standard set by Model Rule 4.2 is an actual knowledge standard, the comment indicates that the lawyer may have a duty of inquiry to determine whether or not another lawyer represents the person when circumstances suggest that this is the case. An ostrich approach is not effective. "[An] inference may arise in circumstances where there is substantial reason to believe that the person with whom communication is sought is represented in the matter to be discussed. Thus, a lawyer cannot evade the requirement of obtaining the consent of counsel by closing eyes to the obvious."[66]

Client Contact with Opposition

The prohibition stated in Model Rule 4.2 falls on lawyers, not on their clients. Nothing prevents a client from speaking with his or her opponent directly. The fact that a party has hired counsel does not limit the activities of that party. Nevertheless, lawyers cannot ethically make an end-run around this rule by using the client as an agent. A lawyer cannot accomplish through an agent what he cannot do himself. Thus, counseling a client not to talk with the opponent is advisable in some situations, particularly if such contact could give rise to a question concerning whether the lawyer encouraged the client to make the contact.

---

64. *Id.* at 1041–42.
65. MODEL RULE 4.2 cmt. 5 (1983).
66. *Id.*

366 ISSUES OF LEGAL ETHICS IN THE PRACTICE OF ENVIRONMENTAL LAW

Government Agencies

In some cases, a lawyer working on a dispute with a government agent may wish to speak with a government representative of the agency involved in the dispute. For example, many environmental lawsuits involve both a retrospective and prospective element. For example, EPA, the Army Corps of Engineers, or another agency may seek both damages and an injunction against an individual or corporation on the basis that its past conduct violates an environmental statute and the same conduct in the future will continue to violate the statute. The client may feel it is important to contact the agency to clear up issues relating to future projects, such as implementation of a mitigation plan under the Endangered Species Act or other environmentally protected legislation. When this is the case, the lawyer will want to contact an agency representative even though that representative is formally represented by counsel.

Comment 1 to Rule 4.2 clarifies the anticontact rule and justifies contact both for issues outside the scope of the controversy and, additionally, when policy decisions could impact the controversy.

> This Rule does not prohibit communication with a represented person, or an employee or agent of such a person, concerning matters outside the representation. For example, the existence of a controversy between a government agency and a private party, or between two organizations, does not prohibit a lawyer for either from communicating with nonlawyer representatives of the other regarding a separate matter.

The comment expressly recognizes the possibility that a lawyer may have a justification for contacting a party relating to government agencies, referring to the possibility of communications authorized by law:

> [P]arties to a matter may communicate directly with each other, and a lawyer having independent justification or legal authorization for communicating with a represented person is permitted to do so. Communications authorized by law include, for example, the right of a party to a controversy with a government agency to speak with government officials about the matter.[67]

---

67. MODEL RULE 4.2 cmt. 1. The District of Columbia Bar has ruled that it is appropriate to contact government lawyers because any citizen can petition the government to be heard or to provide information at any time..

Chapter 10: The Anticontact Rule—Represented Persons   367

Some government lawyers may resist interpretation of this comment to apply to all matters involving a government agency, since that interpretation seems to sweep away the protection in its entirety in the governmental context. One way to resolve the problem arising from the application of Rule 4.2 in innocuous settings is for the parties to agree in advance that lawyers may address particular types of questions to represented entities without contacting the lawyers for each entity. Other government lawyers express the view that lawyers do not violate the anticontact rule when they contact a government official who has the authority to settle the matter at issue.

The ABA Standing Committee on Ethics and Professional Responsibility has expressed its view that the anticontact rule does not prevent a lawyer from communicating with a government official regarding policy matters.[68] In its opinion, the ABA Committee dealt with the question of a private lawyer contacting a government official. The opinion states that Model Rule 4.2 allows a lawyer representing a private party to communicate "about the matter with government officials who have authority to take or recommend action in the matter provided the sole purpose of the lawyer's communication is to address a policy issue, including settling the controversy."[69] Arguably, every controversy with governmental entities involves policy issues of how to handle such matters, including the one currently under consideration. The ABA Committee emphasized that considerations of fair play relate to such contacts even when the anticontact rule does not bar communication with the government official. "In such a situation the lawyer must give government counsel reasonable advance notice of his intent to communicate with such officials, to afford an opportunity for consultation between government counsel and the officials on the advisability of their entertaining the communication."[70]

The parties may agree that counsel has permission to call the various agencies directly without a request to counsel when the information sought is factual or noncontroversial on its face. Of course, a bit of information that may initially appear to be noncontroversial may later develop into a contested point or even a point involved in subsequent litigation. For this reason, the decision of counsel to recommend blanket or generalized agreements presents a difficult choice. If the parties and their lawyers expressly indicate that their representatives may communicate with each other and the parties on stated matters, Rule 4.2 seems to provide no obstacle to communications.

---

68. ABA Formal Op. 97-408.

69. *Id.*

70. *Id.*

Government Agencies (2002 Revision)

A new comment to the revised Model Rule 4.2 emphasizes that the rule does not seek to prohibit the right of citizens to exercise their right to petition the government or other rights. New comment 5 states: "Communications authorized by law may include communications by a lawyer on behalf of a client who is exercising a constitutional or other legal right to communicate with the government."[71]

Contact by Government Prosecutors

Controversy has existed regarding whether prosecutors and investigators may contact employees of represented companies during the investigative phase of an enforcement action.[72] In 1989 Attorney General Richard Thornburgh issued a memorandum that stated standards for interviewing individuals in investigating crimes although the individuals were represented by counsel.[73] In 1994, Attorney General Janet Reno incorporated the approach of the Thornburgh Memorandum in interviewing represented persons.[74] Federal courts held, however, that state rules of ethics apply to Justice Department lawyers[75]

---

71. Model RULE 4.2 cmt. 5 (2002).

72. After a company has been charged with a crime, prosecutors and investigators have, under the Department of Justice policy, contacted employees who are not "controlling individuals" within the company. This rule exempted from interview by the Justice Department only current employees, owners, or members of an organization who hold high-level positions with that organization and those who participate as decision makers in the subject matter of the investigator. *See* John M. Fitzgibbons, *The Tug of War over Ex Parte Contact by Federal Prosecutors*, FED. LAW., June 1995, at 16 ("[T]he Department of Justice has unilaterally declared that its attorneys constitute a unique and elite breed of lawyers whose conduct in these instances is unreviewable"). Federal law now seems to establish that state ethics rules apply to Justice Department lawyers. *See* 28 C.F.R. § 77.1(a).

73. *See* Matter of Doe, 801 F. Supp. 478, 489–93(D.N.M. 1992), *quoting in full* the Thornburgh memo; *see also* Ethical Standards for Attorneys for the Government, 28 C.F.R. pt. 77 (1999); Memorandum from Richard Thornburgh, United States Attorney General, to Justice Department Litigators (June 8, 1989) (reprinted in *In re* Doe, 801 F. Supp. 478, 489–93 (D.N.M. 1992)).

74. *See* 59 Fed. Reg. 39,910 (Aug. 4, 1994).

75. *See* Matter of Doe, 801 F. Supp. 478 (D.N.M.1992) (finding Attorney General Thornburgh's memorandum is not law, that prosecutor may not ignore state codes of ethics, and that prosecutor was not entitled to prosecutorial immunity from state bar disciplinary proceedings); United States v. McDonald Douglas Corp., 961 F. Supp. 1288 (E.D. Mo. 1977) (holding Department of Justice regulations cannot exempt the DOJ's lawyers from state ethics rules).

Chapter 10: The Anticontact Rule—Represented Persons   369

and that government lawyers are not immune from state-bar disciplinary proceedings.[76] The Department of Justice issued a final rule that identified circumstances "under which attorneys employed by the Department of Justice may communicate with persons known to be represented by counsel in the course of law enforcement investigations and proceedings."[77] In 1998, in response to the controversy, the United States Congress passed the Citizen Protection Act (also known as the McDade Amendment), expressly making government lawyers subject to state ethics rules and requiring the Attorney General to make and amend rules of the Department of Justice to ensure compliance with this section.[78] After the Citizen Protection Act took effect, the Department of Justice updated its rules governing lawyer conduct.[79] Almost immediately after passage, the Citizen Protection Act drew fire from federal prosecutors who saw problems with conflicting ethics rules, choice of law issues, and a hampering of the investigative process. Comment 2 to Model Rule 4.2 acknowledges the existence of legal doctrine on the subject of governmental investigations by linking appropriate governmental investigations to the recognized exception for communications that are authorized by law.

> Communications authorized by law also include constitutionally permissible activities of lawyers representing governmental entities, directly or through investigative agents, prior to the commencement of criminal or civil enforcement proceedings, when there is applicable judicial precedent that either has found the activity permissible under this Rule or has found this Rule inapplicable. However, the Rule imposes ethical restrictions that go beyond those imposed by constitutional provisions.[80]

The final sentence of this comment raises issues of line drawing to determine whether a particular investigation complies with both constitutional requirements and, additionally, with the standards set by this ethics rule.

Unrepresented Persons

Environmental lawyers should realize that even fairly sophisticated laypersons may not understand fully the role an environmental lawyer plays. Upon hearing the term "environmental lawyer," some people assume that the lawyer

---

76. *See, e.g.,* Matter of Doe, 801 F. Supp. 478 (D.N.M. 1992).
77. *See* 59 Fed. Reg. 39,910–01 (1994).
78. 28 U.S.C. § 530B (1998).
79. *See* 28 C.F.R. §§ 77.1–77.4.
80. MODEL RULE 4.2 cmt. 2.

is protecting the environment rather than representing an individual client. This assumption can lead to confusion that may prejudice the rights of an unrepresented party. The initial reaction of a layperson who learns that a lawyer practices environmental law is often favorable. Many environmental lawyers have experienced the pleasant (though sometimes short-lived) admiration of a new acquaintance at a cocktail party. The initial response may be followed, however, by the question, "Well, yeah, but who do you work for?" In such cases, the speaker may be a knowledgeable businessperson. A far more serious setting for misunderstanding can occur when the unrepresented party talking with a lawyer has no experience with the law in general or environmental law in particular.

Another type of conflict that is sometimes overlooked is the conflict of interest that can occur when a lawyer deals with an unrepresented person in his role as lawyer for a client. Model Rule 4.3 provides as follows:

> In dealing on behalf of a client with a person who is not represented by counsel, a lawyer shall not state or imply that the lawyer is disinterested. When the lawyer knows or reasonably should know that the unrepresented person misunderstands the lawyer's role in the matter, the lawyer shall make reasonable efforts to correct the misunderstanding.

Model Rule 4.3 creates protection for the unrepresented person, requiring the lawyer to make "reasonable efforts to correct the misunderstanding" when he knows "an unrepresented person misunderstands the lawyer's role."[81] This rule reminds the lawyer that a layperson may have a misconception about the role of the lawyer and may be relying on the lawyer for assistance even though the lawyer does not intend to represent him. This setting can present acute problems, particularly when the unrepresented party is "not experienced in dealing with legal matters."[82] The comment to the rule expressly notes that the lawyer "should not give advice to an unrepresented person other than the advice to obtain counsel."[83]

Model Rule 4.3 limits the advice a lawyer may give to an unrepresented person to the advice to secure legal counsel, prohibiting lawyers from misleading an unrepresented person. It declares that a lawyer must not state or imply that the lawyer is disinterested. "In dealing on behalf of a client with a person who is not represented by counsel, a lawyer shall not state or imply that the

---

81. MODEL RULE 4.3.
82. MODEL RULE 4.3 cmt. 1.
83. *Id.*

Chapter 10: The Anticontact Rule—Represented Persons   371

lawyer is disinterested. When the lawyer knows or reasonably should know that the unrepresented person misunderstands the lawyer's role in the matter, the lawyer shall make reasonable efforts to correct the misunderstanding."[84]

Unrepresented Persons: Environmental Example

The cautious route for environmental lawyers is to explain fully to any unrepresented person his role in the matter at issue. Additionally, the lawyer should advise the unrepresented person to obtain legal counsel in the matter. The question regarding one's dealings with unrepresented persons implicates not only the ethics rules set forth in Model Rule 4.3. It can also result in a holding by a court that the lawyer actually represented not only his own client but (unintentionally) another person by virtue of the expectations of that person. In such a case, the lawyer may have an additional problem. If a court holds that the lawyer accepted a representation by giving advice to an unrepresented party, the lawyer may be (unwittingly and unintentionally) in violation of his obligation to obtain consent of his original client to the representation.

For example, in a Superfund matter, a PRP's lawyer who talks with a landowner of the property involved as a facility in a Superfund cleanup should be cautious. The landowner may be unsophisticated regarding the law generally and CERCLA in particular. In such a case, the prudent course is for the lawyer to limit his conversations with the landowner and advise the landowner to retain other counsel.

Unrepresented Person (2002 Revision)

In response to the Ethics 2000 Commission proposal, the ABA added clarifying language to the prohibition against lawyers giving legal advice to unrepresented persons. Model Rule 4.3, as revised in February 2002, clarifies the context of most concern in this area. That is, it deals with the situation that arises when a lawyer who is representing a client in a matter speaks with an opponent or another person involved in the matter who is not represented by counsel. The revised rule provides in toto:

> In dealing on behalf of a client with a person who is not represented by counsel, a lawyer shall not state or imply that the lawyer is disinterested. When the lawyer knows or reasonably should know that the unrepresented person misunderstands the lawyer's role in the matter, the lawyer shall make reasonable efforts to correct the

---

84. Model Rule 4.3.

misunderstanding. The lawyer shall not give legal advice to an unrepresented person, other than the advice to secure counsel, if the lawyer knows or reasonably should know that the interests of such a person are or have a reasonable possibility of being in conflict with the interests of the client.[85]

This language notes the context of greatest concern, noting that, when a conflict is reasonably possible, the lawyer should restrict his communication with the unrepresented person.

---

85. MODEL RULE 4.3 (2002).

CHAPTER 11

Multidisciplinary Practice

Multidisciplinary practice (MDP) refers to the practice of providing legal and nonlegal services to clients. In a multidisciplinary practice, lawyers work with nonlawyers within the same business entity. Because society is changing, the legal landscape and the way that lawyers practice law are also changing.[1] Some state disciplinary boards and ethics committees are relaxing standards relating to practicing law with nonlawyer professionals.[2] In Europe, the Big Five accounting firms routinely engage in practice with lawyers.[3] Such practice appears to violate the prohibition of Model Rule 5.4 against sharing fees with nonlawyers if the rules of ethics apply to practice of law by lawyers licensed in a state but practicing outside the United States.[4] Additionally, some

---

1. Taudd A. Hume, Comment, *MDPs in Montana: It's the End of the World As We Know It . . . and I Feel Fine*, 63 MONT. L. REV. 391 (2002). Charles W. Wolfram, *Comparative Multi-disciplinary Practice of Law: Paths Taken and Not Taken*, 52 CASE WESTERN RESERVE L. REV. 961, 962 (2002) (noting that "almost all" academics are "more or less in favor" of MDP practice).

2. *See New York Bar Report Recommends Allowing Limited Alliances With Non-Lawyers*, 68 U.S.L. WK. 277 (2000); *District of Columbia Bar Leadership Endorses Rule Amendments to Allow MDPs*, 70 U.S. L.WK. 2805 (2002) (approving the D.C. ethics rules allowing lawyers to practice law within entities controlled by nonlawyer professionals and to share legal fees with them in fully integrated multidisciplinary practices (MDPs)); *see also ABA Ethics Committee Again Proposes Rule on Multidisciplinary Referral Arrangements*, 70 U.S. L.WK. 2740 (2002) (suggesting that under Rule 7.2, lawyers may enter into referral arrangements as long as such arrangements are not exclusive and affected clients are informed of the agreement).

3. *See* Francisco Marcos, *Storm Over Our Heads: The Rendering of Legal Services by Audit Firms in Spain* (May 2000), *available at* http://www.abanet.org/cpr/mdp-add_mdp_papers.html. (visited Mar. 26, 2003).

4. MODEL RULE 5.4 (d). *See also* Robert K. Christensen, Notes and Comments, *At the Helm of the Multidisciplinary Practice Issue After the ABA's Recommendation: States Finding*

374 ISSUES OF LEGAL ETHICS IN THE PRACTICE OF ENVIRONMENTAL LAW

instances of MDP also violate the prohibitions of Model Rule 5.4 against a lawyer forming a partnership with a nonlawyer "if any of the activities of the partnership consist of the practice of law,"[5] and against involvement in a professional corporation in which a nonlawyer owns an interest, acts as a corporate director or officer, or controls a lawyer's professional judgment.[6]

Client demand by sophisticated corporations and other entities has resulted in some firms skating close to the line on the fee-sharing prohibition of Model Rule 5.4. Firms hire accountants, biologists, toxicologists, researchers, and environmental consultants as independent contractors. Some firms hire these professionals as employees. The growing practice by accounting firms of hiring lawyers to deliver services to their clients has made law firms concerned that they will not be able to compete effectively against these large firms. For example, in 1999, the accounting firm of Ernst & Young financed the formation of a law firm by recruiting partners from large law firms.[7]

The debate on MDP is intense.[8] Like practitioners in other areas, lawyers who practice environmental law hold differing views on whether they should be allowed to practice in a firm or partnership setting with nonlawyer professionals. In environmental practice, lawyers often rely on the judgments of accountants, chemists, hydrogeologists, and environmental engineers.[9] Some environmental law firms have affiliated informally with environmental consulting firms. They argue that the association is necessary in the environmental field because of the unique mix of science and law. Many of the legal judgments required in environmental practice involve scientific knowledge and judgment. Because of the need for a close working relationship, environmental lawyers form affiliations with biologists, toxicologists, chemists, and environmental consultants.

Solutions by Taking Stock in European Harmonization to Preserve Their Sovereignty in Regulating the Legal Profession, B.Y.U. L. REV. 375 (2001).

5. MODEL RULE 5.4(b).

6. MODEL RULE 5.4(d).

7. *See* Tom Herman, *Ernst & Young Will Finance Launch of Law Firm in Special Arrangement,* WALL ST. J., Nov. 3, 1999, at B10. In a recent article in *The Business Lawyer,* Professor Daniel Fischel thoroughly analyzes the arguments for and against allowing multidisciplinary practice (MPD). He concludes that opponents to MDP preach economic protectionism hidden within appeals to "professionalism," "lawyers' independence," and "the public interest." *See* Daniel I. Fischel, *Multi-Disciplinary Practice,* 55 BUS. LAW. 951 (2000). *Id.* at 974.

8. For citation to many of the articles on the topic, *see* http://www.abanet.org/cpr/mdp-add_mdp_papers.html (last visited).

9. *See* J. Berton Fisher & William R. Keffer, *Selection, Use and Management of Experts in Environmental Legal Practice,* 33 TULSA L.J. 1003 (1998) (asserting that environmental practice is inherently multidisciplinary).

Chapter 11: Multidisciplinary Practice 375

Perhaps in response to recent debate generated by the proposed multidisciplinary practice rules, some states have made steps toward officially allowing multidisciplinary practice.[10] Additionally, some states are dedicating increased resources to the enforcement of laws prohibiting the unauthorized practice of law. For example, in June of 2000, the New York State Bar Association endorsed principles allowing multidisciplinary practice and also urged enforcement of unauthorized practice laws.[11] The Illinois State Bar Association's Assembly proposed significant amendments to the Illinois Unauthorized Practice Statute, which would give courts authority to issue contempt citations against any nonlawyer who advertised or held himself out as offering legal services.[12] The amendment also provides for a strike force to curtail the unauthorized practice of law (UPL),[13] and allows suit by an individual who suffers harm as a result of unauthorized practice, and provides for equitable relief and a civil penalty of up to $5,000.[14]

Confidentiality

One of the central problems with validating MDP is the difference in approach to confidentiality historically taken by different professions. Critics of MDP see a fundamental conflict between the lawyer's far-reaching duty of confidentiality and the duty of other professionals to disclose client information to prevent injury to third parties or the public.[15] One of the bedrock principles of the legal profession is the lawyer's duty to maintain the confidentiality of client information. By contrast, the primary duty of many other professionals is to the public.[16] For example, in reviewing the client's financial documents, the accountant has a duty to summarize financial information and disclose all information material to the investor's decision to invest, whether

---

10. Joan C. Rogers, *California Bar Task Force Floats Proposal for Amending Ethics Rules to Allow MDPs,* 70 U.S.L.W. 2051 (2001). In July 2001 New York adopted rules permitting associations between lawyers and nonlawyers (N.Y.L.J., July 25, 2001). Additionally, a task force appointed by the California Supreme Court recommended allowing multidisciplinary practice. *See* 17 LMPC Current Report No. 17 (Aug. 15 2001).

11. *Available at* http://www.nysba.org (visited Mar. 28, 2003).

12. *See* 705 I.L.C.S. § 205/1 (2000).

13. *See* http://www.isba.org (visited Apr. 15, 2003).

14. *Id.*

15. *See* Lawrence J. Fox, *Written Remarks Before the Multi-Disciplinary Practice Commission, available at* http:/www.abanet.org/cpr/foxl.html, *cited in* Fischel, *supra* note 7, at 953.

16. For examples of codes of other professions, *see* http://csep.iit.edu/codes/codes.html.

376   ISSUES OF LEGAL ETHICS IN THE PRACTICE OF ENVIRONMENTAL LAW

that information is favorable or unfavorable to the accountant's client. Accountants, as financial auditors, have a duty to the public that transcends their relationship with a client.[17] Similarly, engineers have a duty to act for the public good and to disclose dangers created by a client.[18] The approach of Model Rule 1.6 is to require that lawyers consider the interests of their clients above those of the public. The ability of lawyers to report planned client misconduct may be greater than is often assumed, however. Only six of the states that adopted Model Rule 1.6 accepted the full language of the rule without modification. Most jurisdictions limited the power of the rule's prohibition against disclosure.[19] Professor Fischel argues that the function of lawyers and accountants is more similar than commonly believed.[20] The concept of confidentiality embraced by the Ethics 2000 Commission appears to be more consistent with the obligation of other professionals, balancing the client's right to confidentiality with the right of third parties and the public to be free from unreasonable dangers.[21] The approach of Revised Rule 1.6, adopted by the ABA House of Delegates in February 2002, presents a more balanced approach to protecting both client information and the public.

The differing obligations of lawyers and other professionals relating to the duty of confidentiality and the duty to protect public safety seem to present an intractable problem for working and sharing information about a client. As a practical matter, differing visions of the duty of confidentiality may present a problem regardless of the firm structure employed and regardless of the statement of confidentiality in the Model Rules. This is so because the Model Rules do not constrain other professionals, and the power of lawyers to require other professionals to abide by legal ethics standards is itself an uncertain question—particularly when the standards of legal ethics are in conflict with those governing other professionals. The ABA and other professional organizations continue to scrutinize the issue, particularly in light of stock market losses and legislation responding to the Enron and WorldCom scandals and the public's diminishing confidence in the financial stability of the economy.

The Potential Professional Cognitor

The debate on whether lawyers should enter practice relationships with accountants, architects, and other professionals has heightened recently. The

---

17. *See* United States v. Arthur Young & Co., 465 U.S. 805, 817 (1984).
18. *See* Fischel, *supra* note 7.
19. *See* Irma S. Russell, *Unreasonable Risk: Model Rule 1.6, Environmental Hazards, and Positive Law,* 55 WASH. & LEE L. REV. 117, 172–74 (1998).
20. *See* Daniel R. Fischel, *Lawyers and Confidentiality,* 65 U. CHI. L. REV. 1, 17 (1998).
21. *See* MODEL RULE 1.6, *at* http://www.abanet.org/cpr/ethics2k.html.

Chapter 11: Multidisciplinary Practice 377

American Institute of Certified Public Accountants (AICPA) is working with a consortium of four international accounting associations to establish a new professional designation of "cognitor." The cognitor designation would qualify particular professionals to serve as a type of subcontractor of financial professionals and products.[22] The intent of this movement is to establish a new professional who would provide a range of professional services, from accounting to business law, as an answer to the growing demand for one-stop shopping for professional services. AICPA's draft proposal for designating cognitors states that the specialty requires "an 'acceptable' level of higher education in a field recognized by the credentialing body, at least five years of relevant work experience, and letters of recommendation from two existing credential holders."[23] The group hopes to award the credential in 2002 and projects 700,000 cognitors worldwide within four years. The proposal states that individuals who meet the requirements for credentialing will be grandfathered in through the end of 2004.[24] If passed, the AICPA proposal threatens to weaken the practice of law by allowing the newly recognized professionals (cognitors) to subcontract work from a client to a lawyer, thereby diluting the contact of lawyers with clients. The AICPA proposal comes on the heels of an ABA House of Delegates vote rejecting a proposal to allow lawyers to undertake MDP firms and promises to revive the MDP debate in the ABA.

Commission on Multidisciplinary Practice

In August of 1998, the ABA appointed a 12-person commission to examine the complex issue of MDP and to propose modifications to the Model Rules of Professional Conduct. The Commission considered the potential problems that could be implicated in a rule allowing MDP, including the issues of fee sharing, confidentiality of client information, and conflicts of interest, including imputed disqualification, and the responsibility of lawyers to supervise the work of nonlawyer professionals as it relates to the lawyer's representation of clients. In June of 1999, the ABA Commission on Multidisciplinary Practice recommended unanimously a set of regulations that would allow and control multidisciplinary practice. The ABA House of Delegates rejected the recommendations and voted to retain the current rule subject to further study. In May of 2000, the Commission voted to reject

---

22. *See* Mark Hanson, *A New Credential: CPA's 'Cognitor' Plan Draws Wary Response from Bar,* 87 A.B.A. J. 18 (2001).

23. *Id.*

24. *Id.*

378 ISSUES OF LEGAL ETHICS IN THE PRACTICE OF ENVIRONMENTAL LAW

multidisciplinary practice.[25] Despite the refusal of the ABA House of Delegates to take up the issue, the ABA Commission on Multidisciplinary Practice issued a second report that recommended multidisciplinary practice and allowing fee-sharing with nonlawyers under regulated conditions.[26] Additionally, some state associations have moved toward approving multidisciplinary practice in which lawyers may enter into associations with nonlawyers and may share fees with lawyers under prescribed controls.[27] For example, a 2000 Executive Committee decision of the New York Bar Association recommended approval of multidisciplinary firms.[28]

The concept of multidisciplinary practice is problematic to some lawyers because of problems they see with regard to the core concepts of the legal profession relating to conflicts of interest and confidentiality and fee sharing with nonlawyers. Some lawyers believe that the changes brought by MDP could undermine core principles of the profession and the relationship between the lawyer and client.[29] One of the reasons many lawyers and bar associations disfavor allowing a partnership with nonlawyers is the inevitability of sharing the proceeds of the work, which inevitably results in sharing legal fees between the lawyer and nonlawyer partners in the firm.[30] The fear of control of lawyers by nonlawyers in such settings underlies most objections to proposals on multidisciplinary practice.[31] In July 2000, the ABA adopted Resolution #10F, rejecting fee sharing with nonlawyers and nonlawyer ownership and control of law firms as inconsistent with the core values of the legal profession.[32] Nevertheless, some state associations have

---

25. *See ABA Refuses to Change Lawyer Ethics Rules Unless Further Studies of MDPS Dispel Risks*, 68 U.S. L. WK. 2091 (1999).

26. *See ABA's Multidisciplinary Commission Reasserts MDP Stance in Amended Report*, 68 U.S. L. WK. 2584 (April 4, 2000).

27. *See New York Bar Report Recommends Allowing Limited Alliances With Non-Lawyers*, 68 U.S. L. WK. 277 (2000).

28. *Id.*

29. *See* ABA Commission on Multi-Disciplinary Practice, Report to the House of Delegates (May 11, 2000) [hereinafter ABA Commission, 2000 Final Report], *available at* http://www.abanet.org/cpr/mdpfinalrep2000.html.

30. *See* Michael L. Shakman & Diane F. Klotnia, *Trust Us: How Rules on Referral Fees Influence the MDP Debate*, 14 CBA Record 30 (2000) (arguing that MDP is incompatible with well-established concepts of the lawyer's role and responsibilities to clients).

31. *See generally* Professor David Luban, *Asking the Right Questions*, 72 TEMP. L. REV. 839 (1999) (noting issue of independence of professional judgment in multidisciplinary practice).

32. L. Harold Levinson, *Collaboration Between Lawyers and Others: Coping with the ABA Model Rules After Resolution 10F*, 36 WAKE FOREST L. REV. 133 (2001).

moved toward approving multidisciplinary practice in which lawyers may enter into associations with nonlawyers and may share fees with those nonlawyers under prescribed conditions.[33]

Environmental Practice

Elements necessary for establishing or defending against liability in environmental litigation can only be shown by presentation of scientific data by an expert.[34] For example, a decision regarding whether a mitigation plan for a construction project would provide meaningful protection or a nonfrivolous offer of set-off for wetlands affected by a project is a mixed question involving science and law. Determining whether a discharge is within permitted limits or whether a particular substance should be classified as RCRA waste cannot be made without scientific judgment. If EPA has made an offer to a client that would allow a reduction of a penalty for an environmental violation based, in part, on the client's participation in a Supplemental Environmental Program (SEP), it is likely that the lawyer will need to consult an expert in environmental accounting to determine whether the cost of the SEP is justified in light of the credit EPA is offering. These and numerous other judgments in environmental practice cannot be made by reference to law alone. Scientific data and informed scientific judgment are necessary ingredients of the legal decisions required in the area. For this reason, some environmental lawyers believe that the bar against associating formally with a nonlawyer unreasonably limits the ability of environmental lawyers to provide legal services to their clients in the most efficient and cost-effective way. Other lawyers who practice environmental law believe that the constraints against MDP are appropriate and protective of the profession and clients. The arguments against MDP emphasize the need to protect client information and to avoid the appearance of impropriety.[35]

---

33. *See New York Bar Report Recommends Allowing Limited Alliances With Non-Lawyers*, 68 U.S. L. Wk. 277 (2000).

34. *See* Kim K. Burke, *The Use of Experts in Environmental Litigation: A Practitioner's Guide*, 25 N. Ky. L. Rev. 111 (1997) (focusing on pretrial preparation of experts).

35. Lawrence J. Fox, *Dan's World: A Free Enterprise Dream; An Ethics Nightmare*, 55 Bus. Law 1533 (2000).

CHAPTER 12

Multijurisdictional Practice

Multijurisdictional practice (MJP) is the "legal work of a lawyer in a jurisdiction in which the lawyer is not admitted to practice law."[1] A strict reading of the unauthorized practice standards in most states would restrict legal practice significantly. Many state rules indicate that the lawyer who practices within the state without a license is in violation of the ethics rules. For example, the Tennessee Board of Professional Responsibility addressed the issue of whether lawyers admitted to practice in other jurisdictions but not in Tennessee should be allowed to engage in limited practice within the state.[2] The Board confirmed the general prohibition against lawyers not licensed in Tennessee. It excepted from this prohibition, however, lawyers engaged in limited practice in Tennessee who are admitted in other jurisdictions "(1) when permitted to appear pro hac vice; and (2) when making limited appearances before Federal courts or agencies."[3] The Board also confirmed limited practice by foreign lawyers who have "an active application pending and under consideration for admission to practice in Tennessee" under specified guidelines, including supervision of a licensed Tennessee lawyer with appearances in Tennessee courts under the pro hac vice rule.[4] Similarly, the Pennsylvania Ethics Committee responded to a request by a lawyer regarding whether he must become licensed to practice law in Pennsylvania to appear before state agencies on behalf of his corporate employer. The Pennsylvania Committee observed that legal activities the lawyer de-

---

1. Report of the ABA Commission on Multijurisdictional Practice (Aug. 2002).
2. Tenn. Bd. Eth. Op. 02-F-91(a)
3. *Id.*
4. *Id.*

382 ISSUES OF LEGAL ETHICS IN THE PRACTICE OF ENVIRONMENTAL LAW

scribed require significant knowledge of Pennsylvania law and constitute the practice of law in Pennsylvania. It concluded that the rules of ethics require the lawyer to be licensed in Pennsylvania.[5] When a lawyer who is licensed in one state practices in another in which he is not licensed, he may be violating his state of licensure as well as the unauthorized practice rule of the foreign state. For example, the Missouri Rule states that: "A lawyer shall not practice law in a jurisdiction where doing so violates the regulations of the legal profession in that jurisdiction."[6]

Environmental lawyers present examples of the trend toward national or global practice. The trend toward national and international practice is as pronounced in the field of environmental law as in any other field of the law. Some firms maintain a national practice, representing corporations in the specialized field of Superfund litigation or negotiations with EPA regarding Superfund consent decrees. Some lawyers or firms focus on water law or NEPA or endangered species work and go wherever the client needs them to be. Arguably, environmental law virtually requires multijurisdictional practice. As a matter of necessity, environmental lawyers represent corporations that have holdings and environmental problems in multiple states. Environmental cases present disputes that involve parties in various states. Purchase transactions involving environmental issues may involve property in more than one state. MJP has created controversy in recent years because of a debate among lawyers about the propriety of advising clients about the law of states where the lawyer is not licensed and the decision by some states to sanction lawyers who provide such legal services.[7] The issue of MJP has garnered significant scholarly attention, primarily in support of allowing more practice across state lines.[8] MJP has not been a matter of concern until recent times, probably because traditionally most legal matters arose in one state and were resolved by reference to the law of that state by lawyers who practiced exclusively within that state. MJP is a reality of the legal world today, however, and state advisory committees and disciplinary boards seem to be moving toward relaxing prohibitions against such practice. Representing clients in states outside the lawyer's state of licensure is commonplace, particularly in environmental law and areas of practice that involve corporate clients with far-flung property or business transactions in numerous

---

5. Pa. Bar Ass'n Ethics Op. 91-58.

6. Missouri Supreme Court Rule 4-5.5 (a).

7. *See, e.g.,* William T. Barker, *Extrajurisdictional Practice by Lawyers*, 56 BUS. LAW. 1501 (2001).

8. *See Hofstra Conference Speakers Air Ideas for What Needs Fixing in Legal Ethics*, 17 ABA/BNA LAW. MANUAL ON PROF'L CONDUCT 583 (2001).

Chapter 12: Multijurisdictional Practice   383

jurisdictions. Any lawyer who specializes or practices in a technical area of the law is likely to draw clients from areas outside his or her state of licensure or to represent clients who need or demand representation in more than one jurisdiction.

Unauthorized Practice of Law

The 1983 version of Model Rule 5.5 prohibits lawyers from practicing "in a jurisdiction where doing so violates the regulation of the legal profession in that jurisdiction." The Ethics 2000 Commission and the American Corporate Counsel Association (ACCA) proposed amendments to the rule to allow limited multijurisdictional practice. The profession has consistently regarded the prohibition against unauthorized practice of law as fundamental and necessary to a system of competent representation.[9] Courts have enjoined unauthorized practice.[10] State legislatures have prohibited the unauthorized practice of law and impose penalties on violators.[11] Some states provide for penalties and restitution. All states prohibit the practice of law without being licensed by the state.[12] Many, though not all, states allow limited practice by lawyers under the principle and practice of a pro hac vice appearance.[13] For example, the Tennessee statute on unauthorized practice of law empowers an officer of the state such as the attorney general to seek an injunction,[14] civil penalties,[15] and restitution against violators. It also authorizes an individual to sue the offender for triple the amount paid.[16]

Canon 47, which was adopted September 30, 1937, states: "No lawyer shall permit his professional services, or his name, to be used in aid of, or to make possible, the unauthorized practice of law by any lay agency, personal or corpo-

---

9. On March 28. 2003, the ABA Task Force withdrew its proposed model definition of the practice of law and recommended that each state take up teh task of defining the practice of law. See http://www.abanet.org/cpr/model-def/taskforce_rpt_328.pdf (visited May 7, 2003).

10. *See, e.g., In re* Burson, 909 S.W.2d 768 (Tenn. 1995); Lineberger v. State *ex rel.* Beeler, 129 S.W.2d 198 (1939) (allowing injunction against unauthorized practice as public nuisance).

11. *See, e.g.,* TENN. CODE ANN. 23-3-103 (prohibiting unlawful practice and authorizing penalty in suit by one not licensed by the state).

12. *See* TENN. CODE ANN. 23-3-103.

13. *Id.* (noting that the practice is allowed "as a matter of courtesy" afforded to lawyers of states that afford Tennessee lawyers a similar privilege to appear in its courts).

14. *See* TENN. CODE ANN. 23-3-103(c).

15. *Id.* (authorizing penalty not to exceed $1,000 per violation).

16. *See* TENN. CODE ANN. 23-3-103(b).

384 ISSUES OF LEGAL ETHICS IN THE PRACTICE OF ENVIRONMENTAL LAW

rate." The Model Code prohibits lawyers from aiding unauthorized practice.[17] Model Rule 5.5 prohibits the unauthorized practice of law. It provides: "A lawyer shall not . . . practice law in a jurisdiction where doing so violates the regulation of the legal profession in that jurisdiction." Maintaining current membership by paying bar fees is also important.[18]

Unauthorized practice includes practice by a lawyer in a state in which he holds no license in addition to practice by a nonlawyer. For example, in *Kentucky Bar Association v. Tiller*,[19] the Supreme Court of Kentucky held that a lawyer employed by a debt collection agency aided his employer in the unauthorized practice of law by drafting pleadings when the agency, rather than the lawyer, made the decision to file garnishments and pleadings using nonlawyer personnel of the employer. Despite the fact that a three-month suspension was recommended, the Supreme Court held that the lawyer's license should be suspended for six months for aiding the debt collection company in the unauthorized practice of law.[20] Similarly, the Rhode Island Supreme Court denied fees to a Massachusetts lawyer who represented a client before the Energy Facility Siting Board because the lawyer failed to obtain admission pro hac vice.[21]

Despite the trend toward broad-based practice, problems of unauthorized practice have not been resolved. The profession and courts continue to regard the prohibition against unauthorized practice of law as fundamental to the profession in some way. Judicial decisions have resulted in significant losses to lawyers when courts regard the lawyers' conduct as running afoul of unauthorized practice rules. For example, in *Wellmore Coal Corporation v. Harman Mining Corporation*, the Virginia Supreme Court dismissed a company's appeal of a $6 million judgment based on the failure of lawyers to include a signature of a lawyer licensed in Virginia. The court also held that the lawyer's failure to include the signature of a Virginia lawyer violated the rules on

---

17. Disciplinary Rule 3-101 Aiding Unauthorized Practice of Law provides: "(A) A lawyer shall not aid a non-lawyer in the unauthorized practice of law. (B) A lawyer shall not practice law in a jurisdiction where to do so would be in violation of regulations of the profession in that jurisdiction."

18. For example, Tennessee expressly mandates in its statute that it is unlawful to practice law unless the practitioner's "license therefor is in full force and effect." TENN. CODE ANN. 23-3-103(a). *See also* Richmond Eustis, *Lawyer's Failure to Pay Bar Dues Taints Murder Case Victory*, FULTON COUNTY DAILY REP. (April 19, 2001) (raising question whether "Prosecutor Clinton K. Rucker's failure to pay his bar dues jeopardizes" murder conviction he obtained).

19. 641 S.W.2d 421 (Ky. 1982).

20. *Id.*

21. *In re* Ferry, 774 A.2d 62 (R.I. 2001).

notice of appeal and rejected an amendment to cure this problem.[22] Additionally, the case of *Birbrower, Montalbano, Condon & Frank v. Superior Court*[23] has generated significant controversy in the legal profession nationwide. The Supreme Court of California refused to award lawyer fees to a New York firm that rendered legal services to a client in San Francisco.

Two partners of the New York law firm of Birbrower, Montalbano, Condon & Frank (Birbrower) represented a California corporation, ESQ, in a claim against a Delaware corporation on a contract governed by the laws of California. The Birbrower partners filed a demand for arbitration with the San Francisco office of the American Arbitration Association. They traveled to California, met with and advised their client, investigated the claim in California, interviewed potential arbitrators, and met with the opposing party's representatives. Eventually, with the assistance of the Birbrower lawyers, the claim was settled. ESQ later sued Birbrower in the California courts for legal malpractice, and Birbrower counterclaimed for legal fees. The trial court granted ESQ's motion for summary judgment and dismissed Birbrower's claims for fees.

In reviewing the case, the California Supreme Court assumed that the activities of the New York lawyers constituted the practice of law and focused on the extent to which those activities took place in California. Although noting that attenuated contacts may fall short of unlicensed practice, the California Supreme Court affirmed the trial court decision on the basis that the New York lawyers violated the California statute against the unlicensed practice of law. "Mere fortuitous or attenuated contacts will not sustain a finding that the unlicensed lawyer practiced law 'in California.' The primary inquiry is whether the unlicensed lawyer engaged in sufficient activities in the state, or created a continuing relationship with the California client that included legal duties and obligations."[24] The court noted that a person can violate the statute even without entering the state of California.

> Our definition does not necessarily depend on or require the unlicensed lawyer's physical presence in the state. Physical presence is one factor . . . but it is by no means exclusive. For example, one may practice law in the state . . . by advising a California client on California law in connection with a California legal dispute by telephone, fax, computer, or other modern technological means.[25]

---

22. Wellmore Coal Corp. v. Harman Mining Corp., 568 S.E.2d 671 (Va. 2002).
23. 17 Cal. 4th 119, 949 P.2d 1, 70 Cal. Rptr. 2d 304.
24. 70 Cal. Rptr. 2d 304, 309 (Cal. 1998).
25. *Id.* at 309.

The court declined to "craft an arbitration exception" to the prohibition on unlicensed practice.[26] In response to *Birbrower*, the California legislature in 1998 authorized out-of-state lawyers to represent parties to California arbitrations by associating with California counsel, who must be "the attorney of record," and by filing a certificate agreeing, among other things, to be subject to the jurisdiction of California courts for disciplinary purposes.[27]

The case presents a risk that a lawyer who never physically enters a foreign state may nonetheless violate that state's unauthorized practice rules through "virtual contacts" with the client or by maintaining a "continuing relationship" with the client. The *Birbrower* case may signal a trend toward tighter enforcement of unauthorized practice rules in the interjurisdictional context.[28] Additionally, a lawyer who seeks admission in a state after practicing in the state without the benefit of a license in that state may face a hurdle in the admissions process.[29]

Some courts have rejected the reasoning of the *Birbrower* decision. In *Fought & Co. v. Steel Engineering & Erection, Inc.*,[30] the Hawaii Supreme Court held that an Oregon law firm, which did work in connection with litigation filed in Hawaii, was not engaged in the unauthorized practice of law in Hawaii and was entitled to fees for its work. The court distinguished *Birbrower* on the grounds that (1) the Oregon lawyers did their work in Oregon, not Hawaii, and (2) the client was represented in the Hawaiian courts by Hawaiian counsel. In *Estate of Condon v. McHenry*,[31] a California court allowed fees to a Colorado lawyer who, along with California local counsel, represented a Colorado resident as coexecutor in a California probate proceeding. Both California law and property were involved. The court discussed *Birbrower*, distinguishing it on two points. First, the California Probate Code expressly allows out-of-state residents to serve as executors and entitles executors to lawyers' fees. Second, the California unauthorized practice statute does not prohibit the award of fees to out-of-state lawyers in California probate proceedings.

---

26. *Id.* at 312.
27. California Code of Civil Procedure 1282.4 (1999).
28. John D'Attomo, *The $1 Million Message: Lawyers Risk Fees and More When Representing Out-of-State Clients*, 39 Santa Clara L. Rev. 447 (1999).
29. *See In re* Jackman, 761 A.2d 1103 (N.J. 2000) (imposing 18-month delay on admission of Massachusetts lawyer to New Jersey Bar based on lawyer's unauthorized practice in New Jersey).
30. 951 P.2d 487 (1998).
31. 76 Cal. Rptr. 2d 922 (Ct. App. 1998).

Chapter 12: Multijurisdictional Practice 387

2002 Revisions

Upon receipt and debate of the final report from the ABA Commission on Multijurisdictional Practice, the ABA House of Delegates adopted revised Model Rules 5.5 and 8.5.[32] The House of Delegates adopted the recommendations of the Commission, reaffirming state control over the licensing of attorneys and establishing regulations for MJP. The revised Model Rule 5.5 permits some activities by a lawyer outside the lawyer's home state, including pro hac vice appearances and activities undertaken in anticipation of a pro hac vice admission when local counsel is involved in a substantive way, practice reasonably related to a lawyer's practice in her home jurisdiction, participation in ADR proceedings, and certain practice by in-house counsel. Revised Model Rule 8.5 clarified the "authority of a jurisdiction to discipline lawyers licensed in another jurisdiction who practice law within their jurisdiction pursuant to the provisions of Rule 5.5 or other law,"[33] making clear that state disciplinary boards have jurisdiction over lawyers who practice in a jurisdiction without being admitted in the jurisdiction.

Revised Model Rule 5.5 permits multijurisdictional practice in limited circumstances.[34] First, the revised rule allows lawyers to obtain admission to a tribunal pro hac vice. Second, it permits in-house lawyers admitted in one jurisdiction to perform services for their corporate client or its affiliate in other jurisdictions. Third, it allows lawyers to perform services, such as discovery and investigations, that are related to a matter in the jurisdiction in which they are licensed. Fourth, lawyers gain protection against UPL claims by associating local counsel. The Commission noted that several states have adopted exceptions to unauthorized practice laws that permit occasional interstate practice by an out-of-state lawyer in connection with the lawyer's practice. The interstate practice need not involve a specific matter of a client in the lawyer's home jurisdiction but, rather, may involve a client who contacted the out-of-state lawyer because of that lawyer's national reputation.

---

32. At its meeting in February 2002, the ABA House of Delegates postponed decision on MODEL RULES 5.5 and 8.5 because it decided to await a report by the Multijurisdictional Practice Commission.
33. Report of the ABA Commission on Multijurisdictional Practice (Aug. 2002).
34. *See* http://www.abanet.org/cpr/ethics2k.html.

CHAPTER 13

Pro Bono Representations

All lawyers should strive to improve the legal system and to ensure that all people have access to legal representation necessary to secure their rights under our justice system. The rule has special application and importance in the environmental area, because representation of nongovernmental organizations and other entities seeking to address environmental concerns may stand as representatives of public welfare. "The complexity of environmental law increases the need for legal representation and further disadvantages those individuals and groups who find themselves without the resources to hire a competent environmental lawyer."[1]

Model Rule 6.1 addresses pro bono responsibilities of lawyers. It states: "A lawyer should aspire to render at least (50) hours of pro bono publico legal services per year."[2] The rule encourages lawyers to provide legal services to persons of limited means either without a fee or at a reduced fee. It encourages the same sort of provision of free or reduced-fee services to "charitable, religious, civic, community, governmental and educational organizations in matters which are designed primarily to address the needs of persons of limited means."[3] The rule also encourages lawyers to participate "in activities for improving the law, the legal system or the legal profession."[4]

In recent years, law firms have begun hiring lawyers who specialize in pro bono legal services as a way of meeting the commitment to pro bono work for the lawyers in the firm who may lack the expertise needed to deliver services needed by clients who are unable to pay. Lawyers specializing in

---

1. Robert R. Kuehn, *Shooting the Messenger: The Ethics of Attacks on Environmental Representation,* 26 Harv. Envtl. L. Rev. 417, 418 (2002).
2. MODEL RULE 6.1 (2002).
3. *Id.*
4. *Id.*

390 ISSUES OF LEGAL ETHICS IN THE PRACTICE OF ENVIRONMENTAL LAW

representing victims of domestic violence, homelessness, and immigration provide pro bono in this way. Moreover, it is not unusual for firms to support one or more lawyers who wish to provide pro bono services or reduced billing on particular environmental matters. The ABA Fund for Justice and Education also supports the Center for Pro Bono with donations from ABA members and others.[5]

2002 Revision

The duty to engage in public service is crucial in the environmental area. Environmental lawyers, like many individuals in today's world, recognize the importance of preserving the environment to protect human health, the natural world, and our hope that future generations can continue to inhabit this planet. The 2002 revision of Model Rule 6.1 declares the obligation of every lawyer to engage in pro bono services. "Every lawyer has a professional responsibility to provide legal services to those unable to pay."[6] The rule does not, however, impose a mandatory pro bono requirement of a particular number of hours. The Ethics 2000 Commission considered recommending a mandatory rule for pro bono service. The Commission ultimately stopped short of such a recommendation, and the House of Delegates adopted the Commission's proposal to emphasize the need for pro bono service on a voluntary basis. The 2001–02 Report of the ABA Commission on Billable Hours concluded that the hourly billing system may produce dramatic negative effects, including reduction in the time lawyers are willing to commit to pro bono work.[7]

The revision to Model Rule 5.4 recommended by the Ethics 2000 Commission and adopted by the ABA House of Delegates allows lawyers to share court-awarded legal fees with a nonprofit organization that employed, retained or recommended employment of the lawyer in the matter."[8]

---

5. See www.abanet.org/fje (visited 5/8/2003).
6. Model RULE 6.1 (2002).
7. ABA Commission on Billable Hours, *2001–2002 Billable Hours Report*, *available at* http://www.abanet.org/careercounsel/billable/toolkit/bhcomplete.pdf (last visited Sept. 15, 2002).
8. Model RULE 5.4(a)(4) (2002).

CHAPTER 14

Lawyer Advertising

Solicitation of Clients

Solicitation issues can arise frequently in environmental practice, particularly for lawyers representing plaintiff groups or pro bono groups rather than corporate clients. Even though the lawyer's contact with potential clients in a toxic tort or Superfund matter may seem innocuous, caution is necessary to avoid the risk of violating this bright-line rule by direct contact with potentially responsible parties (PRPs) who are not yet represented in a Superfund negotiation or in discussions with EPA concerning a site. It is important, of course, for all lawyers to be aware of the constraints created by the ethics rules relating to solicitation. Consumers need information about legal services just as they need information about other services available in the marketplace. Traditionally, however, the distribution of information about lawyers has been closely controlled by bar associations. The ABA and local bars relaxed limitations on lawyer advertising during the 1970s as a result of decisions by the United States Supreme Court and antitrust laws. These decisions and laws struck a balance more in favor of dissemination of information than the old bar association rules or the Model Code while retaining the basic concept against direct solicitation by lawyers. Liberalization of norms regarding lawyer advertising may be continuing.[1]

The formulation of the Model Rules relating to advertising and the dissemination of information about legal services regulates advertising but does not bar it. The Model Rules contain significant requirements that a lawyer ignores at his peril. Model Rule 7.1 prohibits lawyers from making false or

---

1. *See* Mason v. Florida Bar, 208 F.3d 952 (11th Cir. 2000) (holding that a lawyer has a First Amendment right to advertise that he received the highest rating available in Martindale-Hubble).

misleading communications concerning their legal services. Model Rule 7.2 verifies that lawyers may advertise their services through a broad range of media.

> [A] lawyer may advertise services through public media, such as a telephone directory, legal directory, newspaper or other periodical, outdoor advertising, radio or television, or through written or recorded communication.[2]

Perhaps the most stringent controls set on lawyer advertising or solicitation relate to direct contact with prospective clients. Model Rule 7.3 sets limits on permissible contact with potential clients, prohibiting many instances of direct contacts. Model Rule 7.3 states that a lawyer "shall not by in-person or live telephone contact solicit professional employment from a prospective client"[3] when "a significant motive for the lawyer's [contact] is the lawyer's pecuniary gain."[4] The rule also includes exceptions to the solicitation prohibition for direct solicitation of individuals with whom the lawyer has a family or professional relationship.

The constraints on written or recorded information are somewhat less stringent than those of in-person or telephone solicitation. Model Rule 7.3 prohibits such contact when the individual contacted (the prospective client) has indicated a "desire not to be solicited by the lawyer," or if the lawyer engages in coercion, duress or harassment.[5] Model Rule 7.3 creates a bright-line rule intended to prevent any direct solicitation by a lawyer.

Lawyers cannot use an agent to solicit clients or to accomplish anything they could not do directly.[6] Model Rule 8.4(a) indicates that professional misconduct includes actions a lawyer takes through the acts of another. The rule states: "It is professional misconduct for a lawyer to: (a) violate or attempt to violate the Rules of Professional Conduct, knowingly assist or induce another to do so, or do so through the acts of another."[7]

---

2. MODEL RULE 7.3(a). The rule also limits the prohibition to cases in which "the lawyer has no family or prior professional relationship" with the person contacted. *Id.*

3. *Id.*

4. *See* related issue of conflicts in representing multiple PRPs at a Superfund site.

5. *See* MODEL RULE 7.3(b). The constraints of subsection (b) also apply to live or telephone contact, but the broad provision of subsection (a) does not apply to written or recorded information.

6. *See, e.g.,* Koden v. U.S. Dept. of Justice, 564 F.2d 228 (7th Cir. 1977) (recognizing authority of Immigration and Naturalization Service to discipline lawyers appearing on matters heard by the INS and affirming penalty against lawyer who employed "runners" to solicit clients and took client funds without providing services).

7. MODEL RULE 8.4(a).

Chapter 14: Lawyer Advertising   393

Model Rule 7.3 also requires that written or recorded information include the statement "Advertising Material" prominently displayed.[8] The Model Rule provides an exception to allow participation in an organization "not owned or directed by a lawyer" that provides prepaid or group legal services and uses the otherwise prohibited methods of contacting individuals such as in-person or telephone contact to attract people to subscribe to the plan. Such a group is exempted from the prohibition on in-person or telephone contact as long as the persons solicited "are not known to need legal services in a particular matter covered by the plan."[9] Thus, plans or groups that are created to solicit clients from a particular disaster are not included in the safe haven of the Model Rule 7.3(b) exception.

Model Rule 7.3 sometimes creates difficult issues for a lawyer seeking to establish a class of plaintiffs in a toxic tort action or to represent similarly situated parties in a Superfund action.[10] In these situations, direct contact would be the most straightforward way to get the information to the potential clients, but, because of the potential for abuse, the rule restricts direct solicitation.

Environmental Example (2002 Revision)

Comment 4 to the Revised Model Rule 7.2 gives guidance on the issue of contacting prospective members of a class in a class action. It states: "Neither this Rule nor Rule 7.3 prohibits communications authorized by law, such as notice to members of a class in class action litigation."[11]

Decisional Law

The United States Supreme Court has made clear that the protections of the First Amendment apply to commercial speech in general and to lawyer ads or solicitations in particular. The decisions on commercial speech relating to

---

8. MODEL RULE 7.3(c) (noting that the term must appear on the outside of an envelope and at the beginning and end of recorded communications).
9. MODEL RULE 7.3(d).
10. *See* Shapero v. Kentucky Bar Ass'n, 486 U.S. 466 (1988) (holding state violates U.S. Constitution by prohibiting lawyers from sending truthful letters to potential clients known to face particular legal problems); Bates v. State Bar of Arizona, 433 U.S. 350 (1977) (holding that a state ethics rule that prohibited lawyers from advertising violated First Amendment). *See also* Vincent R. Johnson, *Solicitation of Law Firm Clients by Departing Partners and Associates: Tort, Fiduciary, and Disciplinary Liability,* 50 U. PITT. L. REV. 1 (1988); John T. Ballantine, Jr., *After Shapero v. Kentucky Bar Association, Much Remains Unresolved About the Allowable Limits of Restrictions on Attorney Advertising,* 61 U. COLO. L. REV. 115 (1990).
11. MODEL RULE 7.2 cmt. 4.

394 ISSUES OF LEGAL ETHICS IN THE PRACTICE OF ENVIRONMENTAL LAW

legal services balance the right of lawyers to advertise and to initiate contact with prospective clients with the right of states to protect their citizens from abusive or harassing conduct.

In the case of *Bates v. Arizona State Bar*,[12] the U.S. Supreme Court held that prohibitions against lawyer advertising amounted to a First Amendment violation. In the *Bates* case, a bar association ruled that lawyers had violated the bar ethics rule against advertising by running an ad in a newspaper that claimed the lawyers provided services "at very reasonable prices."[13] The Supreme Court rejected numerous arguments by the Arizona Bar, including assertions that advertising would result in a loss of professionalism,[14] that the ads were misleading,[15] that advertising would lead to lower quality of legal services,[16] and would stir litigation.[17] To the contrary, the Court found that advertising "may offer great benefits,"[18] noting that the "traditional mechanism in a free-market economy" is to get information to the consumer.[19] The Court acknowledged, however, that limited regulation of speech does not violate the First Amendment "in holding that advertising by attorneys may not be subjected to blanket suppression, and that the advertisement at issue is protected; we do not hold that advertising by attorneys may not be regulated in any way . . . Advertising that is false, deceptive, or misleading, of course, is subject to restraint."[20] The Court left unanswered the question of "defining the boundary between deceptive and non-deceptive advertising."[21] Additionally, the Supreme Court noted expressly that the case did not involve the question of "in-person solicitation."[22]

In its 1988 decision in *Shapero v. Kentucky Bar Association*,[23] the United States Supreme Court validated the practice of lawyers sending direct mailings to potential clients. The *Shapero* holding did not address the issue of in-person solicitation. Thus, the opinion did not overrule the earlier case of *Ohralik v. Ohio State Bar Ass'n*,[24] in which the Supreme Court disapproved

---

12. Bates v. Arizona State Bar, 433 U.S. 350 (1977).
13. *Id*. at 351.
14. *Id*.
15. *Id*.
16. *Id*. at 350–51.
17. *Id*. at 375.
18. *Id*. at 376.
19. *Id*.
20. *Id*. at 383.
21. *Id*. at 384.
22. *Id*.
23. 486 U.S. 466 (1988).
24. 436 U.S. 447 (1978).

Chapter 14: Lawyer Advertising   395

in-person solicitation. In *Ohralik,* the Court upheld an indefinite suspension of an Ohio lawyer who solicited in-person contracts to represent accident victims.[25] Justice Marshall described the lawyer's actions as "classic examples of 'ambulance chasing.'"[26]

The Supreme Court again addressed the issue of solicitation in *Florida Bar v. Went For It, Inc.,*[27] validating a Florida Bar restriction on written communication by lawyers to victims of accidents for 30 days after the accident or disaster. The Court applied an intermediate scrutiny test to judge the restriction, holding that the bar restrictions survived First Amendment scrutiny based on the bar's showing of its substantial interests in protecting injured Floridians from intrusive lawyer conduct and in preventing the erosion of public confidence in the legal profession.

Requirement to Preserve Record

Model Rule 7.2 states that "[a] copy or recording of an advertisement or communication shall be kept for two years after its last dissemination along with a record of when and where it was used."[28] Many states that have adopted this approach have modified the time period for which the lawyer must keep the ad.[29] Some states require that a copy of an ad be filed with a representative of the bar.[30]

Additionally, some states set specific guidelines and limits on solicitation. As the Supreme Court cases discussed above indicate, such controls are constrained by the protection afforded commercial speech by the First Amendment. Some states also require that lawyers file copies of ads with the state

---

25. *Id.* at 469.
26. *Id.*
27. 515 U.S. 618 (1995).
28. MODEL RULE 7.2(b).
29. *See e.g.,* IN. ST. R.P.C. RULE 7.1(e) (requiring advertisement be kept for six years); CT. R.P.C. Rule 7.2(b) (requiring advertisement be kept for three years); N.Y. ST. C.P.R. DR 2-101(f) (requiring lawyers to retain broadly disseminated ads and to file individualized contacts such as letters with the state disciplinary committee).
30. *See e.g.,* FL. ST. BAR RULE 4-7.5(b) (mandating a copy of advertisement be "filed with the standing committee on advertising for evaluation of compliance with these rules ... either prior to or concurrently with the lawyer's first dissemination of the advertisement"); TEX. ST. R.P.C. Rule 7.07(a) (requiring filing with the Lawyer Advertisement and Solicitation Review Committee of the State Bar of Texas); N.M.R. R.P.C. Rule 16-707 (requiring filing a copy of advertisement with the legal advertising committee).

disciplinary authorities.[31] Such limitations are arguably within the sphere of restrictions on lawyer advertising accepted by *Bates*.

Environmental Examples

A lawyer who speaks at an organizational meeting of residents in an area subject to environmental hazards seems different in kind from the sort of overreaching conduct in the *Ohralik* and *Went For It* cases. Nevertheless, the best practice may be for environmental lawyers to contact potential clients initially by mail rather than in person to avoid any charge of improper solicitation of clients. When an existing client requests that his lawyer talk with a neighbor, the client can set up a meeting and ask the lawyer to attend. Such a meeting does not appear to violate the rule against client solicitation, since the lawyer is acting pursuant to a client's request. Simply having a client make the original contact may not be determinative, however. A lawyer should not, for example, direct a client to make contacts with other potential clients. Such action would violate the general rule that lawyers cannot use an agent to solicit clients or to accomplish anything they could not do directly.[32]

Technology

The Internet provides new avenues for lawyer advertising and new challenges for determining the parameters of appropriate advertising.[33] Difficult questions can arise regarding whether Internet communication constitutes the posting of information or the practice of law. When a lawyer provides a legal opinion or advice on the Internet, she must consider whether she is engaging in the unauthorized practice of law. If the recipient of the legal advice or information is in a state in which the lawyer is not licensed, or if the transaction discussed occurs in another state, the lawyer may have violated that state's law on unauthorized practice of law.

---

31. *See* MODEL RULE 1.3 cmt. 3; *see also* Neville v. Vingelli, 826 P.2d 1196 (Ariz. Ct. App. 1991) (imposing duty on lawyer to inform lenders that he was not representing borrower, notwithstanding that lenders initiated transaction); *In re* Halprin, 798 P.2d 80 (Mont. 1990) (disbarring lawyer for failing to act with reasonable diligence and failing to give notice of termination).

32. *See, e.g.,* Koden v. U.S. Dept. of Justice, 564 F.2d 228 (7th Cir. 1977) (recognizing authority of Immigration and Naturalization Service to discipline lawyers appearing on matters heard by the INS and affirming penalty against lawyer who employed "runners" to solicit clients and took client funds without providing services).

33. *See* Louise L. Hill, *Lawyer Communications on the Internet: Beginning the Millennium with Disparate Standards*, 75 WASH. L. REV. 785, 818 (2000).

Chapter 14: Lawyer Advertising   397

Using the Internet to communicate with clients or prospective clients is not necessarily improper. The Nassau County (New York) Bar Association Committee on Professional Ethics recognized the right of lawyers to advertise on Internet sites when it approved lawyer use of a Web site that provided information to the public about particular fields of law, listing one lawyer for each area. Each lawyer listed paid a fee for the listing and was identified online as the "sponsor" of that information. The web site also provided a hyperlink to the lawyers' Web sites.[34] The Committee disapproved the practice of identifying lawyers who pay an additional fee as "lead counsel," but otherwise approved the arrangement. The committee drew the line between listing a lawyer as "sponsor" and as "lead counsel" on the basis that the "lead counsel" designation may mislead consumers into believing that the lawyers listed as "lead counsel" are somehow exceptional. The Committee also disapproved of any hyperlinks that would allow the lawyer and the potential client to engage in a dialogue online, presumably because such a dialogue is analogous or substantially similar to in-person solicitation. The Committee relied on the fact that the Internet site noted that the listing was a paid advertisement. It accepted the use of the term "sponsor" as a term that consumers are familiar with in advertising. The Committee noted that, to avoid unauthorized practice of law in jurisdictions in which the lawyer is not licensed, such sites must include a statement identifying the jurisdiction of licensure of the lawyer.

Answering questions on a listserv or other electronic posting could also lead to unauthorized practice charges. The Ethics Panel of the New Mexico State Bar has advised New Mexico lawyers to avoid this practice. Lawyers could inadvertently enter an attorney-client representation by dealing with specifics of an individual's legal problem.[35] Additionally, the opinion notes that lawyers should guard against unauthorized advertising and unauthorized practice in this setting and against receiving confidential information in this forum for the same reason that receipt of the information can create a difficult fact question regarding whether the lawyer created an expectation that he is accepting a representation.[36]

Internet (2002 Revision)

The 2002 revision to Model Rule 7.2 clarifies the right of a lawyer to use electronic communication to advertise legal services.[37] A comment to Model

---

34. Nassau County (New York) Bar Ass'n Comm. on Prof'l Ethics, Op. 99-3, Sept. 29, 1999.

35. *See* New Mexico State Bar Advisory Opinions Comm., Formal Op. 2001-1 (2001).

36. *Id.*

37. Model Rule 7.2(a) (2002).

398 ISSUES OF LEGAL ETHICS IN THE PRACTICE OF ENVIRONMENTAL LAW

Rule 7.2 praises the Internet as a way of providing information to the public. Comment 3 states: "[E]lectronic media, such as the Internet, can be an important source of information about legal services, and lawful communication by electronic mail is permitted by this Rule."[38] Nevertheless, Rule 7.3(a) restricts solicitation of prospective clients via a real-time electronic exchange. The 2002 revision to Model Rule 7.3 categorizes real-time electronic contact as tantamount to in-person contact and makes clear that real-time electronic contact is prohibited unless the person contacted is a lawyer or has a "family, close personal or prior professional relationship with the lawyer."[39] The revision excluded solicitations to other lawyers from this prohibition.

Stating Specialization

Some states recognize the specialty of environmental law. In such states, the environmental lawyer who has met the state's certification requirements has a right to refer to his specialty in advertisements.[40] However, a lawyer may not assert the status of a specialist in a field of law unless he or she meets the standards for a specialist set by the rules of professional conduct of his or her jurisdiction. Model Rule 7.4, "Communication of Fields of Practice," sets the model standard for advertising specialization in a particular area of practice. If a lawyer is "admitted to engage in patent practice before the United States Patent and Trademark Office,"[41] he or she may claim to be a licensed patent lawyer. Likewise, a lawyer practicing Admiralty law may assert the specialty or claim that he or she is a "Proctor in Admiralty" if that is accurate.[42] A lawyer who has received certification for an area of practice and who practices in a jurisdiction "where there is a regulatory authority granting certification or approving organizations that grant certification," may assert his certification in a particular field by the "named organization or authority."[43] Finally a lawyer practicing in a jurisdiction that has "no appropriate regulatory authority" granting certification may indicate a certification he has obtained but must state clearly that the jurisdiction has no procedure for approving certifying organizations.[44] In jurisdictions that lack a procedure for approving certifying organizations, a lawyer may communicate a certification he has achieved without including the disclosure that the jurisdiction lacks a proce-

---

38. MODEL RULE 7.2 cmt. 3 (2002).

39. MODEL RULE 7.3(a)(2) (2002).

40. *See* CHARLES W. WOLFRAM, MODERN LEGAL ETHICS at § 5.5, 204–05 (1986).

41. *See* MODEL RULE 7.4(a).

42. *See* MODEL RULE 7.4(b).

43. *See* MODEL RULE 7.4(c).

44. *See* MODEL RULE 7.4(c) [option 2].

dure for approving certifying organizations if the organization that provided his certification "has been accredited by the American Bar Association."[45]

Stating Specialization (2002 Revision)

The 2002 revision to Model Rule 7.4 simplified the approach of the rule to the announcement of a specialty. The rule states:

> A lawyer shall not state or imply that a lawyer is certified as a specialist in a particular field of law, unless:
> (1) the lawyer has been certified as a specialist by an organization that has been approved by an appropriate state authority or that has been accredited by the American Bar Association; and
> (2) the name of the certifying organization is clearly identified in the communication.[46]

Solicitation of Clients (2002 Revision)

Although the revision to the Model Rules clarifies the right of a lawyer to use electronic communication to advertise legal services,[47] the revision to Model Rule 7.3 categorizes real-time electronic contact as tantamount to in-person contact and, thus, makes clear that real-time electronic contact is prohibited unless the person contacted is a lawyer or has a "family, close personal or prior professional relationship with the lawyer."[48] The revision excluded solicitations to other lawyers from this prohibition.

---

45. *Id.*
46. MODEL RULE 7.4(d) (2002).
47. MODEL RULE 7.2(a) (2002).
48. MODEL RULE 7.3(a)(2) (2002).

CHAPTER 15

Lawyer Fees

The requirement that a lawyer charge only reasonable fees applies to all lawyers regardless of their area of practice. Nevertheless, the topic deserves special attention in the environmental area because of the extraordinary costs, stresses, and temptations often associated with environmental matters.[1] A recent example is presented in the case of *United States v. Nucor Corp.*, in which a steel company agreed to pay approximately $100 million to settle an action brought by the Department of Justice that alleged violations of standards for air, water, and soil.[2] The level of cleanup costs for Superfund sites, the high penalties charged for violations of environmental laws, and the significant reputational and financial interests at stake in environmental matters create an atmosphere of intensity and even unreality at times. This atmosphere can influence billings, and some lawyers can fall prey to a sense of "anything goes" or "the sky's the limit" when astronomical expenses become commonplace, distorting the lawyer's perception of fairness.[3]

In addition to the extraordinary costs associated with environmental liability, environmental cases often impose extraordinary demands on lawyers

---

1. CUTTING GREEN TAPE, 129–32 (Richard L. Stroup & Roger E. Meiners eds., 2000) (outlining the high costs associated with toxic litigation).
2. *See* United States v. Nucor Corp. 17 F. Supp. 2d 1249 (N.D. Ala. 1998); *see also Steel Company to Pay $100 Million to Settle Air, Water, Waste Allegations*, 32 B.N.A. ENVTL. RPTR. 44 (Jan. 5, 2001).
3. "The annual cleanup bill for sites currently being remediated is enormous. The Department of Energy alone has spent between $5.6 billion and $7.2 billion *per year* on the environmental management of its sites over the past several years. The cost of remediating a typical federal superfund site has been estimated at $27 million." Phillip E. Karmel, *Achieving Radical Reductions in Cleanup Costs*, *in* NEW SOLUTIONS TO ENVIRONMENTAL PROBLEMS IN BUSINESS AND REAL ESTATE DEALS 233 (2000).

402   ISSUES OF LEGAL ETHICS IN THE PRACTICE OF ENVIRONMENTAL LAW

in terms of travel, late hours, the stress of urgent situations, and difficult judgment calls. Lawyers may also risk their time on a case only to learn that the court refuses to award attorney's fees in the matter.[4] Both sets of circumstances may tempt lawyers to seek to recover some of their loss by billing additional time in related matters or by constructing a loose sort of "value billing" in the case at issue. Although courts have recognized the right of lawyers to bill based on the importance of the matter and the exposure of the client to significant liability, such standards do not make it appropriate for the lawyer to build in such charges by adding time to his records.

Like any provider of goods or services, lawyers should only charge fees that are reasonable in relation to the service provided and the circumstances.[5] Jokes about lawyer overbilling indicate the suspicions of the public,[6] and a 1991 survey suggests that the practice is widespread.[7] At any rate, it is safe to say that the perception of lawyers as a group motivated by profit to a significant extent has grown in recent years.[8] In a high-profile case, Webster Hubbell was disbarred because of the practice of overcharging clients.[9] Courts have the power to sanction lawyers for unfair or excessive fees and may reduce or cap a fee award on the basis that the fee is excessive.[10] Even when a fee agreement appears to be reasonable at the time the parties entered the agreement, a court has discretion to judge the agreement based on the effect of the fee at the time it is to be paid.[11]

---

4. *See, e.g.*, S.W. Ctr. for Biological Diversity v. Babbitt, 108 F. Supp. 2d 1209 (D. N.M. 2000) (denying recovery of attorney's fees to environmental plaintiffs seeking designation of a fish as endangered on the basis that the suit did not serve as a catalyst to the Secretary's action of listing the fish as threatened).

5. For a thorough treatment of the subject of lawyer billing, see William G. Ross, *The Ethics of Hourly Billing by Attorneys*, 44 RUTGERS L. REV. 1 (1991).

6. A joke that comes to mind is a 30-something lawyer who protests to St. Peter at the gates of heaven that he died too young, only to be assured that he was in his 70s when he died—based on his recorded billings.

7. Based on a survey of 272 lawyer and 80 corporate counsel throughout the country, Professor William G. Ross reported evidence of significant overbilling in his article, *The Ethics of Hourly Billing by Attorneys*, 44 RUTGERS L. REV. 1 (1991).

8. *See generally* FLEMING & MACKLIN, LAWYERS, MONEY, AND SUCCESS: THE CONSEQUENCES OF DOLLAR OBSESSION (2002).

9. *In re* Hubbell, 896 S.W.2d 440 (Ark. 1995) (accepting Web Hubbell's surrender of his law license in Arkansas).

10. *See In re* Cendant Corp. PRIDES Litigation (Welch & Forbes Inc. v. Cendant Corp.), 243 F.3d 722 (3d Cir. 2001).

11. This point involves both the inherent power of the court to approve or disapprove of the fee and, additionally, general contract law relating to unconscionable clauses. Restatement

Chapter 15: Lawyer Fees   403

The number of disputes relating to lawyer fees has risen dramatically in recent times. To avoid the expense and problems inherent in a fee dispute, fee arbitration, or litigation, lawyers should carefully set forth their billing structure in a letter to the client, preferably a retainer letter, and should be scrupulous in their billing and record keeping. Courts have also disapproved of a delay in producing a writing to memorialize a contingent fee arrangement.[12]

The principle of reasonable fees is axiomatic. It was recognized in the Canons of Ethics. Canon 38, "Compensation, Commissions and Rebates," provided: "A lawyer should accept no compensation, commission, rebates or other advantages from others without the knowledge and consent of his client after full disclosure."[13] The common practice of billing for legal services by the hour may raise issues of fairness.[14] The 2001–02 Report of the ABA Commission on Billable Hours set forth the results of the Commission's study of the effects of the practice of hourly billing on the delivery of legal services and the practice of law. The Commission concluded that the hourly billing system produces negative effects for clients and lawyers alike and recommended that lawyers consider adopting other billing methods such as flat fee, blended hourly rates, monthly retainers, and hybrid models in some types of cases. The Commission report concluded that firms should pursue alternatives to the standard hourly billing practices.[15] At the ABA Annual Meeting in August 2002, a panel on this topic focused on concerns about the adverse effects of an hourly billing model and reasons that firms should consider using alternative models for billing rather than the hourly approach in some types of cases.[16]

---

of the law given lawyers § 34 cmt. c (Unenforceable Fee Contracts); N.Y.C. Ethics Opinion 2003 (2000 WL 33769162, Ill. Ethics Opinion 98-03) (1999), 1999 WL 35560; In the Matter of William J. Gerard, 634 N.E.2d 51 (Ind. 1994) (rejecting lawyer's claim for fees as excessive and fraudulent because the work involving only administrative tasks specific "legal" skills and suspending lawyer from the practice for one year).

12. *See* Starkey, Kelly, Blaney & White v. Estate of Nicolaysen, 773 A.2d 1176 (N.J. Super. 2001).

13. Canon of Ethics, Canon 38.

14. *See* Gillian K. Hadfield, *The Price of Law: How the Market for Lawyers Distorts the Justice System*, 98 MICH. L. REV. 953 (2000) (noting the disturbingly high cost for legal services in the United States and identifying factors that create the current market structure for legal services and possible solutions).

15. ABA Commission on Billable Hours, *2001-2002 Billable Hours Report, available at* http://www.abanet.org/careercounsel/billable/toolkit/bhcomplete.pdf (last visited Sept. 15, 2002).

16. *ABA Panelists Look into Whys and Hows of Moving to Different Fee Arrangements*, 71 U.S. LAW WK. 2143 (Aug. 27, 2002).

404   ISSUES OF LEGAL ETHICS IN THE PRACTICE OF ENVIRONMENTAL LAW

Even for the lawyer who is scrupulous in his record keeping, questions of efficiency are inherent in hourly billing. Despite the widespread use of hourly billing, lawyers should be cautious of the practice and must guard against the incentive it creates to work inefficiently or to take longer than necessary on legal tasks.[17]

> Traditional billing systems distribute risk and reward between law firms and clients in an uneven manner, providing few incentives for efficient legal solutions. The sophisticated clients of today are becoming unwilling to defer complete control of their cases and legal expenses to their attorneys. Clients are now demanding more efficiency; but hourly billing actively discourages efficiency.[18]

Model Rule 1.5 requires that lawyer's fees be "reasonable." It gives a substantial list of eight factors that should be considered in setting a fee. The factors listed include the time and skill required, the customary fees for similar services, time constraints or exigencies, the experience and reputation of the lawyer, and the foreseeability that the employment will preclude other employment.[19] Thus, the rules suggest that fees should not be set based on time alone. Time should be a threshold consideration in that the lawyer should not bill an hourly rate based on a figure that exceeds his actual time.[20] Nevertheless, the overwhelming weight of authority is that lawyers and clients have significant flexibility in setting fees as long as the fees meet the reasonableness standard and the client consents to the arrangement after being fully informed of the terms. The contract between the lawyer and client must clearly indicate the terms of the agreement regarding billing. Nontraditional billing is

---

17. *See* Douglas R. Richmond, *The New Law Firm Economy, Billable Hours, and Professional Responsibility*, 29 Hofstra L. Rev. 207 (2000) (discussing "associate salary wars" and problem of "double billing"); Lisa G. Lerman, *Blue-Chip Bilking: Regulation of Billing and Expense Fraud by Lawyers*, 12 Geo. J. Legal Ethics 205 (1999) (discussing cases of billing fraud).
18. Bradley A. Ullrick, *The Alternative Billing Diner: Serving Up a New Billing Scheme for the Technological Age*, 5 J. Tech. L. & Pol'y 2 (2000) (discussing alternative forms of billing and endorsing fixed-fee billing).
19. Model Rule 1.5(a)(1)–(8).
20. *See Oregon Opinion Disapproves Plan to Bill Multiple Clients for Simultaneous Service*, 71 U.S. Law Wk. 2039 (July 16, 2002) (Oregon State Bar Legal Ethics Comm., Op. 2002-170, May 2002) (concluding that billing multiple clients for services rendered at the same time constitutes misrepresentation by nondisclosure because it charges for more time than the lawyer actually worked).

not improper as long as the fee meets the reasonableness standard.[21] Even if a fee agreement appears to be reasonable at the time the parties entered the agreement, a court has discretion to judge the agreement based on the effect of the fee at the time it is to be paid.[22]

Billing and Collection Practices

In addition to the responsibility of limiting the fee itself based on the reasonableness standard, lawyers must not engage in unreasonable collection practices.[23] Charging a reasonable rate of interest on overdue billings is not improper as long as the client agreed to the practice.[24] The representation agreement should indicate the rates of billing for services and expenses. Courts scrutinize the terms of agreements between lawyers and clients to determine whether the terms of the contracts of employment meet the reasonableness standard and that clients are fully informed of the terms of the agreement. For example, the case of *Lustig v. Horn*[25] held that a retainer agreement that provided for the recovery of lawyer fees and costs for collection was unenforceable because the provision violated the fiduciary relationship between the lawyer and his client.[26] The court noted that courts should presume that a client entered the agreement as a result of undue influence when a lawyer presents a fee agreement to a client after the attorney-client relationship has been established. The court further found that the lawyer failed to meet the burden of rebutting the presumption of undue influence by "clear and convincing" evidence.[27] Nevertheless, the court allowed recovery of the value of necessary services on the basis of quantum meruit.[28] A related point that lawyers should consider in

---

21. ABA-BNA Lawyers' Manual on Professional Conduct Reference Manual, 41:301.
22. This point involves both the inherent power of the court to approve or disapprove of the fee and, additionally, general contract law relating to unconscionable clauses. *See, e.g.*, Restatement (Second) of Contracts § 208 (noting court may refuse enforcement of contract that is unconscionable at time of making or limit enforcement of unconscionable effect); Restatement of the Law Governing Lawyers § 34 cmt c.; *see also* N.Y.C. Ethics Opinion 2003 (2000 WL 33769162), Ill. Ethics Op. 98-03 (1999) (1999 WL 35560).
23. *See* Arthur Garwin, *Bringing in the Fees*, A.B.A. J. 66 (June 2001).
24. *See supra* note 21; *see, e.g.*, City Bar of New York, 2001-02.
25. 732 N.E.2d 613 (Ill. App. 1 Dist. 2000).
26. *Id.* at 619.
27. *Id.*
28. *Id.* at 619–20.

406 ISSUES OF LEGAL ETHICS IN THE PRACTICE OF ENVIRONMENTAL LAW

setting billing practices is the application of statutes relating to the debtor-creditor relationship, such as the Equal Credit Opportunity Act and the Truth in Lending Act.[29]

Lawyers should indicate to the client the fee structure for the particular representation. In a sense, this requirement is more easily met by environmental lawyers than by lawyers in some other fields. Many environmental lawyers work for corporate clients or other sophisticated clients such as large NGOs. For the most part, such clients are comfortable with receiving, negotiating, and entering detailed agreements, including representation agreements that give considerable detail on the terms of the representation. Lawyers should include in the representation letter the type of compensation structure that applies as well as the amount of hourly charges for each lawyer who will work on the case.

Fixed fees are appropriate in some cases. When the tasks involved are of a type that are fairly predictable in terms of the time commitment involved, the lawyer may have sufficient certainty to undertake a task for a fixed fee. Clients sometimes find this arrangement desirable because it gives them certainty regarding the cost of the services. Work that relies on the use of forms that the lawyer has developed or routine tasks of filing or monitoring the progress of administrative matters fall within this category. Some states create a statutory right allowing lawyers to impose a charging lien on the proceeds of a deal or case to secure fees.[30] Nevertheless, these statutes generally do not allow use of the lien when the client needs the file for ongoing litigation.

Advance Fees

Both the 1983 version and the 2002 version of Model Rule 1.5 include a comment noting that lawyers "may require advance payment of a fee."[31] Additionally, however, the comment makes clear that lawyers are "obliged to return any unearned portion" of the advanced fee.[32] In 2002, the ABA Standing Committee on Professionalism, Ethics and Professional Responsibility opined that it is ethical for lawyers to acquire a security interest in a client's property to ensure payment of legal fees, with respect to fees either that are earned or to be earned.[33]

---

29. Analysis of these laws is beyond the scope of this work. *See, e.g., Lawyers Who Don't Demand Prompt Payment of Fees Aren't Creditors under ECOA, TILA,* 70 U.S. LAW WK. 1659 (May 7, 2002).

30. *See, e.g.,* UT. ST. § 38-2-7 (Attorney's lien).

31. MODEL RULE 1.5 cmt. 2; REV. MODEL RULE 1.5 cmt. 4.

32. *Id.*

33. *See* ABA Form. Op. 02-427 (May 31, 2002) (approving use of security interest in client's property to secure payment of fee).

The Committee limited its conclusion to security interests in property that is the subject of the litigation in which the lawyer represents the client.

Lawyer Fees (2002 Revision)

The 2002 version of Model Rule 1.5 reaffirms the requirement that lawyers charge clients only reasonable fees. The revised rule recasts the obligation with regard to fees to a negative, prohibiting the lawyer from making an agreement for unreasonable fees and from "charg[ing], or collect[ing] unreasonable fee or an unreasonable amount for expenses."[34] This change provides detail regarding the lawyer's obligation to charge reasonable fees in the 1983 version of the rules. The revised rule also forbids use of a contingency fee in representing a defendant in a criminal case.[35] It permits the use of a contingent fee in a domestic relations matter, as long as the fee is not conditioned upon "the securing of a divorce or upon the amount of alimony or support, or property settlement in lieu thereof."[36] A comment to the Revised Model Rule 1.5 adopted by the ABA in 2002 underscores the point that contingent fees, like other fees, "are subject to the reasonableness standard" of the rule.[37]

Writing (2002 Revision)

The ABA House of Delegates rejected the proposal by the Ethics 2000 Commission that fee agreements and modifications of fee agreements be required to be in writing. The Ethics 2000 Commission proposal included an exception for regular clients of the lawyer, while the House of Delegates increased the requirements relating to contingent fees to require that such agreements be signed by the client. It rejected the requirement of a writing as a general matter, however. Despite the absence of a rule requiring a writing, many environmental lawyers use a representation letter to set forth the relevant information about the representation. Use of a representation letter is desirable for many reasons. Lawyers can use them to make clear to the client the scope of the representation, the fact that failure to pay the lawyer fees can result in termination of the relationship, and other important details of the relationship.

---

34. ABA MODEL RULE 1.5(a) (2002).
35. MODEL RULE 1.5(d).
36. MODEL RULE 1.5(d)(1).
37. REV. MODEL RULE 1.5 cmt. 3.

408 ISSUES OF LEGAL ETHICS IN THE PRACTICE OF ENVIRONMENTAL LAW

Retainer Agreement

Controversies frequently arise in environmental cases relating to retainer fees—particularly if the retainer is large and the time of the representation was short. Courts take seriously their obligation to monitor and judge the amount of a class counsel fee. In the case of *Zucker v. Occidental Petroleum*,[38] the Court of Appeals for the Ninth Circuit held that the courts have supervisory power over the assessment of attorney fees in class action cases, allowing the trial court to evaluate the fairness of the award without regard to which party objected to the sum. The court affirmed the trial court's reduction of the fee award.[39]

Although courts have validated sizable, nonrefundable retainers,[40] it is prudent for lawyers to specify in the retention agreement the purposes of the retainer and the reasons the parties agree that the retainer is nonrefundable. Courts sometimes use a 25 percent fee as a benchmark for awarding attorney's fees in common fund cases.[41] In the class action suit of *Goldberger v. Integrated Resources, Inc.*, the Second Circuit held that attorney's fees can be calculated for common fund cases using either a percentage method, or the lodestar method in which the number of hours that would reasonably be expended in a case is multiplied by the appropriate hourly rate.[42] This decision is consistent with *Blum v. Stenson*, in which the U.S. Supreme Court recognized as reasonable a percentage of the judgment or fund created for the class in common fund cases.[43] When a court reduces a lawyer's fee from the lodestar amount, it should explain the reasons for the reduction.[44]

Lawyers are generally prohibited from limiting their liability to a client by contract. Model Rule 1.8 prohibits lawyers from entering an agreement with a client that would "prospectively limit[] the lawyer's liability to a client for malpractice unless permitted by law and the client is independently repre-

---

38. *See* Zucker v. Occidental Petroleum Corp., 192 F.3d 1323 (9th Cir. 1999).

39. *Id.* at 1329.

40. *See* Ryan v. Butera, Beausang, Cohen & Brennan, 193 F.3d 210 (3d Cir. 1999); Brobeck, Phleger & Harrison v. Telex Corp. 602 F.2d 866 (9th Cir. 1979) (affirming trial court award of $1 million to lawyer in accordance with retainer agreement in antitrust litigation); *$1,000,000 Retainer Is Valid Despite Ten-Week Employment*, 68 U.S. Law Wk. 1243 (Nov. 2, 1999).

41. *See* Savoie v. Merchants Bank, 166 F.3d 456 (2d Cir. 1999); Goldberger v. Integrated Res., Inc., 209 F.3d 43 (2d Cir. 2000).

42. Goldberger v. Integrated Res., Inc., 209 F.3d 43 (2d Cir. 2000).

43. 465 U.S. 886 (1984).

44. *See* Van Gerwen v. Guarantee Mutual Life Co., 214 F.3d 1041 (9th Cir. 2000).

sented in making the agreement."[45] In a formal opinion in 2002, the ABA Standing Committee on Ethics and Professional Responsibility held that a lawyer retainer agreement may include an arbitration agreement that fee disputes or malpractice claims between the lawyer and client be resolved by arbitration.[46] The ABA Formal Opinion noted the greater use and acceptance of arbitration agreements but indicated that such agreements are subject to "special oversight and review" because of the fiduciary duties that lawyers owe to clients. The opinion also made clear that arbitration agreements are appropriate only when the lawyer fully apprises the client of the "advantages and disadvantages of arbitration" and the client gives "informed consent to the inclusion of the arbitration provision in the retainer agreement."[47]

Similarly, the Maine Board of Bar Overseers Professional Ethics Commission found a retainer agreement permissible that required disputes between the lawyer and client to be referred to binding arbitration.[48] In reaching its decision, the Maine Commission relied on the state's policy favoring arbitration and distinguished arbitration from a limitation of liability by noting that arbitration simply changes the forum for adjudication rather than limiting liability. Similarly, a Michigan court enforced an arbitration clause in a retainer agreement entered by the plaintiff while he was in the hospital.[49] The plaintiff signed the four-page agreement without the benefit of independent counsel. The court relied on the state's policy favoring arbitration and also held the provision of Michigan Rule of Professional Conduct 1.8(h) requiring independent counsel for such agreements did not bind the court.[50] Lawyers should not regard this case as a signal that all arbitration agreements between lawyers and clients are enforceable or that courts will favor such agreements as a general rule.[51] The better and more cautious practice is to use an arbitration agreement only with sophisticated clients who have been fully advised of

---

45. *See* MODEL RULES OF PROF'L CONDUCT, R. 1.8(h).

46. ABA Formal Op. 02-425.

47. *Id.*

48. Maine Board of Bar Overseers Prof'l Ethics Comm., Op. 170 (Dec. 23, 1999).

49. *See* Watts v. Polaczyk, 619 N.W.2d 714 (Mich. Ct. App. 2000); *see also* John Schmitt, *Fine Print Matters: Fee-Agreement Arbitration Clause Bars Malpractice Suit in Court* 87 A.B.A. J. 24 (Jan. 2000).

50. *Watts*, 619 N.W.2d at 715–16.

51. *See* John Schmitt, *Fine Print Matters: Fee-Agreement Arbitration Clause Bars Malpractice Suit in Court* 87 A.B.A. J. 24 (Jan. 2000), *quoting* Ronald E. Mallen, co-author of the treatise *Legal Malpractice*, for the point that the case should be seen as representing "the extreme end of upholding [arbitration] agreements."

410 ISSUES OF LEGAL ETHICS IN THE PRACTICE OF ENVIRONMENTAL LAW

the effect and consequences of an arbitration agreement and have had an opportunity to consult another lawyer regarding use of the particular agreement.

Contingent Fees

Contingent fees are subject to criticism by scholars[52] and are generally disfavored in some contexts.[53] In Formal Opinion 94-389, the ABA Standing Committee on Ethics and Professional Responsibility held that a contingent fee is permissible. It also noted that if the lawyer and client agree, a lawyer may charge a different contingent fee at different stages of a matter.[54]

The weight of authority prohibits the use of contingent fees in domestic and criminal cases, however,[55] and some authorities disfavor the practice generally. For example, the New York Code of Professional Responsibility adopts Ethical Consideration 2-20, noting that lawyers "generally should decline to accept employment on a contingent fee basis by one who is able to pay a reasonable fixed fee."[56] The Ethical Consideration notes, however, that such a fee arrangement is "not necessarily improper for a lawyer, where justified by the particular circumstances" of a civil case "with any client who, after being fully informed of all relevant factors, desires that arrangement."[57] It notes that contingent fee arrangements are "rarely justified" in domestic relations and are condemned in criminal cases.[58]

Many jurisdictions regulate the contingent fee arrangement, requiring that the lawyer reveal in writing the way the final fee will be determined. For example, California requires lawyers accepting a representation on a contingency fee basis to provide the client with a copy of the (written) contract of employment at the time the contract is entered into.[59] The California statute requires that both the lawyer and the client sign the written contract. Additionally, it requires that the writing include (among other things) a statement

---

52. *See, e.g.*, Lester Brickman, *ABA Regulation of Contingency Fees: Money Talks, Ethics Walk*, 65 FORDHAM L. REV. 247 (1996) (arguing against standard contingency fee arrangements).

53. *See* Fasing v. Lafond, 944 P.2d 608 (Colo. Ct. App. 1997) (unsigned contingent fee agreement not enforceable against client as contract or in quantum meruit); WOLFRAM, *supra* n. 56 at 529 (1986); *also see* 1 GEOFFREY C. HAZARD, JR., & W. WILLIAM HODES, THE LAW OF LAWYERING: A HANDBOOK ON THE MODEL RULES OF PROFESSIONAL CONDUCT at § 1.5:501.

54. ABA Formal Op. 94-389 (1994).

55. *See* CHARLES W. WOLFRAM, MODERN LEGAL ETHICS at 535-40.

56. N.Y. ST. CPR EC 2-20 (based on MODEL CODE OF PROF'L RESPONSIBILITY EC 2-20).

57. *Id.*

58. *Id.*

59. CALIF. BUS. & PROF. CODE 6147(a)(2).

of any contingency fee rate agreed to in the contract. The statute also requires that the written agreement indicate whether expenses of the representation will be deducted from the fee.[60]

Contingent Fees (2002 Revision)

Contingent fees are appropriate in limited circumstances. Under the 2002 revision of Model Rule 1.5, even a contingent fee that is appropriate is effective only if set forth in a writing "signed by the client."[61]

Environmental Public Interest Groups

Environmental public interest groups can collect attorney fees for their efforts to force the EPA to act in compliance with certain environmental statutes.[62] This right is part of the private attorney general concept, which is included in many environmental statutes.[63] Citizen suit provisions have a purpose of encouraging private citizens to monitor, report, and litigate violations of the environmental laws. Additionally, they allow action by private citizens against the administrator of EPA or other official bodies who fail to carry out their nondiscretionary duties.[64] For example, in *Natural Resources Defense Council Inc. v. E.P.A*,[65] the court held that a suit by a citizen group against EPA to force compliance with the Clean Air Act (CAA) could recover attorney's fees. The Defense Counsel had prevailed in an action against the EPA under section 307 of the CAA. Like many environmental statutes, the CAA specifically allowed for recovery of attorney fees.

> Under the circumstances it seems fair and sensible that the EPA should be taxed for petitioners' reasonable costs and attorneys' fees. The EPA has been assigned by Congress the task of supervising pollution control. It handles the public funds appropriated for that purpose. To allocate petitioners' reasonable costs and attor-

---

60. *Id.*
61. MODEL RULE 1.5(c) (2002).
62. *See* Coalition for Clean Air v. S. Calif. Edison Co., 791 F.2d 219 (9th Cir. 1992).
63. *See, e.g.*, Clean Water Act § 505(g), 33 U.S.C. § 1365(g) (1986); Comprehensive Environmental Response, Compensation and Liability Act § 310, 42 U.S.C. § 9659 (1995); Resource Conservation Recovery Act § 7002, 42 U.S.C. § 6972 (1995); Clean Air Act § 304, 42 U.S.C. § 7604 (1995).
64. The constitutionality of citizen suit provisions has been challenged as a violation of the Article II presidential duty of enforcing the laws of the United States. *See* Friends of the Earth, Inc. v. Laidlaw Environmental Services, Inc., 120 S. Ct. 693 (2000).
65. 484 F.2d 1331 (1972).

412   ISSUES OF LEGAL ETHICS IN THE PRACTICE OF ENVIRONMENTAL LAW

neys' fees to it is to spread them ultimately among the taxpaying public, which receives the benefits of this litigation.[66]

Payment of Fees as a Sanction

Courts have the inherent power to impose a payment of attorney's fees on a party or lawyer who created unnecessary fees by delaying the other party's discovery or the process of the case.[67] The United States Supreme Court has held that attorney's fees may be awarded as sanctions in cases of lawyer misconduct or failure to comply with discovery requests both under statutory authority and under the court's inherent power and, additionally, that courts have the power to assess attorney's fees against counsel as opposed to assessing the fees against the client.[68] For example, in an environmental matter, *In re Tutu Wells Contamination Litigation*,[69] the Court of Appeals for the Third Circuit upheld sanctions of $120,000 imposed by a trial court against an oil company and its former counsel for discovery violations. In the case of *Stanford v. President and Fellows of Harvard College*,[70] the court ordered Boston's Messing & Rudavsky to pay Harvard University $94,718 in legal fees it expended to move the court for sanctions against the law firm for its attempt to use "informal" discovery in attempts to prove before an administrative judge that its client, Kathleen Stanford, had been passed over for promotions in Harvard University's police department in violation of gender discrimination laws.[71]

Collection

Some firms have computer programs and policies relating to the time and form of billing and the schedule for following up with letters or notices informing clients that their account is past due. Many law firms computerize their billing

---

66. *Id.* at 1334.
67. *See* Wisconsin v. Hotline Industries, Inc., 236 F.3d 363 (7th Cir. 2000) (holding fees awarded to government lawyers under 28 U.S.C.A. 1447 for improper removal of case by other party must be based on actual expenses rather than comparable fees in private practice in the community).
68. *See* Chambers v. NASCO, Inc., 111 S. Ct. 2123 (1991); Roadway Exp., Inc. v. Piper, 100 S. Ct. 2455 (1980).
69. 120 F.3d 368 (3d Cir. 1997).
70. 13 Mass. L. Rptr. 77, 78, 2001 WL 716834 (Mass. Super. 2001) (Cratsley, J.), *reversed* as to Rule 4.2 violation, Messing, Rudavsky & Weliky, P.C. v. President and Fellows of Harvard College, 436 Mass. 347, 764 N.E.2d 825 (2002).
71. *See* Darryl Van Duch, *Harvard Adversary Slammed: Employee's Counsel Sanctioned $94,718*, Nat'l L.J. (Apr. 10, 2001).

Chapter 15: Lawyer Fees 413

process.[72] Some lawyers call clients personally to inquire about the client's satisfaction or lack of satisfaction with the work undertaken on his behalf, especially if the bill is substantial.[73] When the fee is set on an hourly rate rather than a contingency, the lawyer is entitled to payment despite a result contrary to that predicted by the lawyer or hoped for by the client.

Fees in the Environmental Context

There are many cases of high costs in environmental cleanups and high penalties for failure to comply with governmental requirements relating to environmental matters.[74] The cost of remediation of hazardous waste sites in this country is staggering, usually millions of dollars per site. In *F. R. & S., Inc. v. Department of Environmental Protection*,[75] for example, a Pennsylvania court upheld the Department of Environmental Resources assessment of a civil penalty in the amount of $315,000, which was imposed for the failure of the company to meet a deadline set for having in place a cap on a municipal waste landfill. The company missed its deadline by approximately five months. The court affirmed the penalty for the company's failure to complete the required capping project by December 31, 1996, despite arguments by the company that other landfills in the region had missed their deadlines by longer periods of time but had received no penalty or a penalty smaller than that assessed against the company.[76] Lawyers working on matters involving high stakes may be tempted to regard their work as being entitled to a premium. When billions of dollars are spent in any area, it may affect the psychological outlook of the lawyers involved in the matters. It is crucial that lawyers compartmentalize their sense of their input on the case and their billings on the case in order to retain integrity regarding their mission and professional duties rather than being swept away by the magnitude of the issues and money at stake.

Referral Fees: Environmental Practice

In the environmental area, lawyers often refer clients to environmental consultants to do soil testing, to read records and advise clients regarding contamina-

---

72. For a fuller treatment of the subject of billing, *see* Emily Couric, *Smart Money Methods to Setting and Collecting Fees*, J. 66 A.B.A. J. (1985).

73. *Id.*

74. *See* Marianne Lavelle, *EPA's Amnesty Has Become a Mixed Blessing*, NAT'L L.J., Feb. 24, 1997, at A1 (noting need for amnesty because many violations go undetected). *See generally* W.M. VON ZHAREN, ISO14000: UNDERSTANDING THE ENVIRONMENTAL STANDARDS (1996).

75. F.R.&S., Inc. v. Department of Envt'l Protection, 761 A.2d 634 (Pa. Cmwlth. 2000).

76. *Id.*

414   ISSUES OF LEGAL ETHICS IN THE PRACTICE OF ENVIRONMENTAL LAW

tion of property, and to do audits of real estate sales. Whether the consultant pays a referral fee to the referring lawyer depends on local practice. The practice has not been the subject of empirical investigation, and states do not address the issue in a uniform manner.[77] In the 2002 revision, the ABA House of Delegates amended Model Rule 7.2 on advertising to allow lawyers to refer clients to other lawyers or nonlawyer professionals and receive a referral fee under controlled conditions. Rule 7.2 creates a general prohibition against lawyers paying anything for a recommendation. As revised, the rule continues to prohibit referral payments. It allows lawyers to "refer clients to another lawyer or a nonlawyer professional pursuant to an agreement not otherwise prohibited under these Rules that provides for the other person to refer clients or customers to the lawyer, if the reciprocal referral agreement is not exclusive, and the client is informed of the existence and nature of the agreement."[78]

In some jurisdictions, lawyers may ethically accept a referral fee for referring a client to a nonlegal service provider.[79] The cases arising in this area generally relate to lawyer referrals to insurance agents or financial planners. The analysis of these opinions seems equally applicable to the practice of referring clients to other professionals. A joint formal opinion issued by the Pennsylvania Bar Association Committee on Legal Ethics and Professional Responsibility and the Philadelphia Bar Association Professional Guidance Committee held that a referral fee is not a violation of the ethics rules of that state if the lawyer determines that payment of this fee would not diminish the client-lawyer relationship or undermine the lawyer's independent professional judgment.[80] Additionally, the joint opinion noted that to comply with the rule on fees, lawyers who wish to accept such referral fees must give full disclosure to the client and consult with the client regarding the potential conflict. The opinion analyzed numerous factors for consideration by the lawyer assessing whether a referral fee would damage the client-lawyer relationship, including whether the client was fully apprised of the conflict, the level of sophistication of the client, whether

---

77. *See, e.g.*, Utah State Bar Ethics Comm. Op. 99-07 (1999) (allowing referral fees when lawyer meets heavy burden of compliance with ethics rules); Conn. Informal Ethics Op. 94-25 (1994) (allowing referral fees); Arizona State Bar Comm. on Rules of Professional Conduct Op. 98-09 (1998) (holding that Rules 1.7 and 1.8 prohibit referral fees); Mich. Informal Ethics Op. RI-146 (1992) and Mich. Informal Ethics Op. RI-317 (2000) (prohibiting referral fees under Rule 1.7).

78. MODEL RULE 7.2(b)(4).

79. *See* Pa. Bar Ass'n Comm. on Legal Ethics and Prof'l Responsibility, and Philadelphia Bar Ass'n Prof. Guidance Comm., Joint Formal Op. 2000-100, 3/00, *cited in* 68 U.S. LAW WK. 2631 (Apr, 25, 2000).

80. *Id.*

the lawyer recommended outside advice to the client, and the amount of the referral fee in relation to the time and effort spent on the case.

In jurisdictions that have not issued a formal opinion on this matter, the prudent lawyer would seek an opinion from the state's advisory committee on professional responsibility before accepting a referral fee. The ethics opinions dealing with referrals in the financial arena seem likely to control referrals in the environmental area as well.[81]

Fee Sharing

Lawyer codes have traditionally prohibited lawyers from sharing fees with nonlawyers. This prohibition is intended to ensure the professional independence of lawyers. Rule 5.4 is discussed in the section on Multidisciplinary Practice. Rule 5.4(b) prohibits a partnership with a nonlawyer "if any of the activities of the partnership consist of the practice of law."[82] Additionally, Model Rule 5.4 prohibits sharing legal fees with nonlawyers.[83] The rule prohibits "non-lawyers from sharing fees with, being partners in, or holding an entrepreneurial interest in an organization that practices law." In essence, Rule 5.4 prohibits the practice of sharing a business with nonlawyers, since the sharing of fees is essential to a continuing business relationship and could influence lawyer judgments.[84] It allows exceptions for payments to a lawyer's estate for death benefits and for the purchase of a law practice if the lawyer whose practice is purchased is deceased or disabled. The ABA Standing Committee on Ethics and Professional Responsibility clarified the rule in 2001, indicating that it does not prohibit a relationship between U.S. lawyers and foreign lawyers.[85] The rationale of the Committee is that foreign lawyers "who are members of a recognized legal profession do not implicate [the] concerns and therefore should be regarded as lawyers rather than non-lawyers for purposes of Rule 5.4."[86] Commenting on the phrase "member of a 'recognized legal profession,'" the Committee noted that "a person who is specifi-

---

81. *See, e.g.,* California State Bar Standing Comm. on Prof'l Responsibility and Conduct, Formal Op. 1999-154, 8/27/99; *see* U.S. LAW WK. 2631 (April 2000).

82. MODEL RULE 5.4(b).

83. This issue is the topic of discussion in the section on MDP.

84. *See* MODEL RULE 5.4(a).

85. ABA Ethics Op. 01-423 (Sept. 22, 2001) (opining that U.S. firms may form partnerships with foreign law firms).

86. *See* ABA Formal Ethics Op. 01-423; *see also ABA Opinion Advises That Foreign Lawyers May Form Partnerships With U.S. Lawyers,* 70 U.S. L.A.W. WK. 2288 (Nov. 13, 2001).

416   ISSUES OF LEGAL ETHICS IN THE PRACTICE OF ENVIRONMENTAL LAW

cally trained to provide advice on the laws of the foreign jurisdiction and to represent clients in its legal system, and is licensed by the jurisdiction to do so, will qualify as a foreign lawyer."[87] The Committee also reasoned that the safeguard of Model Rule 7.5(b) in this area protects clients.[88] Rule 7.5 allows lawyers not admitted in a firm's home jurisdiction to associate with a firm, as long as the firm "makes known the jurisdictional limitations placed on that individual's ability to practice law in the jurisdiction where the office is located."[89]

Fee Division (2002 Revision)

In February 2002, the ABA House of Delegates approved the revisions to Model Rules 1.5 and 5.4 relating to fees. The 2002 revision to Model Rule 1.5 allows referral fees for competent referrals without the necessity of division of work or joint responsibility.[90] It reaffirms the requirement that lawyers charge clients only reasonable fees. The 2002 version of the Model Rules clarified a point on division of fees that may be applicable to multidisciplinary practice. Comment 7 to Model Rule 1.5, as amended, states that when lawyers arrange for a division of fees from a single billing to a client, the client "must agree to the arrangement, including the share that each lawyer is to receive,"[91] indicating that absent consent by the client, such a division is not permissible. Additionally, the revision states that the agreement "must be confirmed in writing."[92]

The revision to Model Rule 5.4 retained the prohibitions against fee sharing and forming a business entity with nonlawyers that includes the practice of law. The effect of retaining the traditional rules is essentially to reject the movement toward MDP.[93] The prohibition against fee sharing states: "A lawyer or law firm shall not share legal fees with a nonlawyer."[94] The exceptions to the rule do not include MDP. The revision retained the prohibition against forming a practice with a nonlawyer, effectively prohibiting MDP.

---

87. *See* ABA Formal Ethics Op. 01-423.
88. *Id.*
89. MODEL RULE 7.5(b).
90. *See* ETHICS RULE 1.5(e) (2002).
91. MODEL RULE 1.5 cmt. 7 (2002).
92. *Id.*
93. Charles W. Wolfram, *Comparative Multi-disciplinary Practice of Law: Paths Taken and Not Taken,* 52 CASE W. RES. L. REV. 961 (2002) (describing the revision as a "flawed, but perhaps temporary, rejection of the MDP concept").
94. MODEL RULE 5.4(a) (2002).

Chapter 15: Lawyer Fees 417

(d) A lawyer shall not practice with or in the form of a professional corporation or association authorized to practice law for a profit, if:

(1) a nonlawyer owns any interest therein, except that a fiduciary representative of the estate of a lawyer may hold the stock or interest of the lawyer for a reasonable time during administration;

(2) a nonlawyer is a corporate director or officer thereof *or occupies the position of similar responsibility in any form of association other than a corporation;* or

(3) a nonlawyer has the right to direct or control the professional judgment of a lawyer.[95]

The 2002 version of Model Rule 5.4 confirms the ABA's prohibition against practicing in a corporation or business association that includes nonlawyers. Rule 5.4 also disapproves the practice of sharing a business with nonlawyers by its prohibition against sharing of fees with nonlawyers, since the division of fees is essential to a continuing business relationship and could influence lawyer judgments.[96] The rule allows exceptions for payments to a lawyer's estate for death benefits and for the purchase of a law practice if the lawyer whose practice is purchased is deceased or disabled. The revision also allows lawyers to share court-awarded legal fees with a nonprofit organization that employed, retained, or recommended employment of the lawyer in the matter.[97]

---

95. MODEL RULE 5.4(d) (2002) (italics indicating added language).
96. *See* MODEL RULE 5.4(a).
97. MODEL RULE 5.4(a)(4) (2002).

CHAPTER 16

The Lawyer's Role in Working with Consultants

Lawyers frequently work with nonlawyer assistants and with consultants from a variety of fields. In environmental matters, lawyers often need to coordinate the work of the case among a variety of professionals such as biologists, geologists, natural historians, and toxicologists.[1] Consultants and the scientific evidence they gather, analyze, and explain are crucial to legal determinations in environmental compliance and enforcement. Indeed, in some matters, environmental lawyers must have advanced degrees and training in biological sciences or rely on environmental professionals to conduct testing and make the scientific judgments necessary for the monitoring of discharges, safety of work practices, and other scientific determinations.[2] The necessity for environmental lawyers and scientific advisors to work cooperatively can hardly be overstated.

In financial matters, lawyers must often work with the client's financial advisors, accountants, tax advisors, and financial analysts. In family law, lawyers frequently need to interact with and understand the judgments of psychiatrists and other mental health professionals as well as tax advisors and estate planners. Most law firms hire secretaries, law student clerks, and paralegals, generally as employees rather than independent contractors or consultants. Lawyers also hire independent contractors such as consultants and pay them on behalf of the client, passing on the costs of such professionals to the client. Use of employees and consultants by lawyers is accepted practice in the law, both today and traditionally.

---

1. Berton J. Fisher & William R. Keffer, *Selection, Use and Management of Experts in Environmental Legal Practice*, 33 TULSA L.J. 1003 (1998).
2. *See* Mark D. Coldiron & Connie M. Bryan, *Use of Experts in Environmental Litigation and Enforcement Matters*, 11 NAT. RES. & ENV'T 13 (1996).

420   ISSUES OF LEGAL ETHICS IN THE PRACTICE OF ENVIRONMENTAL LAW

Model Rule 5.3

Against this backdrop, Model Rule 5.3 details the responsibilities of lawyers regarding nonlawyer assistants, requiring a protective level of supervision, both in terms of firm policy and individual lawyer responsibility. The rule requires that supervising lawyers "must make reasonable efforts to ensure" that the work of nonlawyers "is compatible with the professional obligations of the lawyer."[3] The lawyer's role of supervising includes giving appropriate instructions to nonlawyer employees who work with the lawyer.[4] With noteworthy directness, the rule states that a lawyer "shall be responsible" for conduct that violates ethics rules if the lawyer orders or ratifies the conduct or knows of the conduct and fails to take "reasonable remedial action."[5]

This rule imposes an obligation on lawyers to take steps to ensure that the conduct of nonlawyer associates is compatible with the rules of professional conduct applicable to lawyers. Because the Model Rules are not applicable to nonlawyers, Rule 5.3 seeks to establish institutional controls relating to the interaction between a lawyer and nonlawyer assistants. It imposes on lawyers a duty to ensure that the professionals who work with them abide by ethical standards of the legal profession, thus protecting the client from disclosure of client information or other infringements by nonlawyer employees, which would constitute a violation of ethics rules. Likewise, the Restatement requires that the lawyer take care to safeguard client information. It requires lawyers to "take steps reasonable in the circumstances to protect confidential client information against impermissible use or disclosure by the lawyer's associates or agents that may adversely affect a material interest of the client or otherwise than as instructed by the client."[6]

Model Rule 5.3 creates layers of protection. First, it states that "a partner in a law firm shall make reasonable efforts to ensure that the firm has in effect measures giving reasonable assurance that the conduct of [nonlawyer assistants] is compatible with the professional obligations of the lawyer."[7] This subsection speaks to firm policies, requiring that firms address the issues of compliance with ethics rules when working with a nonlawyer assistant. The provision suggests that ongoing training must be required to instruct all persons who work with lawyers regarding the requirements of confidentiality and all professional rules. This rule speaks to virtually all persons working

---

3. MODEL RULE 5.3(a).
4. MODEL RULE 5.3 cmt. 1.
5. MODEL RULE 5.3(c).
6. RESTATEMENT (THIRD) OF THE LAW GOVERNING LAWYERS § 60 (2000).
7. MODEL RULE 5.3(a).

Chapter 16: The Lawyer's Role in Working with Consultants 421

with lawyers on behalf of their clients, including secretaries, runners, investigators, paralegals, and law students as well as consultants or other independent contractors.

For a second level of protection, Rule 5.3 speaks to the lawyer with "direct supervisory authority" over the assistant. It requires that the supervising lawyer "make reasonable efforts to ensure the person's conduct is compatible with professional obligations of the lawyer."[8] Finally, Model Rule 5.3 imposes responsibility for the actions of a nonlawyer when the action "would be a violation of the rules of professional conduct if engaged in by a lawyer." The rule imposes responsibility for such conduct on a lawyer who orders or ratifies the conduct or who knows of the conduct and "fails to take reasonable remedial action."[9] By its reference to a standard of "reasonable remedial action," this provision of Rule 5.3 suggests that a third party or client has a cause of action against a lawyer who fails to require assistants to comply with the ethics rules. One who fails to take reasonable remedial action would seem likely to fail the tort law test of reasonable care, and, thus, may be exposed to potential liability if harm results to the client from this failure to act in accordance with the standard of professional reasonableness.

The duty of confidentiality set forth in Model Rule 1.6 seems to be one of the most significant factors in monitoring work by consultants. This duty, as it is conceived by the Model Rules, is in contrast to the duty of confidentiality as envisioned in some other professions. The codes of most nonlegal professionals require disclosure of information necessary to prevent a client from harming the public or third parties. While some states require or allow such disclosure by a lawyer, others prohibit it under the ethics rule on confidentiality. Thus, the differing visions of a professional's responsibility regarding confidentiality may give rise to varying and inconsistent obligations under the rules of ethics of different professions, enhancing the risk of a lawyer's violation of Rule 1.6. For example, if a financial analyst or CPA learns from auditing the records of a company that a part of the company's operation is subject to an agency penalty for failing to comply with environmental regulations, the accountant has a duty to reveal this problem in its public audit.[10] A lawyer of the same client with the same information is likely to be constrained by Model Rule 1.6 to maintain the information as confidential.

---

8. MODEL RULE 5.3(b).

. 9. MODEL RULE 5.3(c).

10. *See generally* Richard W. Painter, *Lawyers' Rules, Auditors' Rules and the Psychology of Concealment,* 84 MINN. L. REV. 1399 (2000) (comparing lawyer and accountant rules on confidentiality and noting the default of secrecy in the law and disclosure in accounting).

422 ISSUES OF LEGAL ETHICS IN THE PRACTICE OF ENVIRONMENTAL LAW

Model Rule 5.3 (2002 Revision)

The 2002 revision to the Model Rules clarified Model Rule 5.3 to make it clear that a lawyer has a duty to use reasonable efforts to ensure that the firm "has in effect measures giving reasonable assurance" that the conduct of non-lawyer assistants "is compatible with professional obligations of the lawyer."[11] The addition makes clear that the duty applies to lawyers who have managerial authority whether or not they are partners in a firm. The point is emphasized by the fact that the rule also declares that a lawyer violates the rule if she orders or with knowledge ratifies conduct that is violative of the Model Rules undertaken by a nonlawyer assistant.[12]

Model Rule 7.2 (2002 Revision)

Environmental lawyers often refer clients to environmental consultants for assessment of the environmental condition of real estate, for assessment of environmental risks such as asbestos in buildings to be sold, and for other specific environmental purposes. Additionally, environmental consultants often refer their clients to lawyers that they have experience with in environmental matters. For example, consultants refer clients to lawyers when litigation may be necessary to protect the client's interest, when legal expertise is needed to negotiate with regulators, or for a wide variety of other legal needs. Rule 7.2 creates a general prohibition against lawyers paying anything for a recommendation. As revised, the rule continues to prohibit referral payments except that it allows lawyers to "refer clients to another lawyer or a nonlawyer professional pursuant to an agreement not otherwise prohibited under these Rules that provides for the other person to refer clients or customers to the lawyer, if the reciprocal referral agreement is not exclusive, and the client is informed of the existence and nature of the agreement."[13] Whether either the lawyer or the consultant pays a fee for a referral is a matter of local practice.

---

11. Model RULE 5.3(a) (2002).
12. Model RULE 5.3(c) (2002).
13. Model RULE 7.2(b)(4) (2002).

CHAPTER 17

The Lawyer Role in Working With the Media

The public often demands to know information about an environmental site because of concerns about the dangers associated with the site that may affect the safety of the public or individuals in the vicinity. The hazardous nature of a CERCLA site or the siting of a recycling plant or other land use means that neighboring residents are likely to oppose the project, especially if they lack basic information about it. Model Rule 3.6, entitled "Trial Publicity," sets forth guidelines and limits on the information lawyers share with the media in relation to matters under investigation or litigation. It makes clear that lawyers have an obligation to avoid prejudicing a client's case by any extrajudicial statement. Moreover, the rule includes a detailed list of the types of information that are not prejudicial.[1]

---

1. MODEL RULE 3.6(b) provides in part:

   (b) Notwithstanding paragraph (a), a lawyer may state:
      (1) the claim, offense or defense involved and, except when prohibited by law, the identity of the persons involved;
      (2) information contained in a public record;
      (3) that an investigation of a matter is in progress;
      (4) the scheduling or result of any step in litigation;
      (5) a request for assistance in obtaining evidence and information necessary thereto;
      (6) a warning of danger concerning the behavior of a person involved, when there is reason to believe that there exists the likelihood of substantial harm to an individual or to the public interest; and
      (7) in a criminal case, in addition to subparagraphs (1) through (6):
         (i) the identity, residence, occupation and family status of the accused;
        (ii) if the accused has not been apprehended, information necessary to aid in apprehension of that person;

The use of the media in today's world goes beyond statements relating to cases in litigation, however. The lawyer who makes use of the media in pursuit of client objectives should scrutinize his motives as well as the potential for adverse effects on the client.[2] Additionally, the lawyer who employs a public relations firm should be cautious in disclosing information and documents to the firm, since such use may constitute a waiver of the attorney-client privilege and the work product doctrine.[3] Consultant files may be discoverable, particularly if the party who seeks discovery can show "exceptional circumstances under which it is impracticable for the party seeking discovery to obtain facts or opinions on the same subject by other means."[4] Courts have held that communication between lawyers and other professionals hired by the lawyer's client are not entitled to the attorney-client privilege.[5] Likewise, when a lawyer provides business advice as opposed to legal advice, his communication with the client on this business advice does not merit the privilege.[6] In some cases, the line between business and legal advice is wavering and unclear. At least one federal court has applied the attorney-client privilege protection to communications between a public relations firm and lawyers when both were hired by a company to attempt to quell a legal crisis.[7] As in any case where a risk of loss of the privilege exists, it is wise to limit the documents that make their way to a consultant's files.

    (iii)   the fact, time and place of arrest; and

    (iv)   the identity of investigating and arresting officers or agencies and the length of the investigation.

2. Jennifer L. Johnson, *Empowerment Lawyering: The Role of Trial Publicity in Environmental Justice,* 23 B.C. ENVTL. AFF. L. REV. 567 (1996).

3. *See* Calvin Klein Trademark Trust v. Wachner, 198 F.R.D. 53 (S.D.N.Y. 2000); *see also* Jeffrey Ghannam, *When Not to Go Public: Documents Given to PR Firms May Not Be Privileged,* 87 A.B.A. J. 22 (Apr. 2001).

4. FED. R. OF CIV, PROC. 26(b).

5. *See, e.g.,* Cavallaro v. United States, 153 F. Supp. 2d 52 (D. Mass. 2001).

6. *See* United States v. Adlman, 68 F. 3d 1495 (2d Cir. 1995) (refusing to apply attorney-client privilege to communications from taxpayer's in-house counsel to accounting firm advising counsel of likely tax consequences of corporate reorganization); *In re* Kidder Peabody Sec. Litig., 168 F.R.D. 459 (S.D.N.Y. 1996) (outside counsel's notes on business issues not entitled to protection).

7. *See In re* Copper Market Antitrust Litigation (Viacom Inc. v. Sumitomo Corp.), 200 F.R.D. 213 (S.D.N.Y. 2001).

Chapter 17: The Lawyer Role in Working With the Media   425

Environmental Example

In environmental matters, a failure to provide the public with information about an environmental site can result in delays and losses to a project—whether it is cleanup of a hazardous waste site under CERCLA or the siting of a recycling plant or other land use opposed by neighboring residents.

> The cleanup and redevelopment of thousands of sites across the country has been delayed and made far more costly due to community opposition to cleanup and redevelopment proposals—opposition that in many cases could have been avoided or overcome by effective outreach efforts to key constituencies, such as local community groups and elected officials.[8]

The importance of including the public and area residents in discussions about an environmentally sensitive project cannot be overstated. In some circumstances, oversight statutes or guidance requires the site manager to give notice to the public and to allow public involvement at the site. In other cases, although no government mandate requires public involvement, transparency of process and involvement of the community may be helpful to both the neighborhood and the corporation or entity undertaking a cleanup or planning a use of a site that may be viewed as undesirable by nearby residents.

> Community involvement is a necessity at some sites and an option at others. At sites already within some formal federal or state superfund or superfund-like cleanup process, community involvement is generally mandatory for significant cleanup decisions. Many state brownfield programs also encourage or require community involvement. . . . Even where the owner has the option of 'going it alone,' a strategic decision must be made as to whether it would be helpful to encourage community involvement in any required cleanup and the ultimate redevelopment of the site.[9]

Today, some public relations firms specialize in environmental issues. They offer their services to companies engaged in cleanup actions and to those that need to provide information to the public regarding an environmental

---

8. Phillip E. Karmel, *Achieving Radical Reductions in Cleanup Costs*, *in* NEW SOLUTIONS TO ENVIRONMENTAL PROBLEMS IN BUSINESS AND REAL ESTATE DEALS, PRACT. L. INST. 281 (2000), *citing* 40 C.F.R. § 3000.430(c).

9. *Id.* at 281.

issue for any reason. Whether to hire a professional to serve as a spokesperson for the company is a difficult decision. Some lawyers speak for a corporate client in such situations. Sometimes a corporate officer or director is chosen as the most knowledgeable and the most credible spokesperson. One commentator suggests that using a lawyer or a consulting firm may backfire. "Perhaps the only persons that the public distrusts more than the management of an industrial facility is the facility's lawyers and public relations firm."[10] Other commentators view the use of public relations firms as valuable, however.[11] Whether a lawyer or others in a corporation serve as spokesperson regarding an environmental matter of public interest, providing accurate and timely information to the public is crucial. The corporate client must provide accurate and understandable information to earn the trust of the neighborhood and the public. Moreover, engaging in dialogue with the public, NGOs, and interest groups can go a long way toward easing the suspicion of the public regarding an environmental project. When open dialogue with the community is possible, greater trust is often the byproduct. The presentation and attitude of the spokesperson is of great significance. Candor and detail are essential attributes for resolving concerns of neighbors about environmental projects.

> Showing up at a public meeting with a fancy, one-sided presentation and a "trust me, I'm a credentialed expert" attitude will not engender public trust—it will only fuel opposition to a project. . . . It is arrogant and meaningless to key a presentation towards the company's assurance to the community that a site or a proposed remediation plan is safe. The community is unlikely to accept the supposition that a site owner has the right to determine whether the community is endangered by a site or a proposed cleanup. . . . The goal is to get the community to decide that a proposed plan is safe; it will not do so merely because a company's engineers and toxicologists provide conclusory assurances that residual risks are "de minimis" or below regulatory "thresholds."[12]

---

10. *Id.* at 283.
11. *See, e.g.,* Tom Weidlich, *Making a Case for PR: Once Estranged, Lawyers and PR Agencies Find They Need Each Other,* 87 A.B.A. J. 24 (Mar. 2001).
12. Phillip E. Karmel, *supra* note 8, 283–84.

CHAPTER 18

Termination and Withdrawal from Representation

A lawyer-client relationship may terminate and a lawyer may withdraw from representation for numerous reasons. Because of the complex nature of many environmental transactions and lawsuits, withdrawal of a lawyer from an environmental matter will often occasion costs for the client. For this reason, a lawyer involved in an environmental action should never take lightly the option of withdrawing from a representation.

The happiest occasion for termination is when the objectives of the client pursued in the representation have been fully accomplished. The termination of representation that falls short of complete achievement of the client's objectives includes both termination by the client and withdrawal by the lawyer. In some cases, a client fires a lawyer; in others, a lawyer fires the client. In all cases, it is paramount that the client's interests be protected to prevent prejudice to the client's interests, whether the interests relate to an ongoing cause of action or any other kind of negative consequence resulting from the end of the relationship. If a case has been set for trial or if some other motion or hearing has been scheduled or needs to be scheduled, the lawyer should seek permission from the court or tribunal to withdraw from the representation. Even when it is the client who terminates the relationship, the lawyer should inform the court of the change in the status quo.

Model Rule 1.16 sets forth the ABA's requirements for lawyer withdrawal. Withdrawal may be a duty or a right, depending on the circumstances. The rule provides the mandatory and permissive bases for withdrawal from representation. Like most of the Model Rules, Model Rule 1.16 is modeled on the framework of private practice rather than in-house counsel or the government lawyer. Nevertheless, the Model Rules apply to corporate and government lawyers. Accordingly, these lawyers, like their counterparts in private practice, may be required under the Model Rule to withdraw from representation as a result of a client's use of the lawyer's services to further crime or a fraud.

428   ISSUES OF LEGAL ETHICS IN THE PRACTICE OF ENVIRONMENTAL LAW

Likewise, conflicts rules apply to prohibit an in-house lawyer from representing opponents to his former employer even after termination.[1] The burden of establishing whether a representation has terminated or continues is on the lawyer rather than the client. In *Stratagem Development Corp. v. Heron,*[2] for example, the court granted a disqualification motion against the plaintiff's counsel, noting that "the evidence concerning the continuation of the lawyer-client relationship was inconclusive."[3] The absence of a clear termination resulted in application of the more difficult standard applicable to concurrent representations.

Mandatory Bases for Withdrawal

Model Rule 1.16 requires that a lawyer withdraw from the representation when continuation would result in a "violation of the rules of professional conduct or other law" and in the obvious cases of discharge by the client or impairment of the lawyer's ability to do his job.[4] A frequent reason for a lawyer's withdrawal is that continuing the representation would result in a violation of the rules against conflicts of interest.

It is clear that a lawyer cannot counsel or assist a client in illegal conduct. When a lawyer knows that a client is using the lawyer's service to engage in illegal conduct, the lawyer must withdraw from the representation to comply with Model Rule 1.16. Moreover, if the lawyer knows that the client plans to proceed with action that will result in a crime or a fraud, Model Rule 1.2(d) may require that the lawyer's withdrawal be "noisy." Model Rule 1.2 prohibits a lawyer from "assist[ing] a client in conduct that the lawyer knows is criminal or fraudulent." A silent withdrawal may assist a client by allowing him to go forward with criminal acts or fraud undetected. If this is the case, Model Rule 1.2 seems to require a noisy withdrawal to avoid assisting wrongful conduct. The prohibition against assisting a client in wrongful or fraudulent activity only applies when the lawyer "knows" that the conduct of the client is criminal or fraudulent. Thus, the standard appears to allow some leeway for lawyer conduct when the state of the law is unclear regarding what constitutes a crime or fraud under the given circumstances. Like Model Rule 1.6, Rule 1.2 relates to future crimes and frauds. It does not prohibit a lawyer from assisting a client in defending against an action charging criminal or fraudulent conduct. Additionally, Model Rule 1.2(d) does not require that the lawyer

---

1. *See* MODEL RULE 1.7 and MODEL RULE 1.9.
2. Strategem Dev. v. Heron, 756 F. Supp. 789 (S.D.N.Y. 1991).
3. *Id.* at 793-94.
4. MODEL RULE 1.16(a).

Chapter 18: Termination and Withdrawal from Representation 429

engage in an investigation in order to confirm or discredit statements that the client has made to the lawyer.

Permissive Bases for Withdrawal

Model Rule 1.16 permits a lawyer to withdraw when the withdrawal "can be accomplished without materially adverse effect on the interests of the client" except when a tribunal orders the lawyer to continue the representation.[5] Model Rule 1.16 also allows withdrawal in six situations despite materially adverse effects to the client.[6] These six categories of cases, which are discussed below, present the rather open-ended tests of Rule 1.16 and give guidance to the lawyer who wishes to withdraw from a representation because she believes her client is in the wrong. Should a lawyer be allowed to withdraw from a representation based merely on a different moral perspective, or should withdrawal be allowed only in situations of gravity, such as a violation of the law? The answer depends on whether the client's actions or the lawyer's reactions to the client constitute the sort of extreme circumstances outlined by the subsection of the rule providing a basis for permissive withdrawal.

Some of these bases present a situation of culpable conduct by the client. For example, the rule allows withdrawal when the client has used or is using the lawyer's services to commit a crime or fraud. The lawyer may withdraw if the client "persists in a course of action involving the lawyer's services that the lawyer reasonably believes is criminal or fraudulent."[7] Similarly, withdrawal is allowed if the client "has used the lawyer's services to perpetrate a crime or fraud."[8] The fact that the client's objective is, in the lawyer's view, "repugnant or imprudent"[9] satisfies another ground for withdrawal. Withdrawal is appropriate when the client fails to make timely payment for services rendered as agreed in the contract for representation. Rule 1.16 states that withdrawal is permitted if the client "fails substantially to fulfill an obligation to the lawyer regarding the lawyer's services."[10] The provision typically relates to a failure to pay. It requires that the lawyer give the client "reasonable warning that the lawyer will withdraw unless the obligation is fulfilled."[11]

---

5. MODEL RULE 1.16(b), (c).

6. MODEL RULE 1.16(b).

7. MODEL RULE 1.16(b)(1).

8. MODEL RULE 1.16(b)(2); *see also* Matza v. Matza, 610 A.2d 702 (Conn. 1992) (lawyer acted appropriately in withdrawing when client engaged in fraud).

9. MODEL RULE 1.16(b)(3); *see also* James P. Hemmer, *Resignation of Corporate Counsel: Fulfillment or Abdication of Duty*, 39 HASTINGS L.J. 641 (1988).

10. MODEL RULE 1.16(b)(4).

11. *Id.*

430 ISSUES OF LEGAL ETHICS IN THE PRACTICE OF ENVIRONMENTAL LAW

A more general basis for permissive withdrawal protects the lawyer from financial hardship, allowing withdrawal from representation when "the representation will result in unreasonable financial burden on the lawyer or has been rendered unreasonably difficult by the client."[12] Finally, a catchall provision allows the lawyer to withdraw for "good cause."[13] The situation posed in the introduction to this section asked whether a lawyer could withdraw because he believes that the client is about to engage in conduct that is criminal or morally wrong. Such a belief appears to form a basis for permissive withdrawal based on the good cause standard. Additionally, the situation may fall within the exception that allows the lawyer to withdraw based on the client's insistence on pursuing a "repugnant or imprudent"[14] objective.

Financial Burden on the Lawyer

A client's failure or refusal to pay a lawyer for services as the contract of employment requires has traditionally been recognized as the basis for a lawyer to withdraw from representation. The Model Rules expand this traditional category somewhat to include recognition of the lawyer's right to withdraw if the representation results in "unreasonable financial burden on the lawyer."[15] This basis for withdrawal appears to be more expansive than the traditional power of the lawyer to withdraw for nonpayment of fees. If the financial burden on the lawyer results from the lawyer's failure to estimate the complexity and time requirements of the matter, however, the issue is problematic. In such a case, it seems inevitable that withdrawal will have a material adverse effect on the interests of the client because the client will be forced to retain another lawyer. If the lawyer seeking to withdraw is correct that the fee quoted to the client is unreasonably low, it seems likely that the client will be unable to find a replacement counsel at the same rate. Thus, even if withdrawal is allowed by the court on the basis of unreasonable financial burden to the lawyer, the client arguably may have a contract action against the lawyer for failure to fulfill his obligations under the contract.

Financial Burden on the Lawyer: Environmental Example

The fact that most lawyers enter contracts based on an hourly rate of pay rather than a project price minimizes the likelihood of withdrawal because of

---

12. *Id.*
13. MODEL RULE 1.16(b)(6). *See* Lasser v. Nassau Cmty. Coll., 457 N.Y.S.2d 343 (App. Div. 1983) (allowing motion to withdraw on basis that client required lawyer to seek approval of another lawyer on all future actions in case).
14. MODEL RULE 1.16(b)(3).
15. MODEL RULE 1.16(b)(4).

Chapter 18: Termination and Withdrawal from Representation 431

financial burden. In such cases, the lawyer continues to have the right to withdraw based on failure of the client to pay.[16] Lawyers who represent environmental plaintiff public interest groups frequently face the problem of personal financial burden as a result of the representation. This fact is a natural outgrowth of the uncertainty of the funding for the representation. Unless public interest groups have wealthy members, they may need to raise funds for litigation in novel ways, such as bake sales, car washes, and marches to attract public attention. Additionally, lawyers representing public interest groups, particularly public interest groups formed on an ad hoc basis to fight a particular development, find that the litigation may be sidetracked or drag on longer than anticipated, resulting in the lawyer losing time for other (paying) cases or in an inability to attract new cases. Lawyers who undertake representation of ad hoc environmental public interest groups often do so because of strong personal commitments. Even when the parties intended that the representation be compensated, the lawyer often cuts the billing on the matter or does at least a portion of the work on a pro bono basis.

Even though a lawyer may have accepted a representation because of strong personal feelings that coincide with those of the groups and with knowledge that part of his efforts might not be fully compensated, the representation may reach the point where the financial burden on the lawyer is too great to allow him to go forward. In such cases, courts face difficult issues in determining whether withdrawal is appropriate. It is quite likely that withdrawal will have a material adverse effect on the client in such a circumstance. The reality of the need for lawyers to earn a living should be something that each lawyer considers before undertaking representation of a client that is likely to face difficulties in funding the litigation or other representation. Securing the commitment of several lawyers who believe in a particular cause is one way of minimizing the risk by sharing the burden of such representations.

Strong Personal Feelings

A lawyer should not withdraw from representation absent a compelling reason.[17] The potential for strong personal feelings exists in environmental cases and can impair a representation.[18] The Model Rules present several bases for

---

16. The basis for withdrawal for nonpayment is set forth in MODEL RULE 1.16(b)(4).

17. This is particularly true when the lawyer is appointed by the court to the representation.

18. *See* C. Baird Brown, *Ethical Considerations in Solid Waste Practice*, C659 ALI-ABA 339 (Jan. 30, 1992) (noting that the commentary of MODEL RULE 1.16 "gives no guidance on what constitutes an objective that is repugnant or imprudent" and noting that moral considerations should be included within the standard).

withdrawal that are fairly open-ended. While the Model Rules clearly indicate that it is the client, not the lawyer, who determines the objectives of representation,[19] the corollary to this power of the client is provided in the lawyer's ability to withdraw because he finds the objectives set by the client to be "repugnant or imprudent."[20]

Strong Personal Feelings (2002 Revision)

A new comment to revised Model Rule 1.10, on the topic of imputed conflicts, gives the example of strong personal beliefs as a clear case where a conflict of beliefs could be a legitimate basis for a withdrawal by a lawyer that would not result in disqualification of other lawyers in his firm.

> The rule in paragraph (a) does not prohibit representation where neither questions of client loyalty nor protection of confidential information are presented. Where one lawyer in a firm could not effectively represent a given client because of strong political beliefs, for example, but that lawyer will do no work on the case and the personal beliefs of the lawyer will not materially limit the representation by others in the firm, the firm should not be disqualified. On the other hand, if an opposing party in a case were owned by a lawyer in the law firm, and others in the firm would be materially limited in pursuing the matter because of loyalty to that lawyer, the personal disqualification of the lawyer would be imputed to all others in the firm.[21]

Environmental Context

Environmental issues often implicate core values of people, including lawyers. The fact that the health or the life of individuals or of the community can be implicated in environmental hazards sets the stage for strong personal feelings. It would not be surprising for a lawyer with young children to have a strong reaction to a person charged with dumping hazardous wastes near the school of the lawyer's children or endangering other schoolchildren or creating less dramatic or direct risks of harm. Moreover, even in cases involving less dramatic facts, it is conceivable that a lawyer's strong personal feelings relating to environmental violations or policies of the client could come within the permissive withdrawal standard.

---

19. MODEL RULE 1.2(a).
20. MODEL RULE 1.16(b)(3).
21. MODEL RULE 1.10 cmt. 3 (2002).

In *Ethical Considerations in Solid Waste Practice*, C. Baird Brown asserts that moral views should be included among the bases for permissive withdrawal, despite the lack of guidance from Model Rule 1.16.[22] He also notes that the withdrawal by counsel in environmental matters often may be less prejudicial than it may appear at first blush. "The fact that representation is generally not before a tribunal will make it easier to withdraw. If you believe your client proposes to do unacceptable harm to the environment or needlessly obstruct public or private action, you can generally withdraw."[23]

Confidentiality

The lawyer's discretion regarding withdrawal from representation is significantly broader than the lawyer's discretion to reveal client information. Some of the most difficult ethical questions may arise from dangers that a lawyer knows about by virtue of knowing client information. Clearly, the duty to maintain the client's confidences survives the termination of the relationship, generally leaving the lawyer bound to hold confidences after the client-lawyer relationship has ended. The ability of the lawyer to reveal client information is unaffected by the right to withdraw. In other words, no matter what the level of significance of the basis for withdrawal, the right of the lawyer to reveal confidences is unaffected by the circumstances. Even if the lawyer withdraws as a result of mandatory withdrawal, as when the representation would result in a violation of law, the duty of confidentiality remains intact. Thus, Model Rule 1.6 remains the primary standard for determining whether a lawyer is permitted to reveal client information.

Impact on Other Parties

The fact that a lawyer withdraws from a representation is likely to have a significant impact on the client. It may also have a significant impact on other parties and individuals not named in the matter. In environmental cases, the stage is set for problems simply because of the large number of parties often represented by one lawyer in environmental cases. In the context of Superfund litigation or allocation procedures, a lawyer may represent dozens or even hundreds of parties. The complex nature of the factual and scientific evidence that the lawyer must understand in environmental matters also makes it difficult to find an appropriate replacement if a lawyer is disqualified by a court or decides he should withdraw.

---

22. C. Baird Brown, *supra* note 18, at 343.
23. *Id.*

434   ISSUES OF LEGAL ETHICS IN THE PRACTICE OF ENVIRONMENTAL LAW

Clearly, a lawyer's withdrawal from an environmental representation may have significant adverse impacts on individuals not part of the cause of action. Many individuals may watch from the sidelines in a matter of great interest to them because they know that an environmental public interest group is going forward with litigation. These individuals may give money to support the cause rather than becoming a party to the action. Likewise, many employees of a corporation may be adversely impacted if the corporation's ability to carry on a defense in an environmental matter or other litigation is compromised by virtue of a lawyer's withdrawal. It is unlikely that courts will be able to quantify or take into account the interests of such third parties, however.

Courts faced with the need to decide whether to grant a motion to withdraw are justified in assessing the impact of the withdrawal on the client, other parties, and the public. A court may refuse to allow a lawyer to withdraw from a representation even though it is satisfied that the lawyer has established one or more of the bases for withdrawal. Model Rule 1.16 recognizes this power of tribunals, stating: "When ordered to do so by a tribunal, a lawyer shall continue representation notwithstanding good cause for terminating the representation." When a lawyer is appointed by a court to represent an indigent party in litigation, a court may also refuse to allow the lawyer to withdraw from the representation. Model Rule 1.16 does not create judicial power. Rather it recognizes the existing power of courts and other tribunals. Absent such a provision in the Model Rule, courts and tribunals would have inherent power to refuse to allow withdrawal.

Moreover, court rules typically prohibit lawyers from withdrawing from litigated cases without the consent of the court.[24] Although Model Rule 1.16 makes no mention of seeking the approval of the court or other tribunal for withdrawal, the comment to the Rule makes clear that the lawyer should seek court approval for withdrawing, at least when the lawyer has been appointed to the case. It states: "When a lawyer has been appointed to represent a client, withdrawal ordinarily requires approval of the appointing authority. See also Rule 6.2. Difficulty may be encountered if withdrawal is based on the client's demand that the lawyer engage in unprofessional conduct."[25]

A lawyer representing a group of 108 plaintiffs addressed a conflict question to the Michigan Standing Committee on Professional and Judicial Ethics as it developed. Six of the 108 clients decided to seek a new lawyer and terminate representation with the existing lawyer. While 102 clients wished to

---

24. *See, e.g.*, New York Civil Practice Law and Rules DR 2-110, 22 N.Y. C.R.R. 1200.15; *see also* Lawrence J. Fox & Jeanine M. Kasulis, *Firing Clients*, LITIGATION 3 litig. 29 (1995).

25. MODEL RULE 1.16 cmt. 3.

continue the representation with the original lawyer, the lawyer had access to the medical records of all the clients, including the six who terminated the representation. Accordingly, the court found that the lawyer had a continuing duty to maintain the confidentiality of that information. Because the individuals in the two groups were in competition for a common insurance fund, the court found that the two groups were in direct conflict with each other and that the lawyer must withdraw.[26]

This situation raises difficult questions. The fact that a lawyer requests withdrawal from a case does not bind a court or other tribunal. It could refuse to grant the lawyer's motion to withdraw from representing the 102 clients. In such a case, the lawyer's duty to the six departing clients is not clear. Must the lawyer attempt to disregard the confidential information that he knows about their cases, or may he use that knowledge to benefit the clients he continues to represent? It seems impossible as a practical matter to disregard or blot out the knowledge. Even assuming that a lawyer could sequester his knowledge about the cases of the six clients and blot it out of his memory, such a limitation on his representation seems to amount to "pulling his punches" to the detriment of his remaining clients. The duty of loyalty to the remaining clients seems to require that the lawyer use his best efforts to secure for those clients the best result possible. Accordingly, requiring the lawyer to continue the representation may force the lawyer into a situation that violates the duty of full and zealous representation.

Withdrawal (2002 Revision)

The 2002 revision to the Model Rules clarified the provision permitting withdrawal by the lawyer from a representation he considers repugnant. The provision, as revised, allows a lawyer to withdraw from representation if "the client insists upon taking action the lawyer considers repugnant or *with which the lawyer has a fundamental disagreement*."[27] The change, noted by italics for the addition, provides a helpful gloss to lawyers regarding permissive withdrawal. The revision deleted the word "imprudent" and supplied the language allowing a "fundamental disagreement" to provide a basis for withdrawal when the withdrawal can be accomplished without material adverse effect on the client. This addition clarifies the right of a lawyer to withdraw when she and the client disagree with respect to fundamental aspects of the representation as long as the withdrawal does not materially impair the client's interests.

---

26. St. Bar of Mich. Standing Comm. on Prof'l and Judicial Ethics, Op. RI-98, 1991 WL 5198777 (1991).

27. Model Rule 1.16(b)(4) (2002) (italics added to show new language).

The 2002 revision to Model Rule 1.16 clarified the obligation of the lawyer to a tribunal when seeking to withdraw. The rule, as revised, states that the lawyer "must comply with applicable law requiring notice to or permission of the tribunal when terminating a representation."[28]

The 2002 revision to Model Rule 1.7 also makes clear that the typical cure for a conflict of interest is withdrawal by the lawyer. "If a conflict arises after representation has been undertaken, the lawyer *ordinarily must* withdraw from the representation, *unless the lawyer has obtained the informed consent of the client under the conditions of paragraph (b).*"[29]

---

28. MODEL RULE 1.16(c) (2002).

29. MODEL RULE 1.7 cmt. 4 (2002) (italics added to indicate new language).

Conclusion

Lawyers today face new questions and old questions in new situations. Developments that have already occurred and those that will come in the future (both legal and technological) call for reassessment of the vision of the lawyer adopted by the Model Rules. As society and the practice of law undergo changes, new issues must be considered in light of the principles of legal ethics. Modern dangers and responsibilities demand reevaluation of norms and laws and even the time-honored concepts of legal ethics.

Although the basic guiding principles of ethics have significant continuity, application of these principles to new problems is by no means easy, perhaps especially in the practice of environmental law. The numerous prescriptive laws applicable to the environmental area make it necessary for lawyers to understand and be able to access and research effectively both the rules of ethics applicable to their conduct and federal and state statutes and regulations relevant to particular hazards. Lawyers should consult the rules regularly in relation to questions occurring in practice. Moreover, each lawyer should strive to develop knowledge about the precepts laid out in the rules and the practical wisdom to apply them.

GLOSSARY

ABA Canons of Professional Ethics—The earlier statement of ethical rules adopted by the ABA on August 27, 1908. The canons were amended numerous times between their original adoption and the subsequent passage of the Model Code.

ABA Model Code of Professional Responsibility—A statement of ethical rules formulated by the ABA and adopted by the House of Delegates on August 12, 1969. The model was superseded by the ABA Model Rules of Professional Conduct. Nevertheless, several states have retained the Model Code as the basis for their ethical rules. Some of these states are currently considering adoption of new rules based on the ABA Model Rules.

ABA Model Rules of Professional Conduct—The statement by the ABA of ethical rules endorsed by the American Bar Association and set forth for the "basis of providing a process for invoking the disciplinary process." The ABA House of Delegates adopted the Model Rules on August 2, 1983, and amended the rules at least 28 times before its comprehensive revision in 2002.

ABA Standing Committee on Ethics and Professional Responsibility—An ABA committee, consisting of 10 members, that issues formal and informal opinions relating to ethics issues under the Model Rules.

Admonition—A private reprimand. *See* ABA Standards for Imposing Lawyer Sanctions 2.6.

Appearance of Impropriety—Rules of ethics in some states require lawyers to avoid the appearance of impropriety as well as impropriety itself. *See* Dillock v. Board, 656 S.W.2d 265 (1983). Generally, such a rule is justified as necessary to promote public confidence in a legal system.

Arbitrary and Capricious—The standard of review often applicable to agency action.

440   ISSUES OF LEGAL ETHICS IN THE PRACTICE OF ENVIRONMENTAL LAW

Beauty Contest—The process of interviewing and evaluating several firms or lawyers to decide which to retain as counsel. Even in such a process, the duty of confidentiality may apply to information gained about the potential client. *See* Bridge Products, Inc. v. Quantum Chemical Corp., 1990 U.S. Dist. LEXIS 5019 (N.D. Ill. 1990).

Board of Professional Responsibility—The name given to most state administrative bodies charged with investigating and prosecuting disciplinary complaints against lawyers.

Canons—Subparts of the Model Code of Professional Responsibility. The nine canons are very brief statements of the ethical principles upon which the ethical considerations are based. Also the title of the ethical standards adopted by the ABA in 1908 and superseded by later standards.

Competence—The foundational duty of a lawyer. Rule 1.1 states the duty of the lawyer to provide competent representation and defines competent representation as requiring "the legal knowledge, skill, thoroughness and preparation reasonably necessary for the representation." *See* Model Rule 1.1.

Cap—One method of remediating a Superfund site where a layer of clay is installed over the top of a landfill that has been remediated.

Categorical Exclusion—Agency action that does not need an environmental impact statement or environmental assessment under NEPA, generally because it is listed in an agency's regulation as the type of action that will not have a significant effect on the human environment.

Chinese Wall—A metaphor for the practice of screening client information from discovery by members of a firm by setting up procedures where all personnel in the firm are warned that a particular member has information about a matter and admonishing all personnel to avoid any discussion or sharing of information about the matter. (See *Screening.*)

Conflict of Interest—A relationship or interest of a lawyer that results in inability to accept or continue a representation of another client or, in some cases, allows the lawyer to continue the representation only with the informed consent of the clients.

Constituents—Individuals through whom an organization acts, such as officers, directors, employees, shareholders, and other individuals authorized to act for an organizational client such as a corporation. *See* MODEL RULE 1.13, comment 2. When working with constituents of a corporation, a lawyer has a duty to advise individuals that the lawyer is representing the corporation rather than the individuals when the lawyer finds that such individuals have interests adverse to the organization. *See* MODEL RULE 1.13 comment 7.

De Minimis—The class of PRPs that have contributed to a Superfund site in amounts of 1 percent (1%) or less of the overall hazardous substances. *See, e.g.,* Martin A. McCrory, *Who's on First: CERCLA Cost Recovery, Contribution, and Protection,* 37 Am. Bus. L. J. 3, fn 201 (1999), *citing* William B. Johnson, Annotation, *Propriety of Negotiated Settlements in Government Cleanup Actions Under Federal Hazardous Waste Statutes,* 114 A.L.R. Fed. 1,78 (1993); Andrew Kenefick, Steve Krchma, Leonard Sorrin, Sara Beth Watson, *Assessing Conflicts of Interest at Multi-Party Superfund Sites: From First Involvement to Litigation,* 4 Envtl. L. 721 n.9 (1998), *citing* 42 U.S.C. § 9622(g)(1)(A).

Denial of Fees—One remedy against a lawyer who has represented clients despite a conflict of interest.

Designated Responsible Corporate Official—The official chosen by the company to certify the accuracy of environmental reports.

Disability—A lawyer may, in most jurisdictions, voluntarily place his license on disability status as a result of physical or mental impairment.

Disbarment—Termination of the status of lawyer and the privileges of practicing law. *See* ABA Standards for Imposing Lawyer Sanctions 2.2.

Discharge (verb)—To release a substance into the environment. In the case of toxic or hazardous substances, such a release may be a violation of the Clean Water Act, the Clean Air Act, and/or the Comprehensive Environmental Response, Compensation and Liability Act. (noun)—The substance discharged.

Discharge Monitoring Report—A report required under the Clean Water Act, the Clean Air Act, or other environmental legislation, requiring a discharger to report to the EPA or some other state or federal agency the effluent or ambient emissions from a plant or other waste source.

Disciplinary Counsel—A lawyer employed by a Board of Professional Responsibility who investigates and prosecutes allegations of lawyer violations and ethical principles.

442 ISSUES OF LEGAL ETHICS IN THE PRACTICE OF ENVIRONMENTAL LAW

Disciplinary Rules—These are subparts of the Model Code of Professional Responsibility. They are stated under each canon and are mandatory rules. A lawyer found in violation of a disciplinary rule is subject to sanctions.

Disposal—Discharge of a substance. Disposal may be through either active conduct or mere passive conduct. Under the Comprehensive Environmental Response, Compensation and Liability Act, some courts have held that passive migration of a hazardous substance constitutes a disposal.

Disqualification Motion—A motion to the court generally by opposing counsel seeking an order disqualifying the lawyer from representing a client in pending litigation.

Disqualification Order—A judicial order holding the lawyer disqualified from representing a party in pending litigation, typically as a result of a motion by opposing counsel setting forth a conflict of interest that is created by the representation.

EIS—Environmental Impact Statement, the report that the National Environmental Policy Act ("NEPA") requires that federal agencies file for all major federal actions significantly affecting the environment. *See* 42 U.S.C. § 4332(2)(C) (2000) (establishing environmental impact statement requirement).

Endangered Species Act—An act passed by Congress in 1973 that provides protection to plants and animals in danger of extinction. "The term 'endangered species' means any species which is in danger of extinction throughout all or a significant portion of its range other than a species of the class Insecta determined by the Secretary to constitute a pest whose protection under the provisions of this chapter would present an overwhelming and overriding risk to man." 16 U.S.C. § 1532(6) (2000).

Environmental Assessment (EA)—An evaluation of property for the purpose of determining whether or not hazardous substances have contaminated the property. Environmental assessments are common today as a requirement for evaluating property that is offered for sale. The Comprehensive Environmental Response, Compensation and Liability Act (CERCLA) has created an incentive for evaluating property prior to transfer. The term "environmental assessment" is also used to refer to an evaluation to determine whether or not an environmental impact statement is required under the National Environmental Policy Act (NEPA).

Environmental Ethics—The philosophical movement that argues for preservation of natural resources and values for their own sake.

Ethical Considerations—Subparts of the Model Code of Professional Responsibility. These are stated under each of the canons of Professional Responsibility. These are aspirations, stating goals for lawyers but not providing a basis for discipline.

FIFRA—The Federal Insecticide, Fungicide, and Rodenticide Act. This Act regulates pesticides. 7 U.S.C. § 136-136(y) (2000).

Formal Opinion—Opinion issued by the ABA Standing Committee on Ethics and Professional Responsibility that is designated as formal because of the Committee's determination that the particular opinion is of "widespread interest or unusual importance." *See* ABA Standing Committee on Ethics and Professional Responsibility Rules of Procedure—Rule 3. The formal opinions are issued in writing by the board on a case-specific basis in response to an inquiry from a lawyer. Generally, boards will not opine on questions relating to the conduct of lawyers other than the inquiring lawyer. The formal opinions are not binding on courts.

Hazardous Substance—Any substance of a pollutant or contaminant that meets the definition under state or federal statute or rule and is regulated because of its toxic, explosive, corrosive, flammable, infectious, radioactive or otherwise hazardous characteristics.

Hearing Committee—A committee appointed by the state's Board of Professional Responsibility, which conducts disciplinary hearings. Generally, the hearing committee consists of three to five lawyers randomly selected from a panel of lawyers appointed by the Supreme Court of the state.

Hot Potato Rule—The doctrine that holds that it is improper for a lawyer to drop a client to represent another client in an action against that client whom the lawyer dropped or dismissed.

Human Environment—All of the environment that could have an impact on persons as well as wildlife. For example, NEPA requires an environmental impact statement to outline the impact of a proposed agency action.

Industrial Waste—Byproducts of chemical or industrial processes that are stored or discarded, including liquid, solid, sludge, or gaseous materials.

444 ISSUES OF LEGAL ETHICS IN THE PRACTICE OF ENVIRONMENTAL LAW

Informal Opinion—Opinion issued by the ABA Standing Committee on Ethics and Professional Responsibility designated as informal based on the determination of the Committee that the opinion does not meet the standard set for formal opinions (that is, that the opinion is of "widespread interest or unusual importance"). The Standing Committee has discontinued the practice of issuing informal opinions.

Informed Consent—A waiver of a conflict by a client after receiving "adequate information about the risks and advantages" of a representation. See Model Rule 1.0(e) (2002); Restatement (Second) of the Law Governing Lawyers § 202. For a client to be capable of giving informed consent, the lawyer must provide full disclosure of information relevant to making the decision to consent.

Inquirer—The lawyer requesting an opinion from the ABA or a state ethics board.

Lawyers Helping Lawyers—A national organization with branch divisions in many cities. This organization seeks to help lawyers, particularly those with substance abuse problems.

Misrepresentation—A statement of law or fact a lawyer knows to be false. Additionally, a failure to make a disclosure may be the "equivalent of an affirmative misrepresentation," in some circumstances. *See* Model Rule 3.3, Cmt. 2.

NGO (Nongovernmental Organization)—NGOs include citizen action groups and environmental public interest groups such as the Sierra Club, the World Wildlife Fund, Ducks Unlimited, and National Resources Defense Council. A synonym is "public interest groups (PIG)." The term public interest group, or PIG, seems to have fallen out of use in favor of the term NGO.

Notice of Violation (NOV)—A written notice to a regulated entity by an agency that indicates that the entity has failed to meet compliance levels of discharge or work practice requirements or is otherwise in violation of statutory or regulatory law. The Notice of Violation is generally followed by a Show Cause Hearing in which the regulated entity bears a burden of establishing that the finding of a Notice of Violation is not justified.

Permit—A document provided by a regulatory agency authorizing specified conduct by the regulated entity. Examples include permits under the Clean Water Act to discharge effluents into the waters of the nation at certain prescribed levels, similar permits setting levels of allowed discharges into the air, and permits under the Endangered Species Act allowing the taking of an endangered or threatened species for justified purposes authorized under the Act.

Positional Conflicts—A type of conflict of interest, also called an issue conflict, which considers the question whether a lawyer can ethically take differing positions on a legal issue on behalf of different clients.

Preamble—The introductory statement of the ABA relating to the rationale for the Model Rules.

Pro hac vice—The legal device by which many jurisdictions allow nonresident lawyers to appear in the courts of the state without obtaining a license in the state. Generally such practice is allowed only when the lawyer is associated with lawyers licensed by that state and does not practice regularly in the state. *See, e.g.,* Tenn. Code Ann. 23-3-103 (noting that the practice is allowed "as a matter of courtesy" to lawyers of states that afford Tennessee lawyers a similar privilege to appear in its courts).

Pro Se Representation—Representing oneself. Individuals may represent themselves without violating unauthorized practice laws. *See* Unauthorized Practice of Law.

Probation—A limitation on a lawyer's practice, generally as a result of misconduct, allowing practice within specific conditions. *See* ABA Standards for Imposing Lawyer Sanctions 2.7.

PRP—Potentially responsible party. An entity subject to liability under the Comprehensive Environmental Response, Compensation and Liability Act (CERCLA).

Reprimand—Declaration that a lawyer's conduct has been improper. *See* ABA Standards for Imposing Lawyer Sanctions 2.5.

RCRA—The Resource Conservation and Recovery Act of 1976. This Act requires that employers implement a hazard communication program and a medical surveillance program in addition to developing safety programs and decontamination procedures for properties contaminated with hazardous waste. The Act regulates disposal activities relating to hazardous wastes, solid waste, underground storage tanks, oil waste, and medical waste. It presents a "cradle-

446   ISSUES OF LEGAL ETHICS IN THE PRACTICE OF ENVIRONMENTAL LAW

to-grave" system, regulating hazardous waste at all stages of its existence from generation to final disposal. Indeed, it regulates waste beyond the grave, in a sense, in that monitoring of the disposal (or grave) continues after the hazardous wastes have been disposed of.

Revolving Door—The phenomenon of government lawyers leaving agencies to undertake private practice is sometimes referred to as the "revolving door" of government practice. The term seems to be a misnomer, since the great majority of the lawyers involved simply go *out* the door to take up private practice after obtaining experience working in a governmental agency such as EPA. These practitioners revolve back in the door not to reappointment in government agency ordinarily but, rather, to appear before a board or other regulatory tribunal of the agency they formerly represented.

Sanctions—Discipline imposed by a board of professional responsibility as a result of lawyer conduct.

Screening—The practice of keeping confidential information known by one or more lawyers in a firm from being communicated to others in the firm. Sometimes referred to as erecting a "Chinese Wall." The 2002 Model Rules defined "screened" as "the isolation of a lawyer from any participation in a matter through the timely imposition of procedures within a firm that are reasonably adequate under the circumstances to protect information that the isolated lawyer is obligated to protect under these Rules or other law." Revised Model Rule 1.0(k).

Scope—Introductory section of the ABA Model Rules of Professional Conduct.

Solid Waste Disposal Act (SWDA)—The Solid Waste Disposal Act has 10 subtitles, including RCRA. SWDA, Pub. L. No. 89-272, 79 Stat. 992 (1965). It was passed in 1965 and amended in 1976 by RCRA. It contains a subtitle on regulation of underground storage tanks, medical waste tracking, and hazardous waste management.

Suspension—Removal of a lawyer from practice for a specific period of time. *See* ABA Standards for Imposing Lawyer Sanctions 2.3.

Terminology—A section of the ABA Rules of Professional Conduct providing definitions. The Ethics 2000 presentation of definitions is set to be included in Rule 1.0.

Toxics—Hazardous substances discharged into the air and water or found in the soil that fall into statutory or regulatory categories of toxicity.

Unauthorized Practice of Law—The practice of law by one who is not licensed to practice within the jurisdiction in which the representation occurs. The unauthorized practice of law occurs when one who is not a lawyer provides legal advice or represents a party in connection with litigation or other legal matters. State statutes prohibit nonlawyers from practicing to protect the public from incompetent legal representation. Unauthorized practice also occurs when a lawyer licensed in one state provides legal services in a state in which he or she is not licensed. Individuals may represent themselves without violating unauthorized practice laws. *See Pro Se* Representation. Generally, ethical rules do not define unauthorized practice of law. It is defined by statute.[1]

Underground Storage Tank (UST)—A below-ground tank used to store gasoline, petroleum products, or other liquid substances. USTs are regulated by state law as part of a delegated program under the Solid Waste Disposal Act. *See* RCRA Part I.

UPL—*See* Unauthorized Practice of Law.

---

1. *See* Haverty Furniture v. Foust, 124 S.W.2d 694 (1939).

APPENDIX A

Acronym List

ABA	American Bar Association
ACCA	American Corporate Counsel Association
AICPA	American Institute of Certified Public Accountants
ADR	alternative dispute resolution
ALAS	Attorneys' Liability Assurance Society, Inc. (provider of malpractice insurance for lawyers)
ALI	American Law Institute
ALJ	Administrative Law Judge
APA	Administrative Procedure Act
CAA	Clean Air Act
CERCLA	Comprehensive Environmental Response, Compensation and Liability Act
COI	Conflict of Interest
CWA	Clean Water Act
DOJ	United States Department of Justice
EA	Environmental Assessment
EAB	Environmental Appeal Board
EIS	Environmental Impact Statement
EPA	United States Environmental Protection Agency
ESA	Endangered Species Act
FIFRA	Federal Insecticide, Fungicide, and Rodenticide Act
FOIA	Freedom of Information Act

FRCP	Federal Rule of Civil Procedure
MDP	multidisciplinary practice
MJP	multijurisdictional practice
MRPC	ABA Model Rules of Professional Conduct of 1983 and 2002
MCPR	ABA Model Code of Professional Responsibility of 1969
NEPA	National Environmental Policy Act
NGO	nongovernmental organization
OCR	Office of Civil Rights of the EPA
PRP	potentially responsible party
RCRA	Resource Conservation and Recovery Act
SEC	Securities & Exchange Commission
SWDA	Solid Waste Disposal Act
UPL	unauthorized practice of law
UST	Underground Storage Tank

APPENDIX B

Frequently Asked Questions

Getting Help

Before launching into particular questions, one should consider the most frequently asked questions by lawyers struggling with an ethics concern is: "Where can I go to get help figuring out this difficult issue?" Because numerous avenues for help exist, there are many answers to this question.

Most big firms have an ethics committee or a partner in charge of ethics compliance. The lawyers on such committees or serving in the capacity of compliance partner are a valuable resource for lawyers facing ethical problems. Additionally, the Boards of Professional Responsibility of most jurisdictions have toll-free telephone numbers and hot lines set up to answer questions and give advice to practicing lawyers. Likewise, most states also have confidential counseling services to help lawyers who are experiencing drug or substance abuse problems or other problems that may affect competency. Several law schools support ethics centers or centers on professionalism, which may provide similar services through telephone or Web site connections.[1] The ABA also provides a service for lawyers who have an ethical problem or question. The ABA ETHICSearch is an online resource for lawyers needing to research an ethics issue. This service is free to ABA members on a preliminary basis. Queries are answered without charge in most cases.[2] A lawyer who needs additional research on a question can authorize the ABA lawyers at ETHICSearch to continue the project at reasonable rates.[3]

---

1. For example, the University of South Carolina School of Law supports the Nelson Mullins Riley & Scarborough Center on Professionalism. *See* http://www.law.sc.edu/profcenter/nmrshome.htm (last visited April 4, 2003).
2. *See* http://www.abanet.org/cpr/ethicsearch/ (last visited April 4, 2003).
3. The phone number for ETHICSearch is 1-800-285-2221.

451

Question 1

Should a lawyer with an ethics problem refer to the ABA Model Rules of Professional Conduct?

Answer 1

The ABA Model Rules provide good background and a good overview of the models presented to the states in 1983 and 2002 as part of the process of updating the rules of ethics beyond the principles set forth earlier in the ABA Model Code. Nevertheless, consulting the rules of the jurisdiction of licensure will give the lawyer a more directly applicable rule to his ethics problem. If the lawyer's problem becomes a dispute and a complaint is filed with the Board of Professional Responsibility, the Board will, of course, apply the rule of the jurisdiction. Although the state rules are based on the ABA Model Rules in most cases, the potential for variation in language exists. The following answers reference some state rules that vary from the Model Rules.

Question 2

Is it ever proper under Model Rule 1.6 to disclose information about a client's past criminal conduct?

Answer 2

Model Rule 1.6 has no exception for disclosing information relating to past conduct even if it is criminal. For example, in *People v. Belge,* 83 Misc. 2d 186 (372 N.Y.S.2d 798), *aff'd* 50 A.D.2d 1088, 376 N.Y.S.2d 771 (1975), the court held that a lawyer was not liable for failing to disclose privileged information given to him by his client about the location of the bodies of his client's victims. A lawyer may be required by law to disclose information in some circumstances, however. Although the 1983 version of Model Rule 1.6 does not address this point specifically, the 2002 version of the rule acknowledges that a lawyer may disclose information required by law. A lawyer may be required by law to disclose information about a client though it is confidential under Rule 1.6 because the information does not fall within the attorney-client privilege. This could be because the client information is not a communication or because the crime-fraud exception applies to the information. For example, evidence is not excludable as a communication if it is eyewitness evidence. The attorney-client privilege protects a client by exempting testimony in a court or other tribunal about a communication with his lawyer. It does not protect communications between a lawyer and client that further an ongoing criminal enterprise, however. In such a case, a prosecutor could subpoena the lawyer to testify about the information if the evidence is essential to the case.

Question 3

Can a lawyer report information if he believes that the client is engaged in a crime or a fraud that will occur in the future?

Answer 3

Whether or not the lawyer is permitted to disclose this information depends on whether the situation fits within one of the exceptions in Model Rule 1.6.

Question 4

What is meant by professionalism within the legal sphere?

Answer 4

"Professionalism" refers to standards of conduct in the practice of law, such as issues of civility and courtesy, for which a lawyer should strive but which should not be the basis for liability.[4]

Question 5

Can a conflict of interest be cured by the consent of the clients to the representation?

Answer 5

Consent is necessary but not always sufficient. In other words, if a conflict exists, it is necessary for clients to consent to a representation for it to go forward. But such consent does not always cure the conflict in the sense of allowing the lawyer to maintain both representations. Other requirements in addition to consent must be met to allow the representation to go forward. In the case of a conflict in which representation of a client is "directly adverse to another client," the lawyer can accept the representation only if he "reasonably believes the representation will not adversely affect the relationship with another client" and both clients consent. In the case of a representation that may be "materially limited" by the lawyer's responsibility to another client, or to a third party, or to his own interests, client consent may cure the conflict only if the lawyer "reasonably believes the representation will not be adversely affected." The rule also notes that with regard to representation of multiple clients in a single matter, the lawyer must explain the "implications of the common representation and the advantages and risks involved."

---

4. *See* ABA Lawyer's Pledge of Professionalism, ABA Section of Tort and Insurance Practice, Lawyer's Creed of Professionalism.

454   ISSUES OF LEGAL ETHICS IN THE PRACTICE OF ENVIRONMENTAL LAW

Question 6

Can a situation arise in which the clients' consent does not cure a conflict?

Answer 6

Yes. Such conflicts are sometimes referred to as "nonwaivable" or "non-consentable" conflicts.

Question 7

Is it true that a conflict can be cured if a firm has a screening mechanism (sometimes referred to as a Chinese Wall) in place to prevent the dissemination of confidential information between lawyers?

Answer 7

Such screening is not a cure in most cases of conflicts. Typically, screening is allowed as a curative measure by which a former government lawyer may affiliate with a law firm. Screening is not a cure for all conflicts, however. Even with the use of such screening, a lawyer who, in her prior job, partici-pated "personally and substantially as a public officer or employee" must not represent a private client in connection with the same matter.

Question 8

If a person represented by counsel voluntarily initiates conversation about the case with another lawyer who represents another party in the lawsuit, is it appropriate for this lawyer to respond and carry on a conversation with that person?

Answer 8

No. The client or witness who is represented by a lawyer does not have the power to waive the No-Contact Rule. The decision to waive the rule can only be made by the lawyer representing that client. Accordingly, if a lawyer knows that the individual initiating conversation about the case is represented, the lawyer should refrain from any discussion of the matter with the represented person.

Question 9

If an individual has been injured, may a lawyer visit that person at home or in the hospital and advise the individual concerning whether he should bring a cause of action against the person who caused the injury?

Appendix B: Frequently Asked Questions   455

Answer 9

Probably not. Model Rule 7.3 prohibits a lawyer from soliciting employment from a prospective client by in-person contact. Even if it is true that the individual who has been injured has a cause of action, the contact of the lawyer in such case is improper. Exceptions exist to this prohibition for relatives.

Question 10

Can a lawyer be disbarred for remaining silent when his client perjures himself on the stand?

Answer 10

Model Rule 3.3 establishes the lawyer's duty of candor toward tribunals. It prohibits a lawyer from knowingly making a false statement of material fact or law or failing to disclose a material fact in its dealings with a tribunal to avoid assisting a client in a criminal or fraudulent act. Model Rule 3.3 also requires that lawyers disclose directly adverse legal authority when that authority is not provided by opposing counsel. The rule prohibits a lawyer from "offer[ing] evidence that the lawyer knows to be false."

APPENDIX C

Sample Letters Relating to Professional Legal Services[*]

Letter Seeking Consent to Concurrent Representation

Esquire
land address
E-mail address

[In-House Counsel]
Current Client
Address

     Re: Potential Representation

Dear X:

I write to give you information about potential representation I have been asked to provide to PRPs (Potential Clients) regarding settlement offers from the Allocator of the Fictitious Superfund sites and, additionally, to solicit your views and judgment regarding whether my involvement in this matter runs counter to the wishes of Current Client in any respect. If you deem the arrangement to be acceptable to Current Client, I also request that you return a signed copy of this letter to me to document your consent on behalf of Current Client to the additional representation described.

  I have received inquiries from some of the defendants recently sued in the litigation relating to the Superfund sites regarding my willingness to represent them in settlement negotiations. The scope of my representation, if I accept the representation, would be settlement solely. I would have no involvement in the litigation itself. Additionally, any representation I would undertake would terminate at the time a settlement offer is accepted by the PRP group or by express agreement on August 15, 2000, whichever occurs first. With the consent of Potential Clients, I will be happy to provide you with a copy of my letter setting forth the terms and conditions of the representation.

---

[*] These samples are provided for discussion purposes and do not present legal advice. The provision of these documents does not constitute the practice of law in any jurisdiction, and the author makes no representation or warranty regarding their suitability or fitness.

458   ISSUES OF LEGAL ETHICS IN THE PRACTICE OF ENVIRONMENTAL LAW

In my judgment, this situation does not present a conflict under the State Rules of Professional Responsibility that guide the conduct of lawyers. The basis for this judgment is that although I represent Current Client in other, unrelated matters, I do not represent Current Client at this site or in any matter related to the site or Current Client's involvement at the site. Additionally, some lawyers who represent PRPs at this site are serving as counsel for other PRPs in the settlement negotiations based on their judgment, and that of their clients, that the clients' interests are served and not adversely affected by such representation. Their judgment may be based in part on the fact that the PRP group is urging settlement with the newly named defendant-corporations.

I recognize my duty of loyalty and confidentiality toward my clients, and I wish never to compromise the interests of Current Client. My analysis of the particulars of the matter under consideration leads me to conclude that my representation of Potential Client does not compromise the interests of Current Client for three reasons. First, my representation of two PRPs at this site will not affect the financial interests of Current Client. The PRP group recognizes that settlement with the numerous PRPs currently not involved in settlement negotiations would benefit the PRPs conducting the feasibility study and remediation at the site. Second, the representation in no way interferes with my responsibilities toward Current Client and will enhance my knowledge in the practical application of one of my primary practice areas, Superfund negotiations. This is an area in which I have represented Current Client in the past. Third, even in the unlikely event that Current Client became a PRP at this site, it is not certain that my representation would present a conflict. As I understand the settlement process implemented in this matter, there are potential reopeners at the site for the possibility of failure of the "fix." Nevertheless, these reopeners would not be affected by the amount particular PRPs have contributed through the settlement process. Rather, the percentage of responsibility would be based on the volume of waste product allocable to each PRP.

My judgment is that my involvement as a lawyer for PRPs in the settlement process at the Fictitious sites would in no way compromise the interests of Current Client. In addition to making my own assessment of the ethical and fiduciary issues, I have discussed this issue with the following ethics experts who also practice in the environmental context: Firm Expert, DOJ Expert. I would appreciate receiving your views regarding this potential representation. A convenient way for you to convey your consent and assent to this limited representation is to sign the additional copy of this letter enclosed and return it to me. Thank you for the careful consideration you have given this question.

Very truly yours,

Lawyer

Corporate Representative

Appendix C: Sample Letters Relating to Professional Legal Services 459

SAMPLE AGREEMENT FOR PROFESSIONAL SERVICES[1]

This Agreement for Professional Services ("Agreement") is made this _____ day of _____, 2000, between [Lawyer] and _____("Client"). In consideration of the mutual promises set forth herein, Lawyer and Client agree as follows:

[Identify Co-Clients, organizational clients, and special roles or powers of representatives of organizational clients in detail.]

1. Scope of Services
Lawyer will perform certain services (the "Services") for Client including ... [describe scope of services and agreed limitations.]

2. Compensation
A. Client shall compensate Lawyer for Services rendered at the rate of ____per hour plus expenses, including travel expenses. Lawyer reserves the right to modify the rate amount upon _____ days written notice to Client [consider timing, e.g., once during each 12-month period following the first anniversary date of this Agreement].

B. Client shall reimburse Lawyer for all expenses and disbursements incurred in connection with the performance of Services, plus reasonable administrative charges, including filing, copying, . . . [include expenses agreed to]

3. Invoices and Payment
Lawyer will submit invoices for Services once a month, which Client shall pay upon receipt. A service charge of -% per month may be added to all accounts not paid within 30 days following the date of receipt of invoice.

---

1. This form agreement draws on an agreement and comments by the late Professor John C. Carter, former faculty member of the University of Memphis School of Law. It relates specific agreements relating to a hazardous waste site as an example of a type of contract within environmental practice. The author makes no warranty regarding the agreement or its usefulness. It is offered as a general document to consider the types of arrangements between lawyers and their clients and does not constitute the practice of law.

460 ISSUES OF LEGAL ETHICS IN THE PRACTICE OF ENVIRONMENTAL LAW

4. Information and Data

Lawyer is not responsible for the quality or accuracy of data or information, nor for the sampling programs or methods from which the data or information was developed, where such data or information is provided by or through Client or third parties. Lawyer shall not be liable for any obligations, claims, losses, damages, penalties, actions, judgments, suits, costs or expenses arising from, related to or in connection with Lawyer's reliance upon, or use of, data or information furnished by Client or third parties.

5. Indemnification and Arbitration

Client agrees to defend, indemnify, and hold harmless Lawyer from and against any and all claims arising from, occasioned by or in connection with (i) the escape, seepage, leakage, spillage, discharge, emission, release or threat of release from the Site of any hazardous or toxic waste, substance or constituent of other substance, and (ii) Lawyer's reliance upon or use of data or information furnished by Client. Client further agrees to submit any disputes arising from the events described above to arbitration between Lawyer and Client as detailed in the attached Appendix. [Consider arbitration for some representations of sophisticated clients. *See* Revised Model Rule 1.8 cmt. 14 and ABA Formal Opinion 02-425 regarding requirements and safeguards for binding arbitration.]

6. Client's Representations

Client represents that it has provided to Lawyer (i) all information in Client's possession regarding any known, potential or possible health or safety hazard existing on or under the Site, with particular reference to hazardous substances, waste or conditions; (ii) all relevant data and information in Client's possession and to the environmental, geologic, and geotechnical conditions of the Site and surrounding area; and (iii) all plans in Client's possession correctly showing the location of subsurface installations, such as pipes, tanks, cables, and utilities.

7. Confidentiality

Each party shall retain as confidential all information and data furnished to it by or through the other party in connection with this Agreement when such information is designated or understood to be confidential, and neither party shall disclose such information or data to any third party except agreement with the other party or as required by law, including statute, regulation, ordinance, judicial order, or governmental agency process.

Appendix C: Sample Letters Relating to Professional Legal Services 461

8. Re-use of Documents

All documents (the "Documents") prepared by Lawyer pursuant to this Agreement are instruments to assist it in the performance of the Services. The Documents are not intended to be suitable for use by any third party or for re-use by Client. Any re-use of Documents by Client or provision of Documents to third party shall be at Client's sole risk and without liability to Lawyer.

9. Term and Termination of Agreement

In addition to all other legal and equitable rights that may be available, either party may terminate this Agreement by ____ days after notice thereof. Otherwise this Agreement shall terminate upon completion and acceptance of Services or by mutual agreement of the parties. A failure to pay for legal services rendered under this contract will result in the termination of this agreement at the end of _____ days after notice by Lawyer to Client that payment has not been received and that termination will occur in the event that payment is not made within a prescribed time period.

10. Assignment

This Agreement may not be assigned by either party without the prior written consent of the other.

11. Waiver of Future Conflicts

[Consider Waiver of Future Conflicts for some clients. *See* MR 1.7 cmt. 22 (2002), ABA Formal Opinion 93-372 (1993).]

12. Client Decisions Regarding Settlement and Other Matters

[Consider terms relating to reports by lawyer, settlement of group claims, and other decisions about representation and voting by members of organizational clients such as public interest groups. *See* Model Rule 1.4 Cmt. 3.]

13. Applicable Law

This Agreement is governed by, and shall be construed in accordance with, the laws of the state of _____.

14. Entire Contract

This Agreement (i) constitutes the entire contract between the parties with respect to the subject matter hereof; (ii) supersedes all prior oral or written understandings and agreements which are merged herein; and (iii) may be amended only by a written instrument signed by both parties.

IN WITNESS WHEREOF, the parties have caused this Agreement to be executed by their duly authorized representatives.

"Client"   "Lawyer"

By: _____   By: _____
              Signature   Signature

_____   _____
           Printed Name   PrintedName

_____   _____
               Date   Date

Appendix C: Sample Letters Relating to Professional Legal Services   463

Letter Terminating Representation

Esquire address
E-mail address

[In-house Counsel]
Client address

>   RE: Completion/termination of Representation Relating
>   to the matter of [. . .]

Dear X:

As you know, we have completed our representation on your behalf in the captioned matter. It has been our pleasure to represent you and your interests in this matter. I hope that you are fully satisfied with the resolution of the issues and the settlement achieved. Additionally, I hope that if you have legal needs in the future, you will feel free to contact me. Thank you for allowing us to serve your legal needs in this representation.

>   Very truly yours,
>
>   Lawyer

Table of Cases

A

Abbott v. Kidder Peabody & Co., Inc., 42 F. Supp. 2d 1046 (D. Colo. 1999), 231, 231 n.158, 246 n.228, 312, 313 nn.230–231

Abell v. Potomac Ins. Co., 858 F.2d 1104 (5th Cir. 1988), 158 n.349

Actel Corp. v. Quicklogic Corp., 1996 WL 297045 (N.D. Cal. 1996), 274 n.59

Adams v. Aerojet—Gen. Corp., 104 Cal. Rptr. 2d 116 (Cal. App. 2001), 252 n.256, 272, 272 nn.52–53

Adlman; United States v., 68 F. 3d 1495 (2d Cir. 1995), 162 n.368, 424 n.6

Advanced Technology Corp. v. Eliskim, Inc., 87 F. Supp. 2d 780 (N.D. Ohio 2000), 33 n.163

Affiliated Ute Citizens of Utah v. U.S., 406 U.S. 128 (1978), 142 n.252

Ahern v. Gaussoin, 611 F. Supp. 1465 (D. Or. 1985), 139 n.236

Airport Car Rental Antitrust Litig., In re, 470 F. Supp. 495 (N.D. Cal. 1979), 273 nn.55–56

Aken v. Business Industry Health Group, Inc., 885 F. Supp. 1474 (D. Kan. 1995), 361 n.48

Alcocer v. Superior Court, 254 Cal. Rptr. 72 (Ct. App. 1988), 322, 322 nn.261–265

Allen v. Academic Games Leagues of America, Inc., 831 F. Supp. 785 (C.D. Cal. 1993), 202 n.10

Allied Realty of St. Paul v. Exchange Nat'l Bank of Chicago, 283 F. Supp. 464 (D. Minn. 1968), *aff'd,* 408 F.2d 1099 (8th Cir. 1969), 282 n.95

American Cyanamid Co. v. Hercules Powder Co., 211 F. Supp. 85 (D. Del. 1962), 69, 70 nn.106–107

American Protection Insurance Co. v. MGM Grand Hotel-Las Vegas, 748 F.2d 1293 (9th Cir. 1984), 363 n.59

Amoco Chemicals Corp. v. MacArthur, 568 F. Supp. 42 (D.C. Ga. 1983), 107 n.80

Anderson v. Dunn, 19 U.S. 204 (1821), 19 n.79

Anderson v. Hale, 2001 WL 417991 (N.D. Ill. Apr. 23, 2001), 133 nn.205–206

Apex Oil Co. v. Wickind Oil Co., 1995 U.S. Dist. LEXIS 6398 (N.D. Cal. 1995), 35 n.173

Armstrong v. McAlpin, 625 F.2d 433 (2d Cir. 1980), *vacated on other grounds,* 449 U.S. 1106 (1981), 267 n.32

Arpadi v. First MSP Corp., 628 N.E.2d 1335 (Ohio 1994), 61, 61 n.57

Arthur Young & Co.; United States v., 465 U.S. 805 (1984), 376 n.17

Atasi Corp. v. Seagate Tech., 847 F.2d 826 (Fed. Cir. 1988), 275 n.62

AT&T; United States v., 642 F.2d 1285 (D.C. Cir. 1980), 162 n.366, 174 n.442

Auric v. Cont'l Cas. Co., 331 N.W.2d 325 (Wis. 1983), 152 n.308

Ausherman v. Bank of America Corp., 212 F. Supp. 2d 435 (D.Md. 2002), 1 n.2

B

Balla v. Gambro, Inc., 560 N.E.2d 1043 (Ill. App.Ct. 1990), 180 n.468

Balla v. Gambro, Inc., 584 N.E.2d 104 (Ill. 1991), 85, 86 nn.173–176, 180, 180 n.469, 181 nn.470–474, 182 n.476, 182 n.480

Banks, In re (State v. Jones), 726 S.W.2d 515 (Tenn. 1987), 278 n.84

Basic, Inc. v. Levinson, 485 U.S. 224 (1988), 142 n.252, 143 nn.254–255

Bates v. Law Firm of Dysart, Taylor, Penner, Lay, Lewandowski, 844 S.W.2d 1 (Mo. Ct. App. 1992), 151 n.297, 154 n.319

Bates v. State Bar of Arizona, 433 U.S. 350 (1977), 393 n.10, 394, 394 nn.13–22

Bennet v. Berg, 710 F.2d 1361 (8th Cir. 1983), 18

Bereano, In re, 719 A.2d 98 (D.C. 1998), 16 n.64

Bereano; United States v., 161 F.3d 3 (4th Cir. 1998), *cert. denied,* 526 U.S. 1130 (1999), 16 n.65

Bieter Co., In re, 16 F.3d 929 (8th Cir. 1994), 162 n.371

Binette v. Dyer Library Ass'n, 688 A.2d 898 (Me. 1996), 151 n.302

Birbrower, Montalbano, Condon & Frank v. Superior Court, 17 Cal. 4th 119, 949 P.2d 1, 70 Cal. Rptr. 2d 304 (Cal. 1998), 385, 385 nn.23–24, 386 n.25

Blue Bell, Inc. v. Peat, Marwick, Mitchell & Co., 715 S.W.2d 408 (Tex. App. 1986, *writ ref'd n.r.e.*), 153 n.316

Blum v. Stenson, 465 U.S. 886 (1984), 408

Boughton v. Cotter Corp., 65 F.3d 823 (10th Cir. 1995), 151 n.303

Bowman v. Two, 704 P.2d 140 (Wash. 1985), 158 n.349

Brennan's, Inc. v. Brennan's Rests., Inc., 590 F.2d 168 (5th Cir. 1979)., 222 n.104

Bridge Prods., Inc. v. Quantum Chem. Corp., 1990 U.S. Dist. LEXIS 5019 (N.D. Ill. 1990), 276 n.69

Bridge Products, Inc. v. Quantum Chemical Corp., 58 U.S.L.W. 2733, 20 Envtl. L. Rep. 20,940 (N.D. Ill. Apr. 27, 1990), 262 n.3

Bridge Products, Inc. v. Quantum Chemical Corp., 1990 WL 70857 (N.D. Ill. 1990), 60 n.53, 65, 65 nn.77–79, 277, 277 nn.74–80, 278 n.81

Briggs & Stratton Corp. v. Concrete Sales and Services, Inc., 174 F.R.D. 506 (M.D. Ga. 1997), 172 n.424

Brinkley v. Farmers Elevator Mut. Ins. Co., 485 F.2d 1283 (10th Cir. 1973), 47 n.3

Brittain; United States v., 931 F.2d 1413 (10th Cir. 1991), 83 n.159

Brobeck, Phleger & Harrison v. Telex Corp. 602 F.2d 866 (9th Cir. 1979), 408 n.40

Brooks v. Zebre, 792 P.2d 196 (Wyo. 1990), 152 n.305

Brown v. Eighth Judicial Dist. Court, 14 P.3d 1266 (Nev. 2000), 202 n.10

Brumley v. Touche, Ross & Co., 463 N.E.2d 195 (Ill. App. Ct. 1984), 159 n.352

Bryan, In re, 61 P.3d 641 (Kan. 2003), 124 n.144

Buckley v. Gray, 42 P. 900 (Cal. 1895), 152 n.304

Burkhart v. Semitool, 5 P.3d 1031 (Mont. 2000), 85 n.170, 86 n.177, 183 nn.486–487, 184 nn.488–490, 186, 187 n.503

Burson, In re, 909 S.W.2d 768 (Tenn. 1995), 383 n.10

Bush; State v., 493 P.2d 1205 (Ariz. 1972), 302 n.180

C

Caldwell v. Bechtel, 631 F.2d 989 (D.C. Cir. 1980), 149, 149 nn.286–287

Calvin Klein Trademark Trust v. Wachner, 198 F.R.D. 53 (S.D.N.Y. 2000), 174 n.441, 424 n.3

Camden v. State of Maryland, 910 F. Supp. 1115 (D. Md. 1996), 361

Campbell Industries v. M/V Gemini, 619 F.2d 24 (9th Cir. 1980), 363 n.59

Canaday v. United States, 354 F.2d 849 (8th Cir. 1966), 68 n.92

Cardona v. General Motors Corp., 942 F. Supp. 968 (D.N.J. 1996), 254 n.268

Caremark International, Inc. Derivative Securities Litigation, In re, 698 A.2d 959 (Del. Ch. 1996), 80 n.146

Carson Harbor Village Ltd. v. Unocal Corp., 227 F.3d 1196 (9th Cir. 2000), 32 n.159

Cavallaro v. United States, 153 F. Supp. 2d 52 (D. Mass. 2001), 424 n.5

Cavallaro v. United States, 284 F.3d 236 (1st Cir. 2002), 162 n.369

CDMG Realty Co.; United States v., 96 F.3d 706 (3d Cir. 1996), 32

Cello-Foil Products, Inc. v. Michigan Mut. Liability Co., 1995 WL 854728 (Mich., Aug. 15, 1995), 310 n.216

Cendant Corp. PRIDES Litigation, In re (Welch & Forbes Inc. v. Cendant Corp.), 243 F.3d 722 (3d Cir. 2001), 402 n.10

Chambers v. NASCO, Inc., 501 U.S. 32, 111 S. Ct. 2123 (1991), 195 n.546, 412 n.68

Chambers v. Superior Court, 121 Cal. App. 3d 893 (1981), 284 n.111

Chen; United States v., 99 F.3d 1495 (1996), 166 n.392

Chevron U.S.A., Inc., In re, 109 F.3d 1016 (5th Cir. 1997), 66 n.80, 66 n.82

Chrispens v. Coastal Refining & Marketing, Inc., 897 P.2d 104 (Kan. 1995), 249

Cinema 5, Ltd. v. Cinerama, Inc., 528 F.2d 1384 (2d Cir. 1976), 213 n.63, 220 n.93

Citizens to Preserve Overton Park, Inc. v. Volpe, 401 U.S. 402 (1971), 50

City of. See name of city

Clagett v. Dacy, 420 A.2d 1285 (Md. Ct. Spec. App. 1980), 158 n.350

Clark v. Sun Refining & Mktg. Co., 1990 WL 91072 (Del. Super. 1990), 131

Clay v. Doherty, 608 F. Supp. 295 (N.D. Ill. 1985), 226 n.121

Clinard v. Blackwood, 46 S.W.3d 177 (Tenn. 2001), 253, 253 n.261, 254 n.264

Coalition for Clean Air v. S. Calif. Edison Co., 791 F.2d 219 (9th Cir. 1992), 411 n.62

Collins v. Binkley, 750 S.W.2d 737 (Tenn. 1988), 151 n.297, 153 n.314, 154 n.319

Collins v. Reynard, 607 N.E.2d 1185 (Ill. 1992), 145 n.267

Colton v. United States, 306 F.2d 633 (2d Cir. 1962), *cert. denied,* 371 U.S. 951, 83 S. Ct. 505, 9 L. Ed. 2d 499 (1963), 68 n.94

Columbia/HCA Healthcare Corp., In re, 293 F.3d 289 (6th Cir. 2002), 164–65, 165 nn.386–387

Comm. on Prof'l Ethics and Grievances v. Johnson, 447 F.2d 169 (3d Cir. 1971), 48 n.8

Commonwealth Ins. Co. v. Stone Container Corp., 178 F. Supp. 2d 938 (N.D. 2001), 208 n.32

Condon, Estate of v. McHenry, 76 Cal. Rptr. 2d 922 (Ct. App. 1998), 386

468   ISSUES OF LEGAL ETHICS IN THE PRACTICE OF ENVIRONMENTAL LAW

Considine v. Compass Group USA, 2001 WL 880531 (Ct. Appeal N.C. 2001), 85 n.171

Cook Consultants, Inc. v. Larson, 700 S.W.2d 231 (Tex. App. 1985, writ ref'd n.r.e.), 153 n.316

Copper Market Antitrust Litigation, In re (Viacom Inc. v. Sumitomo Corp.), 200 F.R.D. 213 (S.D.N.Y. 2001), 424 n.7

Corbin, State ex rel. v. Ybarra, 777 P.2d 686 (Ariz. 1989), 172, 173 n.430

Costanzo; United States v., 625 F.2d 465 (3d Cir. 1980), 71, 72 n.117

Crews v. Buckman Laboratories Int'l, 2001 WL 687137 (Tenn. Ct. App. 2001), 85 n.171

Crews v. Buckman Laboratories Int'l Inc., 2002 WL 1050247 (Tenn. 2002), 86, 87 n.179, 180 n.469, 185, 185 n.496

D

DaRosa v. Arter, 416 Mass. 377, 622 N.E.2d 604 (1993), 150 n.296

David Welch Co. v. Erskine & Tulley, 250 Cal. Rptr. 339 (Cal. Ct. App. 1988), 90 n.4

Davin, LLC v. Daham, 746 A.2d 1034 (N.J. Sup. Ct. 2000), 151 n.299

Davis v. Sun Ref. & Mktg. Co., 671 N.E.2d 1049 (Ohio Ct. App. 1996), 143 n.258, 144 n.260

DCA Food Indust. v. Tasty Foods, Inc., 626 F. Supp. 54 (W.D. Wis. 1985), 65 n.79

Dean v. Dean, 607 So. 2d 494 (Fla. App. 4th Dist., 1992), 163 n.377

Dean v. Harrington, 668 F. Supp. 646 (E.D. Tenn. 1987), 8 n.33

Decker, In re Marriage of, 606 N.E.2d 1094 (Ill. 1992), 164 n.380

Del-Val Fin. Corp. Sec. Litig., In re, 158 F.R.D. 270 (S.D.N.Y. 1994), 290 n.140

DePallo; People v., 2001 WL 735739 (N.Y. July 2, 2001), 115 n.115

Disciplinary Proceedings Against Eisenberg, Matter of, 344 N.W.2d 169 (1984), 201 n.8

Diversified Services, Inc. v. Simkins Indus., 974 F. Supp. 1448 (S.D. Fla. 1997), 34 n.166

Dixon Ticonderoga Co. v. Estate of O'Connor, 248 F.3d 151 (3d Cir. 2001), 26, 26 n.126, 27 nn.127–128

Doe, In re, 801 F. Supp. 478 (D.N.M. 1992), 368 n.73

Doe, Matter of, 801 F. Supp. 478 (D.N.M. 1992), 368 n.73, 368 n.75, 369 n.76

Dondore v. NGK Metals Corp., 152 F. Supp. 2d 662 (E.D. Pa. 2001), 354 nn.15–16

Douglas v. Donovan, 704 F.2d 1276 (D.C. Cir. 1983), 7 n.25

Dresser Industries, Inc., In re, 972 F.2d 540 (5th Cir. 1992), 209 n.41

Duncan v. Board of Disciplinary Appeals, 898 S.W.2d 759 (Tex. 1995), 137, 137 n.224, 137 nn.227–227

Durflinger v. Artiles, 563 F. Supp. 322 (D. Kan. 1981), 155, 155 nn.332–333

E

Easton v. Strassburger, 199 Cal. Rptr. 383 (Ct. App. 1984), 22, 22 n.103, 149 n.284

Edmunds v. Superior Court, 29 Cal. Rptr. 2d 281 (Ct. App. 1994), 23 n.110

Table of Cases   469

Edwards; United States v., 39 F. Supp. 2d 716 (M.D. La. 1999), 303

EEOC v. Waterfront Comm'n of New York Harbor, 665 F. Supp. 197 (S.D.N.Y. 1987), 7 n.25

Eisenberg v. Gagnon, 766 F.2d 770 (3d Cir. 1985), cert. denied, 474 U.S. 946 (1985), 336 n.14

Ellis; United States v., 90 F.3d 447 (11th Cir. 1996), 163 n.377

Employers Ins. of Wausau v. Amcast Indus. Corp., 709 N.E.2d 932 (Ohio Ct. App. 1998), 309 n.216

Environmental Ins. Declaratory Judgment Actions, In re, 600 A.2d 165 (N.J. Super. Law Div. 1991), 362, 362 nn.54–55

Equilon Enterprises, LLC v. Consumer Cause, Inc., 85 Cal. App. 4th 654 (Dec. 18, 2000), 55

Estate of Condon v. McHenry, 76 Cal. Rptr. 2d 922 (Ct. App. 1998), 386

Eureka Invest. Corp. v. Chicago Title Ins. Co., 743 F.2d 932 (D.C. Cir. 1984), 194 n.544

F

Fasing v. Lafond, 944 P.2d 608 (Colo. Ct. App. 1997), 410 n.53

Faucheux, In re, 818 So. 2d 734 (La. 2002), 23 n.111, 312 n.224

Ferry, In re, 774 A.2d 62 (R.I. 2001), 384 n.20

Fina, Inc. v. Arco, 200 F.3d 266 (5th Cir., Jan. 4, 2000), 34 n.165

Financial Technologies Int'l Inc. v. Smith, 2000 WL 1855131 (S.D.N.Y. 2000), 80 n.149

First American Carriers, Inc. v. Kroger Co., 787 S.W.2d 669 (Ark. 1990), 253, 253 n.260, 254, 254 n.266

First City Bancorporation, In re, 282 F.3d 864 (5th Cir. 2002), 19 n.81, 43 nn.11–13

First National Bank of Durant v. Trans Terra Corporation International, 142 F.3d 802 (5th Cir. 1999), 328, 328 n.8

Fisher, In re, 51 F.2d 424 (S.D.N.Y 1931), 69 n.105

Fisher v. United States, 425 U.S. 391 (1976), 162 n.364

Flaherty v. Weinberg, 492 A.2d 618 (Md. 1983), 152 n.307

Flatt v. Daniel, 3 U.S.L.W. 2417, No. S031687 (Cal. 1994), 239

Flatt v. Superior Court, 9 Cal. 4th 275 (Cal. 1994), 252 n.257

Fleming v. State, 270 S.E.2d 185 (Ga. 1980), 302 n.180

Florida Bar v. Went For It, Inc., 515 U.S. 618 (1995), 395, 396

Flynn; State v., 217 A.2d 432 (R.I. 1966), 136 n.217

FMC Corp., In re, 430 F. Supp. 1108 (D.C. W.Va. 1977), 354, 354 nn.18–19, 355 n.20

Folmar v. Elliot Coal Mining Co., 272 A.2d 910 (1971), 146, 146 nn.271–273, 147 n.274

Foran, In re Marriage of, 834 P.2d 1081 (Wash. Ct. App. 1992), 30 n.148

Forti v. New York State Ethics Comm'n, 555 N.Y.S.2d 235 (N.Y. 1990), 280 n.89, 294 n.159

470 ISSUES OF LEGAL ETHICS IN THE PRACTICE OF ENVIRONMENTAL LAW

Fought & Co. v. Steel Engineering & Erection, Inc., 951 P.2d 487 (1998), 386
Fox Searchlight Pictures, Inc. v. Paladino, 89 Cal. App. 4th 294 (Cal. Ct. App. 2001), 183, 183 nn.483–484
Fox Searchlight Pictures, Inc. v. Paladino, 106 Cal. Rptr. 2d 906 (2001), 115 n.115
Friedman v. Comm'r of Pub. Safety, 473 N.W.2d 828 (Minn. 1991), 30 n.148
Friedman v. Dozorc, 312 N.W.2d 585 (Mich. 1981), 158 n.350
Friend, In re, 411 F. Supp.776 (S.D.N.Y. 1975), 99 n.56
Friends of the Earth, Inc. v. Laidlaw Environmental Services, Inc., 120 S. Ct. 693 (2000), 411 n.64
Frost v. Perry, 161 F.R.D. 434 (D. Nev. 1995), 5, 5 n.20, 6 n.23, 9 n.38
F.R.&S., Inc. v. Department of Envt'l Protection, 761 A.2d 634 (Pa. Cmwlth. 2000), 413, 413 n.76
Fusco v. Albany, 509 N.Y.S.2d 763 (1986), 360 n.42

G

General Dynamics Corp. v. Super. Ct., 876 P.2d 487 (Cal. 1994), 85 n.170, 86 n.177, 182, 182 nn.478–480, 183 n.481
General Dynamics v. Superior Court, 7 Cal. 4th 1164 (Cal. 1994), 80, 81 nn.151–152
Georgia-Pacific v. GAF Roofing Manufacturing, 1996 WL 29392 (S.D.N.Y. 1996), 83
Gerald B. Lefcourt, P.C. v. United States, 125 F.3d 79 (2d Cir. 1997), cert. denied, 118 S. Ct. 2314 (1998), 163 n.377
Gerald v. Trunock Plumbing, Heating and Cooling, L.L.C., 768 N.E.2d 498 (Ind. Ct.App. 2002), 275 n.61
Gerard, In the Matter of William J., 634 N.E.2d 51 (Ind. 1994), 403 n.11
Gerrits v. Brannen Banks of Florida, Inc., 138 F.R.D. 574 (D. Col. 1991), 160 n.355
Gionis; People v., 892 P.2d 1199 (Cal. 1995), 320, 320 n.253
Gipson v. Brown, 706 S.W.2d 369 (1986), 253 n.262
Glanzer v. Shepard, 135 N.E. 275 (N.Y. 1922), 152 n.308
Global Van Lines, Inc. v. Superior Court, 144 Cal. App. 3d 483, 192 Cal. Rptr. 609 (1983), 252 n.257
Globe & Rutgers Fire Ins. Co. v. Hines, 273 F. 774 (2d Cir. 1921), 8 n.29
Glueck v. Jonathan Logan, Inc., 512 F. Supp. 223 (S.D.N.Y.), aff'd, 653 F.2d 746 (2d Cir. 1981), 210 n.45
Goebel, In re, 703 N.E.2d 1045 (Ind. 1998), 155, 156 nn.335–337
Goldberger v. Integrated Res., Inc., 209 F.3d 43 (2d Cir. 2000), 408, 408 n.41
Golightly-Howell v. Oil, Chem. & Atomic Workers Int'l Union, 806 F. Supp. 921 (D. Colo. 1992), 85 n.169
Gomez v. Hawkins Concrete Constr. Co., 623 F. Supp. 194 (N.D. Fla. 1985), 144 n.259
Gordon Stafford, Inc.; United States v., 952 F. Supp. 337 (N.D.W.Va. 1997), 83 n.159
Gould, Inc. v. Mitsui Mining & Smelting Co., 738 F. Supp. 1121 (N.D. Ohio 1990), 35 n.172, 299

Table of Cases   471

Grand Jury Matter, In re, 147 F.R.D. 82 (E.D. Pa. 1992), 167, 167 n.399, 173 n.433

Grand Jury Proceedings, In re, 156 F.3d 1038 (10th Cir. 1998), 318 n.243

Grand Jury Proceedings, In re, 680 F.2d 1026 (5th Cir. 1982), 71 n.115, 164 n.378, 166 n.393

Grand Jury Proceedings v. United States, 156 F.3d 1038 (10th Cir. 1998), 81 n.155

Grand Jury Subpoena, Newparent Inc., In re, No. 01-1975 (1st Cir., Dec. 8, 2001), 171 n.420

Grand Jury Subpoenas Dated March 9, 2001, In re, 179 F. Supp. 2d 270 (S.D.N.Y. 2001), 68 n.93

Granewich v. Harding, 985 P.2d 788 (Or. 1999), 152 n.311

Gray v. Rhode Island Dept. of Children, Youth and Families, 937 F. Supp. 153 (D.R.I. 1996), 7 n.25

Great Plains Mutual Ins. v. Mutual Reinsurance Bureau, 150 F.R.D. 193 (D. Kan. 1993), 172 n.423

Greycas, Inc. v. Proud, 826 F.2d 1560 (7th Cir. 1987), 152 n.310

Griffith v. Taylor, 937 P.2d 297 (Ala. 1997), 246 n.226

Guidone, In re, 653 A.2d 1127 (N.J. 1994), 90 n.5

H

Haberstick v. Gordon A. Gundaker Real Estate Co., 921 S.W.2d 104 (Mo. Ct. App. 1996), 149 n.284

Hagerty v. L & L Marine Servs., Inc., 788 F.2d 315 (5th Cir. 1986), 152 n.303

Halprin, In re, 798 P.2d 80 (Mont. 1990), 396 n.31

Halstead v. Murray, 547 A.2d 202 (N.H. 1988), 203 n.15

Hammonds v. Aetna Cas. & Sur. Co., 243 F. Supp. 793 (C.D. Ohio 1965), 20 n.89

Hansen; State v., 862 P.2d 117 (Wash. 1993), 61, 61 n.59, 158, 158 nn.346–348

Hawkins v. King County, 602 P.2d 361 (Wash. Ct. App. 1979), 157, 157 nn.339–341, 158 n.344

Hayes v. Eagle-Picher Industries, Inc., 513 F.2d 892 (10th Cir. 1975), 312, 312 n.226

Haymond v. Lundy, 2000 WL 1824174 (E.D. Pa. Dec. 12, 2000), 19 n.80

Helo Meadows Co. v. Learner Co., 258 F. Supp. 23 (D. Haw. 1966), 282 n.95

Henriksen v. Great American Sav. & Loan, 11 Cal. App. 4th 109 (Cal. App. 1. Dist. 1992), 253 n.262

Henriksen v. Great American Sav. & Loan, 14 Cal. Rptr. 2d 184 (Cal. App. 1 Dist. 1992), 276 n.67

Herber v. Johns-Manville Corp., 785 F.2d 79 (3d Cir. 1986), 151 n.303

Herman v. Crescent Publ. Group, 2000 U.S. Dist. LEXIS 13738 (S.D.N.Y. 2000), 170, 171 nn.418–419

Herman v. Dulles, 205 F.2d 715 (D.C. Cir. 1953), 1 n.3

Heyde v. Xtraman, Inc., 404 S.E.2d 607 (1991), 363 n.59

Heyer v. Flaig, 449 P.2d 161 (Cal. 1969), 152 nn.307–308

Hickman v. Taylor, 329 U.S. 495, 67 S. Ct. 385, 91 L. Ed. 451 (1947), 70 n.106, 171 n.421, 173 n.436

472 ISSUES OF LEGAL ETHICS IN THE PRACTICE OF ENVIRONMENTAL LAW

Holloway v. Arkansas, 435 U.S. 475 (1978), 302 n.180
Horan v. Sun Co., Inc., 152 F.R.D. 437 (D. R.I. 1993), 173 n.433
Horne v. Patton, 287 So. 2d 824 (Ala. 1973), 20 n.89
Horvath; United States v., 731 F.2d 557 (1984), 68, 68 n.96, 68 nn.98–100, 69 nn.101–102
Hoskins v. Droke, 1995 WL 318817 (N.D. Ill. 1995), 85 n.168
Houchens v. Rockwell Int'l Corp., No.93-CI-00158 (Ky. Cir. Ct. May 31, 1996), 21 n.94
Hubbell, In re, 896 S.W.2d 440 (Ark. 1995), 402 n.9
Hughes v. PaineWebber, Jackson & Curtis, Inc., 565 F. Supp. 663 (N.D. Ill. 1983), 276, 277 n.80

I

INA Underwriters Ins. Co. v. Rubin, 635 F. Supp. 1 (E.D. Pa. 1983), 270, 270 n.44, 275, 275 n.62, 276, 276 nn.71–72
Inquiry to Advisory Comm., In re, 616 A.2d 1290 (N.J. 1992), 252 n.258, 281 n.94
In re. See name of party
In re Marriage of. See name of party
In-Store Advertising Secs. Litig., In re, 163 F.R.D. 452 (S.D.N.Y. 1995), 166 n.391
Interstate Commerce Commission; United States v., 78 F. Supp. 580 (D.D.C. Cir. 1948), 8
Interstate Commerce Commission; United States v., 337 U.S. 426 (1949), 8, 8 n.32
In the Matter of. See name of party
Irizarry; State v., 639 A.2d 305 (N.J. Super. 1994), 7 n.25

J

Jackman, In re, 761 A.2d 1103 (N.J. 2000), 386 n.29
Jacobson v. Knepper & Moga, P.C., 706 N.E.2d 491 (Ill. 1998), 86 n.177, 183 n.485
Jacobs v. Schiffer, 47 F. Supp. 2d 16 (D.C. Cir. 1999), 116, 116 nn.120–121, 117 n.122, 189, 189 nn.516–519, 190 nn.520–526, 191 nn.527–528
Jaffee v. Redmond, 116 S. Ct. 1923 (1996), 154 n.324, 154 n.327, 159 n.351
Jaffee v. Redmond, 518 U.S. 1 (1996), 159 n.354
Johnson & Towers, Inc.; United States v., 741 F.2d 662 (3d Cir. 1984), 126 n.157
Jones; State v. (In re Banks), 726 S.W.2d 515 (Tenn. 1987), 278 n.84

K

Kachmar v. SunGard Data Sys., Inc., 109 F.3d 173 (3d Cir. 1997), 85 n.169
Kalamazoo, City of v. Michigan Disposal Services, 125 F. Supp. 2d 219 (W.D. Mich. 2000), 250, 250 nn.245–246, 251 nn.247–253, 264 n.15
Kala v. Aluminum Smelting & Ref. Co., Inc., 688 N.E.2d 258 (Ohio 1998), 252 n.258, 254 nn.267–268
Kashian v. Harriman, 98 Cal. App. 4th 892, 120 Cal. Rptr. 2d 576 (2002), 52
Kasza v. Browner, 133 F.3d 1159 (1998), 9, 9 nn.39–41, 10 n.42

Table of Cases   473

Kelly v. Hunton & Williams, 1999 WL 408416 (E.D. N.Y. 1999), 340, 340 nn.36–38, 341 nn.39–42

Kentucky Bar Association v. Tiller, 641 S.W.2d 421 (Ky. 1982), 384, 384 n.20

Kesselhaut v. United States, 555 F.2d 791 (Cl. Ct. 1977), 290

Keywell Corporation v. Piper & Marbury, L.L.P., 1999 WL 66700 (W.D.N.Y. Feb. 11, 1999); 2000 WL 743970 (W.D.N.Y.), 27, 27 nn.130–132

Kidder Peabody Sec. Litig., In re, 168 F.R.D. 459 (S.D.N.Y. 1996), 424 n.6

Kirkland Const. Co. v. James, 39 Mass. App. Ct. 559, 658 N.E.2d 699 (1995), 150, 150 n.296

Klemm v. Superior Court, 142 Cal. Rptr. 509, 75 Cal. App. 3d 893 (1977), 210 n.45

Koden v. U.S. Dept. of Justice, 564 F.2d 228 (7th Cir. 1977), 391 n.2, 396 n.32

L

Lachman v. Sperry-Sun Well Surveying Co., 457 F.2d 850 (10th Cir. 1972), 147, 147 nn.276–277

Lang v. Reedy Creek Improvement Dist., 888 F. Supp. 1143 (M.D. Fla. 1995), 361 n.48

LaSalle National Bank v. Lake County, 703 F.2d 252 (7th Cir. 1983), 89 n.1, 92, 282, 283 nn.97–103, 310 n.217

Lasser v. Nassau Cmty. Coll., 457 N.Y.S.2d 343 (App. Div. 1983), 430 n.13

Laughlin; United States v., 10 F.3d 961 (2d Cir. 1993), 126 n.157

Lawson v. Nugent, 702 F. Supp. 91 (D.N.J. 1988), 224 n.112

Lemaire v. Texaco, Inc., 496 F. Supp. 1308 (E.D. Tex. 1980), 275 n.62

Leybold-Heraeus Technologies, Inc. v. Midwest Instrument Co., Inc., 118 F.R.D. 609 (E.D. Wis. 1987), 318 n.245

Lincoln Sav. & Loan Ass'n v. Wall, 743 F. Supp. 901 (D.D.C. 1990), 140 n.241

Lindsey, In re, 158 F.3d 1263 (D.C. Cir. 1998), 169, 170 nn.413–416

Lineberger v. State ex rel. Beeler, 129 S.W.2d 198 (1939), 383 n.10

Link v. Wabash R.R. Co., 370 U.S. 626 (1962), 19 n.79

Litton Industries, Inc. v. Lehman Bros. Kuhn Loeb Inc., 125 F.R.D. 51 (S.D.N.Y. 1989), 172 n.422

Lollar v. United States, 376 F.2d 243 (D.C. Cir. 1967), 302 n.180

Lopez; United States v., 115 S. Ct. 1624 (1995), 139 n.237

Lord v. Money Masters, Inc., 435 S.E.2d 247 (Ga. 1993), 49 n.14

Lustic v. Horn, 732 N.E.2d 613 (Ill. App. 1 Dist. 2000), 405, 405 nn.26–28

Lutz v. Chromateux, 725 F. Supp. 258 (M.D. Pa. 1989), 144 n.261

M

Macumber; State v., 544 P.2d 1084 (Ariz. 1976), 72

Manning v. James, Sklar, and Allen, 849 F.2d 222 (6th Cir. 1988), 276

Marcus Bros. Textiles, Inc. v. Price Waterhouse LP, 350 N.C. 214 (N.C. 1999), 22 n.100

Marin v. United States, 814 F. Supp. 1468 (E.D. Wash. 1992), 154 n.321

474   ISSUES OF LEGAL ETHICS IN THE PRACTICE OF ENVIRONMENTAL LAW

Marksman Partners, L.P. v. Chantal Pharmaceutical Corp., 927 F. Supp. 1297 (C.D. Cal. 1996), 142 n.251

Martin v. Lauer, 686 F.2d 24 (D.C. Cir. 1982), 190 n.526

Mason v. Florida Bar, 208 F.3d 952 (11th Cir. 2000), 391 n.1

Matter of. See name of party

Matza v. Matza, 610 A.2d 702 (Conn. 1992), 429 n.8

McCallum v. CSX Transp., Inc., 149 F.R.D. 104 (M.D.N.C. 1991), 362 n.53

McCamish, Lynwood Lesikar & Harriet Lewis Lesikar v. Rappeport, 2000 WL 1281164 (Tex. App. 2000), 149 n.288

McCamish, Martin, Brown & Loeffler v. F. E. Appling Interests, 991 S.W.2d 787 (Tex. 1999), 22 n.99, 149 n.288, 150 nn.290–292, 328 n.6, 333 n.3

McDonald Douglas Corp.; United States v., 961 F. Supp. 1288 (E.D. Mo. 1977), 368 n.75

McEvoy v. Helikson, 562 P.2d 540 (Or. 1977), 153 n.311

McPartlin; United States v., 595 F.2d 1321 (7th Cir.), *cert. denied,* 444 U.S. 833, 100 S. Ct. 65, 62 L. Ed. 2d 43 (1979), 318 n.245, 318 n.246

Meehan v. Hopps, 301 P.2d 10 (Calif. 1956), 35 n.173

Mehaffy, Rider, Windholz & Wilson v. Central Bank Denver, N.A., 892 P.2d 230 (Colo. 1995), 149

Mercer, In re, 652 P.2d 130 (Ariz. 1982), 229 n.141, 230, 230 n.152

Metcalf; State v., 540 P.2d 459 (Wash. Ct. App. 1975), 90 n.12

Micke; United States v., 859 F.2d 473 (7th Cir. 1988), 321

Mid-Atlantic National Bank v. New Jersey Department of Environmental Protection, 474 U.S. 494 (1986), 129

Midboe v. Commission on Ethics for Public Employees, 646 So. 2d 351 (La. 1994), 294 n.158

Moncrete v. Board of Prof'l Responsibility, 25 Tenn. Att. Memo. 32-1 (July 27, 2000), 354 n.14

Montgomery County v. MicroVote Corp., 175 F.3d 296 (3d Cir. 1999), 162 n.370

Morgan v. United States, 380 F.2d 686 (9th Cir. 1967), *cert. denied,* 390 U.S. 962, 88 S. Ct. 1064, 19 L. Ed. 2d 1160 (1968), 68 n.91

Morris, Matter of, 793 P.2d 544 (Az. 1990), 136, 136 nn.220–222

Mourad v. Automobile Club Ins. Ass'n, 465 N.W.2d 395 (Mich. Ct. App.), *appeal denied,* 478 N.W.2d 443 (Mich. 1991), 85 n.167

Murphy, In re, 560 F.2d 326 (8th Cir. 1977), 174 nn.438–439

N

National Wildlife Federation v. EPA, 286 F.3d 554 (D.C. Cir. No. 99-1452, Apr. 19, 2002), 128

Nat'l Mortgage Equity Corp. Mortgage Pool Sec. Litig., In re, 120 F.R.D. 687 (C.D. Cal. 1988), 122 n.137

Natural Resources Defense Council Inc. v. E.P.A., 484 F.2d 1331 (1972), 411, 412 n.66

Table of Cases 475

Nemours Found. v. Gilbane, Aetna Federal Ins. Co., 632 F. Supp. 418 (D. Del. 1986), 1 n.1, 275 nn.62–64

Nevada v. United States, 463 U.S. 110 (1983), 8

Neville v. Vingelli, 826 P.2d 1196 (Ariz. Ct. App. 1991), 396 n.31

Newark, In re City of, 346 N.J. Super. 460 (N.J. Super. Jan. 14, 2002), 7 n.25

Niagara Mohawk Power Corp. v. Stone & Webster Engineering Corp., 125 F.R.D. 578 (N.D.N.Y. 1989), 174 n.440

Niesig v. Team I, 76 N.Y.2d 363 (1990), 163 n.372

Niesig v. Team I et al., 558 N.E.2d 1030 (1990), 361 n.46

Nitla S.A. de C.V., In re, 45 Tex. Sup. Ct. J. 571, 2002 WL 534089 (Tex. Apr. 11, 2002), 72 n.120

Nixon; United States v., 418 U.S. 683 (1974), 8, 133 n.202

Nix v. Whiteside, 475 U.S. 157 (1986), 90 nn.12–13

Nobles; United States v., 422 U.S. 225 (1975), 173 nn.435–436, 175 n.443

North Pac. Lumber Co., State ex rel. v. UNIS, 579 P.2d 1291 (Or. 1978), 165 n.390

Nucor Corp.; United States v., 17 F. Supp. 2d 1249 (N.D. Ala. 1998), 401

O

Occidental Chemical Corp.; United States v., 200 F.3d 143 (3d Cir. 1999), 220

Occidental Chemical Corp. v. OHM Remediation Services Corp., 175 F.R.D. 431 (W.D.N.Y. 1997), 164 n.379, 172, 172 nn.426–428

Ogle v. Fuiten, 466 N.E.2d 224 (Ill. 1984), 152 n.307

Ohrlik v. Ohio State Bar Ass'n, 436 U.S. 447 (1978), 394, 395 nn.25–26, 396

Oklahoma ex rel Oklahoma Bar Ass'n v. Watson, 897 P.2d 246 (Okla. 1994), 34 n.168

Olsen v. Accessory Controls and Equip. Corp., 254 Conn. 145, 757 A.2d 14 (Conn. 2000), 71, 71 n.112, 71 n.114

Olson v. Accessory Controls & Equipment Corp., 757 A.2d 14 (Conn. 2000), 165 n.389, 167, 168 nn.401–403, 173 nn.431–432

Olwell; State v., 394 P.2d 681 (Wash. 1964), 70, 70 nn.109–110

One Wheeler Road Assoc. v. Foxboro Co., 843 F. Supp. 792 (D. Mass. 1994), 129 n.179

Opinion 668 of the New Jersey Advisory Committee on Prof'l Ethics, Matter of, 633 A.2d 959 (N.J. 1993), 361 n.49

Original Grand Jury Investigation, In re, 733 N.E.2d 1135 (Ohio 2000), 133 n.204, 151 n.300

Osborn; United States v., 561 F.2d 1334 (9th Cir. 1977), 194 n.543

P

Parker v. M & T Chems., Inc., 566 A.2d 215 (N.J. Super. App. Div. 1989), 81, 81 n.154, 85 n.168

Paul Oil v. Federated Mutual, No. 97-16190 (9th Cir., Sept. 8, 1998), 329 n.13

Peil v. Speiser, 806 F.2d 1154 (3d Cir. 1986), 143 n.255

476   ISSUES OF LEGAL ETHICS IN THE PRACTICE OF ENVIRONMENTAL LAW

Pennwalt Corp. v. Plough, Inc., 85 F.R.D. 264 (D. Del. 1980), 299, 300 n.177
People v. See name of party
Permian Corp. v. United States, 665 F.2d 1214 (D.C. Cir. 1981), 162 n.366, 164, 164 n.384, 174 n.440
Petition for Rev. of Op. No. 569 of Advisory Comm. on Prof'l Ethics, Matter of, 511 A.2d 119 (N.J. 1986), 280 n.89, 294 n.159
Petition for Review of Op. 552 of Advisory Comm. on Prof'l Ethics, In the Matter of, 507 A.2d 233 (N.J. 1986), 225 nn.115–116
Petroleum Wholesale, Inc. v. Marshall, 751 S.W.2d 295 (Tex. App. 1988), 253 n.261
Pickard Int'l v. Varion Assocs., 670 F. Supp. 1363 (1987), 212 nn.55–56
Poddar; People v., 518 P.2d 342 (Cal. 1974), 154 nn.321–322
Public Service Elec. and Gas Co. v. Associated Elec. & Gas Ins. Services, Ltd. ("AEGIS"), 745 F. Supp. 1037 (D.N.J. 1990), *superceded by regulation Andrews v. Goodyear Tire & Rubber Co., Inc.,* 191 F.R.D. 59 (D.N.J. Feb. 14, 2000), 361 n.49, 364, 364 n.63, 365 n.64
Purcell v. District Attorney for the Suffolk District, 676 N.E.2d 436 (Mass. 1997), 72, 72 n.122, 73 n.123

Q

Quintero v. Jim Walter Homes, Inc., 709 S.W.2d 225 (Tex. App. 1985), 17, 312, 312 n.228

R

Richard Roe, Inc., In re, 68 F.3d 38 (2d Cir. 1995), 175 n.444
Richards v. Commission for Lawyer Discipline, 35 S.W.3d 243 (Tex. App. 2000), 229
Rite Aid Sec. Litig., In re, 139 F. Supp. 2d 649 (E.D. Pa. 2001), 297, 297 nnn.165–166
Roadmaster Industries, Inc. v. Columbia Manufacturing Company, Inc., 893 F. Supp. 1162 (D. Mass. 1995), 337–38
Roadway Exp., Inc. v. Piper, 100 S. Ct. 2455 (1980), 195 n.546, 412 n.68
Roberts v. Ball, Hunt, Hart, Brown & Baerwitz, 57 Cal. App. 3d 104 (Cal. Ct. App. 1976), 153 n.314
Robinson v. United States, 144 F.2d 392 (6th Cir. 1944), 72 n.117
Romo v. Southern Pacific Transp. Co., 139 Cal. Rptr. 787 (1987), 166 n.395
Ronson v. Superior Court, 29 Cal. Rptr. 2d 281 (Ct. App. 1994), 61 n.56
Rosenfeld Const. Co., Inc. v. Superior Court (Sivas), 286 Cal. Rptr. 609 (Cal. App. 5 Dist. 1991), 263 n.9, 272 n.49
Rothman v. Wilson, 121 F.2d 1000 (9th Cir. 1941), 47 n.3
Rowe; United States v., 96 F.3d 1294 (9th Cir. 1996), 80 n.148
Rubin v. Schottenstein, Zot & Dunn, 110 F.3d 1247 (6th Cir. 1997), 158 n.349
Ryan v. Butera, Beausang, Cohen & Brennan, 193 F.3d 210 (3d Cir. 1999), 408 n.40

S

Santa Fe Int'l Corp., In re, 5th Cir. No. 01-40421 (Nov. 7, 2001), 82

Savoie v. Merchants Bank, 166 F.3d 456 (2d Cir. 1999), 408 n.41

Schaffer Equipment Company; United States v., 11 F.3d 450 (4th Cir. 1993), 117, 118 n.128

Schiessle v. Stephens, 717 F.2d 417 (7th Cir. 1983), 270 n.42

Schwimmer; United States v., 892 F.2d 237 (2d Cir. 1989), *cert. denied,* 502 U.S. 810, 112 S. Ct. 55, 116 L.Ed. 2d 31 (1991), 172 n.427

Scruggs v. Roach, 1993 WL 93362 (Tenn. Ct. App. 1993), 338, 338 n.27

Sealed Case, In re, 107 F.3d 46 (D.C. Cir. 1997), 71 n.114

Sealed Case, In re, 676 F.2d 793 (D.C. Cir. 1982), 166 n.394

Servco Pacific Inc. v. Dods, 106 F. Supp. 2d 1034 (D. Haw. 2000), 33 nn.163–164

Shafer Equipment Co.; United States v., 796 F. Supp. 938 (4th Cir. 1993), 331, 332 n.29–31

Shaffer Equip. Co.; United States v., 158 F.R.D. 80 (S.D. W.Va. 1994), 332 n.31

Shapero v. Kentucky Bar Ass'n, 486 U.S. 466 (1988), 393 n.10, 394

Silver Chrysler Plymouth, Inc. v. Chrysler Motors Corp., 518 F.2d 751 (2d Cir. 1975), 214 n.64, 252 n.256, 273 n.58

Silverman v. Ehrlich Beer Corp., 687 F. Supp. 67 (S.D.N.Y. 1987), 7 n.25

Sindona; United States v., 636 F.2d 792 (2d Cir. 1980), 162 n.365

Smith v. Coldwell Banker, 122 F. Supp. 2d 267 (D. Conn. 2000), 120 n.130

Software Tool Works, Inc., In re, 50 F.3d 615 (9th Cir. 1994), 142 n.251

Solid Waste Agency of Northern Cook County v. U.S. Army Corps of Engineers, 121 S. Ct. 675 (2001), 139 n.237

Solow v. W.R. Grace & Co., 632 N.E.2d 437 (N.Y. 1994), 263 nn.10–11, 271, 272, 272 n.48

Spaulding v. Zimmerman, 116 N.W.2d 704 (Minn. 1962), 155 n.330

Stanford v. President and Fellows of Harvard College, 13 Mass.L.Rptr. 77, 2001 WL 716834 (Mass.Super.2001) (Cratsley, J.), *reversed as to Rule 4.2 violation, Messing, Rudavsky & Weliky, P.C. v. President and Fellows of Harvard College,* 436 Mass. 347, 764 N.E.2d 825 (2002), 412

Stare v. Tate, 98 Cal. Rptr. 264 (1971), 176, 176 nn.451–452, 177 n.453

Starkey, Kelly, Blaney & White v. Estate of Nicolaysen, 773 A.2d 1176 (N.J. Super. 2001), 403 n.12

State v. See name of party

Sterling v. Velsicol Chem. Corp., 855 F.2d 1188 (6th Cir. 1988), 151 n.303

Sterling v. Velsicol Chemical Corp., 647 F. Supp. 303 (W.D. Tenn. 1986), *aff'd,* 855 F.2d 1188 (6th Cir. 1988), 146 n.269

Stewart v. Sbarro, 362 A.2d 581 (N.J. Super. Ct. App. Div. 1976), 152 n.311

Stinneford v. Spiegel Inc., 845 F. Supp. 1243 (N.D. Ill. 1994), 85 n.169

Stinson v. Brand, 738 S.W.2d 186 (Tenn. 1987), 153 n.314

Stirum v. Whalen, 811 F. Supp. 78 (N.D.N.Y. 1993), 99 n.56

Strategem Dev. Corp. v. Heron, 756 F. Supp. 789 (S.D.N.Y. 1991), 214, 214 nn.66–68, 258 n.279, 301 n.178, 325, 325 n.279, 428, 428 n.3

478 ISSUES OF LEGAL ETHICS IN THE PRACTICE OF ENVIRONMENTAL LAW

Strategim Development Corp. v. Heron, 1991 U.S. Dist. LEXIS 1474 (S.D.N.Y. 1991), 35 n.172

Strawn v. Canuso, 657 A.2d 420 (N.J. 1995), 149 n.284

Strawser v. Exxon Co., U.S.A., a Div. of Exxon Corp., 843 P.2d 613 (Wyo. 1992), 362 n.53

Superior Air Products Co. v. NL Industries, Inc., 522 A.2d 1025 (N.J. Ct. App. 1987), 129, 129 n.181

Supplee v. Hall, 52 A. 407 (Conn. 1902), 71 n.114

S.W. Ctr. for Biological Diversity v. Babbitt, 108 F. Supp. 2d 1209 (D. N.M. 2000), 402 n.4

Swindler & Berlin v. United States, 524 U.S. 399 (1998), 193, 194 nn.539–543

Swinton v. Whintonsville Sav. Bank, 42 N.E.2d 808 (Mass. 1942), 120 n.129

T

Tarasoff v. Regents of University of California, 551 P.2d 334 (Cal. 1976), 144 n.263, 145 nn.264–265, 154, 154 nn.321–322, 154 nn.325–327, 155 nn.328–329

Tartera v. Palumbo, 453 S.W.2d 780 (Tenn. 1970), 153 n.316

Tatum; United States v., 943 F.2d 370 (4th Cir. 1991), 223 n.111

T.C. Theatre Corp. v. Warner Bros. Pictures, 113 F. Supp. 265 (S.D.N.Y. 1953), 246, 246 n.228

Texaco, Inc. v. Garcia, 891 S.W.2d 255 (Tex. 1995), 249, 250 n.243

Thayer, In re, 745 N.E.2d 207 (Ind. 2001), 230, 230 nn.154–156

TMI, In re, 67 F.3d 1103 (3d Cir. 1995), 149 n.284

Togstad v. Vesely, Otto, Miller & Keefe, 291 N.W.2d 686 (Minn. 1980), 21 n.96, 36, 48 n.10, 61, 108 n.84

Tormo v. Yormark, 398 F. Supp. 1159 (D. N.J. 1975), 45 n.18, 60 n.52, 65 n.75

Torres v. Divis, 494 N.E.2d 1227 (1986), 48 n.8

Transcraft, Inc. v. Galvin Stalmack Kirschner & Clark, 39 F.3d 812 (7th Cir. 1994), 2 n.9

Travelers Indem. Co. v. Gerling Global Reinsurance Corp., 2000 WL 1159260 (S.D.N.Y. 2000), 301 n.178

TSC Indus., Inc. v. Northway, Inc., 426 U.S. 438 (1976), 142 n.248

Tutu Wells Contamination Litig., In re, 166 F.R.D. 331 (D.V.I. 1996), 196 n.552

Tutu Wells Contamination Litigation, In re, 120 F.3d 368 (3d Cir. 1997), 195, 195 nn.548–549, 196 nn.550–552, 197 n.554, 412

Tutu Wells Contamination Litigation, In re, 162 F.R.D. 46, order clarified, 162 F.R.D. 81 (D. V.I. 1995), 196 nn.552–553

U

Udall v. Littell, 366 F.2d 668 (1966), cert. denied, 385 U.S. 1007 (1967), 47 n.4

Unified Sewerage Agency v. Jelco Inc., 646 F.2d 1339 (9th Cir. 1981), 212 n.56, 229 n.141, 229 n.145

United Nuclear Corp.; United States v., 814 F. Supp. 1552 (D. N.M. 1992), 129 n.179

Table of Cases 479

United Shoe Machinery Corp.; United States v., 89 F. Supp. 357 (D. Mass. 1950), 161, 161 n.363

United States Postal Service v. Phelps Dodge Refining Corp., 852 F. Supp. 156 (E.D.N.Y. 1994), 68 n.93, 168, 168 nn.405–406, 169 nn.407–409

United States v. See name of party

United Technologies Corp. v. Liberty Mut. Inc., 1994 WL 879545 (Mass., June, 9 1994), 310 n.216

Upjohn Co. v. United States, 449 U.S. 383 (1981), 133 n.203, 162 n.364, 163, 163 nn.372–375

U.S. Oil & Gas Litig., In re, No. 83-1702-A1-CIV, 1988 WL 28544 (S.D. Fla. Feb. 8, 1988), 152 n.309

V

Van Gerwen v. Guarantee Mutual Life Co., 214 F.3d 1041 (9th Cir. 2000), 408 n.44

Van Jackson v. Check 'N Go of Illinois, Inc., 114 F. Supp. 2d 731 (N.D. Ill. 2000), 263–264, 264 n.13

Van Jackson v. Check 'N Go of Illinois, Inc., 46 S.W.3d 177 (Tenn. 2001), 264 n.14

Viacom Inc. v. Sumitomo Corp. (In re Copper Market Antitrust Litigation), 200 F.R.D. 213 (S.D.N.Y. 2001), 424 n.7

Volberg v. Pataki, 917 F. Supp. 909 (N.D. N.Y.), *aff'd*, 112 F.3d 507 (2d Cir. 1996), *cert. denied*, 520 U.S. 1119 (1997), 86 n.177

W

Wagenmann v. Adams, 829 F.2d 196 (1st Cir. 1987), 224 n.112

Waggoner v. Snow, Becker, Kroll, Klaris & Krauss, 991 F.2d 1501 (9th Cir. 1993), 73 n.124

Walco Invs., Inc. v. Thenen, 881 F. Supp. 1576 (S.D. Fla. 1995), 153 n.312

Ward v. Maritz Inc., 156 F.R.D. 592 (D.N.J. 1994), 175 n.445

Washington State Physicians Ins. Exch. & Ass'n v. Fisons Corp., 858 P.2d 1054 (Wash. 1993)., 343

Watts v. Polaczyk, 619 N.W.2d 714 (Mich. Ct. App. 2000), 409 nn.49–50

Weisman; United States v., 1995 WL 244522 (S.D.N.Y. Apr. 26, 1995), 173 n.437

Weitzenhoff; United States v., 1 F.3d 1523 (9th Cir. 1993), 304

Weitzenhoff; United States v., 35 F.3d 1275 (9th Cir. 1993), 304, 305 nn.196–197

Welch & Forbes Inc. v. Cendant Corp. (In re Cendant Corp. PRIDES Litigation), 243 F.3d 722 (3d Cir. 2001), 402 n.10

Wellmore Coal Corp. v. Harman Mining Corp., 568 S.E.2d 671 (Va. 2002), 12, 384

Westfield Partners, Ltd. v. Hogan, 740 F. Supp. 523 (N.D. Ill. 1990), 52 n.28

Westinghouse Electric Corp. v. Kerr-McGee Corp., 580 F.2d 1311 (7th Cir. 1978), 48 n.9, 48 n.11, 60 n.52, 65 n.75, 211, 211 nn.49–51, 269 n.40

Wheat v. United States, 486 U.S. 153 (1988), 302, 302 n.181, 302 n.186, 303 nn.187–188

Whiteside; State v., 272 N.W.2d 468 (Iowa 1978), 90 n.11

480 ISSUES OF LEGAL ETHICS IN THE PRACTICE OF ENVIRONMENTAL LAW

Wieder v. Skala, 609 N.E.2d 105 (1992), 340, 340 nn.33–34
Willy v. Coastal States Management Co., Inc., 939 S.W.2d 193 (Tex.App. 1996), 187, 187 nn.505–507, 188 nn.508–512
Willy v. Coastal States Management Co., Inc., 977 S.W.2d 566 (Tex. 1998), 188 n.513
Wisconsin v. Hotline Industries, Inc., 236 F.3d 363 (7th Cir. 2000), 412 n.67
Wright by Wright v. Group Health Hosp., 691 P.2d 564 (1984), 361 n.46, 361 n.48

X

X Corp. v. Doe, 816 F. Supp. 1086 (E.D.Va. 1993), 85 n.168

Y

York v. Stiefel, 458 N.E.2d 488 (Ill. 1983), 152 n.307

Z

Zolin; United States v., 491 U.S. 554 (1989), 166 n.396
Zucker v. Occidental Petroleum Corp., 192 F.3d 1323 (9th Cir. 1999), 408, 408 n.39

INDEX

A

Administrative Dispute Resolution Act of 1990 (ADRA), 345–46
Advanced fees, 406–7
Advance waivers, 192, 193, 241–45, 243–44, 317
Advertising, 391–99
  decisional law on, 393–95
  environmental examples of, 393, 396
  false or misleading communication in, 392
  media for, 392
  record of, 395–96
  solicitation of clients in, 391–96, 399
  specialization in, 398–99
  technology and, 396–98
Advice
  about expert witness, 28–29
  to constituent, 75
  environmental practice and, 57–58
  role as advisor, 56–58
  to unrepresented persons, 370
Affidavits of lawyers, 273–74
Agency, government. *See also* Government lawyers
  communication with, 366–68
  representation of, 61–62
Aggregate settlements, 17, 65, 314–15
Agreements
  arbitration, 409–10
  fee, 407
  representation, 59–60
  retainer, 408–10
Alternative dispute resolution (ADR), 56, 345–50
  definition of, 345
  techniques of, 347
  third-party neutrals in, 348–50
American Academy of Matrimonial Lawyers, 111
American Bar Association (ABA). *See also* Canons of Professional Ethics,

ABA; Ethics 2000 Commission, ABA; Model Rules of Professional Conduct, ABA; Standing Committee on Ethics and Professional Responsibility, ABA
  Center for Professional Responsibility, 13
  Commission on Billable Hours, 390, 403
  Commission on Multidisciplinary Practice, 377–79
  Commission on Multijurisdictional Practice, 11, 387
  Committee on Professional Ethics, 16
  Committee on Professional Grievances, 16
  ETHICSearch Web site, 13
  Model Code of Professional Responsibility, 1, 13, 16, 17, 93–94, 95–96
  Standards for Imposing Lawyer Sanctions, 223
American College of Trust and Estate Counsel, 111
American Corporate Counsel Association (ACCA), 383
American Institute of Certified Public Accountants (AICPA), 141, 377
American Law Institute (ALI), 96. *See also Restatement (Third) of the Law Governing Lawyers*
Anticontact rule. *See* Communication with represented persons
Arbitration, 346, 348
Arbitration agreement, 346, 409–10
Attorney-client privilege, 67–73
  confidentiality and, 159–71
  for consultants, 424
  crime-fraud exception for, 71–73, 165–66
  environmental context for, 70–71, 166–69

481

482 ISSUES OF LEGAL ETHICS IN THE PRACTICE OF ENVIRONMENTAL LAW

for government lawyers, 5, 169–71
limitations of, 163–65
for organizational client, 162–63, 169
waiver of, 164
work product compared, 174
Attorney-client relationship. *See* Lawyer-client relationship
Attorney's fees. *See* Fees
Attorneys' Liability Assurance Society, Inc. (ALAS), 223
Attorney work product, 171–75
Audits, environmental, 138

B

Bar associations
peer evaluation by, 12–14
readmission to, 15–16
Boards of Professional Responsibility, 14–15
Business dealings with client, 310–12

C

CAA Amendments of 1990, 129–30
Candor, 327–31
confidentiality and, 114–15, 327–28
environmental example of, 335–36
frivolous claims and, 329
by government lawyers, 117–19
to nonclients, 334, 335–36
to opposing party and counsel, 334
to tribunal, 330–31
Canons of Professional Ethics, ABA, 16
Canon 37, 92, 93
Canon 38, 403
Canon 47, 383
CERCLA. *See* Comprehensive Environmental Response, Compensation, and Liability Act (CERCLA)
Citizen Protection Act, 369
Clean Air Act (CAA), 57–58, 82
attorney's fees under, 411
penalties under, 127, 130
Clean Water Act (CWA), 82
disclosure under, 135
penalties under, 127, 130
trade secrets under, 128

Client. *See also* Consent of client; Former client; Lawyer-client relationship; Organizational client; Prospective client
business dealings with, 310–12
communication with opposing party by, 365
deceased, 193–94
definition of, 59, 211
Hot Potato, 211–15, 257, 258
identity of, 66, 163
objectives of, 49–56
status of, 58–64
as witness, 320–22
Cognitors, 376–77
Committee on Ethics and Professional Responsibility. *See* Standing Committee on Ethics and Professional Responsibility, ABA
Common representation. *See* Simultaneous representation
Communication with client
on Internet, 396–98
organizational client, 77–78, 359, 362–64
Communication with represented persons, 351–72
by agents, 359–60
authorized by law, 356, 360
by client, 365
corporate entities, 359, 362–64
by employees, 359–60
environmental examples of, 358–59, 362–64
former employees, 360–61, 364–65
government lawyers, 366–68
knowledge of representation in, 365
permitted situations for, 352, 356
by prosecutors, 368–69
Communication with third persons. *See also* Communication with represented persons
expert witnesses, 363
unrepresented persons, 369–72
Competence, duty of, 41–42
Comprehensive Environmental Response, Compensation, and Liability Act (CERCLA), 7, 126, 199, 218

disclosure under, 135
disposal definition under, 32–34
reporting obligations under, 125
sanctions under, 126
Confidentiality, 89–198. *See also*
Disclosure of confidential information
attorney-client privilege and, 160–62
of business information, 128–29
candor and, 114–15, 327–28
common law requirements for, 143–47,
153–59
conflicts of interest and, 107, 202
with consultants, 421
for deceased client, 193–94
environmental examples of, 92, 113–14,
119, 122, 124–27, 172–73, 187–91
Ethics 2002 Commission proposals for,
101–2
for former clients, 193
government lawyer obligations for, 4, 5,
116–19
history of rule of, 92–95
in-house counsel obligations for, 179–
91
Kutak Rule and, 94
liability to nonclients and, 147–53
Model Rules approach to, 99–105
multidisciplinary practice and, 375–76
in multiple representation, 194–95, 221–
22
for organizational clients, 73, 108
principles of, 92
for prospective clients, 48, 191–93
reporting obligations for, 124–27
Restatement approach to, 96–99
society's interests and, 91
warn, duty to, 145, 153–59
in withdrawal, 433
of work product, 167, 171–75
Conflicts of interest, 199–259. *See also*
Imputed conflicts
confidentiality and, 107, 202
consent for, 203, 224–28, 236, 241–42,
245, 248, 258
consultation for, 234–35
for criminal defendants, 302–6
curative measures for, 207, 224–28,
232–39, 258–59

with current clients, 209–15
decision to accept representation and,
206–7
declining representation due to, 232–34
directly adverse to client, 205, 207–8,
210–11, 215
disclosure of, 224
disqualification due to, 222–23, 246,
252
for former clients, 245–59
generally adverse interests, 215–16
for government lawyers, 7–10
Hot Potato Rule and, 211–15, 257, 258
issue, 306–18
limiting representation due to, 237–38
loyalty to client and, 201–2, 203–4
materially limited representation, 205–6,
207, 226
Model Rules for, 204–9
nonwaivable, 229–32
for organizational clients, 294–97
positional, 306–18
principles of, 201–3
for prospective clients, 238–45, 316–17
sanctions for, 223–24
termination of representation due to,
236, 258–59
withdrawal from representation due to,
236
Consent of client, 203, 207, 224–28, 258
in advance, 241–42
disclosure of information to obtain,
107–8
environmental example of, 228–29
for imputed conflicts, 272, 289
informed, 206, 226–28, 230
for prospective clients, 242–43, 317
revoking, 228
written, 225, 227, 235, 245
Consultants, 419–23, 424
Consultation, 234–35
Contingent fees, 407, 410–11
Corporate representation. *See*
Organizational client
Court orders, 133–35
Crime-fraud exception, 71–73, 165–66
Criminal acts
confidentiality and, 71–73, 90, 99, 100,
101, 165–66

484 ISSUES OF LEGAL ETHICS IN THE PRACTICE OF ENVIRONMENTAL LAW

disclosure of, 111, 197, 331
as misconduct, 342–43
withdrawal for, 428, 429
Criminal defendants, 302–6

D

Deceased client, 193–94
Diligence, duty of, 42
choice of clients and, 43–44
duration of, 44–46
environmental example, 45–46
prohibited conduct, 42–43
Disciplinary counsels, 14–15
Discipline of lawyers, 1–39
bar associations in, 12–14
for conduct in nonprofessional capacity, 31
for forum shopping, 31–32
for judgment, 30–31
judicial controls in, 19–20
for lawyer-related services, 29–30
for nonlawyer assistant conduct, 28–29
peer evaluation in, 12–14
process for, 14–16
readmission and, 15–16
state boards of professional responsibility in, 14–15
statutory controls in, 18
for taking advantage of opponent's mistakes, 32–34
tort liability in, 21–27
unauthorized practice of law and, 10–12
Disclosure of confidential information, 105–8, 235
client's refusal to disclose, 119–22
to comply with law, 132–35
conflicts of interest and, 107
consent for, 328
consultation with client prior to, 105
by court order, 133–35
for crime, 99, 100, 101, 166
in discovery responses, 195–98
in enforcement, 129–32
in environmental audit, 138
environmental examples of, 106–7, 195
for fraud, 99, 101, 166
for imminent death or substantial bodily harm prevention, 97–98, 197

implied authorization for, 132–33
inadvertent, 175–79
misprision and, 136–37
to obtain consent, 107–8
other laws and, 110–14
permitted reasons for, 97
Securities Act requirements for, 138–43
in self-defense, 90, 105, 122–24, 179–87
state law requirements for, 137
Discovery, 195–98
Disqualification
for conflicts of interest, 222–23
for former client, 246, 252
Hot Potato clients, 213–14

E

Emergency Planning and Community Right to Know Act (EPCRA), 126–27
Employees of lawyer, 419–23
communication with represented person by, 359–60
supervision of, 28–29, 420–21
Endocrine Disruption Hypothesis, 37
Enforcement
any person liability and, 130–32
confidentiality and, 129–32
by court orders, 133–35
owner/operator liability and, 129–30
by state, 137
Environmental audits, 138
Environmental Policy and Conflict Resolution Act of 1998, 347
Environmental Protection Agency (EPA), 142, 199, 218
alternative dispute resolution by, 345
Office of Civil Rights (OCR), 76, 200
Environmental public interest groups, 411–12
Equal Credit Opportunity Act, 406
Ethical Considerations in Solid Waste Practice, 348
Ethics 2000 Commission, ABA, 16, 334
on client consent, 208
on confidentiality, 101–2, 376
on fee agreements, 407
on issue conflicts, 308

Index 485

on multijurisdictional practice, 383
on pro bono service, 390
on screening, 254–55, 258
on third-party neutrals, 349
on unrepresented persons, 371
Ethics in Government Act, 292
Evaluations for third persons, 335, 337
Expert witnesses, 28–29, 363

F

False statements. *See* Misrepresentation
Federal Judiciary Center, 28
Federal Rules of Civil Procedure
Rule 11, 51, 52, 54
Rule 26, 173–75
Rule 26(b)(4)(A), 363
Rule 44(c), 302
Federal Water Pollution Control Act, 137
Fee agreements, 407
Fees, 401–17
advanced, 406–7
billing practices and, 405–6
collection practices and, 405–6, 412–13
contingent, 407, 410–11
disclosure of, 163
division of, 373, 390, 415–17
environmental example of, 413
environmental public interest groups
and, 411–12
fixed, 406
reasonable, 401, 402, 404–5, 407
referral, 413–15, 422
retainers, 408–10
as sanction, 412
sharing, 373, 390, 415–17
Fields of practice, communication of, 398–99
Fifth Amendment, 2
First Amendment, 190, 393–395
Former client, 245–59
appearance of impropriety for, 252–54
confidentiality for, 193
curative measures for, 258–59
disqualification motions and, 246, 252
duties owed, 64
environmental examples for, 249–51, 255
government as, 282–83

Hot Potato Rule for, 257, 258
imputed conflicts and, 252–55
Former employees, 360–61, 364–65
Former government lawyers, 292–94
Forum shopping, 31–32
Fraud
confidentiality and, 71–73, 90, 99, 101, 165–66
disclosure of, 111, 331
withdrawal for, 429
Freedom of Information Act (FOIA), 6, 116, 128, 360
Futrell, J. William, 114

G

Government lawyers
attorney-client privilege for, 5, 169–71
candor by, 117–19
client status for, 61–62
confidentiality for, 4, 5, 116–19
conflicts of interest for, 7–10
consent for, 289
curative measures for, 289–92
current clients of, 281–82
environmental examples for, 286
former, 292–94
former clients of, 282–83
imputed conflicts for, 278–92
lawyer-client relationship for, 7–10
prosecutors, 368–69
regulation of, 3–10
responsibilities of, 6–7
screening for, 290–92
whistleblowing by, 118–19, 188–91
withdrawal by, 427
A Guide to Professionalism Commissions, 14

H

Hot Potato Rule, 211–15, 257, 258
disqualification for, 213–14
environmental examples for, 214–15

I

Imputed conflicts, 261–325
affidavits of lawyers for, 273–74
appearance of impropriety with, 252–54

consent of client for, 258, 272, 289
curative measures for, 272–78, 289–92
disqualification due to, 252, 267–68
environmental examples of, 270–72, 286
exceptions to, 268
firm size and, 268–71
for former client, 252–55
for government lawyers, 278–92
lawyer mobility and, 264–67
for private lawyers, 263–64, 274–78
referrals for, 273
screening lawyers for, 254–55, 258, 274–78, 290–92
Independent contractors, 419–23, 424
Independent professional judgment, 202
Indeterminacy
environmental examples, 36–39
in law, 34
in lawyering, 35–36
Informed consent, 206, 226–28, 230
In-house counsel. *See also* Organizational client
ethical obligations of, 80
termination of, 84, 87, 179–91
whistleblowing by, 188–91
withdrawal by, 427–28
Institute for Environmental Conflict Resolution, 347
Intermediaries, 323–24. *See also* Third-party neutral
Intermediary, 323–24. *See also* Third-party neutral
Internet
communication through, 396–98
inadvertent disclosure through, 175
In the Interests of Justice: Reforming the Legal Profession, 329
Issue conflicts, 308–18
in business dealings with client, 310–12
for current clients, 310–12
in environmental matters, 309–10
for joint defense groups, 317–18
for joint plaintiff groups, 318–24
for prospective clients, 316–17
in settlements, 312–16

J

Joint defense doctrine, 82, 171
Joint defense groups, 317–18
Joint plaintiff groups, 200, 318–24
Joint representation. *See* Simultaneous representation
Judgment, independent professional, 202

K

Kutak Commission, 94

L

Laboratory shopping, 31–32
Lawyer as witness, 319–21
Lawyer-client relationship, 47–87
advice in, 56–58
environmental context for, 55–56, 65–67
existence of, 24, 47–48, 58–64
for former client, 64
for government lawyers, 7–10
objectives of representation, 49–56
for organizational client, 73–87
Lawyer-related services, 29–30
Legal malpractice. *See* Tort liability
Liability. *See also* Tort liability
any person, 130–32
lawyer, to nonclients, 147–53
operator, 129–30
owner, 129–30
Loyalty to client, 42, 47, 201–2, 203–4, 435

M

Malpractice liability. *See* Tort liability
McDade Amendment, 369
Mediation, 348, 349
Misconduct
by lawyer, 342–43, 391–92
misrepresentation as, 328
reporting, 339–43
Misprision, 136–37
Misrepresentation
in advertising, 392
influencing government agency, 342–43
as misconduct, 328

rescission for, 337–39
to tribunal, 330
MJP. *See* Multijurisdictional practice
(MJP)
Model Rules of Professional Conduct,
ABA, 1, 13
history of, 16–18
limiting use of, 20–21
Preamble, 2, 20–21, 30, 110–11
2002 revision, 31, 324
Rule 1.1, 41
Rule 1.2, 30, 49, 109, 122, 135, 176,
237, 315, 428
2002 revision, 243
Rule 1.3, 43, 44–45
Rule 1.4, 77, 233
2002 revision, 233
Rule 1.5, 311, 404, 406
2002 revision, 406, 407, 411, 416–17
Rule 1.6, 3, 48, 87, 92, 95, 97, 99–102,
108–12, 114–15, 120–24, 132–35,
147, 157, 161, 179, 183–86, 190,
191, 288, 327–28, 339, 376, 421,
433
2002 revision, 102–5, 106, 191, 197–
98, 247–48, 262
Rule 1.7, 203, 204–10, 215–16, 225–
26, 229–31, 233–36, 241–42, 247,
264, 265, 267, 281, 285–86, 289,
294, 296–98, 306, 310, 313–14,
319, 321, 324
2002 revision, 64, 107–8, 169, 205,
208–9, 215, 226–28, 231–32, 235,
243–44, 298, 301, 302, 308, 314–
15, 323–24, 436
Rule 1.8, 17, 76, 83, 204, 267, 310,
312–14, 316, 408–9
2002 revision, 25–26, 84, 227–28,
311, 314–15
Rule 1.9, 64, 193, 204, 236, 247–48,
252, 257, 267, 285–87, 289, 319
2002 revision, 64, 66–67, 248, 255
Rule 1.10, 204, 261, 263, 265, 267–68
2002 revision, 268, 432
Rule 1.11, 117, 204, 274, 279–81, 283–
84, 286–90, 310
2002 revision, 117, 284–86, 289, 291
Rule 1.12, 290

Rule 1.13, 73–75, 79–80, 82, 294, 296
2002 revision, 4, 76
Rule 1.16, 427–29, 433–34
2002 revision, 435–36
Rule 1.18, 63, 192–93, 242
2002 revision, 245
Rule 2.1, 31, 56, 58
Rule 2.2, 134, 267, 323–24, 348
Rule 2.3, 134, 337
2002 revision, 337
Rule 2.4, 324–25, 349–50
Rule 3.1, 53
2002 revision, 54–55
Rule 3.3, 114–15, 119, 134, 186, 288,
330
2002 revision, 331
Rule 3.4, 334, 363
Rule 3.6, 423
Rule 3.7, 319–20
2002 revision, 320
Rule 4.1, 327–28, 363
Rule 4.2, 351–56, 358–67
2002 revision, 357–58, 368
Rule 4.3, 370–71
2002 revision, 371–72
Rule 4.4, 335
2002 revision, 179, 335
Rule 5.3, 420–21
2002 revision, 422
Rule 5.4, 373–74, 415
2002 revision, 390, 416–17
Rule 5.5, 10–11, 383–84
2002 revision, 11, 387
Rule 5.7, 28, 29
Rule 6.1, 389
2002 revision, 389–90
Rule 6.2, 434
Rule 7.1, 392
Rule 7.2, 392, 395
2002 revision, 393, 397–98, 414, 422
Rule 7.3, 392–93
2002 revision, 398, 399
Rule 7.4, 398
2002 revision, 399
Rule 7.5, 416
Rule 8.3, 339
Rule 8.4, 328, 341, 356, 391–92
2002 revision, 343

Rule 8.5, 10–12
  2002 revision, 387
Scope, 2, 7, 19–20, 30, 48, 59
Morris K. Udall Foundation, 347
Multidisciplinary practice (MDP), 373–79, 416
  ABA Commission on Multidisciplinary Practice, 377–79
  cognitors, 376–77
  confidentiality in, 375–76
  definition of, 373
  environmental practice and, 379
Multijurisdictional practice (MJP), 381–87
  definition of, 381
  2002 revisions, 386–87
  unauthorized practice of law, 383–86
Multiple representation. *See* Simultaneous representation

N

National Environmental Policy Act (NEPA), 3, 347
Negotiated Rulemaking Act, 346
Negotiation, 56, 348
Neutral, third-party. *See* Third-party neutral
Nonclients. *See* Third persons
Nonlawyer assistants, 28–29, 419–23

O

Objectives of representation
  client determines, 49–56
  limitations on, 50–55, 237–38
  SLAPP suits and, 51–54, 55–56
Opposing counsel/party, fairness to, 334
Organizational client, 73–82
  affiliates, representation of, 299–301
  attorney-client privilege with, 162–63, 169
  client identity in, 74–76
  communication with, 77–78, 359, 362–64
  compliance with laws by, 78–79
  confidentiality with, 73, 108
  conflicts of interest for, 294–97
  environmental examples for, 77–78, 82, 83–87, 294–96, 298–99
  former employees of, 360–61, 364–65

  paying for employee's representation by, 83–84, 297–98
  reporting violations by, 74, 79–82
  representation of constituents of, 296–97
  representation of employees of, 83–84, 297–98
  retaliatory discharge by, 84–87
  termination by, 84–87

P

Peer evaluation, 12–14
Positional conflicts. *See* Issue conflicts
Potentially responsible parties (PRPs), 8–9, 199, 218, 220
Privilege. *See also* Attorney-client privilege
  work product, 171–75
Pro bono representation, 389–90
Prosecutors, communication by, 368–69
Prospective client, 238–245
  advance waiver for, 193, 241–42
  confidentiality for, 48, 191–93
  conflicts of interest for, 238–45, 316–17
  consent for, 241–42, 317
  duties due, 62–64
  initial consultation for, 240–41, 245
Publicity, trial, 423–26

R

Referral fees, 413–15, 422
Referrals, 273
Regulation S-K, 141
Regulation S-X, 141
1990 Remedies Act, 138
Reno, Attorney General Janet, 368
Reporting violations of law, 74, 79–82, 124–27
Representation agreement, 59–60
Representation letter, 407
Rescission, 337–39
Residential Lead-Based Hazard Reduction Act, 126
Resource Conservation and Recovery Act (RCRA), 126
Restatement (Second) of Agency, 233
Restatement (Second) of Torts, 22, 153
Restatement (Third) of the Law Governing

Lawyers, 24, 47, 62, 96–99, 103–4, 106, 113, 191, 201, 217, 229–30, 248–49, 328–29, 352, 356
Retainers, 408–10
Retaliatory discharge, 84–87, 179–91

S

Sanctions, 223–24
  CERCLA, 126
  fees as, 412
  state, 137
Sarbanes-Oxley Act, 18, 73–74, 139
Screening, 258
  court decisions about, 275–78
  devices for, 291–92
  for former judges, 290
  for government lawyers, 290–91
  for lateral hires, 254–55
  for private lawyers, 274–78
  for prospective clients, 192
Securities and Exchange Commission (SEC)
  Regulation S-K, 141
  Regulation S-X, 141
  Rule 10b-5, 141–43
  Rules of Practice, 139
  Staff Accounting Bulletin 92, 141
  Statement of Position 96-1, 141
Securities Exchange Act of 1934, 139, 141–43
Settlement
  acceptance of, 49
  aggregate, 17, 65, 314–15
  communication of to opposing party, 356
  conflicts of interest with, 312–16
  disclosure of, 91, 348
  environmental examples, 315–16
  mass tort, 49
Shared fees
  with nonlawyers, 373, 415–17
  with nonprofit organizations, 390
Shredding the Truth, 329
Simultaneous representation, 208, 218–22
  client identity in, 66, 75
  confidentiality in, 194–95, 221–22
  in environmental matters, 199–200, 218–21, 270–71

Sixth Amendment, 302
Slank, Noreen L., 308
SLAPP (Strategic Lawsuit Against Public Participation), 51–54, 55–56
Solicitation of clients, 391–96, 399
Specialization, advertising of, 398–99
Standing Committee on Ethics and Professional Responsibility, ABA, 13, 335
  Formal Op. 90-358, 191–92, 238, 274, 316
  Formal Op. 91-359, 361
  Formal Op. 92-366, 109
  Formal Op. 92-367, 321
  Formal Op. 92-368, 175, 177
  Formal Op. 93-372, 213, 241, 317
  Formal Op. 93-377, 307
  Formal Op. 93-378, 363
  Formal Op. 94-382, 175, 177
  Formal Op. 94-389, 410
  Formal Op. 95-390, 35, 300
  Formal Op. 95-396, 355
  Formal Op. 96-400, 265
  Formal Op. 97-408, 367
  Formal Op. 97-409, 287
  Formal Op. 98-411, 105
  Formal Op. 99-413, 175
  Formal Op. 99-414, 266
  Formal Op. 00-418, 311
  Formal Op. 01-423, 415
  Formal Op. 01-424, 185
  Formal Op. 02-425, 409
  Formal Op. 02-427, 406
  Informal Op. 86-1518, 175
Strategic Lawsuit Against Public Participation (SLAPP), 51–54, 55–56
Superfund matters, 194–95, 218, 270. *See also* Comprehensive Environmental Response, Compensation, and Liability Act (CERCLA)
Supervision of employees, 28–29, 420–22
Supplemental Standards of Ethical Conduct, 292

T

Termination of representation, 325. *See also* Withdrawal from representation
  communication with party after, 355

for conflict of interest, 236, 258–59
diligence upon, 44
discharge as, 427
by in-house counsel, 84–87, 179–91
Third-party neutral, 348–50
definition of, 324, 349
imputed conflicts and, 324–25
Third persons. *See also* Communication with third persons
candor to, 334, 335–36
duties to, 333–44
environmental examples for, 335–36, 337–39
evaluations for, 335, 337
fairness to, 334
liability to, 147–53
rights of, 335
withdrawal impact upon, 433–35
Thornburgh, Attorney General Richard, 368
Tort liability, 21–27, 145
environment context for, 26–27
limiting, 25–26, 408–9
to nonclient, 147–53
Toxic torts, 144, 199
Trade secrets, 128–29
Trial publicity, 423–26
Truthfulness. *See* Candor
Truth in Lending Act, 406

U

Unauthorized practice of law, 10–12, 375
on Internet, 397
multijurisdictional practice as, 11–12, 383–86
Unitary client theory, 8
Unrepresented persons, 369–72
U.S. Judicial Conference, 2

W

Waiver
advance, 192, 193, 238–39, 241–45, 317
of anticontact rule, 351, 355
attorney-client privilege, 164
Web, communication through, 396–98
Whistleblower's Protection Act, 190

Whistleblowing, 118–19, 188–91
Withdrawal from representation, 427–36
confidentiality in, 433
for conflicts of interest, 236
consent of court for, 434
for financial burden on lawyer, 45, 429, 430–31
impact on other parties of, 433–35
mandatory reasons for, 428–29
noisy, 428
of organizational client, 108
permissive reasons for, 429–33
for repugnant client, 49, 429, 431–33, 435
Witnesses
client as, 320–22
communication with, 363
expert, 28–29, 363
lawyer as, 319–21
Work product, 167, 171–75

Z

Zealousness, 42–43

Also Available from the Section of Environment, Energy and Resources

The Basic Practice Series

The Basic Practice Series is an essential library providing concise information in an easy-to-use format. Each volume focuses on either a specific statute or an area of concentration within environmental, energy, or resources law. Whether you're a new or seasoned professional, you'll find these books to be a quick and necessary resource for understanding the legal fundamentals of these areas.

Titles Available Now Include:

- **RCRA** (Resource Conservation and Recovery Act)
  Product Code 5350094, 2003, 182 pages, 6 X 9

- **CERCLA** (Comprehensive Environmental Response, Compensation, and Liability Act (Superfund))
  Product Code 5350093, 2002, 144 pages, 6 X 9

- **EPCRA** (Emergency Planning and Community Right-to-Know Act)
  Product Code 5350091, 2002, 156 pages, 6 X 9

- **FERC** (Federal Energy Regulatory Commission)
  Product Code 5350095, 2003, 244 pages, 6 X 9

- **TSCA** (Toxic Substances Control Act)
  Product Code 5350082, 2000, 151 pages, 6 X 9

- **FIFRA** (Federal Insecticide, Fungicide & Rodenticide Act)
  Product Code 5350081, 2000, 150 pages, 6 X 9

- **ESA** (Endangered Species Act)
  Product Code 5350083, 2001, 203 pages, 6 X 9

- **Clean Air Act**
  Product Code 5350084, 2001, 245 pages, 6 X 9

Price for each book:
$49.95 Section of Environment, Energy, and Resources Member
$59.95 Regular

1-800-285-2221
www.ababooks.org